A POLITICAL APPROACH TO PACIFISM

Book 2

A POLITICAL APPROACH TO PACIFISM

Book 2

Will Morrisey

Symposium Series
Volume 39b

The Edwin Mellen Press
Lewiston/Queenston/Lampeter

Library of Congress Cataloging-in-Publication Data

Morrisey, Will.
   A political approach to pacifism / Will Morrisey.
      p.   cm. -- (Symposium series ; v. 39a-b)
   Includes bibliographical references and index.
   ISBN 0-7734-8910-X (v. 1). -- ISBN 0-7734-8912-6 (v. 2)
   1. Peace. 2. Pacifism. I. Title. II. Series
JX1952.M62   1996
303.6'6--dc20   95-12482
                                             CIP

This is volume 39b in the continuing series
Symposium Series
Volume 39b ISBN 0-7734-8912-6
SS Series ISBN 0-88946-989-X

A CIP catalog record for this book is available from the British Library.

Copyright © 1996 Will Morrisey

The Edwin Mellen Press   The Edwin Mellen Press
Box 450   Box 67
Lewiston, New York   Queenston, Ontario
USA 14092-0450   CANADA L0S 1L0

The Edwin Mellen Press, Ltd.
Lampeter, Dyfed, Wales
UNITED KINGDOM SA48 7DY

Printed in the United States of America

TABLE OF CONTENTS

BOOK 1

BOOK 2

END NOTES

ENDNOTES

INTRODUCTION

1. See Zampaglione 1973, 316, n.2.

2. See Taylor 1957, *passim*; Young 1987, 306; Martin 1966, 205-206.

3. Brock 1972, 471.

4. See Beales 1931, 6-7; Ceadel 1987, 4-6; and Osgood and Tucker 1967, 327 n.5 for the distinction between secular and religious opinions on peacemaking.

5. Faguet 1908 calls the New Testament "the most pacifistic book that has been written and the only truly pacifist book in all antiquity" (3). Brock 1972 writes that "pacifism in the strict sense of unconditional renunciation of war by the individual is, so far as we can tell, a little less than two thousand years old;" "until roughly the last one hundred and fifty years pacifism in the West was confined to those who stood within the Christian tradition" (3). Zampaglione 1972 attempts to find pacifists in ancient Greece, but his many pages of dilettantish narrative offer little persuasive evidence.

6. A pioneering study is Tomkinson 1940, who finds no "absolute pacifism" in any Chinese "school," mentioning only one strict pacifist, the Mohist writer Sung Tze. Ferguson 1978 discusses opinions on war and peace in a baker's dozen of religions, finding Taoism to be the most nearly pacifistic.

7. Gabriel 1990, 20, 55ff.; Gellner 1988, *passim*.

8. On the connection of war and utility see James 1988, 28.

9. Hirst 1906, 12. Compare Aristotle 1984, I, i, 35; IV, i, 118-119; *Nicomachean Ethics*, I, i, in Aristotle 1941, 935-936.

10. Even in the twentieth century, marked by two devastating world wars and numerous civil wars, 100 million persons were killed in 'peacetime' by governments, contrasted with some 35 million deaths in wars. Seabury and Codevilla 1989 rightly observe that "one of the primordial causes of war is fear of this kind of peace" (6-7). See also Andreski 1968 on 'peaceful' Tokugawa Japan (130).

11. Gentili 1933, I, i, 3.

12. See Aristotle 1984, III, vi, 94; IV, i, 119.

13. See for example Nietzsche 1986, II, i, 220.

14.   E.g., Lothian 1941, 7, 10; Muller 1985, 14, 63. Russett 1972 can conclude that the involvement of the United States in the Second World War was more or less useless, in part because "Russia [i.e., the Soviet Union] replaced Germany as the great threat to European security, and Japan, despite its territorial losses, is once more a major power" (20). Japan as a military oligarchy bent on the imperial domination of Asia by means of military conquest is thus equated with Japan as a commercial republic peacefully extending an economic 'empire' by profits from the sale of goods and services. As for the replacement of Germany by the Soviet Union as the principal threat to Europe, one threat is usually preferable to two.

15.   Sidney 1990, II, xxiii, 214.

16.   Ibid., III, xli, 551.

17.   *Principles of Politics*, XII, 254. On the relation of the political regime of Italian Fascism to war see Ginzburg 1988, 113, and Mueller 1989, 62-63. On Eméric Crucé as "one of the first scholars to realize that the incidence of war might be connected with the structure of society" see Howard 1978, 19.

18.   *The Liberty of the Ancients Compared With That of the Moderns*, in Constant 1989, 309-316.

19.   *Ibid.*, 323-324.

20.   Paine 1961, 402. That this is quite implausible even to a kindly religious pacifist may be seen in Inge 1926:

> The Americans are realizing, rather too late, the danger which besets them from the multitude of Jews, Armenians, Neapolitans, and Russians whom they have allowed to flood their country.... A still more deadly blow to the Puritan tradition has been dealt by allowing many millions of Irish to settle in the country. These immigrants are more dangerous to the solidarity of the American type than are the negroes, because the negroes cannot long tolerate the hard winters of the North and the Middle West. Tuberculosis kills them off (139).

21.   Paine 1961, 505.

22.   Alberdi 1913, 5, 25, 45, 53-60, 102-111, 134-140, 215-236, 257-269, 274-291, 307.

Veblen 1917 somewhat drily concurs with this assessment of 'German' principles and practice:

> It may seem invidious to speak so recurrently of the German Imperial establishment as the sole potential disturber of the peace in Europe. The reason for so singling out the Empire for this invidious distinction − of merit of demerit, as one may incline to take it − is that the facts run that way (202).

23. See for discussion and debate see Babst 1972, Doyle 1983, Doyle 1986, Chan 1984, Weede 1984, Maoz and Abdolai 1989, and Mueller 1989, 21. Also of interest is Rock 1989, who shows how such countries as Great Britain and France avoided war with one another after becoming commercial republics, whereas Great Britain did not avoid war with Germany when the latter was not a commercial republic.

24. Dewey 1946 observes that "the ardent and hopeful idealist" of the nineteenth century "has been proved... wrong":

> It was held that the revolution which was taking place in commerce and communication would break down the barriers which had kept the peoples of the earth alien and hostile and would create a state of interdependence which in time would insure lasting peace. Only an extreme pessimist ventured to suggest that the interdependence might multiply points of friction and conflict (23).

For denials of the claim that republicanism alone would yield peace, see Suttner 1914, 387 (who misstates Kant's view); Key 1972, 22, 74 (whose socialism may prevent her from considering the importance of commerce for peace); Eppstein 1935, 294-296; Wright 1965, 841, 845-846; Andreski 1968, 117; Howard 1978, 83, 131.

25. Proudhon 1861, I, 63-64. Emphasis on original.

26. "Economic Problems of Socialism in the U.S.S.R." in Stalin 1971, 335.

27. Fanon 1968, 313.

28. Inge 1926, 118.

29. Cited in Nicolai 1919, xii. Some twenty years later Norman Angell saw much the same thing: "The worst of the Nazi hysteria and excesses come from the fields and factories, but from the universities" (Angell 1935, 93).

30 Hirst 1906, 344.

31. Foremost among these are Peter Brock's three volumes: *Pacifism in Europe to 1914* (Princeton: Princeton University Press, 1972);

Twentieth-Century Pacifism (New York: Van Nostrand, 1970); and *Pacifism in the United States*: From the *Colonial Era to the First World War* (Princeton: Princeton University Press, 1968). Brock's writings are distinguished by a rare combination of historical knowledge and philosophic acuity. The best short general history of Christian pacifism remains Roland Bainton's *Christian Attitudes Toward War and Peace* (New York and Nashville: Abingdon Press, 1960). On pacifism in America, also see the writings of Charles Chatfield, a most conscientious historian, particularly his *For Peace and Justice: Pacifism in America 1914-1941* (Knoxville: University of Tennessee Press, 1971).

It is fruitless to attempt to understand pacifism without some understanding of the just war tradition. The most substantial recent work in English by an historian is by James Turner Johnson: *Ideology, Reason, and the Limitation of War: Religious and Secular Concepts, 1200-1700* (Princeton: Princeton University Press, 1975); *Just War Tradition and the Restraint of War: A Moral and Historical Inquiry* (Princeton, 1981); and *The Quest for Peace: Three Moral Traditions in Western Cultural History* (Princeton, 1987).

There is a need for a good history of pacifism since the Second World War. Useful if polemical studies of certain pieces of the picture are George Weigel's *Tranquillitas Ordinis; The Present Failure and Future Promise of American Catholic Thought on War and Peace* (Oxford University Press, 1987) and Guenter Lewy's *Peace and Revolution: The Moral Crisis of American Pacifism* (Grand Rapids: William B. Eerdmans Company, 1988). The latter should be read with Michael Cromartie, ed., *Peace Betrayed? Essays on Pacifism and Politics* (Washington: Ethics and Public Policy Center, 1989), which contains Professor Chatfield's measured response to Lewy.

32.   For a statement of historical relativism with respect to pacifism see Fontaine 1965, 114. For a similar statement with respect to just war doctrines see Johnson 1987, xvii. However, Johnson 1975 endorses relativism as an aid to what he takes to be a moral good, namely, the revival of a consensus concerning the criteria for a just war (274); it is not clear whether or not he judges his own conception of moral good to be 'relative.' For a denial of historical relativism by a historian see Troeltsch 1949, 39-48.

For another statement of historical relativism generally see Manicas 1989, 2-4. Manicas may be considered in contrast to what this book argues in many other ways besides. He argues that representative government is an impediment to peace, that only participatory democracy can bring peace because only it can oppose Machiavellian *raison d'état* or the "necessity" of self-preservation (189). He wishes that the 'democratic' or 'small republic' argument had prevailed at the time of the American founding (137-138), and criticizes Kant for endorsing representative government instead of direct democracy

(204). He claims that Marx was a true democrat, and tries to minimize the violence of the anticipated seizure of power by Marxists (232-233). He countenances Marx's supposition that the dictatorship of the proletariat will protect property rights, evidencing the Paris Commune of 1871 (238), that "glorious harbinger of a new society." Manicas concludes that "we are now in the midst of a race between democracy and, because of the possibility of nuclear war, the destruction of human civilization" (390). In this last point he is clearly mistaken, as 'democracy' in his sense been in no way advanced while the threat of global nuclear war has receded.

"There is a sense," Manicas writes, "in which there came to be but two parties in the world after the French Revolution: those who sought to complete the French Revolution and those who believed, not without reason, that the Americans, in 1787, went as far as one could go. The struggle between these two parties is still very much with us" (*Ibid.*, 2). I agree that there is a sense in which this is true, and recommend Professor Manicas' passionate and learned book as a sort of counterpoint to my own, at least on the 'partisan' level.

CHAPTER I

1. "Rabbi Eleazar quoted Rabbi Hanina who said: Scholars increase peace in the world..." – Talmud Berakhot. By "scholars", however, the rabbi refers to scholars of the Law who seek to harmonize apparent contradictions, to demonstrate the wholeness, the coherence of the Law. Such is not always the case in the modern academy. Thomas Jefferson took the optimistic view. When Congress framed the Model Treaty of 1776 for guidance of American ministers overseas, Jefferson sought to improve it by adding a clause on the protection of noncombatants in war: women, children and scholars. See Stuart 1982, 45.

 For a 'throne-and altar' conservative's attack on the American regime, see Molnar 1978, especially 121-141, in which the author professes an inability to discern any essential difference between "the American ideology" and Soviet Marxism-Leninism. See also Molnar 1987, in which the author calls the difference between totalitarianism and the liberal-democratic secularists (with whom he identifies "the American ideology") the difference between a desire to accelerate the modern absorption of human spirituality into physical human nature, and a desire to realize the same purpose gradually. This confuses the enterprise of liberal-democratic secularists with the enterprise of the American Founders.

 For a Marxist critique of the American regime, see Friedrich Engels, Letter to Friedrich A. Sorge, in Feuer 1959, 457-458. American political centrism or moderation, encouraged by the United States Constitution, ethnic pluralism within "the working class," and American prosperity all cause "very great and peculiar difficulties for the steady development of a workers' party."

2. Among conservatives, see Bradford 1979, who dismisses James Madison, Thomas Jefferson, Benjamin Franklin, and Thomas Paine as "deviant revolutionaries," politicians of "unrepresentative sentiments" who did not share the principles of their countrymen. John Dickinson, George Washington, John Adams, and "especially" Patrick Henry better represented the American revolutionists (97).

 Bradford ignores Washington's close collaboration with Madison, and his admiration for the writings of Franklin and Paine. He ignores John Adams' self-described "strenuous" insistence on reference to "the law of nature" in the 1774 Declaration of Rights (*Autobiography* in Adams 1851, II, 370). The final draft of the 1774 Declaration began, "That the inhabitants of the English colonies in North America, by the immutable laws of nature, the principles of the English Constitution and the several charters of compacts, have the following RIGHTS..." These included "life, liberty, and property." Bradford admits that Dickinson opposed the Declaration of Independence, but fails to unearth any serious opposition to the Declaration among the

American revolutionaries. Patrick Henry, who opposed the 1787 Constitution because "there is not an English feature in it," conveniently for Bradford did not write much. Nonetheless, he admits Henry "did employ the conventional language of contract theory and make an occasional bow toward 'natural rights'" – a concept Bradford decries. Bradford claims that by "equal liberty" Henry meant only "the necessity for self-defense and self-preservation," a claim rendering incoherent Henry's most famous declamation, "Give me liberty or give me death!" (101-103).

Bradford asserts, "ours was a revolution to conserve a known regime" (xi): "American colonials had developed their government within the legal context of the established English political forms, minus a titled nobility and a full religious hierarchy" (105). These are very remarkable subtractions, to which the American revolutionaries added the British monarchy and much of English common law. (On this latter point, see Lerner 1987, 60-90, showing how Thomas Jefferson built upon the habits of a citizenry shaped by English law, and introduced innovations). Bradford ignores the substantial body of sermons and political speeches during the colonial period in all regions of America, in which such 'abstractions' as natural law and natural rights were consistently invoked, *along with* the legal rights of Englishmen. See for example Mather 1991, on "the natural rights of Americans as men" (444) and on the English constitution as an imitation of *nature* (446).

Book-battles succeed real ones. The pick-and-choose historiography at work in *A Better Guide than Reason* defends the old Confederacy by dismissing all the American founders whose principles clearly embarrass Confederate principles, and by distorting the remainder. For example, Bradford nowhere mentions Washington's criticisms of slavery. In a letter to Bryan Fairfax dated August 24, 1774, Washington wrote, "we must assert our rights, or submit to every imposition that can be heaped upon us [by the British], till custom and use shall make us tame and abject slaves, as the blacks we rule over with such arbitrary sway" (Allen 1988, 39). This statement vindicating the equal rights of Americans as human beings and the rights of blacks as human beings, and arguing that accretions of custom can debase human nature, surely would have disqualified Washington from Bradford's list of approved American founders, had he noticed it. See also Bradford's distorted summary of Jefferson's comments on blacks in *Notes on the State of Virginia*; Bradford overlooks Jefferson's insistence on the *moral* equality of blacks and whites (51-52).

Predictably, Bradford condemns Abraham Lincoln, although it would have been hard to predict the absurdity of his condemnation. Lincoln resembles Hitler – each "a firm higher-law man" blind to the counsels of experience and the texture of history (56, n.36). Inasmuch as Lincoln won his war, and Hitler lost his, even on the level of experience and history there must have been some notable differences between the two, with Lincoln the rather more practical. As for the inability of "higher-law men" to perceive reality, and the identity of Lincoln and Hitler *as* "higher-law" men, one may note that Jesus of Nazareth also qualifies as a "higher-law man," and Bradford has no open animus against Him. The content of the higher law, not its height, proves decisive in practice.

Bradford's riposte against Lincoln's "A House Divided" speech, in which Lincoln quotes the then-familiar words of Jesus, "A house divided against itself cannot stand," gives the appearance of bluff common sense: *"Houses are always divided in some fashion or another"* (46). No doubt they are; nonetheless, divisions differ. In *The Federalist* 10, Madison distinguishes between factions (citizens "united and actuated by some common impulse of passion, or of interest, adverse to the rights of other citizens, or to the permanent and aggregate interest of the community"), and what Americans today call 'interest groups,' which normally assert their own rights and advantages within the constraints of natural and conventional law (Hamilton, Madison, and Jay 1961, 78-80).

In Matt. 12:25 and Luke II:17, Jesus says, "Any Kingdom divided against itself is laid waste; and a[ny city or] house divided against itself shall not stand [falls]." Lincoln turns "shall not" into "cannot," making this a warning based on practical observation instead of command. Jesus answers the Pharisees, who charge Him with casting out demons by demonic force, "by Beelzebub." Jesus reasons that *if* He casts out demons by demonic force, this reveals Satan's house as divided, unstable, soon to collapse. If however He casts them out "by the finger of God, then the Kingdom of God has come upon you." Lincoln refers to the United States in 1858; "I believe this government cannot endure, permanently half *slave* and half *free*"; it will not collapse but "it will cease to be divided" (Lincoln 1953, II, 461), and become either all slave or all free. The comparison of the spiritual conflict between Satan and God to the moral and political conflict between slaveholding and freedom amounts to a charge of Pharisaism against Lincoln's opponents, including the United States Supreme Court, the Democratic Party, and Stephen Douglas, who "has done all in his power to reduce the whole question of slavery to one of a mere *right of property*" (II, 468).

Bradford's pharisaical sophisms inadvertently point to difficulties with that species of conservatism taking its bearings from the rhetoric of Edmund Burke. This conservatism has many more sober practitioners than Bradford; see for example Kirk 1977, where no partisan axes grind. Still, the problems remain. Neo-Burkeans attempt to rank the American founding as one distinguished event in the vast pageant of Western civilization. This approach proves both all-encompassing and arbitrarily selective. Not the best of all that has been thought or said, but anything that has been thought or said, potentially merits inclusion, and can be made to 'merit' inclusion, because the criteria for classification as 'civilization' cannot really mean anything unless they transcend civilization or tradition. However, the *possibility* of transcending civilization or tradition remains precisely what neo-Burkeans deny. This leaves them vulnerable to arbitrary inclusions and exclusions, despite their desire to respect 'concrete' tradition.

This weakness leads to another. Typically, the celebration of tradition cannot plausibly account for real innovation. Neo-Burkeans cannot really describe the *change* from Judaism and the Roman pantheon to Christianity, although they insightfully describe the continuities. Similarly, when they see the revolution from English constitutional monarchy to American constitutional republicanism, they see constitutionalism abstracted from 'English' and 'American,' from monarchy and republicanism. Neo-Burkean conservatism abstracts continuity from history and subtracts change, trying to explain away change as mere variation on a theme; the theme itself gradually becomes so broad and vague it evanesces, leaving the intellect no criteria for judgment.

'Progressivist' liberals reverse the error, abstracting change from history and subtracting continuity. Former Supreme Court Justice William Brennan suggested the Founders' plural and allegedly contradictory intentions as points along not a tradition but a progression. This progression might have some coherence if it aimed at a fixed point, and 'end of history.' But Brennan's favored *telos*, "human dignity," will "never cease to evolve" (quoted in Jaffa 1987b) the aim of progress never stops progressing or, more accurately receding mirage-like before one's eyes. As with neo-Burkean conservatism, 'progressive' liberalism includes everything and selects anything, because its judgment runs in baggy pants. Jaffa 1987b, in an otherwise telling critique of Brennan's so-called principles, compares this Protean "human dignity" with the Marxist *Zeitgeist*. But Marx does at least sketch an eschaton, communism, positing it as an end whose "demands" will be – no demands at all (Karl Marx and Friedrich Engels, *The German Ideology* [Easton and Guddat 1967, 424-425]). Still, the Marxist definition of communism as "the *real* movement which abolishes the present state of affairs," not "an ideal to which reality [will] have to adjust" (*Ibid.*, 426) – that is, the definition of communism before the 'end of history' – does resemble progressivist liberalism, as Jaffa notes. The very bagginess of the progressivist-liberal *telos* leaves room for humaneness in practice; its theoretical incoherence lets political decency abide, under the cloak of 'pluralism.'

3. McDonald 1979, 129. In his later book, *Novus Ordo Seclorum: The Intellectual Origins of the Constitution*, McDonald expends still fewer words: "The ingredients were incompatible" (McDonald 1985, 8).

4. Selections from *Poor Richard's Almanac*, in Franklin 1987, 1208.

5. See McDonald 1985, 224-225. For a sympathetic critique of McDonald on this and other points, see Morrisey 1987. In finding contradictions in the Founders, McDonald argues that the Constitutional Convention thereby accurately reflected changeable

standards of American society: "Americans reckoned values in the market place and by consensus, unlike the Europeans, who reckoned them through traditional institutions and by absolute standards" (McDonald 1979, 17). There is no reason to suppose that a generation affirming the "self-evident" trust of "certain unalienable rights' did not reckon "values" by an absolute standard. See for example the political sermons in Sandoz 1991.

6. See Wood 1981, 3. For a much earlier expression of this view see Farrand 1913, 201.

7. Griswold 1991, 154a. One difficulty with Wood's argument concerns the status of the state constitutions. Federalists and Anti-federalists alike considered them republican. The federal Constitution left them alone – so much so that Madison proposed an amendment extending to the state constitutions guarantees of equal rights of conscience, freedom of the press, and trial by jury in criminal cases; it failed. (See Storing 1985, 19). Further, the federal Constitution's Bill of Rights, demanded by Anti-federalists and agreed to by Federalists, concerns the unalienable rights of individuals (except for the Tenth), and squarely rests on the principles of the Declaration of Independence.

Wood argues that those state constitutions instituted or reformed during the late 1780's and 1790's partook less of democracy than did the state constitutions of the 1770's. One may concede this without believing the change to be any more than one of institutional emphasis and prudence, not a fundamental departure from principles.

John Quincy Adams, who was by virtue of early childhood education in a position to know, called the 1787 Constitution "the consummation of the Declaration of Independence" (Adams 1837, 44). White 1987 also finds "no fundamental philosophical difference between the Declaration and *The Federalist*" (211).

8. Wood 1972, viii.

9. Wood 1972, 45. For a similar view see Bailyn 1967 and Lienesch 1988, 3-9. The latter is an historical relativist.

10. In *The Federalist* 14 James Madison wrote: "Is it not the glory of the people of America that, whilst they have paid a decent regard to the opinions of former times and other nations" – language deliberately echoing, and more carefully defining, the Declaration's "decent regard for the opinions of Mankind" – "they have not suffered a blind veneration for antiquity, for custom, or for names, to overrule the suggestions of their own good sense, the knowledge of their own situation, and the lessons of their own experience? To this manly spirit posterity will be indebted for the possession, and the world for the example, of the numerous innovations displayed on the American theater in favor of private rights and happiness." This "new and more noble course" went by way of "a revolution which has no parallel in the

annals of human society" (Hamilton, Madison and Jay 1961 [hereinafter cited as HMJ], 104). Alexander Hamilton goes even farther in *The Federalist* 70, "quitting the dim light of historical research, and attaching [himself] purely to the dictates of reason and good sense" (425).

Decades later, James Monroe still affirmed the genuinely revolutionary character of the American regime. "[S]urely no event can be so important, as the establishment of a new system of government, which by its intrinsic merit, and the force of its example, promises to promote so essentially the happiness of mankind." The American revolution "forms the most important epoch in the history of mankind" because "it has introduced a system of new governments better calculated to secure to the people the blessings of liberty, and under circumstances more favorable to success, than any which the world ever knew before" (Monroe 1987, 1).

The American move away from English constitutionalism and toward unmixed republican constitutionalism implied the rediscovery of human nature as distinguished from custom or convention. "Let it be remembered," Madison reminded Congress, "that it has ever been the pride and boast of America, that the rights for which she contended were the rights of human nature" (Address to Congress, April 1783, [Meyers 1973, 32]). Although the Americans aimed their immediate criticisms against the English and the American Tories, the 'left' may confuse natural right with convention as easily as does the 'right.' Madison remarked Robert Owen's utopian-socialist "New Harmony" project with good-humored irony: "Mr. Owen's remedy for [the economic] vicissitudes [of free commerce] implies that labor will be relished without the ordinary impulses to it; that the love of equality will supersede the desire of distinction; and that the increasing leisure, from the improvement of machines, will promote intellectual cultivation, more enjoyment, and innocent amusements, without any of the vicious resorts, for the ennui of idleness. Custom is properly called a second nature; Mr. Owen makes it nature herself" (Letter to Nicholas P. Trist, January 29, 1828 [Meyers 1973, 454]).

While giving somewhat more emphasis to the power of convention, Monroe nonetheless concurred with his senior colleague. "In treating... of government, we must treat of man, for it is for him that the government is formed, and for whom it is indispensable, from the aggregation of a few individuals to the most stupendous masses." Man's "natural endowments, his passions and principles, are always the same;" these are "essentially controlled by moral causes," by which Monroe means both government and civil society (Monroe 1987, 3). As does Madison, Monroe explicitly linked human nature to the need for the protection of unalienable natural rights from natural passions. "The principles and passions of men are always the same, and lead to the same result, varying only according to the circumstances in which they are placed. Self-interest is the ruling passion, whether under free or despotic governments. Highly improved and generous minds will move on a scale correspondent therewith, but a large portion of mankind will look to themselves, and turn every incident of which they may take advantage to their account. It is against these propensities that we have to guard. The principle of the government will go far to infuse a correct spirit into the body of the people, and will have great influence on those who are appointed to high and honorable trusts, provided the people perform, with judgement, their essential duties. A failure, and even a relaxation on their part, may produce the worst consequences." (69).

11. For an account of Penn's "experiment," see Janney 1871, especially 186-187. For an account of Franklin's conflict with Quaker legislators on the issue of defense see Wright 1986, 77-81.

12. *Autobiography*, in Franklin 1945, 717.

13. "The Necessity of Self-Defense," in Franklin 1987, 315.

14. Letter to Jane Mecom, November 1, 1773, in Franklin 1945, 298. Italics in original.

15. Letter to Sir Joseph Banks, July 27, 1789, in Franklin 1986, 1073.

16. Letter to Benjamin Vaughan, October 24, 1788, in Franklin 1986, 1169

17. Letter to Jan Ingehousz, January 16, 1784, in Franklin 1945, 598. Because the inventions of dynamite, the airplane, and the nuclear bomb have all elicited similar hopes, we tend to dismiss Franklin's prediction as naive. As it is. Yet one should also notice that weapons of mass destruction do rechannel war even if they do not end it, and nuclear weapons may have made 'total' wars obsolete, so far. Franklin deserves credit for discovering a partial truth, if not the plain truth.

18. Franklin 1986, 535-539.

19. Thomas Jefferson shared Franklin's view, with an interesting nuance attributable to his reservations about commercial life. Farmers, who stay at home and need no foreign commerce, make "the most virtuous and independent citizens;" they involve themselves in no wars. "But," Jefferson conceded, "the actual habits of our countrymen attach them to commerce... Wars then must sometimes be our lot; and all the wise can do, will be to avoid that half of them which would be produced by our own follies and our own acts of injustice, and to make for the other half of them the best preparations we can." Therefore (following Franklin's argument now) "our interest will be to throw open the doors of commerce, and to knock off all its shackles, given perfect freedom to all persons for the vent of whatever they may choose to bring into our ports, and asking the same in theirs. Never was so much false arithmetic employed on any subject, as that which has been employed to persuade nations that it is in their interest to go to war" (*Notes on Virginia*. Jefferson 1903, II, 240-241). At the beginning of his

presidency, Jefferson put somewhat more emphasis on statesmanship and on the cultivation of good will abroad and virtue at home than Franklin. "My hope of preserving peace for our country is not founded in the greater principles of non-resistance under every wrong, but in a belief that a just and friendly conduct on our part will procure justice and friendship from others" (Letter to the Earl of Buchan, July 10, 1803, Jefferson 1903, X, 401). Statesmanship should have recourse to war only as a last resort: "Peace is our passion.... We prefer trying *ever* other just principles, right safety, before we would recur to war" (Letter to John Sinclair, June 30, 1803, in Jefferson 1903, X, 397). In retrospect, Jefferson found less cause for optimism about the effects of American peaceableness upon other nations. But he still saw prudence in his practice, right in his principles. "It would have been perfect Quixotism to have encountered these Bedlamites, to have undertaken the redress of all wrongs against a world avowedly rejecting all regard to right. We have, therefore, remained in peace, suffering frequent injuries, but, on the whole, multiplying, improving, prospering beyond all example." As a result of this combination of interest and principle – Jefferson called it, with wry exaggeration, "our Quaker system" – "peace has saved to the world this only plant of free and rational government now existing on it." The "happiness and prosperity of our citizens" constitute "the only legitimate object of government, and the first duty of governors, and not the slaughter of men and devastation of countries placed under their care, in pursuit of a fantastic honor, unallied to virtue or happiness; or in gratification of the angry passions, or the pride on administrators, excited by personal incidents, in which their citizens have no concern" (Letter to Thaddeus Kosciusko, April 13, 1811, in Jefferson 1903, 41-43). While the Jeffersonian spirit moved on a higher plane, and was surely warmer than Franklin's ("I have ever cherished the same spirit [of peace] with all nations, from a consciousness that peace, prosperity, liberty, and morals have an intimate connection" [Letter to George Logan, in Jefferson 1903, XIII, 384]) their principles are essentially the same.

The historian Henry Adams regards these principles as reflections of American national character. "In the American character antipathy to war ranked first among political traits.... Although Jefferson carried his pacific theories to an extreme, and brought about a military reaction, the reactionary movement was neither universal, violent, nor lasting; and society showed no sign of changing its convictions" (Adams 1986, 1335-1336). For a recent account of Jeffersonian foreign policy, taking Henry Adams' views in most instances, see Tucker and Hendrickson 1990; the authors distinguish Jefferson from Hamilton more sharply than is necessary; for commentary see Morrisey, 1991. It is at least as probable that prominent Americans (including Jefferson and Franklin) deliberately appealed to, and strengthened, the peaceful inclinations of the American people in the course of the founding.

20.   "The Morals of Chess," in Franklin 1986, 928. Evidence of Franklin's republicanism in chess comes down to us in anecdotal form. Jeremy Bentham recalled a game in a French café. Franklin was losing, but

simply took his opponent's King off the board and pocketed it. As his opponent began to object, Franklin said, "Sir, continue, and we shall soon see that the party without a King will win the game" (Meador 1986, 11). I am indebted to Professor Diana Schaub for bringing this article to my attention. For a republican soldier's contempt for and indignation at an aristocratic or pseudoaristocratic view of war, see Haskell 1958, 32, 109.

21. "General Orders," July 9, 1776, in Allen 1988, 73.

22. "[I]t is doing the people called Quakers no more than justice to say, that (except their declining to share with others the burden of the common defense) there is no denomination among us, who are more exemplary and useful citizens." Washington hoped that "the laws may always be as extensively accommodated to [the conscientious scruples of all men], as a due regard to the protection and essential interests of the nation may justify a permit" ("To the Annual Meeting of Quakers," October 1789, in Allen 1987, 534). The problem of religious warfare will subside as this spirit of toleration − not absolute, but subordinate to national preservation − pervades the society, encouraged by the first President. Contrast Hershberger 1951: "The few Mennonites left in Russia after the [Bolshevik] Revolution seem to have succumbed to the Communist theory, or to have been annihilated" (8).

23. That Washington did not simply expect this result may be seen by the context: "...I cannot avoid reflecting with pleasure on the probable influence that commerce may hereafter have on human manners and society in general. On these occasions I consider how mankind may be connected like one great family in fraternal ties. I indulge a fond, perhaps an enthusiastic idea that as the world is evidently much less barbarous than it has been, its melioration must still be progressive; that nations are becoming more humanized in their policy, that the subjects of ambition and causes for hostility are daily diminishing, and, in fine, that period is not very remote, when the benefits of a liberal and free commerce will, pretty generally, succeed to the devastations and horrors of war." (Letter to Marquis de Lafayette, August 15, 1786), in Allen 1987, 326.

24. "Fifth Annual Message," December 3, 1793, in Allen 1987, 488. Italics added. Notice that Washington did not appeal so much to commercial shrewdness, as did Franklin, but more directly to the clearly perceived need for defense of commerce. Not only will commerce help bring peace; peace will enhance commerce, and peace depends upon military preparedness.

25. Americans "should guard against ambition as against their greatest enemy. We should not, in imitation of some nations which have been celebrated for a false kind of patriotism [he was thinking of Rome, and probably Britain], wish to aggrandize our Republic at the expense of the freedom and happiness of the rest of mankind" ("First Draft of the First Inaugural." April 1789. Allen 1987, 455).

26. "Universal Peace," *National Gazette,* January 312, 1792, in Madison 1962-, XIV, 206-208; *See also The Federalist* 43, on "universal peace" (HMJ 1961, 277). Notice that Madison evinced even more cynicism than Franklin. Whereas Franklin (himself a businessman) regarded success in commerce not a matter of avarice or greed, but a moderate calculating desire for gain, Madison had two passions counteracting each other, with reason, otherwise weak, thus getting its chance to rule. In a much more high-toned statement, Madison claimed that universal freedom of commerce "presents the most noble spectacle, unites all nations, − makes [every man] a citizen of the whole society of mankind − and perfects the good aimed at by the social union and Civil Government." Universal commercial intercourse would establish internal security "by abolishing the causes of external violence and making it [the] interest of all to maintain the peace of all" (Madison, 1912, XII, 68.

Stuart 1982 rejects Madison's argument as "a flight of rhetorical fancy" instancing "the republican myth on war" (65-66). Stuart cites as counter-examples to this myth the several wars the United States engaged in during the period 1776-1815. He fails to notice that only one of these, the one historians call the "Quasi-War" with France of 1797-1801, could be described as a war against a republic. See Nash 1968 for a (necessarily brief) military history; two years into the 'war,' a U.S. Navy captain could capture a French ship and report that his counterpart professed no knowledge of the war: "The French Captain tells me I have caused a War with France; if so I am glad of it, for I detest things being done in Halves." (107)

More plausibly, Stuart argues that the mutual suspicions of the American Federalists (particularly Hamilton) and the Democratic-Republicans (particularly Jefferson) included suspicions of war plans. Hamilton suspected that Jefferson wanted war with England, while Jefferson suspected Hamilton wanted war with France. It is important to add that, on Jefferson's side at least, these suspicions reflected extreme skepticism with respect to the rival party's fidelity to American republicanism itself. The regime question was very much involved.

Stuart follows the highly polemical contentions of Hamlin 1927, who practically denies that defensive wars occur at all, anywhere. The claim of defensiveness constitutes "the war myth of every country" (9). Hamlin discusses six major United States wars, straining to apportion blame equally to both sides in some cases, while squarely blaming the United States in some others. He nowhere finds an American war against another republic, although he implies as much in claiming that both sides in the Civil War "fought to defend the Constitution" (53). Hamlin's arguments are vitiated by historical and cognitive relativism, which allows him to evade questions of political justice − e.g., were the Confederate States right to defend the Dred Scott decision?

27. "Spirit of Governments," *National Gazette*, February 18, 1792, in Madison 1962-,XIV, 233-234. The title of course echoes Montesquieu's *Spirit of the Laws*.

28. "Message to Congress," December 5, 1815, in Meyers ed. 1973, 388. In this message Madison defended Washingtonian as distinguished from Jeffersonian policies for military preparedness — specifically, the need for a disciplined, national army, and, tacitly the need to rely less on the militia. Whereas Jefferson feared a strong national army as a potential instrument of oppression, Madison appealed to the war experience as evidence for the need to enable the political authority of the Union to employ the physical power of the union "promptly and effectually...in the cases designated by the Constitution" (385) — a frequent theme of Washington as both general and president.

29. Monroe 1987 followed Madison in this. Internally, despotism presents a "gloomy" spectacle of "degradation and oppression," whereby the people are "deprived of opportunities of displaying those noble and generous qualities which do honor to the human race." "High qualities are needed" *by the government*. Externally, despotism is a military-imperial menace (70).

30. See Pangle 1988, 278-279: "America is not a traditional society, and therefore its patriotism must be of a strikingly untraditional kind. To a perhaps unparalleled degree, this nation is founded on the contention that patriotism must express more than simply loyalty to one's own, that it must also express loyalty to what is good, and some truly self-conscious awareness of the possible tension between what is one's own and the good....[W]e may rightly assert that what distinguishes American patriotism, in the sense of setting it apart from and above most previous forms of patriotism, is the sternness of its challenge to the *minds* of citizens old and young. American life does not impose moral tests as harsh as those imposed by earlier, and in many ways nobler, republics; it does not require as frequent or as regular sacrifices of life, property, private liberty, and ease; but it calls each and all of us to an intellectual probity, to an education in the great texts of political philosophy, to a quest for self-knowledge as a people, that is perhaps unprecedented."

Dumm 1987 sees some of this, judging it in a much more alarmed (not to say alarmist) manner, as an attempt to "discipline" the minds of citizens. Madison clearly considered republicanism as an attempt to liberate minds, and he thus resembled the thinkers of the Enlightenment. He differed from them, however, in his strong insistence on the permanent power of human passions, and for that reason does not fall into their utopianism.

Compare these scholarly assessments with John Quincy Adams' response to attacks on the American regime by British opinion journals in the 1820's: "In this *warfare of the mind* which we are compelled to maintain, in defense of the character of our country, I hope you will consider me as a follower and a fellow laborer of your own" (Letter to Robert Walsh, Jr., July 10, 1821, in Adams 1913, VII, 116). Italics added.

31.   *The Federalist* 29, HMJ 1961, 208.

32.   *The Federalist* 6 and 7. HMJ 1961, 54-65. John Jay concurred in Hamilton's judgment in *The Federalist* 5. His analogy of North American prospects to European history has no firmer logical foundation.

33.   See John Jay: *The Federalist* 3 and 4. HMJ 1961, 41-45. For further discussion see Tarcov 1990, 102-106; for an opinion contrasting to the argument above, see Garrity, 1987, 87-88.

34.   Letter to John Bannister, April 21, 1778, in Allen 1988, 101. Thomas Jefferson expressed similar views some years later with respect to the Barbary pirates: "[I]t would be best to effect a peace through the medium of war" (Letter to John Adams, July 11, 1786, in Cappon 1954, I, 142).

35.   Letter to Bryan Fairfax, July 20, 1774, in Allen 1988, 35-36. The revolutionary character of the principle, "No taxation without representation," overlooked today, was fully appreciated by English monarchists of the time. Lind 1776 saw that "to have uncontrolled power of legislation, is to be independent" (15); colonists have no right to representation in Parliament under the British Constitution, and to call for representation merely bespeaks the ambition of damagogues playing to a populace of would-be tax evaders (23-32, 64-70). Also see Boucher 1967b, xvi, xxvii 405-427, 435-436 and Boucher 1899, 48-49. The theory of government of the Declaration is "as absurd and visionary, as the system of conduct in defense of which it is destablished, is nefarious," and would be "subversive to every actual or imaginable kind of Government" (119). Also see Boucher 1967b, 504-555. Lind claimed that government exists at the expense of life, liberty, and the pursuit of happiness, not to secure them. To war and to coerce means the end of such rights; government requires the ability to war and to coerce; ergo, securing such rights would make government impossible (120-122). Hutcheson 1776 also derided the Declaration's "absurd notions of government" (10), and argued that the English Constitution did not link taxation to representation (23); Boucher 1967b did the same (xlv). The Declaration commits "the absurdity [of] making the *governed* to be the *governors*" (Hutchinson 1776, 32); Boucher 1967b predicted an American despotism soon after the establishment of a republic (lvi-lvii). More than sixty years later, John Quincy Adams wrote, "The history of mankind had never before furnished an example of a government directly and expressly constituted upon [the] principle of a popular sovereignty" subordinate only to "moral obligations" enunciated in "the laws of Nature's God" (Adams 1837, 20, 24). Boucher 1899 deplored this novelty; after the Revolution he moderated his criticisms, hoping that President

Washington would effectively reconstitute a 'British' order in America (Boucher 1967a, *passim*). In France, a violent monarchist insisted that because "there has never been a large republic before" it was "impossible" to establish one now (Maistre 1974, 65, 67). For a scholarly statement of the problem see Mansfield 1989, xv. Edmund Burke avoided any denunciation of American principles and attempted a reconciliation of American self-government with British imperialism by an appeal to established practices (Burke 1887, II, 9-77, 120-133). Burke's remarks, added to the evidently sincere public and private statements of the Founders themselves stand as the best refutation of Caton 1988, with his accusations of "monumental hypocrisy" on the part of the Founders (353-357).

36.   Letter to Bryan Fairfax, August 24, 1774, in Allen 1988, 39.

37.   "To the Inhabitants of the Island of Bermuda," September 9, 1775, in Allen 1988, 45. Sidney 1990 affirms that "peace is only to valued which is accompanied with justice" (II, iv, 160).

38.   Letter to George Mason, April 5, 1769, in Allen 1988, 23. As a Congressman in the 1790's, as Jefferson's Secretary of State, and even in the first term of his presidency, James Madison urged a policy of commercial measures, primarily tariffs and boycotts, "as an intermediate experiment between negotiation and war" ("Political Observations," April 20, 1795, in Meyers 1973, 296). Such measures worked no better than they have done in subsequent centuries. As with his support for the militia, Madison finally returned to a Washingtonian policy. For a detailed account and a critique of the Jefferson-Madison policy, see Tucker and Hendrickson 1990, 19-21, 28-31, 205-228, 255.

39.   The *Resolution* of Independence, submitted to the Continental Congress by Richard Henry Lee, had been adopted on July 2, 1776. See Hazelton 1906.

40.   Tarcov 1985, 106. Becker 1942 anticipates Tarcov's argument. The Declaration's "major premise...is that every 'people' has a natural right to make and unmake its own government; the minor premise is that the Americans are a 'people' in this sense. In establishing themselves in America, the people of the colonies exercised their natural rights to frame governments suited to their ideas and conditions, while consenting to allegiance to the English king, a consent rescindable if the King violated their natural rights as men and their constitutional rights as Englishmen. Tarcov goes on to associate lives, labor, and fortune with the mutual pledge, at the end of the Declaration, of lives, fortunes, and sacred honor. This is as much a contrast as a comparison, however, because sacred honor need not have anything to do with labor. Nonetheless individuals in the state of nature who form a civil society by means of a social contract might be considered honor-bound to maintain the contract.. A prudent regard for self-preservation is the principal motivation to establish and maintain the

contract; perhaps a sense of honor also supplies needed additional support, after the contract has existed for some time, and memories of the urgent necessity of its establishment grow dim. The question then becomes, To what extent does honor, a refined spiritedness, take an independent status? Tarcov himself supplies the necessary counterbalance to his 'reductionist' conception of politics; see Tarcov 1988. See also Sidney 1990, II, v, 98-99, who supplies historical examples of consent-founded governments.

41.   Some two decades later, Madison wrote: "The fundamental principle of the revolution was, that the colonies were coordinate members with each other, and with Great Britain, of an empire united by a common executive sovereign, but not united by any common legislative sovereign. The legislative power was maintained to be as complete in each American Parliament, as in the British Parliament." The English common law was not binding in America, although of course American legislatures adopted many of the principles of English common law. At the same time, civil society in America never dissolved; American legislatures remained intact, despite the King's actions. See Madison, *Report of the Committee to Whom were Referred the Communications of the Various States, Relative to the Resolutions of the last General Assembly of this State, Concerning the Alien and Sedition Laws*, in Meyers 1973, 316-317.

42.   See, for example, Thomas Jefferson, Letter to Peter Carr, August 10, 1787, in Jefferson 1903, VI, 257. Neither Jefferson nor any of the other principal Founders went so far as to call human beings naturally political, as does Aristotle.

43.   Bradford 1979 baselessly claims that the Declaration's appeal to self-evidentness refers strictly to "common reasonableness" within "the tradition of English law," and "not philosophy." The Declaration merely "completed a conversation concerning the law which had gone back and forth across the Atlantic for many years" (37), a claim that fails to account for the Declaration's stated audience, mankind. One of Bradford's heroes, John Adams, wrote that the Declaration contained "the Reasons which will justify [this mighty Revolution], in the sight of God and Man" [Letter to Abigail Adams, July 3, 1776, in Adams 1851, I, 230]. Wills 1978 sees that the self-evident truths of the Declaration are not self-evident in Locke's sense, thereby independently confirming Eidelberg 1976: "In *An Essay Concerning Human Understanding* (I, ii, 18), only simple ideas, ideas of sensation, are said to be self-evident, e.g., '*White is not* black,' or '*A square is not a circle.*' Ideas such as 'unalienable rights' are far too complex to be self-evident for Locke. Hence it is misleading to regard the Declaration as a Lockean document" (113, n.3). Eidelberg also cites the *Essay* at II, xxviii, 5: "good or evil is drawn on us from the will and power of the law-maker," which may well mean, as Eidelberg concludes, that Locke believes justice to be purely conventional. In the Declaration justice is not conventional. For a left-of-center version of Bradford's argument see Miller 1991, 193-216.

Jaffa 1978 cites a different passage in Locke, *The Essay [on] Civil Government*, 2, 4, where Locke asserts there is "nothing more evident" than that "creatures of the same species and rank...should be equal amongst another without subordination and subjection" (108). (See also Jaffa 1987a, 6). Sidney, it should be added, concurred fully: "Nothing can be more evident than that if many had been created, they had all been equal unless God had given preference to one" (Sidney 1990, I, vii, 24). None of these writers cites both passages and attempts to explain this apparent contradiction in Locke's thought. Thomas Jefferson and Benjamin Franklin, who served on the drafting committee and produced the Declaration, knew both books. Whatever the significance of the contradiction in Locke (a sensible analysis would begin by noting the more philosophic character of *An Essay Concerning Human Understanding*, the more political character of the *Essay [on] Civil Government*), the Signers endorse the 'political' conception of self-evidentness, not the philosophic.

The philosophic conception of self-evidentness, founded upon Locke's well-known contention that the human mind by nature is a *tabula rasa*, comports badly with the Signers' conception of human beings as naturally social animals. A *tabula rasa* has no natural capacity to attempt social relations; according to this thesis, society occurs by chance, and speech is purely conventional or artificial. This view also legitimates propagandistic speech, as one can write anything on a blank slate with no damage to the slate. The Signers by contrast assert that naturally social human beings are made for speech and civil society; the self-evident truths of the Declaration are moral and social truths. Self-evident truths are compatible with the Scriptural concept of conscience, as well as the 'moral sense' teachings of such well-known eighteenth century thinkers as Francis Hutcheson and Thomas Reid, cited by Wills. Wills calls this a "communitarian morality," but this goes too far (Wills 1978, 184); society need not partake of communitarianism, may indeed contain competing elements, without failing to be social.

Jaffa 1965 offers a somewhat different reading. "A self-evident truth is not one which everyone necessarily admits to be true; it is one the evidence for which is contained within the terms of the proposition and which is admitted to be true by everyone who already grasps the meaning of the terms" (177). In this he may follow Sidney 1990, III, xxvi on "axioms" (466). The meaning of any term is based upon abstraction, in the non-pejorative sense, the mind's ability to perceive the general about particulars — 'tree' in the many objects that exist with leaves, branches, trunk, roots. "Freedom of thought is not freedom to deny that two and two is four" (178). Once one grasps the meaning of the abstractions, 'two' and 'four,' the proposition "Two and two is four," is self-evident. This interpretation of self-evidentness opens the Declaration to a meaning that includes Lockean self-evidence but goes beyond it to include Aristotelian logic. There is no evidence to suggest that the Founders intended this broader meaning.

Nonetheless, Jaffa's suggestion points the way toward a defense of the Declaration that does not presuppose acceptance of the Signers' epistemology.

Epstein 1984, 117 remarks Madison's willingness (in *The Federalist* 37) to publicly admit the uncertainty of human perceptions and the ambiguities of language in expressing ideas. Here, Madison's rhetorical purpose was not to affirm shared convictions but to encourage reasoned consideration of the proposed Constitution and to urge patience in interpreting its difficult passages.

Thurow 1976 asks, "What happens if the axioms [or propositions, the word with which Lincoln replaced "self-evident truths"] do not become obvious to everyone?" (74). In Lincoln's time, the equality of "all men are created equal" seemed questionable. In ours, one might add, "all men are created" has seemed more questionable to intellectuals than equality has.

44.   For a discussion of James Wilson's political thought, see Carey 1987. Benjamin Franklin prudently reserved his opinion of Jesus for a private letter written near the end of his life. See Letter to Ezra Stiles, March 9, 1790, in Franklin 1987, 1179-1180. Jefferson wrote, "I am a Christian, in the only sense in which he wished any one to be; sincerely attached to his doctrines, in preference to all others; ascribing to himself every *human* excellence; and believing he never claimed any other." Such details of the New Testament account as the Immaculate Conception and the Resurrection, Jefferson classified as intended or unintended falsehoods by "unlettered and ignorant men." See Letter to Benjamin Rush, April 21, 1803, in Jefferson 1944, 566-570.

For a useful description of how the combination of Christianity and modern political philosophy worked out in one instance, see Dumm 1987, 88-112, on Benjamin Rush's concept of the penitentiary. As seen in the Walnut Street Jail in Philadelphia, the penitentiary used the solitary confinement of criminals as a means of forcing them to re-enact the state of nature, in which labor and civil society look desirable. Rush expected this to reverse anti-social behavior.

Rush's most enthusiastic theoretical formulation of the Christian-modern combination came in a letter to Charles Nisbet: The United States combines "the Kingdom of Christ and the empire of reason and science" (Rush 1951, I, 339). See, however, the eleventh article of the 1796 treaty between the United States and Tripoli: "the government of the United States is not in any sense founded on the Christian religion" (Straus 1887, 68). 'Scriptural' rather than 'Christian' principles prevail. For a theoretical account of the Scriptural and philosophic foundations of the American regime, which does not lose sight of political experience, see Jaffa 1965, 117-122. See also Straus 1887, 26-51, and Destro 1986, 360.

For an example of the confusion that results from failing to see that "All men are created equal" means their endowment with certain unalienable rights, see Kendall 1989. Kendall describes this phrase as "meaningless," closing his eyes to the immediately subsequent clause. He then imagines that the Preamble to the Constitution of 1787, by citing union, justice, domestic tranquility, the common defense, and the blessings of liberty − but not equality − amounts to "an express repudiation of the Declaration's creed that might seem to commit us somehow to equality" (32-33). Define "created equal" as endowment by God of certain unalienable rights, and the problem dissolves. The Constitution, which constitutes a government, seeks to *secure* unalienable rights; it does so by forming a more perfect union, establishing justice, insuring domestic tranquility, providing for the common defense, and so on. Paine 1961 clearly distinguishes natural from civil rights while arguing for the just Foundation of the latter upon the former (306-307). See also Lutz, 1989, 73-79, and Williams 1991, 56.

45. Jaffa 1978 observes that Nature and Nature's God govern but do not create, whereas the Creator-God creates but does not govern (133). "No interpretation of the Declaration which fails to link the God of Nature...with the Creator... can succeed" (108). Jaffa is right to criticize scholars who call the Declaration a Christian document, and to say that the references to Nature and Nature's God bespeak "natural, not...revealed theology" (35). Jaffa does not on this page emphasize the immediately following references to the Creator-God, but these do not presuppose Christianity, either, although they are entirely consistent with it.

Pangle 1988, 21-24 too strongly emphasizes the Declaration's "appeal to the God of Nature rather than to the God of Scripture," thus missing the subtlety of the appeal to both scriptural and modern teachings. Were the Founders, he asks, "not engaged in an attempt to exploit and transform Christianity in the direction of a liberal rationalism?" The sane reply is: Some were, some were not, and there were various degrees to which those that were so committed judged this possible or desirable.

Anastaplo 1789 observes that the Declaration's references to God mirror the Constitution's tripartite division of government: God as legislator, God as judge, God as executive (21).

46. See Hobbes 1962, Pt. I, Ch. 15, on the ninth law of nature, and compare with Pt. I, Ch. 16, on consent. The purpose of consent to despotism is individual and civil security. There is no right to change the form of government, as the sovereign despot is the only legitimate judge of actions and doctrines. Without despotism no civil peace endures (Pt. II, Ch.18).

47. One striking incident of the collaboration of Christian and modern-philosophic statesmanship to settle a potentially divisive religio-

political issue occurred in Virginia in 1784. The Virginia Assembly considered a bill to establish a provision for teachers of religion; if passed, this would have amounted to a religious establishment. James Madison opposed the measure, writing his famous petition "Memorial and Remonstrance." This petition was successful, but "another, still anonymous, petition, based on the fervently Christian argument that the bill contravened the spirit of the Gospel, ran up more than three times as many signatures" (Brann 1984, 13).

On the epistemological link between the perception of self-evident truth and morality, Jaffa observes, "Political freedom would be meaningless if there were not moral freedom, and moral freedom would be meaningless if we were moved to action merely by sense perception, memory, and imagination.... Moral freedom must be based upon a metaphysical freedom of the mind that moves from mere sense perception to reason and from reason to moral choice the comparison of alternative courses of action that constitute moral freedom must follow from a fundamental comparison of ideas. In this comparison, the human mind makes a judgment as to the correspondence of abstract ideas with concrete phenomena" (Jaffa 1987b, 431).

This view contrasts with that of Will 1983, who claims that the Founders viewed moral opinions as strictly irrational: "the modern idea of liberty is grounded on necessity, in the sweep of the strongest passions. Modernity makes a virtue of necessity (and in the process makes a poor thing of the idea of virtue)" (42). Two extreme on the other side are Combee 1988, who claims that "the rock-bottom consensus in Colonial America was a biblical consensus" (88), and Maritain 1957, who calls the United States Constitution "an outstanding lay Christian document tinged with the philosophy of the day" (183).

Jefferson wrote that "the true fountains of evidence [are] in the head and heart of every rational and honest man. It is there [that] nature has written her moral laws" ("Opinion on the question whether the United States have a right to renounce their treaties with France..." April 18, 1793, in Jefferson 1944, 317-319). This "sense of duty" or "moral instinct" is "given to all human beings in a stronger or weaker degree" (Letter to Peter Carr, August 10, 1787, in Jefferson 1903, VI, 257). Notice that Jefferson, when speaking for himself, directly associated natural law with the individual's moral instinct.

For an account of Jefferson's conception of Nature and Nature's God, see Miller 1988, 180 ff., who tries to distinguish natural laws from natural right on the basis of the greater generality of natural laws. Natural laws govern all of nature, whereas natural rights govern human nature only and thus form a subspecies of natural law. It would be more precise to say that God-endowed unalienable rights inhere in *individual* human beings; natural laws, in the Declaration, govern human beings in the collective capacity as peoples. Miller rightly observes that Jefferson rejects Hobbes' contention that relations among peoples are warlike, that the state of nature is a state of war. The "law of nature *and* nation" is a frequent Jeffersonian phrase, and it refers to peaceful or social relations.

John Quincy Adams insisted upon the indispensability of both Christianity and unalienable rights in the maintenance of peace. The atheism of French revolutionists in the 1790's contributed to despotism, because "the transition from infidelity to fanaticism is as easy and as natural as that from unbounded democracy to despotism, a transition of which France is exhibiting" (Adams 1913, III, 427). If the rights to life, liberty, and the pursuit of happiness "are inalienable, they are incompatible with the rights of the victor to take the life of his enemy in war, or to spare his life and make him a slave. If this principle is sound, it reduces to brute force all the rights of man" and "assum[es] that the natural state of man is *War*." The atheistic and despotic doctrine of Hobbes is "equally disclaimed and rejected by the philosopher and the Christian" (Adams 1841, 88-89). See also Adams 1837, 57-62. And see Webster 1991 and Thayer 1991.

48.   Jaffa 1978, 60. Jaffa also observes that America is the first "great political community," as distinguished from a religious community, not to have a myth of autochthony; the natural rights of man as man, not of Americans as Americans, underlie this regime (Jaffa 1965, 130).

49.   By emphasizing naturally and divinely ordained laws governing peoples, the unalienable rights of all human individuals, and the reliance of individuals upon governments to secure those rights, the Signers emphasized politics, and said less than a philosopher might have done about *society*. James Monroe offered a more balanced, better articulated picture than the Signers could do; Monroe did not write against the pressure of events. "All men," Monroe wrote, "are by nature equally free. Their Creator made them so." Man in a state of nature is "at liberty to do what he pleases"; he is "rude, unlettered, and unrestrained." This state is rare, because "Man is by nature a sociable being, and pursuing the impulse derived from nature, clings to his fellow-man." Primitive civil society does have government — given human nature's persistent failings all societies need government. Simple government confines itself "principally to the protection of the virtuous against the vicious, the weak against the strong." In such societies, (Monroe specifically mentioned the American Indian) "the ruler, if there be one, is rather the instrument of the society, than that the members in it are his slaves." (In this Monroe finds confirmation in the studies of Amerindian tribes conducted in the last two decades by anthropologists. See Clastres 1987). In order to achieve "well organized, free, representative government" a civil society's 'civilization' needs to occur; that is, it needs first to grow, thus achieving a social and economic diversity requiring a more forceful government unfortunately tend to despotism. Even the ancient republics, what Aristotle calls mixed regimes, eventually declined into despotism, "overwhelmed by the warlike spirits." But civilization

advances; education elevates the minds of citizens, and property gives them responsibility in management of affairs beyond the household. *Only force can overthrow despotism, the rule of force.* But the successful institution of a popular government requires civilization as well as force: intelligence, private property, independence and morality. Essential to decent popular revolutions is statesmanship: they can succeed "provided that those who take the lead, act with moderation and humanity. Violence and cruelty will be sure to defeat any attempt that will be made." Monroe had seen first hand both the American and the French revolutions, and so spoke with the authority of experience. (Monroe 1987, 24-33).

50.   The Founders followed Sidney 1990, I, x-xi; II, i-vi; III, xxxi. See Jaffa 1965, 176 and Jaffa 1978, 42. See also Epstein 1984 for the contrast between rational consent and "the irregular methods of ancient foundings, where a single lawgiver like Lycurgus used force, superstition, and suicide to initiate his laws" (39). As the civility of civil society advances, government by a more and more rational consent becomes more possible. And see Tarcov 1989, 85.

In the generation after the American Founders, none understood this better than John Quincy Adams. In his *Letters of Publicola*, published during the French Revolution, Adams sharply criticized Thomas Paine for calling "the rights of the majority" unalienable, instead of the rights of human nature (Adams 1913, I, 109). "The principle, that a whole nation has a right to do whatever it pleases, cannot in any sense be admitted as true. The eternal and immutable laws of justice and of morality are paramount to all human legislation" (70). Power does not mean rights − else there could be no right to undertake a revolution. Years later in front of an audience of townspeople in Newburyport, Massachusetts, Adams reaffirmed this principle, holding that natural rights "beyond the reach of organized human power" (Adams 1837, 26), including democracy.

For an example of the difficulties that ensue from the celebration of popular sovereignty with respect for unalienable rights subtracted, see Cooper 1826. Rejecting the equality of unalienable rights, Cooper nonetheless wanted to save "civil liberty," to find for it "another basis" (5). He could not equate might with right, so he did the next thing to it: he equated right with the "happiness" of the people, as it happens to be defined by them at any given time. Therefore, "public utility [is] the criterion by which every law is to be tested" (9). "If any doubt requires to be cleared, go to the people" (21). A South Carolinian, Cooper sought to defend slavery on the basis of a utilitarian version of popular sovereignty − this, decades before Stephen Douglas ran afoul of Abraham Lincoln by playing precisely the same sophistical gambit.

51.   For the *locus classicus* of this view see Sidney 1990, I, i, 8-10. Mansfield 1978 stresses the Declaration's insistence on *individual* rights, underlying the consent of individuals to the just powers of government. Inasmuch as individuality (if not individua*lism*) underlies

reasoning (a group taken as a whole never reasons, although of course individuals within the group may reason together), this insistence was necessary to uphold reasoned self-government, which also entails the reasoned government of oneself. This does not necessarily entail individual*ism*, because reasoning does well to acquire one or more partners, for dialogue (in philosophy) or deliberation (in politics). On the relation between human sociality and reasonableness, especially political reasonableness, see Eidelberg 1976, 6-11. See also Murray 1960, 13, 32-33, 105, 130.

52. "Opinion upon the question whether the President should veto the Bill, declaring that the seat of government be transferred to the Potomac in the year 1790," in Jefferson 1903, III, 60.

53. Becker 1942 claims the Declaration "formulates, in general terms, a democratic political philosophy" (17); this is true only if one takes those terms to be very general indeed. Wood 1972 and Hofstadter 1948, especially 3-17, argue for the democratic character of the Declaration. For a more subtle view see Eidelberg 1976: "We...see in the Declaration a mixture or synthesis of democratic and aristocratic principles, anticipating the 'mixed regime' reflected in the American Constitution" (70n). Also see Lang and Russell, 1991, 7.

54. Robert Goldwin recounts James Madison's later argument that independence from England did not hurl Americans into a state of nature. Civil society remained, the American legislatures remained. The King had been tyrannical, and his overthrow removed *an impediment to* civil society. See Goldwin 1987. For the opposite view, without much supporting evidence, see J. Q. Adams, *Letters of Publicola*, in Adams 1913, I, 73.

55. HMJ 1961, 314. Madison went on to argue, "In a nation of philosophers, this consideration ought to be disregarded. A reverence for the laws would be sufficiently inculated by the voice of an enlightened reason. But a nation of philosophers is as little to be expected as the philosophical race of kings wished for by Plato. And in every other nation, the most rational government will not find it a superfluous advantage to have the prejudices of he community on its side." Madison acknowledged two kinds of reason. Philosophic reason transcends custom, but sees the purposes behind wise custom. Citizen or community reasonableness is primarily moderation and respect for law. It is this latter kind of reasonableness that Abraham Lincoln would strengthen in his "Address Before the Young Men's Lyceum of Springfield, Illinois." "[A]lthough bad laws, if they exist, should be repealed as soon as possible, still while they continue in force, for the sake of example, they should be religiously observed"; "if not too intolerable," they should be endured until change can be effected (Lincoln 1952, I, 112-113) − words that echo this sentence of the Declaration.

56. John Locke, *An Essay [on] Civil Government*, XIX, in Locke 1965, 460-464. The Declaration confirms Locke's assurances that the right of revolution will not be invoked too frequently. See also *An Essay Concerning Human Understanding*, I, 2: "I have always thought the actions of men the best interpreters of their thought" (Locke 1959, 67). Becker 1942 finds this procedure troubling, at least as applied by John Dickinson in his influential analysis of Parliamentary edicts, *Letters from a Farmer in Pennsylvania to the Inhabitants of the British Colonies*, first published in 1767 in the aftermath of the Townshend Acts collecting duties in American ports. Dickinson looked at the intentions of the lawmakers to determine the law's purposes, and at the nature of the law to determine these intentions. Becker calls this "reasoning in a circle" (95). This would be true if the nature of an act or series of acts were *identical* to the intention of the actor. But Locke and the Signers considered acts *revelatory* of intention. Such commonsense conclusions occur in everyone's life, every day. They are not infallible: they are necessary.

57. Letter to Thomas Law, Esq., June 13, 1814, in Jefferson 1903, XIV, 141-142.

58. Becker 1942, 18-22. In *An Essay [on] Civil Government*, Locke distinguishes *unsurpation*, the exercise of a power that another person has a right to, from *tyranny*, the exercise of a power no one can have a right to (XVIII, in Locke 1965, 446). The Declaration's mention of injuries *and* usurpations follows Locke.

59. Eidelberg 1974, 444-445.

60. John Locke, *An Essay [on] Civil Government*, XIX, has several parallel passages (Locke 1965, 461-462, 464-465, 473-475).

61. Tarcov 1988 asks, "How can men give their lives to secure their rights to life?" (142). He argues that spiritedness (what the ancient Greeks called *thumos*), the 'manly' high-heartedness or righteous indignation that cries, "Give me liberty or give me death?" spurs men to risk life — as the desire for comfortable self-preservation cannot. The most civilized form of spiritedness is honor; thus "we can understand more clearly how the Declaration of Independence could culminate in a pledge of sacred honor" (146).

For the classical political philosophers — particularly Plato, Aristotle, Cicero — spiritedness constitutes a necessary psychological element of political element. (See Plato, *The Republic*, 375 a-e, 439e-441e; Aristotle, *Politics* VII, 7; Cicero, *The Republic*, V, iv-viii). This changes with Augustine, who classifies regimes on the basis of the desires they attempt to satisfy (see Augustine 1966 XIX, 231-237). Although not devoid of any concept of honor, Hobbes and Locke follow Augustine more than the classics in this matter.

Tarcov argues that the spiritedness of the Declaration's defense of unalienable rights differentiates it from the doctrines of modern political philosophers. Any attempt to link the Declaration to the classics must proceed along these lines to a considerable degree. Any attempt to link the 1787 Constitution to the classics must follow the suggestion of John Quincy Adams in *Letters of Publicola*: "Many of the laws which are in use to this day in Great Britain, and from thence have been adopted by the American Republics" — e.g., trial by jury — "may be traced back to the remotest period of antiquity" (Adams 1913, I. 87).

Part of the difference between a Thomas Jefferson and a John Locke may well amount simply to the psychological difference between a statesman and a philosopher — the one active and spirited, the other by nature full of daring thought but physically cautious.

62. See Locke, *An Essay [on] Civil Government*, III, in Locke 1965, 321. For the King's purpose under the English Constitution, see Bagehot 1968, 284.

63. Dallas 1815, 34-37. Several lines in this document parallel the Declaration of Independence; see especially pp. 41-51.

64. Thomas Jefferson, Letter to John Adams, October 28, 1813, in Jefferson 1903, XIII, 402. Given the universal character of he rights protected by the American regime, it cannot be the European-ness of these *canaille*, but their character as *canaille*, that prevents them from securing their own unalienable rights in a representative government. *Canaille* in America would have the same corrupting effect, and their presence here would begin a race between the reform of their character and the corruption of republican government. The clergy of the founding era understood this; see for example Colman 1991, *passim*; Sewall 1991, *passim*.

65. See Anastaplo 1986, 1418. As noted above, Anastaplo connects the legislative, judicial, and executive powers of God to the corresponding powers of human government seen in the United States Constitution.

66. Eidelberg 1976, 102-103. Professor Eidelberg and I have borrowed from one another, here. See Wood 1987 for a somewhat different argument — that the Founders deliberately established a democratic regime that would, they foresaw, make such aristocrats as themselves never to be seen again in government.

67. Thomas Jefferson, Letter to John Adams, October 28, 1813, in Jefferson 1903, XIII, 401.

68. James Madison, Letter to Thomas Jefferson, February 8, 1825, in Meyers 1973, 444-445. James Monroe concurred. John Locke, Montesquieu, and Algernon Sidney advocate mixed regimes, admiring the English Constitution above all. Therefore, although Monroe

applauded Locke's critique of Filmer's 'divine-right' monarchism, and Locke's tracing of "the origin of government to its true source the consent of the people and the equal rights of all," he found "little" in Locke "other than the support which he gives to the general cause of liberty, which can be considered applicable to us." The Declaration of Independence, Monroe continued, follows Locke in asserting "the right of the people to change their government at pleasure, and to punish those who violate the laws" (Monroe 1987, 60-61).

Monroe also looked to the structure of the American regime as the primary day-to-day guardian of Americans' unalienable rights.

John Adams adhered to the traditional mixed regime. See Adams 1851, IV, 358, 371. It is possible, although it remains to be demonstrated, that James Madison's apparent deviation from the principles of *The Federalist*, a deviation occurring while Adams occupied the White House, stemmed from apprehensions concerning Adams' well-known preference for a mixed regime, not an unmixed republic. For an overview of Adams' political thought see Webking 1985.

69.   James Madison: *The Federalist* 43, in HMJ 1961, 279. Jaffa 1978, 110 draws attention to this link. One should notice that Madison here conflated the natural/divine-law justification for a people's independence with the government's task of securing Creator-endowed unalienable rights. He could do this because he pointed to the safety and happiness *of society*, not of individuals − to the political task of guarding civil society.

70.   Elliot, 1845, 254. The would-be realist Joseph de Maistre complained "there is too much deliberating, too much *humanity* in this business, and one could bet a thousand to one that the city will not be built, that it will not be called *Washington*, and that the Congress will not meet there" (Maistre 1774, 109).

71.   See Alexander Hamilton, *The Federalist* 15, in HMJ, 110-111. Hamilton thus anticipates the well-known argument of Niebuhr 1932, on 'moral man and immoral society.' Kirk 1977 accurately observes, "A principal difference between the American Revolution and the French Revolution was this: the American revolutionaries in general held a biblical view of man and his bent toward sin, while the French revolutionaries attempted to substitute for the biblical understanding an optimistic doctrine of human goodness advanced by the philosophies of the rationalistic Enlightenment" (24).

72.   James Madison, "Speech to the Virginia Constitutional Convention," in Meyers 1973, 513. In *The Federalist* 51 Madison wrote, "Justice is the end of government. It is the end of civil society. It ever has been and ever will be pursued until it is obtained, or until liberty is lost in the pursuit." Faction in civil society resembles the state of war outside civil

society, "where the weaker individual is not secured against the violence of the stronger" (HMJ, 340).

73. Alexander Hamilton, *The Federalist* 72, in HMJ, 437.

74. Van Buren 1918, 184. He was arguing against the institution of a Bank of the United States. Jeffersonian Democrats persisted in regarding the bank as anti-republican, because it impinged upon the power of the legislative branch to regulate money. Major controversies in the nineteenth century invariably pointed back to the principles of the regime, and success often depended upon convincing the people that one's own side conformed more faithfully to those original principles than did one's opponents.

Madison considered "a dependence on the people" to be "the primary control on the government" (*The Federalist* 51, in HMJ 1961, 322).

75. James Madison, *The Federalist* 55, in HMJ, 346. Madison continued, "Were the pictures which have been drawn by the political jealousy of some among us faithful likenesses of the human character, the inference would be that there is not sufficient virtue among men for self-government; and that nothing less than the chains of despotism can restrain them from destroying and devouring one another." Madison thus implied that some opponents of the Constitution secretly ascribed to the doctrines of the monarchist Hobbes. Monroe 1987 wrote that in America, "Our object is to preserve the sovereignty in the people and give them that agency in the government which will be best adapted to that end, and in those instances in which the agency of a few or of one will be most effectual, to avail ourselves of it, but in a manner which will make them or him perform their duties with fidelity as representatives and servants, without the possibility of their wresting the power from us and becoming our masters" (102).

76. Monroe 1987, 4. The Founders would have known of a still more ancient regime perhaps analogous to their own. Sidney 1989, II, 9 cites the example of the Hebrew commonwealth, with its tripartite division of powers: a Judge of Chief Executive, an Assembly, and a Sanhedrin or 'supreme court.' See also, Straus 1887, who writes, "The form of government outlined by Moses and practically developed under Joshua and his successors, first embodied the principles upon which the rights and liberties of a people should rest and be sustained" (101). Straus cites not only the tripartite division of governmental power, but also the invention of representation, as outlined by Moses in Deuteronomy 1:12-13: "How can I alone bear the load and burden of you and your strife? Choose wise and discerning and experienced men from your tribes, and I will appoint them as your heads." For "experienced" the Ramban has "well-known;" the Septuagint has "prudent."

At Exodus 18:17-24, Moses' father-in-law Jethro recommended this policy, but there is no suggestion of *popular* choice in the first version; Moses appoints the tribal leaders. Moses is God's representative, but the leaders apparently are not elected representatives of the tribes. In Deuteronomy, the tribes choose, then Moses "appoints."

This suggests a Scriptural element not only in the Declaration of Independence but in the Constitution; the American regime's principles and structure owe a debt to Scriptural teachings. However, one should emphasize that the Founders themselves did not cite either Sidney or Scripture in *The Federalist*. The Hebrew Commonwealth and Moses do not appear in those essays, issuing rather from the 'Roman' Publius.

McWilliams 1984 formulates the matter differently. The Bible "has been the second voice in the grand dialogue of American political culture, an alternative to the 'liberal tradition' set in the deepest foundations of American life" (11). This "voice" came 'from below,' not from the Declaration, the Constitution, or, for the most part, from our statesmen. The Biblical voice in America came from the society. "The Declaration's language is designed to be acceptable to deists and orthodox believers alike, but this prudential ambiguity is not enough to make the Creator of the Declaration, 'Nature's God,' the 'distinctly biblical God' who is beyond nature and Lord over it" (21). To which one can only reply, prudential ambiguity is prudential and ambiguous; it neither exclusively rules in nor atheistically rules out the Creator-God. Such language *is* acceptable to deists and orthodox believers alike, as long as both tolerate each other for the purpose of establishing political justice.

McWilliams wrongly classifies religions *as such* as factions in the Madisonian sense; they are factions only when and if they act unjustly. He wrongly claims that Madison assigned to the community only permanent and aggregate interests, not rights; Madison never departed from the Declaration, which begins with an assertion of the right of a people to a separate and equal station among the power of the earth.

This notwithstanding, while McWilliams' interpretation exaggerates the dichotomy between the Founders and American society at the time of the founding, that is all he does. The dichotomy remains. He very tellingly notices that for George Washington religion is primarily civil religion: "It *supports* but does not *define* the moral and civil order" (24). Genuine Biblical religion does not conceive itself as civil religion. Yet even this perhaps goes too far. "Myths justify established orders; the Bible demands that established orders, justify themselves" (15). This is true, and it is precisely what American statesman and clergy demanded of the established colonial order. When they received no satisfactory answer, they joined the battle.

77. James Madison, *The Federalist* 63, in HMJ 1961, 386-387.

78. James Madison, *The Federalist* 37, in HMJ, 241. Monroe 1987 follows Madison: "The principle of election and of representation to certain

offices and in certain stations was well understood and practiced in several of the Grecian republics, but it was never carried beyond a certain limit. It never touched the great powers, or what might be called the share which the people held in the sovereignty of the state" (100). Eidelberg 1968 and 1974 argues that the United States Constitution established a mixed regime, a view that appears flatly to contradict Madison, Monroe, and other Founders. A careful reading of Eidelberg suggests a more subtle view: that the American regime is not a mixed regime in the conventional sense — a regime of 'purely' democratic and oligarchic elements bound together. Rather, it mixes democratic, oligarchic, and other elements more thoroughly, without assigning one branch of government exclusively to any social class. The latter "would be poorly designed precisely because it would be recognized as a mixed regime by virtually anyone!" Eidelberg finds that Aristotle understood this possibility. See Eidelberg 1974, 193-197. Also see Ceaser 1990, 9, 12. The Founders departed from the assumptions of Sidney 1990, III, xxi, who called for a mixed-regime republicanism (444).

79. James Madison, *The Federalist* 10, in HMJ, 82. See also Maritain 1957, 130ff, and, for a pessimistic account, Blalock 1984, 250.

80. James Madison, *The Federalist* 49, in HMJ, 317. This statement clearly separates Madison from the Machiavellian exaltation of faction falsely imputed to the Founders by Caton 1988, 183-289.

81. James Madison, *The Federalist* 58, in HMJ, 360-361. Sidney 1990 describes how Julius Caesar first corrupted the Roman army by requiring unquestioning obedience to himself above family and country and by then inflaming the soldiers' fury so that they would love war (II, xix, 187-188 ; See also II, xx, 193), For a Christian analysis, see Lenski, The Interpretation of St. Paul's Epistle to the Romans, 770.

82. Hendel 1953, 20-21, 80, 128. The resemblance of Hume's account to Madison's critique of factions in *The Federalist* 10 is well-known. Madison however, very sharply distinguishes just from unjust "interests." For an account of the various kinds of "interests" in Madison's thought, see Sheehan 1990. For an account of the relations between reason, passions, and interests in *The Federalist*, see White 1987, 102-106. For the effect of "economic development" on peace, see Boulding, 1962, 324.

83. "[I]n politics, as in religion, it is equally absurd to aim at making proselytes by fire and sword. Heresies in either can rarely be cured by persecution" (*The Federalist* 1, in HMJ, 34). Berns 1984 wittily observes, "it is not possible to be both an American and a martyr" (338). This is not to say that American republicanism abandons religion. To the contrary: George Washington reminded his countrymen of the need for it. "[L]et us with caution indulge the supposition, that morality can be maintained without religion. Whatever may be conceded to the influence of refined education on

minds of peculiar structure, reason and experience both forbid us to expect that National morality can prevail in exclusion of religious principle" (*Farewell Address*, in Allen 1988, 522). In this formulation, religious sentiment serves morality, and thereby guards unalienable rights. In America, religion is 'civil' not in the sense that it enjoys a political establishment but because it does not. By serving civil society, and not by becoming part of the government, religion in America helps to keep the peace.

84. James Madison, Notes for the *National Gazette* Essays, in Madison 1962-, XIV, 163. The prudential calculations bringing Madison to propose the notorious "three-fifths" rule in the United States Constitution, granting slaveholders additional power in the Federal government on the basis of slave populations who could not themselves be represented except by their masters — therefore would not be *represented* at all — are well described in Mee 1987, 165. For an excellent discussion of the reasons Americans of the Founders' generation often failed to see any contradiction between republicanism and slavery, see McDonald 1985, 50-55.

85. Abraham Lincoln, "Annual Message to "Congress," December 3, 1861, in Lincoln 1953, V, 51-52.

86. Abraham Lincoln, "Address at Sanitary Fair, Baltimore, Maryland," April 18, 1864, in Lincoln 1953, VII, 301-302.

87. Jefferson had included a denunciation of slavery, connecting the slave trade with the British King's impositions, in his first draft of the Declaration of Independence. See Becker 1942, 166-167. Becker also observes that this charge was implausible, and argues that Congress therefore was prudent to strike it out (213). Regardless of the historical plausibility of Jefferson's argument, slavery remains at odds with the principles of unalienable rights, and the commerce that guards them. Lincoln said, "without the institution of slavery and the colored race as a basis, the war could not have an existence" ("Address on Colonization to a Deputation of Negroes," August 14, 1862, in Lincoln 1953, V. 372).

88. Eidelberg 1974, 198. In this, as Eidelberg argues, the Founders concurred with Aristotle. On the importance of a moderate self-respect for Americans, see Adams 1986, 149.

Jaffa 1984 exaggerates the difficulties of Madison's agrarianism, calling it self-contradictory because it would make a "majority faction," farmers, a ruling faction, "endowing [it] with all the attributes of transcendent virtue" (208). It was surely unjust of Madison to claim so much virtue for farmers. However, in doing so Madison guarded himself from Jaffa's charge. In the Federalist 10, Madison defines a faction as an *unjust* majority or minority group, one whose passions or interests conflict with the rights of other citizens, or with the permanent and aggregate interests of the community. Though imperfect, farmers did not as a rule deserve that classification.

Abraham Lincoln recognized the utility of agrarian commerce for the promotion of peace. Agricultural fairs in particular make "the bonds of social and political union among us...more pleasant, and more strong, and more durable." Even the man of highest moral cultivation, in spite of all which abstract principle can do, likes him whom he *does* know, much better than him whom he does *not* know. To correct the evils, great and small, which spring from want of sympathy, and from positive enmity, among *strangers*, as nations, or as individuals, is one of the highest functions of civilization," and one to which agrarian commerce contributes (Lincoln 1953, VIII, 472).

On the commercial character of early American foreign policy, see Gilbert 1961.

89.   James Madison, *The Federalist* 14, in HMJ, 101. See also Sidney 1990, II, IX, i, 166.

90.   The Antifederalists feared that the 1787 Constitution "threatened the healthy religious situation as it then existed" by the very size of the republic the Framers envisioned. Antifederalists saw that the United States' size, too great for unified and unifying religious convictions, would need some other, nonreligious or even irreligious, bond to unify it: self-interest perhaps, or force. Truly moral self-government on Christian principles would no longer be possible. Christianity needed small communities if it were to rule. Contradictorily, however, the Antifederalists wanted effective military self-defense and commerce. See Storing 1981, 23.

91.   James Madison, *The Federalist* 51, in HMJ 320-325, conceded that the legislative   branch   in   a   republican   government   "necessarily predominates;" the remedy for this is a bicameralism, providing legislative checks and balances within the large tripartite system, and the executive veto. Hamilton would add judicial review (*The Federalist* 81, in HMJ, 481-491).

White 1987 perceptively observes that Madison used military metaphors of attack and defense throughout his essay (162-163). The three branches are potential enemies, with a need for both the means and the motive for self-defense. The compound republic tames the potentially warlike passions by rechanneling them into a peaceful form of conflict.

92.   James Madison, "A Sketch Never Finished Nor Applied," in Elliot 1845, 109. For the contrary claim that complex political and other "systems" are actually unstable, see Boulding 1962, 40.

93.   Alexander Hamilton, *The Federalist* 31, in HMJ, 197; James Madison, *The Federalist* 46, in HMJ, 299.

94. James Madison, *Report of the Committee to Whom were Referred the Communications of Various States, Relative to the Resolutions of the last General Assembly of this State, Concerning the Alien and Sedition Laws,* Virginia House of Delegates, Session of 1799-1800 in Meyers 1973, 316-317.

95. Monroe, 1987, 4.

96. Monroe 1987, 7-8. Jellinek 1902 contrasts the Declaration with the French Declaration of the Rights of Man and the Citizen: "In America, positive institutions are preceded by the solemn recognition of the rights of individuals;" the people *make* "the right of the state." In France rights *follow* institutions. Jellinek adds that the contemporary German State is "not well-founded," because its founders committed the same error the French did.

97. Monroe 1987, 18.

98. Monroe 1987, 69. This is the "unmixed" republic Madison described. The novelty of the American regime strikes and sometimes confuses commentators to this day. Diamond 1986 argues that human character needs "a comprehensive system of character-forming conditions and restraints − in short, a political community" that enforces a life above mere economic necessity and "passional indulgence" (80. America is not a *regime* at all; it has a "government," only. Madison "depoliticizes" religion and other social issues making "commodious self-preservation...the chief political end" and leaving "the higher human matters...to the workings of society" (94). Diamond concedes that the Constitution's Bill of Rights consists of higher principles that can 'feed back into' the society and upgrade it, but these do not make America a regime in the classic sense.

Cropsey 1986 concurs with Diamond. By limiting our government in the name of individual liberty, we ensure that our regime will be "imperfect." To base government on the consent of the governed means that America must be "powerfully, decisively, complemented or completed by thought" that may be entirely alien to the 'regime' itself − including the very principles of consent-based government and unalienable rights that underlie it.

Tarcov 1985 writes: "The *politeia* [regime] is the form taken by a political community, determined by who rules it. The dominant characteristic of the ruling part determines both the political goal of the whole regime and the personal goals of the individuals in it. This conception reflects the view that political rule is natural. The American conception of a constitution, in contrast, is that of a fundamental law, preferably written in a single document, understood as the expression of the will of the whole people. The Constitution grants powers of government from the natural rights of individuals, not so that some can rule others or form their goals, but so that the remaining rights of all can be more secure" (122).

Eidelberg 1974, in contrast, argues strongly that the "Aristotelian notion of the regime" can be applied, *in modified form* to the American republic (25-35). The modification Eidelberg proposes bases itself on a greater emphasis on individuality; "the modern emphasis on the *individual* (hence, on rights and freedom), and the classical emphasis on the *social* or *political* (hence, on duties and virtue), can be philosophically adjusted to see other in a more comprehensive view" (33). See also *Ibid.* 53-56, 104-113, with particular attention to the critique of Diamond, who exaggerates the materialism and egalitarianism of the Founders. Unfortunately, Eidelberg does not sufficiently address the issue of government's qualified separation from society.

Locke sheds light on the issue. Locke does not separate "society" from "government" to the degree Diamond, Cropsey, and even Tarcov claim. "For the *Essence and Union of the Society* consisting in having one Will, the Legislative, when once established by the Majority, has the declaring, as it were keeping of that Will. The *Constitution of the Legislative* is the first and fundamental Act of Society, whereby provision is made for the *Continuation of their Union*, under the Direction of Persons, and Bonds of Laws made by persons authorized thereunto, by the Consent and Appointment of the People, without which no one Man, or number of Men, amongst them, can have Authority of making Laws, that shall be binding to the rest. When any one, or more, shall take upon them to make Laws, whom the People have not appointed so to do, they make Laws without Authority, which the People are not therefore bound to obey; by which they come again to be out of subjection, and may constitute to themselves a *new Legislative*, as they think best, being in full liberty to resist the force of these, who without Authority would impose anything upon them." Simply put, Locke speaks not of government and society *isolated* from one another, but of *civil society*, of which "the Legislative" is "*the Soul that gives Form, Life, and Unity* to the Commonwealth." Civil Society is thus "a State of Peace, amongst those who are of it, from whom the State of War is excluded by the Umpirage, which they have provided in their Legislative, for the ending all Differences that may arise amongst any of them..." (*An Essay [on] Civil Government*, XIX, in Locke 1963, 455). Americans declared their independence from the British King; their legislatures were already independent, in their view, from the British Parliament. Therefore, *civil* society remained intact. (See above, note 41).

Stevens 1987 argues that for Hobbes and Locke, the regime question had become "secondary:" "The question of *which* regime [human beings establish] takes second place to the question of the coming-into-being in the first place of *some* regime - any regime," of civil society as such rather than in any particular form (270). One should add, however, that the Founders insisted that a particular kind of regime *best maintains* civil society.

Although Diamond, Cropsey, and Tarcov are profoundly right to distinguish the American regime from the smaller, more tightly-knit regimes Aristotle commended, they go too far in saying that America has no regime at all. America *is* powerfully the decisively complemented or completed by thought, but the structure of our civil society reinforces certain kinds of thoughts, thoughts usually consistent with government by the consent of the governed and unalienable rights. It does so by channeling human interests in a way that conduces to peace.

99.   Monroe 1987, 11. "Why did the democratical governments [of antiquity] fail, and why was their existence so transitory? It was because the government was united to the sovereignty in the people, and all the powers, in consequence, regulated in one body [the popular assembly]." (12)   Disorder resulted (see also *Ibid* 85-86). Internal disorder has external effects. As Allen 1990 observes, "The chief means of avoiding war" internationally "is good order at home (164). See also Tarcov 1990, 95.

100.   Monroe 1987, 35-36. Monroe soberly concluded that colonies, emigrant peoples who adapt their native institutions to new conditions, have an easier task when they seek to establish 'American' republics, than do peoples living in older societies, surrounded by formidable enemies.

Jellinek 1902 observes that the history of revolutionary France shows "what dangers can come from the premature adoption of foreign institutions. The Americans, notably, had raised the edifice of their social and political regime in 1776 on foundations that had long existed among them; the French, on the contrary, had overthrown all the foundations among themselves" (46-47).

This begins to resemble neo-Burkean conservatism, but Jellinek (like Monroe, Madison, and the other American Founders) goes on to make the crucial distinction: "Nonetheless, an abyss separates the American declarations [that is, the Declaration of Independence and the bills of rights found in the American states' constitutions] from the English legal precedents." Americans spoke "in the name of the eternal laws of humanity," of nature, not the ancestral/historical rights of Englishmen. One *inherits* English rights, whether they are the popular rights of common law of a monarch's perogatives. Traditional English rights are a patrimony. They are what writers now call 'authoritarian' and also historically relative not universal. Jellinek sees that Locke and Blackstone laid the philosophic foundations for introduction of natural right into English law (47-55).

The examples of Monroe and Jellinek prove that adherence to natural right blends well with Burkean sensitivity to the limits of circumstance.

Neo-Burkeans too often fail to see this, and lapse into historicism. For an eminent Frenchman's attempt to apply the lessons of Burke, of Madison, and of experience to Constitutional building, see *Principles of Politics*, vii, in Constant 1989, 225.

101. Monroe 1987, 42.

102. Monroe 1987, 55. Mansfield 1978 finds this attempt "to find a standard which makes invisible virtue visible so that men can see beauty of soul," to be central to Aristotle's prescriptive account of the mixed regime (5). "Political peace and stability in the mixed regime are built on what can be seen in or inferred from the deeds of the noblest political men...[T]he mixed regime when fully developed is nothing less than aristocracy, and rare if not impossible" (8), and its rarity stems from the invisibility of the human soul.

103. Monroe 1987, 5.

104. Monroe 1987, 64.

105. Monroe 1987, 18.

106. The familiar arguments in *The Federalist* 10 and 51 (which must be read together), receive different emphases by different commentators. Diamond 1987 emphasizes institutions; Eidelberg 1968 and 1974, the essays in Kesler 1987, and Lutz 1988, 82-83, and Sheehan 1990 seek to redress the balance. See also Ceaser 1990, 14-15. Sidney 1990 writes, "Good order once established makes good men, and as long as it lasts such as are fit for the greatest employments are never found wanting" (II, xxiii, 212).

107. James Madison, *The Federalist* 63, in HMJ, 384. Madison cites the Athenians' trial and execution of Socrates as an example of the "tyranny of the people's passions" in pure democracy.

108. James Madison, *The Federalist* 50, in HMJ, 319. White 1987 sees that this amounts to a new twist on the old maxim, 'Divide and rule,' in *The Federalist*, he writes, "Tyranny's vice becomes republicanism's virtue" (201). See also Washington, "Farewell Address," September 18, 1786, on the connection between the cultivation of "peace and harmony" internationally and a policy of "justice and benevolence" at home (Allen 1985, 522-523).

109. See James Madison, *The Federalist* 51, in HMJ, 324-325.

110. The very public assertion of self-evident unalienable rights helps to guard those rights, by fostering the mental attitude immortalized on a colonial flag: "Don't tread on me." Thurow 1976 puts it in the more ample phrases of a scholar's prose: "Public opinion cannot distinguish real inequality from the great pretenders of inequality; however, it can recognize equality. Then the only security against becoming a slave to

others is to deny oneself mastery over others. To claim to be a master asserts an equality which public opinion cannot accurately assay, and hence prepares the ground for one's own enslavement" (53-54).

111. James Madison, *The Federalist* 19, in HMJ, 133.

112. James Madison, "A Sketch Never Finished nor Applied," in Elliot 1845, V, 109.

113. James Madison, *The Federalist* 20, in HMJ, 138.

114. James Madison, *The Federalist* 39, in HMJ, 245-246.

115. Alexander Hamilton, *The Federalist* 15, in HMJ, 108-110. He added: "In an association where the general authority is confined to the collective bodies of the communities that compose it, every breach of the laws must involve a state of war; and military execution must become the only instrument of civil obedience. Such a state of things can certainly not deserve the name of government, nor would any prudent man choose to commit his happiness to it." See also Monroe 1987, 3-4.

116. George Washington, "Farewell Address, October 19, 1796, in Allen 1988, 516. Hamilton had made this argument nine years previously in *The Federalist* 8, in HMJ, 69. In *The Federalist* 15, Hamilton argued that in a condition if disunion "our liberties would be a prey to the means of defending ourselves against the ambition and jealousy of each other." Continual necessity of military services "enhances the importance to the soldier, and proportionably degrades the condition of the civilian." With invasions, citizens' rights must be sacrifices, weakening "their sense of these rights," however self-evident they may be (70-71); recall Monroe's argument about the transition from republicanism to Bonapartism, above, pages 38-39.

117. James Wilson, Speech, June 19, 1787, in Elliot 1845, 209. Thus the Declaration sustains not only the doctrine of unalienable rights, but also the doctrine of federalism, although obviously it was not intended to show how this might work out in practice.

118. James Madison, "Vices of the Political System of the United States," April 1987, in Meyers 1961, 87. He also complains of the low quality of the state legislators.

119. James Madison, "Letter to the *North American Review*, "August 28, 1830, in Meyers 1961, 533-539. In an article published six years later, "Note on Nullification," Madison reaffirmed this argument, saying that the nullifiers confuse a *constitutional* right with a *natural and universal* (unalienable) right. To invoke an unalienable right implies that the state has ceased to avow adherence to the Constitution. To invoke a Constitutional right implies continued adherence to the Constitution. See Meyers 1961, 546 (One may of course do *both*, as the Americans

did in 1776, but this bespoke independence, and a state of nature *between* America and Britain, not in America itself).

120. James Madison, "Note on Nullification," in Meyers 1961, 548.

121. *Ibid.*, 566-567. As Madison pointedly observed, if the United States as a whole were not in some sense sovereign, how could treason be a crime? How could it conduct foreign relations with other states? He concluded, "Thus far, throughout a period of nearly half a century, the new and compound system has been successful beyond any of the forms of Government, ancient or modern, with which it may be compared; having as yet discovered no defects which do not admit remedies compatible with its vital principles and characteristic features. It becomes all therefore who are friends of a Government based on free principles to reflect, that by denying the possibility of a system partly federal and partly consolidated, and who would convert ours into one either wholly federal or wholly consolidated, in neither of which forms have *individual* rights, public order, and external safety, been all duly maintained, they aim a deadly blow at the *last hope* of true liberty on the fact of the Earth" (574).

Madison's final political testament, "Advice to My Country" written ca. October 1834, consisted of a fervent call to maintain the Union: "The advice nearest to my heart and deepest to my convictions is that the Union of the States be cherished and perpetuated. Let the open enemy to it be regarded as a Pandora with her box – opened; and the disguised one, as the Serpent creeping with his deadly wiles into Paradise" (Meyers 1961, 576).

None of the above should be taken to imply the Madison's conception of federalism lacked problems or even contradictions, as seen in Madison's own statements over a career spanning some five decades. For a good statement of the difficulties and a review of scholarly commentaries, see Carey 1987b.

South Carolina Senator John C. Calhoun made the most brilliant attempt to secure the Founders' objective – the establishment of a regime of peace – while compromising their fundamental commitment to universal unalienable rights. Like the Founders, he saw the roots of government in human nature; man is "a social being," who requires society to preserve his existence and perfect his faculties. Society "cannot exist without government" because the individual (though not selfish) desire for self-preservation "pervades all that feels, from man down to the lowest and most insignificant reptile or insect." This yields conflict (Calhoun 1957, 3-5), and the need to govern it.

Unfortunately, the same self-preservative and self-regarding impulses that make government necessary also makes it dangerous. Governmental constitutions – Calhoun sometimes called them "organisms" – must give governments the strength to defend societies from internal and external threats, while limiting governmental power in order to prevent their abuse by all-too-human rulers.

Unlike modern historicists, who use the word "organism" in order to emphasize progress or growth, Calhoun concentrated on the "internal structure" of governments. Stability, not the militant 'advancement' of 'History,' remained his first concern. To achieve stability, he looked at politics realistically: "Power can only be resisted by power − and tendency by tendency. Those who exercise power and those subject to its exercise − the rulers and the ruled − stand in antagonistic relations to each other." A good constitution will insure that "resistance may be systematically and peaceably made" by the ruled when rulers oppress them (11). The right of suffrage is the primary institutional device for such resistance. But suffrage alone could lead to majority-tyranny. Somehow, "the various interests of the community" need protection, so none will dominate the others. Mere majorities do not express the will of the people. Nor can the written guarantees of a 'paper constitution' protect minorities. Only a solid structure of real government will do this, and prevent the degradation of republicanism into despotism, of government by force.

Thus far, Calhoun echoed Madison and the other American Founders. Calhoun departed from their institutional arrangements by proposing a constitution of "concurrent majorities" to supplement the existing structure of separated and balanced powers. Calhoun worried that each branch of government could still be seized by a national majority. With "concurrent majorities" − an arrangement whereby (initially undefined) groups would enjoy *institutional* status in the form of veto-power over the majority's initiatives − reasonable compromises would result. With compromise, "full and faithful utterance to the sense of the whole community, in reference to its common welfare," would prevail (31). "No necessity can be more urgent and imperious than that of preventing anarchy," and this necessity would prevent deadlock between the groups, requiring them to come to peaceful agreement. Calhoun did not explain why a majority, being the stronger party, would not seek anarchy, a circumstance wherein the strongest would most likely prevail. Indeed, the anarchy (so to speak) of the American Civil War conclusively demonstrated that in chaos the strongest prevail.

Calhoun's doctrine resembles the twentieth-century doctrine of "interest-group liberalism," as seen in such writings as Dahl 1956. Calhoun differed, however, in retaining a strong moral foundation; a system of concurrent majorities would promote the virtues of truth, justice, integrity, and fidelity, helping "to form the character of the people" (39). Simple majoritarianism, by contrast, promotes vices: "Neither religion nor education can counteract the strong tendency of the numerical majority to corrupt and debase the people" (40). Liberty and security, in Calhoun's doctrine, are not unalienable rights, but rather means to the development of human faculties. Liberty is not God-endowed but "to be earned." "[I]t is a great and dangerous error to suppose that all people are equally entitled to liberty; liberty, forced on a people unfit for it, would, instead of a blessing, be a curse bringing anarchy." This may well refer to African-Americans living in slavery; Calhoun did not specify how a people might "earn" the "reward" of liberty (42-43).

Calhoun mistook the Founders' understanding of unalienable right. He endorsed the concept of equality before the law, while rejecting the notion of "equality of condition," that is, of equal rights to receiving social and political benefits (43-44). In this the Founders concurred. He denied "that all men are born free and equal" in the "state of nature;" if he referred only to the natural abilities, he would find no quarrel with the Founders. (See, for example, Jefferson's remarks on "natural aristocracy" in his October 18, 1813 letters to John Adams [Cappon 1954, 389]). In saying that men in fact are "born subject" – to parents, laws, and institutions – he did not quarrel with the Founders, either (45). But in tacitly denying the existence of equal, natural (God-endowed) unalienable rights, he broke with the Founders and sided with the slaveholders. Calhoun did not connect equal, unalienable rights with moral and intellectual virtue, and thus descended into a utiliarianism all too ready to sacrifice the rights of some to the advancement of others. In this, paradoxically, he affirmed the exploitation of minorities that he otherwise sought to prevent.

Calhoun admired the Roman Republic and the British Constitution as exemplary systems based upon "concurrent majorities," wherein social groups could check and balance one another by the use of the veto-power. However, these were actually mixed regimes based on social classes – patricians and plebs, aristocrats and commoners. Calhoun would have made North and South into the equivalent of classes; he would have made the United States into a mixed regime. By sidestepping the question of unalienable rights, and by providing institutional security to slaveowners, he might have perpetuated slavery indefinitely.

A Discourse on the Constitution and Government of the United States represents Calhoun's attempt to refound the United States regime, while preserving many if not all of the Founders' intentions. By beginning with the Madisonian understanding, that the peoples of each of the original thirteen states framed and ratified the 1787 Constitution through their representatives, Calhoun offered a reasonable explanation of the Preamble's first and most famous phrase, "We the People" (Calhoun 1883, I, 133). "[S]overeignty resides in the people, and not in the government" (139) – a point the Founders affirmed. Calhoun however rejected Madison's contention that the Constitution makes the government partly federal, partly national, contending that the people *within each state* retained their sovereignty – i.e., that there remain as many sovereign "peoples" in the United States as there are states. The federal government thus represents the states in their corporate character (e.g., in the Senate, with two Senators from each state) and in their popular character (e.g., in the House of

Representatives, whose voting districts never cross state lines). Although the Federal government may rightfully operate on individual citizens directly, and not always through mediating state governments, this in no way dilutes the sovereignty of state populations; the Articles of Confederation provides for such operation as well (150-156).

All of this might have impressed Madison as more a quibble over the word 'national' than a substantive criticism of *The Federalist*'s argument. To this day, there is no doubt that the American people as a whole, the people of a state, or even an individual may rightfully 'secede' from any government that systematically violates unalienable rights. If the United States government decided, for example, to take New Jersey jokes seriously — injuring New Jerseyans' lives, abridging their liberties, and blocking their pursuit of happiness, New Jerseyans would have every right to secede. Even Rhode Islanders would. Although some of us might draw the line at Massachusettsians.

However, Calhoun went on to make an additional claim. "Time and experience" had revealed a flaw in the Founders' design: a majority of the States in both their corporate and popular characters tended to oppress the minority — i.e., free states pressured slave states to abolish slavery, and attempted to prevent the extension of slavery into the western territories. The Federal government thus enjoyed greater power than the Founders had anticipated (238-239). Calhoun feared either despotism or disunion would result. Because "a strong government requires a negative [or veto] proportionally strong, to restrict it to its appropriate sphere" (270), Calhoun reiterated his call for the institution of the concurrent majority.

A man of considerable prudence as well as brilliance, Calhoun foresaw the practical difficulties his proposal would entail. If the states routinely judge the constitutionality of actions by the Federal government, and if all states are 'created equal,' then other states may declare war on states that secede (301). Further, in such a war, victory for the unionists would only strengthen the Federal government still further; Calhoun himself saw the centralizing effects of war, specifically, the War of 1812 (361).

This forced Calhoun back to Madison's position. While the people of each state retain the right to revolution, including secession, the use of right must be governed by prudence in the highest degree. "[T]he possession of a right is one thing, and the exercise of it another. Rights, themselves, must be exercised with prudence and propriety: when otherwise exercised, they often cease to be rights, and become wrongs" (279). The "greatest caution and forbearance" should be exercised here, as the right of nullification is "the most important and delicate right" (479-480), and its threatened exercise should serve to strengthen the Union, not destroy it. Understandably and justifiably pessimistic about the likelihood of the rule of prudence, Calhoun sought a Constitutional amendment to reinforce the concurrent majority by establishing a bicephalous Federal executive — one president representing the North, the other representing the South, each with veto power. "Thus, only, can the Union be preserved, [and] the anticipations of the Founders of the system...be realized" (315, 390 ff.).

The Founders had not anticipated the indefinite perpetuation and extension of slavery. Calhoun believed that the South's "peace, prosperity, and safety" depended upon "the existing relations between the races," the relations of masters and slaves. Abolitionism represented "the spirit of fanaticism," a throwback to the era of religious warfare that the Founders sought to overcome (390). It is easy to see how Calhoun might have believed this. He was partly right: some of the Abolitionists did rant; the end of slavery did injure the South's prosperity, although war, the tactics of so-called Reconstruction, and the greed of Northern financiers did far more damage. Nonetheless, Calhoun was mistaken. Southern whites gradually regained their peace and security after the outrages of 'Reconstruction.' Former slaves attacked former masters far less often than whites attacked blacks. And none of it need have happened, had Calhoun and his fellow-southerners respected the self-evident truth of unalienable right.

122. Alexander Hamilton, *The Federalist*, 16, in HMJ, 114

Monroe 1987 added, "If the members of the legislature lose sight of the nation, and look to their sections only, the system is in utmost danger." Accordingly, "a national policy must be cherished and prevail" even while respecting states' limited sovereignty (17).

123. Abraham Lincoln, "First Inaugural Address," March 4, 1861, in Lincoln 1953, IV, 268.

124. Abraham Lincoln, "Eulogy on Henry Clay," July 6, 1852, in Lincoln 1952, II, 130.

125. At the beginning of the war, Lincoln told Congress that "this issue embraces more than the fate of these United States. It presents to the whole family of man, the question whether a constitutional republic, or a democracy — a government of the people, by the same people — can, or cannot maintain its territorial integrity, against its own domestic foes. It presents the question, whether discontented individuals, too few in numbers to control administration, according to organic law, in any case, can always, upon pretenses made in this case, or on any other pretenses, or arbitrarily, without pretense, break up their Government, and thus practically put an end to free government upon the earth. It forces us to ask: 'Is there, in all republics, this inherent, fatal weakness?' 'Must a government, of necessity, be too *strong* for the liberties of its own people, or too *weak* to maintain its own existence?'" (*Message to Congress in Special Session*, July 4, 1861, in Lincoln 1953, IV, 426).

For an excellent summary of Lincoln's constitutionalism by an historian, see Belz 1988. For a soldier's understanding of the issue of faction as seen in the American Civil War, see Haskell 1958, 157-158. For a thorough discussion of the military implications of commercial republican self-defense as relating to the issue of conscription, see Cohen 1985, especially pp. 119-125, 134-136.

126.   Lincoln 1953, IV, 439. See also Lang and Russell 1990, 7.

127.   Abraham Lincoln, "Annual Message to Congress," December 3, 1861, in Lincoln 1953, V, 490 "Lincoln's message was always peace, but like other messengers of peace, he brought not peace but a sword" (Jaffa 1965, 167).

The British pacifist Henry Richard, by contrast, could see nothing more that "pride and passion" in Lincoln's policy (Appleton 1889, 57).

128.   Alexander Hamilton, *The Federalist* 8, in HMJ, 67.

129.   James Madison, Speech, in Elliot 1845, 257.

130.   John Jay, *The Federalist* 3 and 4, in HMJ, 42-47.

131.   Alexander Hamilton, *The Federalist* 29, in HMJ, argues that "War, like most other things, is a science to be acquired and perfected by diligence, by perseverance, by time, and by practice;" professional soldiers, not part-time militiamen, can learn the science of war (166). James Madison *The Federalist* 41, in HMJ takes the more pessimistic view. Even a small standing army "has its inconveniences." It "may be fatal" on a larger scale. Therefore, a wise people "will exert all its prudence in diminishing both the necessity and the danger of resorting to [a standing army] which may be inauspicious to its liberties" (258); the rule of law itself will help, as will the Constitutional provision for strictly limited terms of budget appropriations for the military.

During the Revolutionary War the militia may have been an economic necessity. Perret 1984 argues that "in an agrarian society that suffered a chronic labor shortage long before the war began there was a strong reluctance to strip the land of men and put them in the army. To go on fighting, Americans had to go on eating" (25).

132.   For an excellent account of Hamilton's thoughts on the relations between war and commercial republicanism, see Flaumenhaft 1976. Hamilton did not suppose that commerce alone led to less warlike conduct; Christianity brought humane sentiments to civil society. Christianity "also led to a new kind of ferocity, the ferocity of...religious zeal" (121). Therefore, Christianity must not be used as a *political* bond. It must be preserved on the level of civil society, so as to influence the government that legislates for society. For government proper, a regard for *natural* rights must suffice; such regard prevents persecution at home and religious warfare abroad.

133.   James Madison, *Helvidius* 1, in Meyers 1961, 265-266. The jibes about English monarchy are of course remarks on Hamilton's political sympathies.

In his *Letters of Publicola* John Quincy Adams contrasted the Constitution's division of responsibility for peace and war — war-declaring in the legislative branch, management of warfare, and of peace negotiations in the executive — with the arrangements in the English and French republican constitutions (Adams 1913, I, 103-106).

134.   James Madison, *Helvidius* 4, Meyers 1961, 276-277. In "Political Observations," his argument for commercial war or boycott, Madison elaborates. "Of all the enemies to public liberty, war is, perhaps, the most to be dreaded, because it comprises and develops the germ of every other. War is the parent of armies, and debts, and taxes are the known instruments for bringing the many under the domination of the few." In war "all the means of seducing the minds, are added to those of subduing the force, of the people." Inequality of fortunes and opportunities for fraud, and "degeneracy of manners and of morals" augment wars's evils. "No nation could preserve its freedom in the midst of continual warfare" (Meyers 1961, 287-288).

On the American understanding of the executive and of executive power see Mansfield 1989, 247-291. Madison is closer, however, to the views of Anastaplo 1989, who emphasizes the primacy of legislative power in the Constitution as "reflect[ing] the proper authority of logos (or reason)" — as distinguished from executive action — "in human affairs" (42).

135.   Monroe 1987, 33. John Quincy Adams hoped that the international balance of powers "would indirectly encourage the growth" of commercial republicanism by "checking the universalist claims of absolutist monarchy" (Lang and Russell 1990, 8).

136.   Van Buren 1918, 485.

CHAPTER II

1. Baldwin 1958, 170. Baldwin remarks that the New England clergy quoted the Bible, writers of classical antiquity, and John Locke ("especially after 1763" [7], but also well before then, as in Elisha Whitfield's *The Essential Rights and Liberties of Protestants, a Seasonable Plea for Liberty of Conscience and the Right of Private Judgment in Matters of Religion, without any control from Human Authority*, published in 1744, a Lockean-Christian tract affirming natural equality of unalienable rights and the liberties based thereon). "Their theology and church policy were legalistic" (13), emphasizing the conventional character of government aiming at the good of the people, founded by the people, and ordained by God. The social compact government parallels, in more exclusively human terms, the covenant between God and human beings that constitutes the Christian Church. Baldwin admits that the proportion of revolutionary to Loyalist clergy cannot be determined (132 and 158-159); she estimates that the revolutionaries were the majority (140).

2. *Ibid.*, 134.

3. *Ibid.*, 171. For a more general survey, see Heimert 1966, especially viii, 15, 387, 445, 479.

4. H. Richard Niebuhr 1959 contrasts the Roman Catholic God of "changeless perfection" with the "forceful reality of power" of God in Protestantism (18-19). Obviously, if Protestantism left matters there, it might serve only destruction. But as Niebuhr sees, God's force primarily creates and always directly or indirectly strengthens creation. In politics, this results in constitutionalism under the sovereignty of God and in no utopian sense. American Protestant settlers "did not think of the Kingdom in the idealistic and utopian terms which became current later;" Governor Bradford, John Cotton, William Penn, and John Winthrop share a "strain of sober thoughtfulness," whether that be Scriptural/legalistic, as with the Puritans, or spiritual and governed by grace, as with the Quakers, or spiritual and governed by grace, as with the Quakers and separatists (46-59). "Connections between the Christian constitutionalism of the constructive Protestants and the political constitutionalism of the seventeenth and eighteenth centuries were intimate and close" (65). The fact of original sin required government; it equally required that government be strictly limited. (79).

    For a brief, pungent survey of American Protestant sermons on military preparedness, see West 1988.

5. Newlin 1962 gives an account of the theology of such liberal clergymen as Charles Chauncy and Jonathan Mayhew, and of such evangelicals as Jonathan Edwards, George Whitefield, and others involved in "The

Great Awakening" of the 1740's. The latter were 'conservative' in their theology, emphasizing Scripture over reason. They were not necessarily conservative politically; evangelicals tended more toward popular government than did many 'liberals.' See also Lutz 1988, 68, x, 16.

6. Nowell 1678, p. 1. The Narraganset Bay War had been fought by the New England Confederation of Puritan colonies against the Indian chieftain King Philip in 1675-76. Quakers had attempted to mediate the dispute, but this was "an impossible mission" because the matter was "a clear case of a 'zero-sum' conflict in which the only solution is the elimination of the claims of one party" (Yarrow 1978, 14).

7. Nowell 1678, 3-4.

8. *Ibid.*, 6.

9. *Ibid.*, 8.

10. *Ibid.*, 9. On civil liberty, Nowell wrote, "God hath not given great ones in the world that absolute power over men, to devour them at pleasure, as great Fishes do the little ones..." (10).

11. *Ibid.*, 11.

12 *Ibid.*, 16.

13. Tennent 1748 a, 11. Tennent cited Grotius' *The Law of War and Peace* several times in this essay.

14. *Ibid.*, 12. Citing Romans 13, Tennent asked, "Can it be reasonably imagined, that a *Magistrate* should show greater Clemency to *Foreigners* and Strangers, than to his own Sons and *Subjects*" – to whom the magistrate is a rightful scourge, if they commit evil (19). The magistrate should "love [evildoers] as fellow Creatures, and compassionate their Miseries from a principle of Humanity; and yet in the mean time he must put them to Death not out of personal revenge, but to promote Justice and the good Ends of Government" (32); lawful war follows this same principle.

15. *Ibid.*, 1748b, 100.

16. *Ibid.*, 24.

17. *Ibid.*, 34.

18. *Ibid.*, 76. Tennent cautioned that defensive war alone cannot bring peace. The fallenness of human nature makes peacemaking difficult, even for the Church. Persecution is "contrary to reason;" the forceful methods needed to establish civil peace do not work for the establishment of religious peace. For that, toleration based upon

humility, charity, and kindness alone suffices. See Tennent 1765, 14-21.

19. Mayhew 1750, Preface (no pagination).

20. *Ibid.*, 24-25.

21. *Ibid.*, 27-28. King Charles I, for example, "had, in fact, *unkinged* himself long before" Englishmen did (47). The 'divine right of Kings' has no Scriptural foundation, and Christianity makes no choice among monarchy, republicanism and aristocracy, rather committing itself to "the happiness of society" under whatever political regime best conduces to the end, under the given circumstances (10).

22. *Ibid.*, 40.

23. Simeon Howard: "A Sermon Preached to the Ancient and Honorable Artillery Company in Boston." In Hyneman and Lutz, eds., 1983, I, 190. Howard's rationalism did not prevent him from acknowledging original sin and its political consequences:

> It is indeed a hard case, that those who are happy in the blessings of providence, and disposed to live peaceably with all men, should be obliged to keep up the idea of blood and slaughter, and expend their time and treasure to acquire the arts and instruments of death. But this is a necessity which the depravity of human nature had laid upon every state. Nor was there ever a people that continued, for a considerate time, in the enjoyment of liberty, who were not in a capacity to defend themselves against invaders, unless they were too poor and inconsiderable to tempt an enemy. (197-198).

24. *Ibid.*, I, 195.

25. *Ibid.*, 196, 208.

26. *Ibid.*, 202-203.

27. *Ibid.*, 208. Howard substitutes "religion" for "Christianity." New England Congregationalists generally shared the just-war views. The Reverend Daniel Shute wrote, "The doctrine of *passive obedience* and *non-resistance* in the unlimited sense it has been urged by some, came not down from above, as it can be supported neither by reason nor revelation; and therefore if any where, may be urged with a better grace by *the rulers of darkness*, in the regions below, upon those who by the righteous decree of heaven, are excluded the common benefits of creation, than by those powers *that are ordained by God* for the good of mankind." (*An Election Sermon*, 1768, Hyneman and Lutz, eds., 1983, I, 126). The Rev. Zabdiel Adams, first cousin of John Adams, conceded "the horrors of war are great; yet, when we come to contrast

them with *slavery*, we find the darkness of the night-piece immediately lessens! Where slavery reigns, nothing good or great can possibly take place." "[W]e cannot resign [reason and freedom], without rebelling against Him Who gave them." (*An Election Sermon*, 1782, in Hyneman and Lutz, eds., 1983, I, 557-558). See also Abraham Williams, *An Election Sermon* (1762) for a statement of the just war as security for equal rights (Hyneman and Lutz 1762, I, 5).

The Reverend Samuel West of Massachusetts campaigned for the ratification of the 1787 Constitution. In 1776 he published the fullest vindication by a Congregationalist clergyman of defensive, just war. The state of nature, he wrote, is a state of equality in the sense that no one has "the right to control another" (*On the Right to Rebel Against Governors*, 1776, in Hyneman and Lutz, eds., 1983, I, 413). "The doctrine of nonresistance and unlimited passive obedience to the worst of tyrants could never have found credit among mankind had the voice of reason been hearkened to for a guide, because such a doctrine would immediately have been discerned to be contrary to natural law," which is from God (414). Self-preservation is "the first law of nature;" liberty is its protection, tyranny its undoing (419). West knows that "Nero, that monster of tyranny, was...Emperor of Rome" when Paul wrote Romans 13. However, the epistle probably dates from the beginning of Nero's reign, when "he was a very humane and merciful prince." Even if this were not so, Paul never enjoins obedience to evil commands; further, he may have been "speak[ing] of magistracy in general," not of Nero particularly, and "tyrants are no magistrates" (428-429, 423). Nonresistants "refuse to defend their persons, their wives, their children, and their country from the assaults of the enemy," but can any rational creature suppose that the Deity can require us to contradict the law of nature which He has written in our hearts, a part of which I am sure is the law of self-defense...?" Nonresistants commit "a sin of omission" (441).

28. Davies 1755, 4.

29. The war promises "all the horrid arts of *Indian* and Popish torture" (*Ibid.*, 3). "Shall *Virginia* incur the Guilt and the everlasting Shame, of tamely exchanging her Liberty, her Religion, and her All, for arbitrary *Gallic* Power, and for Popish slavery, Tyranny and Massacre?" (*Ibid.*, 5). "Now some helpless Children may be torn from the arms of their murdered Parents, and dragged away weeping and wringing their Hands, to receive their Education among Barbarians, and to be formed upon the Model of a ferocious Indian Soul" (Davies 1758, 11). "Can Protestant Christianity expect Quarters from Heathen Savages and French Papists?" – particularly with "the Powers of Hell" as "a Third Party" (*Ibid.*, 18-19)?

30. Davies 1755, 7-8. No self-righteousness enters here; Davies described the war as punishment for Virginians' sins, even though it is just and defensive. "A provoked God intends to scourge us with the Rod of *France*" (Davies 1757, 17). "Repentance, Reformation and Prayer, is

the only way to turn away the Displeasure of God, and obtain His Favour and Protection." If Virginians "attempt this Work with the Pride of imaginary Self-sufficiency, you may be sure Disappointment will be the Consequence" (*Ibid.*, 32-33). Rational, Christian manliness looks finally to the Holy Spirit to guide military spiritedness. "In the name of Jesus, the Captain of your Salvation, I invite you all to enlist in the spiritual Warfare" *as* in the military warfare (Davies 1758, 35).

31. Davies 1755, 9-13. He did not hesitate to suggest the possibility of Apocalypse: "Now who can tell, but that the present War is the Commencement of this grand decisive Conflict between the Lamb and the Beast, *i.e.* between the *Protestant* and *Popish* Powers?" (Davies 1757, 26).

32. Davies 1757, 11-14.

33. Davies 1757, 21-22, 29.

34. Davies 1761, 4.

35. *Ibid.*, 11. "Let *Atheists* and *Epicureans* say what they please, it is an eternal Truth, which all the world will be made to know at last, that *Jehovah* is the Ruler of the Universe..." (Davies 1757, 28).

36. Bemis, 1967, 281. Jay acknowledged the civil-social utility of religion — in a conversation with an atheist, he said, "If there is no God there could be no moral obligations, and I did not see how society could subsist without them" (Letter to John Bristed, April 23, 1811, in Jay 1893, IV, 359-360) — but also upheld the truth of Scripture beyond its utility: "It is to be regretted, but so I believe the fact to be, that except for the Bible there is not a true history in the world" (Letter to Rev. Jedediah Morse, February 28, 1797, in Jay 1893, IV, 225).

37. He reported to President Washington, "The French Jacobins have greatly injured the cause of rational liberty" by committing "massacres, impieties, and abominations" (Letter to George Washington, March 6, 1795, in Jay 1893, IV, 166). "It does not appear probable to me that Europe is very speedily to be blessed with a general and lasting peace," he observed all to justly, "or that the period has already arrived when reason and virtue will govern the conduct of the mass of mankind." Glancing at the French again, he continued, "so many systems which were calculated on the supposed prevalence of reason and virtue, have proved delusive" (Letter to John Hartley, January 8, 1795, in Jay 1893, IV, 153). During the negotiations for the treaty with Great Britain that bears his name, he wrote, "Let us preserve peace while it can be done with propriety; and if in that we fail, let us wage war — not in newspapers, and impotent sarcasms, but with manly firmness, and unanimous and vigorous efforts" (Letter to Colonel Reed, August 14, 1794, in Jay 1893, IV, 50).

38. Letter to John Murray, Jr., October 12, 1816, in Jay 1893, IV, 391. By emphasizing the authority of Jewish *moral* law, and remaining silent on the civil and ecclesiastical aspects of the Mosaic Code, Jay avoided involvement in the controversy over the question of the extent to which Jesus liberated Jews from obedience to the Code. American Calvinists carried over more elements of the Code into daily life than did liberal Christians. Unjust wars proceed from lusts — that is, from the *il*legal. War itself, however, is not essentially sinful or lustful: "the *sin* of waging *any* war is not specified among the numerous sins and offenses which are mentioned and reproved in both the Testaments" (*Ibid.*, 392).

39. Letter to John Murray, Jr., April 15, 1818, Jay 1893, IV, 409-413. Jay thus concurred with Tennent; see above, p. 61.

40. *Ibid.*, 415-416.

41. Letter to John Murray, Jr., October 12, 1816, in Jay 1893, IV, 393.

42. Letter to John Murray, Jr., April 15, 1818, in Jay 1893, IV, 417. Similarly, war admittedly sends to their deaths men spiritually unprepared to die, and so does the system of civil justice. This, Jay argued, does not require the eschewal of war and capital punishment by Christians, as these practices avert greater evils than they produce.

43. *Ibid.*, 418. For another statement of Christian republicanism based upon the Declaration of Independence, see Floy 1841: "A good Christian and a bad citizen are antagonistic terms" in the United States (5-6). The Declaration's principle of equality derives from the Biblical doctrine that "God is no respecter of persons," i.e., of social rank (5-6, 10).

44. Braithwaite, 1919, 415; Brock 1968, 250 ff.

45. Hirst 1923, 390.

46. Brock 1968, 255.

47. Braithwaite 1919, 554. However, Christian spiritualism of seventeenth century England had a noticeable political implications; see Jones, 1932, 4, 51, 147-148.

48. Barbour, 1964, 220. Among those guided by the Holy Spirit a parallel dichotomy emerged. Soderlund 1985 identifies "separate strands of Quaker tradition," one tending toward the legalistic and punitive — inclined to disown those of heterodox views — and those animated more by what she calls "Quaker ideals," with emphasis on tolerance (145-146).

49. *Ibid.*, 182, 197. For an early Quaker attack on the misuse of Christianity as a new version of pagan civil religion, see Crook 1660, 5.

For a defense of spirituality against both rationalism and traditionalism/scripturalism, see Barclay n.d. 63-71. Barclay found "logic and philosophy" to be

> ...an art so little needful to a true minister, that if one that comes to be a true minister hath had it, it is safest for him to forget and lose it; for it is the root and ground of all contention and debate, and the way to make a thing a great deal darker, than clearer. For under the pretense of regulating man's reason into a certain order and rules, that he may find out, as they pretend the truth, it leads into such a labyrinth of contention, as is far more fit to make a skeptic than a Christian, far less a minister of Christ: yea, it often hinders man from a clear understanding of things his own reason would give him...seeing a man, that is not very wise, may notwithstanding to be a perfect logician (292-293).

Barclay objected not so much to "natural logic" or deduction ("I have sometimes used it in this treatise") as to dialectical logic. This technique of "school-divinity" or "heathenish philosophy christianized, or rather, the literal external knowledge of Christ heathenized" has led to contention and carnal wars (294). One reason for the silence at Quaker meetings is, "the devil cannot counterfeit it" (345).

See also Bayly 1676 on the worst danger to Quakers: "...our Vine hath Tender Grapes, that though the Wild Boars of the Forrest cannot so much hurt them, yet the Subtle Foxes of the Desert may (if not prevented by the Wisdom of God) spoil their Resting-Place, which all the Faithful have in God..." (180, misnumbered 176). Finally, see the still earlier statement of Penington 1663:

> Reason left to itself, without the guidance of a Principle of Life, falls below Sense. How cruel, how blind, how selfish, how unrighteous is man, that follows the dictates of his own corrupt reason, without knowing and becoming subject to that, which should enlighten it, and give him the right use thereof! (5).

50. "Oh! that you would awake before wrath awaken you, and put on the armour of God, not relying any longer on men that beat the air, to fight your battles against him who is got into your hearts; but that yourselves as soldiers of Christ may all come to use the spiritual weapons against the spiritual weakness exalted in the temple of God, so that you can neither see nor serve God therein, being filled with wicked and worldly cumbrances." Nayler, *The Lamb's War Against the Man of Sin* (1658), in Barbour and Roberts 1973, 113.

51. Taylor 1697, 182-183.

52. Letter to John Smith (December 13, 1757) in Brookes 1937, 224-225.

53.

> Concerning *Rulers* and *Governors* we believe that there
> ought to be *Rulers* and *Governors* in every *Nation, City,
> Country,* or *Town,* and they ought to be such men as
> feareth God, and hateth every evil way, *who will judge for
> God and not for man....* And we believe that every Law
> of Man ought to be grounded upon the Law of God,
> pure reason and equity being the Foundation thereof,
> and God's witness in every man may answer to it; and
> the Law ought to be known unto all people before
> transgression be charged or punished in any man...
> [Governors and Rulers] ought to be accountable to the
> people, and to the succeeding *Rulers,* for all their actions
> which may be inquired into upon occasion, and that the
> chiefest of these Rulers be subject under the law, and
> punishable by it if they be transgressions, as well as the
> poorest of the people" (Burrough 1660, 4-5).

54. Penington 1653, 4-5. He was rather more pessimistic than was
Madison with respect to the goods political respect to the goods
political regimes can secure, cautioning that God may send travails to
both kinds or regime, "showing the weakness and insufficiency of both"
(5) — and of human inventions generally. "Man so soon as ever he
comes to place of government, his heart is immediately lifted up above
his brother, which temper make[s] him unfit for government, and
prepareth the way to his own ruin... Did *man* ever bring forth
righteousness or peace?" (6). Penington intends this both as a
chastisement to rulers and a chastening of the expectations of the
governed.

55. Braithwaite 1919, 7.

56. For a chronicle of these persecutions, see Besse 1753, who called
persecution "a severe Test upon the Hypocrite and the Earthly-
minded" (iii). The period of persecution in England lasted from 1650
to 1689 when William and Mary approved the Toleration Act; Besse
lists eight points of doctrinal "*Conscientious Nonconformity* [which]
rendered [Quakers] obnoxious to the *Penalties* of the Law" (1). The
exasperation of some authorities may be seen in the story of the
"drunken Priest, who having been told, that *the Weapons of his Warfare
ought to be spiritual,* replied, that *he would fight the Quakers with such
Weapons as he had*" (12).

57. Bellers 1935, 82-83. He continued, "Love contains the whole Armour
of God."

58. George Fox, quoted in Braithwaite 1919, 19.

59. Barclay n.d., 451-453. The distinctions between believing and doing,
and between thought and doing, are similar to those found in John

Locke. See also Fox 1706: who cited the magistrate of Romans 13 as "a Terror and a Discourager of...evil *Workers* and *Works*" (956; italics added).

60.   Braithwaite 1919, 158. An English translation of Locke's *A Letter Concerning Toleration* was prepared by William Popple, a friend of William Penn. See also Besse 1753:

> The more they afflicted them, the more they multiplied and grew. For Religion, next to her own Light and Energy on the Minds of Men, has not a more popular Argument in her Favour than the Patience and Constancy of her afflicted Confessors (iv).

61.   Barclay n.d., 498-500. Barclay listed as acceptable recreations, visiting friends, hearing and reading history, speaking soberly of present or past transactions, gardening, and mathematical "experiments." Fortunately, true love, whether for a woman or for God, occupies one's mind happily and reduces the need for recreation (500) – an insight shared by wives in modern America, deploring their husbands' preoccupation with televised football games.

Penn 1882 condemned luxury and taught, "the best recreation is to do good" (e.g., "visit sober neighbors to be edified, and wicked ones to reform them") (211).

62.   Brookes 1937, 47, 124.

63.   *Ibid.*, 34.

64.   Penington 1661 introduced an important qualification, not shared by most Quakers. He condemned war, but adds,

> I speak not this against any Magistrates or Peoples defending themselves against foreign invasion or making use of the Sword to suppress the violent and evil doers within their borders (for this the present estate of things may and doth require with a great blessing will attend the Sword where it is born uprightly to that end, and its use will be honorable; and while there is need of a Sword, the Lord will not suffer that Governments, or those Governors, to want fitting instruments under them for the managing thereof...). But there is a better state [Penington quickly adds] which the Lord hath already brought some into, and which Nations are to expect and travel towards (8).

Barbour 1964 mistakenly presents Robert Barclay as the Quaker to introduce this distinction between 'advanced' and 'less-advanced'

Christians with respect to the legitimacy of the use of military force (222). See also Braithwaite 1919, 613.

65. Fox 1706, 407; Fox 1911, 161. See also Smith 1675 who writes that wars and contentions come from "lust and pride" (103), and Bayly 1676, 168-170 on the Christian's "New Heart." Bayly also offers a ten-point Scriptural defense of non-resistance (514 ff). Even Penington warns soldiers against "Fleshly wisdom" (Penington n.d., 987).

66. Benezet 1782, 15; Brookes 1937, 386, 356; Benezet 1766, 3-6.

67. Penington 1661, 4-8. See also Smith 1675: "There is nothing stronger than *Love*" (233). Barbour 1964 writes,

> The Friends' great contribution to statecraft was to realize that their own Peace Testimony was not simply a response to actual war but an answer to the deadlock of consciences. Love for an enemy is itself an innate part of Christian commitment, they said unsentimentally (221).

The controversy over the justifiability of defensive war by Christians, and the degree to which Christians should depend upon Providence for their defense, flared again in the 1740's. Finch 1755 qualified Penington's view: "some must be called to begin the great work of peace in the world' (71) and these should be Quaker; however, in the "economy of God" some are also called to lesser degrees of Christian perfection than are the Quakers, and these Christians may fight (94). For these imperfect Christians, the sword is "the outward providential means to preserve thee and others, as well as himself" (100). The anonymous author of *A Modest Plea in Behalf of the People Called Quakers*, published in response to Finch 1746, concurs with Finch's later argument: "The magistrate, or *any other* Person, *not convinced* [of the duty of non-resistance], may *very fitly* fight in Defense of *Life, Liberty*, and *Property*; and it is *even possible*, if not probably, that the outward Sword *thus drawn* in a *good Cause* has been secretly blessed and prospered by the Almighty, and that such an Army formed on these principles may have *often been a Bulwark* and *Security* to those whose *tender Consciences* would not permit them to draw the carnal Sword themselves...." (8-9).

By contrast, Besse 1747, was upcompromising. He was a spiritual perfectionist, claiming that Christ in His advent intended to restore "fallen Mankind into that State of Purity and Peace, wherein [mankind] was at first created" (v). Anything less than complete dependence upon God's Providence betokens rebellion; *self*-preservation and *self*-defense result from "mistaken Pride." Patience, "the Heroism of Christianity," betokens total dependence on and love of God, and "calleth out the *Fear* of Man" (18). Further, Besse believed overcoming evil with good, non-resistant Christian love, to be more effective in this world than retaliation or self-defense. An "*entire*

Dependence on Providence would render the Use of Arms unnecessary" (35). Government and the rule of love should coincide: "The Establishment of *Love* and *Peace answers the End* and *Institution* of Government;" war only "tends to the Subversion of *Society* and *Government*" (50-51). Besse thus shows how entirely spiritualized one's conception of government must be in order to avoid the conclusion that non-resistance entails not martyrdom but a temporally effective way to govern civil society.

68. Brock 1968, 9; Hirst 1923, 163.

69. Janney 1871, 21; Barbour 1964, 245. It is therefore appropriate that some Quakers settled in the Carolina Colony where a constitution written by John Locke was in force; for a succinct account of that constitution, see McGuinness 1989; see also Jonas 1971, 23-24.

70. Penn 1882, 98-100. "Ambition does not only dwell in courts, and senates: it is too natural to every private breast to strain for power" (103); the people too cause wars.

71. Penn 1882, 254; Penn, "To the Inhabitants of Pennsylvania," in Soderlund 1983, 55; Penn, "To Robert Turner" (March 5, 1681), in Soderlund 1983, 54-55; Penn, "Some Account of the Province of Pennsylvania in America," in Soderlund 1983, 59-64. With respect to the American Indian population, Penn compared his intentions with the Roman founder Romulus and lawgiver Numa Pompilius, who "not only reduced, but moralized the manners of the nations they subjected, so that they may have been rather said to conquer their barbarity than them" (59). Indians shall have quality before the law, and equal rights to farm and to possess and enjoy the fruits of their labors — all fundamental principles of the Declaration of Independence some 100 years later (Penn, "Conditions or Concessions to the First Purchasers," in Soderlund 1983, 74).

72. Penn, "The Fundamental Constitutions of Pennsylvania," first draft, in Soderlund 1983, 97-98. Penn was somewhat more restrictive of religious liberty than Fox; Pennsylvania was to enjoy "Christian liberty," tolerating no profaneness about God or Jesus (99). External laws exist for the regulation of the lusts of "such as would not live conformable to the holy law within." Government also has the 'positive' responsibility "to cherish those who do well.... So government seems to me a part of religion itself, a thing sacred in its institution and end" (Penn, "The Fundamental Constitutions of Pennsylvania," final draft, in Soderlund 1983, 120-121). See also Penn 1912: "...so depraved is Human Nature, that without Compulsion some Way or other, too many would not readily be brought to do what they know is right and fit, or avoid what they are satisfied they would not do" (5).

73. Penn, "Frame of the Governments of Pennsylvania," final draft, in Soderlund 1983, 122-125. Algernon Sidney, no Epicurean, nonetheless

described Penn's constitutional system as "Worse than the Turks" in its severity, "not to be endured or lived under" (cited in West 1980, xxxiii).

74. Hirst 1923, 381.

75. Brock 1968 also cites "the increasingly hereditary membership of the Society," which diluted the intensity of Quaker zeal (111). However, it should be noticed that the alternative would have been a loss of membership and an increase in the formally non-Quaker population of Pennsylvania, a trend that would have been even more rapidly fatal to Quaker political influence.

76. Penn's *An Essay Toward the Present and Future Peace of Europe*, published in 1693, argued that peace comes from justice, and justice from government; therefore, Europe should institute a parliament. Penn brushed aside the problem of sovereignty (the states will "remain as Sovereign at home as they ever were" [Penn 1912, 13]), and ignored the problems issuing from differing regimes with opposing conceptions (and misconceptions) of justice, and therefore of (mis)education for virtue. Slightly more sober was Bellers 1710, who advocated both a European parliament and supreme court: "*Europe* being under several Forms of Government, and every country being apt to Esteem their own Form best: It will require Time and consideration among the Powers concerned, to draw such a Scheme as will suit the Dispositions and Circumstances of them all" (92).

77. Brock 1968, 83, 158. Tully, 1977, describes the tensions between the Quaker legislation and the Quaker executive (23-28; 154), resolved in favor of the latter on the grounds of rendering unto Caesar.

78. Soderlund 1983, 278, 10. Janney 1871 looks on the brighter side: "Pennsylvania affords the only example of a state, where the executive power was upheld without military force, justice administered without the use of oaths, and religion sustained without a priesthood or salaried ministry" (550). For a still sunnier opinion see Hauerwas 1989, 138-140. See also Hershberger 1951.

79. Smith 1748, 2, 10, 21-22. The (eventual) American founder who contributed to the debate in the 1740's Pennsylvania was Benjamin Franklin, notably in *Plain Truth: or, Serious Considerations On the Present State of the City of Philadelphia and Province of Pennsylvania* (1748). In this pamphlet Franklin kept his argument on a strictly nonreligious level. Wealthy and defenseless, Pennsylvania doubly tempts military predation, Franklin argued (Franklin 1954-58, Vol 3, 191-192). He was not above playing to racist fears; imagine the miseries, he wrote, "when your Persons, Fortunes, Wives and Daughters, shall be subject to the wanton and unbridles Rage, Rapine and Lust, of *Negroes*, *Mulattoes*, and others, the vilest and most abandoned of Mankind" (198). He reminded pacifist Quakers that public money comes from all, for all; he reminded non-pacifists reluctant to defend nonresistants that militiamen will fight for

themselves as well as for Quakers. And he invoked the prudence of military deterrence: "'Tis a wise and true Saying, that *One Sword often keeps another in the Scabbard*" (203). Fear, prejudice, conscience (of Quakers), self-interest, and prudence: Franklin left few rhetorical strings unplayed. His campaign for a Pennsylvania militia succeeded.

80. Dodge 1854, 101. For a history of the early "peace societies" in America, see Curti 1929.

81. Wells 1810, 14, 34, 66, 100-101. Wells claimed that "the Jewish constitution" gave Israelites "the strongest assurances of peace." "But they departed from it" to make war (65). Mott 1814 paraphrased and at times nearly plagiarized Wells, with one original addition: a warning against the influence of paganism, especially pagan "ideas of virtue" such as "laws of honor," which are a "great means of keeping alive the spirit of war" (29).

82. Dodge 1905, 145, 155-156. See also Dodge 1854, 80: "No one circumstance led me so much to doubt the soundness of the sentiments of my opponents as their general want of faith in the promises and providential protection of God..."

83. Anonymous 1810, 19. This writer was sufficiently unkind to point to Dodge's own safety as an example.

84. Dodge 1810, 15-17.

85. *Ibid.*, 43-44. In *The Mediator's Kingdom* he had loosely paraphrased Matt. 26:52 in writing, "Every political or ecclesiastical body which is defended with the sword will by the sword be destroyed" (146n.), an argument whereby a posited causal nexus makes sense only if the prophecy is authoritative. In *War Inconsistent with the Religion of Jesus Christ* 1815, Dodge ventured to claim that "probably no instance can be found of robbers murdering such *as conscientiously* held to nonresistance. It is resistance that provokes violence; forbearance and good will repress it" (Dodge 1905, 82).

86. *War Inconsistent with the Religion of Jesus Christ*, in Dodge 1905, 32-44.

87. See Dodge 1816. Somewhat more nearly political than Dodge, Whelpley 1818 allowed that the "moral and spiritual kingdom" of Jesus should influence "earthly kingdoms," although not "interfere" with them (24). He had nothing of substance to say about the American regime. He shared Dodge's optimism concerning the prudence of nonresistance, while admitting it has not been tried on a national level (89).

Holcombe 1823a argued that the conscientious refusal to serve in the military finds protection in the United States Constitution's guarantee of the free exercise of religion (9). The remainder of his argument was entirely Scriptural, emphasizing the lack of any Christian injunction to forceful self-defense. Submission or flight are the Christian means of self-defense (Holcombe 1823b, 15-16).

Upham 1836 conceded "that if the code of nature were the only code, which binds its requisitions on the human race, the prospect of universal and permanent peace would be altogether a hopeless one" (86).

However,

> We verily believe in these principles there is a secret power, a hidden but most effective energy, which is but imperfectly understood. If men had the faith to receive it, they would not fail to find, that the panoply of love is more impenetrable to the attacks of adversaries than that of steel" (198).

Upham assumed the progress of Christianity, arts and sciences, representative government, and anti-war sentiment will bring peace gradually to the world (267, 394).

Peabody 1843 went farther: "It is in the very nature of things, impossible for a nation, occupying such a position [unarmed and "in perfect quietness"], to be...assailed" (6). Jesus "transposed" the scale of pagan virtue, replacing courage with Fortitude, resentment with forgiveness, harshness with love. The attempt to combine Christian and pagan virtue, as in the Augustinian teaching for the just war, must always fail (9-10).

Jackson 1846 and Burritt 1956 were for the most part apolitical, citing the Christian love for enemies and arguing its inconsistency with war. Burritt emphasized the active power of Christian love, good humoredly claiming that such brave commanders as Wolfe and Montgomery did not really understand war: "They had not the Gospel knack of taking a city" (56). Burritt recognized that a testing of "that simple and sublime precept of the Gospel, 'overcome evil with good'... requires a capacity of good-will, of forgiveness of injuries, of abnegation of natural instincts, which the population of no town, or province, or state, has ever acquired;" at most, "passive resistance to oppression" has occurred (269). If such a national phenomenon would arise, Burritt did not doubt not that it would be an "irresistible" manifestation of "God's power" (314-315).

88.   Musser 1878, 419-421. "No government can exist without the sword, and occasionally having war; and the idea of having government without it is an absurdity" (460).

89.   *Ibid.*, 424.

90.   *Ibid.*, 440.

91. *Ibid.*, 456, 469. The unconverted

>...enjoy their reward of natural prosperity, comfort and enjoyment of the blessings of life. But it is not possible that they can enjoy the love of God, unless they are converted and receive the Holy Spirit. Neither have they the promise of eternal life.... These men may be officers in government, may be generals in the field, or soldiers in the ranks, and commit no sin in these duties; and will not be condemned for them, any more than they will for any other moral duty they perform. It is asked, 'Is there one law for sinners, and another for Christians?' I say yes! Sinners are under the law of justice, where all men were before Christ came. Christians are under the law of grace and love, where Christ put them. The others are where Christ left them, because they would not obey His call" (*Ibid.*, 454).

92. *Ibid.*, 456, 459.

93. *Ibid.*, 466. Musser also questioned the regime of what Madison would have called pure democracy; it is unclear whether he mistook the United States for a pure democracy: "We are accustomed to boast of our manhood for independence; but I am unable to conceive either manhood or independence in the idea, that because certain men, however high their standing in society, believe, say or do a thing, it must be right" (469).

94. *Ibid.*, 472-473. For a later statement of the traditional Mennonite Position, see Holdeman 1891. Holdeman added a critique of philosophy, beginning with the lapidary sentence, "The philosophers respect evangelical morality, without understanding the grace by which the true believer can keep it" (87). Philosophy alone "could not cause peace and liberty to reign the world," as the French Revolution "proved;" "the religion of reason and atheistic virtue, and vain oppose the torrent of human lusts..." (89). In the end, "religious liberty will become the foundation of universal peace, as soon as the laws shall be made to conform to the Christian conscience, whose faith forbids fratricide" (89), on the grounds that only He who created life has the right to dispose of it (79). Holdeman mistakenly identified the ideology of the philosophers with philosophy itself, and the "atheistic virtue" of the French Revolution with atheistic virtue as such. No competent political philosopher has ever imagined that unaided philosophy could cause peace or liberty in the world; even Plato's ironically-meant polity ruled by philosopher-kings depends upon an obedient guardian-class. Holdeman defined religious liberty as liberty for those who practice true religion, i.e., Mennonite Christianity, and sensibly concluded that this would suffice to bring peace to the world. The question remains whether this is more than sufficient.

Harvey 1921 brought the Mennonite teaching into the twentieth century, without compromising with twentieth-century intellectual fashion. His pamphlet holds interest for one other reason: A Civil War veteran, Harvey admitted that just-war Christianity ("army Christianity") abstains from immoral acts. What it lacks is the sense of the *imitatio Christi*, particularly the need to emulate "His gentleness and His love for all men" (22). "No one can know this until he feels it in his own soul" (24).

For a history of one Mennonite group and its relation to civil government, see Horsch 1931, 133-135. For a later statement of anti-liberal Mennonite constitutionalism, see Gardner 1944, 27-29, 42-44.

For a non-Mennonite example of apolitical Christian pacifism in twentieth-century America, see MacLaren 1900: "No Court of Arbitration can ever prevail to bring this discordant world into unity, harmony and peace, that is not Christ-centric" (183).

95. Worcester 1815, 4. The peace societies were to be formed in all *Christian* nations; in Worcester apolitical Christian pacifism began to blend into a somewhat more political 'movement' pacifism. For a critique of Worcester see Haynes 183-24, who argued that forgiving, nonresistant rulers would scarcely amount to the "terror to evildoers" that is the Pauline magistrate. "There can be nothing more futile to imagine that if governments would forbear to punish, the people would cease to transgress. Therefore, the solemn truth must remain that we must deal with mankind as they *are* and not as they *should* be" (18-20). Compare Machiavelli 1985, 61: "[H]e who lets go of what is done for what should be done earns his ruin rather than his preservation."

Somewhat more nearly political still than Worcester was William Ladd, the founder of the American Peach Society in 1828 and "the chief source of [the peace movement's] vitality" until the early 1840's (Curti 1929, 42). Ladd contended "Every bible society is in fact a peace society" (Ladd 1827, 112), but most of his arguments were secular – moral, social and economic, if not political. He recognized the relatively peaceful character of commerce, finding it to have been the cause of only five of the 286 wars he had studied (26). Love of glory more frequently causes war, whose "continuance" in history "rests *entirely*" on public opinion (10). Early education, the militia system, and war-preparation all influence public opinion to favor war, as does the admiration of women for soldiers. "In a woman's mind" Ladd explained, "the ideas of love and murder are often associated... [T]he intrigues of Mars and Venus are not to be considered barely as a fable of heathen mythology," inasmuch as "it is a law of our nature, that persons of one sex should love those qualities in the other of which they themselves are deficient." As a result, "chivalry as far from being extinct with us," and "not one female writer of any eminence, that I can recollect, has ever employed her pen in favor of peace; though many have busied themselves in exciting a love of military glory" (61-66). Compare Rousseau 1979, 390-391.

George C. Beckwith headed the American Peace Society after Ladd, but was a pacificist not a pacifist, approving "wars strictly defensive" (Beckwith 1845, 5). He considered defensive war no war at all; "self-defense is another thing, quite as distinct from the custom of war as it is from duelling" (Beckwith 1847, 134). Concurring with Ladd that "opinion is now mistress of the world" (*Ibid.*, 244), he therefore assumed the purely verbal rule of a Congress of Nation to be feasible; he had no premonition of twentieth-century-style propaganda, or the use of words as weapons to inspire the use of physical weapons. Appealing primarily to religion ("Our efforts are restricted to countries blest with the light of revelation" [Beckwith 1845, 5]; he wrote that we cannot rely on men of the world, except as occasional coadjutators. "[Peacemaking] is the appropriate work of Christians; and they must do it, or it never will be done" [*Ibid.*, 11]). Beckwith nonetheless was the most nearly political of this group. He attempted so to speak to bring peace to the peace movement, calling for unity among their members despite their doctrinal differences; "union is indispensable to every cause, but to none more than peace" (*Ibid.*, 93). (He did not succeed; in 1838, Henry C. Wright broke with the American Peace Society and founded the more strictly pacifist New England Non-Resistance Society).

> We wish...to influence those who guide the helm of state. How shall this be done? Not one in a thousand of them deems *all* war un-christian. Upon such men it would be quite useless to urge the extreme doctrines of peace; and, if we reach them at all, it must be through its moderate friends and moderate arguments (*Ibid.*, 97).

Beckwith considered modern republicanism pacificist: "The policy of nations has hitherto been essentially belligerent; but popular representation will be averse to this policy, and Propitious to the great objects sought by a congress of nations" (237); contradictorily, he claimed that regime differences would not seriously impede such a Congress, citing the example of the Swiss Cantons, which ranged "from the purest democracy to the stiffest aristocracy" (245). He did not even begin to examine the perhaps induplicable geographical and political reasons for the founding and maintenance of the Swiss confederation.

Beckwith's political superficiality derived from his optimism with respect to religious and civilizational progress. "[U]nder the perpetual advance of Christianity and civilization, mere physical power is every where losing, and moral power gaining social and political influence" (210). His first and last concerns were religious not political. "[F]inally, and more than all, peace would put a stop to the ruin of immortal souls directly occasioned by war" (286). As Machiavelli before him and Nietzsche after him saw,

> ...upon a community of minds impregnated with war-passions, the strongest truths of God's word would fall powerless as moonbeams on ice. Wherever the war-spirit prevails, there would you labor in vain for the conversion of sinners, or the sanctification of Christians (450).

96. Grimké 1832, 4-8.

97. *Ibid.*, 13-17, 26.

98. *Ibid.*, 43-47.

99. *Ibid.*, 54n, 55n. The roughness of this consistency may be seen in the specifically Christian character of Grimké's "Declaration," which contrasts with the nonsectarian Scripturalism of the 1776 Declaration. This, with Grimké's pacifist understanding of Christianity, enabled Grimké to make the political turn away from military defense of unalienable rights.

100. Wayland 1868, 95, 123-124, 128. The first edition was published in 1835.

101. *Ibid.*, 191-192, 203. "The right of property...is the right to use our faculties as we choose, provided we so use them as not to interfere with the similar rights of others" (239).

102. *Ibid.*, 345-347. Wayland 1847 added the rights of intellectual and conscientious freedom to these (8). In this sermon he quoted the Declaration of Independence.

103. *Ibid.*, 355, 367, 392. To maintain peace, Wayland recommended strict justice in foreign relations, kindness and charity to all nations, application for voluntary redress of injuries renouncement of all relations if such application is ignored and, as a last resort, defensive use of force (393-394). This conception of war differs from the conduct of war today, Wayland wrote, because it countenances no vengeance and earnestly seeks to turn "enmity to friendship" after successful self-defense (Wayland 1847, 20). Further, Wayland justified a right to forceful revolution, thus working his way from near-pacifism to a just-war pacifism similar to that of the American Founders: a government that "deprive[es] us of those rights conferred upon us by our Creator...ceases to be a government;" it is "power without authority" (*Ibid.*, 32). As is almost universal among just-war theorists, the word "necessary" makes its appearance at a key point in the argument (20).

104. *Ibid.*, 6.

105. *Ibid.*, 24-25.

106. Blanchard 1848, 5, 3, 19.

107. *Ibid.*, 35.

108. Blanchard 1845, 4-5.

109. *Ibid.*, 13-14, 18.

110. Sumner 1969, I, 4, 14-15, 48, 71, 112.

111. "The Law of Human Progress" (July 25, 1848) in Sumner 1969, II, 251; and "War System of the Commonwealth of Nations" (May 28, 1849), in Sumner 1969, II, 333, 377, 383, 416. Sumner endorsed then-popular plans for international arbitration. See "Stipulated Arbitration, or a Congress of Nations, with Disarmament" (February 22, 1850), in Sumner 1969, III.

112. "Threat of Disunion by the Slave States and its Absurdity," (October 11, 1860), in Sumner 1969, VII. Similarly, the Church of the Brethren's most respected leader, John Kline, protested disunion but could think of nothing to do to prevent it, beyond protest: "The General Government of the United States of America, constituted upon an inseparable union of the several states, has proved itself to be of incalculable worth to its citizens and the world, and therefore we, as a church and people, are heart and soul opposed to any move which looks toward dismemberment." (Quoted in Bowman 1944, 115). Kline prudently confined himself to protest, leaving prophecy to others. Charles K. Whipple, writing on the eve of the war, acknowledged self-defense to be "a natural instinct and a natural right," as is the right to defend those who are wronged (Wright 1860b, 4). But violent self-defense is wrong; "to kill, to wound, and to strike, are acts of offense even more than of defense" (9). The Declaration held life to be an unalienable right; the Founder, to be consistent, would have had to reject both war and the death penalty (13). Slavery also violates the Declaration's principles, and those who would help slaves must still conform to the "hard duties" of nonviolence and love (20). As a practical action, Whipple could only recommend that abolitionists institute shelters for runaway slaves in "the mountains of the slaveholding states," thereby "in a short time draining the whole region of the entire laboring population" (23). Although a sincere friend of American republicanism, Whipple had no practicable advice on how to sustain it. See also Whipple 1860a, for equally airy proposals on "internal defense of a community" against criminals – whose number will be reduced by ninety percent in the next generation, we are assured, if only the state governments would undertake the care of neglected children (25).

113. "Rights of Sovereignty and Rights of War: Two Sources of Power Against the Rebellion" (May 19, 1862), Sumner 1969, IX, 34; "Our Foreign Relations: Present Perils from England and France, Nature and Condition of Intervention by Mediation and also by Recognition,

Impossibility of any Recognition of a New Power with Slavery as a Corner-Stone, and Wrongful Concession of Ocean Belligerence" (September 10, 1863), Sumner, 1969, X, 140-143. For an account of the turn away from pacifism by pacifists during the American Civil War, see Brock 1968, Part IV. As did Sumner, Angelina Grimke wrote, "War is better than slavery" (Brock 1968, 696).

114. See for example *An Essay Concerning the True Original, Extent, and End of Civil Government*, III, 18 in Locke 1963, 320-321.

115. Washburn 1873, 16.

116. *Ibid.*, 16-17.

117. *Ibid.*, 19.

118. *Ibid.*, 25, 32, 36, 43-45. Washburn acknowledged that Rousseau believed life a conditional grant of the state, but characterized Rousseau's language as being "of intensely selfish and scoffing infidelity" − not Christian at all (44).

119. *Ibid.*, 69.

120. *Ibid.*, 65, 88, 109, 117. In pursuing nationalism, "borrowing from the notions of heathen nations," men have committed idolatry, which modern war serves as "human sacrifice." Good government, by contrast, "is but a means to a worldly end," natural justice; the Declaration of Independence enunciates the principle of such government, "the equality of man before the laws of nature" (123-124).

121. Washburn criticized a theologian who called "the blood of traitors...the cement of government." Not the distinction between 'us' and 'them' − whether 'they' are foreign or domestic enemies − but interests and the natural wants underlying them should unite a people under their government. Political union arises not against common few but in common attractions. The 'negative' union of bloodiness occurs where lusts replace wants, reason, and Christianity; such union wins commendation from "the numerous disciples of Cain, the illustrious inventor of this kind of 'cement'" (132-133).

122. *Ibid.*, 141-145. The argument again does not fully address the question of consent: Does he who violates the social contract not therefore *cease* to consent to government, including self-governing republicanism? Is it not therefore his own transgression that government punished forcefully, as God ordains? The question then becomes, If the magistrate is God's minister for good, is death sometimes good for the evildoer? His death is surely good for his erstwhile victims, at least in this-worldly terms. And if we must not snatch life from an evildoer lest he be damned (in life there remains hope of his salvation) the same must be said for these erstwhile

victims, perhaps equally unprepared for death, and surely more numerous than the evildoer.

On the matter of the "tyranny" of the American Civil War, Washburn contended that the Northern states "forgot that our constitution and government are founded in the exact conception in which the South repudiated its allegiance, and for which the North flew to arms," namely, the right to revolution (153). This ignores the representation of the Southern states in the pre-war American government, a right the colonies did not have in the British government. Washburn did go on to acknowledge that Southern claims rested not merely on interests but upon "immortal interests," and he interestingly echoes Madison's (above, p. 42) analysis of the Southern states; "the Southern people [had] the style and feelings of feudal aristocracy" instead of modern republicanism (160-161).

123. *Ibid.*, 178-184. Here Washburn surely glanced at Rousseau's celebrated paradox, that some men must be forced to be free. See *The Social Contract*, I, vii in Rousseau 1959, 18.

124. *Ibid.*, 187-188.

125. *Ibid.*, 203.

126. *Ibid.*, 206. Washburn also insisted that interest would set more or less natural limits on political disunion, since imprudent secession would always injure the seceder. This argument fails for the reasons about to be stated in the text.

127. *Ibid.*, 236.

128. *Ibid.*, 262, 273. Italics in original.

129. *Ibid.*, 281.

130. *Ibid.*, 316, 335-336.

131. *Ibid.*, 382-383, 388.

132. *Ibid.*, 403, 419.

133. *Ibid.*, 456. This comports with his earlier rationalistic overestimation of the power of education.

134. Another example of the reliance upon interest to maintain political union may be seen in Carey 1872. Carey was an economist who considered commercial capitalism to be productive of civilization, "the most perfect individuality and the greatest tendency to union, whether of men or of nations" (416). He added to this the Christian moral law of love, "not more the duty than it is the policy both of men and of nations" (371), and the American practice of self-government (449)

135.   In his address, "The Principles of the Founders," Edwin D. Mead brought political pacifism based on American principles into the twentieth century. Mead clearly associated the Declaration's principle of equality, particularly equality before the law, with peace (Mead 1903, 18). He associated the use of coercion as *ultima ratio* with lawlessness and therefore with the subversion of republican government (61). However, he generally lacked the profundity of the nineteenth-century American pacifists, and never seriously addressed himself to the questions of political union and defense.

136.   One should exercise care in classifying writers under this rubric. Dresser 1849 called the Revolutionary War "fratricidal butchery" and described the growth of slavery as God's punishment for undertaking it (146). But Washburn also considered the *war* to have been evil; condemning the war does not entail condemning the revolution and its principles. Judd 1842, something of an American Tory remnant, believed the British taxes of the 1760's and 1770's to have been just impositions "to meet expenses that had been incurred for [the Americans'] own good, emolument and glory" (7). As for representation, he contended that Americans lacked it while the war was conducted as much as they lacked it under British rule — an odd dismissal of the Continental Congress, which kept General Washington on a rather short fiscal leash throughout. Still, it is not clear that Judd actually rejected the principles of the American republic, as distinguished from their implementation in wartime.

Perhaps as important as the increased distance from the Founder's generation to the formation of an anti-'American' pacifism was the reaction against the United States' war against Mexico in 1846-1848. The best example of this may be seen in Livermore 1850. Deploring that "our Fourth-of-July oratory has inserted in youthful veins the deadly virus of warlike passion" (12), Livermore raised questions about the regime itself. "The old spirit has revived under a new name. We are to have not the tyrant *One*, but the tyrant *Million*, who may be quite as intractable, and quite as subversive of liberty, which respects the rights of conscience" (222).

> The friends of peace had fondly cherished the hope that *pure republics*, the governments of the many as contradistinguished from monarchies and aristocracies, the governments of the one, or the few, would be *pacific*.... But we are disappointed. We see that republics can wage as fierce, brutal, and unjust wars, as feudal and despotic powers. Witness republican France, waging a cruel war against republican Rome to restore the Pope! The example of our wickedness will find in future history but too many imitators. Such cases need not in the least shake our faith in republicanism; but they should convince us of the necessity, if we would have a *true* republicanism, of compounding with it large

admixtures of sound education, *pure religion*, and the spirit of universal brotherhood. The Mexican war has accordingly taught us not to trust to political institutions alone, however free and admirable, for the maintenance of pacific relations among mankind. We must strike a higher key. We must appeal to deeper motives. Men may know their rights in a republic, and still be ignorant of their duties. They may know their duties, and not discharge them (259-260).

Livermore insufficiently distinguished between American and French republicanism. More important, he neglected the distinction between wars of republics against non-republics, which had occurred and would continue to occur, and wars of commercial republics against other commercial republics, which generally speaking had not and would not occur. No other political regime does not attack others of its own kind.

137.   "War and Human Brotherhood," in Channing 1903, 10-11. In this essay Channing appeared to endorse defensive war, distinguishing from "the common instances of war" animated by ambition (13). In his 1816 address, "First Discourse on War," he had contended that "national subjugation is a greater evil than a war of defense...." (Channing 1903, 32).

For a rare statement by a nineteenth-century pacifist basing his argument on strictly libertarian grounds, see Warren 1863, who defined consent as "my sovereign right to control my own" (12), and could therefore claim that the Declaration of Independence should be read as a no-government tract. He objected to war as much for the enforced discipline of military life as for its violence. On the American Civil War, then ongoing, he argued irrefutably that without the Union there could have been no civil war in the first place. He went on to generalize the observation: "Did human beings ever commit any other blunder so great as that of forming themselves into clans of nations?" (60). He did not quite reject politics altogether, proposing that the United States be 'governed' by a "Deliberative Council," with vague powers. Warren differed from the other American pacifists of the time in showing no sign of Christian belief, defining the divine merely as not-human, i.e., winds and tides.

In his 1848 essay *Civil Disobedience* Henry David Thoreau anticipated Warren's argument, though in lightly Christianized form (Thoreau 1966, 224-243). He too attacked representative government and majority rule from the basis of a highly individualistic moralism, and of course detested military discipline. *Civil Disobedience* influenced later pacifism indirectly, its title lending to the mass-movement nonviolent techniques of Gandhi and his admirers. However, it is difficult to see how the real Thoreau could have interested himself in the political organizing required to make 'civil disobedience' effective.

138.   "Lecture on War" (1938), Channing 1903, 75-76, 87, 91.

522

139. "The Passion for Domination" (1828), Channing 1903, 144.

140. Wright 1841, 10-11, 42, 57-58. Unlike Channing, Wright was a true pacifist, rejecting both offensive and defensive war (46). More, he criticized the Quakers for having to do with existing governments, based as they were on appeals to force (Wright 1845, 152-163). In "Does God Ordain Human Governments?" Wright denied that governments were "*approvingly* ordained" (Wright 1846, 12; italics in original), slighting the goodness of the ends governments serve, according to Romans 13. To claim that Paul required Christian obedience to government "only to inculate upon the subject the Christian duty of non-resistance" (12), clearly contradicts the epistle.

141. Wright 1888, 30. Wright dogmatically insisted that disputes "can never be settled" by fighting, that "they are always increased by it" (32). In one story, a boy says he prefers to kill woodchucks instead of rabbits, because the woodchucks fight back, which "makes me angry, and then I can kill them without pity." Wright's moral — "The way to conquer is, *never to fight*" (182) — is somewhat vitiated by the disclosure that the boy persists in killing rabbits.

142. Wright 1846, 6-7. Italics added.

143. Wright 1845, 185, 343-344.

144. Ballou 1910, 216, 3. Ballou distinguished Christian non-resistance from *philosophical* non-resistance (which has its basis in reasoning upon nature), *sentimental* non-resistance (based upon the alleged progress and refinement of human feelings), and *necessitous* non-resistance (the sort required by despots, or "recommended by worldly prudence") (2).

145. Ballou 1860, 22.

146. Ballou 1870-1900, II, 159-161, Ballou 1910; Ballou 1854, 263.

147. Ballou 1860, 9.

148. Ballou 1870-1900, I, 267; Ballou 1854, 79. This assumption led Ballou into some highly ingenious exegesis of Scripture. For example, the "rod of iron" mentioned in Revelations 19:15 symbolizes Jesus' truth, his "rod of correction" (Ballou 1870-1900, I, 269). All apparent references to the "abominable doctrine" of eternal damnation (e.g. Matthew 25:46) were deemed equally symbolic. 'Everlasting' punishment means "everlastingly effectual and salutary." Judgment Day is "a fiction." Ballou was a Universalist and a gradualist (Ballou 1854, 79-82). In all it is undoubtedly more humane to torture a text than a soul. The question then becomes, 'Is God humane?'

149. Ballou 1870-1900, II, 175; Ballou 1910, 78, 88; Ballou 1839, 21. *Human government* is "the will of man — whether of one, few, many or all, in a state or a nation — exercising absolute sovereignty over man, by means of cunning and physical force;" divine government is "the infallible will of God prescribing the duty of moral agents." Therefore, human government, based on force and fraud, "has not original, inherent authority over the conscience." (Ballou 1839, 5-8). The early Christians stood outside government. "This they could do while cherishing a profound respect for the providential ordination and use of these governments, without being dechristianized by them" (Ballou 1870-1900, II, 82-83).

150. Ballou 1870-1900, II, 83-84.

> What has the Christian Church been doing all this time? It has in large part been acting as priestly confessor to the state, to sanctify its iniquities and grant absolution to its sins; especially to justify and consecrate the horrid barbarities of the gigantic war system of the world" (86).

151. Ballou 1870-1900, I, 241.

152. Ballou 1870-1900, II, 179. See also Ballou 1839, 10-11, for a critique of anarchism.

Ballou calls two kinds of Christians unreasonable: the ones Reinhold Niebuhr taught a generation to call 'realists' and also the kind of pacifists Niebuhr criticized. Those who "voluntarily assume the position of disciples of Christ, yet revolt against his lofty precepts are "too high and strict for the world" forget that Christians should not aspire to be of the world.

> On the other hand there are professed non-resistants and friends of peace just as unreasonable as those referred to who make no such profession. They assume that the indiscriminate multitude can be brought to practice that 'love which worketh no ill' as easily as they can be induced to espouse the Temperance, Anti-Slavery, Woman's Rights, and other secular moral reforms. More absurdly still, they call on civil governments, legislatures, and all sorts of milito-political authorities, to act on the highest principles of peace and good will, as if it were possible for them to do this as it is to act on their own lower plane of worldly policy and reserved injurious, death-dealing force. In the very nature of things they cannot do this without a prior regeneration to be attained only through a long process of enlightenment, moral growth, and spiritual development. This gross absurdity exhibits itself to an almost ridiculous extent when in the midst of great wars, governments and military authorities are appealed to in

> deprecatory tones, to stop the tornado of deadly violence at once, 'beat their swords into plowshares,' and inaugurate the reign of brotherhood and peace. The result proposed in such a case is grandly good, but the assumption that it is possible under the circumstances is pitifully puerile if not ludicrous. Christ never contemplated any such instantaneous, wholesale, impracticable method of converting the world from its harm-plotting, war-promoting, death-dealing spirit and habit to the love and practice of kindliness, fraternity, harmony. He began to build his moral superstructure at the foundation, in the renewing of individual characters and lives, by the power of the spirit of peace and love, and not at the apex. So should we (Ballou 1870-1900, II 181-183).

153.   Ballou 1862, 20.

154.   Ballou 1862, 20; Ballou 1910, 47; Ballou 1839, 3; Ballou 1870-1900, II, 91; Ballou 1854, 264; Ballou 1870-1900, II, 187.

> A poor government is better than no government at all, and a government exceedingly faulty in some things is better than anarchy − moral and social chaos. Absolute personal independence, extreme individualism...is an impossibility; were it possible, it would be undesirable as utterly opposed to the genius of Christianity, as obstructive of the operations of some of the strongest impulses of human nature, and as mischievous in its inevitable tendency and effect upon personal character and in society, among the nations and throughout the earth" (Ballou 1870-1900, III, 47).

155.   Ballou 1910, 103-112. Ballou's dichotomous conceptualizing led him to far-fetched speculation on human history.

> Take the worst possible view: resolve all the assailed and injured into the most passive non-resistants imaginable, and let the offenders have unlimited scope to commit all the robberies, cruelties, and murders they pleased; would as many lives have been sacrificed, or as much real misery have been experienced by the human race, as have actually resulted from the general method of self-preservation, by personal conflict and resistance of injury with injury? He must be a bold man who affirms it (Ballou 1910, 103).

Among those who have seen twentieth-century totalitarianism, one must rather be a bold man to deny it.

156.   Ballou 1870-1900, II, 200; Ballou 1854, 165-166.

> What is generically and absolutely natural cannot be
> annihilated or wholly suppressed by any finite power.
> But much that is thus natural can be varied and modified
> as to its form and expression almost to infinity (189).

Thus while "man is a governmental being by nature, as well as a social, intellectual, religious, or otherwise endowed one," the forms of his political life are highly malleable (190-191). Ballou personally recalled his own naturally political inclinations: "Al the young duck takes to water at the first opportunity, so was I disposed to patriotism, politics, and war, from the start" (Ballou 1896, 25-26). This Christian-Aristotelian understanding of human nature also may be seen in Ballou's account of the seven "spheres" of human action: individuality, connubiality, consanguinity, congeniality (friendship), federality (social and political life), humanity, and "universality" ("from the invisible atom to the sun," the angels, and God). (Ballou 1854, 168; compare the argument of Aristotle in Book I of the *Politics*). Ballou combined 'Enlightenment' and Aristotelian motifs with his universalist form of Christianity to form the ideational foundation of a Christian communalism.

157.   Ballou 1854, 25, 302, 177-191. For a late twentieth century version of Ballou's Christian politics, see Hauerwas 1989, who condemns "the corrupt distinction between the public and the private presumed by, liberal political theory" and called the Christ in Church "a political narrative to nations and empires" (133-136).

158.   Ballou 1854, ix, 300-325.

159.   Ballou 1896, 357-359, 342.

160.   Garrison 1885, II 202. He agreed with John Humphrey Noyes, who wrote,

> The signs of the times clearly indicate the purpose of
> God to do his strange work speedily, the country is ripe
> for a convulsion like that of France; rather, I should say,
> for the French Revolution reversed. Infidelity roused
> the whirlwind in France. The Bible, by anti-slavery and
> other similar movements, is doing the same work in this
> country. So, in the end, Jesus Christ, instead of a
> bloodthirsty Napoleon, will ascend the throne of the
> world. (II, 147).

161.   "The American Union," Garrison 1968, 117-119. He attacked the American Founders for their compromise with slavery (Garrison 1885, I, 308).

162.   "The Liberator and Slavery" (January 1832), Garrison 1966, 41-44.

163. Letter to James Redpath (December 1, 1860), in Garrison 1974, IV, 704; Letter to Dr. Samuel G. Howe *et al.* (November 12, 1855).
164. Letter to J. Miller McKim (October 4, 1851), Garrison 1974, IV, 89; Garrison 1885, III, 102; IV 19-23. Garrison criticized Joshua P. Blanchard for believing that the Declaration's doctrine of consent permitted the southern states to secede; he correctly (if again hyperbolically) called this a "stupid and monstrous perversion of the meaning of the Declaration" (Letter to Samuel J. May [August 5, 1863], Garrison 1975-79, I, 163-164.
165.

> It is more and more evident that [Lincoln] is a man of very small calibre, and had better be at his old business of splitting rails than at the head of a government like ours, especially in such a crisis. He has evidently not a drop of anti-slavery blood in his veins; and he seems incapable of uttering a humane or generous sentiment respecting the enslaved millions in our land (Letter to Oliver Johnson [December 6, 1861], Garrison 1975-79, I, 47).

166. "The Practical Working of Nonresistance," Garrison 1968, 86-88; Garrison 1885, I, 219. In "Patriotism and Christianity: Kossuth and Jesus," Garrison disparagingly compared the Hungarian freedom-fighter Kossuth with George Washington; both are "strictly local, territorial, national," unlike Jesus (Garrison 1968m 83). This is false; Washington rather sought universal ends through national action; he intended the 'nationality' of his means to promote not impede universal ends. Thus the quarrel between Garrison and the American Founders remains essentially a quarrel over what is and is not prudent. While saying the spirit of non-resistance and of forgiveness is omnipotent," Garrison did concede that "moral courage, − duty − self-consecration − all have their proper limits" (Garrison 1885, I 507); Jesus Himself commended prudence. Prudence, though prized by Garrison, is not very conspicuous in his rhetoric.

In our time, the Mennonite Hershberger disagreed sharply with Garrison and other 'strong' non-resistants, arguing that the Bible commands us to do justice not to demand it of others. "[I]t is...impossible to believe that Paul would have condoned any revolutionary movement," or any "means of forcing the government's hand." Paul and the other writers of the New Testament command love more than justice (Hershberger 1969, 187).

167. "War Essentially Wrong," Garrison 1968, 95; "To *The Liberator*" (October 15, 1858), Garrison 1975-79, IV, 570; Garrison 1885, III, 473. He nonetheless applauded John Brown's raid (*Ibid.*, 491-492) in its success if not its methods, thus coming perilously close to "jesuitical doctrine." Also, in 1861 he edited *The Abolition of Slavery and the Right of the Government Under the War Power*, a collection of statements by John Quincy Adams, J. R. Giddings, Orester Brownson, and General John C. Fremont, arguing that the United States military

may be used to liberate slaves without violating the Constitution (Garrison, ed. 1861).

168.   Garrison 1862, 44-48, 52. The same goes for the Federal government:

> I do not believe in killing or doing injury even to enemies — God forbid! That is not my Christian philosophy, but I do say, that never before in the history of the world has God vouchsafed to a government the power to do such a work of philanthropy and justice, in the extremity of its danger and for self-preservation, as he now grants to this government. Emancipation is to destroy nothing but evil; it is to establish good; it is to transform human beings from things into men; it is to make freedom, and education, and invention, and enterprise, and peace, and *a true Union* possible and sure (50).

"Slavery," he concluded, " is toryism run to seed" (54).

169.   Letter to Francis W. Newman (July 15, 1864), Garrison 1975-79, I, 222, 223. For his silence on the war power clause after the war, see Garrison 1885, IV. William Lloyd Garrison, Jr. went somewhat farther, defending his father's position with the same argument George Washington used during the Revolutionary period:

> Peace is not merely a cessation from what we term war. Germany and France are not at peace while their enormous standing armies glare at each other across the frontier. Russia is in a state of chronic war, although nominally peace prevails in the Empire. When 'order reigns in Warsaw' it is more deplorable than the fiercest war for human rights.... If the North had been imbued with the true non-resistant feeling, its uprising and appeal to arms would have been a violation of principle and, in theological phrase, 'a falling from grace.' But the North was not imbued with the peace spirit and made no profession of such. It gloried in Bunker Hill and Saratoga, and not to have responded at the fall of Sumter to the President's call, would have been despicable (Garrison 1895, 2).

170.   Brock 1968, 948. For a more left-wing expression of the same point, see Curti 1959, 309.

171.   Hindmarsh 1933 was fairly representative of 'internationalist' thinkers. After deploring "the folly of entrusting world peace and order to the anarchy of unorganized 'sovereign' states," he called for a worldwide "regime of law" backed by sanctions ranging from "moral influences to positive measures of coercion" (3-5). Brewer 1940 wanted a "World Alliance" founded "upon the principles of natural law with due consideration for the frailties of human nature," and a constitution

modeled upon that of the United States. The "super-state" would "compel obedience by force if necessary to preserve peace" (6). He added, sensibly, "If all men and nations were just, force would never have to be used to obtain justice, but unfortunately some men and nations are not just, and armed force is the only authority they will recognize" (51-52). Willkie 1943, a man of scant realism in his assessments of particular statesmen (his account of an interview with Stalin must go down as one of the funniest black comedies ever written), nonetheless cautioned, "unless today, while [World War II] is being fought, the people of the United States and of Great Britain, of Russia and of China, and of all the other United Nations, fundamentally agree in their purposes, fine and idealistic expressions of hope such as those of the Atlantic Charter will live merely to mock us as have Mr. Wilson's Fourteen points" (147). Falk 1975, the dreamiest of them all, designs what he calls "relevant utopias that could be realized" − but were not − by the 1990's (7). Even he admits police powers to his system (11). Page 1957 comes closest to an eschewal of international force in arguing that the United States Supreme Court decisions had never been imposed upon states by an "executive power" (121). Despite and perhaps because of this, the Union had been preserved and strengthened. Page then unwarrentedly extends this argument to international politics, with its serious regime differences.

One of the few substantial contributions to a genuinely American 'internationalist' thought remains Hoover and Gibson 1943. "Military victory alone will not give us peace," they began. "That was proved in 1918." On the other hand, ideals "are only background to be expressed in undertakings of concrete character:"

> The difference between 'aims' and peace treaties is the same difference as that between the Declaration of Independence and the Constitution of the United States. It takes little effort of the imagination to picture the results if, instead of elaborating a Constitution, the Founding Fathers and their descendants had endeavored to govern this country under the terms of the Declaration of Independence (155).

Human beings need effective institutions in order to secure principles.

Beginning "with the defeat of the Kerensky regime in Russia in 1917 and the rise of Communism," and continued by Mussolini in Italy in 1922, the militarist party in Japan in 1931, and Hitler in Germany in 1933, representative government has been under assault and, with it, the only effective means to establish peace. In other countries, too − Austria, Poland, Estonia, Latvia, Lithuania, Yugoslavia, Turkey, Hungary, Rumania, Bulgaria, Greece, and Portugal − a "revolt from Liberalism" occurred. "It is useless to deny that the peoples of many of these countries welcomed the overthrow of freedom." Hoover and Gibson blamed "the faulty structure of these new representative governments" founded after World War I, a structure that encouraged faction. Representative governments that do not find a Madisonian solution to the problem of faction quickly run to extremes politically, while at the same time empowering bureaucracy as the only remaining stabilizing force. Such "ruinous bureaucracies" had provoked the French Revolution for republicanism; whether in the eighteenth century or the twentieth, they bring on a "managed economy" that eventually fails, thus bringing unbearable pressure not so much upon bureaucracy but upon republicanism. The experience of faulty republicanism sours the nation on republicanism itself, and the strongest totalitarian faction takes over, replacing existing bureaucrats with totalitarian bureaucrats (239-243). Hoover and Gibson concluded that political and economic liberty together form the only realistic foundation for peace.

172. Hershberger 1969, 157-159. He also makes telling critique of "Liberal Protestant pacifism" based upon the Social Gospel" of Walter Rauschenbush, which unwarrantedly expects "the Christianization of the social order" through the State. To expect this, one must divinize man, humanize God, or both; the resulting centaur cannot live (184-185).

173. *Ibid.*, 165-166, 176-178. A sample of Hershberger's refreshingly unpretentious advice: "Perhaps the best antidote for a totalitarian state is a society of self-reliant people who know how to do things for themselves" (166).

174. Hoyt 1956, 59-61.

175. Another (much less prominent) example is Ralph T. Templin, a sociologist and social reformer who was a contemporary of Dr.King. Templin saw pacifism in the political and cultural context of the struggle for the survival of democracy and Western civilization. "That which became ascendent in this nation's founding ideology, which made her greatness, attested to her distinctiveness, and validated her mission to all peoples of the world is not today ascendent or predominant" (Templin 1965, 32). Business interests and bureaucracy cause a centralization of power that undercuts the sovereignty of the people which templin, like Madison and Monroe, recognized as the distinctively American contribution to political history. Militarism increases the un-American trend to centralization by "shifting [the] base of security from people to states" (74). Thus "we seem to have lost our original purpose to establish democratic law on all of the earth" (99). On the economic level, Templin admired Sweden, which combines "intelligent planning" with decentralization, according to him (126). "Force-mindedness is un-American" (Templin n.d., 200).

In looking for examples of political methods to be used to bring the changes he advocates, Templin could only point to Gandhian's nonviolent resistance and John Dewey's experimentalism, neither of which has its roots in the thought of the American Founders, and both of which in Templin's formulation, extend the egalitarian principles of the Enlightenment to the sphere of mass physical action for social and economic reform (Templin 1965, 272). Nonviolent resistance, a species of direct-action politics, could weaken attachment to *representative* government. Templin failed to address this issue. Nor did he so much as recognize the problem of political union.

176.   King 1961, 67. To call Gandhian nonviolence a method, does not deny the profundity of the transformation its use can effect on the human soul. As King wrote,

> Admittedly, nonviolence in the truest sense is not a strategy that one uses simply because it is expedient at the moment; nonviolence is ultimately a way of life that men live by because of the sheet morality of its claim. But even granting this, the willingness to use nonviolence as a technique is a step forward. For he who goes this far is more likely to adopt nonviolence later as a way of life (King 1961, 71).

By use of the word "method" I mean to distinguish nonviolent resistance as a political technique, from the reasons for which it is used, i.e., certain political reforms, and second, from the principles that justify those reforms, i.e., unalienable rights.

177.   King 1961, 31-32, 161.

178.   King 1968, 35.

179.   King 1964b, 25, 32, 37, 42, 82.

180.   *Ibid.*, 133.

181.   For an excellent example of King's 'American' constitutionalism, see *An Appeal to the President of the United States for National Rededication to the Principles of the Emancipation Proclamation and for an Executive Order Prohibiting Segregation in the United States of America* (May 17, 1962) in King 1964a. Although he cited Woodrow Wilson's doctrine of presidential leadership (311-312), which was intended to undermine 'American' principles (see Chapter 3, below pp. 105-107), King generally attempted to stay within the Constitutional boundaries of the "supreme law of the land" clause and the "due process" clause. He also clearly saw the relation between the Declaration of Independence, the Constitution, and Lincoln's Gettysburg Address (292-295).

182.   King 1961, 73-76. See de Tocqueville 1945, II, 154-156. It should be noticed that de Tocqueville finds the danger of materialism not merely in 'capitalism' but in democracy itself. In this de Tocqueville ranks as a far more profound political thinker than King. See also King 1968 for

a critique of the "shallow terms" of Marxian dialectic, with its "cold atheism wrapped in the garments of materialism" (89-95).

183.   King 1968, 17, 21-27.

184.   King 1961, 79. Part of pacifist realism is "a tough mind in a tender heart" — King's restatement of Jesus' call for the wisdom of serpents and the harmlessness of doves (King 1963, 1-3). See also King 1968, 140.

185.   King 1961, 173.

186.   King 1967a, 17, 33. If anything, King's faith in the mere enunciation of 'American' principles became too strong. He imagined that because Vietnamese communists had quoted the Declaration of Independence in tracts written in the 1940's, they must have shared those principles (26).

In 1967b, while mistakenly claiming that Jefferson's phrase in the Declaration of Independence really meant, all white men are created equal (77), he strongly criticized the violent ideology of certain Afro-American radicals. "Their Bible is Frantz Fanon's *The Wretched of the Earth*;" King left no doubt that he judged this a poor substitute for the Bible itself. The "Black Power" ideology is "most destructive" in its "call for retaliatory violence," which "will not work" for black Americans and is morally wrong (54-56).

187.   King 1967a, 133.

CHAPTER III

1. Professor George Collins of LeMoyne College, quoted in Chatfield 1971. Collins added, tartly, "ask the natives of India and Uganda their opinion of British democracy."

2. American Friends Service Committee 1951, 32.

3. Douglass 1968, 8, 10, 231. Douglass 1972 continued along the same vein, claiming that "the humanity of the [Vietnam Communist National Liberation Front] goes much deeper than its opponents in the Pentagon" (31), that Leninist parties in Latin America and Southeast Asia are "liberation movements" (18), and that these movements are animated by "love." Indeed, "Marx borrowed his vision from Jesus" (29), and Che Guevara worked for "liberation" as truly as did Martin Luther King (47).

   There are two good, complementary histories of pacifism in twentieth century America: Chatfield 1971, which surveys the movement between the world wars, and Wittner 1969, on the period 1941-1960. Much more polemical but still informative is Lewy 1988, in the 1960's and after; for a thoughtful critique of Lewy, see Chatfield 1989. For a more general survey, not only of pacifism but of internationalism from the First World War to the Great Depression, see De Benedetti 1978.

4. Addams 1907, 3-4. Warner 1905 was an interesting transition-figure, to some extent bridging the gulf between old and new pacifism in America. At first glance, he appeared to combine commercial utilitarian pacifism (3, 83n.1, 91, 101) and Christianity (68-79, 125). But he also occasionally embraced historicist evolutionism (7-8, 28), predicting that history would culminate in a loose confederation of nations, through not a world state (62, 101). He finally did not deny the power of reason to transcend "the particular motives and views" of contending parties (82-83), and insisted that "absolute virtues," such as truthfulness, honesty, sobriety, and physical courage do exist (35, 53); he did not quite make the historicist turn.

5. *Ibid.*, 3, 7-14. Addams quickly drew back from this apparent sentimentalism. "It is not that they are shouting for peace − on the contrary, if they shout at all, they will continue to shout for war − but that they are really attaining cosmopolitan relations through daily experience." This experience, Addams hoped, eventually would "soak up the notion of nationalism" that she believed decisive in spurring warlike passions (18-19). See also Adler 1944, 167, and the praise of Walt Whitman by Somerville 1954, 157-158. For the relation of Addams to Hegelianism see Elshtain 1986, 71-82.

6. *Ibid.*, 27.

7. *Ibid.*, 28.

8. *Ibid.*, 31-32.

9. *Ibid.*, 33-41. "Having looked to the sword for independence from oppressive governmental control, they came to regard the sword as an essential part of the government they had succeeded in establishing" (36).

10. *Ibid.*, 32-33, 56, 63.

11. *Ibid.*, 216-217.

12. *Ibid.*, 90-91.

13. Addams 1922, 53, 65. "Was not war in the interest of democracy for the salvation of civilization a contradiction in terms, whoever said it or however often it was repeated?" (142) Curiously, Addams 'thought dialectically' in the Hegelian manner only when it came to the benefits of peace; in matters of war, she reverted to the old schoolmen's terms of the logic of non-contradiction.

14. *Ibid.*, 174, 230. The militancy of 'German' ideology found a more fitting if not ultimately more successful milieu in the military itself. The Prussian victory over France caused military scholars to become enamored of German military practices, as noticed by such otherwise divergent writers as Kropotkin 1978, 337, and Cohen 1985, 57-59. DeGaulle 1973 tellingly criticized German military practice and the ideological militancy upon which it fed. Upton 1904 presents a fascinating attempt to reconcile the German military system, particularly conscription and the standing army, with 'American' principles (see especially pp. xiii-xiv, 16, 275, 394, 423-465).

15. Bourne 1964, 20.

16. *Ibid.*, 50-52. Bourne faulted German *Kultur* only for its attempt to force reality to conform to 'ideals' instead of using what exists to move closer to 'ideals.' This is the somewhat Anglicized or Americanized historicism of the American 'pragmatist' philosophers – less extreme than 'Germany,' but still essentially 'German.' On the other hand, Bourne wanted somewhat more 'idealism,' rather more radicalism, than John Dewey could offer. See "Twilight of Idols," in *Ibid.*, 55-63, a critique of reformist instrumentalism that would find an echo some forty-six years later in *The Port Huron Statement* of the Students for a Democratic Society.

17. *Ibid.*, 97. In this misconception Bourne followed Beard 1954 (originally published in 1913).

18. *Ibid.*, 93, 102. That Bourne never understood the intentions of the Framers may be seen in one of his last essays, where he wrote, "One of

the larger errors of political insight which the sage founders of the Constitution committed was to assume that the enfranchized watchdogs of property and the public order would remain a homogeneous class" (102). As the tenth *Federalist* argues, the Framers made precisely the opposite assumption, a fact that raises the question of whether Bourne ever troubled to read *The Federalist* at all.

In fairness, it should be noted the Bourne, who died during the influenza epidemic of 1918, published most of his writings at the age of thirty or so. Addams was in her mid-forties when *Newer Ideals of Peace* appeared, in her early sixties when she published *Peace and Bread in Time of War*; her convictions had time to mature.

19. Rolland 1916 forged the most telling critique of 'Germany,' finding Prussian militarism to be the worst form of nationalist imperialism in a world full of nationalist imperialisms (48-51). The "militarization of the intellect" (63), whereby "we speak to them of *Humanity*" but "they reply with *Uebermensch, Uebervolk*" (78), would bring disaster: "Germany will one day realize she has had no more deadly enemy than her own writings" (116). 'Germany' was the most radical instance of a general rule: "Give an intellectual any ideal and any evil passion and he will always succeed in harmonizing them" (110). Rolland identified this as the modern form of the old vice, idolatry. Rolland did not see the advance of 'German' ideology among pacifists, understandably associating it with militarism only. Nor did any American pacifist oppose this ideology at the time of the First World War.

20. Perry 1916, 93, 60-61.

21. Perry 1919, 1, 197-199. "[O]nce the Kantian theory of knowledge is accepted idealism is on a slippery inclined plane with the Absolute waiting at the bottom" (218). This contrasts with the classical 'idealism' of Plato and others, which does not call for a programme of action for 'self-realization,' and thus sustains of politics of moderation.

22. Perry cannot be said to have had a fully-developed sense of moral principles inherent in human nature. His concept of justification, for example, was entirely rhetorical: "[W]e justify our actions in order to gain a wider support for them either within our individual, personal lives or within the social group" (*Ibid.*, 16). Perry's concept of interests potentially has poetic content, but he failed to elaborate on this in his First World War-era writings.

Becker 1942 also identified 'Germany' as one force undermining the reasoned conviction that justice requires the securing of unalienable rights. Savigny's denunciation of the "shallow philosophy of natural law" and his exaltation of conventional law as an expression of a nation's "creative power," exemplified this tendency (263-265), as did von Ranke's progressivism ("It is true that Ranke rejected Hegelianism. But it was the Hegelian history rather than the Hegelian philosophy that Ranke rejected: what he objected to was not so much that Hegel derived a false philosophy from history as that he derived a fantastic history from philosophy" [272]). The systematic subordination of unalienable rights to 'organic society' and 'history' made it "not always easy to tell the difference between rights and wrongs" (273), particularly when injustice is 'justified' as 'historically necessary.' Becker also noted that Darwinian naturalism changed this only by making it materialistic; natural history replaced natural philosophy.

After presenting this analysis, Becker rather surprisingly endorsed historicism in principle, denying noetic status to the laws of nature and of nature's God, and to unalienable rights. "This faith could not survive the harsh realities of the modern world" (279).

See also Kohn 1960, who criticized Bismark for "forg[ing] a new Reich in conscious opposition to liberal democracy" (11). "After 1866 Germany knew neither a true conservatism nor a true liberalism. For Germany Burke and Disraeli were as unthinkable as Gladstone and Mill" (153).

23.   For the best short account of this, see Dennis J. Mahoney: "A Newer Science of Politics: *The Federalist* and American Political Science in the Progressive Era," in Kesler 1987 (especially 250-257). For an independent confirmation of the same thesis, from rather the opposite political viewpoint, see Rodgers 1987, 144-175. See also Friedrich 1969, viii.

24.   Some historians have attempted to make historicism the culmination of 'American' political thought, rather than its negation. For a crude example, see Beard 1954, who claimed that Madison's argument in the tenth *Federalist* rests on an "economic interpretation of history," thus 'proving' that the economic-determinist component of historicism is no European importation. White 1987 convincingly refutes this belief (237, n.2).

Somerville 1954, in the middle of an argument claiming that the Soviet Union's ideology, Marxism-Leninism, is "the extreme opposite" of fascism, alleged that all of the Soviet "republics" enjoy "sovereignty;" that the regime as a whole opposes racial and sexual discrimination; and that "democracy is not some rigid *form* of government" but encompasses ethnic, economic, and social egalitarianism as well (74-82). A few pages later, after pretending that Soviet 'democracy' is at least as plausible as American republicanism, Somerville blithely and contradictorily reversed Lord Acton's famous aphorism by claiming, "All power is an opportunity to do good, and absolute power is the precondition of doing absolute good" (99) – a truth Somerville deployed while ignoring the Madisonian point: If men are not angels, and therefore need government, neither are they gods in whom absolute power may be entrusted. The self-divinization of human beings is of course a typical historicist enterprise.

Equally bizarre is Somerville 1975, wherein early Christianity, the American Revolution, and Marxism-Leninism were presented as essentially the same "politics of survival" (33). Again, Somerville's historicism allowed him to overlook such inconvenient matters as form and content: "The present is a part of history, which means that the present can only be understood as a *process*. History is demarcated by revolutions, and each one is a long and wide process" (xiv). Early Christianity, the American Founders, and Soviet Marxism-Leninism were all revolutionary, *ergo* they are, historically speaking pretty much equivalent (110-112).

Lynd 1968 put a much more sophisticated intelligence at work at the service of a much less crude historicism. He sought "to explore certain intellectual themes which Marxism and native American radicalism share" (vi). Lynd disliked John Locke, the tenth *Federalist* and, of course, capitalism; he endorsed the Marxist-Leninism claim that the state can be made to wither away, after class distinctions disappear. He objected to Locke's psychological determinism and to Marx's economic determinism, preferring the emphasis on conscientious action seen in the small, dissenting Protestant sects of seventeenth-century England and what he takes to be their secular counterparts in England and America — particularly, Thomas Paine (17-30). This too-easy conflation of religious and atheist doctrines brought Lynd to an existentialist/Marxist anarchism, wherein Gerrard Winstanley and Richard Price begin to look rather like the intellectual forbears of Abbie Hoffman.

Lynd attacked commercial republicanism in both its aspects. He denied the obvious egalitarian tendencies of 'capitalism,' failing to see how private property can secure unalienable rights; he rejected representative government as insufficiently democratic failing to consider it as a bulwark against popular passions and, therefore, against tyranny. Defining freedom in the 'German" way, as "self-determining human activity" (46), he therefore could not conceive of self-*government*, and took individual freedom even to oppose in action, laws enacted democratically. With most of the American 'New Left' of the 1960's, Lynd assumed that individual freedom and communalism may be maximized simultaneously, in a stateless society (162), given what he takes to be the fact of universal human perfectibility (104-108).

More honest than Beard or Somerville, Lynd thus presented an openly selective account of American political doctrines, holding up what he rejected as well as what he appropriated. Nonetheless, his progressivist historicism enabled him to synthesize contradictory doctrines without much regard for plausibility.

For an attempt to show analogies between the 'New Left' of the 1960's and the 'left wing' of the Reformation doctrine (particularly Anabaptism), see Gish 1970. For an uncompromising rejection of the analogy between the Christian communalism of one such sect and modern communism, see Horsch 1931, xvi.

For a useful compilation of interviews of 'sixties-era' pacifists, see Finn 1967.

25. For a good summary of Hegel's proposed use of war as an antidote to *embourgeoisement*, see Michael Gillespie: "Death and Desire: War and Bourgeoisification in the Thought of Hegel," in Zuckert 1988, 153-176.

26. Hegel 1966, 8-12. The best study of Hegelian epistemology in English is Rosen 1974.

27. Hegel 1967, 183, 202.

28. *Ibid.*, 807.

29. *Ibid.*, 233-234, 497.
30. Hegel 1973, 225, 22-26. This means, obviously, that "freedom" and "self-determination" in Hegel are really expressions of an all-encompassing necessity, the Absolute Spirit.

31. *Ibid.*, 85, 109, 261.

32. *Ibid.*, 156, 179.

33. *Ibid.*, 121, 188, 216-217. Hegel 1954, 88-89, Hegel 1900, 377.

34. Hegel 1973, 183-186.

35. *Ibid.*, 209. The affinities between the doctrines of Calhoun and Hegel are clearest at this point.

36. *Ibid.*, 295-296.

37. *Ibid.*, 210-212, 215, 217. On this replacement of the Holy Spirit with the "World-Spirit/Mind" or "History," see the warning of Jesus (Matthew 12:31; Luke 12:10; Mark 12:28-29).

38. For an example of the distortions that occur when Hegelian or proto-Hegelian thought attempts to understand the American regime, see Gentz 1959. Writing in 1800, Gentz contrasted the American and French revolutions, very much to the advantage of America. Condemning the French appeal to human rights and to "the chimerical principle of the sovereignty of the people" Gentz claimed that the Americans upheld "real" or purely legal rights (49). They merely defended themselves against British alternations of existing laws.

Gentz admitted that the Declaration of Independence asserts "the natural and unalienable rights of mankind" as "the foundation of all government," and that the Signers asserted popular sovereignty, "that empty pomp of words." But he pretended "they allowed to these speculative ideas, no visible influence upon their practical measures and resolves" — thus overlooking such details as the war itself (70). He falsely claimed that American principles apply to no other nations, justify no other revolutions (81). For Gentz, there is only conventional law, natural passions, and "arbitrary will;" there is no natural right (89).

Gentz represents proto-historicist thought, not historicist thought itself. There is no 'dialectic,' no 'World Spirit' in his writings. He was a sort of Burke devoid of fixed principles, a Machiavellian Burke. The 'Machiavellianizing' of Burke was a needed step toward historicism. See Strauss 1953, 294-323. For other anticipations of histiricism in philosophers before Hegel, see Livingston 1988 on Hume, Horowitz 1987 on Rousseau and Galston 1975 on Kant.

39. R. W. Emerson, "Nature," Emerson 1929, 1, 7-9, 24.

40. R. W. Emerson, "Nature," Emerson *Ibid.*, 17; "The Method of Nature," *Ibid.*, 65. Hegel would never say, "Character is higher than intellect" or praise the Romantic poets ("The American Scholar," *Ibid.*, 31, 35). See also "Circles," *Essays First Series, Ibid.*, 218, and, for un-Hegelian account of the intuitional foundation of logic, see "Intellect," *Essays First Series, Ibid.*, 224. Emerson wanted Hegelian dialectic without Hegelian rationality, and therefore exalted, experience or *praxis* over thought. "Life is not dialectics;" it is for those "who can enjoy what they find, without questioning." This is the point at which Emerson failed, refused, to become a philosopher, remaining a lay preacher or intellectual. "The true *romance* which the world exists to realize will be the transformation of genius to practical power." ("Experience," *Essays Second series, Ibid.*, 256-257, 264). In this Emerson anticipated Karl Marx, as seen by Howe 1986, 21. For Howe's own historicism, see *Ibid.*, 43.

41. R. W. Emerson, "The Transcendentalist," *Ibid.*, 125, 127, 131. To qualify this point, see also "An Address to the Senior Class in Divinity College, Cambridge," *Ibid.*, 47, on the need for a "new Teacher" to assist men in achieving divinity (*Ibid.*, 47).

42. See "Self-Reliance," *Ibid.*, 140: "On my saying, 'What have I to do with the sacredness of traditions, if I live wholly from within?' my friend suggested, — 'But these impulses may be from below, not from above.' I replied, They do not seem to me to be such, but if I am the Devil's child, I will live then with the Devil. No law can be sacred to me but that of my nature."

See also "Spiritual Laws," *Essays First Series*, 167.

43. "Art," *Essays First Series, Ibid.*, 230.

44. "Politics," '*Essays Second Series, Ibid.*, 297. As for Hegel, "What is the best must be the true; and what is true − that is, what is at bottom fit and agreeable to the constitution of man − must at last prevail over all obstruction and all opposition" ("War," *Ibid.*, 1143). See "Man the Reformer" for Emerson's socialist critique of commerce ("a systemic of selfishness" to be overcome by love, "the one remedy for all ills" (71, 78). "The power of love, as the basis of a State, has never been tried;" it is "strange" that no man ever had "sufficient faith in the power of rectitude to try it" (Politics," *Essays Second Series, Ibid.*, 297, 304). This of course raises the problem of political union, as seen in many other socialist writings. Emerson criticized such contemporary communes as Brook Farm, and called for a "union" that would be "inward," whereby each member adhered to his individuality while "go[ing] up and down doing the works of a true member" ("New England Reformers," *Ibid.*, 318) − a solution as ingenious as it is impracticable.

45. "The Conservative," *Ibid.*, 9; "War," *Ibid.*, 1147.

46. "War," *Ibid.*, 1139-1144.

47. *Ibid.*, 1145. Emerson continued, "Whenever we see the doctrine of peace embraced by the nation, we may be assured it will not be one that invites injury; but one, on the contrary, which has a friend, in the bottom of the heart of every man, even if the violent and the base; one against no weapon can prosper; one which is looked upon as the asylum of the human race and has the tears and the blessings of mankind." (1145)

Friedrich Nietzsche, who admired Emerson, adapted this argument (Nietzsche 1986, 380-381).

48. Friedel 1947 observes that as early as the 1820's, "New England had discovered the pre-eminent superiority of German scholarship" (55). One of the earliest German immigrants contributing to American scholarship was Francis Lieber, who was however an anti-Hegelian. Lieber wrote, "The idea of a Constitutional Government, and of liberty founded on firm laws, has never been understood by Prussia. Hegel has done infinite harm to the cause of science. Instead of earnest, thoughtful investigation, and a discreet acknowledgement of previous experience, he is full of arrogance and presumption" (Letter to Mittermaier, cited in Friedel 1947, 112). Although Brown 1951 calls Lieber a product of the German liberalism founded by Kant (7), Lieber in fact endorsed the American concepts of unalienable right consonant with natural right (Lieber 1881, 67, 202) and of popular sovereignty (217 ff.). See also Lieber 1874, 256. One of Lieber's most notable contributions to his adopted country was his "Instructions for Governing of Union Armies in the Field," published at the height of the Civil War, which applied the traditional just-war criterion of proportionality to the conduct of American troops.

John W. Burgess founded the department of political science at Columbia University in 1880, envisioning "the prospect of great, genuine institution of pacifist propaganda" owing to an Hegelian triumph of reason (Brown 1951, 107). Burgess claimed that "Aryan" nations (the nation being a concept based on language, not biology) had the "highest talent for political organization" and are thus "authorize[d] to lead all others" (Burgess 1893, I, 2, 4). The State, which consists of both nation and government, "represents the highest good," and is "all-comprehensive," determining the content of "so-called" laws of God and nature (I, 42, 52-53). Individuals' rights derive from the state, not vice-versa. See Rodgers 1987, 166-170, for a good discussion of Burgess' influence. "[T]he state is *a* product, nay *the* produce, to history," which progressively "makes humanity more divine" (I, 67), and eventually will issue in peace.

Mulford 1887 also presented an Hegelian picture of the nation as an "organism." and individuals as mere "members of a living body" (9-10). He acknowledged his debt to Hegel (vi, 22, 54). Individual rights are subordinate to the nation (75). Although he rejected both slavery and confederacy, Mulford otherwise admired John C. Calhoun's organicism (212). Mulford re-Christianized Hegelian doctrine not with Emerson's notion of "a nation of lovers" but in a much more orthodox manner; he made Hegel's dialectical "Absolute Spirit" into divine providence (358), and called Jesus Christ "the only and actual king" (412).

John J. Lalor's *Cyclopedia of Political Science* contains articles contributed by American English, German, and French scholars. Generally, the French took natural right more seriously than the others. "Natural Law" is classified under "Fictions," an article that dismissed "so-called natural rights" and assured readers that "the sphere of fiction must steadily diminish as that of inductive and positive science advances and as man's mind becomes stronger, clearer, and more discerning" (Lalor 1895, II, 183-184). The attack on natural law in the American regime was popularized by Bentham, whose positivism strongly influences much Anglo-American jurisprudence to this day: see Onuf and Onuf, 1990, 71.

For an early statement of American Hegelianism, see Hurd 1968, 6-7, n.2, 47. On the replacement of the 'American' model of republicanism with the 'German' nationalist model among European republicans, see Billias 1990b, 34-35.

49. For an excellent brief account of Wilson's principles of political leadership as distinguished from traditional statesmanship, see Eidelberg 1974, 279-311. Ceaser 1979, 170-212 confirms Eidelberg's account and adds substantial evidence, with particular emphasis on Wilson's conception of party leadership.

50. *Diary* (June 19, 1876), Wilson 1966-1986, I, 143.

51. *Diary* (July 6, 1876), *Ibid.*, I, 149. See also the entry of July 9, 1876, *Ibid.*, I, 151.

52. Wilson 1898, 2, 19-20.

53. Wilson 1898, 369, 438, 454, 467. See also "The Modern Democratic State," Wilson 1966-1986, V, 63. See also "The Causes of the Civil War" and "The Doctrine of State Sovereignty and the War," Wilson 1966-1986, I: "Wars are seldom fought about abstract theory," such as states' sovereignty, Wilson claimed (356).

   Wilson is well known for advocating the adoption of English institutions in the United States, notably cabinet government; see *Congressional Government*, written 1879 (Wilson 1966-1986, I, 572), and Wilson 1898, 388. For the 'Englishness' of the American regime, see also Wilson on James Madison and the 1787 Constitution — the former allegedly more English than American, the latter "a great organic product, a vehicle of life as well as a charter of authority." Jefferson, however, "was not a thorough American [or Englishman] because of the strain of French philosophy that permeated and weakened all his thought," which was "un-American in being abstract, sentimental, rationalistic, rather than practical." Abraham Lincoln was "the supreme American of our history," Wilson claimed, although of course Lincoln admired Jefferson above all previous American statesmen except Washington, precisely because of Jefferson's 'abstract' principles. (See Wilson, 1896, 191-193, 198, 206). The American Founders, Wilson insisted, "planned no *revolution*: they did not mean to invent an American government but only to Americanize the English government...." ("Democracy," Wilson 1966-1986, VII, 350). Notice how Wilsonian progressivism so closely resembles the neo-Burkean conservatism of such late twentieth-century writers as Bradford and Kirk (above, pp. 1-5), except, of course, with respect to the evaluation of Lincoln.

54. *The Modern Democratic State*, Wilson 1966-1986, V, 76. "The historical view of government is in any case the only fully instructive view...." (65) See also 63, 71, 75. "Individual rights" are "peers to the rights of the state," Wilson claimed here, without elaborating any independent foundation for them (80). For a statement of Wilson's historical relativism see "Machiavelli," Wilson 1966-1986, V, 461.

55. *The Modern Democratic State*, Wilson 1966-1986, V, 85; "Democracy," *Ibid.*, VII, 357, "The Study of Administration," *Ibid.*, V, 360-364.

56. *Ibid.*, 368, 377.

57. "Leaders of Men," Wilson 1966-1986, VI, 659; "Prince Bismark," Wilson 1966-1986, I, 313.

58. "Leaders of Men," Wilson 1966-1986, VI, 659. "What a lesson it is in the organic wholeness of Society, this study of leadership!" Wilson

exclaimed, adding that leadership precludes "rashness" or "raw invention" (670).

59.   Addams 1922, 58. Otherwise, Addams' sentimental historicism and Wilson's rationalist historicism dovetailed nicely, except, finally, on the question of absolute prohibition of military force — a disagreement perhaps deriving from the difference between certain kinds of sentiment and reason.

60.   "Socialism and Democracy," Wilson 1966-1986, V, 561-562.

61.   "Democracy," Wilson 1966-1986, VII, 348; "Memorandum: Philosophy of Politics," Wilson 1966-1986, XI, 239.

62.   "Democracy and Efficiency," Wilson 1966-1986, XII, 7. "We printed the SELF large and the *government* small in almost every administrative arrangement we made" at the time of the founding. "[T]hat is still our attitude and preference" (16), he wrote in an essay published in 1900. There is little or no sense in Wilson's writings that American institutions were designed to secure individual rights by governing the selfishness of individualism.

A recent statement of the historicist conception of rights may be seen in an essay by Yale Law School professor Owen M. Fiss. "Rights," Professor Fiss believes, "are not premises but conclusions. They emerge through a process of trying to give concrete meaning and expression to the values embodied in an authoritative legal text." Thus "adjudication is an interpretive process through which rights are created and enforced" ("Two Models of Adjudication," Goldwin and Schambra 1985, 36). Emergence, process, "concrete meaning," values, creativity: It is rare to see so many of historicism's key terms compressed into two sentences.

63.   The historicist alternative to Wilson's historicism has of course been the radical Hegelianism of Karl Marx and his admirers. Herreshoff 1967 correctly sees that Emersonian individualism and Marxist socialism have a "cognate character;" both link revolution to "consciousness," both use "alienation" as a descriptive term, rating *praxis* over theory, and both predict the triumph of socialism. To oversimplify, whereas Emerson put 'self-culture' before social progress, Marx reversed this. (18 ff). Nineteenth century American Marxists generally admired the American revolution as a move forward in History's dialectic (166); claimed that "the only difference" between contemporary America and Europe was "that over there the bourgeois is monarchist and over here republican" (63); and opposed war when it tended by further the 'imperialism' of the bourgeoisie but not when it pushed 'History' forward (166) — as notably, in the American Civil War.

Marx himself examines the American regime in his review-essays on Bruno Bauer's studies of the theologico-political question as it affected

German Jews. By the 1840's, "some" of the free states in North America" had succeeded in entirely secularizing 'the Jewish question' ("Bruno Bauer, *The Jewish Question*, Braunschweig, 1984" in Easton and Guddat 1967, 222). The very existence of any religion at all "implies a defect" in a socio-economic system; mere political emancipation of Jews cannot solve these 'deeper' problems. Real freedom implies freedom *from* religion as such (223), which will only occur when mankind progresses beyond the "abstract, limited, and partial" advantages of solely political freedom and eliminates private property with its class contradictions. (On the matter of the abolition of religion, Marx cites Hegel's *Philosophy of Right*). The American regime makes the citizen "an imaginary member of an imagined sovereignty," a participation in "the sophistry of the political state" (226). Emancipated Jew and republican bourgeois alike unwittingly participate in the sophistical self-contradictions of capitalism. "*Political* emancipation is indeed a great step forward. It is not, to be sure, the final form of human emancipation, but it is the final form *within* the prevailing order of things" (227); real revolution is still to come. Quite tellingly, when Marx criticizes 'bourgeois' statements of unalienable right – because they express the liberty of egoistic man, man separated from other men and from the community," man "viewed as an isolated monad" (235) – he quotes the 1791 French Declaration of the Rights of Man and the Citizen along with two American state constitutions; he never mentions the Declaration of Independence, which begins with an acknowledgment of "a decent Respect to the Opinions of Mankind" and ends with a mutual pledge of lives, fortunes, and sacred honor.

Both Jew and bourgeois worship the "worldly god" of money; what they need is emancipation from money, an emancipation that would dissolve the "dull mist" of "religious consciousness" ("Bruno Bauer, 'The Capacity of Present-Day Jews and Christians to Become Free,' Twenty-One Sheets," in Easton and Guddat 1967, 243). In America, the commercial society par excellence, politics has become the slave of "financial power" (245), as indeed has every other form of activity.

Marx's incapacity to see the real liberation entailed in commercial republicanism, and his visionary belief that all human conflict can end if only private property can be abolished, exemplify the distortions of Hegelian 'dialectic' when introduced to political thought. Although Marx proudly insists, "My dialectic is not only different from the Hegelian, but is its direct opposite" – because for Marx it is *matter* that underlies 'ideas,' *its* 'dialectical' movement that causes the dialectics of the mind to proceed (Marx 1906, 25) – Marxist dialectic is still dialectical, a subspecies of Hegelian doctrine or historicism. The materialization of Hegelianism is one way to democratize it, although in a different way than those offered by Emerson and (much more ambiguously) by Wilson. Marx would *use* 'theory' as a material force: "But theory becomes a material force once it has gripped the masses" (Toward a Critique of Hegel's Philosophy of Law [Right]: An Introduction," Easton and Guddat, 257). This begins to remove the distinction between theory and propaganda, as 'good' theory becomes theory that 'works,' theory that actually grips and moves "the masses" toward Marxist ends. Like Hegel, Marx insists upon the priority of social or 'organic' life to individual life; his materialization of Hegelianism makes this priority *economic*, a project of effecting material, 'dialectical' change. Hence Marx's famous aphorism, "The philosophers have only *interpreted* the world in various ways; the point is, to *change* it" (*Theses on Feuerbach, Ibid.*, 402). Marx goes so far as to imagine that material dialectics will entirely overcome individuality, so that "the conflict between the individual sensuous existence of man and his species-being is transcended" ("Bruno Bauer, 'The Capacity of Present-Day Jews and Christians to Become Free,' Twenty-one Sheets," *Ibid.*, 248). On the relationship of Marxian materialism to 'democracy' or egalitarianism, see also "Critique of Hegel's Philosophy of the State," *Ibid.*, 173, 175-176. Trotsky 1918 understood that Marxian materialism reverses Hegelianism to the extent that "Might is the mother of right," and not vice-versa (226).

The Marxist variation of historicism has had considerable influence in twentieth-century pacifists in America and elsewhere, as will become clear in the discussion below.

64. "Peace Without Victory," Frisch and Stevens 1973, 288-291. Although none of Wilson's "Fourteen Points" explicitly affirmed the need for republican institutions, Wilson did implicitly call for parliamentarism in postwar Germany. He vitiated this realism with his call for "open covenants of peace, openly arrived at" − the former indispensable to consent, the latter nonsensical − and by an historicist claim that "the moral climax of this the culminating and final war for human liberty has come" − nothing else than an 'end of history' democratically dressed ("The Fourteen Points Speech," *Ibid.*, 292-294).

65. A second-generation American, Rauschenbusch received part of his education in Germany. One admiring biographer writes that Rauschenbusch's "encounters with German scholars who taught that economic institutions were historical and relatively freed him from the crippling abstractions of the classical economists" (Robert D. Cross: "Introduction," Rauschenbusch 1964, xi). Cross associates Rauschenbusch with John Dewey, Charles Beard, Thorstein Veblen, Oliver Wendell Holmes, Woodrow Wilson, and Walter Lippman − all turn-of-the-century intellectuals who shared an "historical understanding" of human life (xiv).

66. Rauschenbusch 1964, xxi, xxiii, 14-15. Neither the Hebrew prophets nor the early American colonists actually were egalitarians; Raushenbusch was obviously reading his own wishes into their writings.

67. "Humanity" is defined as: the need for food; word; and the struggle with nature and with "hostile men" to feed the young struggle with nature and with "hostile men" to feed the young (*Ibid.*, 1) − none of which are distinctively human characteristics.

68. *Ibid.*, 45, 214.

69. *Ibid.*, 49.

70. *Ibid.*, 59.

71. *Ibid.*, 69. Rauschenbusch criticized the "apocalyptic hope" of the early Christians, judging Jesus' 'organic' or gradualist view to be sounder. Compare Wilson, above p. 136.

72. *Ibid.*, 67, 73, 89. On Jesus the religious revolutionary, see *Ibid.*, 73; on Jesus the social revolutionary, see *Ibid.*, 85-86. See also 247, where Rauschenbusch cautioned that social equality does not entail natural equality.

73. *Ibid.*, 186, 191-194.

74. *Ibid.*, 203.

75. *Ibid.*, 260, 327, 346.

76. Historicist pacifism of course does not stand as the only pacifism in America after 1900. Two other major schools are the moralists (Christian and secular), continuing a tradition dating almost to the first settlers, and what might be called 'movement' or 'semi-political' pacifists (also coming in Christian and secular varieties). Moralist pacifism carried on the oldest of pacifist traditions: 'movement' pacifism usually owes some debt to historicism.

    Among moralists, Darrow 1903 dismissed politics, including democratic politics, as the realm of force and fraud (16, 18). His naivete may be seen in his belief that "no nation, however powerful, would dare to invite the odium and hostility of the world by sending arms and men to conquer a peaceful, productive, non-resistant land" (27) — the example of English settlers in Tasmania should have sufficed to disprove this — and that "the most ambitious [rulers] have abandoned their dreams of world power and are content to exploit a portion of the earth" (33) — this, eleven years before the beginning of the First World War. Darrow contradicted his own moral revulsion at force by endorsing psychological determinism (95); in this he departed from the teachings of his master, Leo Tolstoy. For a confrontation between Darrow's shaky but decent moralism and an anti-pacifist form of dialectical materialism, see Darrow and Lewis, 1911, wherein Darrow rightly predicted that if Marxists succeeded, "You would be just where you were in the French Revolution, where as soon as they got rid of the heads of the nobility they commenced cutting off each other's heads" (112). The American Revolution, which did not devour its children, went unmentioned by both debaters.

Holmes 1916 contradictorily criticized the Declaration of Independence for justifying the use of force (46), then exclaimed, "Let Germany come here to America today as she came to Belgium yesterday — what of it? The Declaration of Independence would defy her sword, the Constitution resist her 42-centimeter guns, the memory of Lincoln shame her panoply of arms" (290). It is safe to say that, whatever else the memory of Lincoln might shame, a panoply of arms is not among them, unless one is a loyal partisan of the old South, or a pacifist to begin with.

Thomas 1974 presented a humanitarian-Christian argument almost devoid of political sense ("The enemies of democracy know well that freedom can no longer be defended or promoted by war.... Communism in Russia might have experimented with industrial and political democracy, if the fear of war had not been an ever present reality, the most potent of all reasons for accepting governmental tyranny" [279-280]). He based political democracy strictly on individual morality (286), going so far as to assert, "Unlike war the refusal to cooperate with tyranny can never destroy the values of democracy" (287) — a point that overlooks the need for people who uphold "values," people who may well end up dead under tyranny.

Hughan 1942 dismissed the possibility of an enemy invasion of the United States on the peculiar ground that Americans are rich (8). She helpfully recommended a pledge by all public officials to die instead of surrendering — a leftist version of the quaint 'loyalty oaths' that came into vogue in the 1950's. Brinton 1943 offered a touching argument from nature: "Nations have, significantly, taken as their emblems the fiercer, more aggressive animals — lion, eagle, bear. But Christianity has for its symbol the Lamb, gentlest of creatures. Lions, eagles, bears are becoming extinct. Not so lambs." (54) This fails to note that the most intelligent predator, sitting at the top of the ecological 'food chain,' finds lambs most flavorsome, and so breeds them for their nourishing flesh. Thus, while New Zealand's population of lambs nears ten times its population of humans, the 'turnover' among the woolier citizens far exceeds that among unfeathered bipeds.

Cousins 1945 inaugurated 'nuclear pacifism,' the pacifism that limits just-war doctrines to those modes of warfare that do not make use of weapons of mass destruction. Cousins attempted to think politically, calling for "a common world sovereignty" to end war. But in citing *The Federalist*'s argument for a union of American states, he overlooked the Constitutional stipulation that all those states were to be republics; he included non-republican and even virulently anti-republican regimes in his plan for world confederation (27-32).

Long 1950 admitted that nuclear weapons put secular pacifism into question:

> The implications of the atomic bomb for this type of pacifism are serious. The idea of overcoming evil with

> nonresistance may have had some validity in times when warfare meant hand-to-hand combat. It has little meaning when warfare consists of wiping out entire cities with a single bomb, possibly by remote control.... [This] underscores the fact that disavowal of force is a sure road to neither peace nor justice, and that pacifism cannot be defended as pragmatically realistic. (66-67)

However, he mistakenly described "an armed truce" among the major countries with nuclear weapons as untenable (72). He retreated to less assailable ground by writing, "Existence is not the ultimate value," and Christianity exalts martyrdom (110). Long 1968 admitted that non-nuclear war could occur in the 'nuclear age,' while cautioning readers against taking "the nuclear stalemate...for granted" (9). Long 1983 moved toward a somewhat more politic appreciation for the American regime, suggesting that the Hebrew *Shalom* means not only peace but "the general welfare," as cited in the Preamble to the United States Constitution (61).

Day 1959 preferred the traditions of various urban ethnic groups to the "bourgeois mediocrity" of 'America' (14) − in this she followed Addams. Her mentor, Peter Maurin, embraced "a Utopian, Christian communism" (Day 1963, 22); where was little of Addams' historicism in either Maurin or Day, who adhered to Christian reconciliation not 'dialectic,' material or otherwise. Their avowed utopianism freed them from the need to think politically.

Mills 1968 claimed that "genuine repentance and turning to God would be an invincible security for America" (22); Snow 1981 agreed (51, 71). Zahn 1967 presented analysis of post-Nazi Germany that depended exclusively on 'cultural' trends, with no sensitivity to the importance of political regimes (59-65). Hesburgh 1989, while rejecting a comprehensive pacifism on grounds of practicality (10), adopted pacifism limited to the refusal to use weapons of mass destruction. As do most of the moralists, be glided away from the regime question as soon, and insofar as, he promoted pacifism. The abolition of nuclear weapons "will not leave us with a perfect world. It will at least give us a chance for survival in the fact of other imminent threats: greenhouse effect, ozone depletion, pollution of the oceans, tropical diseases that affect hundreds of millions of people, world hunger, and over population, to mention a few" (15) − not one of which is political.

'Movement' or semi-political pacifism knows how it wants to proceed, but does not know its destination too precisely. 'Movement' pacifism emphasizes process, not results, and comes close to viewing the immediate affects of process *as* result. 'Movement' pacifism attempts to answer the problem posed, famously, by William James in his 1910 essay, "The Moral Equivalent of War." James, who has read his Hegel, concedes that "The military feelings are too deeply grounded to abdicate their place among our ideals [note the anti-Hegelian equation of feelings with ideals − much closer to Emerson and Marx] until better substitutes are offered than the glory and shame that comes to nations as well as to individuals from the ups and downs of politics and the vicissitudes of trade" (James 1967, 660-661). Commerce and republicanism, alone or together, do not quite satisfy the human soul. A "sort of double personality," deploring *and* exalting "military instincts and ideals," has resulted. "So long as anti-militarists propose no substitute for war's disciplinary function, no *moral equivalent* of war...they fail to grasp the full inwardness of the situation" (666). Describing himself as a "pacifist" (663), James offers his antidote to "a simple pleasure-economy" of peace. He proposes that youth be conscripted in "an army enlisted against Nature" (669), conquering social as well as physical inertia and transforming the world into — exactly *what* is not too clear, except that it will be humane. (Bourne 1964 followed the Jamesian program [145-146]).

One obvious problem with the moral equivalent of war is that these warriors cannot defend themselves. Freeing mankind to pursue the subpolitical humanitarian goals of better health care and more livable factory conditions presupposes a solution to the political problem. As Duffield 1933 noted, this is precisely what pacifists have failed to do; they quarrel, even amongst themselves, "exist[ing] in a state of perpetual internecine feud" — an Hobbesian war of all against all, without the blood, except when nonpacifists go on the offensive (689).

This is the familiar problem of finding a means or method of establishing political union, while avoiding hedonism and sidestepping the inevitably divisive controversy over political ends and political regimes designed to secure those ends. To many pacifists the doctrines of Mohandas K. Gandhi seemed to untie this Gordian Knot. Case 1923 outlined varieties of pacifist theory, citing the need for union (in Case's 'modern' language, "organization" [8]) among diverse pacifists. Case admitted that pacifists have and often will fail (231-232, 248), detailing numerous successful and unsuccessful nonviolent protests. Gandhi's methods promised a higher ratio of successes than any other, in Case's judgment. He concluded that "Non-violence, therefore, whether it takes the form of *persuasion* or *coercion*, seems too idealistic and exacting to accomplish the every-day work of the world. Yet both these methods are of the greatest value when kept within the bounds set by the emotional limits of human nature." (407).

Gregg 1966 (first published in 1934), brought to America the passion of a Gandhian disciple, not dispassionate scholarship. This can be seen in his belief that "human unity is *actual* in man's universal *capacity* to think, feel, will, understand, act, and to apprehend spiritual truths" (9, italics added). Gregg's conflation of actuality and capacity suggests perhaps the most succinct self-description of utopian assumption that could be formulated: What can be, *is*. With this belief at hand, the problems associated with establishing and sustaining union among human beings seem to dissolve into the question of finding the right method or technique. "Human unity is a power that can overcome all differences of race, nationality, ideology, or culture" (9); the conviction that human nature is constant transforms itself into the belief that this unity can not only recognize itself but *act* upon its self-recognition in a manner that will successfully preserve both human nature and its self-recognition. "Action," Gregg claimed, may indeed be considered a mode of thought...a sudden uprush of creative energy from the subconscious." Gregg's Gandhiism thus issued in a sort of Christian Nietzscheism: "It may *create* new *values*" (63-64, italics added). The Eastern reluctance to accept the principle of non-contradiction here dovetailed with the historicist dialectic that 'synthesizes' opposites. Gandhi was the Roman Caesar with Christ's soul. Gandhians practice "moral jiu-jitsu;" causing "the attacker to lose his moral balance" (43-44).

> If you want to conquer another man, do it not by outside resistance but by creating inside his own personality a strong new impulse that is incompatible with his previous tendency. Reinforce your suggestion by making it an auto-suggestion in him, so that it lives by his energy instead of by yours. And yet that new impulse is not to conflict directly with his former urge, but to divert and blend with it and absorb it, so as to use the full psychological energy of both impulses. (53)

Oddly, despite the Eastern and historicist tendency to synthesize opposites, 'movement' pacifists seldom recognize the use of war *and* nonviolence — a common enough phenomenon in history, whereby the military conqueror eventually wins the allegiance of the conquered, and 'assimilates' him. Gregg was not exception, falsely claiming that "the children of a conquered nation will not accept the doctrines of foreign conquerors" (128), and preferring to dream of conquered populations assimilating their conquerors. This led him to extremes of sentimentalism, as when he recalled, in a postwar edition of the book, the Nazis' permission to Quakers to do relief work within Germany: "Even Nazi hearts could be touched by long-continued kindness" (90).

Gregg echoed the Jamesian hope for a stern, disciplined, as it were spirited nonviolence: "Struggle is a part of the very meaning of life" (95). Nonviolent struggle will "secur[e] a power that is much greater and more satisfying" than that attained forcefully (102). This is a pacifist version of Nietzsche's will-to-power. It is a kind of horrifying absurdity, but not *only* an absurdity, given the historicist assumptions underlying Gregg's Gandhiism, that he compared Gandhi to Lenin (123). By complying with "certain principles," Gregg claimed, one can "tap the spiritual power pervading the entire world" (143). Gregg was rather latitudinarian in specifying what, or who, this "power" is (157). Folk songs and dancing, group meditation, and storytelling will establish human unity, as will community service. "A method, not a dogma" (174), nonviolent persuasion and coercion submerge the content of convictions beneath a wave of process, a wave that aspires to erase all the shorelines of politics.

Aside from Martin Luther King, who for the most part integrated Gandhian techniques into the framework of 'American' principles and institutions, several pacifists in the 1960's re-examined Gandhiism, with varying degrees of optimism. Sibley 1968, after blaming "the non-German world" for Hitler's election, admitted that non-violent resistance would not have been likely to work after 1933: "No method and no technique of social conflict can perform miracles" (368), and "commitment to non-violence does not mean that we can dispense with political wisdom (371). Miller 1964 went further, conceding "it would be moralistic to assert that violence can have no other effects but disaster," while quickly adding that violence is "unstable and risky" (42-43). *Contra* Gandhi, he noted that "meat, alcoholic beverages and sex have not proved to be stumbling blocks for...leaders or cadres of non-violence" (169). While decrying "the twin forces of hedonistic materialism, bourgeois and Communist, that are ranged against us" (213), he never leaped from moral criticism to expectation of victory for the forces of goodness. The examples of nonviolence resistance that presented generally showed the limited efficacy of nonviolent resistance in politics. Seifert 1965 gave a cautiously optimistic account of the use of nonviolent resistance against military occupation (153-156). Gandhi, Seifert judged, had "underestimated the pervasiveness of sin" and the power of technology in totalitarian hands (157-158). He also observed, however, the totalitarianism may leave even less scope for violent resistance than for nonviolent, at least among conquered populations (14), leaving nonviolent resistance the only, albeit remote, chance for overthrowing a well-established totalitarianism 'from within.' Further, the destructiveness of modern weapons makes revolution 'from outside' less reliable than ever. On this latter point, Seifert was right only with respect to those totalitarian regimes protected by weapons of mass destruction.

Two scholarly studies of the relationship between nonviolent resistance and democratic politics are by Singer 1973 and Johnson 1976. Singer confirms the oft-made observation that nonviolent resistance works better in democratic regimes than in others; however, he prefers direct democracy to representative government (106 ff.), a preference that may stem from his sympathy for nonviolent direct-action. Johnson rightly sees that "nonviolence is more closely aligned with the concerns of contemporary rhetorical thought than classical thought" (115) — a fact he views most indulgently, because he has no real knowledge of classical thought. He believes that "while the classical scholars [e.g., Plato, Aristotle, Cicero] developed a human standard of discourse it did not extend beyond the borders of the city-states" (a claim that overlooks Aristotle's and Xenophon's knowledge of such regimes as Persia's, and entirely ignores Epicurean and Stoic thought) "beyond the wealthy and well-educated" (a claim that ignores the example of Socrates) "nor beyond the male sex" (a claim that ignores Diotima) (51).

For a critique of 'movement' pacifism or nonviolent resistance from a Christian point of view, see Hershberger 1969, 191-202. *Nonresistance* should not be confused with nonviolent *resistance*; Hershberger judged nonresistance to be Scriptural, nonviolent resistance unscriptural. Hershberger quite consistently rejected Christian participation in government (243).

77. The pacificist-anarchist Emma Goldman and the militarist Homer Lea exemplified these extremes. Each took selective glances at the American Founders, in order to find precedents for a favored ideology: Goldman called the Jeffersonian motto, 'that government governs best that governs least' as the "real Americanism" (Goldman n.d., 4); Lea reduced the original "principles of the Republic" to "militant patriotism" (Lea 1909, 25). After correctly predicting that Wilson would lead the United States into the European war, Goldman imagined that an "American militarism" would be "far more terrible than German or Prussian militarism could ever be," because "nowhere in the world has capitalism become so brazen in its greed and nowhere is the state so ready to kneel at the feet of capital" (Goldman n.d., 2). Class war underlies "all other wars" (9). As do other material-historicist writers, Goldman identified 'natural law' or 'human nature' with physical needs and desires human beings share with animals (Goldman 1969, 64). She denied that any country "outrage[s]" personal liberty more than does America, "the stronghold of the Puritanic eunuchs" (180).

Lea took a more Hegelian view, contrasting the spiritedness embodied in patriotism, "political virtue," to "commercial vanity" (5, 25-26, 44).

> In considering the future of this Republic one must do so, not from the closets of its politicians, not from its alleyways with their frenzied crowds, not from theorists or feminists, for these are but the feverish phantasms and sickly disorders of national life. It must be regarded from the heights of universal history and empirical knowledge which appertains to national existence. (23)

Whereas pacifists would see in improved communication and transportation the beginnings of 'one world,' Lea saw only faster invasions (34, 37-38). Standing armies bring not war but peace (88-89). He could not conceive of patriotism among immigrants; he could only conceive of it as the 'organic' love of one's land of birth (128). He went so far as to assert, "the preservation of the Constitution is not more vital than the inviolability of the Monroe Doctrine" (103) − a wonderful example of the historicist depreciation of form or structure in favor of movement or force, in this case the (rather remote) threat of military invasion. War is evolutionary (82).

In sum, the errors of Goldman and Lea sprang from their historicist antipathy to commerce, their historicist denigration of the power of stable republican institutions to secure unalienable rights − which power they either despised (Goldman) or ignored (Lea). They would extract 'civil' from 'civil society' − the one in the name of anarchic individualism, the other in the name of military discipline. Both are 'militants'; therefore, neither is 'civil.' Historicism is 'thought-militant,' whether pacifist or bellecist.

78. Karsner 1919, 25, 35. On the alleged similarities of Bolshevik revolutionaries to the Americans, see 27; on Debs' historicism, see 31. On capitalism and prisons, see 40-41; on capitalism and prisons, see Debs 1927, 23 ("prison in our modern life is essentially a capitalistic institution," he wrote, as Stalin consolidated his gulags in Soviet Russia).

79. *Ibid.*, 190. Roger Baldwin had an even larger blind spot, as evidenced by his article, "Pacifism and the Criminal: in Allen 1929: "In Soviet Russia the Bolsheviks, despite a government even stronger than the Tsar's, in their whole approach to the problem of crime minimize the law's violence" (86); he took at face value "the official attitude of the Soviet regime," namely, "no more police, no more prisons" (87). Pleased that "the death penalty has been abolished throughout the Soviet Union for all crimes except armed robbery and political offenses" (87) — the latter ground for execution did not cause him even to blink — he concluded that "the whole spirit of the Soviet penal codes is just what pacifists desire" (88).

80. Page 1931, 38-46.

81. *Ibid.*, 240-241.

82. *Ibid.*, 226-227, 274, 275-293. He did admit that Soviet communism glorified class war (271), but failed to see any possibility of the internationalization of such war, once a given country or alliance of countries became a 'proletarian dictatorship' seeking the overthrow of 'international capital.'

83. *Ibid.*, 297-357.

84. Abrams 1933 surveyed American pastors, finding that only about ninety of them, nationwide, retained their pacifist convictions during the war (195). (Because Quakers do not have pastors, they were necessarily excluded from the survey). Abrams typified the then-current fascination with the use of propaganda and 'symbols' to manipulate public opinion. Arnold 1935 is perhaps the best-known analyst; Lasswell 1927 concerned himself with the use of propaganda in the world war. These writers carried on the 'German' tradition of political science. Abrams, for example, believed the American flag and the Declaration of Independence, the Cross and the Bible, to be essentially as propaganda symbols with little principled content, allied in the promotion of nationalistic war. (Nor did he mean this merely as a criticism of the misuse of manipulation of these symbols: the Bible is "the greatest war book known to man" [251]). Given this cynicism, it is ghastly, yet, in retrospect, not surprising to see him end his study by

deploring "the current wave of hysteria over Hitler" (256), believing it just another manifestation of propaganda-manipulated passion.

Van Kirk 1935 surveyed the "peace policies of the larger and more influential religious bodies in the United States" (x), omitting Roman Catholic and Jewish congregations, reporting that "it begins to appear as though the unholy alliance between Christianity and militarism were being broken up" (5); "pacifism is sweeping through the church today as it has not done for centuries" (8). Christian pastors evidently accepted the Marxist claim "that economic competition among nations is a cause of war," that "economic imperialism" seeking "the perpetuation of profit-seeking capitalism" yields war (49). To this Marxist *analysis* they wedded a Christian-utopian call for a world wide "mental revolution in which the peace ideal is made regnant in the thought processes of oncoming generations" (91) — a Christian version of Hegel's end of history.

Carter 1956 argued that the mid-1930's saw a split between the pacifistic original form of the Social Gospel and a more thoroughly Marxist and therefore non-pacifist form (154). For a stern critique of the Social Gospel from a Biblical perspective, see Horsch 1924, who attacked "the so-called historical method" (60) of Biblical exegesis and warned, "Modernism demands a democratized God," a God who turns out to be the people self-deified (143).

It is important to notice that not all Christian objections to war and to commercial republicanism issued from an historicist critique of 'capitalism.' John J. Hugo, an associate of Dorothy Day, began with a critique of *modern* war ("the negation of Gospel law" because it is 'total' war [Hugo 1944, ii]), deploring modern war's "purely economic cause" (iii). He rejected modern political movements:

> Liberalism is another iniquitous system which, like Communism and Nazism, must likewise be opposed by Christians.... It is just as great a moral evil as the others; it is also a moral evil nearer home...[in] the countries we call democratic....[F]rom its womb came that neo-paganism which, in turn, spawned Communism and Nazism. (iv)

All modern ideologies rest on idolatry, the love of creatures not the Creator; carnal love being the cause of war according to Scripture, all modern ideologies cause war. Hugo went so far as to call war itself "a wholly unnecessary evil" caused by the failure to love God with one's whole heart (12) — mistakenly supposing that God gives grace to everyone. Although he judged the Second World War "Capitalistic and Imperialistic" (19), his (unsubtle) analysis arose not from historicism but from a critique of all modern political thought, including historicism. In a subsequent essay, Hugo shrewdly undermined the traditional Roman Catholic doctrine of the just war. "The affirmation of the possibility of a just war is a starting point for

554

true Christian pacifism," he began; "ultimately, a denial for the possibility of just war involves a denial of human rights" (vi). He firmly rejected "the widespread moral relativism which looks upon human rights as a gift made by society to individuals or as the product of mere custom" (vii) − organicism.

However, Hugo then argued that although "war *as such*" − that is, as it exists in the mind − can be justified, a just war *in practice*, is "morally impossible" (xix). This is especially true of modern wars, "proceeding from the evils and inner tension of Industrial Capitalism" (xix). A "perfect Christian would suffer death rather than commit a deliberate venial sin;" hence "the Gospel makes war impossible" (85). To those who reject Gospel perfectionism, Hugo replies, "if you say that sin is unconquerable, that war is inevitable, that you concede victory to the devil over Christ" (88). Here Hugo ignored the teaching of *Revelations*, that sin *is* unconquerable in the world as a whole, until the return of Jesus.

85. "Saints for This Age" (1962), Muste 1967, 414.

86. *Ibid.*, 418, 424.

87. Muste 1940, 172, 126. The Creator-God is a worker-God, and Jesus was, appropriately, a carpenter (2).

88. "Sketches for an Autobiography" (1957-1960), Muste 1967, 21, 38; Muste 1947, 130.

89. "Pacifism and Class war," Muste 1967, 180-181; Muste 1947, 208. Muste did not, however, continue to assume economic determinism; economic inequality is *"one of* the taproots of war," not the only taproot (Muste 1947, 208; italics added).

90. Muste 1940, 45; "Pacifism and Class War," Muste 1967, 183; "Sketches for an Autobiography," Muste 1967, 133-135, 169. "I have to *experience* ideas, rather than *think* them," Muste wrote (136). This inability kept his feet on the ground as he matured, but it made him a poor prophet.

91. Muste 1940, 1-2, 130.

92 Muste 1947, 51; Muste 1940, 5-6. Muste criticized the movements for democratic social change for slighting the importance of religion-based morality and for blaming evil simply on the socio-economic system. Genuine majority *consent* − meaning, *moral* agreement − will be necessary for a genuine revolution (Muste 1940, 64).

93. Muste 1947, 208: Muste 1940, 63. Americans are often pharisaical, and this is "the worst sin" in the Christian ("Who Has the Spiritual Atomic Bomb?" [1965], Muste 1967, 486. See Also Muste 1947, 59: The Pharisee is "in many respects a good and religious man," but one who separates himself from others. "[I]t needs to be said over and over

again in these days, that one of the crucial obstacles to peace in the world is American self-righteousness, our feeling that we never sought anything but peace, that our invention and building of a nuclear arsenal was in the interest of peace" ("The Civil Rights Movement and the American Establishment" [1965], Muste 1967, 461). Much of Muste's most interesting rhetoric over his long career consists of attempts to avoid the extremes of unjustly denigrating 'American' principles and institutions, and of tolerating pharisaical smugness in the 'American' class par excellence, the bourgeoisie. Muste's historicist ambitions made this balancing act all the more difficult, as he wanted the acrobat not only to stand on the tightrope, but to walk on it. In modernity, "the balance of power in deciding whether a people shall turn toward reaction or toward social progress rests with certain sections of the middle class — farmers, the better paid workers, technicians, small business people, professional people" (Muste 1940, 79). Leftist denunciations of democracy and glorifications of violent class warfare will turn the bourgeoisie toward fascism; leftist denunciations of religion will alienate Christian and Jewish congregations (80). Thus Muste attempted to solve the problem of faction within the progressive 'movement' by an appeal to political effectiveness or realism. On the moral component of this — Muste's insistence on rooting out pharisaism not only in the bourgeoisie but in the 'movement' itself — see Muste 1940, 70. As a communalist, Muste needed a much more exacting religious standard to provide the basis of political union than did James Madison. Muste's 'low but common ground' is therefore rather higher than Madison's, and also more exclusive, much more difficult to achieve.

94. Muste 1940, 103-105.

95. Muste 1940, 107-109; Muste 1947, 98. Muste gave no evidence of support among the American Founders for a future world government.

96. Muste 1940, 74-77. But see also *Ibid.*, 90, where Muste focused blame on the Bolshevik Party's "high-handedness and brutality" during and immediately after the regime's founding.

97. Muste asked, "Why should we expect that men who have embraced a purely materialistic philosophy of life, who do not believe that there are objective moral standards, who have no genuine respect for the individual but only for 'the mass,' who believe in dictatorship — why should we expect such men, for all the admirable qualities some of them may have, to be able to help the masses to build a fair and stable order?" (Muste 1940, 87)

98. *Ibid.*, 182-186. "There is no basis for justice in a naturalistic or materialistic philosophy" (Muste 1947, 108).

99. "The True International" (1939), Muste 1967, 209.

100. "The Fall of Man" (1964), Muste 1967, 449. Muste agonized over the question of pacifist collaboration with Communist Party and Communist-front organizations. Compare "Communism and Civil Liberties" (1949) with "Crisis in the World and in the Peace Movement" (1965), Muste 1967, 326-330, 467-477.

   Here, the decisive factor against or for collaboration is the presence or absence of Stalinism in the Soviet Union.

101. "Korea: Spark to Set a World Afire?" (1950), Muste 1967, 346.

102. "The Problem of Discontent" (1905), Muste 1967, 177-178.

103. "Return to Pacifism" (1936), Muste 1967, 210; Muste 1940, 12-15; Muste 1947, 63-71, 87.

104. Muste 1940, 23-25; Muste 1947, 46.

105. Muste 1940, 29, 88, 115, 116-125.

106. Muste 1940, 148.

107. Muste 1940, 148. Muste also argued that "under modern conditions" conquerors cannot benefit from conquests. He used the example of France's attempts to exploit the Ruhr farmlands of Germany. "The only way to get milk out of a cow is to permit her to become strong, France discovered" (158). Muste overlooked France's commercial republicanism, which wanted milk from cows. Other regimes might prefer beefsteak. Still others, such as the one dominated by the vegetarian Chancellor Hitler, had no use for cows at all.

On violence, Muste was uncompromising. It "must be ruled out of transactions in the realm of moral, i.e., human life" because it treats men as objects, not as men (71). It is morally better "to have atomic bombs dropped on you than to drop them on others" (74). It is morally better to do nothing violent in the face of violence against others than to try to defend them violently (75). Because "repentance is a unilateral business" (112), Americans should disarm unilaterally. On this moral ground, Muste's argument is unassailable, if the premises are correct – that is, if he correctly understood Christian Scripture as commanding no use whatever of lethal force. Unfortunately, he persisted the claiming practical, this-worldly benefits for pacifism. The slogan, "Violence begets violence and not something else" (104), simply overstates the case; here Muste's moralizing impulse impeded historical perception. His hope that pacifism would probably work, even immediately, reflected the same noble prejudice: "War comes because two nations pursue certain policies" – obviously; "it is the inevitable result of these policies" – or at least the result. "Then," Muste hypothesized, "one nation radically changes its course" – in the direction of total disarmament. "Will not the other be affected by that?" (119). Most likely it would. But, to trade rhetorical question for rhetorical question. In what way would it be affected? Would it too disarm? Or would it seize a possibly unique opportunity to master, not love, its neighbor? A good answer will require prudence — the serpentine virtue Jesus would combine with dovelike harmlessness. Muste lacked a teaching on prudence.

108. Muste 1947, 84-87.

109. Muste 1940, 55-56, 138-139, 170; "The World Task of Pacifism" (1941), Muste 1967, 217 ff.; "War Is the Enemy" (1942), Muste 1967, 266; "Where Are We Going?" (1941), Muste 1967, 256; Muste 1947, 12, 19, 34-35; "Germany — Summer 1947" (1947), Muste 1956, 301; "Korea: Spark to Set the World Aflame" (1950), Muste 1967, 347; "Of Holy Disobedience" (1952), Muste 1967, 371 ff.; "Who Has the Spiritual Atom Bomb?" (1965), Muste 1967, 500. Of all these predictions, only the prediction that an international organization would not bring peace was unqualifiedly correct. Even the (rather obvious) prediction that an Allied victory in the Second World War would strengthen Communism (Communist Russia was, after all, one of the victorious allies), must be qualified by observing that commercial republicanism, its 'decadence' often decried, derided, or celebrated in the 1930's, also benefitted noticeably from the defeat of rightist totalitarianism as a world-historical force.

110. When political realities happened to match Muste's moral teachings, Muste prophesied accurately. It would be hard to surpass Muste's comment in his 1964 essay, "Rifle Squads or the Beloved Community": "To base the tactics of the civil rights movement on the assumption that a traditional [i.e., violent] revolution is imminent in the United States is either mad or criminal" (Muste 1967, 434).

111. "Getting Rid of War" (1959), Muste 1967, 393; "What the Bible Teaches about Freedom" (1943), Muste 1967, 294. See Weigel 1989 for a brief discussion of historicist influences on American pacifism resulting in "a collapse of eschatology into apocalyptic" (75). Prudence, not apocalyptic is more appropriate to politics (Ibid., 81). Compare Jones 1932, 107, on Gnostic politics.

112. Thomas 1941, 11.

113. "The Christian Patriot" (1917), Thomas 1974, 47 ff.; "Speech at Mass Meeting of the Soldiers, Sailors and Marines Protective Association" (1919), Thomas 1974, 145.

114. Thomas 1923, 3, 8, 128-142. Thomas also cited "brutalities" against conscientious objectors; see 143-164.

115. Thomas 1931, 96, 116. On Hitler's rightist totalitarianism, see Thomas 1934, 50.

116. Thomas 1931, 105.

117. "Fight Fascism" (1934), Thomas 1974, 160-161; Thomas 1934, 16, 43, 207, 223-224.

118. Thomas 1935, 167; 187. In this, his last major pacifist work, Thomas again wrote of "the capitalist-nationalist system" (130) as the cause of war, which he tended to do whenever he lost focus on the regime question.

119. "The Pacifist's Dilemma" (1937), Thomas 1974, 168.

120. Thomas 1941, 5, 8, 27, 43, 98, 109, 177. The "once and for all" proof of socialism's potential comes only one page before a mediation of the *im*permanence of "historical judgements" (28); in Thomas as in Muste, *one* is more impressed by the latter.

121. Thomas 1944, 32, 172. Thomas rightly identified Stalinism as "the most comprehensive and amoral dictatorship on earth" (77) at a time when much of the American left still admired our war-ally. He correctly predicted in "aggressively imperialistic" Soviet Union in the years to come (79). He retained his illusions about Marxism; Communists in the United States "have been following Marx not Machiavelli" (167) — an overdrawn distinction if ever there was one. He continued to warn of possible "fascism" in the United States (139).

    The invention of nuclear weapons impelled Thomas to call the "collective suicide" of humanity "most likely," given the tensions between the United States and the Soviet Union (Thomas 1959, 13, 18). This time, he called not for unilateral disarmament by the United States, but mutual disarmament (43), i.e., temporary dependence upon armaments.

122. Wittner 1969, 15-16. Wittner mistakenly dates Niebuhr's critique of pacifism from 1934; *Moral Man and Immoral Society*, with its clear reservations concerning pacifism, appeared in 1932. Niebuhr did not begin explicitly to justify international war until 1937, around the time Norman Thomas did — i.e., in response to the civil war in Spain, with its clash among almost every significant political ideology of the twentieth century: rightist 'authoritarianism,' commercial republicanism, and both 'rightist' and 'leftist' totalitarianisms.

123. Niebuhr saw the tension between 'American' and 'German' principles before the United States intervened in the First World War. In an article published in the July 1916 issue of *The Atlantic* titled "The Failure of German Americanism," Niebuhr argued that "German-Americans...had failed in two ways: they had neither embraced American principles nor expressed allegiance to the best traditions of their own homeland," namely liberal progressivism in politics and religion (Fox 1985, 44). Fox observes that Niebuhr became a pacifist in reaction to the war, after the war was over (79).

124. "The Use of Force," Allen 1929, 16-17, 19, 25.

125. Niebuhr 1932, xi-xii, 30.

126. *Ibid.*, 3, 6, 11, 16, 91, 95. Within every nation, power thus tends to destroy its own purpose by violating the social peace it seeks to secure, and "by robbing the common may of his basic privileges which might bind him to his nation" (11). Notice that Niebuhr silently rejected the concept of natural *right*. Niebuhr's suspicion of power ran so deep that it extends to God: "Since supreme omnipotence and perfect holiness are incompatible attributes, there is a note of rational absurdity in all religions" (53); Niebuhr 'saved' the religions by emphasizing the feebleness of reason and the power of love. Except for the rejection or neglect of natural right, all of this is anti-Hegelian.

127. *Ibid.*, 73.

128. *Ibid.*, 14, 113-116, 137, 144, 148-255, 270-271. Niebuhr also rejected the scientific pretensions of Marxism-Leninism, regarding it rather as an "apocalyptic vision" (155). He rejected the Marxist prediction that power-relationships someday will cease (160 ff.). See also *Ibid.*, 184, for a discussion of the *analytical* limitations of Marxism, although Niebuhr stopped short of rejecting the Marxist prediction of capitalism's inevitable decline. He did uncompromisingly reject the feasibility of a 'temporary' revolutionary dictatorship of the proletariat.

129. *Ibid.*, 170-172, 234-235. It is this radical egalitarianism that caused Niebuhr to make the foolish claim that utilitarians, with their "compromises with human selfishness" probably pose as dangerous a threat to "the life of society" as the doctrines of Lenin (262).

130. *Ibid.*, 238, 242-247, 266-267.

131. Niebuhr 1934, ix, 3-4, 53, 70-74.

132. *Ibid.*, 11, 13. While criticizing Marxism (128-131), Niebuhr adhered to the Marxist prediction of a 'proletarian' revolution, claiming that "the pure methods of democracy will never suffice to arbitrate the conflict" between oligarches and proletarians (157). This false prediction follows from Niebuhr's discounting or neglect of political institutions.

133. *Ibid.*, 209.

134. *Ibid.*, 217-218, 223.

135. *Ibid.*, 246-247, 251-252. Niebuhr concluded,

> The liberal soul produces neither warriors nor saints, heroes nor rebels, and it is ill at ease when confronted with their fury and their passion. The manifestations of

life which reveal its darkest depths and its sublimest
heights leave the liberal soul in baffled confusion (262).

The liberal soul therefore needs Christian spirituality and a touch of
Christian pessimism, to ward off the dark seductions of political
extremism.

136.   "The Anarchy of the World," Niebuhr and Eddy, 1936. Leaving aside
        the problem of a morally relevant natural law, it is clear that Niebuhr
        was mistaken in implying that nature is anarchic. Even the Second
        Law of Thermodynamics, which states that all things tend toward
        increasing entropy and decreasing energy, works in an orderly or lawful
        way; mathematicians have shown that such 'anarchic' events as
        explosions actually follow measurable patterns.

137.   *Ibid.*, 5, 7, 10, 11. Italics added.

138.   *Ibid.*, 11-12, 14.

139.   Niebuhr 1940, x.

140.   *Ibid.*, 1-32. Or, as Niebuhr puts it later in the book, "The Socialists
        have a dogma that this war is a clash of rival imperialisms. Of course
        they are right. So is a clash between myself and a gangster a conflict of
        rival egotisms." (168-169).

141.   *Ibid.*, 39, 47, 56-57, 83, 99, 124. Niebuhr perceptively noted modern
        scientists' ignorance of the conditions of their own free inquiry: "The
        five hundred American scientists who recently presented a memorial
        to the President favoring neutrality in the name of scientific
        impartiality seem not to have the slightest idea that scientific freedom
        is dependent upon the vicissitudes of political history." (171)

Niebuhr also remarked the commonsense mistrust of a republican
people for anti-republican governments:

> The common people are no fools. In fact they react with
> a wholesome common sense to the problems of the day.
> The fools were the intellectual leaders of our democracy
> who talked utopian nonsense in a critical decade in
> which the whole of western civilization faced its hour of
> doom (72).

On the matter of 'capitalist' failure to oppose rightist totalitarianism,
Niebuhr was of course correct. But he might have blinked in
astonishment, at first, before grinning sarcastically at the sight of
'capitalists' rushing to support failing leftist regimes with loans and
investments, a practice that Occidental Petroleum and other
corporations had merely pioneered in his own time. Perhaps Niebuhr
credited capitalism with too much Machiavellianism and too little
greed.

142.   *Ibid.*, 49.

143.   *Ibid.*, 86.

144.   *Ibid.*, 59, 622. In American religious life, Calvinism earned Niebuhr's praise for its insistence on the perennial reality of sin. The political thought of the American Founders and the theology of American Calvinists both resisted utopianism: "Sin in history is not finiteness and particularity. Sin is the false eternal and the false universal." (63).

Niebuhr continued to avoid rational*ism* by insisting on the limits of reason with respect to the discovery of the meaning of human life. When directed at teleological questions, reason "mistakes the image of God in man for God Himself" and thus tend toward idolatry, indeed toward "implicit or explicit self-glorification and deification" (206). "Once known, the truth of the gospel explains our experiences which remain inexplicable in any other level" (214). This explains much of Niebuhr's skepticism with respect to Christian natural law; it is too much the product of reason, and reason is too weak to be very useful in the quest for absolute principles.

> The fact that the content of the natural law as Catholicism conceives it differs so widely from the content of the natural law as the eighteenth century conceived it, though the contents of both are supposed to represent 'self-evident' truths of reason, must make the critical student skeptical.... Both fail to appreciate the perennial corruptions of interest and passion which are introduced into any historical definition of even the most ideal and abstract moral principles. (Niebuhr 1944, 69-70)

145.   Niebuhr 1940, 144-152.

146.   Niebuhr 1944, 119. "The conception of human nature which underlies the social and political attitudes of a liberal democratic culture is that of an essentially harmless individual" (18), Niebuhr imagined. He conveniently ignored the political philosophy of Montesquieu, which may more accurately be described as a quest for remedies for individuals' harmfulness, and he misconceived Adam Smith's doctrine of the "invisible hand" (25), which does not presuppose individual harmlessness but rather sets one selfish man against another, for the common good. Niebuhr claimed that John Locke restricted social conflict to matters of self-preservation while ignoring grander conflicts (27-28). Niebuhr overlooked Locke's obvious knowledge of such conflicts; the Glorious Revolution, after all, occurred in his lifetime. Niebuhr underestimated the extent to which Locke may have sought deliberately to dilute grand conflicts. As Niebuhr stated later in the book, "It must be admitted that toleration in religion" — on which topic Locke wrote a short book — "could probably not have been achieved in

any modern democratic society had there not been a considerable decay of traditional religious loyalties," given the melancholy fact that "religious humility as a rarer achievement than religious indifference" (130).

147. *Ibid.*, 55, 57, 89. A similar non-explanation, equally revealing of Niebuhr's incomplete understanding of the American founding, may be seen in this remark on American 'international lawyers': "America has produced so many pure constitutionalists in international political theory partly because American history encourages the illusion that the nation was created purely by constitutional fiat and contract" (166).

As any reading of the Declaration of Independence will show, the "nation" or people of America were not "created" by a fiat, constitutional or otherwise. Their representatives declared the independence and devised a constitution designed to secure the unalienable rights of an *existing* people.

148. *Ibid.*, 40-41.

149. *Ibid.*, 180-183.

150. *Ibid.*, 5.

151. Niebuhr 1964, II, 1-4. Niebuhr thus overlooked the historicism of Hegel, who quite obviously believes himself a sort of rational Christ, wherein history has ended and all stands (rationally) revealed.

152. Niebuhr mistakenly charged that Platonism, like Brahmanism, does not consistently sustain its anti-historical character, because Socrates in Plato's *Republic* centrally calls for the rule of the polis by philosopher-kings, and the need to drag philosophers back to the cave of conventional society (*Republic*, 473d). This reading ignores Socratic, and Platonic, irony; the polis to be ruled by the philosopher-kings exists only in *logos* — in speech, beyond history and its changes. Socrates and Plato never for a moment suppose that philosophers will actually rule a real polis, though they might, for reasons of their own, agree to advise a ruler.

153. *Ibid.*, 20-26.

154. *Ibid.*, 36. The real meaning of human life overflows "the 'system' of meaning which the human mind always prematurely constructs with itself as the centre" (38 n.1). This is the mistake of legalism, whether Jewish or 'natural,' wherein men seek a premature sense of security and righteousness — premature because the Messiah has not yet finished His work (40-41). Niebuhr 1949 called "the culminating error in modern man's misunderstanding of himself" the attempt to conquer *human* nature by technological means. "The self as creator does not master the self as creature by the extension of scientific technics" (12).

155. Niebuhr 1964, II, 46-49, 63, 68, 72, 86, 89, 180. Oddly, Niebuhr 'overlooked' Hell, claiming that evildoers are not to be destroyed, that Christ bears their evil (46). Niebuhr identified the notion of unmitigated historical progress to "the Renaissance" (166), although he also sees such tendencies in such later Christian sects as the Quakers, Anabaptists, and Puritans. "It is a good thing to seek for the Kingdom of God on earth; but it is very dubious to claim to have found it" (178).

The genealogy of historicism is of course complex. For the purposes of this study, Hegel has been taken as the originator of historicism because he contends that all thought and belief before his own advent was strictly relative to its own historical period. Although previous philosophers had proclaimed or implied the superiority of their own thought to that of their predecessors, to accuse a previous thinker of error is not identical to calling him historically relative. The latter claim is in one sense more generous − it allows Plato, Aquinas, Machiavelli to be right 'for their period' − and in another sense more severe − Socrates did not and could not ascend from the cave of opinion to the sunlight of truth. The mere love of wisdom, Hegel believes, has been transformed into wisdom itself in his own thought, and in no other. See Niebuhr 1949, 1-2 for an account of the "very unclassical view of history" adopted by Renaissance writers, who conceived of the course of human events as "spirals of advance."

156. Niebuhr 1964, II, 129-241. Niebuhr singled out Marxism as one of "the late fruits [of] the soil of Renaissance thought" (243). All progressivist ideologies imagine the Kingdom of God "an immanent force in history" (245); compare with Voegelin 1952, III, 124-126, 131, 152, 167-170 and Voegelin 1978, 103-113.

157. Niebuhr 1964, 246, 252-258. Niebuhr further distanced himself from an anti-political prejudice he once shared with many historicists: "The modern belief that social power is the most basic form, and that all other forms are derived from it, is erroneous" (261). Political life is primary. The abolition of private property in Communist regimes merely establishes a new kind of oligarchy, a 'statism' of the left (262, n.4), because in any case concentrations of economic power persist. The decentralization of power democracy effects does restrain oligarchic elements; it does not abolish them (263).

Niebuhr 1949 held that modernity fuses "the fulfillment of life through the extension of reason" (he calls this a classical Greek idea) with confidence in "historical growth" (67). Modernity "exaggerate[s]" the growth of human nature in history and "add[s] the second mistake of identifying freedom with virtue" (69). Marxism exemplifies these errors (87, 160-161).

158. Niebuhr 1949, 207.

159. Niebuhr 1964, II, 260, n.2.

160. Niebuhr 1953, 28. In fact, mutual fear among the American states may have been one factor in the establishment of the Union. See *The Federalist* #4 (HMJ 1961, 45-50).

161. *Ibid.*, 17, 26. Niebuhr unwittingly demonstrated the limits of Burkean or neo-Burkean thought when he claimed that "There may be a larger deposit of Christian wisdom in the traditional communities of Europe than in a nation like ours in which the viewpoints of the Enlightenment won a unique triumph and colored even our Christian inheritance: for a combination of the visions of the Enlightenment and the optimism of sectarian Christianity, developed in the expansive conditions of a nation with an advancing frontier and an expanding economy, have tended to obscure the realities of history and to identify Christianity with pure 'idealism' rather than with a sense of responsibility in the actual conditions of human existence." (66-67)

   If this were the case, European politics would display more realism and more Christianity than the United States does. Not so, in either case, as the last two centuries of history testify so amply.

162. *Ibid.*, 96, 103. Niebuhr should have noticed the importance of humility in Judaism. See Eidelberg 1983, 48-60.

163. *Ibid.*, 135. See also 171-173.

164. Niebuhr 1952, 5, 11, 21-22.

165. *Ibid.*, 24-30, 33, 69-71.

166. See Grose 1984, 4-8 for a fairly conventional account of "American Israel" rhetoric in early America, an account that confirm Niebuhr's, although with a bit more shading. For the actual use of the analogy by a real Puritan, see Bradford 1952, especially Chapter IX. Bradford clearly saw the parallels between pilgrims and Jews as a source not for pride but for thankfulness to God.

167. Becker 1942, 212-213.

168. Niebuhr 1952, 32. See also Niebuhr and Heimert 1963, 109. Similarly, Niebuhr failed to see in George Washington's association of the fate of liberty with the fate of the American people, the sense of responsibility Washington brings to this assertion, which is far from a piece of oratorical flattery.

169. *Ibid.*, 75-77, 89, 106, 1-7.

170. *Ibid.*, 96. Niebuhr nonetheless did appreciate Abraham Lincoln, "whose awareness of the element of pretense in the idealism of both sides [in the Civil War] was rooted in his confidence in an over-arching providence whose purposes partly contradicted and were not yet

irrelevant to the moral issues of the conflict" (171). That "Christian realism" need not be Christian, may be seen in Mayer 1944, who argued that pacifists commit "the fallacy of angelism" (8) — "mistak[ing] men for angels" (5) — whereas fascists mistake men for beasts. "If men are animals, they must be expected to use force, justly or unjustly. And if men are political animals, all objection to war is political objection" (11). Many objected to American participation in the Second World War on the political (if chimerical) ground that "the system of wars is taking [the United States] inexorably down the road" to tyranny. (11)

171. Niebuhr 1958, 30-31.

172. Niebuhr 1952, 172; Niebuhr 1958, 19.

173. Niebuhr 1958, 42.

174. Niebuhr 1959, 13-29.

175. Niebuhr 1959 explicitly alluded to the American Civil War: "[I]t has not struck the imagination of the nation that in a crisis force was necessary, and was used, to preserve the unity of the nation" (34). See also *Ibid.*, 181.

176. Niebuhr and Sigmund 1969, vi.

177. Muste 1947, 91, 95.

178. Muste 1940, 37.

179. Muste wrote:

> The only real 'answer' to what neo-orthodox theology has to say about human corruption and moral impotence has to be given our lives, individual and corporate, by the Church of Christ and by the members of the Church. And who is equal to that challenge? As someone remarked recently, at the close of a long discussion when a feeling of deep humility had settled on the group. "That's where Niebuhr has us!" ("Pacifism and Perfectionism," Muste 1967, 318).

180. "We are warranted, therefore, in humbly asking those of our fellow-Christians who frame, or accept, elaborate and distorted doctrines about man's general inability to do the will of God and adhere to the ethic of the gospel, whether they are in this way rationalizing their own disinclination to obey the gospel at some very specific point — in not renouncing war, for example, when deep in their hearts they know there is no longer any way in which it can be reconciled with the gospel" (*Ibid.*, 320-321).

181. Raven 1940, 21-25, 34-40, 72.

182. Raven 1951, 21, 35, 63-66.

183. Raven 1951, 72 ff. Raven began to see this distinction when he wrote, "The fact is that justice as we know it in the system of ordered law belongs to a different category of social ethics from the Christian religion" (58-59), classifying individuals into types ('murder,' 'thief' etc.) instead of taking them as individuals to be saved by Jesus' Word. Raven did not go on to imagine anything other than the simple overcoming of the system of ordered law, including the principles of just war.

184. Hinshaw 1954, 3-5, 13. Hinshaw mistook the double standard for a medieval artifact; the double standard − really an articulated single standard − dates to the New Testament (Romans 13).

185. *Ibid.*, 17-19.

186. Hinshaw 1956, 2-3, 32-36. Hinshaw did not unreservedly condemn military resistance. He metamorphosed the double standard:

> For a man who sincerely believes that he ought to take up arms against the enemy, to be negligent in what he thus considers to be his duty, is to weaken the foundation of character itself. And that foundation of integrity is more important ultimately than the content of a particular ethical choice.... [T]hose who believe they should fight actually should do so as long as they have political responsibility for the nation. We approve what impels them even though we cannot sanction the action itself. This is hard for some pacifists to understand, but early Friends had no difficulty on this point. (23-24).

187. *Ibid.*, 37.

188. *Ibid.*, 41.

189. Rutenber 1950, 2-3, 5.

190. *Ibid.*, 22-27.

191. At 42-43 Rutenber argued that a people cannot make war then establish a lasting peace, as seen in the aftermath of the Second World War, when the United States and the Soviet Union engaged in indirect warfare (Korea then, other places later). Because the United States was at peace, and remained at peace, with the countries it had actually fought, Rutenber's true observation cannot be said to be very telling.

192. *Ibid.*, 50 n.27, 51 n.27, 74-75.

193. *Ibid.*, 92-97.

194. *Ibid.*, 103.

195. *Ibid.*, 102.

196. *Ibid.*, 122-130.

197. For the best Biblical exegesis provoked by Niebuhr written by a pacifist see Macgregor 1960. Macgregor's interpretations of Scripture will be considered on the Second Part of this book.

198. Merton 1968, 3-6, 13, 39. Elsewhere Merton produced an argument similar to that of Hugo 1944, xix (above, footnote #84), that a just war "might" be possible today, but that in practice the theory is "irrelevant" (Merton 1980, 90).

199. Merton 1968, 19-20, 27-29.

200. Merton, 1966, 71, 208.

201. Merton 1968, 48 ff., 194-195. "In such a situation, who needs atheists? The unbelief of the believers is amply sufficient to make God repugnant and incredible" (197).

202. *Ibid.*, 200. Merton did not forgo sardonic humor in describing some manifestations of modern thought:

> Einstein was a great prophet of the now dead age of liberalism. He emerged with the disconcerting kindness and innocence of the liberal, came forth from the confusions of his day to produce for us a little moment of clarity, and also, as an afterthought, he left us the atomic bomb (Merton 1966-85).

Merton concluded, "We are no longer living in a Christian world" (Merton 1980, 13). See also Merton 1966, 209.

203. Hobbes 1962, 100, 129.

204. Merton 1980, 50-67.

205. Merton 1968, 64, 112, 148-149.

206. *Ibid.*, 123-131, 167-174; Merton 1980, 77. After making one series of predictions, Merton concluded, fairly enough, "we'll see" (Merton 1968, 166). We did; he was wrong.

207. Merton 1980, 229.

208.   For more specimens, see McSorley 1979 ("Experts judge that by 1985 thirty-five nations will have nuclear weapons" [132-133]): and Sider 1979 ("responsible scientists believe that there is at least a 50 percent chance of nuclear war" by 1993 [183]).

Perhaps the most spectacular of recent works of 'prophetic' Christian pacifism has been Aukerman 1981, who demonized 'the State' and exalted Christian communitarianism with breathtaking simplism. Aukerman turned the Niebuhrian argument against just-war thinkers, claiming that such theorists fail to see human sin "within ourselves," and self-righteously kill in self-defense (21). Self-defense by war is self-justification, and self-justification is self-righteousness. "In the United States the God-and-country patriotism that sees America implicitly or explicitly as the New Israel lies in continuity with the collective presumption that the New Testament writers recorded and struggled against" (29). "Thought-control" techniques in 'democracies' exceed those in communist regimes (52); this thought-control serves as an instrument of nationalist of self-worship or idolatry, as does war, "the chief ritual of nationalist religion" (56). "Because of this idolizing, any nation-state is inherently totalitarian" (55), and overtly or covertly "contrary to the dominion of the messianic king," Jesus (84). The United States is worse than the Soviet Union, exploiting "the world's poor" more and deluding itself with pseudo-Christian self-righteousness (106). Indeed, "the communist takeover of the United States has already occurred" because "the worst in communism — the readiness to resort to any means and to sacrifice any number of people to what is proclaimed as the public interest — has come to dominate the national posture of the United States" (144). A small example of this may be seen in the 1972 presidential election, when Senator George McGovern's campaign was "blocked by manipulation of the public." Had McGovern won, "there might have been resort to assassination" by the United States "military elite" (165). More generally, "In the nuclear era, reliance on nationalist defense is doomed, and a country's true defenders, its only sure early warning system, are those who cry out to the nation who turn back" (195), those who live in "Shalom communities" where "worship is the vital center of the life together" (203). "The greatest danger is not nuclear holocaust but God's impending judgement" upon a people willing to use nuclear weapons (197).

It might be tempting to dismiss all this as paranoiac ranting. But it should be noticed that some such comprehensive fear of the ordinary events and institutions of political life will likely inhere in any attempt to meld moralism and foresight. 'Prophetic' speech will fail every time the prophet does not serve as a conduit for the Creator's power, because only an all-powerful Creator can ensure that the prophecy 'comes true.' Aukerman might reply that we are no longer in ordinary political times, that nuclear weapons require an 'apocalyptic' response:

> The framers of the Constitution of the United States recognized human fallenness and the dangers that go

with the exercise of power by government leaders. They set up elaborate checks and balances to prevent undue concentration of power in the executive branch of government. But now the only real checks and balances over against the monstrous thermonuclear power held by the President and the other top national security managers in the executive branch are those provided by rival governments. Such checks and balances were for Hitler too the only decisive ones. (86)

This is where Aukerman's demonological view of politics misled him. In history, the United States enjoyed nearly twenty years of unquestioned nuclear superiority; as late as the Cuban missile crisis of 1962, a United States nuclear strike would have devastated the Soviet Union with no chance of counterstrike endangering the people of the United States as a whole. During that time, the United States used nuclear weapons only twice, and then in order to end a war not to start one. Aukerman failed to recognize how such governmental institutions as balanced, separated powers can help to build an ethos of moderation. In his analysis of Romans 13, Aukerman predictably sidestepped Paul's explicit statement that the magistrate's sword should, and can, service as a terror to evildoers, not to the good (95-99). Once that is admitted, the question of political regimes, which channel the ambitions of political men and shape citizen character, begins to matter very much, and no loose talk of 'the nations' taken as a homogeneous lump will be countenanced.

209. See, for example, Wiesel 1968, 209-212.

210. Yoder n.d., 14-19.

211. Yoder 1976, 111-112. Given Paul's intense missionary and evangelical concern, along with his authoring of Romans 13, Yoder's criticism is empty.

212. *Ibid.*, 56, 125-127.

213. *Ibid.*, 35-38, 47, 111-112.

214. *Ibid.*, 19.

215. Yoder 1971, 14-18, 59-62, 69, 79.

216. *Ibid.*, 83.

217. *Ibid.*, 128, 165-166, 181. For an elaboration of the claim that just-war theory's alleged failure in practice, due to its lack of precision and its manipulability of self-interested men, see Yoder 1984, especially 57-71, 74-82.

218. Yoder 1983, 41.

219. *Ibid.*, 38-39.

220. Hauerwas 1985, 16.

221. Jesus mentions His church very much in passing, and then only in response to Peter's expression of faith in Him as the Christ (Matthew 16:15-20). Hauerwas thus violated his own exegetical precept, that "religions, like languages, can only be understood in their own terms" (5).

222. Hauerwas 1985, 65.

223. *Ibid.*, 67-72, 76.

224. *Ibid.*, 111.

225. *Ibid.*, 122-125.

226. *Ibid.*, 125-127.

227. *Ibid.*, 130.

228. *Ibid.*, 163-166, 197.

229. "Persuasion versus Force" (1916), Bryan 1917, 95-97.

230. "Memorial Day at Arlington" (1894), Bryan 1909, II, 387-388.

231. Taft and Bryan 1917, 112, 155; "Imperialism" (1900), Bryan 1909, II, 34.

232. "America's Destiny" (1899), Bryan 1909, II, 11-13. Imperialism "is the one tree of which the citizens of a republic may not partake. It is the voice of the serpent, not the voice of God, that bids us eat" ("Naboth's Vineyard" [1897], Bryan 1909 II, 8). He criticized the Republican Party for abandoning Lincoln's principles and "accept[ing] the European idea and plant[ing] itself on the ground taken by George III, and by every ruler who distrusts the capacity of the people for self-government or denies them a voice in their own affairs" ("Imperialism" [1900], Bryan 1909, II, 30-31). See also *Ibid.*, 36-37, 47.

233. Bryan 1917, 7; "America's Destiny" (1899), Bryan 1989, II, 15; "The White Man's Burden" (1906), Bryan 1909, II 219; "Imperialism (1906), Bryan 1909, II, 35-49. See also "At the Peace Conference" (1906), Bryan 1909, II, 230: "All movements in the interest of peace have back of them the idea of brotherhood."

Unlike many historicists, Bryan disliked historical determinism, which he associated with the American imperialists who spoke of the 'Manifest Destiny' of the United States: "Destiny is the subterfuge of the invertebrate, who, lacking the courage to oppose error, seeks some plausible excuse for supporting it" (*Ibid.*, 47). Also unlike many historicists, Bryan opposed socialism on the grounds that is "does not take human nature into account" — that is, Bryan thought human nature a stable essence, not a changing historical phenomenon ("At the New York Reception" [1906], Bryan 1909, II, 88).

234. Bryan 1917, II ff.; Taft and Bryan 1917, 75, 111-112. A national referendum on war or peace would replace Congressional declarations of war, except in case of invasion.

235. "The St. Louis Convention" (1904), Bryan 1909, II, 52-54; Bryan 1917, 95-97, 109.

236. Taft and Bryan, 1917, 28-29, 40, 45-46, 52, 89, 98-102, 139-140.

237. Sharp 1973, v, 7, 112.

238. *Ibid.*, 8-9. For Clausewitz's understanding of political power, see Clausewitz 1976, 78-81, 85-87, 92, 117-119, 148-149. Clausewitz's reply to one such as Sharp might be, "The fact that slaughter is a horrifying spectacle must make us take war more seriously, but not provide an excuse for blunting our swords in the name of humanity. Sooner or later someone will come along with a sharp sword and hack off our arms" (260).

239. Sharp 1973, 25, 28, 35, 63-72.

240. *Ibid.*, 454.

241. *Ibid.*, 455, 557.

242. Sharp 1980, 24-25, 41, 48-49, 92-93, 109-111.

243. *Ibid.*, 127, 134. Sharp warned the radical left that

> Those who envisage that they could become some kind of incongruous 'Gandhian Jacobins' and, while a clear minority, impose their will on the majority, are obviously ignorant of the nature of nonviolent action and are harboring ideas which are irresponsible and dangerous....If a policy is to be permanently secured by nonviolent means it can only be done by building up conviction in its rightness among the population to the point where it has majority support. (128)

244. *Ibid.*, 158-159, 192, 197-199, 208.

245. *Ibid.*, 197-199, 323, 376.

CHAPTER IV

1. See Legnano 1917, cxciv, 354. On the character of this city, see Origen 1973a, x, xvi, 393: "Every soul that possesses by nature some elevation and some acuteness to perceive the things of the mind is a citizen of that city."

2. See Students for a Democratic Society 1969, 3-4.

3. *Ibid.*, 5-8, 12.

4. *Ibid.*, 15.

5. See Berns 1969, 25 ff.

6. Mansfield 1979, 10.

7. Machiavelli 1985, XV, 61.

8. Machiavelli 1950, II, xxviii; III, iv, 407. See also *Ibid.*, III, vi, 423. For the theological significance of this, compare *Ibid.*, III, i-iii with Machiavelli 1979, VIII, 37 and see Mansfield 1989, 126-127.

9. *Ibid.*, III, xxii, 478.

10. See *Antichrist* 2, in Nietzsche 1968, 570-573, and Mansfield 1989, 136.

11. Machiavelli, 1950, II, ii, 285-288; II, xiv, 321; II, xvi, 328.

12. Machiavelli 1985, XVII, 65. See also Cox 1987 *passim*.

13. Machiavelli 1985, XII, 48-50; XXIV, 97, XXIV 103. For the underlying significance of this thought, including its theological implications, see Machiavelli 1985, XIII, particularly the story of David and Goliath, and compare I Samuel 17, 39-52; notice what weapon is absent from the latter account, and what person is absent from the former. See also Machiavelli 1950, I xix, 174; I, xx, *passim* and II, xxx, 388.

14. Machiavelli 1985, VI, 24; XIV, 58.

15. For one of them, also involving guilt and the issue of peace, see Machiavelli 1950, III, xxxii, 505.

16. Machiavelli 1985, XVII, 66-67, 72.

17. Machiavelli 1985, XVIII, 70; III, 10. Compare Cervantes 1949 II, xi, 576: "I perceive now that one must actually touch with his hands what appears to the eye if he is to avoid being deceived." On the other hand, Machiavelli would never write, earnestly, as Cervantes does at II,

lxxi, 972, that "ever since [Quixote] had been overcome in combat he had talked more rationally on all subjects." See also Eidelberg 1983, 281-282, 367 n., who however, emphasizes the use of the hand to strike while overlooking the use of the hand seductively to caress.

18. Machiavelli 1985, V, 21: "In republics there is greater life, greater hatred, more desire for revenge." Therefore, he argues, "in truth there is no secure mode to possess [conquered states] other than to ruin them" (V, 20). To bring peace to one newly-acquired state, Machiavelli recalls, a duke assigned "a cruel and ready man" and gave him full power. This man "reduced it to peace and unity." The duke then established a court of law, thereafter having his cruel man killed, satisfying and stupefying the people. Machiavelli quietly notes that he himself served as counselor to this duke. (Machiavelli 1985, VII, 29-32).

19. Machiavelli, 1950, I, xxxvii, 208-209, II, x, 309-310; II, xxiii, 358; III, xvi, 463 ff.; III, xv, 487. However, he adds, the republic *government* should be wealthy.

20. Machiavelli 1950, II xxv, 371.

21. Machiavelli 1950, I, v, 128.

22. See 2 Timothy, 4-5.

23. Machiavelli 1965, Preface, 3-4, I, 13; I, 25; II, 64 (these last are the midpoints of Book I and of Book II); I, 29; I, 40-41; IV, 129; VI, 164-165.

24. *Ibid.*, II, 79. For a comment on the overall intention here, see Mansfield 1983, 855, and Mansfield 1989, 129-130.

25. Nehemiah 4.

26. Deuteronomy 18.

27. Genesis 4:8. See Dannhauser 1983, 35.

28. Genesis 32:29.

29. Psalm 11:5; Joel 3:10; Isaiah 2:4; Micah 4:3. The Christian pacifist Lasserre 1962 admits, "There seems no doubt that the expression 'Thou shalt not kill' refers explicitly to individual murder, not to capital punishment or war." He immediately adds that "the Old Testament can never be normative in the sphere of ethics." (169). Lasserre criticizes John Calvin for "giving the same authority" to both Testaments (58). See also Childress 1982, 69.

30. See Gottwald 1979, who cites Exodus 15:21, Judges 5:1, and I Samuel 2:1. Christian pacifists often claim that Israelites warred without moral

evil only because God commanded them to do so (Gurney 1833, 138; Yoder 1972, 81, n.4, 83; Lind 1980, 23, 38, 73). Martin Luther makes the needed finer discriminations: God, he writes, "makes a choice of men and arranges everything as though they were to rely upon their own powers and arms in battle, like other nations. This He does in order to hide himself under the outward mask and win the victory secretly through faith in His Word, that Israel might not seem to be tempting God when it fought bare and unarmed. Now it learns to bear arms indeed and to use the equipment of war, but not to trust in it. He wants to conquer, not *through* arms and equipment but *under* arms and equipment, that faith, which is of things not seen (Heb. ll:1) may thus have a place and that they not tempt God by neglecting what God gave outwardly for use in war." (*Lectures of Deuteronomy*, Luther 1956, IX, 203).

31. Deuteronomy 25:17-18; Hirsch 1974, 5, 9, 27. "[N]owhere did Judaism project nonresistance to evil as the noblest ethical good" (64). Christian pacifists often reply to such arguments by positing the notion of "progressive revelation" or, more precisely, "progressive appropriation" of revelation by human beings (Dakin 1956, 11). Dakin mitigates his own argument by preferring some earlier prophets to some later ones, and by misinterpreting the story of Jonah as a parable against revenge – overlooking the fact that God falsifies Jonah's prophecy of the destruction of Ninevah only because the Ninevites repent, not because they should not have been punished had they remained unrepentant (Jonah 3:5-10). More consistent are Cadoux 1919, 178 ff. and Heering 1932, 1 – the former emphasizing humanity's progress, the latter emphasizing the progress of revelation itself, or more precisely, of the Holy Spirit in the world. Cadoux's argument dates back at least as far as the anonymous fourth-century tract *Dialogus de Recta Fidei* (cited in Cadoux 1919, 218). Heering's argument was adopted, then abandoned, by Augustine, who appropriates parts of the Mosaic law for Church use (see Brown 1964, 113-114). Heering overlooks the fact that there is no 'progress' in the sequence of prophetic statements in the old Testament. Isaiah 2:4 comes well before Joel 3:10, for example.

32. Eidelberg 1983, 11-13.

33. Voegelin 1954-74, I, 374.

34. Soloveitchik 1983, 19-28, 64.

35. Zimmerman 1979, 10-14, 21-22, 26; 286.

36. Soloveitchik 1983, 31-36. In reply to this, Nietzsche charges that the Old Testament God invented was in order to divide peoples, disrupt science, and exalt priests (*The Antichrist*, #48, Nietzsche 1968, 629).

37. Lasserre 1962 is wrong to claim that "everywhere in the Old Testament human life is cheap, and the best believers have scarcely felt any scruples about shedding blood" (60).

38. Proverbs 8:13.

39. II Samuel 12. Xenophon 1968, *passim*.

40. Eidelberg 1983, 216-218; Breuer 1974, 32-35, 43, 91.

41. Voegelin 1954-74, I, 241.

42. Lind, a Christian pacifist, takes the extreme antimonarchical position (Lind 1980, 32-34, 149, 167-174) linking the kings of Israel with militarism (114). See for contrast Voegelin 1954-1974, who argues that the "pacifism" of the Israelites, as distinguished from Israel, increased under monarchy, when "wars were conducted by professionals" (I, 210-211). Gottwald 1979 goes farther, suggesting that the Israelites' holy wars served as means of "selective expulsion of kings and upper classes and the selected expropriation of resources such as metals" (550).

43. Gottwald 1979, 544-545.

44. Deuteronomy 9:4-12.

45. Exodus 23:4-5, 23-24. This kind of teaching allows Martin Luther to write that the ancient Jews "had the same spirit and faith in Christ as we have, and were just as much Christians as we are" (Luther 1956, XLV, 97); as those Jews wielded the sword, they are to be emulated by good Christians, as long as Christians understand that wielding the sword righteously will not bring salvation. Anscombe 1961 concurs: Jesus does not substitute a higher or more spiritual religion for Judaism; Judiasm equally requires its adherents to "seek not revenge" (Leviticus 19:17-18). See also Leviticus 19:33-34, where God commands love for resident aliens. For contrast see the Christian nonresistant Chelcický 1964a, who claims, "If [Christ] had wanted people to cut each other up, to hang, drown, and burn each other, and otherwise pour ut human blood for his Law, then that Old Law would have stood unchanged, with the same bloody deeds as before." (139-140).

46. Fast 1959, 40, 51.

47. H. Windische writes, "After the manifestation of Christ and the outgoing of the first Christian mission, Judaism had nothing more to say to mankind" (cited approvingly in Heering 1943, 4).

48.   ...on account of their disbelief in Jesus and all their other insults to him the Jews not only will suffer at the judgement which is believed to be coming, but also have already suffered *more than others*. What nation but the

576

Jews along has been banished from its own capital city
and the native place of its ancestral worship? (Origen
1965, viii, 72-73).

George Fox agrees, writing to the Jews, "had you obeyed the Law of
God, you had not gone into Captivity" after Jesus came, bringing "a
kingdom of peace" (Fox 1661, 37).

49. Micah 3:9-10, 7:2.

50. Dymond 1855 writes, "An appeal to the Hebrew Scriptures is
     frequently made when the precepts of Christianity would be too rigid
     for our purpose" (45). Rowntree 1900 observes, "It is rare, when
     Christian wars are attempted to be defended, that their advocates do
     not resort to the pages of the Old Testament" (8). Hoyt 1956 argues
     that Israelites fought wars because Israel was of the world; because
     they were "not a regenerated people as a whole" (although they had
     their saints); and because it was under the Law, not under grace (73).
     He does not adequately show why the formulation and promulgation
     of the Law was not an act of grace. Hershberger 1969 contends that
     "the various Old Testament commands of God requiring killing, such
     as the commands to slay the Amalekites, to hew Agag to pieces, and to
     kill the giant Goliath, were *permissive commands* given to a sinful, lean-
     souled people who had chosen to live on the lower, 'sub-Christian'
     level" (33-34). He continues, "whereas under the old covenant God
     made a concession to the hardness of men's hearts [Matt. 19:18], under
     the new covenant He gives His children a new heart so that they are
     able to accomplish that which men of a stony heart did not accomplish
     under the old covenant" (46). The laws of God henceforth were
     written on Christian hearts instead of stone tablets, and "the civil law of
     Moses [war] brought to an end that the moral law might be fulfilled"
     (46). "[N]owhere in the New Testament are members of the kingdom
     of God given any part in the execution of God's wrath" (44).

51. See DeGaulle 1973, *passim*.

52. White 1978 perceptively observes that while the tyrant of the ancient
     world might "exist in any walk of life," as he is simply "a man afflicted
     with many passions," the modern tyrant is "afflicted with,
     fundamentally, only one passion, the lust for power" (33). One might
     call the ancient tyrant polytheistic in his atheism, the modern
     monotheistic in his atheism, or self-idolatrous.

53. "Machiavelli allows his anger at God to become anger at the good"
     (Platt 1987a, 20). Nietzsche conceived of the Renaissance as a
     "revaluation" of Christian morality and "the triumph of life;" he blamed
     the "German monk," Martin Luther, for overturning this wholesome
     revaluation (*The Antichrist*, 361, in Nietzsche 1968, 653-654). Does
     Nietzsche perceive the *ressentiment* in the Machiavellian Renaissance?
     Or does he choose nobly to overlook it?

54. See Legnano 1917, *passim*. Mr Docksman excludes Legnano's provision for duelling.

55. Suarez 1944, XIII, i, 3, 802; iv, 1, 816.

56. See Bacon 1986b, 3; Gentili 1933, III, 15; Maritain 1957, 24.

57. Bainton 1960, 15. Bainton identifies three Christian "attitudes toward war:" pacifism, traditionally associated with withdrawal from the world, the just war, associated with qualified participation in worldly matters, and the holy war, associated with Church dominance over the world. Swift 1983 questions the inclusion of holy war and, by implication, just war in the Christian tradition, saying there are no such things for Christians as sacred prostitution or sacred homicide (22). This assumes that 'war' is equivalent to prostitution and homicide or murder rather than, say, sexual intercourse and man-killing; that is, Swift's argument assumes its own conclusion.

58. Legnano 1917, x, 225.

59. Warner 1805, xiv-xv; Parsons 1813, 3-4.

60. Boorne 1846, 6-8. Walsh 1916 calls a declaration of war "the abrogation of morality − a license to kill, lie, covet, steal and perform every sin...." (42) He especially condemns "the murderous raptures of the non-fighters," including "the cowardly swagger of the music hall, the prostitution of the pulpit to the heathen deity," and "the pedagogue pouring hate into the helpless ear of innocent childhood" (45).

61. See "Bellum baudquaquam lachrymosum," in Erasmus 1972, 297; and "The Blasphemy of John of Leiden," Simons 1966, 43-46; Boorne 1846, 8. "For though the Church of Christ do walk in the Flesh, yet the Apostle saith, We do not War after the flesh...." ("A Distinction betwixt the Wars and the Weapons and the Arms and the Armor in the Old Testament and the New," Fox 1706, 845).

62. Hauerwas 1983, 74. See also Barbour 1964, 71; Green 1952, 92, 95-96.

63. "Now to love one another, is not to war with one another, and to love Enemies, that is [Jesus'] Command, and so not to war with them, nor strive, nor fight...." ("To all that Profess Christianity, Are these Following Particulars," in Fox 1706, 252).

64. Green 1952. Green goes on to raise the question of why so many Christian pacifists are "people who have been nurtured in certain religious beliefs" (92) − i.e., taught by parents and coreligionists, not directly by the Hold Spirit.

65. The Apostles "had the true knowledge of true Zeal, that wrestleth not with Flesh and Blood, but with Spiritual Weapons against the Rulers of Darkness and Spiritual Wickednesses; but the blind Zeal wrestles with

Carnal Weapons, against Flesh and Blood, with the Beast's Mark on their Fore-Head and Right Hand, and with the Dark Power's Strength in a Notion and outside Profession, without the Power and Spirit of the Prophets, Christ and the Apostles, and such do not know what Spirit they are of, neither have they rule over their own Spirits; but are like unto a City whose Walls are broken down, that is an Heaps: And pray you *Christendom* see whether your walls are not broken down?" ("Possession above Profession," Fox 1706, 509).

66.   George Fox 1660, 3. Fox continues, "we shall freely give up our Bodies as a sacrifice, rather than disobey the Lord" (4). See also Origen 1960, 331-337; Eusebius 1961, 211; Augustine 1950, vi-vii, 321-325; Alighieri 1966, III, xiv, 204-205; Bernard of Clairvaux 1954, I, 64; Grebel 1975, 60; Margret Fox 1660, 5-7; Bayly 1676, 167; Windass 1964, 5-6. Penn 1882 writes that Alexander the Great and Julius Caesar

> vanquished others, not themselves; Christ conquered self, that ever vanquished them; of merit therefore the most excellent prince and conqueror. Besides, they advanced their empire by rapine and blood, but he by suffering and persuasion; he never by compulsion, they always by force prevailed. Misery and slavery followed all their victories; his brought greater freedom and felicity to those he overcame. In all they did, they sought to please themselves; in all he did, he aimed to please his Father....(38).

67.   Barbour 1964, 209.

68.   See Barclay n.d., 520. "And whereas we are a People accused to raise up a new War, it is False; for dwelling in the Word, it takes away the Occasion of Wars, and gathers our Hearts together to God, and unto one another, and brings to the Beginning before Wars were...." ("To all who love the Lord Jesus Christ, mercy and Peace be multiplied unto you" [Fox 1706, 25]).

69.   See Nuttall 1958, 51.

70.   Enz 1972, 69; Hornus 1980, 68 ff.

71.   See Barbour 1964, 252.

72.   *Phaedrus* 66, Plato 1937, I, 450. This assertion is part of an edifying speech that rhetorically denigrates the body and claims immortality for the soul.

73.   *Republic* 373d-374e, Plato 1968, II, 50-51. Machiavelli of course represents war itself as necessary, not as the product of the overreaching of necessity. Weber 1958 contends that war led to progressive widening of political boundaries in Europe, as the Roman Empire replaced the small city-states, to be replaced in turn by

Christian cosmopolitanism (99-103); at the same time, a countervailing trend of political independence (eventuating in modern nationalism) also fed on the military spirit (120). Osgood and Tucker 1967 claim that "the whole astonishing explosion of modern Western civilization is linked with a distinctive bellicosity in its organized political life" (4).

74. Dodge 311. He continues, "Accordingly nature wished man to owe the gift of life not so much to himself as to loving kindness."

75. *Ibid.*, 315, 318. The origin of war in hunting is affirmed in O'Connell 1989, 10. For observations concerning the relationship of hunting to wars of conquest, see Crèvecoeur 1957, III, 47-51.

76. "Man is a battlefield within himself: reason is at war with the passions and these are in conflict with each other;" this conflict within souls causes conflicts among souls and the bodies souls animate (*Querela pacis indique gentium ejectae profligataeque*, Erasmus 1986, XXVII, 297-299). See also Fox 1661, 31, and Bayly 1676. Dymond 1892 claims that "People do not often become soldiers in order to serve their country, but to serve themselves" (22), and that military glory is nothing but folly and iniquity (29). In this he follows Barclay n.d., who classifies war with games, sports, and theatrics as activities that make men forget the fear of God that is the beginning of wisdom. Woolman 1922 contends that pride yields vanity, which yields "Imaginary wants," which "prompt men to Exert their power in requiring that of others, which themselves would rather be excused from," which begets "Hard thoughts," which ripen into malice, which becomes vengefulness, which inflicts pains and spreads desolation (269). Clarkson 1806 contrasts the pridefulness of warriors with the meekness of Christians (74); see also Jefferson 1832, 3-4; Dymond 1855, 403-404; and Hershberger 1969, 1. The latter adds "Certainly no environment is more favorable for the perpetuation of the nonresistant faith than is the rural community" (226).

77. Dodge 1905, 81. Platt 1983 notes, "The Ancients used music to temper already excited warriors; the Moderns use music to excite their own warriors or frighten the enemy's" (68 n.10).

78. Homer 1967, I, 11, 568-569, I, 581; XXIV *passim*. This reading contrasts with that of Simone Weil in her essay "Reflections Concerning the Causes of Liberty and Social Oppression" (Weil 1973, 68-69), and with Van Braght 1950, 353.

79. "No weapons of self-defense will be so efficacious as Christian meekness, kindness and forbearance, the suffering of injuries, the absence of revenge, the return of good for evil, and the ever-operating love of God and man" (Gurney 1845, 148). Hauerwas 1983 claims that truth "has no need to resort to violence to secure its own existence (115), overlooking the retaliation of God against the rebellious angels. See Luke 10-18, Romans 16-20.

80. Parsons 1813, 4.

81. Homer 1967, *11*, 233-384.

82. *Alcibiades I*, 112a-d, in Pangle 1987, 186-187. See also Aron 1966, 365-366.

83. "O Friends, do not Rule with your own Reason!" (Fox 1659, 1).

84. Aristotle 1985, VII, xv, 1334a; Burckhardt 1979, 217-218.

85. Legnano 1917, XI, 229. Legnano overlooks evasiveness and mentions only hunting.

86. Matt. 4:19; Mark 1:17.

87. "...though the consequences of Cromwell's massacres in Ireland were an enduring legacy of Anglo-Irish animosity, the consequences of Charlemagne's massacres in Saxony were, curiously enough, the opposite; the Saxons were soon the most loyal supporters of the Frankish monarchy." (Barraclough 1958, 6).

88. Colet 1965, 86-87. Scargill 1815, 9, 12.

89. See Platt 1983, 54, 126; Cantor 1976, 86.

90. See Aristotle's observation that foreign war "made evident the weakness of the laws" in Crete (Aristotle 1984, II, x, 1272b).

91. Fortune "exerts a powerful influence, as well as in other matters, especially in war, effects great changes from trifling causes" (*Commentaries on the Civil War*, Julius Caesar 1887, 354).

92. "*Testa collisa testae,*" Erasmus 1972, 297.

93. Augustine 1966, IV, iii, 13.

94. Barth 1961, 452. He concludes that people do not "become better in war;" most become far worse (454). Stratmann 1928 admits that "War may be a short cut, *if it does not last long,* to a moral and religious awakening; but if it continues for long it is full of danger to religion and morality," causing souls to "break down and become Godless" (37). See also Macgregor 1960: "The moral universe in which we live is so constituted that when man asserts his independence of God, his right, if he so wills, to live for self alone, then he finds that his way of living tends to call forth a similar way of living in other men" (55).

95. "*Dulce bellum inexpertis,*" Erasmus 1972, 308.

96. Cadoux 1940, 30.

97.   "*Dulce bellum inexpertis*," Erasmus 1972, 321.

98.   Cadoux 1940, 30.

99.   Comenius n.d., 33.

100. Augustine 1964, V, #229, 152-153.

101. *The Kingdom of God Is Within You*, Tolstoy 1960, 221-222, 224. See also MacNamara 1841, 166-167, 180-184; he calls for Christians to "place reliance on the Almighty" in prayer, good actions, and, if circumstances warrant, remonstration with invaders (197). M'Cree 1845 exclaims,

> What honor would accrue to this country from a proclamation of forgiveness to an offending people! It would give us true fame. It would bring all nations to our feet. It would place the throne of our Queen on an immovable basis. It would surround us with barriers more impregnable and permanent than mountains of brass, and cliffs of iron. We *are* renowned for our commerce, famous for our inventions, celebrated for our enterprise, admired for our science, and feared for our prowess — oh! let us be *loved* for our mercy (12).

Calhoun 1946 sharply distinguishes between fear of God and fears of men, of life, and death; the latter fears "can be disastrous" (5).

102. Woolman 1922, 211. Woolman amplifies this thought as follows:

> It requires great self-denial and resignation of ourselves to God to attain that state wherein we can freely cease from Fighting when wrongfully Invaded, if by our fighting there were a probability of overcoming the invaders. Whoever rightly attains to it, does in some degree feel that Spirit in which our Redeemer gave his life for us, and, through Divine goodness many of our predecessors, and many not living, have learned this blessed lesson; but many others having their Religion chiefly by Education, and not being enough acquainted with that Cross which Crucifies to the world, do manifest a Temper distinguishable from that of an Entire trust in God. (207)

103. Fry 1904, 28-29. She goes on to comment "a *passionate* conviction, of the practicability of the way of peace which Christ came to teach, and which he died in making plain to us" (40). She goes so far as to claim that the lack of forceful sanctions for international agreements makes agreement stronger, because moral force is more powerful than physical force (34): human beings are like a child who "is only overcome when he is brought to recognize that, since the command

was no mere whim but part of a law too large for him to comprehend, he has injured his own inmost being by disobedience" (30). Byrd 1960 writes that Quakers "make no distinction between public affairs and private affairs" (30); "Fundamentally, there is nothing singular about the relationships among the nations"(43).

104. Field 1945, 33-38. Field adds that many Romans were "searching for a new and satisfying religion, and many religions were being tried" (33); this led to a certain saving ambivalence that enabled Christianity to survive and spread.

105. In Plato 1980, I, 638a, 17, Socrates notes that victory in war may merely reflect the greater size of the victorious country.

106. John 16:13.

107. "These things I have spoken to you, that in me you may have peace. In the world you will have tribulation, but take courage; I have overcome the world" (John 16:33). Ferguson 1974 writes that "...our proper understanding of the New Testament as a whole can only be built up out of the accurate interpretation of its component parts.... The gospels are in fact build up out of isolated passages: each of these is technically known as a *pericope*...or 'cut out.' These were preserved in the Church for various reasons...." (viii)

Different Christians emphasize different aspects of Scriptural interpretation: The guidance of the Holy Spirit-animated conscience as against the mere 'letter' of the Word (Fox 1911, 73, 89; Barclay n.d. 78, 91, 94-95); the guidance of the letter, given the defects of the human conscience (Hershberger 1969, 313); the need for rational thought about Scripture and the urgings of spirit (Cadoux 1940, 47; Jones 1919, 396); the emphasis on the historical context of Scriptural utterances (Green 1952, 97; Scheiders 1983, 91-94), an emphasis that need not require a belief in historical *relativism*. Authors who claim a "progressive development" of human understanding of Scripture swim in hazardous waters, tending either toward secularist progressivist historicism (Jones 1919, 379, 396) or else raising the question of why Jesus' self-understanding as presented in the New Testament should be authoritative. Bowman 1945, 94 does not even consider this question.

108. Bainton 1960, 13. Cadoux 1940 writes that God's will "does not lend itself to complete and precise formulation in any written document long or short;" a particular, practical issue can only be resolved by heeding the general sense of the Christian community, the utterance of the Christian heart, the character and teaching of Jesus, the Christian doctrine of the character of God, and the nature of the results (60).

109. Dymond 1892, 53, 59-60.

110. Parsons 1813, 18.

111. Ephesians 6:15; John 8:32. Vincent 1903, I, 353 observes that "Satan" derives from a Hebrew word meaning "to lie in wait" and "to oppose" – a stealthy enemy. For Christianity as spiritual warfare see also I Timothy 1:18-19; II Timothy 2:4; 2:22; II Corinthians 6:7; 10:3-6.

112. "Fear is not in love, but perfect love casts out fear, because fear has to do with punishment, and the fearing one has not been perfected in love" (I John 4:18).

113. See Matthew 10:39. Also see Hauerwas 1983, 12.

114. See Daniel 8:25 and Acts 24:2. For articles on these words see Kittel 1964, 400-420.

115. Matthew 18:22. See Origen 1973b and Vincent 1903, I, 105. Pollard 1946 argues that "all war is civil war, worse indeed, it is fratricidal strife" Cainite (4).

116. Luke 3:14.

117. See Barclay n.d., 520; Parsons 1813, 19.

118. Barclay n.d., 520; Dodge 1905, 99; Harnack 1981, 71. Porteous 1929 tells the story of forty Christian theology students from Oxford University who, while living in Jerusalem, served as police volunteers in repelling a direct and personal attack by Moslems upon Jews (184). Although a Quaker and a nonresistant, Porteous defends this as a police action, not an act of war.

119. Matthew 3:17; Vincent 1903, I, 26.

120. For Jesus as "our captain of the faith," see van Braght 1950, 357, 391.

121. Matthew 2:6; Luke 2:14; Vincent 1903, I, 269.

122. Hebrews 9 and 10; compare Exodus 24:8.

123. Matthew 9:18-26.

124. Cadoux 1925, 57.

125. John 8:3-11; Lasserre 1962, 190-192.

126. Luke 2:14.

127. Kersey 1815, 81.

128. Vincent 1903, I, 35-36. "Peace" as a greeting is also a blessing (e.g. John 14:27) and blessing transmits divine vitality even as cursing withdraws it. (See Josephine Massyngbaerde Ford, "Cursing and

Blessing as Vehicles of Violence and Peace in Scripture," Reid 1986, 22). Although Jesus tells the disciples to bless those who curse them, the disciples themselves do curse their enemies (*Ibid.*, 25 e.g. Peter to Simon Magus, Acts 8:20).

129.   Matthew 5:9. Vincent 1903, I, 151, observes that Matthew is the only apostle to use the word *eirenopoioi*.

130.   Matthew 5:44. See Scott 1800, 4 and Fry 1904, 68-70 for pacifist interpretations of this passage, the latter arguing, somewhat paradoxically, for the boundlessness of the law of love, i.e., for the boundlessness of a regulation, for an infinite finitude.

131.   Letter to Marcellinus, Augustine 1964, III, 46. Augustine 1961 b, XXII, 301, applied this specifically to the precept, "Turn the other cheek."

132.   Letter to Publicola, Augustine 1964, I, 230. See also Thomas Aquinas 1963, 2a2ae, 40, 1, calling for nonresistance or resistance depending upon prudential assessment of the circumstances with an eye to the common good and the good of enemies, and *Ibid.*, 108, 4 on the law of love as "inward readiness of mind."

133.   Luther 1956, XXI, 107, 110-113. See also Thomas Aquinas 1963, 2a2ae, 188, 3: *Jacobi Paleologi ad scriptum fratrum Racoviensium de bello et judiciis forensibus Responsio*, cited in Kot 1957, 54 ff; Vann 1939, 23-24, 39-43.

134.   Grotius 1925, 72; Finch 1746 *passim*; Howard 1983, 193-194; Lewis 1980, 49-50; Ramsey 1982, 143-145 Bruce 1983, 70-71; Harries 1986, 14. The Quaker historian Bainton 1960 concurs, writing that 'Turn the other cheek' means "not that one should not defend one's life, but that one should not resent indignity" (61). The Old Testament commends turning the other cheek in this spirit (Lamentations iii, 30).

135.   Cadoux 1919, 24; Yoder 1972, 120, 130-131; Hauerwas 1983, 61-63.

136.   Ferguson 1974, 14.

137.   Romans 12:17-21.

138.   Romans 3, 17-23; Romans 4, 13; Romans 5. See also Lactantius 1973, V, xx, 157.

139.   Matthew 6, 33. "The too-common and well-known distinction between political and moral right: or, in other words, between political expedience and Christian duty, is a distinction dangerous in the extreme, not founded on truth, and of a most pernicious tendency to morality in general...." (Scott 1800, 8).

140. Thus Ananias and Sapphira are punished, but by something like a miracle, or perhaps terror, not physically by Peter himself (Acts 5:1-11). I Corinthians 5:1-5 refers to the destruction of the flesh of a sinner by Satan, permitted by Paul so that the soul may be saved by Jesus Christ. It is not clear what Paul means by "delivering" the sinner to Satan, although this could mean corporal or even capital punishment.

141. Romans 12:18; Howard 1983, 192.

142. Luther 1956, XXI, 39, 76; Grotius 1925, VII, 70. Augustine 1961d, XX, 27 cites Luke 12:48 as proof that "sin can be punished in love rather than be left unpunished." However, this is actually an example or parable, not a direct endorsement of corporal punishment or war.

143. Yoder 1970, 29. Yoder, a pacifist, is summarizing the view of Karl Barth. On the distinction between force and violence, see Vann 1939, 20, Lewis 1940, 65-66, 86.

144. Thomas Aquinas 1975, III, 146.

145. Van Bragt 1950 cites Matthew 5:39, 44; Romans 12:14; I Peter 3:9; Isaiah 2:4; Micah 4:3; Zechariah 9:8-9. The last three passages from the Old Testament may be considered indecisive on the grounds that Jewish law permits war and capital punishment.

146. II Corinthians 10:6-8. Suarez 1944 claims that this means that physical means of punishment may be used.

147. Legnano 1917, lxxx, 280.

148. Luke 12:46-51.

149. Hebrews 11:31, 34. Stratmann 1928 argues that God's commands to make war, recorded in the Old Testament, prove that war can be moral, "as God cannot approve of anything immoral even to gain the most holy ends" (81). However, Stratmann immediately notices that God's will makes an otherwise immoral act moral, as when He commands Abraham's sacrifice of Isaac.

150. Two of these parables occur in Matthew 21:33-46 and in Matthew 22:1-14 — involving the destruction of murderers and the burning of a wicked city, both intended as images of God's impending punishment of the chief priests and Pharisees. Three more parables occur in Luke's Gospel: "When the strong man, having been well armed, guards his palace, his goods are in peace; but when one stronger than he overcomes him, the armor upon which he had relied is taken, and [the victor] distributes his arms" (Luke 11:21-22); "[W]hat king, going to encounter another king in war, will not sit down first and deliberate whether he is able with ten thousand to meet him who comes against

him with twenty thousand?" (Luke 14:31); the nobleman whose citizens (*politai*) reject him, orders them slain (Luke 19:27).

151. Thessalonians I, 5:2-3. Cadoux 1919, 39, makes this argument.

152. Ramsey 1983, 524.

153. Luke 10:30-37. See Churchill 1948, 53, II, 320; Bainton 1960, 63; Ramsey 1983, 142-143; O'Connor 1983, 112.

154. Matthew 22:21.

155. Dymond 1982, 72. However, see Romans 13:6-7, in which Paul evidently associates payment of taxes with support of rulers as servants of God.

156. Lasserre 1962, 92; Cullmann 1970, 47.

157. Luther 1956, XL, 99. He cites Titus 3:1, and comments that

> "...as far as body and property are concerned, they are subject to worldly rulers and owe them obedience. If worldly rulers call upon them to fight, then they ought to and must fight and be obedient, not as Christians, but as members of the state and obedient subjects."

The passage itself reads, "Remind them to be subject to rulers, to authorities, to be obedient, to be ready for every good deed."

158. Matthew 21:12. See Bacon 1918, 9-19; Stratmann 1928, 88.

159. Origen 1973a, raises doubts about the authenticity of the story itself, because Jesus' only weapon, a small whip of cords, and his reputation, were so slight. Origen suggests that Jesus' "divine nature... was able to quench, when He desired to do so, the rising anger of His foes "(X, xvi, 395), who otherwise could have overpowered Him. Holmes 1916 offers the excuse that Jesus' outburst resulted from stress; He was "tired, worn, hunted," and angry (169). Bacon 1918 refutes this, observing that the entry into the Temple was carefully planned (9-10). For statements of the argument in the text, see Cadoux 1918, 35; Macgregor 1960, 17; Bowman 1945, 92; Lasserre 1962, 48; Yoder 1972, 49; Ferguson 1974, 2; and Cassidy 1978, 45.

160. James 1:20; 4:1; Galatians 5:21-22; Ephesians 2:3, 14-22. See also Dymond 1892, 57 (following Barclay *n.d., passim*); Hirst 1906, 74.

161. *Phaedo* 66, Plato 1937, I, 450; Grotius 1925, 79.

162. The wry Grotius styles it thusly: "Because the Church at that time was without the backing of public authorities, for its protection God had called forth that supernatural power; that power, again, began to fail at

about the time when Christian emperors came to the support of the Church, just as the manna failed when the Jewish people reached fertile lands" (*Ibid.*, 78).

163. E.g., in Luke 11:45.

164. Acts 23. See also I Corinthians 9:7.

165. Letter to Marcellinus, Augustine 1964, III, 47-48. See also Augustine 1961 b, 301; Letter to Boniface, Augustine 1964, IV, 268.

166. Matthew 8:9. Anscombe 1961 argues, "On a pacifist view, this must be much as if a madam in a brothel had said: 'I know what authority is, I tell this girl to do this, and she does it....' and Christ had commended her faith" (55).

167. Vincent 1903, I, 52.

168. Chelcický 1964, 154-155. MacNamara 1841, citing Hebrews 11:31, writes that "Rehab, the harlot of Jericho, was commended by Paul for her faith, manifested in receiving the spies, but no one will justify her profession on that account" (91). The story of Rahab in Joshua 2, does not suggest that she will continue in her profession after the Israelites conquer Jericho. Harnack 1981 addresses the issue by attempting to minimize the importance of the centurion's status as a centurion, a difficult interpretation to sustain given the attention drawn to this fact in the story itself (70).

169. Acts 10:1-8, 24-48.

170. Lenski 1961, *Interpretation of the Acts of the Apostles, passim*; Barclay n.d., 521; Dymond 1892, 69; Lasserre 1962, 54; Cadoux 1919, 19.

171. Bowman 1945, 92; Hollenbach 1983, 26; Trocmé 1973, 96. Grotius 1925 claims to take the silence or lack of sanction as tacit approval of military force (65), as do Madan 1805, 15, and Helgeland, Daly, and Burns 1985, 29.

172. *Ibid.*, 1985, 23-25, 54.

173. Grotius 1925, 84; Thomas Aquinas 1963, 1a2ae, 188, 1-3.

174. Eppstein 1935, 47.

175. Tertullian 1973b, xi, 100; Bowman 1945, 92.

176. Dymond 1892, 69; Paupert 1969, 55-59.

177. Matthew 26:52; Tertullian 1973b, xii 99; Dymond 1892, 62.

178. John 18:11; Matthew 26:52; Augustine 1961d, II, xviii, 55.

179. Warner 1805, 20.

180. Letter to Vincent, Augustine 1964, II, 62; Augustine 1961b, xxii, 299; Caspary 1974, 134 ff.; Thomas Aquinas 1963, 2a2ae, 40, Hubmaier 1971, 281, 295, 301-302; Luther 1956, XLV, 92-93; XLVI, 30; Suarez 1944, I, iii, 802; Grotius 1925, 80; Madan 1805, 7-9, 15; Lee 1943, 18-38. Thomas Aquinas 1963 also argues that Jesus told Peter to sheath his sword because Peter represented "all bishops and clerics;" because "different functions are better and more efficiently carried out by different persons than one," and because war "seriously prevent[s] the mind from contemplating divine things, praising God, and praying for people, which is what clerics are called to do," clerics "are forbidden to fight in war, not because it is a sin, but because it is unbecoming their persons" (2a2ae, 40, 2). Luther 1956, XLV argues that Jesus' prophecy is a command for capital punishment of murderers (84-91). Kautsky 1953 advances the Marxist-revolutionary hypothesis that the original story "told of a *coup de main* in the course of which Jesus was taken prisoner;" later, pious editors could not erase the whole story, so "they blunted its point." Kautsky adds that the Mount of Olives, where the incident occurs, is "the best place from which to make an attempt on Jerusalem" (312-316).

181. John 18:36.

182. Hubmaier 1971, 281; Luther 1956, XLVI, 97; Howard 1983, 192.

183. Tennent 1748b, 35 ff.; Harnack 1981, 29 n.2; Cullman 1956, 32-34.

184. Lasserre 1962, 39. Barclay n.d. cites Ambrose's suggestion, that the sword is intended for purposes of bluff, but not to be used, and Origen's claim that the language is purely symbolic (521-524). Dymond 1892 flounders conspicuously and finally is reduced to contending that the command cannot be meant literally because it contradicts the rest of the New Testament, with the exception of the sayings of John the Baptist, which are not authoritative (74-75). Cadoux 1919 speculates that "Peter may have put on a sword without Jesus noticing it" (31, n.2). Bowman 1945 explains that "the disciples were not far enough away from their old habits and customs to follow the ideal of Jesus completely" (92). Fast 1959 observes that even the peaceful Essenes of the period carried swords to ward off bandits (72). Macgregor 1960 agrees, but also offers the possibilities that Jesus speaks "seriously, but metaphorically" ("It is enough," in this reading, would be an expression of exasperation) or "literally, but ironically" (i.e., Jesus intends the comment as "a wistful reminder of the utter futility of armed resistance") (24). Lasserre 1962 hypothesizes that Jesus may have the Apostles mistaken for criminals, in order to ensure that He would be executed as their ringleader (38), as is consistent with Isaiah 53:12 on the suffering servant who, "numbered among the transgressors," nonetheless "bore the sin of many, and interceded for the transgressors."

185. Romans 12:20-21. See Clarkson 1806, III, 77; Jefferson 1832, 11.

186. Grotius 1925, 77.

187. Luke 19:42.

188. Xenophon 1962, *Constitution of the Lacadaemonians*, viii, 163.

189. Romans 3:23; Romans 13:1-4; I Peter 2:13-17; I Timothy 2:2; Acts 22; Matthew 24:12. See Calvin 1982, 78, and Barth 1944, 27. Grotius 1925 argues that to pray for kings implies that kings can be saved and remain kings; this is not necessarily the case, however (64).

190. Bainton 1960, outlines three such responses: that of Anabaptists, who teach that the State is ordained by God for sinners, to be administered *by* sinners whom Christians should obey within the limits of conscience but abet; the Lutheran teaching, that the state is ordained by God for sinners, and Christians should participate in its functions to prevent it from collapsing; the Calvinist teaching, that the state is ordained by God for sinners, and Christians should participate in its functions not only to preserve the law but to foster righteousness and faith (58 ff.). For the early Christian responses to "Caesar," see Aland 1968, 115-127; Hornus 1980, 28, 51; Swift 1983, 23.

191. Tacitus 1942, *The Annals*, XV, 380-381.

192. See Octavius Felix 1973, xxix, 191; Origen 1965, 500; and Letter to Emeritus, Augustine 1964, II, 18-19. Cullman 1956 cites the suggestion of A. Deissmann in his 1923 study *Licht vom Osten*, that the number "666" means "Caesar-Is-God" (82-83). Cullman observes that the "exousiai" or "powers that be" in Romans 13 are both temporal and angelic, some good, some evil; "as long as they remain in bondage to Christ, however, they stand in God's order" (69). See also Lasserre 1962, 82-87. Kallas 1965 argues that these tensions or contradictions evidence textual corruption, but other scholars do not go this far.

193. Macgregor 1960, 86; Lenski 1961, *The Interpretation of St. Paul's Epistle to the Romans*, 777; Lasserre 1962, 183-187; Yoder 1972, 198-202, 204, n.12, 206-213; Ferguson 1974, 7, 82-90; Glidden 1948, 21-24. Trocmé 1973, 147 claims that Paul's strictures refer only to the Roman Empire, not to any subsequent governments; he gives no substantial argument for this assertion (147).

194. Van Braght 1950 makes this argument, and it stands as a clear statement of the traditional Anabaptist position. Secular authority, he writes, is not mentioned by Paul as being "among the officers of the church, nor that Christ taught His disciples such a thing, or called them to it; but, on the contrary, that He enjoined them to follow Him in His defenseless life and cross-bearing footsteps, prohibiting all revenge, not only that with arms, but also to return failing for sailing, and on the

contrary, commanding to pray for one's enemies, to do good unto them who do us evil; and much of a similar nature which is connected with the office of magistracy; hence we are afraid to fill such offices in our Christian calling" (36-37). Tertullian 1973a adjures Christians to pray for the Emperor's safety and for "brave armies," but not to participate in governmental or military affairs (xxx, 42). Chelcický 1964b teaches that "The Apostle set the faithful under the manifest pagans for worthy reasons, but he did not join the two together in the faith. The worst thing is that this paganism is accepted into the faith and is joined with it, and has already corrupted the faith...." (173) Warner 1805 writes, "The intricate maxims of courts, the mysterious schemes of ministries, bear no resemblance to, and can have no alliance with, the simple principles of religion, and the plain morality of Christ" (25), a remark that might be compared with Woodrow Wilson's celebrated attempt to achieve "open covenants, openly arrived at" among nations. See also Cadoux 1919, 211-215; Scott-Craig 1938, 95-96; Cullman 1956, 53; Douglass 1968, 208; Hershberger 1969, 20-22.

In opposition to Christian non-participation in government, see Sidney 1990, III, vii, 358-359.

195.   Yoder, 1972, 204 n.12; Irenaeus 1973, xxiv, 552; Harries 1983, 56.

196.   Thomas Aquinas 1963, 2a2ae, 19, 3; Suarez 1944, iv, 6, 818. Maritain 1935 follows the Thomistic tradition in writing,

> Force is necessary in civil communities because of men who are violent and inclined to vice but it has a pedagogic office and ought to lead in the direction of freedom. It is only a substitute for those creations of freedom that we call virtues. The good man like the Prince has no contact with the bloody hand of the law; he knows only its kind eyes....(79).

197.   Luther 1956, XXI, 23-25; XLV, 94-95, 105 (note that he assumes Paul must have meant that every *body* is subject to the magistrate, although Paul's word is "soul"); XLVI, 95-96. In the latter passage Luther compares capital punishment and just warfare to surgery, "amputat[ing] a leg or hand, so that the whole body may not perish." See also Grotius 1925, 67; Finch 1746, 14-18, 42; and Madan 1805, 19-21.

198.   Thomas Aquinas 1963, 2a2ae, 104, 5-6; Sidney 1990, I, iii, 15-16, II, xxiv, 219-220, III, iv, 339-340, viii, 359-365, III, x, 372-380, III, xii, 384, Vann 1939, 29; Cullman 1956, 55-57, 89. Luther agonizes over the problem of the right to revolution, at first prohibiting it on the grounds that even an unjust authority cannot harm the soul, and rebellion involves judging one's own case. Luther 1956, XLIV, 92-101, XLV, 62-63. The latter permits it on the grounds that "self-defense against the bloodhounds [i.e., the Papists] cannot be rebellions" (XLVI, 20, 34-35).

199. Acts 8:27-39; 13:7-12. See also Calvin 1982, 88-91.

200. Barclay n.d., 458; Mansfield 1989, 114-116.

201. Luke 16:14.

202. See Luther 1956, XXI, 170, 186, XLVI, 78; Figgis 1921, 57; Potter 1973, 57. Troeltsch 1949 writes that Calvinism unites "systematic conscious effort" with "an utter absence of interest in the results of effort" (II, 619).

203. Thomas Aquinas 1a2ae, 92, 1; Calvin 1960, IV, xx, 1487; Eppstein 1935, 352-355.

204. Hornus 1980 observes that Augustine does not originate this doctrine, which may be seen in Philippians 3:20 (109).

205. Augustine 1966, I, i, 13; xxxv, 139, II, xxi, 225-227, XIV, i, 261; XV, i, 425; XXII, xxix, 357, xxx, 377-379. See also Luther 1956, XLV, 80-91; Samuel Przypkowski, *Animadversions*, cited in Kot 1957, 184-186; Murray 1960, 289-292.

206. Augustine 1966, XVIII, 365-367; XIX, 141, 157, 163-167, 237-239. See also Stevenson 1987, 19-21, 60, 63; Luther 1956, IV, 35; Calvin 1960, IV, xx, 1485-1486; Gentili 1933, V, 28; Finch 1755, v; Maritain 1935, 186. Augustine also warns that no part of the earthly city will "be able to rule lastingly over those it was able to subjugate victoriously" (XV, iv, 425).

207. Augustine 1966, XIX, lists peace of the body; peace of the irrational soul (when appetites are sated); peace of the rational soul (ordered agreement of knowledge and action); peace of body and soul; peace between man and God; peace between individual (an ordered agreement of mind); domestic or civil peace; and the peace of the heavenly city (175).

208. Samuel Przypkowski, *Animadversions*, cited in Kot 1957, 189-201. On the distinction between *exthroi* and *polemioi*, see the most helpful article by Gottfried 1991, 283.

209. Thomas Aquinas 1949, 9-12, 23-24; Thomas Aquinas 1963, 1a2ae, 95, 2-96, 5; Calvin 1960, IV, xx, 1493-1494; *Pacem in Terris*, Gremillion 1976, 204; *Gaudium et Spes, Ibid.*, 309-312. For a more superficial treatment, see National Conference of Catholic Bishops 1983, 77-78.

210. Ferguson and Pitt-Watson 1956, 42-43, 51.

211. See Calvin 1960, IV, xx, 1497-1500, 1516; Stratmann 1928, 90-92; Murray 1960, 268-270; Swift 1983, 134, 160. As is so often the case, Martin Luther urges Christians most emphatically: "If you see that there is a lack of hangmen, constables, judges, lords, or princes, and

you find that you are qualified, you should offer your services and seek the position, that the essential governmental authority may not be despised and become enfeebled or perish" (Luther 1956 XLV, 95).

212. Scott-Craig 1938, 59; *Mater et Magistra: Christianity and Social Progress* in Gremillion 1976, 164-168.

213. Tolstoy 1960, 497, 511-522. Tolstoy claims that the universalization of professed Christianity, so that all countries "have the same basic principles today" (514), means that there are no longer any "material or moral grounds" for patriotism or war. This view, dubious in 1894 when Tolstoy published it, quickly became incredible in the decades following. It is essential to Tolstoy's claim that patriotism is nothing but artifice.

214. Hirst 1906, 508.

215. deGivry, 1924, 2-6, 9-15, 21-25, 79-80.

216. Dodge 1905, 110-111; Chalmers 1816, 30.

217. Tolstoy 1960, 513. See also Dymond 1892, who condemns patriotism as a kind of national pride "irreconcilable in its nature with the principles of our religion" (14) because it is excessively particularistic:

> Christianity is designed to benefit, not a community, but the world. If it unconditionally encouraged particular patriotism, the duties of a subject of one state would often be in opposition to those of a subject of another. Christianity, however, knows no such inconsistencies; and whatever patriotism, therefore, is opposed, in its exercise, to the *general welfare of mankind*, is, in no degree, a virtue." (Dymond 1892, 36n.)

Dymond fails to notice that the American Founders acknowledged this point by guiding their 'particularistic' actions in accordance with universal principles.

218. *Institutio principis christiana*, Erasmus 1986, XXVII, 214, 219, 236-243; Chalmers 1816, 14-15; Jefferson 1832, 14; Allen 1946, 11-13.

219. Erasmus 1972, 344-348; Erasmus 1986, XXVII, 305-307; Tolstoy 1968, 159-160, 192.

220. Heering 1943, 133-134.

221. *Ibid.*, 168.

222. Kagawa 1936, x, 47-58, 154, 195-196.

223. Plato 1968, IV, 436b-c: "The same thing won't be willing at the same time to do or to suffer opposites with respect to the same part and in relation to the same thing" (115). This statement of the principle of non-contradiction occurs in the context of the search for an answer to the question 'What is justice?' In some respects, justice is understood as 'minding one's own business,' that is, first, the identification or classification of distinct parts of the human soul and of distinct kinds of human souls, and then the arrangement of those parts so that each 'does its part,' functioning for the good of the whole. The principle of non-contradiction serves as the basis of language itself, and of any reasonable politics; politics is then primarily a matter of speech and not of deeds; deliberation should precede actions, and govern them.

224. "It is incorrect...to say that the goods that this city covets are not good, since through them even the city itself is better after its own human fashion. Thus to gain the lowest kind of goods it covets an earthly peace, one that it seeks to attain through warfare; for if it is victorious and no one remains to resist it, there will be peace, while they opposed one another and struggled in their wretched poverty for the things that both could not enjoy at the same time. When, however, the victors are those who were champions of the more righteous cause, who can doubt that the victory in that case justifies joyous celebration and that the peace that resulted is desirable?" (Augustine 1966, XV, iv, 425-427).

225. Price 1790, 7, 26-27, 37-38.

226. See Augustine 1964, III, 43; Stratmann 1928, 110-112, 120; Eppstein 1935, 6; Murray 1960, 286-288; *Gaudium et Spes: Pastoral Constitution on the Church in the Modern World*, Gremillion 1976, 314; Mansfield 1989, 113-114.

227. Alighieri 1949, I, xi, 14-15; xiv, 20. See also Fortin 1981, 101, 127. Ramsey 1983 cautions that "a world public authority, organized to solve the crisis that has come upon the use of power, and an authority powerful enough to subdue the problem of nuclear weapons, would necessarily be tyrannical unless there is a genuine world community based on common values and a common understanding of justice" (200). Notice the modern emphasis on institutions instead of a ruler's virtues.

228. *Joinville's Chronicle of the Crusade of Saint Louis*, Marzials 1965, I, 139-143. See also *Nicomachean Ethics*, IV, iii, 1123b-1125b, in Aristotle 1968, 991-995.

229. Augustine 1966, XVIV, viii, 283; xiii, 309; Luther 1956, XLV, 119-126.

230. Luther 1956, XLV, 113.

231. See Aristotle 1984, II, ix, 1269b, 74; Ovid 1963, XII, 303.

232. Justin Martyr 1973b, I, 271.

233. I Corinthians 13:4-8.

234. Vincent 1903, II, 135-136. See also Tolstoy 1970, 26-29; Kagawa 1929, 59.

235. As does Caecilius in Minucius Felix 1973, 177.

236. Ferguson 1974, 93. See also Lee 1943, 38.

237. Kittel 1964, I, 55; Kagawa 1929, 168; Bowman 1945, 80-83.

238. Nygren 1941, I, 86-97, 170; Ferguson 1974, 94.

239. Nygren 1941, I, 145-147.

240. Quakers come the closest to claiming that God's love may literally perfect men, purify them of all sin. But see Barclay n.d., 18, Barbour 1964, 128, 138-158, for some qualifications. For the more traditional view see Stevenson 1987, 89-95.

241. Raven 1948, 9-10.

242. Augustine 1966, IX, v, 169; XV, xxii, 545; Augustine 1961c, XV, 48, XXVIII, 56; Thomas Aquinas 1963, 2a2ae, 44, 7.

243. Romans 13:10. For a more rationalistic account by a Jewish scholar, see Eidelberg 1983, 34-35, 260-270. Breuer 1974 confuses Christian love with *eros* (290). Nygren 1941 claims that Paul's example shows the gulf between Jewish and Christian Law; the Jewish conception of righteousness "had led him as far away from God as possible," and "it was the Way of the Law itself that had landed [Paul] in sin" (I, 81-82), resulting in pride in his own righteousness. This evidently distorts the Christian teaching, which is not that such Jews as Saul observed the Law too well, but that they observed the letter and not the spirit of the Law.

244. Jefferson 1832, 7; Gurney 1845, 141; Dymond 1855, 227, Macgregor 1960, 67-69, 77.

245. Nygren 1941, I, 23-24, 29, 130-137, 163 ff. See also *Ibid.*, II "At the manger of Bethlehem reason receives its doom," because unaided human reason cannot ascend to God (486). Paul evangelizes not in the wisdom [sophia] of speech" but in "the word of the Cross" (I Corinthians 1:17-18). Also, see de Rougement 1983, 70; Soloveitchik 1983, 39-45. On the divine gift of joy, see Hauerwas 1983, 147.

246. "The naturally right kind of love" is "to love in a moderate and musical way what's orderly and fine" (Plato 1968, 403a, 82). "Love is a finder, always" (Ovid 1983, IV, 83).

247. See Nygren II, 232-252, for a discussion of Augustine in this light. Mysticism is perhaps the most striking example of the attempt to synthesize *agape* and eros; see Eidelberg 1983, 93; Jones 1923, 211-215, 309-311. "Erigena is one of the few who realize that behind the ecclesiastically approved term 'amor' the *eros* of Plato and Neoplatonism is concealed" (Nygren 1941, II, 434).

248. McWilliams 1973 writes, "'Make love, not war,' is sensible only if we do not ask, 'to whom?' Love becomes specific becomes limited, potentially scarce, and perhaps the most prolific source of war men know" (79). For the most astute dissection of romantic love, in particular the metamorphosis of Christian martyrdom into masochism, see de Rougement 1983, 51, 234. De Rougement associates Romanticism with the modern German philosophers Hegel and Fichte (51n., 265). In this he may go too far. Granted that happiness is "essentially alien to romance" (194), then why did Hegel marry, and commend marriage, in a sort of comic imitation of his own dialectic? And if romance is nothing but a subspecies of eroticism, how did the erotic/philosophic Aristotle stay so resolutely unromantic?

249. Brunner 1945, 114-115.

250. John 12:42-43.

251. Ovid 1963, II, 55.

252. Clement 1973b, 15 ff.

253. Ramsey 1983, 499.

254. Alighieri 1966, I, iii, 46-47. Neither Catholic nor Calvinist, Field 1945 takes the view that Hell cannot be a manifestation of love, but only of veiled or unadmitted hatred (69).

255. Augustine 1966, I, 15; IX, 45. The conquest of Canaan by the Israelites was undertaken "to stamp out the pagan practice of sacrificing the innocent for the sake of the guilty" (Eidelberg 1983, 136). Following *The Antichrist*, 40, Eidelberg implies that Jesus of Nazareth's sacrifice represents a return to paganism (Nietzsche 1968, 616). For statements of an Augustinian concept of Christian or loving retaliation, see Stratmann 1928, 40-43 (who, however, denies the doctrine's applicability to modern warfare); for statements by pacifist Christians who nonetheless grant the Christian character of righteous indignation, see Cadoux 1940, 100; Macgregor 1960, 38; Fast 1959, 99. Thomas Aquinas 1963 states the matter somewhat differently: "By its very nature each thing hates its contrary in so far as it is its contrary. But enemies are contrary to us precisely as enemies, and it is this that we ought to hate in them, for we should grieve to see them so. But as men, capable of eternal happiness, we should love them" (2a2ae, 25, 8).

256. Erasmus 1972, 327; Dymond 1892, 57; Tolstoy 1905, 389; Tolstoy 1970, 32; Walsh 1916, 247, 254; Glidden 1948, 38; Farmer 1948, 63-64; Windass 1964, 151-158; Collins 1966, 11-12; Lasserre 1962, 26; Ferguson 1974, 13. Beaumont 1808 decries "a sort of temporizing, half-bred, mule-christians, who confound and paralyze simple and honest hearted [Christians]" by "consecrat[ing]...in the name of the Prince of Peace...instruments of destruction, and pray for the *success* of *bloodshed* and *devastation*" (164).

257. Haskell 1958, 65, 69; Allen 1946, 20-21; Blunden 1956, *passim*; Andreski 1968, 9; Gray 1970 *passim*. See also Voltaire 1962, 251-252 and, significantly, Gandhi 1958-84, III, 222-223. For the distinction between killing in war as a choice *to* kill, as distinguished from killing in war as a choice to do one's duty, defend one's country, etc., see Grisez and Boyle 1979, 390-393; in the second case, "the morality of the deed is affected by the fact that the young man has not voluntarily taken or accepted a stance incompatible with a sincere and unrestricted love of all of the basic human goods including life." Bainton 1960 makes a somewhat Machiavellian point: "One may conclude that although a war may be fought in sorrowful love, it can never be won in this mood. Those who entertain such a disposition are few, and wars are the affairs of the masses" (248). Pacifists and Machiavellians often agree on the character of war, if not on its desirability.

258. Cadoux 1940, 73. Following Stratmann 1928, cited above, Cadoux denies that the conditions of modern war permit such a response (74).

259. Ambrose 1916b, I, xxvii, 22; I, xxviii, 23; I, xxix, 24; Swift 1983, 102-103. Ramsey 1961 argues that early Christian nonresistance and later Christian justified-war doctrines reflect the same "basic strategy" of "responsible love and service of one's neighbors in the context of the common life" (xvii).

260. Augustine 1961b, xxii, 303-304; Augustine 1966, XV, 351; Augustine 1964, III, 46-47; Thomas Aquinas 1963, 2a2ae, 108, 1-4; Suarez 1944, I, iii, 802; Grotius 1925, 75-76; Finch 1755, v; Lewis 1980, 42-43; Bennett 1962, 94; Eidelberg 1983, 273; Harries 1986, 2-8; Ramsey 1988, 100.

261. Lasserre 1962, 24-25.

262. *Ibid.*, 28.

263. Herodotus 1942, 547.

264. Cicero 1955, I, 20; II, 111. Penn 1882 associates the sentence "it is better to be loved than feared" with Pythagoras (296).

265. Lincoln 1953, I, 273.

266. Xenophon 1947, Vol. II, VIII, vii, 439.

267. Ellul 1976, 208, 213, 154; Fox 1661, 39; Denck, quoted in Jones 1914, 30.

268. Augustine 1961b, XIX, 248-249; Stevenson 1987, 78-82; Thomas Aquinas 1963, 2a2ae, 123, 3-10.

269. For the experience of conversion, see Barbour 1964, 1-2; Brinton ca. 1941, 5, and Brinton 1958, 6-8. For the other points in this argument Darby 1908, 32, 75-87, 100; Hodgkin 1915, 47-56; Cadbury 1918, 86-87, 93; Kagawa 1929, 42; Cadoux 1949, ix; Macgregor 1960, 158; Hartill 1948, 50-53; Yoder 1972, 114; Ferguson 1974, 104-105 (who adds, "Good Friday is transmuted into Easter," although "not necessarily in three days"). Augustine 1964 writes, "God showed in the rich and far-famed Roman Empire how much can be achieved by natural virtues without true religion, so that we might understand how, with this added, men can become citizens of another state whose king is truth, whose law is love, whose measure is eternity" (III, 50).

270. MacKenzie 1961: "If Britain disarmed completely, I do not believe that any nation in the world would dare to take advantage of her material weakness, because her moral strength would be overwhelming" (142). See also Cadoux 1940: "...[I]t may yet take some unarmed or martyr-nation a vanquisher of the fleets and armies of its foes" (17); and see Gollancz 1959, 135. The more naturalistic argument of Dymond 1855 — that the plunderer "who feels a confidence that his own life will not be taken may conduct his plunder with comparative gentleness" (228) — is even less plausible and encouraging.

271. Walsh 1916, ix-x; Scheiders 1983, 101.

272. *Ibid.*, 103. For philosophers, of course, death is no tragedy at all. See *Phaedo, passim*, Plato 1937, I.

273. Nygren 1941, I, 65-70, 75. For a 'softer' version, see Jones 1914, xliv-xlix. Gray 1970 observes that suffering "has very limited power to purge and purify;" it "appears to improve characters already strong and sensitizes consciences already awake; with others it produces most often the opposite effect" (218). If so, then Hell would be *eternally* just for its residents in one sense: it would confirm them in their own corruption.

274. Hans Denck, *Widerruf*, quoted in Jones 1914, 26.

275. *Sophist* 222c-223b, Benardete 1984, II, 10-11.

276. Matthew 4:19. Notice that the sophist appeals to wealthy youths, whereas Jesus appeals to the poor youths. And consider the effects of the Christian appeal, described by Origen 1965:

> If [Jesus] was a mere man, I do not know how he
> ventured to spread his religion and teaching in all the
> world, and was able to do what he desired without God's
> help and to rise above all the people opposing the
> spread of his teaching – kings, governors, the Roman
> Senate, rulers everywhere, and the common people.
> How is it possible for a natural man with nothing more
> than that about him to convert such a vast multitude? It
> would not be remarkable if only some of the intelligent
> people were converted. But there are also some of the
> most irrational people and those most subject to their
> passions, who on account of their lack of reason are
> changed to a more self-controlled life with greater
> difficulty (II, lxxix, 127).

277.   Origen 1965, VI, ii, 316-317; VII, lix-lxvi, 445-449.

278.   Origen 1965, I, lx, 12; x-xi, 13-14. Origen also writes "The existence of certain doctrines, which are beyond those which are exoteric and do not reach the multitude, is not a peculiarity of Christian doctrine only, but is shared by the philosophers. For they had some doctrines which were exoteric and some esoteric" (I, vii, 10). Christian esotericism originates in Judaism, in which the names of things are given in accordance with "a consistent system, which has principles known only to very few" (I, xxiii-xxv, 22-27).

279.   See Fortin 1972, 13.

280.   See Origen 1965, iv, 318; xxxviii, 480; Lactantius 1973, II, iii, 44; III, i-iv, 69-71; III, ix, 77; III, xv, 84; III, xviii, 89; IV, ii-iii, 102; Augustine 1964, III, 123; Augustine 1966, III, i, 3-5; iv, 19-21; ix-x, 23-45, VI, i, 283-285; Alighieri 1966, II, iii, 46-47; van Braght 1950, 6-7 (contrast with *Ibid.*, 14). Breuer 1974 writes that reason, being confined to nature, cannot comprehend the laws underlying nature; philosophers are "blind to the disparity between the sixth and the seventh day," that is, between God's laws of creating and God's laws of nature when God rests (126-128). Machiavelli also makes this distinction between the constituting and the constitution, but assigns the role of Creator-God to man, or more precisely to those rare men who are the founders of new modes and orders.

281.   See Augustine 1966, IX, xiii, 203; Fox 1796, 693; Holcombe 1823, 27; Cochrane 1972, 97, 237-238, 402, 480; Fortin 1972, 26; Wilhelmsen 1978, 63; Hauerwas 1983, 24-31. Nietzsche dissents, asserting that Pascal "believed in the corruption of his reason through original sin when it had in fact been corrupted only by Christianity" (*Antichrist*, I, 15, Nietzsche 1968, 527). There have been attempts to combine classical naturalism with Christianity; see Irenaeus 1973, xv, 479; Thomas Aquinas 1963, 1a, I, 5). Modern political philosophy is more ambitious still, seeking rigorous laws or 'methods' for ruling secular

society, methods that enable man to 'create' his world and even himself through self-lawgiving or 'autonomy.' See Horwitz 1962, *passim*.

282. Cropsey 1977, 224-229.

283. "A heathen who accepts the seven commandments and observes them scrupulously is a 'righteous heathen,' and will have a portion in the world to come, provided that he accepts them and performs them because the Holy One, blessed by He, commanded them in the Law and made known through Moses, our teacher, that the observance thereof had been enjoined upon the descendants of Noah even before the Law was given. But if this observance thereof is based upon a reasoned conclusion he is not deemed a resident alien, or one of the pious of the Gentiles, but one of their wise men" (Maimonides 1963, VIII, 230). Maimonides goes on to discourage non-Jews from studying *halakha* (X, 237 ff.).

284. Augustine 1966 asks, "What difference does it make in what direction or by what route the hapless condition of man launches its expedition in search of a blessed life, if divine authority does not show the way?" (XVIII, xii, 19).

285. Charney 1988, 78. See also *Symposium* 221, in which Alcibiades describes Socrates in war, "as he is in the streets of Athens, stalking like a pelican, and rolling his eyes, and making very intelligible to anybody, even from a distance, that whoever attacked him would be likely to meet with a stout resistance." Alcibiades adds, "this is the sort of man who is never touched in war" (Plato 1937, I, 343).

286. Vattel 1916, v-vi. Augustine 1966 observes that "it is the love of truth that prompts the search for holy leisure, while it is the compulsion of love that makes men undertake a righteous activity in affairs" (xix, 205). Erasmus warns against the wrong kind of leisure, urging a limit on the number of monasteries, colleges, and barracks (*Institutio principii christiana*, Erasmus 1986, XXVII, 267).

287. For the vigorousness of the buzzard, see *The Birds*, Aristophanes 1962, 150. Origen 1965 adds that buzzards reproduce without copulation, even as philosophers do (xxxvii, 36 and Plutarch, *Moralia* 28bc). Blotner 1974 notes that the American novelist William Faulkner longed to be reincarnated as a buzzard: "Nothing hates him or envies him or wants him or needs him. He is never bothered or in danger, and he can eat anything" (II, 1595). Dunne 1990 notes that American buzzard species are members of the stork family, a group often associated with reproduction and childbirth (17). For the close association of philosophers with childbirth, see *Theaetetus* 149-151, Plato 1937, II, 150-153.

288. Thomas Aquinas 1a2ae, 102, 6. See also M'Cree 1845: "It is a lamentable thing to hear a professed disciple of the Prince of Peace defending war. One might almost fancy, that he delighted to dwell on

Mount Sinai, or to gloat with a vulture's eye on the horrors of a field of battle, in preference to worshipping on Mount Zion, and learning lessons of mercy" (14).

289. Julian 1962, III, 365. In the *Timaeus* (xxiv) Athena is described as a lover of both war and wisdom as distinguished from the folly of divination (Plato 1937, II, 10). For an attempt to reconcile philosophy and divination see Sidney 1990, II, ii, 83-84.

290. The responses of nonphilosophers to philosophers are indeed diverse, perhaps confused.   Minucius Felix 1973 dismisses "Socrates the Athenian buffoon" (xxxviii, 197); Augustine 1966 calls Hermes Trismegistus (the Greek name for Thoth, the Egyptian god of letters) the first philosopher (XVIII, xii, 19); Jones 1923 claims that "Socrates belongs to the order of the prophets" (58). Erasmus 1986, XXVII, 214 and Gibbon n.d., II, xlvii, 811 offer sharply contrasting views.

291. Contrast Lewis 1980:

> What does war do to death? It certainly does not make it more frequent; 100 percent of us die, and the percentage cannot be increased. It puts several deaths earlier, but I hardly suppose that that is what we fear. Certainly when the moment comes, it will make little difference how many years we have behind us. (31).

Assured of eternal life, the Christian seeks fulfillment in the City of God and will not hesitate to engage in conflict, whether as a warrior or a martyr.

292. Augustine 1964, I, 55; Augustine 1966, X, xxix, 39; XII, viii, 37; xiv-xxi, 80-101; XIX, iv, 127-139; XXI, xiv-xv, 81-87; compare with Eidelberg 1983, 46, 53-54, 61-62, 111-119, 227. It was perhaps something like this conviction, exacerbated by his observations of modern philosophers, that impelled Comenius n.d. to urge a gathering of English and Dutch ambassadors, "Ye have with you doubtless theologians, guardians of your consciences; take them too into your councils, that ye may be attentive not only to that which *Machiavelli or Papinianus* saith, but also to that which *Christ and Moses* say" (121). See also Simons 1966, 545-547 and Erasmus 1972, 331.

293. *Gorgias* 483, Plato 1937, I, 543,; Mark 8:34-38; Romans 6:5-7; Colossians 3:5-10; Saxonhouse 1983, 1962.

294. Mansfield 1978, 7; Cropsey 1977, 271.

295. Origen 1965, V, xliii, 298.   On the distinction between Jews and Christians, less marked than that between philosophers and Jews or philosophers and Christians, see *Ibid*., lx, 310.

296. II Corinthians 4:4-5; Romans 8:6-30; Colossians 2:8; Ephesians 3:17-19; I Corinthians 1:17, 20, 24; 2:3-15; 3:3, 19; 4:20; 8:1; Philippians 4:7-9; Justin Martyr 1973 a, cx, 254. See also Origen 1965, lxv, 116; lxxii, 121, and Lactantius 1973, V, xx, 157 (on the Christian sacrifice of the fleshly intellect); VI, v, 167; vi-xix, 168-186.

297. Origen 1973a, VI, i, 349; v-vi, 354-355; X, ii, 381; Origen 1973 b, II *passim*; Origen 1965, III, xxxviii, 154; VII, xi, 404, xviii, 409. In the thirty-third paragraph of the sixth chapter of Book X of his *Commentary on the Gospel of John* — thirty-three being the traditional age of Jesus of Nazareth when sacrificed — Origen writes, "What other continual sacrifice can there be to the man of reason in the world of mind, but the Word growing to maturity, the Word who is symbolically called a lamb and who is offered as soon as the soul receives illumination," (Origen 1973b, 376). See also the thirty-third central section of Book V of Origen 1965, on the apocalypse and also the commentary on Origen in Nygren 1941, in which Origen is observed to teach that the word *eros* was replaced by the word *agape* by Christians only in order to avoid, by means of a "protective disguise" (I, 173), the misinterpretations of the vulgar.

298. Augustine 1966, II, i, 145; Jacob Boehme, *Aurora*, quoted in Jones 1914, 172.

299. Origen 1973a, I, xlii, 320; Origen 1973c, IV, i, 357-375. Unfortunately, Origen's example of a literally 'impossible' passage in need of allegorical understanding is Matthew 5:39, which he claims, presents the physical impossibility of being slapped on the right cheek by another's right hand; this is easily explained literally by observing that the right hand easily explained literally by observing that the right hand can hit another's right cheek if it is the back of the hand.

300. Origen 1965, IV, xxxi, 208. Robert Barclay rather more grudgingly admits reason to his theology (Barclay n.d., 292-294).

301. Augustine 1966, XI, xxvii, 539.

302. Clement of Alexandria 1973c, II, i, 271.

303. Fortin 1972, 16-18.

304. Nietzsche 1986, 11.

305. Hackett 1979, 109.

306. Augustine 1964, I, 3.

307. Augustine 1966, IV, xxxi, 119; VI, ix, 3470349; VII, xv-xvii, 429-435.

308. De Quincey 1897 deplores Plato's "affectation of a double doctrine: esoteric, the private and confidential form authorized by his final

ratification; and exoteric, which was but another name for impostures with which he duped his calumniators" (VIII, 45-46). De Quincey complains that it is impossible to sustain this "double doctrine" consistently; that it is sophistical and therefore unSocratic; that it conceals, in its "cumbrous superfluity of words" (the dialogue form), "a philosophy by no means remarkable for its opulence in ideas:"

> Never was there an instance in which vanity was more short-sighted. It would not be possible by any art or invention more effectually to extinguish our interest in a scheme of philosophy — by summarily extinguishing all hope of ever separating the true from the false, the authentic from the spurious — than by sending down to posterity this claim to a secret meaning lurking behind a mask. If the key to the distinction between true and false is sent down with the philosophy, then what purpose of concealment is attained? Who is it that is duped? On the other hand, if it is *not* sent down, what purpose of truth is attained? Who is it, then, that is *not* duped? (46-47)

De Quincey thus mistakes philosophy for doctrine, a quest for a gift. To conceive of truth as a gift instead of the object of a quest will accustom intellectuals to read in order to learn a set of opinions instead of reading in order to think. The peaceful 'war' of dialectic will be replaced by a cycle of subjection to and rebellion against received opinions. See also Jones 1914, 133, 140. And see Caspary 197, Introduction, *passim*, in which an otherwise excellent commentary is marred by insufficient consideration of the various intended audiences of Origen's writings. For the opposite view see Julian 1962, II, 75-87, 105-121.

309. Clement of Alexandria 1973e, II, i, 299-303; ii, 304-305; xii, 313; xix, 322-323, xxiv, 336.

310. Romans 9:20-24; Matthew 10:16. For an account of Jesus' careful silences, see Schweitzer 1968, 102-111.

311. Augustine 1964, IV, 145.

312. *Annals*, Tacitus 1942, I, 419. Price 1790 closely associates knowledge with virtue encouraged by religion and political liberty. "Virtue without knowledge makes enthusiasts; and knowledge without virtue makes devils; but both united elevates to the top of human dignity and perfection" (16-17).

313. Justin Martyr 1973c, i-x, 163-165. Justin calls for punishment of false Christians, who are known by their actions not their words (xvi, 168). "[T]hose who have lived reasonably are Christians, even though they have been thought atheists;" Christians thus include Socrates, Heraclitus, and "men like them," as well as Abraham and Ananias (xlvi,

178). The advent of Jesus brought "right Reason" more fully into view than ever, although Jesus was "partially known even by Socrates" (Justin Martyr 1973c, ix, 191). These teachings of Justin Martyr should be contrasted with the actual teaching of Socrates: "Unless the philosophers rule as kings or those now called kings and chiefs genuinely and adequately philosophize, and political power and philosophy coincide in one place, while the many natures now making their way to either apart from the other are by necessity excluded, there is no rest from ills for the cities, my dear Glaucon, nor I think for human kind, nor will the regime we have now described in speech ever come forth from nature, insofar as possible, and see the light of the sun" (*Republic* 473 d-e, Plato 1968, 155-156). The amalgamation of Platonism and Christianity thus may be said to produce a 'popular' or democratized Platonism. This should be contrasted with Yoder 1972, who describes Christianity as a form of communalism based upon commands not reason. There is no 'human dignity' by nature; man is not to strive for liberty, as he is strictly a subject of God. The 'democratic,' indeed "revolutionary" character of Christianity inheres in its insistence on addressing socially and politically subordinate persons as moral agents whose souls can be saved (173-174).

314. Romans 1:20-32.

315. Augustine 1964, II, 167. Clement of Alexandria 1973c claims, in contrast, that God hates no one; His reproaches are kindly (I, viii, 225-226). This leaves the problem of eternal punishment open to question. Origen 1973c refuses to take Biblical expressions of God's anger literally, and asserts that punishment in Hell is not eternal (II, ii, 278; v, 280); Ballou 1854 shares this 'universalism,' calling eternal damnation an "abominable doctrine" and ingeniously describing 'everlasting' punishments as "everlastingly effectual and salutary" (79-92). One can only admire the humanity of these writers, who prefer to torture a text than a soul.

316. I Corinthians 13:12.

317. Lactantius 1973, iv-v, 261-262; XVII, 274-275; XXIII, 279. See Zahn 1983 for a much 'softer,' and less Scriptural, account of God as entirely nonviolent (121-124). And see "Epistle of Methetes to Diognetus" in Roberts and Donaldson 1973, I, vii, 27, and Wilson 1923 (26, 36, 50). See Huxley, 1937 for a condemnation of the concept of a personal God, a God who commands, and a defense of the impersonal Deity of Buddhism (280, 284, 380-381).

318. Enz 1972, 9-12.

319. Mark 10:34. See also Matthew 12, 50; Hebrews 12:11; Acts 17:29-31. Fiorenza 1983 claims that the God of Jesus of Nazareth is not a Father but Sophia, a woman (132-133, 140), but gives little convincing evidence.

320. Clement of Alexandria 1973c, IV, 211; XII, 234-235; Clement of Alexandria 1973a, I, 173; X, 203. See also Luther 1956, XLV, 100.

321. Ferguson and Pitt-Watson 1956, 40.

322. Clement of Alexandria 1973a, XI, 204; Ferguson and Pitt-Watson 1956, 19-23, 34-37, 48-50; Bowman 1945, 72; and Macgregor 1960, 37.

323. Ferguson and Pitt-Watson 1956, 29-31. See also Ramsey 1988, 111-112, who writes that "Christology is the heart of the matter." On the issue of the *imitatio Christi*, Stratmann 1928 writes:

> It is untrue to say, as the Quakers do, that as Christ was not a soldier, no Christian must be a soldier. For Christ would not tell His followers to do anything he did not do Himself. Christ was not a merchant nor was he married, but what is true is, that the Christian must have the Mind of Christ and Christian patriotism must be something that Christ can bless (196).

See also Ingram 1939, 53, and Thompson 1959, 27.

324. Raven 1948, 4-5; Fast 1959, 191, 196-198, 205; Trocmé 1973, 147; Ferguson 1974, 102-103.

325. Yoder 1972, 16-20, 244. The Cross is not "a peculiarly efficacious technique...for getting one's way," Yoder writes; obedience not calculation is behind it.

326. Maimonides 1963 calls Jesus one of "the children of the violent" prophesied in Daniel 11:14. He explains this surprising claim as follows: "All the Prophets affirmed that the Messiah would redeem Israel, save them, gather their dispersed, and confirm the commandments. But [Jesus] caused Israel to be destroyed by the sword, their remnant to be dispersed and humiliated. He was instrumental in changing the Torah and causing the world to err and serve another beside God" (V, ix, xxiii). By 'caused' Maimonides refers to Jesus' prophecy of the destruction of the Temple in Jerusalem, perhaps. The Apostle John writes that certain Jews attempted to kill Jesus in Jerusalem for two reasons. Jesus broke the Sabbath, and Jesus called God "Father," thus "making God equal to himself" (John 5:18).

327. Matthew 11:25-27; John 14:6.

328. Matthew 13:57.

329. John 5, 46-47; 7:17.

330. Colossians 1:15-20. For a different conception see Origen 1965: "We affirm that [Jesus'] mortal body and the human soul within Him

received the greatest elevation not only by communion but by union and intermingling, so that by sharing in His divinity He was transformed into God" (III, xli, 156). This conception is clearly more erotic/philosophic than that of Paul.

331. Clement of Alexandria 1973c, V. 248; Macgregor 1960, 133-137, 156; Lasserre 1962, 14-17, 69. Athanasius 1961b writes: "...those barbarians who have an innate savagery of manners, while they still sacrifice to the idols of their country, are made against one another, and cannot endure to be a single hour without weapons: But when they hear the teaching of Christ, straightway instead of fighting they turn to husbandry, and instead of arming their hands with weapons they raise them in prayer, and in a word, in the place of fighting among themselves, henceforth they arm against the devil and against evil spirits, subduing these by self-restraint and virtue of soul" (liii, 64). See also Dakin 1956, 114-115 and Dresner 1961, 174-177.

332. Irenaeus 1973, xxvii, 352. Irenaeus is evidently not a strict nonresistant, however, as he mentions "military and kingly pursuits" without censure (xxxii, 408). Heretics can also call for peace, although they will not achieve it; see Schall 1983, 29-32, for the distinction between true and false peace.

333. Yoder 1972, 39-45. See also Thomas Aquinas 1963, 1a, 23, 5.

334. Wilhelmsen 1978, 145.

335. Augustine 1966, V, xxii, 253. Augustine contends that all physical things have "an internal law of peace" bringing them into their own "places where they should be in the natural order" (XII, v, 23) – a conception he borrows from Greek physics. Human beings, by contrast, have free will and can misuse their own nature; because their "lapses are not inevitable but willful, the punishment that follows is righteous" (XII, viii, 37), and this punishment may involve war. Augustine should of course add that the punishment must 'fit the crime.'

336. Thus Fox 1659 can argue that if the English had "been faithful to the power of the Lord God" they would have conquered Spain and Rome (1-5), nonviolently.

337. Augustine 1966 makes this charge against Cicero (V, ix, 167-169).

338. *Ibid.*, ix-x, 175-187.

339. Schweitzer 1960 writes that Jesus "was not a teacher, not a casuist; He was an imperious ruler" (403). On the "amazing slaughter" at the end of days see Howard 1983, 193.

340. Luke 21:22; Romans 14:17; Revelation 2:27; 19:12; 20, 21.

341. II Thessalonians 2:10-11.

342. I Thessalonians 5:2-3; Mark 9:1; Luke 17:20-21, 37; Matthew 24:28.

343. Revelation 22:12; Matthew 10:23; 16:28; 2 Peter 16-19. Gibbon n.d. makes note of these prophecies (I, xv, 402), as does Voltaire 1962, 344. Schweitzer 1960 presents an historical survey of theological research on this issue, concluding that Christianity has been 'de-eschatologized' and thereby distorted by attempts to ignore the evidence (360). Schweitzer's study was published in 1906; some forty-five years later he reaffirmed his conclusion: "Though frequently proclaimed by the prophets as imminent, the coming of the Kingdom was constantly deferred. In the course of time the thought must have forced itself upon their minds that there was a problem here" (Schweitzer 1968, 32). See also *Ibid.*, evidence, criticizes Schweitzer's research on some points, but shares the view that Jesus "expected the Kingdom to come in the near future" (118); see also *Ibid.*, 152. Fortin 1989 argues that "the New Testament has no genuine political teaching of its own," that the apostles believed none was needed "because all or most of them were convinced that the end of time was near" (38-39).

344. Wilson 1914, 40-41, 52; Macgregor 1960, 141; Cullmann 1956, 89; Topel 1982, 91-93; Bruce 1983, 109, 154; Harries 1986, 17; Yoder 1986, 287.

For the different view of the early Quakers, see Burrough n.d., 1-7, and Braithwaite 1912, 356. Cadoux 1919 accepts the view that early Christians were "largely obsessed and deluded by mistaken eschatological hopes," but were nonetheless superior to modern Christians in their energy and sincerity (2-3).

345. Yoder, 1972, 109-110, n.10. See also Wilder 1939, 12, 54, 196-197, 227, for a variety of explanations all of which smack of special pleading. Jeremias 1971 cites Luke 18:6-8, claiming that God can shorten or lengthen men's period of waiting for the end-time, but these passages suggest a short wait. Hauerwas 1983 claims that the Kingdom *has* come, *is* present, whenever Christians follow Jesus (83-90). This does not address the problem of the Parousia, however.

346. See Schweitzer 1968, 154-155, 167-171, 180, 183.

347. Cadoux 1925, 12-13, 16-18; Eppstein 1935, 5; Yoder 1972, 233-238; National Conference of Catholic Bishops 1983, 18-19.

348. *Gaudium et spes*, Gremillion 1976, 315.

349. Cadoux 1919, 137.

350. Roberts 1915, 62-63; Yoder 1972, 250; Trocmé 1973, 66.

351. See Ramsey 1961, 128; Martin 1966, 68; Weigel 1988, 17. The latter deplores the "collapse of eschatology into apocalyptic." He does not remark the close relationship of this collapse to the secular doctrine of historicism – most prominently, Marxism. See Engels, "on the History of Early Christianity," in Feuer 1954, 168-194, and Kautsky 1953, 325. For a gradualistic Christian apocalypticism, see Raven 1948, 13.

352. Cadoux 1919, 45-47; Cadoux 1925, 615; Heering 1943, 41-43; Macgregor 1960, 33; Ferguson and Pitt-Watson 1956, 47; Fast 1959, 69.

353. Cullman 1956, 4; Cullmann 1970, 13, 19-20. See also Lasserre 1962, 217-218.

354. Matthew 18:3; 19:14. But contrast with I Corinthians 14:20.

355. Troeltsch 1949, I, 138.

356. Martin 1966, 203.

357. Geyer 1986, 303.

358. Niebuhr, H. Richard 1959, 158-159, 165, 179, 186. For a secularist's account see Lynd 1968, 31-36, 92-96, 131-153.

359. Bainton 1960, 120. Gentili 1933 writes prudently, "To attempt by force what cannot be done by force is madness," and proposes initiating holy wars only against nations that are atheistic; since none are (though there are idolatrous nations), there should be no holy wars (IX, 38-41; SSV, 123-125).

360. Figgis 1960, 20; Heering 1943, 97; Byrd 1960, 12-13.

361. Heering 1943, 133-134, 180.

362. Figgis, 1921, 111. For this reason Troeltsch 1949 observes, "In reality Christianity seems to influence social life in two ways: Either, on the one hand, it develops an idealistic anarchism and the communism of love, which combines radical indifference or hostility towards the rest of the social order with the effort to actualize this ideal of love in a small group; or, on the other hand, it develops along social-conservative lines into an attitude of submission to God and His Will, so far as the world is concerned, combined with a strong independence of an organized community which manages their own affairs, which, as its range of influence increases, finds that it cannot ignore secular institutions, but that it must do its utmost to utilize them for its own purposes." (I, 82).

   See also *Ibid.*, 87. Byrd 1960 regrets that Quakers "have consistently failed to bring into their own affairs that spirit of unity which they urge upon the nations" (201).

363. Potter 1973, 27, 31-32. See also Weigel 1988, 16-18.

364. Heering 1943 avers that "In the last resort, the disarmament question too, like every one of life's serious questions, is a matter of faith" (217). Heering mistakenly supposes that "general disarmament will only get a chance [under] the stimulus of national [i.e., unilateral] disarmament" by the commercial republics (195).

365. Matthew 7:3-5; Luke 6:41-42. Heering 1943 warns that commercial republics "should not be sidetracked [in disarmament] by 'the Red peril'"; he blames armament on the "strong alliance between capital and the army" (207-208). Ferguson 1974 claims that Judgment Day will see the punishment of whole nations, and that the failure of Western nations to feed the starving means those nations "are living in hell, and shall be until we disarm and use our resources for the service of those in need" (52). The purpose of repentance, as distinguished from self-denigration, is to make oneself worthy of receiving the Holy Spirit and thus to speak prophetically; see Soloveitchik 1983, 110, 128-130.

366. For a critique of the claim that war is amoral, see Murray 1960, 91.

367. Finch 1746, 24. Gremillion 1976 observes that Catholic "social teaching" since Pope John XXIII moved from a "static" natural law conceptions "toward human rights and fulfillment of human capacities, promoted by man's innate worth" (8). The fulfillment of human capacities as the task of ethics is of course the topic of the *Nicomachean Ethics*, Aristotle 1941.

368. Contrast with the first use of the word 'just' in the New Testament. Mary "was found" to be pregnant by the Holy Spirit; Joseph was told in a dream by an angel of the Lord that "the thing in her, begotten of the Holy Spirit, is Holy." Had he not been told this, Joseph would have "dismissed" Mary, but secretly, not publicly, because he is a "just" (*dikaios*) man who does not want to "hold her up as an example" (Matthew 1:18-19). Stratmann 1928 insists, "Morality must not adapt itself to men, but men to morality, even if the accepted point of view has to be broken down" (75).

369. Finch 1746, 24.

370. Harries 1986, 67.

371. Dymond 1892, 24, 93-95; Hirst 1906, 77; Ferguson 1974, 39; Lackey 1989, 17-18.

372. Luther 1956 observes that "the Hebrew word for peace is nothing less than well-being" (XXIV, 177).

373.   Plato, *Laws*, I, 628d-628e, Pangle 1984, 7. Aristotle 1984 criticized
        Spartans for failing to see that "warlike virtue" is only "a part of virtue,"
        that while they "preserved themselves as long as they were at war, they
        come to ruin when they were ruling [an empire] through not knowing
        how to be at leisure..." (*Politics*, II, ix, 1271 b). Russell 1975 mistakenly
        describes Aristotle as "unable to distinguish a just war from a merely
        successful one" (4). In fact Aristotle writes that "the beginnings of wars
        are not always just" (*Politics* I, 6, 1255a), that "injustice is harshest
        when it is furnished with arms" (I, 2, 1253 a). It is "possible to
        dominate unjustly," and warlike virtues and equipment are for the sake
        of peace, not vice-versa (VII, ii, 1324b-1325a; VII, xiv, 1333a). Military
        training should be practiced "not for the sake of reducing to slavery
        those who do not merit it, but in the first place in order that they
        themselves will not become slaves to others," for the benefit of the
        ruled, and for the punishment of those who deserve it (VII, xiv, 1333b-
        1334a). See also the "Life of Caius Marius," Plutarch n.d., 494-521, and
        also the lives of Pompey (*Ibid*, 755) and of Galba (*Ibid.*, 1271).

374.   Cicero 1955, I, iv, 13. Cicero criticizes Plato's philosophers for merely
        avoiding injustice and failing to perform acts of justice (I, ix, 29). He
        considers war as last resort of negotiation fails, insists on treating the
        conquered justly (the empire is a protectorate, not a dominion), and
        requires the honoring of promises with no treachery. Soldiers are to
        be legally sworn into service. (I, xi-xiii, 37-45; I, xxiii, 81; xxiv, 83; II,
        viii, 195; III, xxix, 385-387).

375.   Mansfield 1989, 25-71.

376.   Augustine 1966, XIX, xx-xxvi, 205-237.

377.   For a commentary on Augustine's teaching, see Stevenson 1987, 37-45.
        For applications of this teaching, see Stratmann 1928, 48-65; Murray
        1960, 252-263; Ramsey 1983, 151; Brundage 1986, 72; Harakas 1986,
        259-264. Ambrose 1961b contends more strongly that justice "is
        binding, even in war" (I, xxix, 24).

378.   Heering 1943, 35-37; Hershberger 1969, 214; Lasserre 1962, 165-176,
        212; Hauerwas 1983, 112-113.

379.   See Royden 1915, 35. Hirst 1923 writes, "Peace principles do not
        involve a neutrality which apportions equal condemnation to every
        belligerent, any more than religious toleration involves the view that all
        doctrines are equally false" (291).

380.   Dymond 1855 writes:

        The possession of political liberty is of great importance.
        A Russian may enjoy as great a share of personal
        freedom as an Englishman; that is, he may find as few
        restrictions upon the exercise of his own free will; but he
        has no security for the continuance of this. For aught

that he knows, he may be arbitrarily thrown into prison tomorrow; and therefore, though he may live and die without molestation, he is politically enslaved. When it is considered how much human happiness depends upon *the security of enjoying happiness in future*, such institutions as those of Russia are great grievances; and Englishmen, though they may regret the curtailment of some items of civil liberty, have much comparative reason to think themselves politically free (245).

Dymond cautions, "Republicanism opens more wide the gates of ambition" than does other regimes (262); on balance, however, he prefers republicanism. For nonpacifists who take a similar view, see O'Brien 1967, 1-2, and Harries 1986, 131, 143.

Several pacifists have argued for the equivalence of republican and despotic regimes. Gollancz 1959 writes:

When I was [in the Soviet Union] in 1937, at the height of one of the terrors, the man on the street seemed to be enjoying himself in much the same way as we do in the West.... Life goes on, love goes on, sea and country and rivers are still there, children play about, there is even laughter and fun: those are things you cannot kill, even if you want to unless you kill a whole people. (139)

He adds, "The ballet is superb" (140), and concludes:

Here it is in a sentence. Under a Soviet occupation there would be *life*: a nuclear war would mean death: and the man who chooses death rather than life is a blasphemer, not, if you prefer, against God, but against his own proper nature. (141)

Gollancz thus endorses a sort of spiritualized Hobbesianism. See also Geach 1961, 99-101

381. Lasserre 1962, 209.

382. Heraclitus 1967, 485, 489, 491.

383. *Cratylus* 440, Plato 1937, I, 229.

384. *Laws* VIII, 832c, Plato 1980, 223.

385. *Rhetoric* I, 4, 1359b-1360, Aristotle 1941, 1337-1338; Aristotle 1984, V, iii, 1303b; VI, vii, 1321a.

386. Augustine 1966, XIX, xiii, 177-179; Eppstein 1935, 225-229; Gremillion 1976, 70.

387. Demosthenes tells the Athenians in his oration "On the Duties of the State,"

> ...by arms must your enemies be vanquished, by arms the safety of the constitution must be maintained. Voting will not make your soldiers victorious, but they who by soldiership have overcome the enemy provide you with liberty and security for voting and doing what you please. In arms you should be terrible, in courts of justice humane. (Demosthenes 1967, 241).

388. *Statesman* 276, Benardete 1984, III, 27. For commentary see *Ibid.*, 103, 141.

389. Augustine 1966, IV, 17.

390. Augustine 1964, I, 230; III, 282-296; Augustine 1966, XIX, xvi, 193. Rousseau 1986 on this point concurs, to some extent, with his great rival: "[P]ity for the wicked is a very great cruelty to men" (IV, 253). Augustine 1961a cautions that God's will, "concerning erring men, as far as they should be amended rather than destroyed "(I, 129); early in his career he argued against capital punishment on this ground (Augustine 1964, II, 142). However, after seeing the citizens of Hippo converted from Donatist heresy to "Catholic unity" through "the fear of imperial laws," he began to recognize the (as it were) sacred utility of force (*ibid.*, 72-73), arguing that "nothing can cause more complete death to the soul than freedom to disseminate error" (203).

Synesius of Cyrene 1926 appears to agree with Augustine and Rousseau: "The man who remains unpunished for longstanding sins should be deemed the most unfortunate, as one cared for neither by God nor man" (XLI, 117). However, as usual with that writer, there are limits pointed to, with irony:

> Torturers are wonderfully efficient in exposing shams. These men possess iron nails which have the force of learned syllogisms, so that whatever is made manifest when they hold sway, this is truth itself (118-119).

391. Heering 1943, 137-139.

392. Anscombe 1961, 46-47; Schall 1983, 41.

393. Arendt 1970, 44-45. Ellul 1969 rejects this distinction because force or violence is as necessary to life as "digestion or falling bodies or gravitation;" it is amoral. He therefore refuses to distinguish between commercial republicanism and tyranny except to call the one "masked violence," the other unmasked (84-104). "If we are free in Jesus Christ," he continues, "we shall reject violence precisely because it is necessary," that is, un-free (130). A Christian may use violence, but consciously, knowing that he sins and may be forgiven (137). The

obvious untenability of the latter teaching perhaps forces Ellul 1976 to reject violence entirely, calling it satanic (57-58); he also rejects the flesh as "the power of man in his opposition to God" (134). In this he approaches Manicheanism. Shinn 1972 disagrees with Ellul on commonsense grounds (237); Schall 1983, without mentioning Ellul, attributes such views to nihilism (36).

394. Thucydides 1934, V, xvii, 331-334. See also Livy 1962, IX, 189; Augustine 1964, 269-270. For commentaries on Augustine see Fortin 1972, 31-32 and Swift 1986, 62-64. See also *De Ivri Belli*, paragraphs 466-467, Victoria 1917, 187; Gentili 1933, I, xiii, 59 (the central chapter of Book I is also the symbolic number of atheism); I, xiv, 61-65; Vattel 1916, I, 235; III, 246; VIII, 279; XII, 305-306; Howard 1983, 191; DeQuincey 1897, 373-381; Tucker 1960, I, 90 n.92.

395. The *locus classicus* of this argument appears to be *Querela pacis indique gentium ejectae profligatae*:

> But I have long been hearing the sort of excuse clever men produce for their own wrongdoing. They protest that they act under compulsion and are dragged unwillingly into war. Pull off your mask, drop your pretences, examine your own heart, and you will find that anger, ambition, and folly brought you to war, not any constraint — unless you define constraint as something not altogether to you liking! Such trappings are for the people; God is not to be fooled by pretence (Erasmus 1987, XXVII, 310).

See also Arnobius 1973: "It is better to suffer wrong than to inflict it, that we should rather shed our own blood than stain our hands and our conscience with that of another" (I, vi, 415). Clarkson claims that wars are not necessary because one Quaker at the head of each country on one continent would spell the end to wars on that continent (III, 79-80, 92); he fails to consider the possibility of civil wars. See also Scott 1800, 3-4; Beaumont 1808, 177, 182; Kersey 1815, 88; Jefferson 1832, 23; Richard 1846, 1-5, 8; Gurney 1847, 147; Dymond 1892, 49, 105, 120-127, 143; deGivry 1924, 6-7; Markus 1961, 66-67. Nonpacifists need not assert an absolute right to self-preservation in order to sustain their position; see Finch 1755, 12.

396. Ramsey 1988, 104. See also Morris 1949, 200-201; Hollenbach 1983, 14-15, 18; Hollenbach 1988, 130-132.

397. War was long recognized as conducing to inequality (see Fustel de Coulanges n.d., III, xv, 209; *Commentaries on the War in Gaul*, Julius Caesar 1887, 28). Justice requires a kind of equality that war itself cannot provide; justice in turn serves greater ends (*Nicomachean Ethics*, V, vi, 1134a; X, vii, 1177b, Aristotle 1941, 1013, 1104-1105). Note that the topics of war and philosophy are associated.

398. Suarez, 1944, IV, vii, 19-20. Ramsey 1983 makes a related point: "It is always disheartening to hear Christian people say that the norms governing the domestic use of force do not apply between nations. International relations are a moral jungle, it seems to them; and *non sequitur par excellence*, only 'peace and non-violence' can be applied there" (188). Ramsey argues that international relations lack not morality but legality — hence the need for just war doctrine.

399. Xenophon 1947, I, iii, ii, 259 ff.

400. See National Conference of Catholic Bishops 1983: "Deterrence reflects the radical mistrust which marks international politics" (55).

401. Erasmus 1972, 337; Russell 1975, 304-305; Russell 1986, 94-95; Tucker 1977, 15, 115-119.

402. Calhoun 1946, 14-16.

403. Cyprian 1973, I, vi, 277; Athanasius 1961a, XLVIII, 577.

404. Cobden 1973, 5-11, 197-205; Dymond 1892, 19; Hirst 1923, 291. These are among the many nineteenth and early twentieth century writers who called for international arbitration as a substitute for balance-of-power diplomacy. The limitations of this approach may be seen in Eppstein 1935, who concedes that when Christians defended themselves "against the attacks of pagans and heretics" and Moslems, "the question of arbitration, mediation or the submission of the dispute to an independent tribunal could hardly arise" (149), given the as it were non-negotiable differences between the warring parties. But, by the mid-1930's, Eppstein contended, wars occurred among Christians or between Christians and their colonists; therefore, such international institutions as the League of Nations and the Holy See could effectively discourage excessive rearmaments. This view proved over-optimistic.

405. Thomas Aquinas 1963, 2a2ae, 40, 1. Bacon 1968b characteristically mentions justice while emphasizing the need for sufficient forces and provisions, and the prudent choice of strategies (2). De Givry 1924 denies that Jesus of Nazareth or the early Church provide any foundation for a just war doctrine (95-100). Some historians distinguish 'just war' from the crusade (see especially Bainton 1960, *passim*). Walters 1971 argues convincingly that the crusade was considered a kind of just war by the major Catholic and Protestant just war theorists (417).

406. Childress 1982, 92.

407. McCormick 1978, 35. See also National Conference of Catholic Bishops 1983, 31. Earlier formulations restricted the ruler's responsibilities strictly to the goods and harms to the ruler's own

country; see *A Work on the Three Theological Virtues*, IV, viii, Suarez 1944, 821; Vattel 1916, III, 291; O'Brien 1967, 86.

408. See for example the critique of Barth, Yoder 1970, 40, 92-93. Yoder unwisely extends this criticism to military budgets; "[I]f modern states are spending in many cases over half their budgets on an activity which is foreign to their real nature, then must the Christian not...ask how such a state can be the 'justice-state' which is worth defending?" (106). This calculation overlooks public spending by local and subnational governments; it also ignores the enormity of the evils from which some "modern states" have defended themselves. See also Sheen 1961, 145 and Hollenbach 1983, 50, 61, 143.

409. See Lewis 1980, 39-43. Lewis writes, "The doctrine that war is always a greater evil seems to imply a materialist ethic, a belief that death and pain are the greatest evils." For the difficulties involving the incommensurability of certain conflicting goods and evils, see Ramsey 1978, 72-79.

410. According to Xenophon 1947, the father of Cyrus the Great observed, "the words you say will have more power to convince, when you can abundantly prove that you are in a position to do both good and ill" (I, i, vi, 95). One learns that right use of causing pain in youth by hunting; children are not to be taught his, as they would be corrupted, unable to distinguish evil from evils. See also *On Hunting*, Xenophon 1967; Xenophon 1855, V, viii, 178; Thomas Aquinas 1963, 1a2ae, 79, 3-4. Aquinas contends that "anger in some sense involves reason," if it "wills evil to its object not precisely as an evil but as good under a certain aspect;" this differs from hatred, which "consists in applying evil for evil" (*Ibid.*, 1a2ae, 46, 4-6). See also Luther 1956:

> If people were good and wanted to keep peace, war would be the greatest plague on earth. But what are you going to do about the fact that people will not keep the peace, but rob, steal, kill, outrage women and children, and take away property and honor? The small lack of peace called war or the sword must set a limit to this universal, worldwide lack of peace which would destroy everyone (XLVI, 98).

De Rougement 1983 describes the man of supreme passion or unreason, who decides he "wishes to be his own god." Reasoning cannot avail against this man. "Such a man's passion can be overcome only by killing him before he can kill himself, and in some other way than he wishes to die" (299).

411. Stein 1961b, 38. Potter 1973 disagrees: "An act of war may be 'evil' in the sense of entailing great suffering, but if it can be judged to be the 'lesser evil,' it is tragic but obligatory. A lesser evil is not 'evil' in the sense of being morally 'wicked'" (40).

412. Vann 1939, 7; Childress 1982, 56; Johnstone 1986, 311, 320-322.

413. See O'Toole 1941, 4-5.

414. *De Ivri Belli*, paragraphs 446-448, Victoria 1917, 178-179; *A Work on the Three Theological Virtues Faith, Hope, and Charity*, VII, xvii-xix, Suarez 1944, 848, 849; McCormick 1978, 30-35.

415. Cadoux 1944, 34.

416. Anscombe 1961, 57-59; Ramsey 1983, 316-327, 399-400, 410-419.

417. Wells 1967 almost makes this point but gets carried away with polemical ire (160); see also Gollancz 1959, 126-137. Murphy 1979 points out that a simple dichotomy of civilian and soldier is problematic, because a soldier might be 'forced' to fight, while the civilian may be a warmonger. In practical terms, the relevant distinction is combatant and noncombatant (347-350). Murphy's analysis is seriously vitiated by his tacit equation of rights with sentiment (359-363). See also Mavrodes 1979, 331-337. Just-war theorists Lewis 1980, 43 and O'Brien 1967, 60-61, 83, sidestep Simon Liteson's argument by describing the deaths of innocent civilians as a lesser evil on a scale of good and evil.

   Russell 1986 notes that "Augustine betrayed no sense of outrage at the killing of noncombatants, for after all, as sinners they were being punished for sins in some other connection unrelated to the war" (89). This argument does not address the charge of evil intention in the killer. Russell goes on to argue that such justice-*to*-war arguments as the need to attempt to preserve civilian lives make no sense without the justice-*in*-war arguments that must form part of any coherent justification of war. Without *ius ad bellum, ius in bello* "becomes morally stranded, terrifying to contemplate, and intractable to consider" (92).

418. Calhoun 1946, 8; Page 1948, 154-157; Stein 1961, 29; Ellul 1969, 6; Wells 1979, 270; National Conference of Catholic Bishops 1983, 49-50, 61; Hehir 1986, 148, 154. The just-war theorist O'Brien 1967 agrees that the attempt to justify as 'incidental' the damage that would be done by strategic nuclear weapons overwhelm the principle of 'double effect' (31, 57). Struckmeyer 1979 asserts that "the sheer magnitude of destruction which can be wrought by contemporary warfare does not by itself warrant a contrast between past and present" wars (275); the Chinese killed millions in war, as did the Mongols. This is true, but neglects the fact that those ancient warriors could have spared many innocent victims, whereas a modern government armed with weapons of mass destruction can only spare the innocent by refraining from their use.

419. Boyle 1986, 329, 335.

420. Finnis, Boyle, and Grisez 1987, 73-79, 92, 118-119.

421. *Ibid.*, 132-134, 138-140.

422. The authors above argue implausibly that a strategy designed to retaliate only against a rival's rulers and soldiers would target individuals who are guiltless of the *nuclear* attack (149). This of course is true in many wars; no one claims that the same soldiers who invaded your country will be the ones killed in your counterattack. Nonetheless, all must be judged part of the enemy's military force, and therefore legitimate 'targets' in terms of just-war doctrine.

423. Wells 1967, 105; Ramsey 1983, 187; Finnis, Boyle and Grisez, 75.

424. *Reflections Theologicae* XII, Victoria 1917, par. 320, 122; Gentili 1933, I, v, 28; Vattel 1916, III, iii, 243.

425. See Figgis 1921, 65. Thomas Aquinas 1963 writes, "To attack one's enemies in order to keep them from committing sin is licit, and this not only for their own good but for the good of others" (2a2ae, 83, 9). More 1946 gives a specific example. His Utopians will attack a people who "hold a piece of ground void and vacant to no good or profitable use, keeping others from the use and possession of it" (II, 60-61). The Roman Catholic "zelant," Zebedaeus, in Bacon 1968a, argues that "when the constitution of the state and the fundamental customs and laws of the same (if laws they may be called) are against the laws of nature and nations, then, I say, a war upon them is lawful" on the grounds that he who defaces God's image ("Natural Reason") in himself "divests himself of [his] biblical right to rule over brute Creation" − to say nothing of other human beings. Examples of such constitutions are pirates, nomads, the Assassins, the Munsterites, and tribes that practice human sacrifice (30 ff.). Vattel 1916, II, 245-246 concurs, as does Bacon 1918, 26-27. See also Ramsey 1983, 24, 35, and Childress 1982, 157.

426. Wells 1967, 44.

427. *Alcibiades I*, 109a-112d, Pangle 1987, 182-187.

428. See Maimonides 1963, XIV, Treatise V, iv-vii, 216-227; Zimmerman 1986, 119-131; Gibbon n.d., I, i, 8; Augustine 1961b, xxii, 301; *De Ivri Belli*, Victoria 1917, par. 421, 167; Luther 1956, XLV, 103-104; XLVI, 118-122; Victoria 1917, par. 386-408, 151-161; *Ibid.*, par. 429-435, 170-173; Bacon 1968b, 4; Gentili XVIII, 83, XIX, 86-90; Vattel 1916, III, xiii, 310; Finch 1746, 2-4, 12-14; Hackett 1979, 108; Ramsey 1988, 88.

429. Holcombe 1823a, 43. See also Anonymous 1798, 16, 30.

430. *Institutio principii christiana*, Erasmus 1986, XXVII, 282-283; *Panegyricus ad Phillippum Austriae ducem*, Erasmus 1986, XXVII, 54-

57.

431. See Henry Richard, quoted in Appleton, 67, 69-70.

432. Vattel 1916, III, iii, 253; IV, iv, 356. See also Luther 1956, XLV, 125.

433. An example will be found in Pseudo-Aristotle 1987, 2-3.

434. Legnano 1917 recognizes this: "Should the Church declare war against the Jews? We must say not, since everywhere they are prepared to serve, and do not persecute, Christians. Otherwise of the Saracens, who do persecute Christians" (lxx, 274). Victoria writes, thinking of the Spanish conquest and persecution of American Indian tribes, "Unbelief does not destroy either natural law or human law, but ownership and therefore they are not destroyed by want of faith" (*Reflectiones Theologicae* XII, Victoria 1917, par. 323, 123). Luther 1956 puts matters with characteristic bluntness:

> Christians are not so commonplace so many can assemble in one group. A Christian is a very rare bird! Would to God that the majority of us were good, pious heathen, who kept the natural law, not to mention the Christian law! (26).

As discussed in footnote #386, above, Augustine took a different view, arguing that wrong habituation must be broken by force, which, while not itself an especially effective moral guide, can exert a helpful influence on moral development. See for discussion Brown 1964, 111-112.

435. Woolman 1922, 214.

436. See Augustine 1964, I, xxi, 95; IV, 160; V, 7: Augustine 1961b, xxii, 300-301. Note that Augustine sides with Machiavelli against Cicero on the question of whether a ruler should be loved or feared: "[R]uling a province is different from ruling a Church; the former must be governed by instilling fear, the latter is to be made lovable by the use of mildness" (Augustine 1964, III, 10). Thus may be said to have prepared the way for Machiavelli, who quietly discarded the Church as a specifically Christian institution and subordinated it to government.

On the issue of authority to wage war, see also Legnano 1917, xiv, 234. For historical discussion, see Russell 1975, 68, 84, 230.

437. *A Work on the Three Theological Virtues Faith, Hope and Charity*, Suarez 1944, VI, viii-xi, 832-834; Vattel 1916, III, iii, 247; xi, 303. The limits of knowledge can also afflict the ruler, and the same teaching applies; see Johnson 1975, 179.

438. Johnson 1975, 20.

439. Eppstein 1935, 126. See also Dymond 1982, 154-160. Walsh 1916, 172-180.

440. Augustine 1961b, 301.

441. *De Ivre Belli*, Victoria 1917, par. 436, 173; see also "The First Sermon preached to King Charles, at St. James," April 3, 1625, in Donne 1953-62, VI, 245.

442. See Ellul 1969, Chapter I, *passim*; Hollenbach 1983, 31.

443. Thucydides 1935, II, vi, 107-108. See also Palmer 1982 for commentary. Aron 1966 calls antiquity "the age of courage" (253); its vestiges may be seen in the speech of Roland at the Battle of Roncevaux, refusing reinforcements: "I'd rather die than thus be put to shame; If the King loves us it's for our valor's sake" (Anonymous 1969, LXXXVI, 94).

444. Aristotle 1941 identifies five false kinds of courage: that of the citizen-soldier, which rests upon penalties and honors; that of the professional soldier, which rests upon experience; passion; sanguinity; and ignorance of danger (*Nicomachean Ethics* III, viii, 1116a-1117a). Bacon 1968b contends, "the Spaniard's valor lieth in the eye of the looker on; but the English valor lieth about the Soldier's heart. A valor of Glory, and a valor of natural courage, are two things" (70).

445. Zuckert 1988, 2. Critics of Christianity often assert that it teaches slavery by calling spiritedness sinful, and therefore removing the psychological foundation of freedom, the inclination to resist tyranny. See Julian 1962, III, 387 and Nietzsche 1968, 589-600. For commentary see Platt 1987. Also see Goltz 1918, who argues that our modern conception of courage is deeply rooted in Christianity," animated by self-denial fidelity, and self-sacrifice. However, the courage of a general remains as it was in antiquity: the contempt of death that is natural to a certain kind of man (76).

446. Walsh 1916, 110-111, 149.

447. Synesius of Cyrene 1926, 193.

448. Walsh 1916, 67-69. For an 'ancient' critique of soldiering, see Plautus 1968.

449. Colet 1965 teaches that "the Christian warrior's prowess is his patience, his action is suffering, and his victory, a sure trust in God; a confidence that is either justly suffering, or patiently enduring, the evil" (87-88); "patience itself is true fortitude" (98). Fry 1904 writes, "only those who are in league with eternity can allow their work to await the test of time" (53). Macgregor 1960 cites the example of Jesus of Nazareth, whose "fellow-countrymen are to pursue the policy of reconciliation and peace with the foreign ruler, even at the risk of temporary

submission to injustice" (47). Yoder 1972 observes, "what Jesus renounced is not first of all violence, but rather the compulsiveness of purpose that leads men to violate the dignity of others;" Jesus taught the "readiness to renounce our legitimate means" (243-244). See also Dymond 1892, 31; Scott 1800, 9; Parsons 1813, 7-8; Ferguson and Pitt-Watson 1956, 9, 47; Kelsey 1956, 94-96; Vining 1956, 144-148; Lasserre 1962, 211; Yoder 1972, 97-100; Hauerwas 1983, 138.

450. Bacon 1981, 28.

451. Tertullian 1973d, Hornus 1980, 214.

452. *Alcibiades* I, 133c-133d, Pangle 1987, 217; North 1966, 3 ff.

453. Augustine 1961d, I, ii, 5; I, xix, 24; Augustine 1968, 79.

454. Augustine 1966, i, 259; Thomas Aquinas 1963, 2a2ae, 29, 1-3.

455. Comenius n.d., writes:

> If the disagreement be caused by a difference in government, monarchy or aristocracy, there should be recalled for the renewal of accord the words of the apostle: The powers that be are ordained of God (Romans 13, 2). For if the powers that be are ordained of God, then not only the power of monarchy proceedeth from him, but also that aristocracy; yea, and of democracy. Therefore let them not seek to hinder, much less to destroy, but rather to help one another; and let accord reign between the members of the body....
>
> [B]oth one and the other are beautiful; if only kings would rule their subjects with moderation and behave in a friendly manner toward their neighbors, and if republicans would live in accord among themselves, neither dangerous nor oppressive to anyone, but rather recommending themselves by their readiness to serve. (53-57).

456. *Ibid.*, 59.

457. Thucydides 1934, I, iii, 38.

458. Xenophon 1968, III, ii, 175; IV, iii-5. Pericles tells the Athenians, "...where the chances are the same, knowledge fortifies courage by the contempt which is its consequence, its trust being placed, not in hope which is the prop of the desperate, but in a judgement upon existing resources, whose anticipations are more to be depended upon" (Thucydides 1934, II, vii, 118). Ambrose 1961b calls prudence "the first source of duty" (I, xxvii, 22). Christine de Pisan calls prudence

"the mother of virtues," without which other virtues would be vices (*Le Livre de la Paix*, I, v in Willard 1958, 66).

See also Tasso, 1992, 171-187 on the superiority of prudence to courage; Eidelberg 1977, 2-3. La Fontaine 1965 teaches that "force has the best of any argument," but he also teaches that "bloodthirsty minds are small" (I, x, 21).

459.   Matthew 10:16. The nonresistant Rowntree 1900 writes that Jesus and the Apostles "well knew that the Gospel, when allowed to operate on the hearts of men, would strike at the root of every abuse and corruption in human society; and they chose rather to wait patiently, as in the parable of the leaven, till it bore its legitimate fruit, than on every occasion to run counter to the opinions and prejudices of men, at a time when almost every human institution, but especially in heathen lands, was based on principles fundamentally opposed to the benign spirit of the Gospel" (15). Ellul 1969 exercises his habitual irony on this topic as well: "[C]ontrary to widely held opinion, faith in the Holy Spirit does not mean that we may act imprudently" (82).

460.   Origen 1973b, X, xxiii, 429; Thomas Aquinas 1963, 2a2ae, 45, 6; Gentili 1933, XII, 53; Ferguson and Pitt-Watson 1956, 13-16; Murray 1960, 275.

461.   Cicero 1955, I, 9. See also I, 69-70 and Cicero 1880, I, 10. Complementarily the *supremely* ambitious political life must be in a sense philosophic (*Ibid.*, I, 29-33).

462.   Thomas Aquinas 1963, 1a, 49, 3; 2a2ae, 47, 1-16; 50, 4. For commentary see Walters 1971, 61-62. Ingram 1939 criticizes Christian pacifism as deficient in prudence:

> The weakness of the perfectionist case is that it ignores the distinction between these absolute principles and the manner in which they can be applied to the world in which we live.... [I]f we were able to carry out Christ's moral teaching as an exact law, we should discover that, because of the complicated system in which we are placed, we were producing results very different from those at which we should be aiming or which Christianity itself envisages (60).

As an example, Ingram cites the system of slavery, which Christian principles oppose but which Jesus did not directly attack, knowing that "the moment had not come for any attempt to abolish slavery, that several developments would have to take place before society would be ready for that further step towards the attainment of a community of free and equal persons" (62). This is true as far as it goes, but overlooks the fact that Jesus of Nazareth and his apostles did not keep slaves; similarly, a nonresistant Christian might recognize the unlikelihood of abolishing war here and now while nonetheless refusing to go to war. See also Lewis 1940, 22-27 for a Marxist critique. On the need generally prudently to direct political authority, see Synesius of Cyrene 1926, 261; Aron 1966, 8; Novak 1986, 127.

463. Thomas Aquinas 1963, 1a, 79, 12-13; 1a 2ae 13, 1; 15, 2-3; 17, 1-3; 19, 3-5, 94, 2.

464. Lewis 1980, 33-39. For the opposite view see Sutherland 1946, 2-5.

465. Erasmus 1986, XXVII, Epistle Dedicatory.

466. Erasmus 1986, XXVII, 253-255.

467. Johnson 1975, 159.

468. Aron 1966, 584-585, 609, 634, 781.

469. Luke 16:8; see also Thomas Aquinas 1963, 2a2ae, 55, 2 ff., on "astuteness." Contrast the praise of vulpine astuteness in Machiavelli 1985, XIX, 79. See also Eidelberg 1983, 253-257, who, however, goes too far in tarring "the whole philosophic tradition" as "a license to murder" because it allegedly does not lay down specific laws prohibiting murder, which in fact it does. See *Nicomachean Ethics*, II, vi, 1107a, Aristotle 1941, 959.

470. Bainton 1960 complains that Aquinas makes justice "depend upon a fallible forecast" of whether the damage caused by a contemplated war will not exceed the injury to be sustained by submission (106). See also *A Work on the Threefold Virtues Faith, Hope, and Charity*, Suarez 1944, XIII, vi, v, 830; Dymond 1855, 253; Dymond 1892, 99; Tolstoy 1960, 43 ("Ninety-nine percent of the evil in the world results from such reasoning," he calculates); Walsh 1916, 9-13. Blainey 1988 writes that prudence is least effective in calculating the duration of a war; miscalculations in this have characterized every war since the year 700 (294).

471. For example see Stein 1961b on nuclear deterrence. Stein claims that "unrestricted prudence can no longer find its way around, even on its own terms" (138-139). Nuclear deterrence is "inadequate even in military terms...impotent on the ideological plane" and "recklessly intemperate in its accepted risks" (149). Conceding that "unilateral disarmament also is absurd" in prudential terms, Stein concludes that neither side can establish the prudence of its own case. Therefore, prudence should be strictly subordinated to "moral law" (150). Some three decades after Stein's claims, one must question whether nuclear deterrence is inadequate, impotent, or recklessly intemperate, or that prudence has lost its way. For views similar to Stein's, see Gollancz 1959, 14; Markus 1961, 74; Gottwald 1961, 64-70; Sampson 1965, 179-181; Geyer 1982, 37-38, 53-55.

472. Allen 1946, 4-5. In war, Allen contends, "consequences are...far more difficult to foresee than elsewhere" (9).

473. Grisez and Boyle 1979, 397. See also Finnis, Boyle, and Grisez 1987, 241-243, 251, where the authors almost insensibly slip into equating deterrence of war with war itself. The authors' claim — that "to become willing to do and become anything that may be required to achieve some 'greater good' or prevent some 'greater evil'" will lead to the sacrifice of "personal individuality and stable identity" — is undeniable. However, this does not however establish that military deterrence, even nuclear deterrence, deserves classification as 'anything,' or that anything claimed to be a greater good is in fact greater. Nor do the authors establish that, because prudential reasoning cannot compare goods with mathematical precision, it therefore cannot perceive any difference at all (See *Nicomachean Ethics*, I, iii, 1094b, Aristotle 1941, 936; II, 2, 1103b, 953. For the same point applied to the issue of nuclear deterrence, see McCormick 1983, 172-173, 180.

The authors also claim that there is finally no such thing as moral choice, because if one course of action is judged unqualifiedly superior, morally, it necessarily must be taken. Wrong 'choices' occurs only because some non-moral value is confused with a moral value; "one could have no *rational* inclination toward any alternative if there were an unqualifiedly greater good available" (255-260). This analysis fails to distinguish the two components of choice, deliberation or prudential reasoning and desire. Deliberation may well involve the foreseeing of consequences; one might well consciously desire an immoral consequence, after careful moral deliberation. Thus Milton's Satan: "Evil be thou my good" Milton 1962, IV, 1.110, 86.

474. Finnis, Boyle, and Grisez, 1987, 371 ff. The authors also appeal to a more worldly 'consequentialism': "Look with both eyes, unblinkingly, and you will see that Marxism and the secularism of the liberal democratic societies have turned the heritage of Christendom into a house divided against itself and polluted with the blood of the innocent" (380). Nuclear deterrence, they claim, "corrupts" the commercial republics by "nurtur[ing] pleasure-seeking and greed" (383). They offer no substantial evidence linking nuclear deterrence to pleasure-seeking and greed.

475. Cadoux 1940, 106-118; 130-132; 157-159. Cadoux claims that pacifism has no weakness as a doctrine; rather, pacifists are ineffective because they are so rare. It is also likely that the rarity of pacifism results from its lack of experienced success in the everyday lives of most people.

476. Sidney 1990, II, xxiii, 210. Seifert 1961 concedes that "Too simple a moralism may result in international crimes" (114); see also the nonpacifist Anscombe 1961, 53. Perhaps most tellingly, the Christian pacifist Windass 1964 writes, "Significant progress is made only when

convenience and morality enter into a secret conspiracy" (162). Thus Windass opposes *unilateral* disarmament on the grounds that "the futility of violence, which is in essence to do with the nature of violence itself, is only *evident to the world* through the balance between the great opponents," the United States and the Soviet Union (164). For a 1930's leftist version of the anti-pacifist argument from political consequences, see Fischer 1938. See also the exchange between just-war theorists Lefever 1961 and Ramsey 1961.

477. Johnson 1975, 13. The contrary view is usually expressed in a much more anecdoted manner, e.g., Dakin 1956, 89.

478. Thomas Aquinas 1963, 1a, 22, 1-2.

479. See the debate between the theologians Szlichtyng and Wolzogen, as summarized in Kot 1957, 176-180. For the nonresistant position, see Scott 1800, 20; Beaumont 1808, 174-175; Douglass 1968, 920 for the just-war position, see Stevenson 1987, 103 (on Augustine) and Faulkner 1981, 47 (on Richard Hooker). Both sides agree with Origen 1965, I, xlvi, 55-56, who describes Herod's attempt to destroy the infant Jesus as an attempt to *conquer* Fortune; this is of course the Machiavellian project (Machiavelli 1985, XXV).

480. Reilly 1986, 216.

481. Hollenbach 1983 addresses this point as it relates to nuclear deterrence. The policy "threatens precisely what it seeks to avoid," using "irrationality as a tool of political reason" (65). Hollenbach distinguishes "between the intent to use nuclear weapons and the intent to deter their use" by that threat, as "no simple logical argument can be made from the illegitimacy of use to the moral evaluation of the intentions involved in deterrence" (73). "The real question for moral judgment is whether a concrete strategic option will actually make the world more secure from nuclear disaster or less so" (74).

482. Ramsey 1988, 122-123.

483. Thomas Aquinas 1963, 1a 2ae, 3, 5-8.

484. Heering 1943, 89, 93.

485. See Jones 1914, xxxvi-xxxvii and Sibley 1949, 11-12, 17, for statements of Christian pacifist revolutionism.

486. Troeltsch 1949, writes:

When Church and State became allies there were surprises on both sides. The State hoped to include the Church among its supporters, and it found itself confronted with the sovereign authority of a purely spiritual power. With the help of the State the Church hoped to come to a satisfactory conclusion on the question of unity, and in admitting the influence of the State she admitted a disturbing element, a foreign body, which under certain circumstances, was useful, and in others disintegrating, but which in any case was always an alien influence (I, 211).

Martin 1966 observes that "politics are based on consensus within disunity, but since the sect is based on acute cleavage it can envisage only rule by flat or withdrawal, neither of which are political in the liberal sense of the word" (59) — or, one might add, in any decent and workable sense of the word.

487. Sattler 1975, 74.

488. Roberts 1915, 22, 30.

489. Jesus "restored...the laws of rule and government which had been corrupted, by subduing all enemies under His feet, that by this means...He might teach rulers themselves moderation in their government" (Origen 1973c, III, 5, p. 343).

490. Cullman 1970, 41-44; 50-52; Fast 1959, 14, 34-35.

491. See Glidden 1948, 16-17; See also Glidden 1948, 16-17; Paupert 1969, 63, 67; Yoder 1972, 23, 59-63; 112.

492. Chelcický 1964a, 151-152. See also Ludwig Wolzogan, who contended, "God does not wish Christians to be free from persecution. Lasting peace is a very great foe of godliness; hence it is proper to hate it. A Christian king would do away with real martyrdom, and the place of Christian courage would be taken by martial courage" (Kot 1957, 174).

493. Augustine 1966, XIX, xvii, 197-199. Yoder 1972, not without political ambitions for Christianity, nonetheless denies primary Church responsibility for the rule of civil society (246-248). Paupert 1969 goes so far as to urge a "return of government" (132-133); rather, Christians should act "in such a way that the difficulties and inherent dangers of the specific system are reduced or eliminated and the evangelical potentialities linked with it are brought to fruition" (134). See also *Ibid.*, 135-169.

494. Simons 1960, 603.

495. Van Braght 1950 commends Christian deference to rulers (32) while condemning involvement in government or even in commerce (9-10).

496. Chelcický 1964a, 140-144, 156-157. If civil authority

> ...intentionally inclines itself to be compassionate and does not torment the unwise people who do not understand mercy, and if it abandons what it ought to do by virtue of its office, it will multiply future complaints to

itself and about itself. For love does not succeed with those who are not under love but under fear; if the fear be taken away, then there will be many injuries done and complaints will multiply. Power thus ruins itself with mercy, and it will not be esteemed if it does not use force. Power is for those who are without God's yoke and who do not belong under love, so that they may intimidate the unwise people with cruel power (159).

Chelcický actually makes the same accusation against the Roman Catholic Church as did Machiavelli; it is guilty of "soft effeminacy" in its government (162). For commentary, see Kaminsky 1964, 119; Wagner 1983, 76. Brock 1957 misunderstands Chelcický as an exponent of "philosophical anarchism" (39, 43). Chelcický is neither philosophic nor anarchistic. Better is Brock 1973, 35 ff.; note especially the perceptive observation of the close association of political indifferentism with rural life.

497. See Cadoux 1940, concerning the Second World Wars:

I do not expect the country at large to be able to pledge itself to adopt my method, and I am therefore ready to recognize as a second best its adoption of the only means of checking Hitler which as a community it knows — namely, by force of arms. I am quite sure that it will be much worse for the world if Hitler wins the war than if the Allies win it. I therefore have a conscientious objection, not only to fighting myself, but to obstructing the Government and my fellow-citizens generally in doing what they believe to be right.... [P]robably the most urgently needed political service the pacifist can render during war is to work so far as he possible can for the conclusion of a really healing peace (210).

See also *Ibid.*, 167-179. See Brock 1972 for a more typically optimistic Quaker critique of Mennonism (67-71, 228, 483-486). Yoder 1972 speaks of governments and other "structures" rather as old-fashioned men speak of women: "*We cannot live without them. We cannot live with them*" (146). (Italics in original).

498. Barclay n.d., 451-453; Hoyt 1956, 17, 24, 43-52, 63-39; Lasserre 1962, 99-120 (who, however, stops short of endorsing war, on the grounds that it is entirely disorderly [129-130]); Hershberger 1969, 53-55.

499. Origen 1965, VIII, lxxiv, 509-510; Cadoux 1940, 179; Bowman 1944, 240; Barth 1961, 464.

500. Hoyt 1956, 81.

501. See Barbour 1964, 70; Barclay 1879, 71; Jones 1919, 599-600. See also Simons 1960, 118; Van Braght 1950, 402; Barth 1961, 458-459.

Lasserre 1962 lists ten characteristics of a "just and humane political order, based upon the Decalogue (158-159); however, he refuses to sanction war, even for non-Christians.

502.   Acts 11:18.

503.   Those who deny it include Bennett 1962, 93 and Lasserre 1962, 138. Those who affirm the Biblical teaching include Bogue 1813, 55-64; Kersey 1815, 87; Wells 1831, 89 (his example, however, is the Chinese nation); Gurney n.d., 3-4; Dymond 1855, 241; Hershberger 1969, 309-311; Zahn 1983, 126 (who, however, utterly neglects the argument of Romans 13 in order to deny any principled distinction between public and private orders).

504.   Origen 1965, VIII, lxxv, 510; Johnson 1975, 245-246.

505.   Origen 1965, I, i, 7; Bowman 1944, 44.

506.   John 15:19; Acts 2:44-45; II Corinthians 8:12-15; Nuttall 1958, 81; Macgregor 71; Ramsey 1988, Chapter 5, *passim.*

507.   See Barth 1944, 29-34.

508.   Ellul 1976, 379 n.1.

509.   Leo Tolstoy is of course the best-known exponent of this view. Tolstoy 1960 argues for a sort of historicism, claiming that the truth of Christianity will be proven as human beings outgrow "the State" (281-283). His argument against "the State" consists of an *ad hominem non sequitur*; "all men in power assert that their authority is necessary to keep bad men from doing violence to the good, thus assuming that they themselves are the good who protect the bad" (288); no important philosopher or Church writer has made any such assumption, and it is the argument, not the one who makes the argument, that is decisive. As any historicist must do, Tolstoy refuses to show what form his dreamed-of stateless society will take (Tolstoy 1909, 86). For commentary see Stratmann 1928, 148; Hershberger 1969, 189. For a contemporary statement of Tolstoyism, see Sampson 1966. Sampson claims that "conservatives" make "the appeal to Nature," to limitations of human being, in order to justify government and war (7). He associates the concept of nature or limit with original sin, and therefore argues that "conservatives" assume that there are two human natures, one justly the master, one justly the slave (9-10).

Alternatively, some "conservatives" claim that human nature is unitary but violent, implying that "the whole creation was a monstrous and diabolic joke" (11). Sampson contends that there is no human nature; the 'nature' or essence of human beings is "psychic freedom" (111). Unfortunately, psychic freedom can be thwarted by "human egoism" (146). Human beings seek power as "compensation" when freedom is thus denied them, and this *libido dominandi* yields governments and wars. Political rights, so-called, are merely expressions of "the metaphysics of egoism" (149-150). "The heart of the Machiavellian metaphysic is the insistence that there is a fundamental, unchanging human nature which prescribes the same limits to human behavior at all times and places" (154). There is no justice to be found in politics, which is the realm of coercion and inequality.

Unlike real Christianity, which affirms real limits to human nature both 'fallen' and 'redeemed,' Sampson's romantic christianism depends heavily on imagination. In attempting to explain how free human beings fell victim to egoistic machinations — why so many people are "weak and easily ruled" by governments (232) — he blames poverty of imagination (234). This analysis enables him to call our problems tractable to re-imagining. As in so much of post-Christian utopian thought, imagination replaces grace — the inevitable corollary to the assumption that divine grace is merely imagined.

510.   Socinus, quoted in Kot 1957, 87.

511.   Warner 1805, vi; Stephen 1890, 135-140.

512.   Wolzogen writes, "Today the world is filled with so many crimes that it is hard to restrain them by sword and gallows. Let the State then rather have for king a Turk, a Jew, or a pagan, who would be warlike and pay heed to external justice" (Kot 1957, 175). The Quaker writer Barclay n.d. writes of "nominal" Christians who are magistrates:

> ...while they are in that condition [of nominal Christianity], we shall not say, that war, undertaken upon a just occasion, is altogether unlawful to them. For even as circumcision and the other ceremonies were for a season permitted to the Jews...because that Spirit was not yet raised up in them, whereby they could be delivered of such rudiments; so the present confessors of the Christian name, who are yet in the mixture, and not in the patient suffering spirit, are not yet fitted for this form of Christianity, and therefore cannot be undefending themselves until they attain that perfection (525).

See also Kellerman 1901, 42.

513.   Hershberger 1969, 243. He adds, "Let those who aspire to nothing higher perform the task of magistracy, the police, and the military. There will always be more than enough people ready to fill these positions...." (243) Hirst 1923 describes the list of Quaker statesmen as "short but noteworthy:" William Penn and John Bright. Bright was not a pacifist with respect to civil society; he made speeches in parliament defending the Union in the American Civil War (273-277).

514. Brunner 1947, 461-463. He adds, "Whenever Christians, in the exuberance of their joy in the faith, have thought that they could found a commonwealth on family lines, eliminating the element of political coercion altogether, experience has taught them otherwise" (461). Brunner calls for "a realistic type of pacifism," as it is "the duty of Christians to think politically in matters concerning the State" (697-698, n.10).

515. Origen 1965, V, xxxvii, 293. "The written code of cities" should be made as consistent as possible with "the ultimate law of nature," which "Probably derived from God."

516. *Ibid.*, IV lxxxi, 248; lxxxv, 251.

517. Lasserre 1962, 81; Strauss 1973, 34.

518. Augustine 1966, I, xix, 89-91.

519. Augustine 1966 writes that "no one can have true virtue without true religion, that is, without true worship of the true God, and...there is no true virtue where virtue is subordinated to glory. However, those who are not citizens of our eternal city...are more useful to the *earthly* city when they have their own kind of virtue than if they did not have even that" (V, xix, 243-245). This concept of limited virtue and justice may be the best response to the concern of Weigel 1988, who asks if such contemporary pacifist concepts as 'first violence' (e.g., the deliberate disregard of unalienable rights) and 'second violence' (justified rebellion against those who disregard such rights) do not "subject the rigor of the pacifist argument to the death of a thousand cuts" (10). The problem is rather the false conceptions of rights and of justice (often based upon the puerilities of Frantz Fanon), coupled with the imprudence of pacifists who deal naively with contemporary ideologues and tyrants.

There is, however, a considerable practical problem with the Christian concept of law, a problem well stated by Eidelberg 1983:

> [B]y eliminating [Christians would say, simplifying and getting to the foundations of] the coherent and comprehensive system of laws of the Torah, Christianity was forced to adopt the patchword laws of pagan nations, laws which could not but conflict with and eviscerate the unguarded teachings of the Nazarene or of his disciples. Hence Christianity was and still is compelled to render unto Caesar the things that are Caesar's and to God the things that are God's, when in truth, nothing in a monotheistic universe belongs to Caesar (145).

The latter assertion misreads Christianity, which never teaches that 'Caesar' does not finally belong to God. However, Eidelberg is right to raise the concern that, given the delay of the *Parousia*, the 'radical' or root-Judaism that is Christianity may lack sufficiently precise guidance for the everyday life of ordinary people. In this respect, orthodox Judaism is better built for the long haul. But there is another side to the coin: Christianity's very imprecision makes it more easily adaptable to the variety of non-Jewish regimes, bringing a sort of Jewish wisdom to 'the gentiles.' Orthodox Judaism can rule, but rarely gets the chance; Christianity cannot rule, but often gets the chance.

520. See, for example, Bowman 1944, 29.

521. Cited in Ceadel 1987, 149. Compare Strauss 1964, 64.

522. Ellul 1967 claims that 'democracy' has brought no "substantial" charge to France, that "there are more differences between the American state of 1910 and 1960 (despite the constitutional sameness) than between the latter and the Soviet state (despite the constitutional differences)" (10). Both are subservient to "the technological structure," with technician-bureaucrats ruling in all important respect (39). Both seek "happiness" through "efficiency" in centralized organizations (70). Ellul uncritically accepts Hegel's dubious claims about the 'impersonality' of bureaucracy. Ellul mistakenly assumes that technology can only centralize power, and he underestimates the extent to which bureaucrats justifiably fear and dislike 'the politicians' who pay them to do what they do. To some extent, Ellul's strictures are rhetorical jabs intended to spur his readers to enrich their private lives including their religious lives (202-221). See also Ellul 1976, 373-383, 393-397. Ellul hopes to employ Christianity in much the way commercial republicanism employs commerce – to reduce political passions. Unlike Christianity and much of commercial republican doctrine, however, Ellul denies all moral status to political life, a misreading of Romans 13.

523. Kautsky 1953, discusses the origins of Christianity from a Marxist viewpoint:

> Whatever one's position may be with respect to Christianity, it certainly must be recognized as one of the most titanic phenomena in all human history. One can not resist a deep feeling of wonder when one thinks of the Christian Church, now almost two thousand years old and still vigorous, more powerful than the governments in many countries (3).

524. Paraphrasing Cadoux 1919, 67.

525. Bainton 1960, 53-54.

526. Bainton 1960, 67 outlines these three arguments. Harnack 1981 argues that early Christians opposed military service for both reasons, anti-idolatry and nonresistance (62-67).

527. Helgeland 1986, 36. The same has been true of some Christian clerics since that time.

528. Gibbon n.d. gives five causes of the early Christians' success: their zeal; their doctrine of a future life; the miraculous powers ascribed to them; their pure and austere morals; and the union and discipline of the Christian republic, "which gradually formed an independent and increasing state in the heart of Rome" (I, xv, 383). See also *Ibid.*, I, xv, 414; xx, 640-641; xxi, 685. On the warlike potential of proselytizing zeal, see Huxley 1937, 104 and Faulkner 1981, 50.

529. For statements of modern pacifists, see Leeds 1876, *passim*; Clarkson 1806, III, 56; Cadoux 1925, 113-121; Hornus, 1980, 16, 168-169. For statements by nonpacifists, see Lee 1943, 51-56; Swift 1983, 29. For the most detailed analysis by a 'democratic' historian, see the nonpacifist Johnson, 1987, who calls Cadoux's account "both dead wrong and misleading in its depiction of the historical evidence" (9). Johnson argues that there was "pluralism" in the Church on the issue of war, that six major Christian theologians, all of them nonresistants, who wrote during the period 200-315 A.D., did not represent the Church as a whole (19). It must be said that Johnson's discussions of two of these theologians minimize the nonresistant character of their writings. Tertullian 1973c reports that in the lower grades of military service, "there is no necessity for taking part in sacrifices or capital punishments," a circumstance that to some extent excuses military service by Christians who, since Jesus of Nazareth's disarming of Peter, have gone unarmed (XIX, 73).

530. Tatian the Assyrian 1973 actually condemns only the assumption of military *command* XI, 69); Athenagoras 1973 condemns putting human beings to death, "though justly," explicitly mentioning gladiatorial spectacles and abortion, but not war (XXXIV, 147). Cadoux 1919, in discussing Justin Martyr, ascribes this refusal to issue an outright condemnation of soldiering to prudence. Justin "would needlessly have prejudiced the Emperor against his main plea, viz. for toleration, if he had *gone out of his way* to say that, if ever the attempt were made to compel Christians to serve in the legions, they would refuse to obey the Emperor's orders" (Cadoux 1919, 103). See also Zampaglione 1973, 255:

> The pagan cults formed the very basis of the civilization of the old world. On them rested the social structure which reflected and translated into legal institutions and political rules their vision of the world. To desire the disappearance of these cults was surely tantamount to preaching the destruction of the state....(255)

531. Origen 1965, II, xxx, 92: "[H]ow could this teaching, which preaches peace and does not even allow men to take vengeance on their enemies; have had any success unless the international situation had

everywhere been changed and a milder spirit prevailed at the advent of Jesus?" (92). See also Caspary 1979, 131-132.

532. See for example Ambrose 1961a, II, xvi, 241-242. Ambrose cites the Old Testament.

533. Eusebius Pamphilus, 1961b, XX, 579; XXVI, 580; 1961c, i-v, 581-586; xvi 606; 1961a, I, iii-v, 482-483; I, xxiv, 489; II, iii, 500-501; IV, iii, 555; Lactantius 1973b, *passim*; Eusebius 1961, X, vii, 379-383; ix, 386.

534. Augustine 1961a, I, xxviii, 490. Compare with Julian 1962, I, 95-97; II, 397; Voltaire 1962, 341; Gibbon n.d., I, xx, 639-640; Ferguson 1974, 67.

535. Helgeland, Daly and Burns 1985, 72. Swift 1983, II *passim* discusses the changing social and political context in which Christians found themselves during and after Constantine's reign. See also Harnack 1981, 99-104, and contrast with Cadoux 1919, who claims, "It is evident from many quarters the settlement was accepted only gradually and with an uneasy conscience" (261).

536. Momigliano 1964, 9-15; Wilken 1984, 117-125. Jones 1964 gives a slightly different account, arguing that the Christian emperors elevated Christians into a "new nobility more subservient to their wishes" than the old, and giving new meaning to the phrase, "exalted those of law degree" (35-36).

537. Chelcický 1964a, 145-146; Kellerman 1901, 53-67; Hobhouse 1909, 111-119; Raven 1948, 8; Hoyt 1956, 90-94; Bainton 1960, 86-87; Lasserre 1962, 93-94; Douglass 1968, 199 ("When Constantine raised the cross above his troops, raised before the Christian Church the same temptation which Satan had set before Christ on the mountain with the sight of all the kingdoms of the world;" Ferguson 1974, 67).

538. Scott 1800, 14; Clarkson n.d., 19; A. Cleveland Cox, in Roberts and Donaldson 1973, VIII, 3.

539. Figgis 1921, 35; Scott-Craig 1938, 49; Ryan 1952, 3; Helgeland, Daly, and Burns 1985, 2; Harries 1986, 63. See also B. Schopf: *Das Totungsrecht bei den Fruhechristichen Scheriftstellern*, cited in Aubert 1965, 115.

540. Hornus 1980, 186-187.

541. Russell 1975, 36-39.

542   Pagels 1988, 64-65, 98-116.

543. Zampaglione 1973 discusses Manichaeism in this regard (297); see also Bainton 1960 on Cathars (115); Brock 1972 on Cathars, Waldensiians, and Lollards (26-31). De Rougement 1983 associates these groups with the Anabaptists and Mennonites (175-176).

CHAPTER V

1. Sharp and Jenkins 1990, 7. Childress 1971 defines civil disobedience as "a public, non-violent, submissive violation of the law as a form of protest" (11).

2. Sharp and Jenkins 1990, 7. The authors observe that nonviolent resistance is not exclusively the possession of pacifists. Nonviolent resistance, in their (modern Western) view, is primarily "an effective *means* of action" (emphasis added). The success of nonviolent resistance in the late 1980's would not have surprised Gandhi:

   > Just as violence has its own technique, known by the military science, which has invented means of destruction unheard of before, non-violence has its own science and technique. Non-violence in politics is a new weapon in the process of evolution. Its vast possibilities as yet unexplored (Gandhi 1958-1984, LXVI, 269).

3. See "Letter from a Birmingham Jail" in King 1964, 82-84. On the related issue of civilian-based national defense against a foreign occupier, Carter 1967 writes, "the best kind of political experiences for resisting an oppressive regime is probably a tradition of free political activity, including numerous voluntary associations, individual economic independence, and decentralized political institutions" (282-283).

4. Weiner 1988 observes that

   > ...the British colonial model of tutelary democracy has been more successful than other colonial models in creating democratic institutions and processes in newly independent countries. Almost every country that has emerged from colonial rule since the Second World War with a continuous democratic experience is a former British colony. Not a single newly independent country that lived under French, Dutch, American, or Portuguese rule has continually remained democratic. (24-25)

5. Parekh 1989b, 12-20, 45-47. The English-educated Gandhi, Parekh complains, "had too little knowledge of Indian history to be able to trace the sources and development and even identify the character of Indian degeneration" (51). Singer 1972 reports the claim of a very patriotic Indian and devout Hindu who traced foreign corruption as far back as 500 years (88). Von Schlegel 1849 laments, "The history of India since the time of Alexander the Great certainly presents little more than a series of foreign conquests and internal revolutions" (508).

6. Nanada 1985, 45-48. Since independence, the habit of self-congratulation has migrated to some Indians; Singh 1981 describes "Indian Independence" as "by far the most momentous event of the current century," worldwide (4).

7. Edwardes 1986, 31. Edwardes adds the important point that the growing popularity of pseudoscientific claims of racial superiority, imported to Britain from continental Europe, and thence to the British in India, may have added to Indian resentment and strengthened Indian nationalism (135).

8. *Ibid.*, 34, 61-65. On Britain as a "bourgeois empire" see *Ibid.*, 257. On the Indians' lingering hostility towards Christianity as an agent of imperialism see Gandhi 1958-1984, IV, 407 and Andrews 1930, 85-89.

9. For a concise yet comprehensive account of Churchill on imperialism see Emmert 1989.

10. Churchill 1931, 10, 46-47. See also *Ibid.*, 106, 120-121.

11. *Ibid.*, 30, 35, 40, 62, 120.

12. *Ibid.*, 111.

13. *Ibid.*, 96-97, 126.

14. *Ibid.*, 10, 26, 73, 103-104. It was in this context that Churchill fulminated, famously: "It is alarming and also nauseating to see Mr. Gandhi, a seditious Middle Temple lawyer, now posing as a fakir of a type well-known in the East, striding half-naked up the steps of the Vice-regal palace, while he is still organizing and conducting a defiant campaign of civil disobedience, to parley on equal terms with the representative of the King-Emperor" (94).

15. *Ibid.*, 34.

16. *Ibid.*, 30, 122.

17. *Ibid.*, 47, 81, 120.

18. *Ibid.*, 125, 136-137.

19. *Ibid.*, 112.

20. Grenier 1983, 72-75. Holmes 1953 claims that "it was the influence of Gandhi through the discipline of thirty years gone by, that prevented the spread of the conflagration" from northern to southern India (91). This suggests that Gandhiism both indirectly inflamed and directly limited the inflammation of murderous sectarian passions.

21. See Lamb 1968, 3; Edwardes 1986, 257.

22. Gandhi 1958-1984, I, 295. The British class system was of course more rigid than the young Gandhi believed; in contrast to the Indian caste system, however, it must have seemed a model of social fluidity.

23. Puri 1987, 48.

24. Gandhi 1958-1984, XXIX, 173.

25. *Ibid.*, 140; Andrews 1930, 220-221. Andrews adds that Gandhi appreciated English susceptibility to arguments appealing to conscience (350).

26. Puri 1987, 90-93; Andrews 1930, 234.

27. Brown 1972, 13-15.

28. Gandhi 1958-1984, XLIII, 19.

29. See Reynolds 1956 for a brief discussion from an anti-imperialist viewpoint. Reynolds made a claim that would become fashionable some years later: "The great issue of out time...is not the so-called East-West conflict, but the great moral issue of white domination of Africa [where Britain and France still had colonies] and other parts of the world" (5). The "so-called" conflict between commercial republics and socialist oligarchies outlasted colonialism by decades, although many of the economic disputes associated with colonialism could persist in 'North-South' relations for decades to come.

   It is important to observe that the same debate between English constitutionalism and anti-constitutionalism played out among Indians. Brown 1972 concludes, "the more ardently constitutional men were, the fiercer was their opposition to [Gandhi's] satyagraha" (110).

30. Taylor 1920.

31. Taylor 1921, 876-877.

32. Taylor 1922, 55.

33. Anonymous 1921, 586.

34. Hoyland 1922a, 73. Hoyland gave as an example the Indian Congress Party's criticisms of 'Untouchability,' which marked "an incredible advance towards the ideals of the kingdom of God, and is directly attributable to Mahatma Gandhi" (74).

35. Hoyland 1922b, 233.

36. Hoyland 1922c, 305. Hoyland later wrote that Gandhi was "in no sense of the word a statesman," but was "disastrously incompetent" in his political calculations (Hoyland 1923b, 632).

37. Hoyland 1923a, 151.

38. *Ibid.*, 153.

39. Hoyland 1923b, 631-632.

40. Hoyland 1929a, 668.

41. Hoyland 1929b, 924.

42. Hoyland 1929b, 924-926; Hoyland 1929c, 949.

43. Hoyland 1929d, 967. Hoyland called Gandhi's campaign for de-industrialization "impracticable" (1929h, 1107).

44. Hoyland 1929e, 989.

45. Hoyland 1929d, 967.

46. Hoyland 1929f, 1009-1010.

47. Hoyland 1929g, 1057.

48. See Alexander 1928a, 1928b, and 1929, who is primarily concerned with presenting a sketch of Gandhi's virtues and explaining his programme, and Ratcliffe 1929, who writes a short biography and emphasizes Gandhi's affinities to Quakerism − particularly his aversion to litigiousness, his pacifism, and his "passionate application of religion to everyday life" (915).

49. Sorabji 1922 deplored the nonreligious character of English education in India, saying it had left many young men "either agnostic or frankly atheistic;" she contended that India needed Christianity in order to "become fit to govern itself" − a claim Hoyland did not make (281-282). Dobson 1925 cautioned that Indians were "not political realists:"

   > There is a disposition to look upon self-rule as a *terminus ad quem*, rather than as a long and difficult journey. The word *swaraj* [self-rule] exercises a magic fascination which might prove fatal. For after *swaraj*, what then? (283)

   For another sampling of opinion see the correspondence section of *The Friend*, Vol., LXIX, No. 50, with letters from John W. Harvey, Horace G. Alexander, and John W. Graham (1156).

50. Singha 1924, 807.

51. Graham 1928, 256-257.

636

52. Graham 1929, 1157.

53. *Ibid.*, 1157.

54. See *The Friend*, Vol LXX, No. 22 (May 30, 1930).

55. Anonymous 1930a, 566.

56. *Ibid.*, 567-568. Emphasis in original.

57. *Ibid.*, 569.

58. Watkins 1924, 27; Anonymous 1930b, 141-142. Watkins distinguished among *passive resistance*, exemplified by the Rev. John Clifford's campaign against the 1902 Balfour Education Act (primarily involving tax withholding — the resisters "did not mob Mr. Balfour"), *conscientious objection* ("the invention of a few cowards who tried to escape the khaki during the war"), and Gandhian "non-cooperation" (27-28). By contrast, Shoran S. Singha called Gandhi a "real follower of Christ" practicing "the tenets of Christianity" without, of course, accepting Christian doctrine. Gandhi made the Gospel "more real" and "more understandable and attractive" to Indians (Singha 1925, 221-222). Sharp 1979 provides a good account of Gandhi's antecedents. They include the 1905 Russian Revolution, a Chinese boycott of United States goods, and a boycott in Bengal against British partition (33-41); this is to say that many antecedents were non-Christian.

59. Hoyland 1930, 144.

60. Graham 1930, 146. Graham also made the Jeffersonian claim that "political liberty for a vast illiterate population is a mockery" (145). The American branch of the Fellowship of Reconciliation did not address this point in extending its "definite support" for Indian independence (American F.O.R. 1930, 151).

61. Pollard 1930, 148-149.

62. For an extreme statement of political disaffection by a European pacifist who admired Gandhi see Hobhouse 1949, who detests the "false civilization" of the West so much that he refuses to differentiate between republics and despotisms (92) or, when he does so, scorns republics more ("the great Western democracies [so-called]" are more dangerous than communist states" [106]). As the republics continue to "try to serve God *and* Mammon" (102), engaging in "competition for material wealth and domination," wars against communism "will merely intensify the general poverty and oppression," Hobhouse mistakenly predicted (106). A satanic world-tyranny would result, to be overthrown apocalyptically by nonviolent resistants (107-108).

63. Brock 1972 sees that "the idea of nonviolent resistance to wrong and non violent coercion to achieve the right...does not appear as a definite concept in the history of pacifism, except at a very embryonic stage, until the nineteenth century, although its practice 'nonintentionally' dates back millennia" (476). His examples — Garrisonian "nonviolent direct action:" and Tolstoyan "conscientious objection" — did not, however, achieve the comprehensive and articulated form seen in Gandhi.

64. Gandhi's first published articles appeared in an English Vegetarian publication in 1891, two years before he went to South Africa, and not without political calculation: "The Vegetarian movement will indirectly aid India politically," he wrote to a friend, "inasmuch as the English Vegetarians will more readily sympathize with the Indian aspirations (that is my personal experience)" (Gandhi 1958-84, I, 87). Hunt 1986 is highly informative on this issue. The young Gandhi had "no meaningful contact" with any orthodox Christian church; European acquaintances were almost exclusively Nonconformist British Protestants or non-Christian cultists. The latter included the Theosophists, "the first of the modern Western cults showing strong Hindu influence," synthesizing Victorian evolutionism with Asian religions, and the London Ethical Society, an offshoot of William H. Salter's Ethical Society of Chicago, a form of "rational humanism" claiming that all religions teach fundamentally similar doctrines (8ff.). See also Gandhi 1958-84, VI, 273 ff. Gandhi also had associations with the Esoteric Christian Union, founded by a former Theosophist, Edward Maitland, who presented an allegorical interpretation of the Bible as a prescription for the inner development of the human soul; in this schema, to 'find the Christ' means to realize the highest human potential. (See Gandhi 1958-84, I, 139). Gandhi's closest Christian friend was C. F. Andrews, an Anglican who gave up his ordination vows; he also had many friends among Quakers who, as demonstrated by the above discussion of their reactions to Gandhi, often did not accept many of the New Testament's Christological teachings. See also the account in Green 1986, 65 ff.

This is not to deny that Gandhi quickly learned to appeal to Christian principles for political purposes. See for example his 1894 letter arguing for the franchise for Indians in South Africa (Gandhi 1958-84, I, 136-137),

65. Sharp 1979, 91. Sharp draws three distinctions between Gandhi and the Western pacifists of the time: Gandhi had political objectives extending far beyond conscientious objection to war; Gandhi accepted the necessity of conflict and struggle, not simple negotiation, conciliation, and arbitration; Gandhi called for action by masses of people including nonpacifists. Hunt 1986 distinguishes Gandhian nonviolent resistance from the Rev. John Clifford's "passive resistance" campaign in the wake of Lord Balfour's 1902 Education Bill establishing a national school system in England. First, Gandhi formulated a constructive program of village development and

education to supplement his campaigns of civil disobedience. Second, Gandhi had long-range goals and could therefore compromise on nonessentials. Finally, Gandhi seldom threatened his opponents with divine sanctions and used moral indignation sparingly – perhaps in part because he could not invoke the same god, exactly (146-147).

66. *Antichrist*, xlii, in Nietzsche 1968, 617.

67. *Ibid.*, xlviii, 619.

68. *Ibid.*, lx, 652.

69. Chatfield 1976, 56. "Nowadays Peace is a Power" intones Hirst's Mr. Truelove (Hirst 1906, 226). For a recent statement see Boulding 1989.

70. "The irony of radical sectarianism is that [despite its insistence on Church-state separation] it points toward an involvement of the Church in society in perhaps even more thoroughgoing and fundamental ways than that of the 'Constantinian' Church" (Johnson 1987. 109). This is true, but it is also true of the Christianity of the Book of Revelations; apocalypticism is the style of much older (and non-'Mennonite' or non-separatist) nonresistant Christianity. See Lanza del Vasto 1972, 7-10.

71. There is still disagreement over the *rational* status of nonviolent resistance. Wilson 1918 takes a view close to Gandhi's. The world, he contends, can be "made rational" (12); "spiritual activism" (22) is "stronger, more certain in action, and more efficient than returning injury for injury" (32) because God and His world are finally on reason's side: "...if the interests of men and nations are bound to clash, the militarist is right; if the final truth of the Universe is that it is not and cannot be a Universe at all, but that it is in its nature at best an equilibrium of opposing forces and opposing wills, at worst a general free fight; then the Pacifist is a dangerous sentimentalist and ought to be silenced." (131)

Lanza del Vasto 1972, in contrast, deplores reason as the force that "arms for war" (12); spirituality is distinct from and even opposed to it. This is perhaps more a Christian than a Gandhian view.

72. Tertullian 1973a, XXXVII, 45. See also Cassidy 1978, 77-84. John Donne agrees, calling obedience "one ingredient in all Peace" ("First Sermon Preached to King Charles, at St. James" (April 3, 1625), Donne 1953-1962, 19, VI, 254); "*Obedience* to lawful Authority is always an *essential* part of Religion" (258). He adds, "Keep the Law, and the Law shall keep thee" (259). It should be noted that Donne is preaching this *to a king*, i.e., to one who might most be tempted to circumvent the law.

73. Iyer 1973, 8. For the confirmation of this point by a man who knew Gandhi personally, see Jones 1948, 27-29.

74.   Rolland 1924, 121-222, 247. Holmes 1976, 224, concurs.

75.   Winslow 1949, 314-316. See also Page 1930, 691-693.

76.   Sikes 1976, 348. Christians were not the only Westerners to find in Gandhi a tonic. Cousins 1953 recalls that "futility" had been "the fashion of my generation. Gandhi proved that "there was scope for free will and conviction in the shaping of society, that history could be fluid, not fixed, if men were willing to transcend their egos in order to merge themselves with the larger body of humanity." The examples of Gandhi and Tagore led Cousins back to Emerson (3-4), i.e., to democratized Hegelianism.

77.   Holmes 1953, 26-27.

78.   *Ibid.*, 31. See also Holmes 1976, 224.

79.   Holmes 1976a, 608, 610; Holmes 1976b, 220. See also Holmes 1953, 58. For similar views expressed by an Indian Christian see George 1939, 22-28; 46-47 and George 1976, 335-340.

80.   Jones 1948, 8, 11.

81.   *Ibid.*, 51, 59. "[H]ow shall I defend that distinction? I don't. I leave it undefended. But it is the nearest statement of the facts I know." (59).

82.   *Ibid.*, 60-64. For the same criticisms stated more sharply see Thomas 1969, 235-236.

83.   Jones 1948, 65-69. Gandhi also entertained the suspicion that the Untouchables found Christian missionaries' material goods attractive (Thomas 1969, 214).

84.   *Ibid.*, 77, 85, 157.

85.   See also Pickett 1953, 311 ff., 394-395, 409.

86.   Hoyland 1949, 125.

87.   *Ibid.*, 133, 137, 140, 145.

88.   Jones 1971, 5, 15.

89.   Puri 1987 writes that Gandhi

       ...had no use at all for the pacifism of Quakers or conscientious objectors or war resisters as an ideology of protest on grounds merely of conscience. Contrary to the pacifist position, his indeed was the stance that in a conflict there should always be ardent and constant participation rather than withdrawal or apathy (21).

Gandhi "was not advocating, Quaker-fashion, the slow building up of a society through the transformation of individuals one by one" (Chatterjee 1983, 6)

90.   Quoted in Pickett 1953, 85.

91.   Wilson 1918 called for an international, democratically elected parliament. He acknowledged that this would be hard to achieve without democracy in each member-state, but viewed the future optimistically: "the growth of democratic sentiment in all countries has been so marked of late that it does not seem likely that this factor in success will be lacking when the League of Nations come to be formed" (114).

On the need for Christianity, see Wilson 1918, 125.

92.   Byrd 1960, 43-45; 56-59; 60-62; 84. See also Hubbard 1974, who veers toward political mysticism:

> If, instead of using the mind, instead of thinking, instead of referring everything to the standards of the intellect, we suspend this continuous argument in our head and became still, then we have a new awareness. We are aware of a sense of unity with the whole creation...(71).

Yarrow 1978 takes a more calculating stance. The Quaker policy *treats* the two sides in a conflict even-handedly, but this does not mean that Quakers fail to *see* that one side may be more in the right. Even-handedness is a technique, a means of "maintaining contact with both sides" in order to reach reconciliation (273). Yarrow acknowledges a trend away from conciliation toward confrontation of oppressive 'power structures,' and urges caution (290-293). He observes that Quakers' activity in the Vietnam War, "which involved visits to both sides, would be a better case study of American Quaker confrontation with the American government, rather than conciliation between opposing national forces" (xxvi.)

93.   Byrd 1960, 173.

94.   Jones 1971, 69-70. She continued:

> I'm glad the eyes of the world are focussed on Russia because this country is going to point the way, I believe, not to the communism that the rich capitalists are so afraid of, but to the freedom that our pseudo-democracy prattles about but doesn't practice... Bolshevism! It's nothing but a name to which people in their ignorance have attached a poisonous label. The time will come

> when workers in factories and mills in the United States who are oppressed by these rich men are going to rise up and smite them. (70-71)

95. Yarrow 1978, 52-55, 96-98, 140. Warren contended that "Christian churches were basically healthier under the hostile regime of East Germany than under the protective regime of the West" (123). He failed to call for increased hostility to Christian churches in the West as a means of restoring their political health. He also conceded that decentralized Quaker organization and Quaker beliefs were viewed with more suspicion in the East (128), but did not claim that such suspicion acted as a tonic to Quakerism there. Persecution, evidently, was healthy only for other people's churches.

96. Hershberger 1969, 191-195. Hershberger does not resist adding, "From its beginnings Quakerism was characterized by nonviolent coercionism rather than nonresistance" (202).

97. Maritain 1935, 168-170. Maritain published his book years before India achieved independence, not without violence and the threat of violence. The 1989 revolution in Czechoslovakia is an even purer example qualifying, if not utterly refuting, Maritain's understandable skepticism.

98. Maritain 1957, 69-70, 177-178.

99. Regamey 1966, 33, 55, 102-104, 125.

100. *Ibid.*, 162 n.1, 185-187, 201, 242, 252-253. Regamey warned that violence "in fact eludes the expectations and control of those who have recourse to it" (242), a point that O'Brien 1967 makes about non-violence as well (331).

Häring 1970 sought to bring the revolutionary intentions of the 1960's into Catholic political thought. His claim that nonviolent resistance is animated by "the purest form of power," namely, "that of love and truth," is Gandhian. However, he considers the attempt to assassinate Hitler during the Second World War as justified (7-9).

101. Cunningham 1910, 49-50, 216.

102. Cunningham 1915, 1, 117-123, 167-168, 181. Collins 1966, writing with full knowledge of Gandhi's career, made the same argument Cunningham did. While supporting a policy of nuclear disarmament he nonetheless opposed the philosopher Bertrand Russell's call for civil disobedience aimed at obtaining it. "[T]he rule of law in international affairs is unlikely to be ushered in by a breakdown of the rule of law in Great Britain" (336).

103. Iyer 1973, 317-328.

104. Ramsey 1988, 74.

105. Ramsey 1961, 77-78, 84, 97, 104, 111, 117.

106. Barth 1944, 5-6; Barth 1961, III, 430-433. Collins 1966 shared Barth's reservations: "It is because I cannot subscribe to absolutist dogmas about human behavior that I am not an absolute pacifist" (274). Because he supported an armed international police force he could endorse the Korean War under the auspices of the United Nations (270 ff). See also Yoder 1970, 29-40.

107. For further exposition and commentary see Yoder 1970, 46-50. Writing in 1936, Albert Einstein contended that nonviolent resistance "could not be used [effectively] against the Nazis in Germany today" (Letter to Hans Thirring, August 12, 1936, in Einstein 1960, 261). "It is no exaggeration to say that the British and, to some extent, French pacifists are largely responsible for the desperate situation today because they prevented energetic measures from being taken at a time when it would have been relatively easy to adopt them" (*Ibid.*, 273).

108. Brown 1972 reports that "the First World War transformed Gandhi into a political leader in his native land." More precisely, the War enabled him to lead by democratizing Indian politics; imperialists partially democratized Indian politics in order to strengthen Indian loyalty to Britain (123).

109. Kaunda 1980, 16, 23, 24, 31-35. Kaunda himself, he writes, was seen by English imperialists as "a rational alternative" to violent men whose "very existence often guarantees [the pacifist's] effectiveness" (52-53).

110. *Ibid.*, 37-39.

111. *Ibid.*, 41.

112. *Ibid.*, 44.

113. *Ibid.*, 58-59.

114. *Ibid.*, 60.

115. *Ibid.*, 26, 62-63. Shridharani 1934 calls a Buddhist king, Asoka, who lived in India circa 300 B.C.E., "the first politician to apply nonviolence to affairs of state." Asoka's empire "went to pieces" some time after his death, after foreign invasion (178). Kaunda added, "Whenever someone tells me that war never settles anything, I ask him to show me the *Kraal* of Shaka Zulu or introduce me to the Governor-General of Portuguese East Africa or tell me how the Third Reich is getting along" (78-79). Nakamura 1974 notes, "even Gotama Buddha himself could not do anything when invasion occurred" (176); a king must rule according to the maxim, "By killing one, makes many others live" (178). See also Walzer 1977, 331-334.

Kaunda refused to attempt to reconcile Christian love of neighbor with killing one's neighbor (a "moral absurdity" [98]) but also refused to reconcile Christian love of neighbor with effectually allowing him to be killed by another neighbor. "[I]f what I actually do in no way eases his burned, how can my action be an expression of that strong thing Jesus called love?" (88).

Kaunda also acknowledged that to preach revolution, including nonviolent revolution, as Gandhi, Martin Luther King, and he himself did, will "encourage a slave to think and act like a man;" this in turn will lead some of these 'new' men to violence (129).

116.   *Ibid.*, 101, 137, 141, 184.

117.   Iyer 1973 observes, "More books and essays have already been written about Gandhi than about any other figure in world history except the founders of the great religions" (5). What follows is an attempt not to refute any of that commentary but to add a slightly different perspective to it, a perspective informed by an interest in the nexus of religious principles, political philosophy, and statesmanship. Several outstanding book-length studies have considered Gandhi from one or more of those three 'angles.' Iyer 1973 gives a clear, comprehensive, well-proportioned depiction of Gandhi's political thought, comparing it to the doctrines of political philosophers (particularly Kant). Parekh 1989a and 1989b gives initial vent to a superficial anti-imperialism, but quickly settles into a valuable comparison of Gandhiism and traditional Hinduism. Brown 1972, 1977, and 1989 are models of intelligent political history, indispensable to the serious study of Gandhi as a statesman. On the relationship of Gandhiism to Christianity, Jones 1948 is the most thoughtful. Borman 1986 subjects Gandhi's teachings to searching philosophic critique, bringing to his task a rare combination of analytical power and familiarity with Hindu texts. Also of interest are Bondurant 1958, Varma 1965, and Roy 1984.

In studying Gandhi's writings, scholars who cannot read the original language in which they appeared, Gujarati, must exercise due caution and modesty, but reportedly need not give way to despair. Parekh 1986 faults the standard translations but adds, "more satisfactory translations will not radically change our view of him" (172).

118.   Bondurant 1958, 146. Much earlier, Doke 1909 tried to capture this paradox by writing, "Mr. Gandhi is a practical dreamer" (66). See also Tahtinen 1964, 14-15.

119.   Byrd 1960 writes,

> Experience is the final authority for Friends. Not doctrine, not scripture not ecclesiastical fiat, and not logically established theory, but direct, personal experience (5).

120. Chatterjee 1983, 3.

121. The great souled man "thinks himself worthy of great things, being worthy of them" and particularly demands great honors conferred by good men in reward for his "greatness in every virtue." (*Nicomachean Ethics*, IV, iii, 1123b-1125a, in Aristotle 1941, 995-995.

122. Gandhi 1958-1984, LVI, 172.

123. Grenier 1983 notes Gandhi's "strong sense of expediency" (67). Sharp 1979 argues that many Indians regarded nonviolent resistance as nothing more than a set of prudent tactics useful for gaining independence and not as a way of life, as Gandhi did (124). Nanda 1985 observes that "Gandhi found there was a limit to the number of patriots who could be persuaded to plunge into the non-violent fight for freedom, and open themselves to the risks of broken limbs, broken homes and broken careers" (68). For the older, more sentimental view of Gandhi as a pure 'idealist,' see Rolland 1924, 4.

124. Gandhi 1958-1984, XX, 500-501.

125. Gandhi 1958-1984, LXIII, 374; LXV, 81; Varma 1965, 124.

126. Gandhi 1958-1984, XXVII, 113, XVIII, 31, XXXII, 402. Brown 1972 calls this "the way of adamant resistance judiciously mixed with conciliation" (93). Panter-Brick 1966 calls Gandhiism "Machiavellianism redeemed," a "new Machiavellianism." Gandhi eschews Machiavellian force and fraud, denies that "effectiveness" need sacrifice "morality," and contends that truth and love are effective *forces* in politics (3-11). She notes that although nonviolent resistance "rejects violence, it does not renounce illegality." "From this midway position [Gandhiism] therefore draws a double advantage: illegality remedies for it the inadequacy of constitutional means of action, while the non-violence lays it less open to repression" (25). For a less Machiavellian and more moralistic account see Horsburgh 1968, 21-22, 28, 45.

127. Gandhi 1958-1984, LVII, 165. This prudent selectivity extended beyond events to the interpretation of Hindu scriptures; Varma 1965 sees that Gandhi's nonviolence abstracts from the overall teaching of Hinduism (129 ff.).

128. Gandhi 1958-1984, LXVIII 425.

> Sages of old mortified the flesh so that the spirit within might be set free, so that their trained bodies might be proof against any injury that might be inflicted on them by tyrants seeking to impose their will on them. And if India wants to revive her ancient wisdom and to avoid the errors of Europe, if India wishes to see the Kingdom

of God established on earth instead of that of Satan which has enveloped Europe, then I would urge her sons and daughters not to be deceived by fine phrases, the terrible subtleties that hedge us in, the fears of suffering that India may have to undergo, but to see what is happening today in Europe and from it understand that we must go through the suffering even as Europe has gone through, but not the process of making others suffer (XVII, 489).

129. Gandhi VII, 442; XXIII, 24. Bennett 1958 cautions that the Christian political pacifist "usually fails to take account of the special responsibilities of government as a trustee for a nation which is not pacifist in convictions and therefore incapable of following a pacifist strategy consistently" (169). Childress 1971 acknowledges that the disinclination of nonviolent resisters to anti-social lawbreaking may not stop others, who are so inclined, from leaving restraints behind after witnessing the nonviolent (234-235, 242). Clearly, Gandhi recognized these problems.

Where Gandhi's teaching has been more tellingly questioned is in its claim to practice politically effective suffering. Varma 1975 regards the "vast sea of Indian population," Indians' "numerical strength," as decisive in the struggle against Britain. "Hence I feel skeptical of the wonderful potency attributed to suffering by Gandhi" (219).

Brown 1972 attributes Gandhi's successes primarily to his "ability to make ordinary people feel that he appreciated and cared about their particular problems" (68) and thus to build an effective political organization among "people who had probably never heard a political speech before" (93). No other political figure in India — surely none of the British, and also none of the self-styled Marxists — could command such broad, local support (248-2721). Brown also cites the disadvantages of Gandhi's strategy, mostly with respect to lack of unity or factionalism (192, 240-241, 346-348).

130. For comments on Gandhi's patience, see Rolland 1924, 61-65, and Iyer 1973, 212. The psychologist Erik Erikson deplores Gandhi's celibacy as a "barrier" between Gandhi and "today's and tomorrow's fighters for peace;" Erikson calls for an "enlightened eroticism" — whatever that may be (Erikson 1969, 100). Bondurant 1958 nearly begins with the assurance that "it is not necessary to subscribe to the asceticism so characteristic of Gandhi nor to his religious notions in order to understand and to value the central contribution of his technique of non-violent action" (vi). See also Parekh 1989b, 209-210. The funniest response was that of birth control advocate Margaret Sanger, who, upon being told by Gandhi of the superiority of self-control to birth control, insisted that sexual activity is a "spiritual need" (Gandhi 1958-1984, LXII, 159). For a more sympathetic view see Huxley 1937, 365.

131. Gandhi 1958-1984, I, 165-166; Iyer 1973, 33. Gandhi associated materialism with flesh-eating, capitalist accumulation, and war, vegetarianism with spirituality and peace; he claimed that the Book of Isaiah's vision of the lion dwelling with the lamb presupposed universal vegetarianism (II, 290 ff.). Gandhi's claims concerning health could lead him to beliefs not only false but peculiar: "As the Europeans indulge in sensual pleasures more than the Colored peoples, their lives are shorter" (IV, 419); "vaccination is a filthy remedy...one of the poisonous superstitions of our time" (XII, 111). See also the stricture of Thomas Jefferson: "I fancy it must be the quantity of animal food eaten by the English which renders their character insusceptible of civilization" (Letter to John Adams, September 25, 1785, in Cappon 1959, 70).

132. Gandhi 1958-1984, XXX, 461.

133. Gandhi 1958-1984, LXVII, 195-196.

134. *Ibid.*, 196. For commentary see Horsburgh 1968, 41; Borman 1986, 30-31, 41-49; Parekh 1989a, 178-182. Edwardes 1986 reports that Hindu tradition teaches that sexual abstinence (for example) causes the male body to assimilate its own semen, producing energy (184-185). One social consequence of Gandhian asceticism would have been a campaign against pornography (see Gandhi 1958-1984, XLIII, 20).

135. See Roy 1984, 41.

136. See for example Holmes 1953, who described the "sense of awe" that seized Gandhi's audiences, a present of "more than royalty" (42). That one need not share Holmes' (or Gandhi's) religious convictions to feel this authority may be seen in the remarks of Friedrich Nietzsche, who writes, "Wherever on earth the religious neurosis has appeared we find it tied to three dangerous demands: solitude, fasting, sexual abstinence." Men of secular power have bowed before the saint, sensing "the superior force" of the saint's conquest and fearing it (*Beyond Good and Evil*, III, xlvii, Nietzsche 1968, 251).

137. Gandhi 1958-1984, XXVII, 439; Iyer 1973, 35. Edwardes 1986 calls Gandhi's "idealization of poverty and the poor" extremely damaging to India in the long run. If he means that Gandhiism discouraged the development of commerce, he may be right, inasmuch as commerce requires a moderated desire for material goods. If he means that Gandhiism was unrealistic about he effects of poverty, he is wrong. It is true that Gandhi taught that "the economic crisis would be relieved if people love poverty" (XLVIII, 406), but poverty is not famine.

138. Shridharani 1939 perceptively observes that "Gandhi stands in sharp contrast with those who regard struggle as the fundamental law of creation" (252). See also Strauss 1953, 64-66.

139. Gandhi 1958-1984, XIV, 63; LXI, 291. See also Tähtinen 1964, 60-61; Puri 1987, 78.

140. Gandhi 1958-1984, XXVIII, 21; XXXI, 291-292. Gandhi goes so far as to claim that tigers, wolves, snakes, and even germs can be overcome by fearlessness (XXVIII, 48; LXI, 293).

141. Gandhi 1958-1984, LXI, 265. See also LXI, 17-19.

142. Gandhi 1958-1984, X, 50-52. XV, 2. Sharp 1979 too rigidly separates "moralistic" and "political" acts when he discusses Gandhi's concept of courage (99-106, 123).

143. Gandhi argues that

> Independence by non-violent means can therefore never mean an interval of chaos and anarchy. Independence by non-violence must be a progressively peaceful revolution such that the transference of power from a closed corporation to the people's representatives will be as natural as the dropping of a fully ripe fruit from a well-nurtured tree. (Gandhi 1958-1984, XXIII, 27).

144. Gandhi 1958-1984, I, 33; VIII, 272; LXII, 29-30. Satyagraha contrasts with duragraha or hate-force; *duragraha* prevents progress, trapping its practitioners in a cycle of retaliation. In Judeo-Christian terms *duragraha* is pagan-cyclical; in Hindu terms *duragraha* prevents the soul from escaping the wheel of temporal existence, of birth, death, and rebirth (XIV, 64). This notwithstanding, military resistance is far preferable to cowardice:

> ...military training is intended for those who do not believe in satyagraha. That the whole of India will ever accept satyagraha is beyond my imagination. A cowardly refusal to defend the nation, or the weak, is ever to be shunned (XIV, 65).

One who "take[s] part in war" may "yet whole-heartedly try to free himself, his nation, and the world from war" (XXIX, 279). "If a man remains unconcerned with defeat or victory, knowing that they are a part of life, he commits no sin in fighting;" nor does he earn any merit (XXXII, 116-117). See also XIV, 438, 475 on the unreadiness of the Indians (in 1918) for full practice of nonviolent resistance; for Gandhi's acceptance of violent resistance in such imperfect circumstances, see XVIII, 132, XXVII, 51-52, XXXVIII, 271; LXI, 266.

145. Gandhi 1958-1984, XXVI, 489; LXIII, 319, XXIX, 95; LXXXIV, 89. Gandhi argues that violence fails to get to the roots of injustice:

> If I kill a man who obstructs me, I may experience a sense of false security. But the security will be short-lived. For I shall not have dealt with the root cause. In

> due course other men will surely rise to obstruct me. My business therefore is not to kill the man or men who obstruct me but to discover the cause that impels them to obstruct me and deal with it. (XLV, 229)

See also Sharp 1979, 128; Chatterjee 1983, 76.

146. "The central fact of Hinduism...is cow-protection" because the cow symbolizes "the entire sub-human world" (Gandhi 1958-1984, XXI, 248-249). Gandhi said he would accept being eaten by a crocodile: "You see, our life does not finish with the death of our body," and it is better to die nonviolently than to live in fear or anger − to live 'on the wheel' (XXIII, 108). Plant life also must not be destroyed; fruits and vegetables may be eaten, (after preserving the seeds?), but not the whole plants (XLI, 210). Gandhi recognized the practical disadvantage of nonviolence towards some animals:

> Monkeys are a very intelligent species. They understand us immediately. I had seen in Vrindavan that in an Indian locality they would fearlessly continue to destroy things, while in the area occupied by Europeans there is no trace of monkeys because they are afraid that they would get a beating if they went there (XXXVII, 33).

Tähtinen 1964 correctly claims that "the crucial difference between supporters of ahimsa and its critics is the limit to which ahimsa is extended." His example is ill-conceived, however. "If ahimsa were not practiced in the family circle, it would be fatal to the child" (164). This is true only so long as it is recognized that a child who took advantage of parental ahimsa might be fatal to itself, its siblings, or even its parents.

147. Gandhi 1958-1984, LIX, 89; LXI, 291; Iyer 1973, 204.

148. Gandhi 1958-1984, IV, 418.

149. Gandhi 1958-1984, LXII, 28-29, Varma 1965, 195-214.

150. See Tähtinen 1964, 17, 23; Iyer 1973, 184; Lanza del Vasto 1974, 13. Thomas 1969 is therefore wrong to identify ahimsa with Christian love, agape, (208), which more nearly resembles satyagraha.

151. Gandhi 1958-1984, XIII, 519; XVIII, 133; XXVI, 141; XLVIII, 407; Rolland 1924, 12, 19, 21; Lasserre 1962, 213-215; Tähtinen 1964, 137; Horsburgh 1968, 128-130, 134; Sharp 1979, 43.

152. "Nonviolence is a dormant state," Gandhi wrote. "In the waking state, it is love" (Gandhi 1958-1984, XIII, 521).

153. Chatterjee 1983, 89, 129. Nanda 1985 contends:

One can be an atheist or agnostic, and still practice satyagraha. But it is easier for men of religion to accept the assumptions on which satyagraha rests: that it is worthwhile fighting, and even dying, for causes which transcend one's personal interests, that the body perishes, but the soul lives, that no oppressor can crush the imperishable spirit of man, that every human being, however wicked he may appear to be, has a hidden nobility, a 'divine spark' which can be ignited (73).

154. Gandhi 1958-1984, VIII, 61; LXII, 28; Datta 1961, 76-84; Horsburgh 1968, 56; Iyer 1973, 122; Parekh 1989b, 147-148. Childress 1971 writes, "the appropriate criteria for evaluating civil disobedience coincide to a great extent with traditional just war criteria such as good cause, good motives and intentions, exhaustion of normal procedures for resolving disputes, reasonable prospect of success, due proportion between probable good and bad consequences, and right means" (204).

Childress believes that he disagrees with Gandhi on this point, attributing to Gandhi the conviction that all nonviolent acts are good in principle (202). It is more likely that Gandhi would refuse to classify as genuinely nonviolent the noninjurious acts Childress classifies as nonviolent but unjust − i.e., the abuse of police officers by demonstrators, impatient or ill-considered demonstrations, etc.

155. Gandhi 1958-1984, LXVIII, 188; Andrews 1930, 347; Bondurant 1958, 9. Shridharani 1939 finds four similarities between nonviolent resistance and war: both assume that a mass action "precipitating and emotional crisis" is necessary for "certain radical social changes" both are *direct* actions, usually both offensive and defensive; both require organization, discipline, and strategy; both associate willingness to suffer or to risk suffering with the acquisition of political authority (278-283). For a list and classification of various kinds of force human beings exert upon each other − "individual" and "collective," "coercive" and "non-coercive," and (among the coercive) "injurious" and "non-injurious," see Cadoux 1940, 15 ff.

Gandhi's "moral equivalent of war" differs noticeably from that proposed in William James' essay of the same title (in James 1967). James conceives of "moral" war as socially-directed work aimed at the conquest of nature and of various social disorders. His project is modern-scientific, not spiritual.

156. Sharp 1979, 173. Gandhi called nonviolent resistance "the only course law-abiding and peaceful men can adopt without doing violence to their conscience" (Gandhi 1958-1984, VII, 211).

157. Gandhi 1958-1984, XIX, 245.

158. Parekh 1989b, 143. See also Erikson 1969, who translates satyagraha with the metaphor "the leverage of truth" (198) — recalling Gandhi's interest in *jiu-jitsu*. And see Horsburgh 1968, 35, 57-58, 123-124.

159. Bondurant 1958, 193. Bondurant distinguishes Gandhi's teaching from modern historicism, as seen in Hegel and Marx, because Gandhiism is not deterministic and is therefore insistently moral, not scientific or pseudoscientific (192). As Chatterjee 1983 good-humoredly notes, "Ghandi shocks his Western readers by often pointing out the *irrelevance* of history" (6). Iyer 1973 writes:

> Gandhi's way of countering the doctrine that the end justifies the means was by asserting not merely that unworthy mean could belittle a great end but also that evil means can never, as a matter of principle, lead to good ends.... His reason for believing this to be wholly and always true was his metaphysical conviction that the whole world is governed by the law of karma, that there is a moral order (*rta*) at the heart of the cosmos. (368)

Iyer argues that to suppose the opposite, that a 'lesser evil' can lead to a 'greater good,' is "no less non-empirical" than Gandhi's claim (368-369). However, one must observe that it is common-sensical to suppose so, whatever 'empiricism' may tell us.

160. Gandhi 1958-1984, LXIII, 320; Tähtinen 1964, 49. The conclusion of Gandhi's sentence — that each succeeding war will outdo the preceding one in ferocity — does not follow logically. Gandhi also argues, "If Love was not the law of life, life would not have persisted in the midst of death" (320-321). It suffices to observe "Love" need not be *the* law of life — and surely not the kind of love Gandhi means — for life to persist. Varma 1965 sees that Gandhi's teaching leads to a moral version of the law of the conservation of energy: "Nothing good is ever lost in a spiritual universe" (65-66). See also *Ibid.*, 58-60. See Iyer 1973, 72-78 on the importance of vows in Gandhi's universe.

161. Varma 1965 writes,

> ...while the Greek philosophers put the primacy of the *polis* and the Roman thinkers stressed the *civitas* as the methodological postulates of their inquires in social and political realms, Gandhi started with the Atman [soul] — man as a subjective entity, and hence in spite of the presence of conflict dreamt of eventual cosmopolitanism and internationalism (68).

See Iyer 1973, 114-116 for the social character of this individualism.

162. Gandhi 1958-1984, XLVIII 405; LV, 121; LXIII, 262, Erikson 1962, 412; Iyer 1973, 231-232. Parekh 1989a offers some illuminating remarks about Gandhi's recasting of the genre of autobiography,

hitherto attempted only in the individualistic West; Gandhi's new kind of autobiography called attention to Gandhi's life *as* a series of experiments with (radically non-individual) truth (259-263). See also Borman 1986, 61-62.

163.   Gandhi 1958-1984, XLIX, 157; Richards 1982, 1.

164.   Gandhi 1958-1984, IV, 94, 408; LVI, 171; LXIV, 422; Varma 1965, 40-50; Horsburgh 1968, 33; Parekh 1989b, 72-78. Datta 1961 argues that Gandhi was closer to conceiving of God as a person than as the "Indeterminate Absolute" of the more intellectual forms of Hinduism (7, 21-24) but this is by no means clear from Gandhi's writings. Borman 1986 cites another difficulty; the problem of evil. If God creates evil within man in order to induce man to practice virtues, the universal exercise of virtue would then cancel the meaning of all creation (150). "Without Truth life is meaningless, and with Truth life is unnecessary" (9-10). It may be, however, that the Hindu quest for Nirvana or God is precisely to make life and its cyclical motions "unnecessary" − that is, to put an end to God's creation and return to God.

165.   Parekh 1989b, 193. See also Iyer 1973, 370.

166.   As does Nietzsche's Zarathustra; see Dannhauser 1974, 247. See also Varma 1965, 5.

167.   Gandhi 1958-1984, IV, 122; VIII, 217, 241; X, 139; XXXII, 256, XLI, 88; Gollancz 1959, 178; Varma 1965, 77; Iyer 1973, 269.

168.   Gandhi 1958-1984, XLVIII, 369.

169.   Borman 1986, 135. Iyer 1973 notes that Gandhi tended "to confuse intentions with consequences" and therefore made "excessive claims for the harmlessness of nonviolent cooperation" (252-283) as well as formidable claims for the success of nonviolent resistance − which, if it "does not make a direct appeal to the soul of the oppressor," could at least "arouse public opinion." Gandhi observed that the crucified Jesus triumphantly inspired "hundreds of Christians" to nonviolence (Gandhi 1958-1984, XLVIII, 278). Iyer goes on to observe that even if nonviolence fails to arouse public opinion, "it could at least purify the sufferer," bringing him (now in Gandhi's words) a joy that "surpasses all other joys" (Iyer 1973, 290).

170.   Roy 1984, 68.

171.   Gandhi 1958-1984, XXXIX, 20-21. Aristotle does not believe that the good man could make the world his friend in the true sense (*Nicomachean Ethics*, VIII, iii, 1156b, in Aristotle 1941, 1061). For Socrates' career of salutary annoyance and public reticence, see *Apology* 30-33 (Plato 1937, I, 415-416).

172. Gandhi 1958-1984, XIV, 53; 298; Iyer 1973, 383. For the place of patriotism as one component of Gandhi's religion, see Gandhi 1958-1984, IX, 179; for an optimistic account of the feasibility of universal adherence to Gandhiian principles, see *Ibid.*, XVII, 154.

173. "[T]he truth seems to have been important in ancient Hindu thought, but primarily for what the truth can do for one, particularly with respect to liberation from the unwelcome cycles of rebirth." Knowledge thus "tends to be regarded as having magical properties" (Anastaplo 1985, 274). See also Schlegel 1849, 467-481. Compare Nietzsche, *Beyond Good and Evil*, sections 9, 229, 230 (Nietzsche 1968, 206, 348-352). For a similar teaching operating within or perhaps playing off the Christian tradition see Boehme 1969, II, 256-258.

174. Gandhi 1958-1984, XVIII, 25, 132; XXIX 6, LXVIII, 300. See also Childress 1971, 176-180 for exposition and some reservations.

175. Gandhi 1958-1984, LV, 142. See also LXI, 266.

176. Gandhi 1958-1984, LXVI, 105. Andrews 1930 reported that "Little birds and squirrels and other tiny animals, which we call 'wild' in the West, are so tame in India that they never fear at all the presence of mankind." (33)

177. Gandhi 1958-1984, XIV, 64.

178. Gandhi 1958-1984, LXVIII, 204-205, 277; XXXVII, 362. Gandhi did not hesitate to assert that Hitler, despite his extremism ("the tyrants of old never went so mad as Hitler seems to have done," and "he is doing it with religious zeal" [LXVIII, 138]), could be stopped by nonviolent resistance, either by its effect on Hitler's own soul or by its effect on the Germans who could overthrow him (LXVIII, 277). Further, if Great Britain, the United States, and France would disarm, he wrote in April 1939, "Peace will reign in the universe" as the German and Italian rulers would "dare not go to war," fearing to alienate their people (LXIX, 178). Earlier, during the 1938 Italian invasion of Abyssinia, Gandhi claimed that "the moral force" of British renunciation of imperialism and adoption of satyagrahic justice "would stagger Italy into willing surrender of her designs" (LXII, 29). A year earlier still, Adolf Hitler advised Britain's Lord Halifax

> All you have to do is shoot Gandhi: if necessary shoot some more Congress [Party] leaders. You will be surprised how quickly the trouble will die down. (Harries 1986, 44).

Gandhi anticipated this possibility, if not with respect to Hitler then with respect to the Japanese. In April 1942, considering the possibility of a Japanese invasion of India, Gandhi wrote:

> It is conceivable that they will exterminate all resisters. The underlying belief in such non-violent resistance is that the aggressor will, in time, be mentally and physically tired of killing non-violent resisters.

If extermination nonetheless occurs, a moral victory will obtain; nonviolent resisters "will have won the day inasmuch as they will have preferred extermination to submission" (LXXVI, 5). On Hitler, see Sampson 1965, 175, and Douglass 1968, 91, both of whom endorse Gandhi's views.

179. Mr. Pyarelal quoted in Douglass 1983, 1. Douglass enthusiastically agrees, claiming that "you can bring the whole world to your feet" by using the Gandhian "law" because "there is a loving, caring will at the center of reality which is as objective and concrete as a physical law" (2). See also Gregg 1966, 272-273. For a descriptive account see Borman 1986, 25, 30, 95-110.

180. On the potential of the many who are poor, Gandhi wrote: No king can remain in power if he sets himself against the people. I have taken it as the chief mission of my life to prove this (XIV, 328-329). See also XVII, 483; XXIII, 9; Douglass 1968, 12-13. As for women, "If they would realize the nobility of nonviolence, they would not consent to be called the weaker sex" (XLVIII, 407).

Gandhi admitted that Jews were in serious danger from Hitler, correctly predicting in 1938 that "the calculated violence of Hitler may even result in a general massacre of the Jews" in the event of war. However, "for the godfearing, death has no terror," and "no Jew need feel helpless if he takes the nonviolent way." Gandhi conceded that Jews "have not been actively violent in their own persons" against the Nazis, but "they called down upon the Germans the curses of mankind, and they wanted America and England to fight Germany on their behalf;" they had not attempted true nonviolent resistance (LXVIII, 139, 202-204).

181. Gandhi 1958-1984, LXI, 266.

182. Ingram 1939 writes that the Scandinavian nations "have no potential influence, their moral influence counts for little, precisely because they have no military forces of any consequence behind them" (73). A Marxist-Leninist, Ingram imagined that a pacifist order would occur after socialist economies became widespread (89).

183. Field 1945, 27-30.

184. Brock 1972 cites the destruction of Tolstoyan nonresistant by Stalin (457 ff.).

185. Sharp 1979, 15. Sharp has since recanted (see above, footnote #2), claiming that Poland and Czechoslovakian 'totalitarians' were

654

overthrown by nonviolent resistants. But those 'totalitarians' were not genuinely 'totalitarian' at all, permitting an independent Catholic Church in Poland and an anti-Soviet underground in Czechoslovakia.

186. Aron 1966, 631.

187. Boserup and Mack 1975, 90, 130-138.

188. Smoke 1987, 53.

189. Platt 1981, 273.

190. Doke 1909, 41. Osgood and Tucker 1967 observe "It is only by denying, whether implicitly or explicitly, the ends men have sought through war, or by minimizing the significance of the ends that have often prompted men to war, that proponents of nonviolence can largely ignore the supreme difficulties in replacing war with nonviolent methods of conflict resolution" (332).

191. Gandhi 1958-1984, XXXIII, 93.

192. "[W]hen Indians were spinning and weaving their own cotton, they were well off and happy," Gandhi contended. "From the day on which they attempted to sell their cotton to Lancashire, they have become increasingly lazy and poor" (XXIII, 239).

193. Gandhi contended that mass violence originated not in the masses but in intellectual elites who manipulate the masses (Sharp 1974, 94). See also Huxley 1937, 349 and Mashruwala 1946, 42-43.

194. Gandhi 1958-1984, XXVIII, 190; XXXV, 455; LIX, 42; Morris-Jones 1960, 28; Iyer 1973, 356.

195. Gandhi 1958-1984, XIII, 219; XXVIII, 22-23; Andrews 1930, 118-120, 130; Parekh 1989b, 57-59. Gandhi wrote:

Swadeshi [self-sufficiency] is the only doctrine consistent with the law of humility and love.... My patriotism is both exclusive and inclusive. It is exclusive in the sense that in all humility I confine my attention to the land of my birth, but it is inclusive in the sense that my service is not of a competitive or antagonistic nature (XIII, 224).

196. Xenophon 1970.

197. Gandhi 1958-1984, XIX, 278; XXVIII, 188-189, XLVIII, 229; LXXXVII, 326; Rolland 1924, 57; Erikson 1969, 11-12. It is now widely understood that technology produces more jobs than it eliminates; technology does increase wealth, but not only for the few. Gandhi's error is serious but not fatal, inasmuch as he would still reject

the commercial economy that has generated technological advances. Einstein 1960 rejects Gandhi's anti-technological stance as "mistaken" because "machine production... is here to stay and must be accepted" (261).

198.   Gandhi 1958-1984, XLVIII, 441.

199.   Gandhi 1958-1984, LIX, 318-319. Gandhi approved of state ownership only as a last resort in extreme and particular circumstances, not as an economic regime. "We know of so many cases where men have adopted trusteeship, but none where the State has really lived for the poor" (319).

200.   Gandhi 1958-1984, LIX, 264. On the need for "the guiding influence of...institutions" see XIII, 313; on the limitations of government institutions see LXI, 7, where Gandhi rejects recourse to government action with respect to the seduction of students by teachers. Gandhi differed from Tolstoy in his refusal to demonize and reject government altogether, although Brock 1972 exaggerates in saying that Gandhi had a "*much* more positive attitude toward the state and the nation" than did Tolstoy (468, emphasis added). Tolstoy's extra measure of individualism may stem from his Christian roots.

201.   Osgood and Tucker 1967, 320. To these authors, pacifism fails to be political because those who refuse the means cannot ensure the ends of political life (325-331).

202.   Gandhi 1958-1984, XIII, 221, 234; XVIII, 196; XLIII, 131. In the latter passage Gandhi employs a judicious ambiguity, saying that "Jesus's whole preaching and practice *point* unmistakably to non-cooperation" (emphasis added). See also Doke 1909, 90; Varma 1965, 85-94; Iyer 1973, 40-50, 60-61. Iyer criticizes Gandhi for the "importation of the religious spirit...into Indian politics," which, in Iyer's judgment, increased fanaticism despite Gandhi's own respect for all religions. "In our century we can see all too clearly how easily and often the best becomes the enemy of the good" (378-379).

203.   Gandhi 1958-1984, XXIV, 314.

204.   In violent conflict,

> The sword makes men equal. After fighting with one another like so many bulls, till they all get exhausted, the opponents salute each other and become friends. Anyone who shows weakness will humiliate himself. (XVII, 105).

In satyagrahic conflict, one side wins without pride in its own heart or humiliation in the heart of the adversary, because "ascendancy is accepted not out of fear but out of love, and so both become equals" (XVII, 105). It is not clear why love should entail a conviction of equality among lovers. See also Varma 1965, 231-235; Iyer 1973, 90-92; Parekh 1989b, 199. Parekh claims that Gandhi believed the human mind itself to be "an essentially plural, federal and non-hierarchical structure of autonomous and interacting faculties, each with its own distinctive mode of operation and way of knowing," with the rational faculty laying down "the minimum, not the maximum" in terms of standards of conduct (*Ibid.*, 74). This may or may not be an imposition of late-twentieth-century epistemology upon Gandhi.

205. On equality before the law, see Gandhi 1958-1984, LXIII, 262. Economic quality should be governed by the slogan, "Distribution can be equalized when production is localized" (XLVIII, 165, 167).

206. Gandhi 1958-1984, XVII, 44; Rolland 1924, 46; Varma 1965, 172-175. Gandhi opposed Untouchability as an illegitimate addition to the caste system, nor did he admire the elaborate system of sub-castes within each of the four original castes. *The Bhagavad Gita* confirms Gandhi's view (Anonymous 1972, XVIII:41-44, 118-119); for discussion see Anastaplo 1985, 269-271. Nehru claimed that Gandhi called the attack on Untouchability a surreptitious attack on the caste system as a whole (Nanda 1985, 26), but this may be Nehru's own 'twist.'

207. Gandhi 1958-1984, XIII, 91-95, 227-232; Varma 1965, 295, 296.

> The doctrine of satyagraha is not new; it is merely an extension of the rule of domestic life to the political. Family disputes and differences are generally settled according to the law of love. (XVIII, 153)

For the contrast between Gandhi's commune-ism founded upon "metaphysical idealism" and Lenin's communism founded upon dialectical materialism, see *Ibid.*, 327-331. For a Gandhian communalism adopted to Christian circumstances, see Doke 1965, 11, 18-29.

Gandhi thus attempted to meet the kind of criticism made by Boserup and Mack 1975, and who criticize what they call the "positive" conception of nonviolent resistance as distinguished from the "pragmatic" conception. "Pragmatic" nonviolence confines resistance to usefulness: nonviolence is a method, "an instrument of power." "Positive" nonviolence seeks "the overriding unity of the contenders" to political power, requiring the "complete reorientation of the public's view of the opponents" and tends to dissolve the polarization that is "the perquisite for the collective actions against the opponent" (13-23).

> It is hard to escape the impression that wherever positive means (conversion, etc.) are recommended in the literature, the author is in fact thinking of...isolated pairs of individuals and ignoring the social and psychological context. It seems that the conversion of groups is never considered in the literature...(28)

In established groups, nonviolent resistants inevitably will be regarded with suspicion by some group members (32), undermining the unity upon which success will depend.

Gandhi might reply that his ashrams, founded upon vows not birth, will establish themselves within existing villages and earn the villagers' trust before undertaking nonviolent resistance against some evil. Further, Gandhi's own practice refutes the contention that 'positive' nonviolent resistance cannot polarize a community for the purpose of collective action. The question for nonviolent resistants will always be 'Can you convert *enough* people to reach "critical mass," (so to speak)?' And, 'Is it likely that you will reach "critical mass" throughout the world and forever?'

208.   Gandhi 1958-1984, XXXIV, 314.   Gandhi associated India's "republican" character with its ability to survive "every shock hitherto delivered" (XIII, 221) with its ability to assimilate waves of conquerors. Here again, he offered no definitions or explanations. Diwaker n.d. reports that "democracies and republics, like that of the Vrijis at the time of the Buddha (sixth century B.C.) were working in India centuries before Christ and probably some of them were earlier than the Greek republics" (41). According to Diwaker, ancient Indian democracies formally resembled those of Greece, with "full and frequent assemblies" (44). But minorities in these democracies enjoyed freedom "to convert the majority to their own view by every peaceful and moral means but never by violence and forces open or implied" (43). Gandhi could also make it seem that he admired Western political traditions, as in his conversation with the prominent English political philosophy scholar Ernest Barker, who came away with the impression that Gandhi mixed "a great Indian tradition of devout and philosophic religion" with "the Western tradition of civil and political liberty in the life of the community" (Barker 1949, 61). Gandhi would appeal to the tradition of whomever he met, in the apparently sincere belief that each tradition was in some sense true. This practice also had rhetorical advantages that Gandhi could not have overlooked.

209.   Gandhi 1958-1984, 388, 389. Notice that in discussing nonviolence as a unifying governmental spirit Gandhi compares it to the law of gravity, not to the 'revolutionary' and explosive '$E=MC^2$' of Einstein.

210.   *Ibid.*, 389-390.

211.   Gandhi 1958-1984, LXIX, 122-123; LXXII, 29, 60; LXXII, 26-27; LXXVIII, 2. See also Mashruwala 1946, 5-6; Varma 1965, 257; Santhanam n.d. 47-48; Roy 1984, 74-75. For a similar if somewhat less harshly critical view, see Lanza del Vasto 1974, 57. Gandhi mistakenly predicted that General Douglas MacArthur's forceful imposition of commercial republicanism upon Japan, including the labeling of some Japanese as "war criminals," would provoke rebellion (LXXXII, 151).

212. Gandhi quoted in Andrews 1930, 144. Rolland 1924 reports that
      Gandhi "considers 'mobocracy' the greatest danger that menaces
      India" (95).

213. Gandhi 1958-1984, XC, 510.

214. Gandhi 1958-1984, XLVII, 91.

215. Gandhi 1938-1984, XLV, 329; XLVII, 92. See also Tewari n.d., 21-29;
      Parekh 1989b, 113-116, 120-123. The latter makes the interesting
      point that Gandhi regarded cooperation, not consent, as "the basis of
      the state" (123). 'Consent' was too purely verbal for Gandhi, whose
      techniques of nonviolent resistance largely consisted of actions.
      Varma 1965 contrasts Jeffersonian "popular sovereignty" with
      Gandhi's insistence on "moral authority...obtained through the
      adherence to spiritual norms and values" (265), ignoring Jefferson's
      understanding of consent as founded upon God-endowed unalienable
      rights. Jefferson may rely more upon nature as intercessary between
      God and consenting human beings, but "moral authority" is surely
      upheld. Varma is, however, correct to write that "Gandhi would be
      thoroughly opposed to the Hegelian and Austinian concepts of
      sovereignty and law" (277).

      Iyer 1973 reports Gandhi's concern that nonviolent resistance will be
      needed in republican governments when good men fail in their efforts
      to employ constitutional procedures (320); Gandhi expressed concern
      that such actions might undermine the rule of law in such republics
      (325). Childress 1971 tries to work out principles and practices
      whereby this inconvenience might be avoided (109-110, 114-127, 140-
      144. 211-219). Childress particularly objects to any civil disobedience
      that would directly impede democratic processes themselves.

216. Andrews 1930 writes that Gandhi's "conservative orthodoxy...has been
      his strength with the masses of common people" who "have been able
      to understand him through this avenue of familiar Hindu Scriptures"
      (60). Unlike so many Indians educated in English schools, Gandhi "is
      not *déraciné*" (61). See also Shridharani 1939, 166; Varma 1965, 80.

217. Bondurant 1958, 105, 111-114. Bondurant singles out the social
      character of Gandhi's enterprise as its least traditionally Hindu
      element. Parekh 1989b goes further: "Gandhi redefined almost every
      major category of philosophic Hinduism in activist, social and worldly
      terms" without reducing the religion to "mere social service or
      morality" (109). When accused by traditionalist Hindus "of being a
      crypto-Christian trying to Christianize Hinduism" Gandhi thought it
      wise to backtrack;" this was "a tactical retreat not a change of mind"
      (Parekh 1989a, 23). Parekh ascribes the conflict to Gandhi's dual task
      of defending Hindu tradition (inculcating self-respect in people shaken
      by British imperialism) and of criticizing and reforming Hinduism as it
      existed in his lifetime (32).

218. Doke 1909, 89; Iyer 1973, 135. Doke 1909 describes nonviolent resistance as

> ...inherent in Indian philosophy. In old time, it was called 'to sit *dhurana* [in mourning].' Sometimes a whole community would adopt this method toward their Prince (83).

Bondurant 1958 reports, however, that Gandhi metamorphosed this traditional act, making it more thoroughly nonviolent by eschewing vengefulness (118-119).

219. "I decline to be bound by any interpretation [of Hindu scriptures], however learned it may be, if it is repugnant to reason or moral sense" (Gandhi 1958-1984, XXI, 246). This evidently contradicts Gandhi's assertion of the priority of revelation over reason. Traditional Hinduism suspects reasoners of atheism (Anonymous 1882, 31). See also Bondurant 1958, 121. Parekh 1989b rightly insists that for Gandhi both reason and moral sense are practical, confirmed by experience, and hence "scientific" (85-96).

220. Gandhi 1958-1984, XXI, 515; XLIX, III; Bondurant 1958, 117-118.

221. See Chatterjee 1983, 8 and Parekh 1989b, 40. Characteristically modern Western forms of synthetic epistemology require prior 'warfare' — theses and antitheses clashing, often with considerable *Sturm und Drang*, as in Hegel and Marx. Gandhi's practice resembles their theorizing, complete with a quite Marxian sketchiness about the promised eschaton, but he holds back from personal violence for himself and his fellow satyagrahis, a self-denial nowhere to be found in modern philosophers.

222. Gandhi 1958-1984, XIV, 477; XXV, 85-96; Iyer 1973, 100-109, Puri 1987, 59.

223. The *Laws of Manu* describe the King as "a great deity in human form" (Anonymous 1882, VII, 217). The King rules through fear of punishment according to the law.

> If the King did not, without tiring, inflict punishment upon those worthy to be punished, the stronger would roast the weaker, like fish on a spit.... The whole world is kept in order through punishment, for a guiltless man is hard to find; through fear the whole world yields the enjoyments [that it owes]...provided that he who inflicts [punishment] discerns well. (VII, 219-220).

"A king who is both sharp and gentle is highly respected" (VII, 238). See also Parekh 1989b, 112.

224. Gandhi 1958-1984, V, 49, XXV, 168, LXIV, 20; LXXI, 179, Doke 1909, 7; Varma 1965, 79 (including footnote 1 where, significantly, Varma cites John Locke); Parekh 1989b, 83. Datta 1961 claims that India had long seen "a subtle unity beneath her apparent diversity" of religious sects, "a wonderful unity of moral outlook" (4-7).

225. *Koran*, III:1-12. See also Averroes 1973, 170, 175. The *Koran* is both 'good news' (for believers) and a warning (to unbelievers) [XLI:1-5].

226. *Koran* II, 108-109, 213; III, 110-115; V, 51.

227. *Koran* VIII, 38-43; IX, 122-128.

228. *Koran* II, 190-193; XVII, 33; XXIII, 95-99; XLI, 33-36; XLII, 36-43; LX, 7-9.

229. IV, 95; VIII, 12-18.

230. See for example Averroes 1974, I, 25.10-26.30; I, 28-32.30; II, 60.20-65.5; Averroes 1977a, 51; Averroes 1977, 66, 70, 74-77; Alfarabi 1969, iii; V, 58; X, 66-67; Alfarabi 1973a, 41; Alfarabi 1973b, 67-78.

231. Gandhi 1958-1984, XIII, 518 (emphasis added). This was not always his view. In 1905 he ascribed Islam's strength in India to its rejection of caste and "the power of the sword" (IV, 376).

232. Gandhi 1958-1984, XVII, 46; Andrews 1930, 53-64.

233. Brown 1977, 145-148; Bondurant 1958, 131, 141.

234. Gandhi 1958-1984, XXV, 19; LXXXVII, 424. His pointed question to another socialist deserves repeating, also: "How do you seek to oppose the 'introduction of religious issues into politics' if you regulate and control all religious endowments?" (LVIII, 37).

235. Gandhi 1958-1984, LVIII, 36.

236. *Ibid.*, 36-37.

237. Gandhi 1958-1984, XXV, 531; XXXVIII, 380; XLVIII, 334, 429; LVIII, 37; LXVIII, 112-114; LXXXIII, 27; LXXXV, 367. Gregg 1966 rejected any 'popular front' collaboration with communists or fascists on Gandhian grounds (289). See also Mashruwala 1960, 42, 66; Varma 1965 ("I do not concur with Lenin's thesis that the socialization of the means of production will effectuate a change in human nature" [70]); Horsburgh 1968, 47. Green 1986 recalls Marx's scorn for non-European civilizations (122).

238. Green 1986, 128. For Nehru's endorsement of Marxism, admiration of Lenin, and his consequent sympathetic but critical opinion of Gandhi, see Nehru 1961, 229-236, 258-259, 318-326, 348-351.

239. As Maritain 1957 observes, in 'totalitarian' states nonviolent resistance "can be reduced to nothing by the pure and simple annihilation" of the would-be resistants (71). Bondurant 1958 disagrees, claiming that "satyagraha may, in fact, be the only possibility open to an oppressed people in this age of highly technical means of oppression;" it is "doubtful" that modern tyrants "could prevent word-of-mouth propagation of an idea" in instances in which there has been "some previous understanding of its meaning and effectiveness" (226-227). Experience shows that this is true and not true: true in the sense that careful, patient reconstruction of a civil society can lead to well-timed revolution after hollowing out the tyrants' system; false in the sense that nonviolent resistance can succeed against a well-designed, vigorous modern tyranny. When Horsburgh 1968 insists that nonviolent approaches "have met with some response even from hardened Nazis" (60), one can only reply that the response was insufficient.

240. Gandhi 1958-1984, XIV, 299, XIX, 95; XXIII, 105.

> According to the teaching of Mohammed this would be considered a Satanic Civilization. Hinduism calls it the Black Age (X, 21).

241. Gandhi 1958-1984, XXIX, 14; LXXXVII 192. Zoroaster, the Buddha, Jesus, and Mohammed exemplify Eastern moral wisdom. "And then what happened?" Gandhi asked. "Christianity became disfigured when it went to the West." Christianity became Roman or Constantinian.

242. Gandhi 1958-1984, XXVI, 488.

243. Gandhi 1958-1984, VIII, 289, 337; X, 21; XIII, 521-522; XXV, 19, XLII, 291.

244. "Let it be remembered that western civilization is only a hundred years old, or to be more precise, fifty," he wrote in 1908 (Gandhi 1958-1984, VIII, 374). The Indian Mutiny had occurred in 1857. He distinguished modernity from "Christian progress" (VIII, 244).

245. Gandhi 1958-1984, XIV, 66; XXXII, 164; Rolland 1924, 50; Iyer 1973, 85; Parekh 1989b, 28-34, 72-80. Varma 1965 appears to cast the net somewhat broader, writing that "Gandhi represented the defiance of Western power politics based on the theories of Thrasymachus, Machiavelli, Hobbes, Cecil Rhodes, and Treitschke" (32); Gandhi might reply that Thrasymachus exemplified no appreciable part of ancient Western *civilization*. Green 1986 rightly links Gandhi's anti-modernism to Gandhi's political symbiosis with Indian villagers (130).

246. Gandhi 1958-1984, XXI, 516. If invaded, Indians would "defend ourselves against all aggressors" through suffering nonviolent resistance.

247. Gandhi 1958-1984, LXXXVII, 192-193.

248. Gandhi 1958-1984, VIII, 244.

249. Gandhi 1958-1984, XXXII, 16. See Parel 1971 for an ingenious if implausible attempt to synthesize Gandhi and Machiavelli. Singer 1972 optimistically predicts coexistence and mutual adaptations of Indian tradition and modernity, denying that tradition and modernity are dichotomous. He manages this argument in part by carefully substituting the word "Indian" for "Hindu" in key passages (245 ff.) and also by remarking that 'modernized' Indians (e.g. Brahman industrialists) *believe themselves* to be good Hindus (315-316).

250. Breig 1976, 343-346.

251. Edwardes 1986, 248-257.

252. Gandhi 1958-1984, LXII, 202; LXVIII, 7.

253. Liberation theology should not be confused with the 'political theology' movement of postwar Europe, developed by Johannes Metz, Jürgen Moltmann, and Wolfgang Pannenburg. Ellul 1969 criticized this movement as too 'modern,' too much a mere reaction to earlier trends in modernity:

> A while ago, people made the monumental error of saying that democracy, liberalism, competitive capitalism were all expressions of Christianity. Today they make the same monumental error for the benefit of socialism. (32)

Ellul judged it "very likely [that] the Prince of this world also had a finger in revolutions" (54-55), even well-intentioned socialist ones. Leftist Christian revolutionaries selected the poor they loved, excluding Tibetans overrun by Communist Chinese, Khurds oppressed in Iraq, and others whose afflictions do not stem from 'capitalists' (67). Ellul called the claim "that revolution is *prerequisite* to reconciliation" a "monstrous" theological error (73).

254. Boff and Boff 1987, 7, 89, 93; Gutierrez 1988, 30-32.

255. Comblin 1979, xii; Gutierrez 1988, xiv. Because Latin American countries differ one from another, local variations of liberation theology occur; see Levine 1988, 156.

256. Castro 1969, 90.

257. Bonino 1983, 4, 8-9; Lopez 1969, 131-134; Levine 1988, 241-243; Gutierrez 1988, 52-53; Assmann 1987, 44; Boff and Boff 1987, 67-68. On the CELAM conference see Pottenger 1989, 10-20. Boff 1982a describes liberation theology as the most recent in a sequence of liberations: the liberation of reason (Galileo); the liberation of the citizen (Rousseau); the liberation of the spirit (Hegel); the liberation of the proletariat (Marx); the liberation of life (Nietzsche); the liberation of the *psyche* (Freud); the liberation of industrial man (Marcuse); the liberation of women (feminists); and finally the liberation of theology. Bidegun 1989 goes on step farther, 'liberating' liberation theology from the domination of male theologians. For a parallel movement among North American theologians see Cox 1969, 17-22, seeking to replace the 'East-West' conflict between communists and 'capitalists' with a movement toward reconciling the 'North-South' conflict between 'developed' and 'undeveloped' countries (17-24). The fact that Latin American political economies are not commercial or even 'capitalistic' but mercantilist should be obvious to any reader of Adam Smith, a writer liberation theologians do not read (see Novak 1986, 3a, 58, and Soto 1989). In fairness, however, liberation theologians contend not so much that Latin America is fully 'capitalist' but rather that it is exploited by foreign 'capitalist.' Assmann 1987 writes, "I am beginning to doubt the Marxist principle that capitalism is always linked to pure profit" and is therefore always necessarily exploitive (60).

258. Assmann 1987, 38; Rochietti 1989, 115. One of the ablest among the feminist liberation theologians, Rochietti associates the defense of life with "defense of our motherhood," a "communal and political function" set against impoverishment and political repression" (115).

259. Comblin 1979, 15; Boff 1986, 1; Boff 1988, 35, 50-51.

260. Segundo 1976, 51; Segundo 1978, 34-37, 48-51; 65-70; Boff 1988, 20, 43-44, 55. Fortin 1959 muses. "If the [materially] poor are really closer to God, I suppose one should think twice about robbing them of their poverty" (42).

261. Segundo 1976, 7-8, 1-3; Segundo 1978, 129; Boff 1978, 28-31, 38.

262. Assmann 1975, 47, 57, 77, 80-81; Segundo 1978, 128-129; Boff 1987, 157, 161-162; Boff 1985, 77-79, 85; Boff 1987, 1-2, 253-356; Bonino 1983, 115-117. None of the male liberation theologians goes so far as Tamez 1989b, who charges "Logic, too, has been imposed upon us: not only by theology, but by Western thought in general" (5). Boff more cautiously contends that "all knowledge must be conceived in terms of the absolute mystery called God," a mystery that is not, fortunately, absolutely absolute, thanks to divine revelation. Humanly speaking, we never see a *human being* "walking down the street" — only a man or a woman. Psychologically, sociologically, and historically, both the person perceived and the perceiver are a man or a woman, limited beings not fully human beings. Only in Jesus the

Christ are all human beings − Jew and Greek, slave and freeman, male and female − one (Galatians 3:28) (Boff 1987, 28, 47-53).

263. Boff 1982a, 6-7; 11-19; 160n.12. This account is obviously based on the historical theses of Martin Heidegger. In his 'German' account of theological epistemology, Boff makes a move that few contemporary Christians would endorse; he claims that agapic love "radicalized [the] basic impulse" of Eros, purifying Eros (36). This abandons the sharp distinction between agape and eros implicit in the Bible and uncovered in this century by Nygren 1941. The implications of this, move for Boff's conception of Christianity are profound; see below, footnote 265.

264. Boff 1988, 69, 75, 82.

265. Gutierrez 1988, xxxiv-xxxix; Assmann 1975, 74-75; Segundo 1976, 1-2; Boff 1988, 14; Boff and Boff 1987, 9-12, 20; Isaac-Diaz and Tarango 1988, 1; Berryman 1987, 85-86. Boff 1987 add:

> Aristotle used to say that friendship could not be possible between divinity and human beings because of the differences in nature. The philosopher could not have imagined the emergence of God in warm, receptive human flesh. (89)

In fact Aristotle could indeed imagine, as Greek mythologists did before him, the emergence of gods in warm, receptive flesh − and not only human flesh. Zeus and the other gods have a decided proclivity for such embodiments, and evidently share many human (all-too-human) passions. It is true that *Aristotle*'s 'God,' the "unmoved mover" is no person; see *Physics* VIII, vi, 260a, in Aristotle 1941, 376.

"God has made himself known so that the human could become God (Boff 1978, 197). This hubristic formulation, following the teachings of the psychologist Carl Jung (203) − before him, Dun Scotus (204), after him, Teilhard de Chardin − reminds one of nothing more than contemporary 'New Age' claims − perhaps most ominously in Boff's claim that "there are other spiritual beings who carry out [the] sacerdotal function [of cosmic priests giving glory to God] better than human beings (*Ibid.*, 216). The invitation to Godhood belongs rather to demons than to angels in orthodox Christianity.

266. See Schall 1982, 50-62.

267. Freire 1974, 19-22, 57-60, 66-73, 76. "The evangelical Christian is concerned when he sees that the Freirean anthropology assigns no proper place to the Scriptures and man does not appear as a sinner" (Nuñez 1985, 61). See also *Ibid.*, 165-167 on the affinities between Marxist and liberation-theology 'praxis.' The resemblance of much of this to the pedagogy of the democratic-socialist American educator John Dewey should not be overlooked, although both might find it

somewhat embarrassing. In fact both derive their doctrines from Hegel, then liberally season it with an emphasis on 'praxis.' Both are concerned to avoid the 'bureaucratism' (to say nothing of the monarchism) of Hegel and the leftist-totalitarian tendencies of Marxism. Bizarrely, Berryman 1987 claims that Freire reflects "Western philosophy" as such, from the Greeks to Sartre (37).

268.   *Ibid.*, 40, 76-81, 82 n.7, 167. On Marx see *Ibid.*, 90, n16. As is consistent with this inconsistency, the book itself while stressing 'dialogue' and 'concreteness,' in fact consists of the most hortatory sort of monologue stuffed with 'abstract' language and arguments rather like one of Fidel's eight-hour orations. Freire associates monologue with propaganda accusing leftist propagandists of unwittingly imitating the habits of commercial society. "[C]onviction cannot be packaged and sold" (54).

269.   *Ibid.*, 93-95.

270.   *Ibid.*, 97-118.

271.   For a North American version of this project but much more nearly Christian, see Schaull 1969; see also Ruether 1972, 4-9, and Weigert 1989. More interesting because more thoughtful and more firmly based in experience, is Bing 1989; significantly, Bing notices that the techniques work better in Richmond, Indiana, albeit in a very limited way (53-54), than they do in Jerusalem, where they evidently do not work much at all (58).

272.   Jean-Francois Revel: *Ni Marx, Ni Jésus*, Paris: Editions Robert Laffont, 1970. See Revel 1971.

273.   Comblin 1979, 37. See also Barbé 1987:

> The miserable have nothing to live by and the affluent
> no longer know why they live. To the first Marx opens
> his mouth to speak; to the second, Nietzsche. (32)

Barbé wants liberation theology to go beyond Marx and Nietzsche.

For an example of a Marxist who seeks to attach himself to liberation theology and also nonviolent resistance see Bonpane 1985, 6-7, 19-20, 35.

274.   Gutierrez 1988, 8, 10, 18-21, 55, 249 n.51.

275.   Boff and Boff 1987, 26-33, 85-88. See also Assmann 1975, 39.

276.   "Instead of examining the specific concrete and historical possibilities of religion and theology, Marx takes the easy way out of disqualifying religion in general insofar as he views it as an autonomous and ahistorical monolith" that is "merely ideal" (Segundo 1976, 17; see also

666

Ibid., 59). "Marx never studied the question of religion, he just picked up Ludwig Feuerbach's critique; he had no notion of gospel transcendence" (Barbé 1987, 15).

277. Segundo 1985, 99.

278. Colossians 3:9-11; Gutierrez 1988, 56-81; Berryman 1987, 59.

279. Gutierrez 1979, 17; Bonino 1983, 119-123; Boff 1988, 18; Kirk 1979, 68, 162-163.

280. Segundo 1985, 108-110.

281. Assmann 1975, 85-86; Assmann 1986, 134; Barbé 1987, 15-16.

282. Segundo 1978, 117; Boff 1978, 265, 271. While Christian motif may reassure many readers, it should be noted that Boff goes on to cite not Scripture but Maurice Merleau-Ponty's apologia for Stalinist Marxism, *Humanism and Terror* (322, n.6), which may well impel readers to reflect upon the potential dangers of "prophetic denunciation and horatatory proclamation" by 'committed' persons (271).

283. Miranda 1986, 160; Segundo 1985, 111; Barbé 1987, 64.

284. Reding 1987, 31, 39, 46, 73-75, 83, 101, 106, 113-115, 131.

285. Berryman 1987, 144.

286. Among many recitations of the facts see Cuadra 1990 and Navarette 1990. For 'the God that failed,' see Crossman 1949.

287. Boff and Boff 1987, 87. Berryman 1987 leaps to the defense by denying that Cuba has been an economic failure; if true, this would make it unique among Marxist regimes. However, it is not true.

288. Ratzinger 1988, 257.

289. Comblin 1979, 64-79. The science of geopolitics was developed at the Geopolitics Institute of Munich and popularized in England by Halford J. Mackinder and in the United States by Alfred Thayer Mahan, "who established the theoretical bases for the American imperialism President Theodore Roosevelt was creating" (70). See MacKinder 1962 and Mahan 1892. It should be needless to observe that both MacKinder's and Mahan's concepts have been used to oppose the imperialist expansion of Germany during two world wars; 'German' ideas may of course be employed to thwart German historical ambitions. For Mahan's early association with Theodore Roosevelt see Millis 1956, 156. Chapter Three above describes how the 'German' ideology played itself out on the American 'left.' Post-World War II America may be seen to have combined 'left' and 'right'-wing 'Germanism' in the American context.

The literature on the 'national security state' is vast; for a brief summary of current left-democratic opinions, see Raskin 1989. Far more thoughtful are Lord 1989b and (with respect to the Brazilian experience) Stepan 1988.

290. Comblin 1979, 125, 132, 147-148. Comblin somewhat oversimply associates 'German' statism with the political philosophy of Thomas Hobbes (Comblin 1979, 77-78, 89-90, 102-104, 121). He overlooks Hobbes' individualism and focuses only on Hobbes' interest in "power;" he therefore misses the importance of the individualist variant of modern political philosophy seen in Locke and Montesquieu.

291. Berryman 1987 summarizes Comblin's thesis concerning the "national security state" while studiously avoiding any mention of the critique of 'Germanism' (118-122). This may be because Berryman wants to redeem Marxism for "critical use" (139).

Yoder 1990 clearly intends to distinguish liberation theology from 'German' developments (289-290). He prefers to associate liberation theology with the various Protestant sects of the British reformation; "the logical moves are parallel" to those made by Puritans, Levellers, Diggers, and Quakers (291).

This in turn enables him to associate liberation theology with the forces that generated modern English Constitutionalism:

> This entire puritan experience is formative in all English-speaking political science and philosophy of government. The failure of Cromwell's success has permanently vaccinated Anglo-Saxons against cheap promises of greater justice based on an easy change of regime. On the other hand, Anglo-Saxons remember the success of the 'Glorious Revolution' of 1688/89, which established without violence what by now is the oldest civil regime in Western history, perhaps the oldest in world history, the mother of democracies. (291).

Because, until now, the Latin Catholic world has not had this experience, liberation theology seems new. "The parallel is not a matter of genetic dependency" − no liberation theologian cites George Fox or Gerrard Winstanley − "but rather a recurrence in a new setting of something that was done before" (292).

Yoder's thesis is perhaps a touch too edifying. Liberation theology remains more political and activist than the *pacifists* among the English Reformers were. Gandhian nonviolent resistance rather than Christian nonresistance (even in its Quaker form) was closer liberation theology than was anything in England.

292. Assmann 1975, 29-35; Segundo 1976, 71, 80-117; Gutierrez 1985, xii; Boff 1985, 119; Boff 1986, 39; Boff 1988, 15, 37, 43, 84; Levine 1988, 253. The contention that political *theology* traditionally seeks to legitimize the status quo is not entirely true (the example of Augustine should suffice) and does not mean that political *philosophy* traditionally seeks to legitimize the status quo, a contention that would be insupportable.

293. Boff 1988, ix, 2.

294. Boff, 1978, 171-174; Boff 1987, 196-201; Boff 1988, 14-16; Boff and Boff 1987, 62. As is so often the case, Boff 1988 then cites Fidel Castro's claim, "History will absolve me," and the "Sandinista Hymnal" as examples of a tradition of liberation to be completed by Christianity (16-18). See also Freire 1974, who speaks in quasi-religious terms about the "real humanist" for whom "conversion to the people requires a profound rebirth" (46-47) and Ruether 1972, who describes liberation theology as theology that "takes as its base the entire human project" in overcoming the "'oppressor-oppressed' relationship" (1-3).

295. Castro 1969, 92-93; Assmann 1987, 51; Barbé 1987, 22; Gutierrez 1985, 94; Gutierrez 1988, xx-xxvii; Boff 1982a, 49-50; Boff and Boff 1987, 3-4, 50-61. Burtchaell 1988 questions the claim that "suffering is...almost exclusively...a result of oppression" (267).

296. Assmann 1986, 133; Gutierrez 1985, 1-4, 12; Boff 1982a, 69-78; Boff 1988, 27-30.

297. See Ruether 1972, 11-13, who acknowledges the latter problem, and Nuñez 1985, who remarks it 257).

298. Topel 1982, 8-10; Berryman 1987, 49. For an extended treatment of the Book of Exodus by a liberation theologian see Gutierrez 1988, *passim*. This appropriation of the Exodus story has come under sharp criticism from several writers who find the analogies imperfect. Nunez 1985 observes that ancient Israelis depended far more on God, far less on their own actions, than liberation theologians say. Further, the Israelis never revolutionized Egypt; they left it (190). Burtchaell 1988 cautions that "the land of milk and honey was seized by fire and sword" (273). Klenicki 1988 objects that liberation theologians substitute Latin American Christians for Jews, effectively denying contemporary Jews "a continued theological and historical role" in the contemporary State of Israel (5-6). Yoder 1990 calls the Exodus story potentially "triumphalistic" and thus "unable to sustain the devotion of suffering peoples in nontriumphal settings, where freedom is not just around the corner" (286-287). Liberation theologians should correct this by mentioning the Exile, the Diaspora, and the Cross; some have (288).

299. Castro 1969, 98-99; Segundo 1978, 25; Barbé 1987, 6; Gutierrez 1988, 134-135.

300. Segundo 1978, 1; Gutierrez 1988, 104; Boff 1978, 275, 281-287; Boff 1982a, 128, 131-139. Boff curiously urges love of all of God's creation, including "the negative," a formulation that ignores the adjuration to love the sinner but hate the sin.

301. See Topel 1982, 156.

302. Latin American Episcopal Council, "Medellin Document on Peace," in Rosso 1986, 14-16.

303. *Ibid.*, 17.

304. Segundo 1978, 127.

305. Segundo 1976, 88, 157-172. See also Ronald Muñoz, cited in Fontaine 1987, 166. For other statements of conditional acceptance of violence, see Assmann 1975, 98; Assmann 1986, 130; Boff 1979, 113-114. Boff argues for the strictest conditions and eventually moves toward nonviolence. The more clearly Marxist writers of course endorse revolutionary violence; see Freire 1974, 40-42; Bonpane 1985, 41.

306. Bonino 1983, 117, 125-128. Pottenger 1989 evidently follows Bonino; see 143-144, 156, with a discussion of Segundo on 146-149.

307. Galilea 1979 calls violence "certainly the most radical challenge facing Latin America," a "collective kind of sin" that is only destroyed by an *imitatio Christi* (174-177).

   Comblin 1979 regrets "the myth of the guerrilla, of the *faco guerrillero*, of total revolutionary action" that arose in Latin America during the 1960's; this myth ends either in an explosion of violent deaths or in a passive waiting for the revolution to occur 'by itself' (24). Tamez 1989 contrasts 'male' combativeness seeking conquest and domination with 'female' combativeness seeking justice nonviolently (6).

308. See Gutierrez 1988, 201 n.38.

309. Gutierrez 1985, 14, 64-65; Gutierrez 1988, xxx, 159.

310. Barbé 1987, 33, 39. Barbé regrets the abandonment of nonviolent resistance by Nicaraguan priests Miguel d'Escoto and Ernesto Cardenal (62).

311. Boff 1978, 47-51, 88, 102-103, 290; Boff 1982a, 96-100, 151-153; Boff 1982b, 7-8; Boff 1985, 50, 59-64; Boff 1988, 12; Boff and Boff 1987, 62. Barbé 1987 agrees that Christians who turn violent show "a fatal germ of mistrust with regard to grace" (73). He also insists, serpentinely, that "nonviolence is not suicide" (135). Life should be risked only in a "calculated" way (138), with "a shrewdness that will not be spoon-fed with fairy tales" (138). Prudence and goodness complement each other:

If goodness is all that one has, one will be plucked like a
pear. If one is merely prudent, one will also be cruel.
(138)

The "powerful and rich" fight with their weapons (141); the powerless
and poor should fight with theirs — losing, while doing so, fewer lives
"than in a conventional war" (138). In all of this "Gandhi was a
forerunner of surpassing genius" (144). Violence is not "always
avoidable" (147). But it is always evil, even when unavoidable.

312. Gutierrez 1988, 67, 69-71; Assmann 1987, 59-60; Topel 1982, 138-145;
Miranda 1986, 161; Isaac-Diaz and Tarango 1988, xvii, 5, 78, 89.
Miranda *op.cit.* cites Mark 10:21-25; Luke 8:1-3; John 12:6; 13:2; and
Acts 2:44-45; 4:32-35 in support of Christian communism. The first
ecclesial base communities were founded in the mid-1950's (Boff 1988,
9). They have, therefore, "no necessary link to any theology of the
political" but rather arose as a response by the Church to a shortage of
priests. Lay preachers organizing villagers for Bible study and other
instructions were judged by Church authorities to be preferable to no
pastoral care at all (Yoder 1990, 286). Liberation theology in many
respects responded to and grafted itself upon the ecclesial base
communities.

313. Boff 1982a, 46-47, 94-95; Boff 1988, 19.

314. Boff 1985, 127; Barbé 1987, 113, 127, 150.

315. Boff 1982a, 90; Boff 1982b, vii; Boff 1986, 4-6; Novak 1986, 182-188;
Gutierrez 1988, 18; Levine 1988, 251-252, 257-259; Burtchaell 1988,
267.

316. Segundo 1976, 43-44; Boff 1985, 161; Alves 1986, 93; Barbé 1987, 66.

317. Geyer 1982, 200.

318. Kaufman 1985, 23.

319. Muller 1982, vii, xiii, 8, 10, 20, 30, 46, 58, 74-75, 123-126.

320. *The Antichrist*, xlii, in Nietzsche 1968, 616-617.

321. Alves 1986, 95-96, 100-105.

322. Boff 1978, 64.

323. *Ibid.*, 235-236 (italics added).

324. *Ibid.*, 237, 244, 250, 257-258, 321, n. 13; Boff 1985, 10, 46, 89-93, 98-
102.

325. Ruether 1972, Chapter 6.

326. Jesudesan 1984.

327. *Ibid.*, 130-131.

328. For a critical survey of 'New Age' doctrines from a Christian viewpoint see Marrs 1987, especially 13, 39, 58, 93, 101-102 (on the paradox of egalitarianism and 'leadership'), 102, 117, 127-128. Marrs might not be surprised to learn that Gandhi associated with Theosophists while in England.

A standard, sympathetic account of 'New Age' beliefs and practices is Ferguson 1980, who endorses Gandhian satyagraha (199-201) and cites with approval such circles as the Alchemists, Gnostics, Cabalists, Hermetics, and American Transcentalists (24-48). Bailey 1978 presents not a regime analysis but a mystico-astrological classification of various nations and their supposed historical roles, assigned to them by a "Hierarchy" of spiritual beings whose "directing center" is "Shamballa" (24). Sounding rather like Hegel, she asserts that "Humanity itself is rapidly arriving at the point where its *united will* will be the determining factor in world affairs and this success of the evolutionary process" (36). Kueshana 1982 offers "the first open discussion of the ancient Brotherhoods and their far-reaching influence in the civilizing of mankind;" these "world-wide interlocking organizations," whose members "have traditionally withheld their identity from non-members in order to avoid certain persecution for holding highly idealistic views," are now announcing their presence as part of a program to respond to "the urgency of the world dilemmas of our time" (5-6). George Washington, Benjamin Franklin, Thomas Jefferson, and James Madison were all "under the guidance of the Masonic inner court," (67) and indeed "all the major and minor Prophets of the Old Testament were Brothers, and all the authors in the New Testament, except Saul of Tarsus...." (69). Armageddon is scheduled to begin in 1998; by 2001, only ten percent of world population will survive — fortunately, these will be "emotionally mature individuals" ready for genuine democracy (296). Satin 1977 appears to be a sort of apostle of the New Age to the New Left, rejecting old-Left dialectics for "intuition and imagination" (27) and claiming that wars and other forms of aggression will cease because deprivation, threats, and resentment will disappear in the New Age (49ff.). He admires Gene Sharp's writings on nonviolent defense: "New Age people wouldn't want to defend themselves in any other way" (61). Spangler 1984 sets for himself the challenge of making New Age beliefs seem normal; he sets forth a 'soft' version of Nietzschean life-worship and downplays apocalyticism.

Probably the most influential 'New Age' spokesman is the United Nations bureaucrat Donald Keys, who teaches that "the world *will* organize as a community or human life will perish" (3). Again somewhat like Hegel, he claims that "Planetary humanity is a new organism where the nations are the organs and we the participating individual cells" (14); "when the transformed seeker becomes a knower, then he or she becomes a powerful force for human unification" (100). The United Nations, as "a key nerve center for forming of the global organism" (16), must be strengthened sufficiently to disarm the nations. This will require the elimination of national sovereignty by "the periodic 'pooling of sovereignty' with respect to specific tasks and agencies when their effective functioning is seen as critically essential to national and world interest. There will be no magic moment when the world organism springs to life; more probably there will be a series of little-noticed events when one or another aspect of planetary management has quickened" (44). "We have an informal network at the UN of persons who are committed, aware, and striving to bring the new world to birth" (59); in a process Keys calls "transformative infiltration," certain "members of the new constituency are taking responsibility to work within existing institutions and to rekindle in them goals expressed by their originators but now often neglected, as well as to open new, creative directions" (90). These practitioners of "the politics of consciousness" (79) will contribute to the construction, "millenia in the future," to "a post-human society" in which "the good and the right would be intuitively arrived at" (81). Post-human society will be hierarchic, as egalitarianism is "a distortion of the truth," and democracy is "based on assumptions which cannot be regarded as fully accurate" (81).

329.   Nietzsche 1986, 380-381. See also Gray 1970, 226-233. Note well that the Nietzschean doctrines of the will-to-power and the eternal return might be traceable to Hinduism, via the doctrines of Schopenhauer (see Schopenhauer 1974). Note also that Emerson and Thoreau shared the interest in Hindu doctrines seen in several of their German contemporaries.

330.   Barbé 1987, 30. The same dilemma occurs in some contemporary feminist arguments. Spretnak 1982b conflates body, spirituality, and mind into "life-force" (xv), ending with a conception of politics as power that is fundamentally identical with that of Machiavelli and Hobbes (xxiii). See also Starrett 1982, 190. This leads some feminists to the logical conclusion of self-deification (e.g., Starhawk 1982, 51). The paradox that results in practice is the same as in Gandhi: An ideology that presents itself as universally 'inclusive;' non-adversarial, and anti-dualistic nonetheless chooses its enemy (in Gandhi's case imperialism, for feminists 'partriarchy') and treats it very much as an evil 'foreigner' or 'other' (e.g., Starrett 186-190).]

CHAPTER VI

1. Einstein 1960, Letter to Benedetto Croce, June 7, 1944, 327. Einstein goes on to say that while the philosopher may be destroyed by other people, "they can never offend him!"

2. Gentili 1933, I, v, 28. Even the Stoic Seneca commends just wars (29); it is the theologians – Cyprian, Tertullian, Lactantius, who oppose war as such most strongly. Erasmus, whom Gentili also cites, evidently opposes war even while giving lip service to the contemporary Church orthodoxy of just war doctrine, but Erasmus deduces pacifism from his Christian faith, not from conventional opinions or from natural intuition and reasoning.

3. Lewis 1940, 121. Lewis then quotes (without attribution) Machiavelli on the fate of unarmed prophets.

4. Joad 1939, 231.

5. Nicolai 1919, 3, 177 (emphasis added). To reject the distinction between offensive and defensive war would betoken the rejection of the philosopher's personal defensive war against persecution.

6. Grotius 1925, III, i, 608. It is a measure of Grotius' philosophic inclinations that he cites the example of Jesus of Nazareth along with that of Socrates. For Bertrand Russell's view of "lies and hypocrisy," see his letter to Lady Ottoline Morrell, August 17, 1918, cited in Clark 1976, 7.

7. Anonymous 1837, 38-39, 92.

8. See Rosen 1989, 4-19.

9. This is the Baconian project; for an astute commentary on Bacon's *Advertisement Touching a Holy War*, see Weinberger 1981.

10. All of Dewey's educational writings, simultaneously commending scientific experimentalism, egalitarianism, and 'progress,' attempt to establish such an ever-revolutionizing tradition, which unfortunately descends quickly into a moral relativism that destroys its own inquiring spirit. See Eidelberg and Morrisey 1992, 106-122.

11. "A, B, C," in Voltaire 1962, 564-574.

12. Russell, 1915, 27; Russell 1917a, 38-39; Russell 1936, 51, 134, 142-143, 151-152; Clark 1976, 255, 466. Russell mistakenly supposed that the case of Denmark proved his point with respect to the Germans' fear: "As the Danes have almost no armed forces, it does not matter to the Germans what their opinions are; and as they have no Empire, they

have no possessions that might afford a field for the investment of German capital. In this way they are defended by their very defenselessness" (Russell 1936, 136). As it happened, the Danes' defenselessness did not defend them from the Nazis. For Russell's ambiguities on this issue, however, compare *Ibid.*, 89 and 108.

The claim that any war would destroy Western civilization itself became fashionable in the 1930's. "Who in Europe does not know that one more war in the West and the civilization of the ages will fall with as great a shock as that of Rome?" English Prime Minister Stanley Baldwin asked (Page 1937, 16). Thus war itself was represented as the enemy, not any political regime such as Nazi Germany (see Russell 1936, 213-214). This removal of regime politics from prudential consideration resulted in near-disaster for England, and in disaster for republics closer to Germany. For an extreme example of misplaced 'internationalism' yielding complacency toward the Nazis, see Blum 1932, 42-46.

13. Joad 1939, 61, 109-110.

14. I have conflated statements from two letters, one to Alfred Nahan dated July 20, 1933, the other to the French Secretary of the Defense Committee of the League of Conscientious Objectors, August 28, 1933; see Einstein 1960, 229-230. Einstein drew back from his call for preemptive war in a letter to F. M. Hardie in November 1933 (*Ibid.*, 246). As late as December 1930 Einstein had been claiming that "uncompromising war resistance" was good and necessary ("The Two Percent Speech," *Ibid.*, 117).

15. Statement to the Hunter College chapter of the American Student Union, March 31, 1937, Einstein 1960, 274.

16. Letter to a Missouri University student, July 14, 1941, Einstein 1960, 319.

17. Letter to Seiei Shinohara, February 22, 1953, Einstein 1960, 585 and 588.

18. Cotta 1985 defines violence as "unruliness," a denial "at the root [of] the dialogical nature of [human] existence" (66). Cotta describes three "modes" of measure of moderation: acting *with* measure (i.e., a measured state of the soul); acting *in accordance* with measure (i.e., acting in a measured way); and acting *for the purpose of* measure, for a specific, concrete purpose, not for some absolute 'ideal' or 'value' that excuses any crime. Action in accordance with all three of these "modes" of measure can be forceful but still lawful and law-enhancing (*Ibid.*, 86).

19. Boulding 1962 defines "conflict" as "a situation of competition in which the parties are *aware* of the incompatibility of potential future

positions and in which each party *wishes* to occupy a position that is incompatible with the wishes of the other" (5). See also *Ibid.*, 277-283.

20.   *Ibid.*, 24. See also Clark 1988, 24.

21.   For recent examples, see Hoffman 1981, 97-98 and Clark 1988, 12.

22.   Nardin 1983 presents a sophisticated version of this argument. "The classic maxim 'Let justice be done though the heavens may fall' is simply a hyperbolic way of expressing the outlook embodied in the conception of morality and law as essentially restraint-oriented (practical) rather than end-oriented (purposive)" (14). Nardin accordingly prefers international law, "a legal order without a state" (69), to the more ambitious schemes of world government or a quasi-sovereign 'league of nations.' "There exists no Olympian standpoint from which the diverse principles of obligation of different practices can be rationalized *sub specie eternitatis*" (252). Nor can there be, because there exists a variety of incommensurable standards by which 'should' statements can be derived, including morality, law, and interest. If we claim that, say, moral statements should rule over statements of 'ought' deriving from law or from interest, one commits a tautology, "a reassertion from within the authoritative practice of morality that the considerations of its practice are authoritative" (253). When law and morality conflict, "I can do the thing that is legally right or the thing that is morally right, but I cannot do that which is right without qualification." While "it is legally right to act legally and morally right to act morally, there is no criterion independent of those principles to tell us what to do. The idea of a single coherent scheme of principles according to which all conflicts of principle can be reconciled is a chimera" (253). This means for example that God (and His Law) is a chimera.

But even granted his atheistic/agnostic or secular terms Nardin's argument is mistaken. For who is the 'I' who considers the 'shoulds,' legal and moral? Nardin tacitly acknowledges that this 'I' *must* choose between these 'shoulds,' if they conflict, by choosing the legal 'should' over the moral. The choice of the legal over the moral means that the choosing 'I' is, as academic philosophers say nowadays, metalegal and metamoral. Practically speaking, one cannot not choose, as not-choosing is effectually a choice. The 'must' of some 'should' means that behind every 'aught' there is an 'is,' in this case a conception of the human good. When Nardin prudently warns that a morality that refuses to "work toward a modus vivendi" with law, a "reconciliation of competing demands, because such a refusal will leave morality at risk of "rendering itself irrelevant to experience through rigidity" (254), he can do so only by assuming some over-arching 'should' and its corresponding 'good' that the 'I' perceives or at least seeks. The 'I' need not be "Olympian" so to perceive. ("Olympian" is scare-language, rhetoric). Hence the need for a concept of nature, including human nature.

23. See Lackey 1989, 4.

24. Nietzsche 1986, I, 194. The goddess Athena is "a lover of both war and of wisdom" (*Timaeus* xxiv, in Plato 1937, II, 10).

25. Perry 1915 writes, "If one is prepared to renounce the existent world and the achievements of history, one may perhaps escape the need of war" (824). Novikov 1911 observed that there were "individuals in France who from sheer epicureanism would be willing to give up Alsace-Lorraine" (60n.).

26. See for example Muller 1985, ix, 172.

27. Lackey 1989, 10.

28. See Morrisey 1984, 108-109.

29. Cadoux 1940, ix, 227; Huxley 1937, 40.

30. Lewis 1940, 35-36, 123-129. Nietzsche 1986 charges that the good can grow only out of the good and upon the basis of the good" (II, ii, 327). Novikov 1911 quite rightly objects to war on the grounds that "If the same spirit of concord had been displayed beforehand, an agreement would have been reached" and no war would have occurred (19). But this is merely to see that justice need not always lead to war, not that no wars are just.

31. Novikov 1911, 44.

32. Gargasz 1922, 35.

33. Richardson 1960b, 120.

34. Lewis 1940, 59-63, 77.

35. Horsburgh 1968, 7.

36. *Ibid.*, 18.

37. Cady 1989, 44. This claim requires Cady to assert that wars to end war, killing for peace, conscription to defend freedom, and armed coercion to foster peaceful cooperation cannot possibly work (49). However, except for wars to put and end to war itself, an evidently utopian project, such actions can do help to produce their intended effects.

38. Huxley 1937, 10.

39. Perry 1915, 825.

40. Grotius 1925, I, ii, 52-54; II, i, 170-173; Vattel 1916, III, i, 235-236.

41. Grotius 1925, II, xx, 462-475.

42. Rousseau 1979, IV, 253. Cropsey 1977 distinguishes "what makes justice good" from "what makes it obeyed" (174) but denies that the harshness of what makes justice obeyed need overbalance the goodness of justice: "A moral law that brings the obedient to death and shame and guarantees the success of its violators is not to be discussed at length by men with practical responsibilities" (176).

43. Hirst 1906, 19-20.

44. Smith 1976, II, 260: Heering 1943, 92.

45. Grotius 1925 writes:

> The fact must also be recognized that kings, and those who possess rights equal to those of kings, have the right of demanding punishments not only on account of injuries committed against themselves or their subjects, but also on account of injuries which do not directly affect them but excessively violate the law of nature or of nations in regard to any persons whatsoever. For liberty to serve the interests of human society through punishments, which originally, as we have said, rested with individuals, now after the organization of states and courts of law is in the hands of the highest authorities, not, properly speaking, in so far as they rule over others but in so far as they are themselves subject to no one. For subjection has taken this right away from others.

> Truly it is more honorable to avenge the wrongs of others rather than one's own, in the degree that in the case of one's own wrongs it is more to be feared that through a sense of personal suffering one may exceed the proper limit or at least prejudice his mind (II, xx, 504-505).

46. Godwin 1946, 184-185, 338-342, 363-366.

47. Proudhon 1927, II, 127-130, 183-195. As usual Proudhon goes too far in his 'dialectical' presentation, insufficiently distinguishing the "right of force" as the forceful defense *of* right from a quasi-mystical "right of force" as a right *constituted* by force; for the latter see his discussion of the Melian dialogue of Thucydides (*Ibid.*, II, 142-143).

48. Horsburgh 1968, 27; "the debate between believers in armed force and believers in non-violence is a debate about human psychology and sociology as well as about morality" (27).

49. See Joad 1939, 65. They may also have more resources that attract rivals, or their geopolitical circumstances may invite attack. Angell

1939 asks pointedly, "Was it really fear of Abyssinian armaments which caused Italy to launch her war, poison-gas and all, upon Abyssinia?" (85).

50. Cadoux 1940, viii.

51. Cady 1989, 79, 91.

52. Hume 1985, I, iv, 32. See also II, xii, 468.

53. Boulding 1989, 44, 77-78, 109-110, 153. Germaine de Staël's view is more balanced. In modern republics public opinion is "submissive to the slightest demonstration of force" but "at the same time [public opinion is] the only invincible power. It cannot be conquered because it does not fight." The mind of the modern republican "cannot be made to change...for it wants only its well-being" (*The Circumstances that Ended the Revolution and the Principles that Founded the Republic in France*, in Berger 1965, 121). Russell 1915 adds that "The doctrine in non-resistance, as I hold it, is only applicable to wars between civilized states" (27). Carter 1967 concurs: "The unity and determination of any resistance movement is likely to depend a good deal on the measures or type of regime being opposed" (275); "the best kind of political experience for resisting an oppressive regime is probably a tradition of free political activity" (282). Liddel Hart 1967 judges nonviolent resistance effective with "opponents whose code of morality was fundamentally similar" (206).

54. As does Lewis 1940, 186. See also Roberts 1967, 10. Russell 1917a disagrees: "The same courage and idealism which are now put into war could quite easily be directed by education into the channel pf passive resistance" (46). But if the "courage and idealism" and unity of nonviolent resisters is only equal to that of attacking soldiers, the nonviolent resisters will be outmatched, having no weapons. Further, is armed resistance not less difficult to organize and sustain at a high degree of unity that is nonviolent resistance. See Perry 1916, 84-86.

55. On the contrary, Sun Tzu's tactics resemble those of Machiavelli's fox:

> Plans and projects for harming the enemy are not confined to any one method. Sometimes entice his wise and virtuous men away so that he has no counsellors. Or send treacherous people to his country to wreck his administration. Sometimes use cunning deceptions to alienate his ministers from the sovereign. Or send skilled craftsmen to encourage his people to exhaust their wealth. Or present him with licentious musicians and dancers to change his customs. Or give him beautiful women to bewilder him (114).

Because "heart is that by which the general masters," he will do everything that "robs the enemy of his heart and of his ability to plan" (108).

56. On the Ruhrkampf see Sternstein 1967; on the Norwegian resistance see Skodvin 1967.

57. See Jones 1967, 19 and Roberts 1986, who calls Gandhi's recommendations "dogmatic and indiscriminate in character" (264).

58. The best known advocate of civilian defense in the United States today is Gene Sharp. For discussion see Chapter Five above, *passim*.

59. Hume 1985, I, v, 39-40.

60. Simmel 1963, 293.

61. Briffault 1963, 105-106; Clastres 1987, 323. Clastres clearly rejects the contention that hierarchic command and coercion *within* a tribe are inevitable – just the opposite (7-13, 23-25, 28-46). He does contend that they are *natural* in the sense that they are forms of power or violence. But they are not the only possible forms of power; *social* or non-hierarchic power is less violent in its day-to-day exertions, although it is indeed violent in its first manifestation, the rites of initiation (184-188).

62. "[W]e used to make war to eat one another; but in the long run all good institutions degenerate" (*A, B, C,* in Voltaire 1962, 590). Lorenz 1966 observes that the "heavily armed carnivores" actually avoid preying upon their own kind; human beings, omniverous and ineffectually armed physiologically, unfortunately lack such "reliable inhibitions" (241).

63. Mumford 1972, 323, 327.

64. See Lévy-Bruhl 1966, 383; de Jouvenel 1962, II, v, 80; III, viii-ix, 178.

65. Thucydides 1934, 4. See also Clastres 1987, 206-210.

66. Clastres 1987, 212.

67. Thucydides 1934 asserts that "the acquisition of wealth" led to the establishment of the first tyrannies (10). On population see Clastres 1987, 213; on foreign intercourse see Lévy-Bruhl 1966, 392. Compare Rousseau 1968 on the singularity of the village of Neufchatel (62), and see de Jouvenel 1962, III, vi, 91-102. Some writers associate militarism with the establishment of agriculture, on the grounds that "There was not much point in one hunting-gathering band conquering another, for there was really nothing to conquer" (Boulding 1989, 221-222); see also Gellner 1988, 153-156. Angell 192-38 remarks the anti-capitalist character of Nazism, with its "glorification of the peasant" (73). By

contrast, the views of Thomas Jefferson are well known; see also Jefferson's political enemy but sociological ally Boucher 1967b, 27, 170.

68.   Maistre 1974, 59-60. It is likely that de Maistre here mocks not Jefferson but the French Republican anthem, *La Marseillaise*, which speaks of the blood of citizens fertilizing the fields of *la patrie*.

69.   Maistre 1965, 253-254.

70.   Bernhardi 1914, 18-26. Bernhardi emphasizes the anti-individualistic, anti-hedonistic/materialistic virtues of war, following de Maistre in his loathing of the bourgeosie. Nietzsche 1986 takes a somewhat more moderate view. After saying that military conscription squanders "men of the highest civilization," he draws his balance sheet:

> Against war it can be said: it makes the victor stupid, the defeated malicious. In favor of war: through producing these two effects it barbarizes and therefore makes more natural; it is the winter of hibernation time of culture, mankind emerges from it stronger for good or evil (I, 162-163).

Notice that Nietzsche's (as it were) moderation here derives from his primitivism; he implicitly rejects evolution, progressivism, and therefore associates war with a return to the roots, not the full development of the tree.

71.   Russell 1962 writes that "it is probable that, on balance, wars in the past have done more to increase than to diminish the numbers of the human population of the planet" (12); mankind's future wars would do no such thing, he quickly insists. Lewis 1940 questions the survival value of pacifism ("The German Social Democrats were peaceful enough. Where are they now?" [186]) but does so in the context of a Marxist argument for the eventual possibility of peace. Wells 1967 readily labels war as natural; his view of human nature as partly characterized by "sadistic impulses" forms part of a call for the overcoming of nature (173). Hocking 1923 urges that "pugnacity is the instinctive agency of readjustment," and therefore natural, but "the last conquest of pugnacity, before reaching the ideal state, would be the conquest of itself" (368-369). *Criticism* would replace it.

72.   Wilson 1914, 130; Inge 1926, 90.

73.   Nicolai 1919, 67. Anti-bellecists need not be any less racist than bellecists. The pacific Inge 1926 opines, "I do not think that the Americans have ever fully recovered from the Civil War of 1861-1865," in whose aftermath "the numerical loss was made good by immigrants of a type somewhat inferior to the splendid descendents of the English and Dutch colonists" (90). Huxley 1937 argues, contradictorily, that war is anti-evolutionary because it kills the young and the strong, and

that "the most valuable traits are not necessarily the most warlike" (101); obviously, if the most valuable traits are not the most warlike, then war *is* 'evolutionary' because it kills the most warlike. The unwarlike might then encourage the warlike to war, all for the sake of the ascent of man.

74. See Richardson 1960b, who estimates that wars resulted in only 1.6% of all deaths between 1820 and 1949, worldwide. Modern man may be less warlike than his ancestors (141-167). Lackner 1984 asserts that "about 95 percent of all beings lead peaceful lives, dying when their biological clocks run down;" this statistic is produced in order to show that "forcible selection of the fittest through the [violent] struggle for survival" is an unproven dogma (ix-x). Angell 1913 simply asks, "If militarism is so virile, why is Latin America so squalid?" (228-229).

75. "The tendency toward war is as much a part of man's nature as it is a part of nature of rivers to inundate their banks from time to time; and just as artificial means are required to avoid inundations, so man must adopt artificial measures to avoid wars" (Letter to a United States Army Officer, February 1946, in Einstein 1960, 369). More subtly, Einstein remarks that the "ability to think is also part of human nature" (Interview with Robert Trout, CBS radio, May 28, 1946, *Ibid.*, 378).

Lorenz 1966 concurs: "Humanity would indeed have destroyed itself by its first inventions, were it not for the very wonderful fact that inventions and responsibility are both the achievements of the same specifically human faculty of asking questions" (242). Aggression, intra-species "fighting instinct" (ix), can and should be rechanneled away from war (57). The sociobiologist Wilson 1978 also recognizes the biological foundations of human aggression while insisting on their capacity to be rechanneled (101-102, 119). See also McGuinness 1987, vii, xiv and compare with her argument on p. 312.

One anthropologist, Greenhouse 1986, observes that anthropologists' writings "tend to share a fundamental premise that war is a form of social pathology;" she considers this premise a "bias:" "The fact is that war is not always and not only an accident or a function of sociocultural breakdown in international relations" (49).

Among twentieth-century philosophers, John Dewey argues that human nature defined as "the innate needs of man" does not change. Physiological needs, the needs for companionship, for "exhibiting energy," for mutual cooperation in "aid and combat alike," for esthetic satisfaction, and the need "to lead and to follow" are permanent, or more precisely, as long-lasting as the species itself (Dewey 1946. 184). However, human nature defined more ambitiously as a particular set of beliefs or a pattern of behavior can and does change (186). "Combativeness" is "a constituent part of [unchanging] human nature;" war is only "a social pattern," like slavery. Wars are "changeable *manifestations* of human nature" (186-188, italics added). Dewey endorses William James' quest for the rechanneling of the combative instincts (188-189).

76. Kropotkin 1972 opposes this thesis to that of Hobbes (84) and to Hobbes' nineteenth century descendants Herbert Spencer and Thomas Huxley. Kropotkin also discusses animal life at some length (17-82), anticipating Lackner 1984, who states that "cooperation is not the exception, but the natural rule among most animal species" (5). On the sociality of human nature see also Trotter 1922, 125-132, 162-167. Wright 1965 adopts the Rousseauan opinion that "natural man, timorous for his life and sympathetic to humanity," can only be induced to go to war by means of convention, training (96). How the natural man became subject to such unnatural chains is left to the imagination.

77. See Godwin 1946, 7-14; Faguet 1908, 12; Angell 1913, 181-214; Aron 1966, 365-366; Andreski 1968, 217. The anthropologist Goldschmidt 1986 writes,

> Man is not naturally aggressive (pace Lorenz) any more than he is naturally given to mutuality (pace Prince Kropotkin). Humanity has the capacity for aggressive behavior that can be institutionalized through social supports. Once this motivation for warriorhood is institutionalized, however, it takes on a life of its own (8-9).

78. In this they follow such writers as Godwin 1946, 86, 273, and Nicolai 1919, 10. The modern originator of the radical malleability thesis is of course Rousseau, although he is anticipated by Locke 1990, VII, 173-201.

79. Huxley 1937, 105.

80. Ligt 1938, 24, 38-39.

81. Genovés 1972 denies "that man 'is' this or that one thing for all eternity" (ix), yet a few pages later identifies "peace" as "the first law of Nature" (17). After denying that animal behavior can be an accurate guide for human behavior on the grounds that only human beings have "culture" (ix), Genovés conspicuously notices that intra-species combat among animal species is "seldom mortal or even dangerous" 44). He smuggles morality into his science by averring, "The only *proper* attitude to take toward the almost infinite diversity of cultures is one of gratitude and humility" (129). "In the end," he admits, "it is easier to seek facts that confirm our convictions than to change these convictions" (153). Evidently so. For an even more polemical treatment see Huyghe 1986.

82. Mead 1912, 119; Trotter 1922, 219; Wright 1965, 1291, 1302; Fornari 1974, xii, xvi, 163; Eckhardt 1976, 6. The latter concedes that some (revolutionary and egalitarian) violence is acceptable (*Ibid.*, 20-25;

most violence, however, is an unacceptable manifestation of "egoism," which he also associates with alcoholism, Friedrich Nietzsche, and Barry Goldwater (5).

Somewhat less subjectivist is Richardson 1960a, who tries to account for war in terms of stimulus and response. "The chief stimulus to falling deeply in love is any sign of love from the other person" — Richardson must have been extraordinarily lucky in love — "just as the chief stimulus to becoming more annoyed is any insult or injury from the other person" (19). Loving initial actions and loving responses to hostility will therefore elicit returned love. This is Christianity without martyrdom, and Richardson offers no evidence to buttress his optimism.

83.   Sidney 1990, III, xix, 432.

84.   *Politics* II, ix, 1270b, in Aristotle 1984, 76.

85.   Weston 1957, 79 n. 20. See also Hobbes 1962: "The end of worship amongst men, is power" (265).

86.   *The Proficience and Advancement of Learning*, I, in Bacon 1955, 194. Hobbes 1962 calls philosophy "the knowledge acquired by reasoning, from the manner of the generation of any thing, to the properties; or from the properties, to some possible way of generation of the same; to the end to be able to produce, as far as matter, and human force permit, such effects, as human life requireth." Geometry, *method*, and not prudence, is required to understand and to move nature (III, xlvi, 478). Religious prophets prophesied "with a purpose to make those men that relied on them, the more apt to obedience, laws, peace, charity, and civil society;" "Miracles failing, faith also failed" (*Ibid.*, II, xii, 90, 96). The modern philosophers imply that scientific method can produce an unfailing series of 'miracles,' founded upon accurate predictions (or even more ambitiously the fulfillment of the scientist-king's will by the manipulation of malleable nature) and thereby rule. Among the modern sciences is political economy: "Philosophy, with the aid of experience, has at length banished the study of alchemy; and the present age, however desirous of riches, is content to seek them by the humbler means of commerce and industry" (Gibbon n.d., I, xiii, 316).

87.   On fathers as the generators of life see Fustel de Coulanges n.d., I, iv, II, i, vii-viii.

88.   For one who sees the difference, see Eisler 1988, 105.

89.   *Critias*, cxxi, in Plato 1937, II, 84.

90.   Filmer 1949e, 199-203, 206-229; see also Filmer 1949f, 90.   For Filmer's citation of Bodin's *Republic*, II, i, where the same argument

occurs, see Filmer 1949a, 304. For an excellent summary of Filmer's overall doctrine see Tarcov 1984, 10-34.

Boucher 1967b associates republicanism with paganism and the incessant warfare of ancient times. "The spirit of contention, and the spirit of war, belong not to the character of Christians" (6). Burke 1961 famously warns of the threat to civil peace posed by the modern French republican insistence that consent is "the *only* principle" of political legitimacy (25). With respect to the royal succession after the 1688 revolution, Burke writes that Parliament in its Declaration of Right "threw a politic, well-wrought veil over every circumstance tending to weaken the rights, which in the meliorated order of succession they meant to perpetuate" out of a moral necessity to avoid further bloodshed and further danger to England's "religion, laws, and liberties" (29-30).

91. Filmer 1949f, 53-57, 67, 90-94. See also Filmer 1949a, 295-297 and Filmer 1949d, 259. Filmer very understandably attacks Aristotle both for his concept of natural right and for his qualified approval of the mixed regime. He finally does not "much blame" Aristotle for these errors because unaided human reason cannot find its way back to Scriptural first principles (Filmer 1949a, 203-206; see also Filmer 1949e, 193-198; Filmer 1949f, 78-80.

On majority tyranny, see also Boucher 1967b, 516-517. For a recent defense of Filmer, attacking Lockean consent, see Clark 1989, 71ff.

92. Filmer 1949f, 57-58, 63, 262-263, 267; 1949d, 261-263. Filmer writes that the Hebrew word for 'family' derives from a word signifying a prince or lord (Filmer 1949f, 75-76).

93. Filmer 1949e, 289, italics added.

94. Filmer 1949a, 289; Filmer 1949f, 61-62.

95. Filmer 1949f, 84-85. See also Filmer 1949e, 189. "The sin of the children of Israel did lie, not in desiring a king, but in desiring such a king, like as the nations round about had...." (Filmer 1949d, 257). God "is both King and Father of us all" (Filmer 1949e, 233).

96. Filmer 1949e, 188. See also Boucher 1967b, 504-505.

97. Filmer 1949a, 277.

98. Filmer 1949f, 105; Filmer 1949d, 258.

99. Filmer 1949c, 157, 172; Filmer 1949d, 260; Filmer 1949f, 104, 109-113. See also Boucher 1967b, 489.

Burke 1961 does not go so far. While describing obedience to the king as obedience to "the law in him," and insisting that "civil confusion" is no proper remedy against "arbitrary power," (41-42), he asks readers not to confuse his views with those of the "exploded fanatics of slavery" who asserted the divine, hereditary, and unfeasible right of monarchs. "These old fanatics of single arbitrary power dogmatized as if hereditary royalty was the only lawful government in the world, just as our new fanatics of arbitrary power" – the French revolutionists and their British admirers – "maintain that a popular election is the sole source of sovereignty" (38).

100. Filmer 1949b, 267, 269-271; Filmer 1949e, 235; Boucher 1967b, 398, 508, 539-546, 593. In contrast, Burke 1961 vindicates the right to revolution, albeit as "the very last resource of the thinking and the good" (43). The affirmation of "the rights of Englishmen" as distinguished from the 'rights of man' rests finally not on traditionalism but on nature; Burkean traditionalism perceives the good "not by [means of] the superstition of antiquarians, but by the spirit of philosophic analogy" (45-46); England's "artificial institutions" are in "conformity to nature," as is the English citizen's adherence to them. Reverence for the old is natural; nature is the ancient foundation of sound tradition (46-47).

101. One of the oldest political stories is that of Atlantis. In Plato's *Critias* we hear of the "days of old" in which gods governed human beings by persuasion not force, where "military pursuits were common to men and women" – hence the warlike goddess Athena – "a testimony," the speaker claims, "that all animals which associate together, male as well as female, practice in common the virtue which belongs to them without distinction of sex" (*Critias*, cviii, cx, in Plato 1937, II, 73-74). This is not yet a matriarchal story; for this we go to "the founders of modern anthropology" (Briffault 1963, 27).

Although anthropology and archeology have established the existence of matriarchy, the way the facts are used is no more scientific than is the way of patriarchalists. Part of this may be due to the current state of knowledge; the "long history of women opposing war" – and of "women warriors" – "is only now being unearthed" (MacDonald 1987, 2). But, as Plato understood, much has been irrevocably destroyed (*Critias*, cx, in Plato 1937, II, 74); many of the spirited arguments on matriarchy have a decidedly speculative air. Eisler 1988, who has reviewed the historical accounts, claims for example that there are "indications of antiwar activism by women in ancient Greece" (115) – this on the 'evidence' of Aristophanes' *Lysistrata* alone. Even more dubiously, she claims that it was Socrates' advocacy (according to the *Republic*) of equal education for women that got him in trouble with the Athenian *demos* (*Ibid.*, 117). If this is how texts written in historical times are to be treated, one worries about the accuracy or speculative flights concerning pottery, paintings, architecture, and the other remnants of matriarchalism. It may be that prehistoric women and men enjoyed "a fantasizing, intuitive and mystical consciousness" to go along with their mastery of engineering and architecture. It is a certainty that modern writers on the subject have such a consciousness to go along with their antiquarian interests. It is perhaps an irony that today's academics believe written texts to be impossible to interpret, 'undecidable,' while paintings stand as strong evidence for political object-lessons.

102.   Reardon 1985, 92-94; Elshtain 1989, 126; Ruddick 1989, 57.

103.   Ruddick 1989, 18. Eisler 1988 offers a much more 'modern' list: creativity, freedom, individualism, and social reform (139-141) − the agenda of the feminism of autonomy instead of the feminism of maternity. See also Reardon 1985, 26.

104.   Ruddick 1989, 42-43; Elshtain 1983, 343-345.

105.   To overlook this is an 'Hegelian' error; see Strauss 1968, 213.

106.   Seabury and Codevilla 1989, 88.

107.   Wollstonecraft 1988, 14.

108.   Briffault 1963, 53, 59-61, 96-98, 431; see also Hobbes 1962, II, xx, 152 and Stone 1978, 11. Briffault was an economic determinist with Marxist sympathies; rather in anticipation of Stalinist genetics, he attributed physical differences between the sexes "largely" to the effects of the division of labor (98). If this were so, men and women today would resemble one another quite closely. It is not so.

109.   Schreiner 1914, 41, 49, 52-54. For a view that encompasses men as well as women, see Woolf 1963, 11. Schreiner claims, "No woman who is a woman says of a human body, 'It is nothing!'" (44). However, more recent matriarchalists endorse abortion (Eisler 1988, 167) and lesbianism (Ruddick 1989, passim). Yet surely mothering first requires generation and cannot 'abstract' from generation; it cannot ignore the fact that 'reproductive freedom' means freedom *not* to reproduce. Thus the original, natural source of maternal authority, the power to generate life, disappears beneath the rhetoric of autonomy and even of population control.

This abstraction is all the more curious because it comes after an attack on rational or 'abstract' thought. After citing Schreiner and Jane Addams on "the history and cost of the human flesh" (186), Ruddick asserts that "the philosopher" is fearful of childbirth; "the idealization of reason in Western philosophy may be in part a defensive reaction to the troubling complexities of birthing labor" (191). She associates philosophic abstraction with war, which kills and suffers (as philosophers analyze and are killed for it?) but "does not give birth" (204). She overlooks the example of the self-described philosophic midwife, Socrates. It would be closer to the truth to charge that *modern* philosophy, with its scientific method, proposes to take the place of natural generativity.

110. Briffault 1963, 319.

111. Graves 1970, 110.

112. Briffault 1963, 285-287, 357-359; Lévy-Bruhl 1966, 316; Stone 1978, 129. Briffault adds that the deities worshipped as "Great Mothers" had no husbands; they were virgins in the original meaning of the term: "not a woman who had no sexual experience, but one who was independent" (375).

113. Elshtain 1987, 206, 224-225; see also Briffault 1963, 106-107.

   Some modern feminists endorse defensive war (Wollstonecraft 1988, 145; Key 1972, 95). Key deplores women "egging men on to war" (235). Proudhon 1927 notices the same inclination: "Women can love the man of work and industry like a servant, the poet or the artist like a gem, the wise man like a rarity; the just she respects; the rich obtain her preference: Her heart is with the *militaire*" (I, 59).

114. See Briffault 1963, 64, 99-100, 203, 280-282, 287, 357; see also Stone 1978, 132. On the Amazons see Kirk 1987, 27-28. Eisler 1988 admits that the matriarchs of ancient Crete fought wars, while insisting that they did not "idealize warfare" − this on the evidence that their paintings feature no "grandiose scenes of battle or of hunting" (35-37).

115. Eisler 1988, 54-56, 63.

116. Stone 1978, xiii, 20, 67-68, 94-95; Eisler 1988, 43-46.

117. Stone 1978, 156, 182-188. Stone goes so far as to charge that the priestly tribe of Levites, who urged the destruction of goddess-worship, were not Semites by Aryans:

   > If this hypothesis bears up under further investigation, we must certainly view the events of the Second World War, and the atrocities enacted upon the Hebrew people of the twentieth century by the self-styled Aryans of Nazi Germany, not only as tragic but ironic. The researches and excavations of the Hittite culture have been carried on primarily by German archaeologists throughout this century. It was sometime before and directly after the First World War that *nasili* was slowly beginning to be accepted as the real name of the Hittite language and Nesa, of Nasa, their first capital. The original name of the Hittite invaders may have been Nesians or Nasians. Nuzi became the capital of the Indo-European nation of Mitanni. One cannot help but wonder how much Adolf Hitler was affected by the reports of these finds, which may have found their way into the popular media of the times. Was it these accounts that caused him to change his name from

Schickelgrüber to Hitler, which in German would mean
something like "teacher of Hit?" Strangely enough one
more connection between the Hittites and the Hebrews
is the Hebrew use of the word *nasi* for prince....(127)

Eisler 1988 more cautiously concedes that the "politically motivated"
(85) Jewish Bible has some good in it (94). Daly 1985 prefers Stone's
general stance and extends it to Christianity, claiming that the
Antichrist is not evil but "a fuller stage of conscious participation in the
living God;" "the Antichrist and the *Second Coming of Women* are
synonymous" (96). For a Christian feminism see Fiorenza 1983, 105,
132. For an anthropologist's account see Briffault 1963, 370-371.

118. Lackner 1984, 65.

119. Woolf 1963, 6-10; Yudkin 1983, 263-265; Stephenson 1983, 291;
Horstock 1983, 283-285; Daly 1978, 355-361; Daly 1985, 114, 120;
Eisler 1988, xvii, xx.

120. Reardon 1985, 1-17, 23-24, 30-32, 44, 49-59. Pacificist rather than
pacifist, Woolstonecraft 1988, 37 and Elshtain 1987 still share these
reservations against 'masculine' warlikeness. Elshtain associates this
concept of masculinity with Plato's warrior-guardians, Machiavelli, and
Rousseau (56-63); she ignores Machiavelli's Lady of Forli when
discussing Machiavelli's women.

The emphasis on technology-as-conquest causes Eisler 1988 to
minimize the differences between "capitalist" and "communist"
"nations" (xiv, 154). Rowbotham 1972 prefers Maoism (188), which
she believes to be feminist and egalitarian, despite noticeable evidence
to the contrary.

121. Reardon 1985 follows Jane Addams in rejecting the emphasis on
political structures and praising "living organic notions of
transformation" (84) − Hegelianism democratized. She mistakenly
claims that the "masculine preoccupation with the public and
structures...has aborted the transformative potential of most twentieth-
century revolutions" (90), when in fact the word 'abstract' has been a
term of abuse, 'concrete' a term of praise among 'masculine' minds
since the late eighteenth century.

122. Brown 1988 claims that the body is "the locus, vehicle, and origin of our
freedom" (196), the active part of human beings. Machiavelli's well-
known preference for touch (whereby one can grasp and manipulate
nature) over a sight (reason) or hearing (prophecy) thus finds a new
echo in Brown's kinder, gentler Machiavellianism − as she herself
more or less sees (209-210). This kind of feminism does not abandon
but rather varies and extends the Machiavellian-Cartesian project.

Other feminists present a more measured view of androcracy. Eisler
1988 observes that male domination was gradually tamed in Greece by

philosophers and by democracy (111-112). Socrates, she knows, learned from a woman. See also Fiorenza 1983 on Epicureanism (214).

123. Stone 1978, 32; Eisler 1988, xvi-xvii, 13-14, 24-25. Stone, however, also claims that matriarchal/matrilinear societies were governed by assemblies probably comprised of elders (130-131) — "a more communal attitude toward power" than that manifested in one-man rule, to be sure, but rather less egalitarian than government by either elected or randomly selected representatives. The superior egalitarianism of commercial republicanism can be seen in Mill 1911, 79, 91-96.

124. Eisler 1988, 164. See also Capra and Spretnak 1985, *passim*, for the "four pillars" of the "Green" political movement in (then) West Germany. These are ecology, social equality, participatory democracy, and nonviolence.

   The relation of pacifist feminism to what is now called 'deep ecology' may be seen in Rifkin 1991. If the earth is a living being symbolized as a mother whose name is Gaia, and the environmental damage caused by war amounts to a form of rape, then we have a resurrection of the old Goddess religion in a new form.

125. Eisler 1988, 105-110. Eisler's name for her regime is "gylany" — "gy" standing for women, "an" for men.

126. Briffault 1963 writes:

   The desire to dominate takes different forms in men and women. Woman's ambition is not to exercise physical compulsion, but to bend the will of others to her desire, to overcome not physical but psychical resistances. Her object is to have her way. The man, however, delights in the display of power, is flattered by hostile envy and desires his power to be felt and known. (106).

127. Mill 1911 — a man, admittedly, but far from insensitive to women's rights — criticizes the politics of compassion and motherly care. "The influence of women counts for a great deal in two of the most marked features of European life — its aversion to war, and its addiction to philanthropy" (192). These "excellent characteristics" need limitation, however, given "the ultimate evil tendency of charity or philanthropy which commends itself to [the] sympathetic feelings," namely, the weakening of "the very foundations of the self-respect, self-help, and self-control which are the essential conditions both of individual prosperity and of social virtue" (194). Undiluted admiration for mothers (Great or human) leads to "notions of good" consisting solely of "blessings descending from a superior" (195). In historical societies this superior has been a male head of household or a male-dominated government; to rebel against these in the name of motherhood, even of

690

a kind of all-encompassing egalitarian mother-spirit that pervades all of society, merely shifts the source of the *secular providence*. Society as a whole becomes the final authority, with the consequent danger of majority tyranny.

128. Wollstonecraft 1988, 15.

129. Eisler 1988, xxii, 104, 198.

130. MacDonald 1987, 3; Eisler 1988, 190; Capra and Spretnak 1984, xix, 169-170; Reardon 1985, 16, 19-22.

131. Eisler 1988, 193; Ruddick 1989, 77, 166-168. Woolf 1963 less ambitiously concedes that women "have no weapon with which to enforce our will" except "the weapon of independent opinion based upon independent income" (13-17, 40); for commentary see Pierson 1987, 218-220. Recall also the argument of Hocking 1923, cited in footnote 71, above.

132. Ruddick 1939, 138-139.

133. Elshtain 1983, 342.

134. *Ibid.*, 342; Elshtain 1987, 3-8. Whereas Wollstonecraft 1988 insists that "for man and woman, truth, if I understand the meaning of the word, must be one and the same" (51), feminists today often endorse value relativism and epistemological pluralism, effectively ensuring continued and intensified conflict; see Ruddick 1989, 9-16. "Temperamentally I am a pluralist," Ruddick announces (127); yet feminists persistently write and act with more temper than pluralism; without some universal criterion of truth beyond ever-varying 'praxis,' nihilism and its attendant evils, including war, will follow inevitably.

135. Grotius 1925, II, ix, 311-312.

136. *Ibid.*, 1925, I, iii, 103ff.; II, vi, 260.

137. Montesquieu 1989, I, x, 142. Nicolai 1919 cites Montesquieu as part of an argument claiming that wealth, order, and health increase in "every subjugated nation," and that victory enervates the conqueror. Montesquieu does not go so far into pacifism.

138. Sun Tzu 1963 argues for self-preservation as an end, and war as a means to that end (63); by contrast, Locke 1965 sharply contrasts the just use of executive power with tyranny, defending a right to revolution (*Second Treatise*, xi, 411; xiii, 419, 448; xix, 463. Cox 1982 sees this as the seed of nationalism (125). See also Montesquieu 1989, I, ii, 10; Hume 1970, "Of Public Credit," 103; Hume 1985, II, xiii, 489-490; Sidney 1990, II, vii, 117; Burckhardt 1979, 308; Green 1967, 165; Angell 1935, 34-36; Walzer 1977, 230-231, 326.

139. Sun Tzu 1963, 73. For the assertion that is the only truly important object, see Goltz 1913, 79; for an untenable attempt to combine cynicism and idealism, see Guevara 1969, 6-8.

140. Proudhon 1861 asserts that the "pretended science of the rights of man" consists of nothing but "fictions" (6). See also Bernhardi 1914, 30-35 (consonant with his Machiavellian endorsement of wars of national unification, *Ibid.*, 42); Meinecke 1957, 25-31, 38; Aron 1954, 77.

141. Meinecke 1957, 38-49. Thus in 1576 Innocent Gentillet could proclaim, "Neither the Christian in him, nor the knight, wanted to have anything to do with the cold monster of raison d'état" (cited in *Ibid.*, 56). The English Christian minister Inge 1956 writes:

> Machiavelli was the pioneer. Our Francis Bacon professes the same creed: his international ethics differ in no way from the principles expounded before and during the way by German professors. Hobbes, too, says quite plainly that the state can do no wrong. Fichte, in his famous lectures at Berlin after Jena, proclaims the unlimited right and duty of every nation to destroy its neighbors....(311-312).

142. See Machiavelli 1985, xvii; compare Sun Tzu 1963, 128-129. On the use of the enemy's fears see *Ibid.*, 109-110; on the use of one's own troops' fears see the description of an officer's response to his own retreating troops at the Battle of Gettysburg: "On some unpatriotic backs of those not quick of comprehension, the flat or my sabre fell not lightly, and at its touch their love of country returned, and with a look at me as if I were the destroying angel, as I might have become theirs, they again faced the enemy" (Haskell 1958, 104). For a tyrant who confused fear with love and eventually suffered for it, see Mussolini 1928, 138, 308-310.

143. For a critique of Hegelianism along these lines see Meinecke 1957, 344-350; Heering 1943, 99-115. For an attempt for effect this synthesis see Bernhardi 1914, 47-49.

144. Haskell 1958 writes, "Many of the [Confederate] officers were well dressed, fine, proud gentlemen, such men as it would be a pleasure to meet, when the war is over;" "pity and sympathy were the general feelings of us all," and he records his "respect" for "my brave, though deluded, countrymen" (120, 151). Walzer 1977 observes that an enemy "alienates himself from me when he tries to kill me, and from our common humanity." But "the alienation is temporary, the humanity immanent" (142).

145. Walzer 1977, 7-8; Buenode Mesquita and Lalman 1990, 174-175.

146. Nardin 1983, 178, 194. It should be added that although Nardin rejects that he calls "positivism" based upon national sovereignty, he upholds a different form of positivism: one based upon international "practice" (286-287). See also *Ibid.*, 8-12. This "practice" is ruled by necessity; a practice of common respect for international rules, manners, procedures, etc., exists, Nardin claims, among those "who are not necessarily engaged in any common pursuit but who nonetheless *have to* get along with one another" (12, italics added). Nardin questions the existence of human rights as entities independent of rules (294-300). However, it quickly becomes clear that his endorsement to the rules itself depends upon something beyond the rules, namely, prudence (303-304). And what does prudence serve, if not the good? Surely not the rules alone, else we descend into circularity.

147. Proudhon 1861, I, 23, 49-57; see also Burke 1982, 20-21; Constant 1989, 163-164.

148. In antiquity, Proudhon writes, "The assimilation after conquest is the first duty of the conqueror, I say also the right of the people conquered" (Proudhon 1927, III, 203). France's modern wars were useless and unjust, as no assimilation occurred (206-208). "Force, by itself, knows no doctrines," but the human use of force never abstracts from human purposes (217). This is so much so that Proudhon can insist that "the universal conscience" is "more powerful than the police of kings or the wisdom of jurists," that the conduct of any war should not be "left to chance, abandoned to the ferocity of the soldier;" "all that can assure the sincerity and honorableness of the struggle" is good (220-225).

149. Spengler 1929, I, ix, 302-309. Reilly 1986 accurately distinguishes between ancient and modern or Machiavellian tyranny:

> In the ancient world, tyranny was limited by the reach of the tyrant's will: It was a moral disorder. In modern ideology, this disorder is not only moral, it is intellectual and metaphysical (222).

Spengler 1929 associates the "Will-Culture" with Descartes and Kant, noticing that "Plato never felt, as Kant was driven to feel, the ego as center of a transcendent sphere of effect" (Spengler 1929, 311).

150. Hegel 1954, 88-89; see also Rosen 1974, 14, and Hoffman 1989, 95-100, 117.

151. Pangle 1973, 136-137, 227-238. See also Rousseau 1979, IV, 329.

152. Camus 1958, 11.

153. For recent discussions of this point that focus on epistemology instead of the 'state' of nature, see Hoffman 1986, ix-xvi, 10-20, 33, and Hoffman 1989, vii-viii. "Eternal" self-preservation, absent divine grace,

can only mean the long-term preservation seen in art, including new-philosophic writings, that gain lasting glory for their authors.

154. See Shelley 1966, "A Philosophical View of Reform," on the connection of "the new spirit in men's minds" seen in Bacon, Montaigne, Locke, Spinoza, and Hobbes with the American regime (234). On Lockean consent and conquest see Johnson 1975, 240, and Lowenthal 1988, 130-135. Montesquieu 1989 calls the right of conquest "a necessary, legitimate, and unfortunate right, which always leaves an immense debt to be discharged if human nature is to be repaid" (II, x, 142); it is a right to use, not to destruction; for commentary on Montesquieu see Voltaire 1962, 550. Roosevelt 1990 finds a similar teaching in Rousseau (60). Nonetheless it is clear that a conquest of a smaller nation by a *mass* army might be more in line with republican consensualism, if the mass army takes care to couch its ambitions in humanitarian rhetoric.

155. Fried 1916, 85-90; Russell 1917, 32-34; Joad 1939, 39. Walzer 1977 more prudently observes that "it is the success of coercion," not its failure, "that makes war ugly" (35). It should be noted that an older and more historically well-versed Bertrand Russell admitted that "it is a curious fact that military conquest very often produced in the conquered a genuine loyalty towards their masters" (Russell 1960, 13-14).

156. "Little is gained by conquest if it is followed oppression" (*Life of Cnaeus Julius Agricola* in Tacitus 1947, 689). A recent student of Rome concurs; see Arendt 1971, 125-138. See also La Boétie 1975, 64-68; Montesquieu 1968b, I, 27; IV, 52; VI, 75; Montesquieu 1989, I, iv, 34; I, v, 59; Green 1967, 169.

157. On Aristotelian kingship see Mansfield 1989, 23-25, 45-54; on the Roman dictatorship and mixed government see *Ibid.*, 76-85.

158. Fustel de Coulanges n.d., IV, vii.

159. Filmer 1949d, 239-243.

160. Hobbes 1962, II, xx, 155.

161. *Ibid.*, I, xiv, 110. Walzer 1970 observes that "individual bodily security is the only ultimate in Hobbes's system and the search for that security can never be forsaken or transcended" (85).

162. Hobbes 1962, I, xiii, 98-100. See also Smith 1965, I, ii, 15. It is not sufficiently appreciated that Sigmund Freud derives his politics from Hobbes.

> Human life in common is only made possible when a majority comes together which is stronger than any separate individual and which remains united against all

separate individuals. The power of this community is then set up as 'right' in opposition to the power of the individual, which is condemned as 'brute force.' This replacement of the power of the individual by the power of the community constitutes the decisive step of civilization. The essence of it lies in the fact that the members of the community restrict themselves in their possibilities of satisfaction, whereas the individual knew no such restrictions. (Freud 1962, 42)

163. Hobbes 1962, I, xv, 115; II, xxi, Hobbes 1971, 159. See also *Tractatus Theologico-Politicus* I, xvi, in Spinoza 1951, 200.

164. Hobbes 1962, I, xvi, 127; II, xvii, 132; II, xviii, 141. With respect to monarchy Hobbes 1990 makes the same point: "all men are fools which pull down anything which does them good before they have set up something better in its place" (155). See also *Tractatus Theologico-Politicus*, I, xix, in Spinoza 1951, 249-256. For a statement objecting to Hobbesian absolutism see Constant 1989, 178-179.

165. Hobbes 1962, II, xx, 151, 154; II, xxi, 159. Hobbes 1990 gingerly draws out the theological implications: God "gives all the kingdoms of the world," he begins piously, "which nevertheless [!] proceed from the consent of people, either for fear or hope" (12). See also Hume 1985, II, xii, 474, 482 and Smith 1989, 64. Maritain 1957, 29-45, well understands the anti-theistic substance of Bodin, Hobbes, and Rousseau.

166. Hobbes 1962, I, xiv, 110; Hobbes 1990, 152.

167. Hobbes 1990, 193.

168. Hobbes 1962, II, xxi, 165. On the subject's 'right' to attempt to escape the death penalty see Hobbes 1990, 50.

169. *Ibid.*, II, xxvii, 231, 234; II, xxx, 260. For recent examples of Hobbesian argument see Narveson 1965, 73, and Hungerland 1989, 35-36.

170. Bodin 1962, I, i, 1; I, viii, 84; II, ii, 185; Hobbes 1962, Introduction, 19. For commentary see Mansfield 1989, 151-158, 168. For an historical example of a Bodinian-Hobbesian monocrat who "liked to subjugate nature by art and treasure" see Saint-Simon 1901, 311.

171. Hobbes 1962, I, iv, 35; II, xxvi, 198-199; II, xxx, 255. See also Hobbes 1990, 44.

172. *Ibid.*, II, i, 129; II, xvii, 132; II, xix, 148.

173. Hobbes 1962, II, xix, 144; II, xxi, 161, 167; III, xlvii, 506. Nietzsche 1986 similarly denies that tyranny, justice, and the rule of law differ in kind: "to be a lawgiver is a more sublimated form of tyranny" (I, 123).

174. Hobbes 1990, 45. On Hobbesian utilitarianism see Nicolai 1919, 417-426. German *Realpolitik* descends directly from Hobbes, as Nicolai sees. On the Baconian and Cartesian origins of Hobbesian materialism and utilitarianism, see Proudhon 1927, II, 113-122.

175. Hobbes 1990, 77, 112-117, 175.

176. Andreski 1968 observes that "monocracy has a levelling effect on social stratification" (101). Germaine de Staël reports on Napoleon Bonaparte's policy of "annihilat[ing]" individuality and reducing civil society to "a mass" (*Considerations on the Principle Events of the French Revolution*, III, iv, in Berger 1965, 45).

177. Hobbes 1962, I, v, 43, 46; II, xxxi, 270. For commentary see Mansfield 1989, 170-178. Mansfield tellingly remarks that Hobbes opposes method to prudence but actually draws upon his own prudence in establishing his method; method cannot justify itself. In view of the foregoing, Nardin 1983 surely emphasizes the wrong aspect of Hobbes' system in claiming that "Hobbes did not challenge the traditional understanding of the law of nature as a set of principles that could be known by reason and thus defended rationally" (230, n. 7). Hobbes conceives of both nature and reason in an entirely different way than, say, Aristotle does.

178. The *philosophe* Mercier de la Rivière writes:

> Euclid is the true type of the despot. The geometrical axioms which he has transmitted to us are genuine despotic laws; in them the legal and the personal despotism of the legislator are one and the same thing, a force evident and irresistible; and for that reason the despot Euclid has for centuries exercised his unchallenged sway over all enlightened peoples. (Quoted in Bruun 1927, 28).

179. Machiavelli, 1965, IV, 128. See also *Ibid.*, II, 79.

180. Hobbes 1962, I, vi, 50-54; I, x, 73; I, xi, 80-81, 86; I, xii, 90.

181. Hobbes 1990, 2-11, 16, 21-22, 50. Both Catholics (through their use of Aristotle) and Presbyterians (through their university study of Greek and Roman political history) incline to republican sympathies and inculcate seditious opinions in their sermons (*Ibid.*, 16-17, 23-26, 42-44). "The Universities have been to this nation, as the wooden horse was to the Trojans" (40); they are "the core of the rebellion" (58). The combination of philosophy and theology yields "the advancement of the professors" not the advancement of learning; Hobbes so loathes the resultant priestcraft, throughout human civilization from the Druids to the Persian Magi, from Egyptians and Jews to Indian fakirs and Ethiopian witch-doctors, that he muses on how much better it

would have been to kill 1,000 Presbyterian ministers than to allow 100,000 Englishmen to die in civil war (*Ibid.*, 95).

182. *Ibid.*, 43-46, 144; Hobbes 1962, III, xlii, 394.

183. Hobbes 1990, 58-63. Walzer 1977 emphasizes the sovereign's need to fix the meaning of legal terms, including religious terms; epistemological peace precedes civil peace (11-12). Griswold 1989 emphasizes obedience to the sovereign and the polemical critique of much "commonly received dogma" (25). But the rhetoric defending a minimalist Christianity probably had a stronger influence on subsequent writers who were most influential.

184. Hobbes 1990, 58. For a slightly earlier, somewhat different version of this strategy, see Grotius 1925, II, xx, where the philosopher sets down four principles of "true religion, which is common to all ages" (510), principles that are later reduced to one, namely, that God exists, and is one (515).

185. Hegel limits his monarch more strictly than does Hobbes. Hegel's is a constitutional monarch. "[T]he monarch's part is merely to set to the law the subjective 'I will'" (Hegel 1973, 289, n. 171). "This 'I will' constitutes the great difference between the ancient world" — where nature was treated "as a power which...expressed what was good for men" — "and the modern, and in the great edifice of the state it must have its appropriate equivalent" (*Ibid.*, 188, n. 170). This "will with the power of ultimate decision" (*Ibid.*, 176) alone can bespeak the State's unity, speak for its sovereignty ("the ideality of all particular authorities" within the State [180]). As for Hobbes, an elective monarchy will not do. "[T]o be independent of public opinion is the first formal condition of anything great or rational in life or in science" (*Ibid.*, 205). The monarch wills existing laws, unless he happens also to be a "great man," the kind of man who "tell[s] his age what it wills" (*Ibid.*, 295). Hegel here presents a perhaps ennobled version of the Machiavellian prince, not so much a peace loving, war-fearing Hobbesian. Hegel differs from both Machiavelli and Hobbes in his emphasis on organization; superior organization is the real conqueror in human history (Hegel 1954, Pt. I, Sec. iii, Ch. iii). He praises a bureaucracy prevented from tyranny by the sovereign monarch above it and the corporations below it (Hegel 1973, 193).

186. Gibbon n.d., I, xv, 417.

187. Howard 1983, 152; Richardson 1960b, 237. Richardson immediately cautions his readers not "to hastily blame Christianity" for this, before going on to observe that the frequency of wars among Christians was greater than those among other religions, although not to a statistically significant degree (239). Voltaire 1962 writes that "Hobbes was considered to atheist; he led a tranquil and innocent life; the fanatics of his time deluged England, Scotland, and Ireland with blood" (102).

188. Grotius 1925, Prolegomena, 20. Crucé 1972 regards religions as "a mere pretext" for war in most cases (8); Voltaire 1962 considers ambition, greed, and "artificial" religion as causes (196, 302-305).

189. Burckhardt 1979, 88-89.

190. For an excellent discussion of Socratic thought on religion see Ahrensdorf 1989. Consider Burke 1961, writing not of religions but of superstitions:

> Wise men, who as such, are not *admirers*...are not violently attached to these things, nor do they violently hate them. Wisdom is not the most severe corrector of folly. They are the rival follies, which mutually wage so unrelenting a war...(174)

As superstitions inevitably "engage the immoderate vulgar" on both sides, often compelling the unsuperstitious to choose sides, a wise man or woman "perhaps...would think the superstition which builds, to be more tolerable than that which demolishes" (175). Even more modestly, a wise man or woman might prefer the one that demolishes the least of the best.

191. Voltaire 1952, 268. He adds, "Even the law is impotent against these attacks of rage; it is like reading a court decree to a raving maniac."

The first article in the *Philosophical Dictionary* is "Abbé," "Father;" from the 'patriarchal' beginning Voltaire moves finally to "Virtue," which he defines as "Doing good to your neighbor" (*Ibid.*, 495). Voltaire intends to relegate the cardinal virtues of prudence, courage, moderation, and justice and the theological virtues of faith, hope, and charity to the private realm, leaving exclusively sociable virtues in the public realm. This provided a foundation for toleration and peace without cultivating social indifference or "our garden" (as in *Candide*). "Virtue among men is a trade of kindnesses" (495); brotherliness replaces fatherliness. The question for Voltaireans will always be: 'Can there be brothers (or sisters) without fathers (and mothers)?' Voltaire himself concedes that religion is "absolutely necessary" in order to sustain oaths (Voltaire 1962, 102). For a more recent, and much more pious, version of this stance, recall the British socialist and pacifist George Lansbury, "first and foremost a Christian," who believed that "man through the omnipotence of modern science could do for himself what hitherto he had asked God to do for him" (Maaranen 1981, 208). The metaphor of light employed by Hobbesian philosophers was of course employed previously by Christians, e.g., John 3:19-21.

192. Russell 1960, 100-101.

193. For an early statement in favor of religious toleration within Christendom see More 1946, II, 101. For a brief account of Spinoza's

alliance with a sect of sincere Christians devoted to an 'inward' religion, see Jones 1914, 124ff. Locke 1968 is a work of seventy-seven paragraphs whose thirty-third paragraph cites Jesus' command to forgive an enemy seventy times seven times (87).   Locke also commends an 'inward' Christianity of Christians who war against their own vices according to "the faith that worketh, not by force, but by love" (*Ibid.*, 59); physical wars of persecution do not save souls and "make use of arms that do not belong to Christian warfare" (63). He goes so far as to identify the spirit of toleration with Jesus (*Ibid.*, 89) and to urge (qualifying if not openly contradicting the express teaching of Jesus at Matthew 7:13-14 and John 14:6; c.f. also Acts 4:12) that there are "several paths" in "the same road" to salvation, and "it is doubtful which is the right one" (*Ibid.*, 93). This 'inwardness' applies not only to individuals but to nations, as Vattel 1916 argues: "True zeal will apply itself to make a holy religion flourish in the countries where it is received and to render it helpful to the moral life of the citizens; and while awaiting the dispositions of Providence, either in the form of invitations from foreign Nations or a clearly divine mission to preach abroad, it will find enough to do at home" (II, 133).

On moral relativism see Locke 1959:

> [T]he greatest happiness consists in the having of those things which produce the greatest pleasure, and in the absence of those which cause any disturbance, any pain. Now these, to different men, are different things...Men may choose different things, and yet all choose right; supposing them only like a company of poor insects; whereof some are bees, delighted with flowers and sweetness, others beetles, delighted with all kinds of viands, which having enjoyed for a season, they would cease to be, and exist no more for ever (II, xxi, 352).

The error here is Locke's equation of different *tastes* in human beings with different *species* of insects, thereby implying that tastes make different human groups *as* different as different natural orders of insects. Lackner 1990 echoes Locke in saying, "A multifarious being like homo sapiens should adopt tolerance as 'second nature,' in the truest sense" (55). Murray 1960 notices that this discussion of 'free will' occurs in the context of Locke's chapter "Of Power," and draws out the moral implications (III, 303-310, 323-329). De Jouvenel criticizes "the idea that toleration could be ensured by moral relativism" as "one of the strangest intellectual illusions;" evidently, as Jaffa 1975 observes, extreme skepticism in morality as in epistemology, "devours itself, leaving dogmatism unchallenged in the world" (236).

194. Griswold 1989 rightly sees that the solution preferred by Socrates in Plato's *Republic* — to "change the self-interested part of human nature" (26) through strict education, eugenics, communism, and civic religion — is politically infeasible, and that Plato's Socrates knows this. Montesquieu 1968a, cxxxv, Montesquieu 1968b, xx, 190, Hume 1985, I,

viii, and perhaps especially Smith 1965, V, i, 740-766 for the neo-Hobbesian solution to the violence of religious sectarianism. These philosophers would prevent the worst religio-political factionalism by means of "the principle of divide and conquer" (Cropsey 1977, 81).

195. See Grotius 1925, II, i, 182; Montesquieu 1989, V, xxv, 489; Voltaire 1962, 482; Mansfield 1965, 6-8, 178 (on Burke). Brock 1972 describes how Mennonite wealth and the increasing toleration of Mennonites in seventeenth-century Holland caused Mennonite pacifism to decline and Mennonite internal divisions increase, even as persecution of Mennonites decreased (162ff). See also Hershberger 1969, 84-87. These tendencies have not gone unnoticed among some twentieth-century Christians, e.g. Heath 1915, 72; Stratmann 1928, vii-ix; H. Richard Niebuhr 1959, 84.

196. Locke 1968, 65-71, 83-87, 99, 103-115, 127-135. Troeltsch 1949 observes that "the most versatile individualistic rationalism, purely utilitarian and sectarian in character...can be abstracted as it stands from the religious setting of Locke's theory" (II, 638). The Socinians had anticipated many of Locke's formulations; in England Socinians had been expelled in 1660. See Kot 1957, *passim*, and Brock 1972, 137-138.

Characteristically, Voltaire 1962 restates Locke's secularism in more vigorous tones: "Priests are to a state something like what teachers are to citizens' households; they are there to teach, pray, and set an example; but they cannot have any authority over the master of the house, at least until it has been proved that the man who pays the wages must obey the man who receives them" (432-433). Paine 1961 denounces both religious intolerance and toleration — "Both are despotisms" — in favor of "UNIVERSAL RIGHT OF CONSCIENCE." The marriage of Church and State produces a bad-tempered "mule animal;" "take away the law-establishment, and every religion reassumes its original benignity." Paine describes (whether or not he believes) "original" religions, "religions in their nature," rather as Rousseau describes human-individuals in his state of nature: "mild and benign" (323-326).

See also *Principles of Politics* in Constant 1989, 275-284; Green 1967, 170-171 and Burckhardt 1979, 165.

Locke's argument is vulnerable at two places. Although "light can be no means accrue from corporeal suffering alone" (71) — Machiavelli endured torture without any noticeable increase in piety — corporeal suffering may serve to prepare the mind for receiving otherworldly ministrations. This is tacitly admitted when Hobbesians argue that physical comfort can lead the mind away from other-worldliness. Second, the hedonism implicit in Locke's claim, "I cannot be saved by a religion that I dislike" (99) overlooks the example of Saul on the road to Damascus, and many others.

197. Rousseau follows Machiavelli and Hobbes in blaming Christianity for dividing the citizenry: "All that destroy social unity is worthless; all institutions that set man in contradiction to himself are worthless" (*Social Contract*, IV, viii, in Rousseau 1950, 134). "Jesus came to set up on earth a spiritual kingdom, which, by separating the theological from the political system, made the State no longer one, and brought about the internal divisions which have never ceased to trouble Christian peoples" (*Ibid.*, 131). As does Locke, Rousseau approves of surreptitious Socinianism for the clergy (Rousseau 1968, 13-14) but without Lockean disestablishment. Vattel 1916 also takes a Machiavellian or quasi-Machiavellian view, although in Vattel one senses a certain real moral elevation not to be found in the Florentine (I, xii, 53-67). Vattel endorses an established but tolerent Church in each country. It should be noted that Vattel draws an interesting conclusion from his refusal to absolve the churches from public authority: He will not exempt them from taxation (*Ibid.*, 65).

198. Burke 1961, 22-24, 103-108, 112-136, 159-168. Brunner 1947 finds that the twentieth century sees a crisis in marriage or private life and a crisis in government or public life due to "the severance of the order of the state from all connection with the eternal world," leading either to state absolutism or to "unrestrained individualism" (440). The pacifist Suttner 1914 laments that while "religious hatred is conquered," "national hatred" remains (417).

Other Christian writers, on both the 'left' and the 'right' politically, who have attacked the Lockean settlement include Boucher 1967b, who calls government by consent a "hazardous" principle likely to lead to civil unrest and irreligiosity (484-489), O'Toole 1941, who deplores "Masonic liberalism" for its privatization of "religion and morals" (36), Iglehart 1941, who condemns the "pagan" and "secular" character of "modern life," wherein "Man and his work stand at the center, self-sufficient, self-regarding, self-worshiping," and violent (127), and Maritain 1957, who attempts to reconcile Roman Catholicism with liberal democracy (162-177).

199. Crucé 1972 writes that "it is not tolerance to forgive the wicked; it is cruelty, because impunity will make them more daring and will foment their malice" (63). Vattel 1916 essays a witty reversal: "Far from disturbing a philosopher in his opinions, public officials ought to punish those who accuse him publicly of irreverence" (I, xi, 49). Even Voltaire warns, "You know that toleration is the principle of the government of China, and of all those of Asia; but isn't that toleration fatal when it exposes an empire to being overwhelmed by fanatical opinions?" (138

200. Augustine 1964, III, 163. See also Hobhouse 1909, 67.

201. Ferguson 1974, 17.

202. Adams 1986, 1344.

203. Fried 1912, 88-89. Among Fried's 'proofs' of the Kaiser's pacifism: Wilhelm II had been sent a copy of Norman Angell's popular book, *The Great Illusion*, and "is stated to have read it with great interest, and to have been deeply impressed by it" (17). Fried then triumphantly summarizes Angell's pacifist argument. A similar combination of sycophancy and hope may be seen in the dealings of 'intellectuals' with tyrants of all political hues, particularly in the eighteenth and twentieth centuries.

204. Montesquieu 1989, II, ix, 132; Nietzsche 1986, II, ii, 383. Nietzsche predicts or hopes that this quarantine need last only a hundred years. Benjamin Constant presents the balanced view that is in fact similar to Montesquieu's considered opinion:

> One needs an absurd party spirit and a profound ignorance to wish to reduce to simple terms the choice between republic and monarchy: as if the former were merely the government of many, and the latter simply that of one. Reduced to these terms, the one does not ensure peace, while the other cannot grant liberty...[W]ho could deny that in England, for the last 120 years, people have enjoyed greater personal safety and political rights than France ever acquired by its attempt at a republic, whose shapeless and imperfect institutions spread arbitrary power and multiplied the number of tyrants? (*The Spirit of Conquest*, II, Constant 1989, 85-86, n. 1)

205. See Herodotus 1942, VII, 417; Aristotle 1984, V, xi, 174-175; Boétie 1975, 58-62, 68-85; Sidney 1990, II, xxi, 197-201; *The Spirit of Conquest*, II, in Constant 1989, 116-126. In his thirteenth section Constant describes the baleful effects of despotism upon religion, whose independence despotism fears (127-129).

206. Sidney 1990, III, xxxix.

207. Paine 1961, 315, 362, 384-385. Paine here follows Aristotle 1984, V, ix, 174.

208. *Second Philippic*, in Demosthenes 1967, 170; Sidney 1990, III, xxiii, 451-454; Vattel 1916, I, 28-31; *The Spirit of Conquest*. II, in Constant 1989, 114-115.

209. Grotius 1925, II, xxiv, 573.

210. *Second Treatise*, III, in Locke 1965, 320-321. See also Boétie 1975, 45-50; Rousseau 1979, I, 481 n. 2; for a more recent statement see Hollenbach 1983, 21. See also Staub 1989, who demonstrates the connection between tyranny and genocide.

211. *Judgment on Perpetual Peace*, in Rousseau 1927, 105; Voltaire 1962, 513; Sidney 1990, III, xxi, 445-446; Paine 1961, 396-397; Godwin 1946, 142-143; Anonymous 1837, 8-29, 53, 156-157, 168 (on Machiavellianism); "A Philosophical View of Reform," (in Shelley 1966, 260. De Givry 1924 too complacently supposes that no wars at all would ever occur without tyrants or "monarchs" (134-135).

212. *The Spirit of Conquest*, II, in Constant 1989, 132-133; Sidney 1990, II, xi, 136-143; Paine 1961, 406-408. See also Aron 1966, 67 and Waltz 1967, 309.

213. Grotius 1925, II, 346.

214. Nardin 1983, 284. Nardin 1983, 284. Nardin further contends that peace is therefore "a juridical rather than a natural condition," and a condition enjoyed only when "realized and preserved through political artifice and on the basis of law." This is indeed the opinion of Hobbes and Kant, the authors Nardin cites, both of whom believe nature to be thoroughly entropic, at least with respect to human intentions.

215. Grotius 1925, I, iv, 138, 149, 158; see also Sidney 1990, III, xvii; Vattel 1916, I, iv, 21-26.

216. Boétie 1975, 50-58; Sidney 1990, II, xxiv, 221-225; II, xxix, 285-286; III, xi, 382. Sidney ignores or minimizes the possibility that a people might destroy itself in factional strife during a revolution, even as Grotius tends to minimize the dangers of a perpetuated tyranny.

217. Paine 1961, 270, 315-317.

218. Godwin 1946, 144-145; Adler 1944, 43, 64. See also Aron 1966, xiii-xiv, 32. Godwin and Adler do not sufficiently consider the resentment felt by tyrannical personalities for commercial republicanism itself as a cause of civil and international strife.

219. Herodotus 1942 calls the Greeks dangerous because they contend for honor not money (596); see also "Of Commerce" in Hume 1985, 259. See Hirst 1906, 30, and Russell 1960, 95-96, on the relation of commerce to mutual understanding and knowledge. See Saint-Simon 1901, III, 73-74, 252 on the anti-commerical luxury and warlikeness of non-republican governments. *The Spirit of Conquest*, II, on Constant 1989 contrasts the ancient republicans ("with the exception of Athens") pursuing "satisfactions in their public existence," to modern commercial republicans, more cautious, less spirited, more 'private' (103-105); see also Voltaire 1962, 509, 518-519. On the bourgeois virtues see Eidelberg 1974, 198; on the bourgeois God see Mansfield 1989, 196.

220. Tocqueville 1945, II, 266-267.

221. *Ibid.*, II, 337. Tocqueville also worries that the very interdependence fostered by commerce will make wars rarer but more intense, as "the interests are all so interlaced" (II, 297). He was right to foresee world wars, wrong to assume that the *republics* would fight among themselves. So far, at least, Howard 1978 is persuasive in arguing that most warlike passions manifested in commercial-republican souls have owed their origins to the fading spirit of aristocracy (63-63).

222. Rousseau correctly observes:

> It is a great error always to value the gains and losses of sovereigns in money; the amount of power they aim at is not measured by the millions they possess. The prince always rotates his projects; he would command in order to enrich himself, and enrich himself to command; he will sacrifice by turns the one to the other in order to acquire whichever of the two he lacks: but it is only in order to succeed finally in possessing both together that he pursues them separately; for to be the master of men and things he must have at once empire and money (*Judgment on Perpetual Peace*, in Rousseau 1927, 109)

For a balanced view see Vattel 1916, I, 76, 241, commending the defensive military spirit of Switzerland.

223. Cicero 1970, I, 65, 75; Paine 1961, 413-416.

224. See Herodotus 1942, V, 401-408; *Second Treatise*, V, in Locke 1965, 340 (compare and contrast with Cox 1982, 171-173, 175-179); Sidney 1990, II, xiv, 155 and (on Xenophon) II, xviii, 176-178; Haskell 1958, 2, 13-14.

225. Montesquieu 1989, III, xix, 332; Paine 1961, 381, 410-411; Godwin 1946, 160-179; Mansfield 1989, 198.

226. Smith 1965, V, i, 659.

227. Smith 1965, V, i, 660-669; DeGaulle 1934, *passim*.

228. Sidney 1990, II, xxii, 202-206; III, xl, 545. See also Seabury and Codevilla, who ridicule "the magic kingdom of modern upper-middle-class American life," whose denizens hide from the hard realities of military defense by the whole citizenry (3-9)

229. See Voltaire 1962, 549 (equating soldiering with slavery); "A Philosophical View of Reform," in Shelley 1966, 253; *The Spirit of Conquest*, I, 62-64; Walzer 1977, 28-32.

The practice of mass conscription, associated with the French Revolution rather than the American regime (see O'Toole 1941, 40-44, 53; Horsch 1927, 28-29), clearly cannot fully be reconciled with republicanism (or commerce) except in circumstances of national emergency. Conscription and strong nationalism (as distinguished from patriotism) emerge historically in France, conceptually in Hegelianism, as Elshtain 1987 sees (108, 114, 118).

230. Sidney 1990, III, xxvi, 259. See also Lewis 1940, 135-149; Aron 1954, 257-261, 320-324; Aron 1959, 73; Jouvenel 1962, III, viii, 141-153; Michnik 1985, 5.

231. Strauss 1964, 64. See also Lewis 1981, 57.

232. Montesquieu 1989, I, xx, 338. On the egalitarian and anti-'feudal' character of ungoverned commerce see *Ibid.*, I, iv, vi; Smith 1965, I, xi, 238; IV, v, 508; Cropsey 1977, viii, xii. That commercial equality can lead to affluence, then to luxury and inequality, see Montesquieu 1989, I, vii, 100; Montesquieu 1968a, xix, 218. That "the spirit of extreme equality," on the other hand, can lead to envy, corruption, and finally despotism see Montesquieu 1989, I, viii, 114-115.

233. Smith 1965, III, iv, 385; IV, iii, 460; *The Spirit of Conquest*, I, in Constant 1989, 52-57, 65, 140-141; Cobden 1973, I, 13; Angell 1913, ix-xi, 30, 53-57, 269-283. Montesquieu 1989 credits the Jews, a then-stateless people, for having "invented letters of exchange, and in this way commerce was able to avoid violence and maintain itself everywhere, for the richest trader had only invisible goods, which could be sent everywhere and leave no trace anywhere" — evading the exactions of princes fawned upon by theologians fascinated by Aristotle (IV, xxi, 389). Much of modern anti-semitism, from Marx's essay "On the Jewish Question" to Hitler's venomous writings, is *also* an attack on commerce. Hirst 1906 has one of his characters suggest that "the Jews have had a long and lucrative revenge on their persecutors" by loaning money to warlike gentiles (440-441).

234. Cobden 1973, I, 36, 79, 102, 106. Lee 1943 gives "the great panacea" a religious cast: "Although the religious leaders did not always recognize this, it was the supplanting of military by economic forces in the modern state which made possible the kind of social progress which has come to be regarded as the work of the Kingdom" (206).

235. Montesquieu 1989, IV, xxi, 389. The conviction that warfare amounts to commercial folly can be traced at least as far as the Renaissance. Burckhardt 1951 reports that "when the Florentines wished to form an alliance with Venice against Filippo Maria Visconti, they were for the moment refused, in the belief, resting on accurate commercial returns, that a war between Venice and Milan, that is, between seller and buyer, was foolish" (46).

Erasmus' essay "*Dulce bellum inexpertis*" provides an early statement of the claim that war is unprofitable (Erasmus 1972, 326, 343). See also Crucé 1972, 14; Paine 1961, 447-452 (extending the argument to the unprofitability of conquest and imperialism); Bentham 1939, 25, 38 (dismissing any military threat from France not too long before the rise of Napoleon); Rowntree 1900, 43, 62 (coupling commerce with civilization and Christianity); Russell 1917a, 82 ("There is more hope of preventing war in the future by persuading men of its folly than by urging its wickedness"). Howard 1978 ascribes the modern 'peace movement' itself to habits inculcated by international commerce (36); Chickering 1975 finds that membership in the Germany 'peace societies' formed in the 1890's was drawn primarily from the commercial classes (81).

236.   Anonymous 1837, 62. Foch 1931 deplores the conduct of France's rivals prior to the Great War:

> The Germany of 1914 would never have resorted to war
> if she had properly estimated her own interests. No
> appeal to arms was necessary: she had only to continue
> an economic development that already was penetrating
> every country in the world (xlvii).

Foch blames Germany's error on the spirit of Prussia, a state that served as "cradle of militarism and of a philosophy both marked by rabid positivism" (xlviii), yielding the belief that "Victory was certain, and victory made all things legitimate" (xlix) — i.e., a typically modern synthesis of Cartesian method and Machiavellianism.

237.   Crucé 1976, 24-25. See also Vattel 1916, I, 40, 90; II, 121-124.

238.   Smith 1965, III, iii, 325. Constant, thinking of Napoleon and perhaps also of the French Revolution, warns, "Woe betide those who, believing themselves invincible, throw down the gauntlet to the human race, and claim to carry out through it, since they have no other instrument, upheavals of which it disapproves and miracles for which it has no wish" (*The Spirit of Conquest*, I, Constant 1989, 49); see also Angell 1913, 263-264. For a statesman who believes economics more important than politics see Harold Macmillan's favorable contrast of himself with de Gaulle (Macmillan 1972, 113-114).

239.   Tucker 1893, 405. See also Paine 1961, 404-405; Cobden 1973, 216; Fried 1916, 31. Hitler 1943 associates "economic pressure" with "blackmail," so long as "the necessary unscrupulousness is present on the one side, and sufficient sheeplike patience on the other" (48). For a critique of commercial libertarianism as a means to peace see Waltz 1965, 81-97.

240.   Smith 1976 writes, "Fortune never exerted more cruelly her empire over mankind than when she subjected those nations of heroes" — the so-called primitive nations — "to the refuse of the jails of Europe, to wretches who possess the virtues neither of the countries which they come from, nor of those that they go to..." (V, 33); see also Smith 1965, IV, vii, 570). Smith exempts thinly populated and unpopulated territories from this stricture (Smith 1965, IV, vii, 531-532). John

Stuart Mill also expects nations of "barbarians" from non-aggression guarantees because conquest will "likely" benefit them and because "barbarians will not reciprocate," anyway ("A Note on Non-Intervention," Mill 1963, 374-377). For a more resolutely anti-imperialist stance see Walsh 1916, 293-294, 313-341.

241. "Tradesmen, not being used to the open air and not doing any hard work but enjoying all pleasures, grow soft in spirit and their bodies are weakened and rendered unsuitable for military labors" (Thomas Aquinas 1949, 77); see also Chelcický 1964a, 166; Woolman 1922, 400-401; O'Toole 1941, 48-49; Jouvenel 1957, IV, xiv, 246. In *The Principles of Politics*, VI, Constant contrasts the "constant and progressive" spirit of landed property; the landed proprietor "depends on nature and is independent of men." Commercial and industrial property "instills less regularity into [the owner's] life," and simultaneously less practicality, less peaceableness, and less patriotism (Constant 1989, 217-220). Bernhardi 1914 follows Hegel in commending the military spirit as an essential countertoxin to bourgeois decadence (9-21, 116-117). Equally anti-bourgeois but also resolutely pacifist is the Christian de Givry 1924, 183-184, 198-210. Writers such as de Givry, Huxley 1937, 158, and Murry 1937, 15-17, 35, 45-51, 91 associate commerce of 'capitalism' with the acquisitive spirit of conquest; they are evidently influenced by the Marxist-Leninist critique of imperialism.

Perhaps most interesting is Hume 1968, who begins by seeming to claim that the end of politics and war, justice, could be replaced by a sufficiently prosperous commercial economy, which would enable human beings to practice the generosity they preach (III, ii, 495). Unfortunately, human "narrowness of soul" puts present desires ahead of future interests; government serves the needed purpose of inventing justice and making it a more immediate interest (III, ii, vii, 537), of regulating the conflict of one man's avarice with another.

242. See Richardson 1960b, 20-21 and Bacon 1968b, *passim*.

243. Bacon 1968b rather wickedly argues that

> ...Money, no doubt is the principal part of the greatness of Spain; for by that they maintain this veteran army; and Spain is the only state of Europe, that is a money-grower. But in this part, of all others, is most to be considered the ticklish and brittle state of the greatness of Spain. Their greatness consists in their treasure; their treasure is their Indies; and their Indies (if it be well weighed) are indeed but an accession to such as are masters at sea (71-72).

A war by Great Britain, a master of the sea, upon Spain, no such master, "is likely to be a lucrative and restorative war," even though "wars are generally causes of poverty" (73).

244. See *The Spirit of Conquest*, I, Constant 1989, 69-70; Ramsey 1983, 234; Foch 1931, xxiv. As an example of this weakness in a 'proletarian' economic man instead of a 'bourgeois' economic man, recall the statement of British Labour Party leader Sir Stafford Cripps in 1936:

> I do not think it would be a bad thing for the British working classes if Germany defeated us. It would be a disaster for profit makers and capitalists but not necessarily for the working classes (cited in Ceadel 1987, 74).

245. Aron 1954 suggests that this secret political passion animated many of the nineteenth-century European imperialists, who excused conquest as a means to expanded trade (56-73).

246. Roosevelt 1990, 32-38, 54-55; *A Discourse on the Origin of Inequality*, in Rousseau 1950, 225, 242, 263, 275; Plattner 1979, 77. That this is only one strand of Rousseauan thought may be seen in the fact that the good citizen of *The Social Contract* appears nowhere among the acquaintances of the Solitary Walker of the *Reveries*, nor does the Solitary Walker step into the democracies commended in *The Social Contract*. Anarchism would universalize the Solitary Walker, or, more radically still, try to draw him out of his solitude into a free community of like-minded souls.

247. Paine 1961, 304. Like Rousseau, Paine himself is no anarchist, advocating instead a minimalist government (398-400). Rothbard 1973 claims that "libertarians" such as himself differ from anarchists on the issue of human nature. Anarchists believe that the abolition of government will change human nature whereas libertarians do not (243-244). This is not necessarily the case. There is no principled theoretical difference between liberatarianism and anarchism; either can claim to liberate human nature from governmental entrapment.

248. Burke 1982, 6-10, 31-95. Burke's argument is of course an ironic presentation of doctrines associated with Bolingbroke. Burke's real view — that "a certain quantum of power must always exist in the community, in some hands, and some appellation" and that this fact makes the extreme egalitarianism anarchy would require unworkable — may be seen in Burke 1961, 156. For a serious presentation of Burke's ironic argument see Rothbard 1973, 48. For the same argument, with a Christian flavor, see *The Kingdom of God Is Within You*, in Tolstoy, 1960, 175-176, 198-205, 226-231m 374 (on the baneful character of all government), 276, 290-293, 310-317 (on the contradiction of the Christian with the secular consciousness). For the non-Christian element in Tolstoy's project, see his teaching, "The Kingdom of God can only be reached by effort," a "violent effort" at that, a sort of self-conquest (*Ibid.*, 428, 443-444). This is clearly an instance of erotic not agapic love, the latter not sustained by human efforts so much as divine 'efforts' within human beings. However, see Tolstoy 1904, 49, for a more nearly Christian stance.

249. Fornari 1974, 191-202; see also Rothbard 1973, 26.

250. Kropotkin 1978, 208-209.

251. Tolstoy 1904, 13, 37-42; Tolstoy 1968, 15-16. In Tolstoy the conquering Christ replaces conquering 'Science' (*Ibid.*, 27).

252. Rothbard 1973, 11, 23, 26. Rothbard adds that "most libertarians are not pacifists" (48) in individual relations, as the individual retains the right to forceful self-defense against force. They are pacifists in opposing the *organized* violence — both interstate violence and government violence directed against disobedient citizens or subjects. War is "mass murder" by the government (49). A "world libertarian society" would have no wars because it would have no governments to fight them; "*all* problems will be local police problems" (249). In the meantime, the United States could prudently become a libertarian society. "Being no longer a nation-state, which is inherently threatening, there would be little chance of any country attacking us" (248). Those who worried could pay for nuclear deterrence with voluntary contribution (250). American guerrillas, again volunteers, would ruin any occupying force (287).

253. See for example Ferrero 1933, 137-138.

254. "Patriotism and Government," in Tolstoy 1960, 548, 569. Christianity "is simply a teaching of life corresponding to the age and the state of material development humanity has now reached, and which it must therefore accept" (*The Kingdom of God Is Within You*, in Tolstoy 1960, 135).

255. Tucker 1893, 70-71, 80. It is true that Tucker calls passive resistance "the only resistance which in these days of military discipline resists with any result," but he insists on reserving the "dynamite bomb" for "emergencies" and denies "any limit on the right of the invaded individual to choose his own methods of defense" or any immunity from retaliation to the invader (413, 428).

256. "The Spirit of Revolt" in Kropotkin 1927, 35-42. It may have been his considering these historicist anarchists that prompted Rothbard to claim that anarchists deny the existence of any stable human nature (footnote #247). Kropotkin does indeed reject natural right for "the modern philosophy of evolution," calling wars nothing more than historical accidents ("Anarchist Communism: Its Basis and Principles," in Kropotkin 1927, 47). Kropotkin's anarchism is also noticeably more egalitarian and communitarian/socialist than Rothbard's libertarianism, although this difference may be partly a matter of rhetorical emphasis ("Anarchist Communism," in *Ibid.*, 61; "Anarchist Morality," in *Ibid.*, 85-98; "Anarchism: Its Philosophy and Ideal," in *Ibid.*, 119, 133, 140-141).

257. Stirner n.d., 5, 386-387. "All wisdom of the ancients is *the science of the world*, all wisdom of the moderns is *the science of God*" (99): In this Stirner shows that he understands himself as part, perhaps the culmination, of the Machiavellian project.

258. *Ibid.*, 68. Hegelianism is "the triumph of *philosophy*." "the omnipotence of mind," and therefore to be rejected (78). "[T]hinking and thoughts are not sacred to *me*, and I defend *my skin* against them as against other things. That may be an unreasonable defense; but, if I am duty bound to reason, then I, like Abraham, must sacrifice my dearest to it!" (158). Stirner's "dearest" is of course not a beloved son but his own beloved person or "self."

259. *Ibid.*, 84. The "new monarchy" of republicanism is "a thousand times severer, stricter, and more consistent" than the old regime (107).

260. *Ibid.*, 46.

261. *Ibid.*, 113.

262. *Ibid.*, 115-131, 322.

263. *Ibid.*, 159.

264. *Ibid.*, 165, 178-180, 189-193. "Fichte speaks of the 'absolute' ego, but I speak of me, the transitory ego" (190).

265. *Ibid.*, 196.

266. *Ibid.*, 295. The criminal's mistake is to seek *others'* possessions instead of his own (211).

267. *Ibid.*, 218-219.

268. *Ibid.*, 270.

269. *Ibid.*, 306-311. Stirner cannot claim, therefore, to be quite so far removed from bourgeois, utilitarian doctrine as he wants to appear.

270. *Ibid.*, 311.

271. *Ibid.*, 312.

272. *Ibid.*, 223.

273. *Ibid.*, 335.

274. See Durkheim 1951, *passim.*,

275. Adler 1944, 37, 69-75; Seabury and Codevilla 1989, 33.

276. Joad 1939 criticizes the 'German' notion of 'the State' as "a moral being with a personality to develop and a purpose to fulfill" (131). Lewis 1940, 182, fails to credit Joad with recognizing the need for a (non-personal) state; in fact Joad does advocate one such state, the world-state (Joad 1939, 155). Lewis is better in his criticisms of anarchism as utopian (Lewis 1940, 134).

On the theoretical contradictions and practical inadequacies of anarchist pacifism see Aron 1966, 323-329. Howard 1983 observes, "A failure to take the strategic approach may place one at the disposition of somebody who does" (47).

277. Grotius 1925, II, xvii, 433.

278. *The End of All Things.*, in Kant 1963, 83. Kant downplays Christianity's rather prominent system of rewards and punishments, making Christianity into a prefiguration of Kantianism.

279. Michelet 1973, 159. Michelet presses his argument to the point of claiming that the individual soul's passionate and reflective parts cause more discord than the various elements within a good democracy (147). Michelet also claims that the French Revolution replaced God with Man (259).

280. *Essay on Christianity*, in Shelley 1966, 197, 206. Simone Weil describes her ideal society, which, despite her antipathy to technocracy, turns out to be the familiar Enlightenment-dream of a world without competition or secrets, with freedom and equality for all; she cites approvingly Rousseau, Shelley, and "above all, Tolstoy" ("Reflections concerning the Causes of Liberty and Social Oppression," in Weil 1973, 98-107).

281. Martin 1966, 88-96.

282. Read 1943, 1. Read lists Jesus of Nazareth, Lao-Tse, Zeno, John Ruskin, Prince Kropotkin, William Morris, Tolstoy, Gandhi, and Eric Gill as exemplary practitioners of the 'politics.' Read's politics are so unpolitical that they prevent him from distinguishing between the United States and the Third Reich (*Ibid.*, 6), except insofar as democracy is "more dangerous" than fascism (13).

For a Christian politics so lacking in theological content that it might as well be secularized, see Murry 1941, *passim*. Specifically, Murry sighs, "The world being what it is today, the only possible basis for a Christianity that is genuinely universal is an absolute repudiation of the warfare between the nations" (123).

For a recent American example of secularized-Christian politics, see Carter 1976, 149; Carter 1977, 41 (on Tolstoy), 109, 128-130, 181-182; Carter 1984, 245 (on negotiating with the Soviets). For commentary see Morrisey 1984b, *passim*.

283. Boulding 1962, 95.

284. Nietzsche, 1986, I, 192.

285. See *The End of All Things.*, in Kant 1963, 82 on the self-contradictory character of a secular *command* to love; see also Faguet 1908, 184-209; Lewis 1940, 234-235.

286. For a similar argument see Strauss 1965: "The liberal state cannot provide a solution to the Jewish problem, for such a solution would require a legal prohibition against every kind of 'discrimination,' i.e., the abolition of the private sphere, the denial of the difference between state and society, the destruction of the liberal state" (6). Although the loving state might be very different from the liberal state, it would need liberty just as much, albeit liberty of a different kind.

287. Thucydides 1934, II, vi, 104-106.

288. Aristotle 1984, II, vii, 65.

289. Pangle 1973, 219.

290. Howe 1978, 39.

291. *A Discourse on the Arts and Sciences*, in Rousseau 1950, 161. See also *A Discourse on Political Economy*, Rousseau 1950, 298; *A Discourse on the Origin of Inequality*, Rousseau 1950, 269; *Social Contract*, I, viii; II, vii, in Rousseau 1950, 19, 38; Rousseau 1968, 17, 67, 117, 134-135; Rousseau n.d., 590 (on Hume).

292. Hugo 1887, 394.

293. *The Social Contract*, III, xv, in Rousseau 1950, 93. See also Gibbon n.d., I, i, 9; I, iii, 53.

294. Gildin 1983 observes that for Rousseau the philosopher may rule only very indirectly in the form of the Legislator; the Legislator aims not at providing the best regime but a legitimate regime (145). The 'best regime,' philosophic self-rule, is for solitary walkers only; only it is truly free.

295. Hence Constant's title, *The Spirit of Conquest*, describing "the invention of a pretext for war previously unknown, that of freeing peoples from the yoke of their governments, which were supposed to be illegitimate and tyrannical" (Constant 1989, 65 n. 2). Although in the eighteenth century the spirit of conquest had abated, in the nineteenth century it emerged "more imperious than ever," requiring not merely the "general obedience" of the conquered but their conformity to new patterns of life public and private (72-73). At the bottom both of French republican demagogy and Napoleonic despotism lay "the will to

tyranny" (74). "Variety is life, uniformity, death" (77); "the natural order of things takes revenge on the outrages that men attempt against it, and the more violent the suppression, the more terrible will be the reaction to it" (78). See also Tocqueville 1959, 140, 149, and Ferrero 1933, 123-129. Russell 1936 also decries "wars of principle" and "the principle of nationality," in which he sees an analogue in Marxist "class war" (113).

The French Revolution borrowed none too discriminately from both Rousseau and 'Enlightenment' writers. Its failure to achieve liberty, justice, or peace has occasioned polemical exchanges to two centuries, the best of which remains that between Burke and Paine. Burke 1961 "most heartily wish[es] that France may be animated by a spirit of rational liberty" (15) but denies that reason or liberty will survive a politics of rationalism abstracted from circumstances: "The circumstances are what render every civil and political scheme beneficial or noxious to mankind" (19). The attempt to wipe out existing institutions and customs and "begin anew" will yield licentiousness instead of liberty, the rule of "bold and faithless men" (49-50). Such ambitions are an "unnatural" attempt to remake men and women beyond the efforts of God, nature, previous education and longstanding habit (51-52). The Revolution succeeded only in elevating incompetence to power, itself an unnatural act, though alas not an uncommon one (53-59). "[T]hose who attempt to level, never equalize" but only put themselves "at war with nature" — an unwinnable war (61-62).

Burke never denies the existence of natural rights. He denies that they can govern without intervening institutions, customs, and laws (religious and political) that habituate and educate citizens to act in a manner that accords with natural rights (*Ibid.*, 71-75). Too frequent, directly appeals to such rights stir revolutionary and cruel passions, yielding tyrannical reaction — a constant state of war (76-91), of Machiavellianism (94). Burke's famous social contract among the living, the dead, and the unborn is intended not to replace human nature but to perfect it (110); this contract sustains a mixed regime, the rights of private and especially landed property, and an established church not because these institutions supersede natural rights but because they alone give such rights concrete if imperfect embodiment. See also *The Spirit of Conquest*, II, in Constant 1989, 150-154. To do otherwise is to employ brute force instead of the "social means" that conduce to genuine peace, means they are slow but surer than "violent haste" in "defiance of the process of nature" (Burke 1961, 180-186). (See also *The Spirit of Conquest*, II, in Constant 1989, 150-154). In empowering a unicameral, elected representative legislature at the expense of executive and judicial independence the revolutionaries combine the worst of Rousseau with the worst of modern republicanism; they elevate democracy but retain the impersonality of representative government and a money-economy (200-226). The large citizen-army has no discipline; "you have got the wolf by the ears" (227). "The last reason of Kings" — sending in the troops — "is always the first with your assembly" (243). In its quest for justice, militant or thumotic democracy will destroy liberty and peace because "moderation will be stigmatized as the virtue of cowards; and compromise as the prudence to traitors" (264).

Paine 1961 incorrectly claims that Burke denies to nations the right to revolution (276). Paine responds thumotically in defense of thumotic democracy: "It is the living, not the dead, that are to be accommodated," and the social contract serves only those alive to reaffirm or readjust it (278-281). If violent excesses have occurred, the French revolutionaries learned them from the masters they rightly overthrew, who had initiated "government by terror" (295).

> These outrages are not the effect of the principles of the Revolution, but of the degraded mind that existed before the Revolution, and which the Revolution is calculated to reform...Never were more pains taken to instruct and enlighten mankind, and to make them see their interest consisted in their virtue, and not in their revenge, than what has been displayed in the Revolution of France. (296)

The Declaration of the Rights of Man and the Citizen "is by reciprocity, a Declaration of Duties also" (353). Paine predicts that the Declaration "is of more value to the world, and will do more good, than all the laws and statutes that have yet been promulgated," making "revolution" "diminutive of its character;" the events in France mark nothing less than the beginning of "a regeneration of man" (353).

Hereditary rights are accidental; wisdom or prudence does not rule by accident; ergo, hereditary rights are unwise. (Paine does not show that respect for some accidents is necessarily unwise). Moreover, government by the wise is a usurpation; it is not self-government of the nation as a whole (356-357). The nation can become enlightened or wise if the wise will only step aside and let the nation learn. Exercise of self-government will develop the intellectual and moral virtues of all, yielding "a gigantic manliness" (379-433). In the sweep of Paine's world-historical eschatology, "prejudices are nothing," except impediments; "I do not believe that monarchy and aristocracy will continue seven years longer in any of the enlightened countries of Europe" (392-393). On all political subjects "men have only to think, and they will neither act wrong not be misled" (393). If they really want peace, the old regimes will simply step aside (394, 433-434, 446).

They did not. Inasmuch as a decent regime will remain decent, if less so, under the pressures of war, Burke's later arguments concerning the latter years of the French Revolution tellingly refute Paine's optimism. Burke denies that England can make peace with "the Republic of Assassins" ("On the Overtures of Peace," in Burke 1887, V. 246). Ceasing to resist militarily will bring no security to Englishmen because "we are at war with a system which by its essence is inimical to all other governments, and which makes peace or war as peace and war may best contribute to their subversion" (*Ibid.*, 245, 250). The French republic consists of armed willfulness (*Ibid.*, 250, 267); to be at peace with such a regime is to become its accomplice or else its victim (*Ibid.*, 326). The Jacobins are "a set of fanatical and ambitious atheists," military in principle, maxims, spirit, and actions ("On the Genius and Character of the French Revolution as It Regards Other Nations," in Burke 1887, V, 345, 375). Thumotic or "irritable" philosophy no longer philosophizes; it seeks to conquer, violating the very natural rights and "eternal peace" it "pretends to secure" ("On the Rupture of the Negotiation..." in Burke 1887, V, 397, 443). *Philosophe*-politicians assassinate fathers or kings and establish a tyrannical oligarchy animated by "that dread maxim of Machiavelli, that in great affairs men are not to be wicked by halves" ("Fourth Letter on the Proposals for Peace with the Regicide Directory of France," in Burke 1887, VI, 43). There is a kind of appeasing English politician, in whose veins "the milk of human kindness" runs instead of blood, who "is nothing but a curd" (44), lacking the "wisdom and fortitude" to defend a good constitution against French republicanism (100). This politician cannot fight a war for genuine peace, and would leave England vulnerable to perpetual war in the name of perpetual peace

See also Faguet 1908 on the tension between democracy and parenting (142, 154).

Rousseau himself would have appreciated Burke's critique of political abstractions or ideologies. "Abstractions are painful and unnatural operations," he writes; "a thinking man is a depraved animal." Reason and its highest use, philosophy, "isolates" men, and thus serves as a poor bond for a political community (*A Discourse on the Origin of Inequality*, in Rousseau 1950, 204, 217, 226); see also Plattner 1979, 34-42.

296. *The Spirit of Conquest*, II, in Constant 1989, 102, 106-112; see also *The Liberty of the Ancients*, in Constant 1989, 318-322. Hegel shares Rousseau's ambition to combine or 'synthesize' ancient and modern; for commentary see Smith 1989, 6-8. On the relationship between 'Enlightenment' and nationalism with particular reference to Rousseau and Hegel see Smith 1971, 15, 56, 72, 170, 191; on nationalism and democracy see Ligt 1938, 3; on nationalism and secularism, Kohn 1964, 3.

297. Mill 1951, 156-171, 217. "What is to be learned from the middle class," asks Michelet 1973 in his usual rhetorical mood. "As for the salons, I never left them without feeling my heart shrunken and chilled" (5).

298. Ruskin n.d., 66-67. War "is the foundation of the high virtues and faculties of men" (70).

299. Sorel 1967, 54, 76-77, 86-90, 104, 115.

300. Nietzsche 1986, I, 176.

301. "The Moral Equivalent of War," in James 1967, 668-669. The youths "would have paid their blood-tax," James insists, but it is difficult to see how blood-tax can be paid without the real risk of shedding blood. Mining, dishwashing, construction work, and James' other recommendations may teach "our gilded youths" how the other half lives, and help them "get the childishness knocked out of them," but these jobs are still only jobs, these tasks only work not battles (669). A sweat-tax is not a blood-tax. One might also glance suspiciously at James' vision of martial socialism whose citizens will be "conscious of our work as an obligatory service to the state" by which "we should be *owned*, as soldiers are by the army" (670).

As an unwitting *reductio* of James' argument, it would be hard to excel Morris R. Cohen's suggestion (made to James himself when Cohen was a university student) that baseball is the moral equivalent of war. ("He listened sympathetically and was amused, but he did not take me seriously enough. All great men have their limitations" ["Baseball as a National Religion," in Cohen 1946, 335]).

See also Russell 1917b, 99-112; Russell 1960, 8-11; Gray 1970, 216. Obviously, Gandhi's nonviolent resistance offers a more likely potential for this kind of project; see Horsburgh 1968, 19-20.

302. The American Civil War diarist Rebecca Harding Davis well describes the revolutionary character of some wars:

> There was one curious fact which I do not remember ever to have seen noticed in histories of the war, and that was its effect upon the nation and individuals. Men and women thought and did noble and mean things that would have been impossible to them before or after... We no longer gave our old values to the conditions of life. Our former ideas of right and wrong were shaken to the base. The ten commandments, we began to suspect, were too old-fashioned to suit this present emergency. (Davis 1984, 57-58)

Liebknecht 1972 agrees that some wars "let loose the revolutionary forces which create a powerful social and political tension within individual states and bringing it to the snapping point" (148); unlike many revolutionaries, however, Liebknecht prefers not to use war as a means to revolution, as on balance he finds militarism conducive to the kinds of revolution he does not want.

303. Benda 1959, 21-29, 79. The academic becomes an intellectual Callicles, and "disinterested intelligence" disappears; an "apology for Machiavellianism has inspired all the German historians for the past fifty years" and also "very influential thinkers" in France (*Ibid.*, 42, 50).

Huxley 1937 concurs: "[O]ne word is common to all the dictatorial vocabularies and is used for purposes of justification and rationalization by fascists, Nazis, Communists alike. That word is 'historical'" (74).

304. Voltaire 1962, 161-166. On Rousseau's incipient historicism see Horowitz 1987; on Kant's see Galston 1975.

For acknowledgment of Hegel's influence see Huxley, 1937, 75; Merleau-Ponty 1964, 63; de Jouvenel 1962, I, iii, 51; Berdyaev 1960, 27-28, 95, 107.

305. Barth 1944 calls it "a monumental disgrace to all Protestantism that the monster of National Socialism could be born in the very cradle of the Reformation" (15). It should be noticed that Martin Luther's theology resembles the ideologies of Marxism and Nazism in their 'providential' or telic-historicist character. To notice is not to blame, it also should be noticed.

The historicist alternative to telic historicism is historical relativism, the doctrine that each epoch is relative not to the 'end of history' but to every other epoch. This logically entails nihilism, spirited or dispirited.

306. Hegel 1973, 212-216; Hegel 1954, 11, 21-22; Hegel 1966, 309. See also Nietzsche 1974, I, 79.

307. See Rosen 1974, 56, 236-273.

308. Hegel 1973, 85, 155-156, 252. Hegel does share with the Machiavellian social contract theorists the belief that reason must be built into the natural world by human will (*Ibid.*, 160, 167).

309. On Hegel's historicist account of war generally see Elshtain 1987, 75. On the putatively consciousness-raising character of violence see Hoffman 1989, 71, and Smith 1989, 197-203. On Hegel's concept of war as an antidote to *embourgeoisement*, see Smith 1989, 159-164.

Proudhon adapts historicist dialectic to a kind of pacifism. War "is one of the powers of our soul," with "deep roots" in "religious, juridical, esthetic, and moral sentiments of peoples" (Proudhon 1927, I, ix, 70-71). "War is the oldest of all religions: It will be the last" (74). Victory in war produces right in the "savage state" (II, ii, 87-89). But today war's reality contradicts its 'idea' (III, iii, 227).

> Heroism is a beautiful thing; but heroism is finished.... I esteem force; it gloriously inaugurated on earth the rule of right; but I do not want it for a sovereign (Proudhon 1861, I, 24).

Proudhon wants "not an abolition, but a transformation of war" (*Ibid.*, I, 69-70) into the "constructive antagonism" of a peaceful but "dynamic" society (Hoffman 1972, 269-271).

The commercial republican Constant appears to endorse historicism with respect to war, claiming that war is "man's nature" during "certain stages in the history of mankind" (*The Spirit of Conquest*, I, Constant 1989, 51). But Constant finally describes justice as "belong[ing] to all ages" and liberty as the preparation for "every sort of good" *Ibid.*, II, 157).

310.   Marx 1963, 106-110. The same is true of philosophy, even of Marxist philosophy:

> ...philosophers do not grow out of their time like mushrooms; they are the fruit of their time, of their people whose most subtle, precious and invisible sap circulates in philosophical ideas. The same spirit that builds philosophical systems in the brain of the philosopher builds railroads by the hands of the workers ("Religion, Free Press, and Philosophy," in Easton and Guddat 1967, 122).

The "spirit" is in fact entirely the result of material causes, though these are complex and not merely economic, even if they are based upon economics and biology. Marxism differs from all other philosophies hitherto only in that it has been formulated at a time when the real causes of human history revealed themselves – another instance of historicism's secularization of Western religions. See also "The Three Sources and Three Component Parts of Marxism," in Lenin 1968, 21.

311.   Marx, "Critique of Hegel's Philosophy of the State," in Easton and Guddat 1967, 171. On the relation between Marxism and extreme nationalism see Read 1943, 43.

312.   Marx and Engels, "Manifesto of the Communist Party," in Feuer 1954, 4, 26.

313.   "The Historical Destomy of the Doctrine of Karl Marx," in Lenin 1968, 18; *The State and Revolution*, in *Ibid.*, 267; "The Tasks of the Youth Leagues," in *Ibid.*, 613-616; "The Three Sources and Three Components of Marxism," in *Ibid.*, 20. See also Liebknecht 1972, 49 (on retaliation in history) and Merleau-Ponty 1969, 43, 52, 56 (on the inter-relationship of historical events and the beliefs and choices of human individuals).

314.   See Bertrand Russell in Russell and Nearing 1924, 67-68. Contrast also the more or less historicist beliefs of Russell 1917b (especially 37-39, 248) with the much more skeptical Russell 1960, with his sharp critique of Hegel's "farrago of nonsense" and of Marx's ill-conceived imitations thereof (93).

315. In her "Reflections Concerning Technocracy, National-socialism, the U.S.S.R. and Certain other Matters," Simone Weil writes in an attempt "to make militants think" (Weil 1973, 25). Lenin's epistemology of partisanship, she argues, leads directly to bureaucracy, to a ruling class with ruling beliefs or dogmas masquerading as science (30-31). See also her "Is There a Marxist Doctrine?" in *Ibid.*, 190-193.

316. Luttwak 1987 observes that "the entire realm of strategy is pervaded by a paradoxical logic of its own, standing against the ordinary linear logic by which we live in all other spheres of life" (4). For example, 'If you want peace, prepare for war,' makes sense as a strategic motto, in circumstances when you know in advance that the other man may well be a deadly enemy. In ordinary private or public life, including international relations, it can only offend.

317. For one of the best descriptions of this twofold seductiveness, see Koestler 1949, 20, 35-45. For examples of the kind of mythic world a devoted Marxist can construct for himself see Somerville 1954, 74-76, 99 (on Soviet 'democracy'); Somerville 1981, 9-10 (for an utterly fanciful account of the 1962 Cuban missile crisis); Lewis 1940, 204-211, 160, 232 (on the wonders of the Soviet policy under Stalin and its "system of security" among "the nations it embraces"). For the illusions of sincere democrats who accepted Soviet propaganda too easily see "Address to the Jewish Council for Russian War Relief," in Einstein 1960, 322-324 and, far more comprehensively, Wallace 1970, *passim* — the latter surely the *locus classicus* of social-democratic illusions in the post-World-War II period.

318. Wright 1949, 140-141.

319. *Ibid.*, 122-126. On 'Socialist Realism' as a work of the imagination, see Fischer 1949, 205-206.

320. Nietzsche 1986, I, 12-13; II, 322-325; Polin 1974, 66-70. To leave Nietzsche at the level of physical violence is to overlook his celebration of a spiritual form of the will to power, as noticed above, Chapter Five, p. 407. See also Nietzsche 1974, I, 87; *Beyond Good and Evil*, I, 206.

321. Barrès 1976, 159-162. Heidegger advances a similar national determinism; for commentary see Hoffman 1986, 57-58.

322. Nietzsche 1974, V, 318 (sharing the Hegelian esteem for Napoleon); *Zarathustra*, I, Prologue, in Nietzsche 1968, 125; *Zarathustra*, IV, "On the Higher Man," in *Ibid.*, 399.

323. Nietzsche 1974 writes, "We simply do not consider it desirable that a realm of justice and concord should be established on earth" (328). See also *Zarathustra*, I, "On War and Warriors," in Nietzsche 1968, 159; *Zarathustra*, II, On Human Prudence," in *Ibid.*, 256 (on the over-dragons of the future).

324. Mussolini 1964, 349-364. Contrast, however, with Mussolini 1928, who writes that "there is no revolution that can change the nature of man" (191-192).

325. Hitler 1943, 284-287.

326. *Ibid.*, 172, 212-213, 380, 384, 455-456.

327. Speech, April 12, 1922, in Hitler 1941, 22. Notice that Hitler leaves his audience the blank space to fill: the annihilation of 'the Jew.'

328. *Notes* (1888) #481, in Nietzsche 1968, 458. On Mussolini's descent into a "fantastic world" of his own devising, see his associate Mezzasoma's comments cited in Hibbert 1962, 277. It should be observed that much more pleasant and peaceful utopias can be dreamed on much the same intellectual foundation. These utopias are no less mad perhaps but much less malicious. See Cotta 1985 on the anarchism of Walter Benjamin (105-112) and the 'New Age' pipedreaming of Smoke 1987, 87-97. The latter quite appropriately quotes with approval several German philosophers of the nineteenth century and bows to modern physics and "Eastern religious philosophies."

   Camus 1955 takes the measure of these ideologies:

   Nature is still there, however. She contrasts her calm skies and her reason with the madness of men. Until the atom too catches fire and history ends in the triumph of [scientistic] reason and the agony of the species. But the Greeks never said that the limit could not be overstepped. They said it existed and that whoever dared to exceed it was mercilessly struck down. Nothing in present history can contradict them. (137)

329. See Grotius 1925, II, xxvi, 425; Sidney 1990, II, xvii, 173; *Reviews of Herder's Ideas for a Philosophy of the History of Mankind*, in Kant 1963, 41; *The End of All Things*, in *Ibid.*, 71-19. Nietzsche 1974 argues that prophetic "infallibility" comes from psychological insight, not foreknowledge of events as such (297). The historian Burckhardt 1979, 43-44 and the Christian Weil 1973, 169-170 firmly reject secular prophesying. The military strategist Sun Tzu 1963 realistically observes that "What is called 'foreknowledge' cannot be elicited from spirits, nor from gods, nor by analogy with past events. It must be obtained from men who know the enemy situation," that is, from spies (145-149).

330. Quoted with admiration in Somerville 1975, 135. The scientistic claims of Nazi racism and of Soviet economics form the most demonstrably fraudulent part of materialist historicism. The pseudoscientific character of Marxism especially offends Bertrand Russell, who

deplores the "impatient philosophy," the 'religious' "militant certainty" calling itself science that Bolshevism sets against the genuinely scientific "skeptical temper" of the West (Russell 1920, 5-6, 41, 117-119; see also Russell and Nearing 1924, 38). Russell objects to Marxist scientism not because it flows from the Baconian project of the conquest of nature, which he endorses, but because it flows from that project in the wrong direction, in a 'churchy' and dogmatic, non-experimental way (Russell 1920, 113-135).

For much the same criticism by a Christian, see "Reflections concerning the Causes of Liberty and Social Oppression," in Weil 1973, 38-48; "Fragments, 1933-1938," in *Ibid.*, 147; and "Is There a Marxist Doctrine?" in *Ibid.*, 171-172.

Finally, for a poet's criticism see Spender 1949, 260.

Generally speaking, scientism animated by passions ordinarily associated with religious certitude will set fire to Baconian ambitions, yielding an even more uncompromising imperial war, one that threatens science itself.

331.　"A Talk with the Defenders of Economism," in Lenin 1968, 46. That this readily leads to warfare may be seen in Lenin's subsequent defense of the purge as a means of strengthening the militant Party (49).

332.　Koestler 1949, 61, 71-74.

333.　Liebknecht 1972, 89.

334.　Trotsky 1936, 10-11, 24-25, 28. Trotsky compounded his folly by calling the Soviet Union the first "worker state" in history, temporarily deformed by Stalinist bureaucracy (28-29).

335.　Murry 1932, 9, 41.

336.　Fanon 1968, 312-316.

337.　Speech, January 1, 1939, in Hitler 1941, 585. Hitler introduces this prediction with the portentous sentence, "Today I will once more be a prophet."

338.　Arendt 1971 complains that the masses of people in the twentieth century are so atomized socially and so gullible ideologically that common sense no longer sways them:

> They do not believe in anything visible, on the reality of their own experience; they do not trust their eyes and their ears but only their imagination which may be caught by anything that is at once universal and consistent in itself.... Totalitarian propaganda can

outrageously insult common sense only when common sense has lost its validity. (351-152.)

In fact this state of mind describes the propagandists far more accurately than the so-called masses. The people of Europe *did* 'believe in' visible things; they saw war and depression; some of them believed in Lenin and Hitler, even more felt and saw crushing power wielded by those tyrants.

339. Marx's famous command not to understand the world but to change it finds its aristocratic-individualistic counterpart in Nietzsche 1974, who calls actions "incomparably personal, unique, and infinitely individual," whereas conscious thoughts are common, herdlike, *communicable* (299). A Nietzschean rabble-rouser is thus a contradiction in terms, but several did arise: "truth is valueless so long as there is lacking the indomitable will to turn this realization into action!" Hitler exclaimed, prior to informing his audience that Jesus of Nazareth "was greatest not a sufferer but as fighter" against "Jewish poison," overturning the money-changers' tables in the Temple (Speech, April 12, 1922, in Hitler 1941, 25-26). This is the 'Christianity' that forms "the unshakable foundation of the morals and moral code of the [German] nation" (Speech, March 3, 1933, in *Ibid.*, 157). See also Mussolini 1928, 244, and, on the same phenomenon on the 'Left,' Koestler 1949 ("We [intellectuals] craved to become single-and simple-minded" [50], succeeding all too well).

340. Cotta 1985, 15.

341. Hobbes 1990, 126.

342. Marx 1906, III, vii, 257.

343. *Ibid.*, I, iii, 149; IV, xiii, 363; xiv, *passim*; "On the Jewish Question," in Easton and Guddat 1967, 247; "The Manifesto of the Communist Party," in Feuer 1959, 23.

344. Marx 1906, IV, xiii, 358; *"Left-Wing" Communism – An Infantile Disorder*, in Lenin 1968, 518ff. Russell 1920 reports that Lenin "spoke as though the dictatorship over the peasant would have to continue for a long time, because of the peasant's desire for free trade" (39).

345. Trotsky 1936, 7-9; Ligt 1938, 48; Sartre 1968, 14. See, for a similar 'analysis' from a democratic socialist, Dewey 1946, 124, 175. Fischer 1949 remembers that "Russia's basic aspirations became more attractive to me after a look at the dull 'normalcy' of the Harding-Coolidge era in the U.S.A. and the aimlessness of Europe" (202).

346. Mussolini 1928, 131, 147, 167, 281. See also Hitler 1943, 209.

347. Speech, September 3, 1933, in Hitler 1941, 205; Speech, December 10, 1940, in Hitler 1941, 889.

348. On the supposed links between 'capitalism' and Jews, see Speech, April 12, 1922, in Hitler 1941, 16-18; Speech, July 28, 1922, in *Ibid.*, 28-29; Speech, April 13, 1923, in *Ibid.*, 54; Speech April 24, 1923, in *Ibid.*, 57. On the 'internationalist' Jewish state "universally unlimited as to space," a parasitical "state within states" as "the mightiest counterpart to the Aryan," see Hitler 1943, 150, 300-304. See also Drumont 1970, predating Hitler by decades, on the "mercantile, covetous, scheming, subtle, and cunning" Jewish profiteers contrasted to the "enthusiastic, heroic, chivalrous, disinterested, frank and trusting" "Aryan" creators (92).

349. Speech, August 17, 1934, in Hitler 1941, 23-24; Hitler 1943, 93, 126, 234, 320-327, 382, 401-406, 447 (on liberal and Marxist majoritarianism).

350. Hitler 1943, 383. If "the superior intellectual ability and elasticity" of the human race were "lost to the absence of their racial bearers," the Aryans, and the Jewish communist and bourgeois elements were to seize control of states worldwide, those states might bring on "the destruction of the human race" (*Ibid.*, 391). It is easy to formulate a National-Socialist 'analysis' of the world's peril after the Second World War, as Bolsheviks and plutocrats brandished nuclear weapons at each other.

351. *Ibid.*, 153.

352. *Ibid.*, 391.

353. See Burke 1961, 63-66, 169-170, 176. For two rather more cynical views see Nietzsche 1986, I, ii, 383-384 (on the potential for a middle-class anti-capitalist, but unsocialist, parliamentarism) and Hirst 1906, 227 (on the greater humanitarianism of Bismarck as contrasted with Frederick the Great, and the low-but-solid means by which it was effected).

354. Speech, April 12, 1922, in Hitler 1941, 21; Speech, July 28, 1922, in *Ibid.*, 29-31; Speech, September 12, 1923, in *Ibid.*, 67-68; Speech, January 1, 1932, 97, 99; Speech, September 3, 1933, 205-206; Speech, September 14, 1936, 405; Hitler 1943, 78-82.

355. "Critique of Hegel's Philosophy of the State," in Easton and Guddat, 173; "On the Jewish Question," in *Ibid.*, 227; "Critique of the Gotha Program," in Feuer 1959, 127; "The Class Struggles in France," II, in *Ibid.*, 317.

356. "Our Programme," in Lenin 1968, 33-35; "Marxism and Revisionism," in *Ibid.*, 30; *Two Tactics of Social Democracy in the Democratic Revolution*, in *Ibid.*, 59-62, 77-78, 82; "A Caricature of Marxism and Imperialist Economism," in *Ibid.*, 73-74. Trotsky 1918 follows the same line with respect to Germany (104, 108, 139, 143, 153-159).

357. "Critique of Hegel's Philosophy of the State," in Easton and Guddat, 176; "On the Jewish Question," in *Ibid.*, 241. Christianity, Marx writes, first posited the division of 'state' from 'society,' a division the bourgeois order has secularized (*Ibid.*, 247).

358. *Two Tactics of Social Democracy in the Democratic Revolution*, in Lenin 1968, 139.

359. *Ibid.*, 141. See also *The State and Revolution*, in Lenin 1968, 326.

360. Trotsky 1936, 59.

361. *Ibid.*, 59-62. It is a matter of consistent astonishment to historicists that the proletarians continue to insist on the reality of the 'formal' rights and institutions of commercial republicanism; for example see Steel 1967, 212, on Latin America.

362. Speech, December 10, 1940, in Hitler 1941, 879.

363. Hitler 1943, 615.

364. "An Open Letter to Boris Souvarine" (December 1916), Lenin 1966, XXIII, 196-198; "Bourgeois Pacifism and Socialist Pacifism" in *Ibid.*, XXIII, 177-192.

365. *Imperialism, the Highest Stage of Capitalism (A Popular Outline)*, in Lenin 1968, 242, 261; "Report on the Party Programme," in Lenin 1966, XXIX, 165, 168; Trotsky 1918, 21-29; Liebknecht 1972, 13-20 (with, however, the acknowledgment that capitalism and militarism "fear and hate each other" and merely regard one another as "a necessary evil" against the common enemy, socialism [40]); Ligt 1938, 57-64; Ingram 1939, 50; Lewis 1940, 164-166, 171; Wells 1967, 204, 230. The argument reaches its absurd extreme in Fanon 1968, who claims that "Europe is literally the creation of the Third World" (102) and Nkrumah 1969, who calls for "true independence" of 'Third World' nations from Europe – in a book published in Moscow by International Publishers (8-11).

366. See Aron 1954, 56-58; Aron 1966, 265-276; Brown 1987, 61ff.

367. For the most recent and comprehensive statistical analysis see Dye and Ziegler 1989.

368. In one of his last pronouncements, Lenin claimed that the international bourgeoisie were playing a "diplomatic game" with the Soviet Union in order to open an invaluable market:

> We know perfectly well what lies at the bottom of this game, we know that it is trade. *The bourgeois countries must trade with Russia*; they know that unless they

> establish some form of economic relations their
> disintegration will continue in the way it has done up to
> now. ("The International and Domestic Situation of the
> Soviet Republic," in Lenin 1966, xxxiii, 214)

This was so obviously the reverse of the truth that recent years have
seen charges that some 'socialist' economies (e.g. Cuba) lag because
'capitalists' refuse to trade with them, denying needed markets *to the
'socialists.'*

369. Speech, September 8, 1934, in Hitler 1941, 287-288.

370. Elshtain 1987 describes Marx, Engels, and Lenin as 'philosopher'-
warriors who downplay or even ignore the role of women in revolution
(80-85). Guevera 1969 insists that a woman "can work the same as a
man and she can fight" before admitting his preference for using
women as messengers, cooks, and teachers (86). Nkrumah 1969
observes sententiously that "the degree of a country's revolutionary
awareness may be measured by the political maturity of its women"
(91); their roles will be in the fields or propaganda, education,
medicine, driving ("we cannot afford to *waste* a single *man* on non-
combat duties" [94, emphasis added]), food preparation and
distribution.

371. Speech, July 28, 1922, in Hitler 1941, 40; Speech, September 18, 1922,
in *Ibid.*, 46; Speech, September 12, 1923, in *Ibid.*, 69; Speech,
December 11, 1933, in *Ibid.*, 230; Speech, November 18, 1940, in *Ibid.*,
871; Hitler 1943, 57, 65, 96, 112, 408, 458. Ferrero 1933 predicts that
"the frenzy that appears to be dragging Germany towards a social
revolution...will be much more disastrous for Europe than the Russian
revolution" (12).

372. Mussolini 1928 described Lenin's appeal with some envy:

> The power of Lenin – I admit it – had assumed a
> quality of potency only paralleled in mythology. The
> Russian dictator dominated the masses. He enchanted
> the masses. He charmed them as if they were
> hypnotized birdlings. (112)

Hitler 1943 observed that "the psyche of the great masses is not
receptive to anything that is halfhearted and weak" (47), and Orwell
noticed the consequences in Germany: "Whereas socialism, and even
capitalism in a more grudging way, have said to people 'I offer you a
good time,' Hitler has said to them 'I offer you struggle, danger, and
death,' and as a result a whole nation flings itself at his feet" ("New
Words," Orwell 1968, II, 14). Andreski 1968 argues that "the sense of
power which one can enjoy when dropping a vote into the ballot-box is
rather negligible, compared to one's vicarious enjoyment of power
through identification with the powerful dictator or the victorious
nation" (72).

373. Nietzsche 1974, V, 292; Hitler 1943, 132.

374. Hitler 1943, 396. "We all sense that in the distant future humanity must be faced by problems which only a highest race, become master people and supported by the means and possibilities of an entire globe, will be equipped to overcome" (*Ibid.*, 384).

375. "Critical Notes on *The King of Prussia and Social Reform*," in Easton and Guddat 1967, 350.

376. Marx 1963, 41.

377. "One of the Fundamental Questions of the Revolution," in Lenin 1929 XXI, 170; "The Russian Revolution and the Civil War, in *Ibid.*, XXI, 230.

378. Trotsky 1918, 223-226; Trotsky 1936, 144-157. See also Liebknecht 1972, 165, on the citizen-army.

379. Guevara 1969, 4, 33. The history-bearing vanguard must always, in guerilla warfare, kill the 'point man' of the enemy force; "the moment arrives when nobody wants to be in the vanguard" of the bourgeois army (65-66).

380. Fanon 1968, 35-43, 80, 88-94, 207, 222, 235, 246; Sartre 1968, 17, 21-28. Fanon is particularly interesting because he combines Marxist class-struggle with racialism (*op. cit.*, 212-214, 235).

381. Merleau-Ponty 1969, 107-117, 127-128. See also Fanon 1968: "[V]iolence, like Achilles' lance, can heal the wounds that it has inflicted" (30).

382. Strauss 1964, 129. Gollancz 1959 observes that historicist tyranny has, "hidden deep down in it, a powerful element of attractiveness for the spiritually weak" (103).

383. Speech, September 16, 1930, in Hitler 1941, 89-90; Speech, January 30, 1937, in *Ibid.*, 408; Speech March 18, 1938, in *Ibid.*, 470; Speech, November 8, 1938, in *Ibid.*, 554-555; Hitler 1943, 91, 111, 392-395. For a more 'statist' opinion, see Mussolini 1928, 276-281, and Rocco 1964, 343-348. The Italian Fascists adopted the statist opinions of Hegel; Hitler is in this matter much closer to Marx, both in his emphasis on societies and nations and in his thoroughgoing materialism.

384. "On the Slogan for a United States of Europe," in Lenin 1968, 156; *State and Revolution*, in Lenin 1968, 267, 281-283, 297-298, 329; "Can the Bolsheviks Retain State Power?" in Lenin 1968, 384.

385. *State and Revolution*, in *Ibid.*, 328-329.

386. *Ibid.*, 337; "The Congress of Peasant Deputies," in Lenin 1929, XVIII, 221; "Six Theses on the Immediate Tasks of the Soviet Government," in Lenin 1966, XXVII, 316-317; "Report on the Party Programme," in *Ibid.*, XXIX, 184. See also Trotsky 1936, 44-49, 119-120; Stalin 1971, 159-172, 186-187; Stalin 1939, 47-54; Fanon 1968, 184-185; Nearing, "First Affirmative," in Russell and Nearing 1924, 19-25.

387. Russell and Nearing 1924, 41. See also Russell 1920, 26-30. Russell claimed that democracy could not work at present in Russia and that the Bolsheviks were "performing a necessary though unamiable task" (*Ibid.*, 110-111).

388. "Fear of the Collapse of the Old and the Fight for the New," in Lenin 1966, XXVI, 401.

389. Mussolini 1928, 121, 228.

390. Speech May 1, 1935, in Hitler 1941, 307; Speech, May 21, 1935, in *Ibid.*, 311, 319; Speech, December 10, 1949, in *Ibid.*, 875.

391. Hitler 1943, 134.

392. Speech, January 1, 1939, in Hitler 1941, 584; Speech, April 1, 1939, in *Ibid.*, 627; Hitler 1943, 134-136. It is worth noting that in his prewar speeches Hitler pretends to seek peace as the end of war; in *Mein Kampf*, however, he writes that "Mankind has grown great in eternal struggle, and only in eternal peace does it perish" (Hitler 1943, 135).

393. "The Socialist Revolution and the Right of the Nations to Self-Determination," in Lenin 1968, 160-162. See also Liebknecht 1972, 142.

394. "The Persecutors of Zemstvo and the Hannibals of Liberalism" in Lenin 1929, 154. Proudhon 1861, I, anticipates Lenin in "regard[ing] the partisans of perpetual peace" who defend the existing regimes "as the most detestable of hypocrites" (70). Engels of course also anticipates Lenin; for a good summary see Gallie 1978, 67-88. See also Merleau-Ponty 1969, xviii-xix.

395. Speech, October 14, 1914, in Lenin 1929, XVIII, 71-72; "On the Slogan for the United States of Europe," in Lenin 1968, 155-156; *Socialism and War: Attitudes of the Russian Social-Democratic Party towards the War* (with G. Zinoview), in Lenin 1929, XVIII, 219, 245; "The Military Program of the Proletarian Revolution," in Lenin 1966, XXIII, 77-85; "The 'Disarmament' Slogan," in *Ibid.*, 95. "War is the continuation of the policies of a class," Lenin writes, adapting Clausewitz; "to change the character of the war, one must change the class in power" ("Report on the Political Situation," in Lenin 1929, XVIII, 207).

See also Russell 1920, 31-34; Lewis 1940, 8-9; Brezhnev 1978, 310, 313; Fanon 1968, 147; Guevara 1969, 15-16; Nkrumah 1969, 1923, 52-59.

396. "Report on the Review of the Programme and on Changing the Name of the Party," in Lenin 1966, XXVII, 130.

397. Letter to G. V. Chicherin, February 16, 1922, in Lenin 1966, XLV, 474-475.   See also "Political Report to the Central Committee of the R.C.P.," in *Ibid.*, XXXIII, 264; Trotsky 1936, 16-21, 130; "The Growing Crisis of World Capitalism and the External Situation of the U.S.S.R.," in Stalin 1971, 314.   For an example of the sort of pacifist easily exploited, see Horsburgh 1968, 167. Russell 1936, is less naive:

> The pacifist...can have only a very restricted field of cooperation with the convinced Communist. Before any considerable measure of cooperation becomes possible, it will be necessary to convince Communists that a modern war between national States is not the road to their millennium. (195).

Kissinger 1957 formulates Lenin's strategy succinctly:

> To the non-Soviet world, peace appears as an end in itself, and its manifestation is the *absence* of struggle. To the Soviet leaders, by contrast, peace is a *form* of struggle. (328).

398. *The Social Contract.*, II, viii, in Rousseau 1950, 42. Ferrero 1933 traces the rest of the genealogy with respect to the 'left:' "Though it would be an exaggeration to call Robespierre a forerunner of Lenin, one might well regard Lenin as a Russian Robespierre, brought up on Karl Marx instead of Rousseau, a Robespierre who contrived to die in advance of Thermidor" (169).

399. For a restrained account by a former National Socialist, see Raushning 1939, particularly 59-97, "The Permanent Revolution."

400. "Where to Begin?" in Lenin 1968, 38-39; *State and Revolution*, in *Ibid.*, 281; "Can the Bolsheviks Retain State Power?" in *Ibid.*, 378, 384; "Theses and Reports on Bourgeois Democracy and the Dictatorship of the Proletariat," in Lenin 1966, XXVIII, 464; Letter to D. I. Kursky, May 17, 1922, in *Ibid.*, XXIII, 358. For propaganda purposes to a United States audience Lenin equated Bolshevik terror with that employed by the British "bourgeoisie" in the Glorious Revolution and by the French "bourgeoisie" in 1793 ("Letter to American Workers," August 20, 1918, in Lenin 1966, XXVIII, 71).

401. Trotsky 1918, 219. For Marxist-Leninist terrorist-apocalyptic as "a Christian heresy" seen Aron 1954, 116, 128. For estimates of persons killed in Stalin's 'permanent revolution' see Conquest 1991.   For approbatory commentary on the use of terror by Soviet tyrants see Merleau-Ponty 1969, 34-36, 97-98. Merleau-Ponty traces the "element of violence and Terror" in Marxism to the Hegelian dialectic thereby

"Each self-consciousness aims at the destruction and death of the other" (103). For critical commentaries written very near the beginning of the regime, years before Stalin's accession to supreme power, see Russell 1920, 178.

402. Kautsky 1973, 1-2, 114, 119-120.

403. Trotsky 1936, 23-24, 73, 77-82; Trotsky 1930, 474. Considering Trotsky's murder by Stalin's agents some years later, one recalls Joseph de Maistre's mockery of certain ideologues: "[W]hen a philosopher justifies evil by the end in view, when he says in his heart, *Let there be a hundred thousand murders, provided we are free,* and Providence replies, *I accept your offer, but you must be included in the number,* where is the injustice?" (Maistre 1974, 32).

404. Russell 1920, 4.

405. *Ibid.,* 147-149. Russell not only anticipates the rise of rightist national socialism here, but also the pressure placed on commercial republicanism by the necessity of establishing strong domestic and foreign security agencies that will by their very nature operate at and beyond the edges of law.

406. In *The Spirit of Conquest* Constant distinguishes despotism, which "rules by means of silence, and leaves man the right to be silent," with "usurpation," which "condemns him to speak" and "pursues him into the most intimate sanctuary of his thoughts, and, by forcing him to lie to his own conscience, deprives the oppressed of his last remaining consolation" (Constant 1989, 96-97). Anticipating the Moscow Purge Trials some 120 years in advance, Constant writes that "the despot prohibits discussion and exacts only obedience; the usurper insists on a mock trial as a prelude to public approval" (*Ibid.,* 95).

Nietzsche also understands this, although he uses the term 'despotism' differently:

> [Socialism] desires an abundance of state power such as only despotism has ever had...[I]t requires a more complete subservience of the citizen to the absolute state than has ever existed before, and since it can no longer even count on the ancient religious piety toward the state but has, rather, involuntarily to work ceaselessly for its abolition — because, that is, it works for the abolition of all existing *states* — socialism itself can hope to exist only for brief periods here and there, and then only through the exercise of the extremist terrorism. (Nietzsche 1986, I, 173-174)

See also Tucker 1893, 8; Russell 1960, 29-32; Murray 1960, 232.

407. On "the Regiment of Terror" see Kautsky 1973, 207-218 and Kropotkin 1927, 252-254. On compulsory labor see Kautsky 1973, 169. On 'socialist' oligarchy see Russell 1920, 143; Kautsky 1973, 34-43; Ferrero 1933, 39; Gide 1949, 183-184; Fischer 1949, 212; Aron 1954, 341ff.; Aron 1966, 256. Russell 1920 already sees the regime of police and spies (80) and the failure of Soviet agriculture (169-173).

408. Russell 1920, 140.

409. Spender 1949 writes that "The Communists told me that [love, pity, and the passion for individual freedom] were 'bourgeois.' The Communist, having joined the Party, has to castrate himself of the reasons which made him one" (272) – a very dialectical process, no doubt, but scarcely one well-designed for historical success in the long run. See also Koestler 1949, 29-30; Aron 1954, 147; Aron 1966, 501.

410. Even a simple matter of the denial of any right to travel freely within the country tends toward political disunion. In commercial republics ethnic enclaves gradually shrink or dissolve altogether as individuals pursue careers elsewhere; without the liberty to travel, ethnic groups 'freeze' in place (except those who are forcibly transferred, resented and resentful). Ethnic passions persist, spurred rather than restrained by the rhetoric of nationalism emanating from the central government.

411. Maritain 1957, 71.

412. *The Spirit of Conquest*, II, in Constant 1989, 139. On the Soviet empire see Aron 1954, 219, and Michnik 1985, 25-28, 46-49, 53.

413. Letter to the Executive Secretary, American League Against War and Fascism, November 15, 1937, in Einstein 1960, 276.

414. Johnson 1987, 183. See also Hoffmann 1965, 62-73.

415. If "benevolent precepts of nature were everywhere observed, ...profound peace would reign upon the earth." "But the inordinate passions and self-interest of men will prevent them from ever realizing [the beautiful dream of a World Republic]" (Vattel 1916, II, i, 117-118).

416. *Perpetual Peace*, in Beck 1963, 92; Kant 1964, 86-100, 118-120. See also *Conjectural Beginning of Human History*, in Beck 1963, 59, 62-63.

417. *An Old Question Raised Once Again: Is the Human Race Constantly Progressing?* in Beck 1963, 152. Human *in*equality if a "rich source of evils but also of *everything* good" (*Conjectural Beginning of Human History*, in *Ibid.*, 64, italics added).

418. *Perpetual Peace*, in Beck 1963, 106-114; *Conjectural Beginning of Human History*, in *Ibid.*, 66-68; *Idea for a Universal History from a Cosmopolitan Point of View*, in *Ibid.*, 13-18.

419. *Ibid.*, 18-19.

420. *Ibid.*, 19-20. See also Sidgwick 1909, 89; Friedrich 1969, 50-75; Bok 1989, xiii, xiv, 25, 66 for arguments deriving from Kant, although Friedrich tries to synthesize Kant with Marx, quite implausibly (12, 236-239), and presumably with a hope toward some future convergence of the United States and Soviet regimes. For a Christian pacifist critique of Kant as the proponent of an inadmissible "double morality, fatal to the earnestness of Christianity" because he counsels "resignation" in the face of sin, see Heering 1943, 129-132.

421. *Perpetual Peace*, in Beck, 1963, 117-127; *Conjectual Beginning of Human History*, in *Ibid.*, 57-58. See also Friedrich 1969, 154-155.

422. Friedrich 1969 makes this claim (23-24, 86-91, 203). See also Hoffmann 1989, 50-51.

423. Galston 1975, 203. For an example of this stance, untroubled by Kant's own hesitations and ambiguities, see Friedrich 1969, 29-30. For an attempt to replace 'unjust war' with 'aggressive war' see Pompe 1953. "Today 'war' with 'aggressive war' see Pompe 1953. "Today 'war' is either a sanction or a crime" (38); the crime of aggression is an act that threatens another country's territorial integrity or political independence (113). Pompe supposes that this criterion makes it easier for impartial spectators to judge a country's use of force. Experience shows that this is false, as ambitious rulers will define 'aggression' as they please, even as they earlier defined justice as they pleased. 'Aggression' turns out to be no more clear-cut than justice.

424. Aron 1966, 241.

425. *Perpetual Peace*, in Beck 1963, 115-116.

426. *Idea for a Universal History from a Cosmopolitan Point of View*, in Beck 1963, 22-26.

427. *Conjectural Beginning of Human History*, in Beck 1963, 65.

428. *Perpetual Peace*, in Kant 1963, 93-97. "None of the ancient so-called 'republics' knew this system [of representative government], and they all finally and inevitably degenerated into despotism under the sovereignty of one" (*Ibid.*, 97).

   Einstein 1960 consistently requires republicanism as a precondition to peace, criticizing the United States political system only insofar as it has itself adopted the institutions of centralizing bureaucracy. See his letter to Kurt Hiller, September 9, 1918, 23; his interview with Leo Lania, September 19, 1933, 234; and his letter to A. J. Muste, January 23, 1950, 519.

See also Hirst 1906 ("When the civil distractions of Russia are healed *and tyranny expelled*, and when a decent government has been established in Macedonia, Europe will be free from the scourge of war" [16-17]); Mead 1912, 49, 99; Jaspers 1961, 108-112; Friedrich 1969, 159-162.

429.   See Gallie 1978, who however mistakenly claims that Kant's was "the first significant attempt" to address these issues (13-14). The ambiguity of Kant's regime theory manifested itself in his endorsement of the American *and* French revolutions — the latter even after the Terror; see Friedrich 1969, 180.

430.   Nardin 1983 downplays Kant's regime advocacy, perhaps in an attempt to sidestep the serious regime differences that have led to wars in the twentieth century (309-324). So in rather more sentimental fashion does Bok 1989, 27-30, 79-101, 115-117. The invention of nuclear weapons and the terror they occasion may give a certain unphilosophic but understandable impetus to these evasions. For contrast see Hirst 1906, 341.

431.   *Perpetual Peace*, in Beck 1963, 99-101. Friedrich 1969 mentions that the Covenant of the League of Nations stipulated republicanism; he fails to observe that the United Nations Charter has no such provision (42). Jaspers 1961 remarks the consequence of this omission: the United Nations had become a propaganda platform without any capacity to resolve major conflicts. The failure of the League, by contrast, resulted from the failure of commercial republicanism in post-World War I Europe.

432.   Rousseau 1927, 83ff. The heterogeneity of regimes in Rousseau's federation would add to its vulnerability, as "there is the danger that the league may disintegrate as the rival factions struggle for power" (Friedrich 1969, 44). Rousseau's strongest argument against aggression by states outside Europe is their foreseeable weakness for decades to come. He has no good argument against Friedrich's objection.

433.   Hegel 1973, III, iii, 210.

434.   Friedrich 1969, 33; Gallie 1978, 24; Jaspers 1961, 96-103. Friedrich himself rejects Kant's argument and proposes a "comprehensive world state," without satisfactorily addressing the objections (44-46).

435.   Schmitt 1976, 61-79. Schmitt overdraws his portrait of "liberalism." *Contra* Schmitt, neither the American Founders nor Kant supposed that human nature was simply good, nor did they seek to abolish politics. The American Founders and Kant are omitted from Schmitt's list of genuinely political thinkers, which includes Machiavelli, Hobbes, Bossuet, Fichte, de Maistre, Donoso, Cortés, Taine, and Hegel.

436. Kant 1964, 112.

437. *Ibid.*, 112-113. See also Proudhon 1861, I, 12-23, 36, 62; Proudhon 1927, I, 51-54; Nietzsche, *Thus Spoke Zarathustra*, I, v, 129-130; Burckhardt 1979, 217-218; Faguet 1908, 108-127. On Hegel see Gillespie 1988, 163-170.

438. In contradistinction from this argument, Proudhon 1927, III concludes that the "double face" of war, derives from the contradiction between war as an idea or 'ideal' – the heroic struggle for justice – and war as a practice – dirty, brutal, rapacious (313-328). Sidgwick 1909 explains the contradiction in terms of the good intentions of both sides, the belief of each that he "contend[s] on behalf of legitimate interests" (91).

439. Novikov 1911, 62.

440. Proudhon 1927, I, 58, 61-62.

441. See Gibbon n.d., I, vii, 166 on the affinities of military government with both tyranny and democracy; Mussolini 1949, 111-112 and Jaspers 1967, 34 on the successes of minority war-factions (111-112); and Walsh 1916, 207, on the militaristic tendencies of the popular press. Finally see Goltz 1913 for a statement by a militarist against commercial republicanism and for a monarchy buttressed by an hereditary aristocracy and a peasant class (466-467).

442. Coulton 1916, 286. Compare "Message to Congress in Special Session," July 4, 1961, in Lincoln, IV, 426.

443. As an example of this kind of thinking in a polemical mode, see Coulton 1916, 54, 68, 72, 183, correcting the pacificist excesses of Angell 1913; see also Angell 1938, *passim*, and Angell 1939, 3-10, 48, 72-75, correcting the ideologically spawned illusions of 'intellectuals' between the world wars.

444. "Why I Am Not a Pacifist," in Lewis 1980, 44. Angell 1938 observes that "Democracy is not indispensable to good government but liberalism is," that fascists "are much more the enemy of liberalism than of democracy," being democratic themselves "in the sense of being demogogic, of relying so much on mob passion" (50-51). See also Jaspers 1967, 91.

445. Lewis 1980, 34-35.

446. Lauterpacht 1970, II, 24.

447. Herodotus 1942, VII, 541. Wright 1975 acknowledges that until a world government is instituted some day "far in the future," international law "will remain largely law within states" (29).

448. Montesquieu 1989, II, x, 138.

449. Grotius 1925, III, xxv, 860.

450. See Lauterpacht 1970, II, 327 (on Grotius) and also Falk 1970, 17. Falk claims that "centralization of authority over principal instruments of international violence appears to be necessary" to prevent war; this will require a "revolutionary" reordering of "world politics" beyond the level of interactions among 'nation-states' (18-23). Falk further believes that only the French and the Leninist revolutions "attained such a magnitude as to have relevance for the conduct and character of world politics" (60). See Barkun 1968 for the more prudent claim that political 'charisma' and millenarianism tend to reject law as such, and therefore will continue to fail the relevancy test with respect to the advancement of international law (154-160).

451. Lauterpacht 1970, I, 9.

452. See Brierly 1963, 1, 48, 52; Kelsen 1968, 85; Hoffmann 1968, 22. Ferrero 1933 observes that it is not enough, for example, to outlaw war; to become an effective law, the outlawry of war "must become an active reality" (149), a possibility Ferrero courteously questions.

453. Waltz 1965, 107.

454. In *Perpetual Peace* Kant excepts civil war from his general condemnation of forceful foreign interference with the constitution or the government of any country (Kant 1963, 89). In "A Note on Non-Intervention" Mill writes that nonintervention, if respected by "free states" but not by despotism will come "to this miserable issue, that the wrong side may help the wrong, but the right must not help the right" (Mill 1963, 383). It is of course a matter for astonishment that Americans, who owe their independence to the French Navy, could object on principle to military intervention in the internal affairs of another country.

455. Vattel 1916, I, 7, 14-16, 18; II, 131-132, 137. See also Letter to Charles C. Burlingame, April 9, 1938, in Einstein 1960, 278. If law is not contract but only formalized command, as in Hobbes, then international law does not exist, there being no international commander on earth (see Lauterpacht 1970, I, 11).

456. Though a warm defender of international law, Moynihan 1990 undercuts his own argument by confusing right with conventional law (4-5) and by denying the existence of laws of nature (17-19). While insisting that international law is needed to regulate the "profusion of ethnic and regional conflicts" in the world (13), Moynihan dismisses the only principles that might serve effectively to guide those statesmen who seek to moderate the passions that cause those conflicts.

457. *Prolegomena*, in Grotius 1925, I, 9-12.

458.   *Ibid.*, 13.

459.   *Ibid.*, 18-19, 21; III, i, 599-600; xi, 741, 746, 754, 770. See also Vattel 1916, II, xii, 162.

460.   *Theologico-Political Treatise*, XVI, in Spinoza 1951, I, 200-201; *Political Treatise*, III, in *Ibid.*, 301. Compare Hobbes 1962, II, xxx. Lauterpacht 1970 outlines Spinoza's indebtedness to a tradition beginning with Machiavelli, continuing with Bacon (who "did more than anyone else to transplant the ideas of *The Prince* to English soil"), and Hobbes, then extending after Spinoza to Hegel (whose statement 'the real is the rational, and the rational is the real' "is only another formulation of Spinoza's conception of the *jus naturale*") and Fichte (II, 346, 368, 372-373, 381-382).

461.   Vattel 1916, Preface, 5a; I, 3-6.

462.   Lauterpacht 1970, I, 16, 29, 69, 75-76.

463.   Brierly 1063, 22-24, 49-50, 56-68, 71 (emphasis added). As Bueno de Mesquita 1981 observes, even war is not "an irrational act of passion" but most usually acts prompted by calculated (even if miscalculated) intention (ix, 4-5, 19-21).

   One attempt to avoid Machiavellianism and natural right alike may be seen in Nardin 1983, who argues that because law is by definition binding, international law must be binding; the binding character of international law has nothing to do with such questions as whether it is "morally valid, expressi[ve] of the wills of states, or instrumental to the realization of desirable ends" (219). The law is the law. This argument sidesteps the question of whether anything that is *called* law really *is* law, and therefore binding. Law cannot be defined without reference to the universe outside the law, a universe that includes ethics and politics.

464.   *Perpetual Peace*, in Kant 1963, 133.

465.   Vattel 1916, Preface 9a-12a.

466.   Lauterpacht 1970, I, 17ff.

467.   *Ibid.*, 20, 165-170; Nardin 1983, 161; Moynihan 1990, 177.

468.   Luard 1962, 130-147; Nardin 1983, 126-144, 161-177; Moynihan 1990, 132.

469.   Hoffmann 1968, 22-27.

470.   Wright 1975, 29.

471. E.g., Richardson 1960a, 228. Sidgwick 1909 already sees that in conflicts of principle "there may be an unsuperable difficulty in finding an arbiter on whose impartiality both sides can rely" (99) — to say nothing of finding a conflict in which both sides want impartiality in an arbiter. As a result, as Thompson 1959 notes, few significant international disputes have been arbitrated, and most of these were disputes between commercial republics (62).

472. Vattel 1916, II, 225. He adds, "Independence and impunity are a touchstone which makes known the alloy of the human heart" (226). See also *Ibid.*, II, 135-141.

473. Singh 1986, 10.

474. Clemenceau 1930, 272. Nardin 1983 observes that the League of Nations' efforts for peace were "completely shattered" by "the revolutionary attempt of the Communist and Nazi movements to reconstruct European society along entirely new lines;" no "common framework of principles" could obtain under those circumstances (103-104).

475. See Hembleben 1943, *passim.* This is not of course to suggest that all disagreements are principles, or even that all disagreements on principle are sincere.

476. Alighieri 1949, I, ii, 6; viii, 11; xi, 14. The preference for a secular world-ruler instead of a pope or other priestly world-ruler suggests the rule of philosophy not revelation; see Fortin 1981, 101.

Johnson 1987 acutely observes that Dante does not depend upon the virtue of the world-ruler but upon his position; "This is a *structural* solution to the problem of how to create a good state" (116).

477. See Crucé 1972, 54 and Gargaz 1922, *passim.*

478. Montesquieu 1989, IV, xx, 352. Commerce conquers nature in the sense that it ranges beyond geographic and climatic limits; natural boundaries of countries no longer have the same importance (*Ibid.*, xxi). Rousseau recognizes this also, without much liking it. He prefers the peace that would result from a world of small, self-sufficient, and defensive countries modeled to the Swiss republic. He rejects the hope that the Swiss model and the commercial model could be combined, although to some extent twentieth-century Switzerland has accomplished that (see Roosevelt 1990, 177-180).

479. See Strauss 1953, 197; Mead 1912, 48ff.; Boulding 1962, 228, 331-334; Wright 1965, 3-6.

480. Boulding 1962, 228, 331-334; Boulding 1985, 59, 130. Wright 1965, 3-6.

481. See Thompson 1988, 5. The dates of these wars are 1494-1517, 1580-1609, 1688-1713, 1729-1815, and 1914-1945.

482. *Judgment on Perpetual Peace*, in Rousseau 1927, 129, 131. See also Perry 1915b, 830-831; Russell 1936, 85, 88; Murry 1948, 37, 39; and Aron 1954, 170. Of these, Perry, Russell, and Murry judge the risks worth the prize.

483. Fried 1916, 12-13, 16, 37, 120; Angell 1935, 36-37, 119, 124, 258-259; Joad 1939, 14; Cadoux 1940, 221; Lothian 1941, 12-36; Murry 1948, 82 ("The tragedy of the modern world is that there is no Caesar" — i.e., no world-emperor — for Christians to 'render unto'); Luard 1962, 65, 104, 122; Waltz 1965, 186; Galtung 1980, 3, 107.

484. *A Discourse on Political Economy*, in Rousseau 1950, 290, 293; *Social Contract*, II, iii-iv, vii, in *Ibid.*, 26-30, 37-42; Rousseau 1968, 24. Notice how in Rousseau the 'Legislator' replaces natural law; peace becomes a humanly willed harmony (Mansfield 1965, 214).

485. Angell 1943, 75; Wright 1975, 27.

486. Murry 1948, 13-15.

487. Joad 1939, 188-198.

488. *Ibid.*, 199.

489. See for example Russell 1962, 80.

490. E.g., Angell 1939, 298; Einstein 1960, 21, 445. Lothian 1941 adds to this a geopolitical strategy for controlling the oceans (46-47). For a pacificist military strategy see also Angell 1935, 272-273.

491. *A Project of Perpetual Peace*, in Rousseau 1927, 5-7, 21-25, 39-41, 63ff. See also McNamara 1841, who more simply but no less naively urges rulers worldwide to "*legislate for peace!*" (317).

492. Paine 1961, 274. Adler 1944 writes, "I think we are in a position to be more optimistic than Kant" (176) and predicts a rapid movement toward constitutional government, to be followed by "democratization of the world" (187). Luard 1962 imagines a "foreseeable future" in which "international authority will be imposed by consent" — a flavorsome paradox — "rather than by coercion" (128). For an elaborate effort in this direction see Brown 1987, 221ff.

493. Holcombe *et al.* 1975, 4, 4-8.

494. See for summary Smith 1989, 149-151, and Aron 1954, 263, 275, 331. Weber 1958 observes that bureaucracy is historically a feature of the Eastern regimes, particularly China (120). This fact is consonant with the interest in Eastern beliefs and practices seen in Hegel and other

'German' thinkers. Notice that some historicist thought, with its emphasis on metaphors of 'flow' and its distaste for structure, nonetheless envisions the consummation of human striving in bureaucracy. Marx of course is an exception to this, although his followers fell into bureaucracy when Marxian eschatology proved false.

495. See Weil 1973, 3-9, 13-16; Kissinger 1962, 300-307; Olsen 1982, 41ff. For an attempt to bring bureaucracy under more traditional control see Lord 1989.

496. Hollins 1989 calls any "substantial transfer of sovereignty in the peacekeeping field from the national to the global level" under the auspices of the United Nations unworkable, at least in a period of strong nationalist sentiment (180). Gellner 1988 calls both centralization of power *and* local independence untenable; as a result, the world is something of a muddle and will remain so indefinitely (270).

Luard 1962 cites the "insuperable dilemma" faced by any centralized government designed to enforce peace: "Either the forces it creates are so powerful that individual powers or groups will demand to exert veto power over their use; or they will remain only so powerful that they can never effectively challenge the forces of the individual nations" (124). Existing 'nation-states' solved this problem on a much smaller scale — usually by conquest (*Ibid.*, 125).

497. See Proudhon 1927, III, ix, 292-293 and Schmitt 1976, 53-57, who argues that political life requires real friends and real enemies, and it is in the divisions that thus arise that both liberty and real purpose develop. Benda 1959 draws the conclusion: A united humanity would still need an enemy; finding none on earth, it would choose God as its enemy.

> Thereafter, humanity would be unified in one immense army, one immense factory, would be aware only of heroisms, disciplines, inventions, would denounce all free and disinterested activity, would long cease to situate the good outside the real world, would have no God but itself and its desires, and would achieve great things; by which I mean that it would attain a really grandiose control over the matter surrounding it, to a really joyous consciousness of its power and grandeur. And history will smile to think that this is the species for which Socrates and Jesus Christ died (163).

See also Waltz 1965, 228; Berns 1984, 71-75; Schell 1984, 43-44. Nietzsche 1986, I, 25, argues for the need of diverse national goals as a precondition of culture.

498. See Strauss 1964, 228-231.

738

499. See Einstein 1960, 260, 349, 439, for a "supersovereignty" restricted to "the field of security." See Russell 1936, 187; Russell 1960, 5-7, 67; Russell 1962, 80-81, 86, for a cautious but essentially optimistic advocacy of a worldwide social democracy.

500. Roberts, Schmidt, and Streit 1987, 91. This organicism was the fundamental flaw of the League of Nations, which "failed *because* of its general principles" (121, n. 1). See also Maritain 1957 on the "Hegelian roots" of political organicism (192).

501. Roberts, Schmidt, and Streit 1987, 92, 107.

502. Maritain 1957 attempts to overcome this difficulty by avoiding a world sovereignty, preferring a "world political society" with a "supreme advisory council" whose authority would be moral not political (199, 214).

503. Plato 1980, I, 626a, 4. Tacitus 1947 writes that the Arabs "hated the Jews with the usual hatred of neighbors" (657). Goltz asserts that "wars are the fate of mankind, the inevitable destiny of nations," and that "eternal peace is not the lot of mortals in this world" (470). See also Aron 1959, 18, and Waltz 1965, 238.

504. Russell 1917a, 3, 11, 19, 193. Russell later contradicts himself, saying that hatred in wartime "springs only from blindness, not from any inexorable physical necessity" (*Ibid.*, 26). Gray 1970 argues more coherently, claiming that hatred and fear, and the consciousness of being hated and feared, corrupt the human soul, destroying "our higher impulses and potentialities" (229). Insofar as he makes a secular argument, however, he cannot show that this makes being hated and feared unexceptionally worse than being killed or conquered.

505. Hegel 1967, 378; Hegel 1973, 20, 26, 66-67; Hoffman 1989, 11, 23-26, 132-139, 144-149.

506. *The Saint Petersburg Dialogues*, VII, in Maistre 1965, 245.

507. *Thus Spoke Zarathustra*, in Nietzsche 1968, 159, who adds, "War and courage have accomplished more great things than love of neighbor."

508. Rule 1988, 265-266. The pacifist Richardson 1960b observes that "indignation is so easy and satisfying a mood that it is apt to prevent one from attending to any facts that oppose it" (xxxv). The factors that increase indignation and spur countries to fight and to fight on, he writes, are unjustified killing on the part of the enemy, the deaths of eminent citizens, and the fear that war deaths are but the prelude to some greater evil (11-12). While it is easy to see how such indignation may be impervious to facts, it is also easy to see that it might respond justly *to* facts — i.e., the enemy's killing may be unjustified, eminent citizens may indeed have been killed, and war deaths may indeed

presage an intent to tyrannize. See also *Oration on the Crown*, in Demosthenes 1967, 104; Clausewitz 1976, 149, 605.

509. Burckhardt 1979, 124, n. 1, 216. See also Briffault 1963, 130. Andreski 1968 writes:

> No culture is possible without normative codes, and these cannot be upheld unless deviations from them are condemned; therefore, foreigners who do not observe them must be looked down upon. The liberal intellectuals who think they are perfectly tolerant are mistaken (13).

As Faguet 1908 observes, the pacifist perception that evil is ascribed to 'the other' not because of his otherness but because he is foreign, and the "love of the similar for the similar" is accurate as far as it goes but not sufficient (13-14). 'The other' may in fact be evil. See also Lord 1982, 190-196; Hoffmann 1981, 4, 11; Gellner 1988, 272-278.

510. Maistre 1974, 97; Schmitt 1976, 26-53; Molnar 1981, *passim*; Mussolini 1928, 205; "The Fascist Decalogue," in Cohen 1962, 392. Strauss 1965 identifies the problem with this remoralization: "Whoever affirms the political as such, respects all who are willing to fight; he is quite as tolerant as the liberals, but with the opposite intention" (350). See also Benda 1959, 92-101, and compare with his parallel critique of "mystic pacifism" (149-150).

511. Milne 1934, 25. Veblen 1917, less high-minded, takes the immateriality of "national honor" as evidence of its non-existence (28-29). See also Fried 1916, who imagines that hatred "is merely a discovery of diplomacy, which creates national moods in order to cite them as justification for its own errors" (118). For a middle ground between the "ferocity" of bellecism and the disembodies honor of pacifism see Hume 1985, II, 274-275.

512. See Perret 1989, 72, and Gray 1970, 47-50. Gellner 1988, writes:

> There is a fundamental distinction between production and coercion. They have a radically distinct logic. They cannot be treated as parallel. The political and economic histories of mankind, though intertwined, are not carbon copies of each other (176).

Whereas the productive work of economic life can mean the differences between life and death as much as the coercive work of war, economic competition is peaceful, not usually aiming at the physical destruction of the competitor. Unlike economics, political life does not end toward moral relativism or "agreement at any price" (or, to put it in another way, agreement at cash value); see Strauss 1968, 348, and Andreski 1968, 26. See also Hirst 1906 on "true patriotism" (54).

513. Nietzsche 1986, I, 183.

514. See Proudhon 1927, I, 63-68; Key 1972, 13. Even Mussolini 1928 cites "that universality of enjoyment with which boys the world around make friendship by battle and arrive at affection through missiles" (6). (For the biological link between friendship and aggression see Lorenz 1966, 148). Churchill praised Germany's General Rommel in Parliament during the Second World War and wrote:

> ...some people had been offended. They could not feel that any virtue should be recognized in an enemy leader. This churlishness is a well-known streak in human nature, but contrary to the spirit in which a war is won or a lasting peace established (Churchill 1948-53, IV, 67).

See also Gray 1970, 86.

Axinn 1989 recalls the similar spirit of the American Founders:

> The Declaration [of Independence] reminds us that an enemy today is a human whom we hold to be capable of peace and friendship with us. But that peace and friendship is, in the words of St. Augustine, "not just yet." An honest soldier can know that the enemy is human and also know that the enemy must be attacked ferociously. A dignified soldier has that duel knowledge; a fanatic does not (38).

Greenhouse 1986 shows how American soldiers in the Vietnam war could fight without hatred and thus affirm both their humanity and their citizenship: "the ideals that create harmony on the local level — discipline and faith — are exactly the same ones that bring soldiers to war" (58) and, it is important to add, out of war.

See Kecskemeti 1984 for the severe problems caused by the insistence on 'total victory' or 'unconditional surrender' by the enemy: "Permanent peace rests on a weak foundation indeed if it depends on the undying memory of a just chastisement" (240).

Both the pacifist Crucé and the bellecist Goltz agree on the importance of political not military rule; see Crucé 1972, 16-19, and (more grudgingly and with reservations) Goltz 1913, 140-142.

515. Key 1972, 57. Faguet 1908 concurs that "people who cease to be patriotic while others remain patriotic is simply a people who want to die;" patriotism makes both the imperialism of war and the imperialism of peace intenable (392-397). Patriotism is true pacifism, bringing with it a relative peace that defends itself and thus "does not invite conquest to advance" (*Ibid.*, 400).

516. Maistre 1974, 80; Gellner 1988 argues that "logical and social coherence are inversely related" (61) in part because "Men may quake before a high god, but they will not quake before a high concept" (89). Hobbesian cosmopolitanism "destroy[s] the moral basis of national defense" and therefore fails to contribute to any stable peace (Strauss 1953, 197).

517. Nicolai 1919, 250-300. See for contrast Jaspers 1961, 293.

CHAPTER VII

1. Nietzsche 1986, I, 188-189.

2. Montesquieu 1968a, Letter 106, 197.

3. "An Old Question Raised Again: Is the Human Race Constantly Progressing?" in Kant 1963, 139.

4. See Hume 1985, II, xi.

5. Churchill 1948-53, III, 200. See also Proudhon 1927, III, vi, 254-256; III, viii, 282-283; Ruskin n.d., 75-77.

6. Goltz 1913, 19-20.

7. "The Twentieth Century − Its Promise and Its Realization," March 3, 1949, in Churchill 1974, VII, 7801-7804.

8. Ferrero 1933, 1.

9. *Ibid.*, 2.

10. *Ibid.*, 14, 18-19, "Kill, kill: movement is all, and direction is of no importance" (*Ibid.*, 24). See also *Ibid.*, 53-55, 73.

11. Hirst 1906 calls Germany "almost the only modern society in which militarism gives the tone to society" (107), adding that "war has certainly lost its glamor for the soldier," who is "every year...more at mercy of chemists and mechanics" (153). "I doubt it can be said that even animal courage is fostered by modern war, though doubtless it makes tremendous demands on the nerves" (*Ibid.*, 51). See also Russell 1917, 106-107; Page 1937, 3-5; Angell 1935, 18.

12. See Blunden 1956, *passim*; Vann 1939, 47-50.

13. Jaspers 1961, 47.

14. See Jaspers 1961, 45-47; Elshtain 1986, 84, n. 28, 106.

15. Gray 1970, 134.

16. Goltz 1913, 10.

17. Elshtain 1986, 107. Elshtain is describing the ethos of bellecist bureaucratic scientism, not its false opposite, 'movement' pacifism. She does however recognize that unlimited love of the human race is as much an abstraction as unlimited hatred of an enemy (*Ibid.*, 107-108).

18. Horsburgh 1968, 1-15. "The paradox of contemporary civilization is that beyond a certain point the individual's security begins to vary inversely with the power embodied in the systems meant to insure that security" (Holmes 1989, 3); see also *Ibid.*, 4-7, 17, 25. This argument is also made by Margolis 1986, 159-161.

19. See Bloch 1972, xxx-xxxi, on the suicidal character of future wars, with accurate predictions of trench warfare, stalemate, mass mobilization and mass attrition (41) − the latter caused by shells "thrown with unexampled rapidity to unheard-of distances" (159). Severe economic disruptions and resentment of conscription will foment "popular discontent" and make "subversive principles" more popular (348, 356).

20. Russell 1936 denies that any future world war could be won and predicts mob panic during air raids (123-124). He mistakenly claims "the war, as it has now become, is not a method by which *any* good thing can be preserved" (129) − only a few years before the Battle of Britain. See also Ligt 1938, 55. Such claims of course become more plausible after the invention of nuclear war; see Russell 1962, 96; Arendt 1970, 3; Crosser 1972, 1, 7. For an excellent literary survey see Russell 1975, especially 7-22.

21. See Brodie 1959, 307-311; Knorr 1966, 141-144. Crosser 1972 alleges that "if a war is to break out in which the United States military forces are to be engaged, it is by the logic of history and the dialectic of military technology bound to become a nuclear confrontation" (7). The falsity of this claim should teach one to suspect any sentence in which "the logic of history" and "dialectic" are trotted out to do the work reserved for sturdier horses. For a similar example see Caldicott 1986, 166.

22. Proudhon 1927, II, vii, 268.

23. Several writers are quick to remark that the wars antiquity, conducted by politics whose philosophers first formulated the doctrine of just war, yielded enormous casualties and, routinely, the enslavement of the defeated. See Aron 1959, 80 n. 138; Struckmeyer 1979, 275; Child 1986, 39; Seabury and Codevilla, 10, 15. Brodie 1959 even challenges the claim that the limited wars of the eighteenth century were not bloody (30), although he does concede the restraint of the constitutional monarchs (32).

24. Goltz 1913, 12. He adds, "If obstinacy and persistency were displayed equally by both sides, the end of the struggle would only be conceivable after general devastation and pauperization had completely exhausted the physical, and long suffering the moral, forces" (405). "But," he concludes, "it will rarely come to this extreme measure, and in the case of the prosperous nations, perhaps never" (465).

25. See Haskell 1958 on the Battle of Gettysburg, "this great iron battle of missiles" (89). Despite Haskell's brave remark that his men "lay under

the heaviest cannonade that ever shook the continent, and among them a thousand times more jokes were cracked than heads were cracked" (90), one must recall that Haskell himself was killed at the Battle of Cold Harbor, not long thereafter.

26. See de Gaulle 1973, *passim*, and Brodie 1959, 55-67. For evidence that a modern war that *is* strategically sound (as least on the winning side) should not be regarded with any complacency, see Fussell 1989, 3-10, 26, 138. Rather less jaundiced but also unromantic is Gray 1970, 142-160. For the malign psychological effects of modern warfare see Gabriel 1987, 3-4, 38, 43.

27. Kissinger 1957 writes:

> It is...no longer possible to speak of military superiority in the abstract. What does 'being ahead' in the nuclear race mean if each side can already destroy the other's national substance? What is the strategic significance of adding to the destructiveness of the nuclear arsenal when the enormity of present weapons systems already tends to paralyze the will? (132-133).

See also Crosser 1972, 137; Kennedy and Hatfield 1982, 14; Wieseltier 1986, 38.

28. See Knorr 1966, 82-84, and contrast with *Ibid.*, 101. Knorr rightly judges this danger to be remote.

29. Kissinger 1957, 9.

30. Mueller 1989, 4. By May 15, 1984, "the major countries of the developed world had managed to remain at peace with each other for the longest continuous stretch of time since the days of the Roman Empire" (*Ibid.*, 3). See also Nye 1990, 179-180 and, for a Marxist perspective, Kardelj 1960, 35-37, 57-58.

31. Aron 1966, 278.

32. This view opposes that of Russett 1970, who suggests that "the greatest risk from possessing a needlessly big military force is the temptation to use it too readily" (183): not so, if your enemy's military force is also needlessly big. On 'arms races' generally see Maoz 1990, 31-32, 41. For the somewhat different but related concern that technical failure poses a great risk in complicated military systems, see Caldicott 1986, 131-135 and Wallace 1990, 121-122; this problem evidently has been surmountable so far, leading one to suspect the more urgent formulations of it.

33. Lifton and Markusen 1988, 70-71, 74. See also Ruston 1984, 62; Russett 1983, 48; Geyer 1982, 25. Aron 1959 traces this "naive" opinion to the aftermath of the First World War, when "pacifists

believed that the cause of war had been an armed peace," that "by abolishing the instruments of warfare one would automatically abolish the will to fight," in a large part by taking the profit out of it (18). This sort of thing went well with the assumption, common at the time, that people were naturally harmless beings somewhat unaccountably led astray by faulty institutions and clever but base propagandists.

34.   Caldicott 1986, 74.

35.   See Aron 1954, 229; Richardson 1960a, 10, 70.

36.   See for example Payne 1983, 66-67, on the ambitions of the German rulers prior to the First World War.

37.   Luard 1962, 43. See also *Ibid.*, 29; Luttwak 1986, 162-163; Luttwak 1987, 186; Smoke 1987, 29; Martino 1988, 56-57. "The basic problems of disarmament are political" concludes Geyer 1982, 139. Jaspers 1962 observes that tyrannies can never accept arms control *in principle*, but only as a tactic (16-17).

38.   On this confusion see the clear-sighted analyses of Howard 1983, 17-18, 21-22; Payne 1983, 62-69; Waltz 1990, 741.

       A most interesting historical case study is Perrin 1979, an account of Japan's voluntary eschewal of guns in favor of the traditional swords in the year 1597. Although Perrin concludes that this episode proves that technological progress is not inevitable but is governed by political considerations, he also shows the exceptional character of the circumstances in Japan, namely, the social and political interests of the Japanese aristocracy and warrior class, for whom firearms represented a contemptible decline in the test of martial virtue (*Ibid.*, 23-25, 37). An additional circumstance was the isolation of Japan from outside predators, enabling rulers to rule without international pressures. Under such circumstances 'arms control' takes on a very different coloration than it does in modernity.

39.   Herodotus 1942, IX, 688.

40.   Schell 1983, 103; see also *Ibid.*, 105-106. Dickinson 1925 threatens, "If mankind does not end war, war will end mankind" by means discovered by modern science, "the principal hope of mankind" but also "the principal menace" (11).

41.   See, respectively, de Givry 1924, 177; Lasserre 1962, 9; O'Donovan 1989, 23.

42.   Russell 1917a, 17; Brodie 1959, 5. See also "The Nobel Prize for Literature," December 10, 1953; "The power of man has grown in every sphere except over himself" (Churchill 1974, VIII, 8515).

43.   For a useful, brief summary see Nietzsche 1986:

> The machine of itself teaches the mutual cooperation of hordes of men in operations where each man has to do only one thing: it provides the model for the party apparatus and the conduct of warfare. On the other hand, it does not teach individual aristocracy... (II, ii, 366).

The product of the "highest intellectual energies," the machine "releases a large quantity of energy in general that would otherwise lie dormant" but does not provide instigation to enchantment, to improvement, to becoming the artist." Hence it "makes men *active* and *uniform*," finally sapping the very energies that produced it. (*Ibid.*, 367).

44. Thus in a book written in the same period as his warnings on nuclear war, Bertrand Russell deplores the "modern techniques" that "have made possible a new intensity of government control" 'justified' by appeals to equality at the expense of liberty (Russell 1960, 23).

45. See Weart 1988 for a discussion of Isaac Newton as the quintessential scientific alchemist and for an account of the 'last man' of Cousin de Granville and of Mary Shelley, in works written in the early part of the nineteenth century (15-64).

A most informative account of "the cult of the super-weapon" in the United States will be found in Franklin 1988. The steamboat inventor Robert Fulton, Franklin contends, was "the first person to articulate the modern ideology for rationalizing superweapons" on Baconian and militant-republican grounds as early as 1797 in a pamphlet "To the Friends of Mankind." Later figures in this line were Thomas Edison, whose work on the Naval Consulting Board in 1915 sought to inspire the development of technological means for a war to end all wars (*Ibid.*, 70-76), and air power enthusiast Billy Mitchell (*Ibid.*, 97-107). Franklin's book is vitiated by its claim that 'superweapons' are somehow the necessary result of "industrial capitalism," a thesis that overlooks the lively interest in such weapons displayed by the enemies of 'capitalism.'

46. Helen Caldicott's vaporings on this topic are too notorious to require any commentary; see Caldicott 1980 and 1986, *passim*. Cohn 1989, a Harvard University Medical School Psychologist, recounts her time spent with defense technocrats, deploring their "elaborate use of abstraction and euphemism" to conceal the murderous effects of many nuclear weapons (41-42), their "militarization of ... mind" (62). "Technostrategic discourse functions more as a gloss, as an ideological curtain behind which the actual reasons for these decisions hide," reasons having nothing to do with science of objectivity and everything to do with reified sexual potency, political power-hunger, and the love of death (63-64). Cohn offers no real evidence of (as it were) sexually loaded talk by these men, although she does demonstrate her own obsession with sexual imagery (e.g., 43). She baselessly claims that

military jargon is a language for *"white* men" (58, italics added), and ends with a peroration about "creating compelling alternative visions of possible futures" to be "invent[ed]" by "conversations" between "rich and imaginative alternative voices" (64). The amoral character of the 'abstract' or technostrategic mind is in a way perfectly mirrored by the fulminations of the morally outraged; neither party can understand or speak to the other. See also Santoni 1984, 13-14; Lifton and Markusen 1988, 226-228.

The limitations of trying to 'invent away' the realities that technostrategy seeks to grasp may be seen even more clearly in Solomon 1988. A literary critic, Solomon discusses the Heideggerianism of Jacques Derrida, who claims that the age of nuclear weapons is "the absolute *epoche*" the end of absolute or objective knowledge. Solomon does his best to sympathize with this claim, but by the hundredth page or so he begins to worry that nuclear weapons themselves have an embarrassingly *real* look to them, and are not to be 'deconstructed' out of existence by linguistic gamesmanship. "Such a deconstruction of the present, of the dynamic propensities and historical actuations of lived experience, has the practical effect of paralyzing decision in the face of a historical present such as that to which the nuclear referent can be said to refer" (*Ibid.*, 217). "Can be said:" now that is a cautious touch. Solomon, a last man of the bourgeoisie, contemplates Heidegger, a last man of the romanticism, and backs gingerly away, paying his respects all the while:

> ...while there is certainly nothing wrong with pursuing an antirealistic, antirationalist, or antimimetic line of approach when analyzing literature, the extension of antirealistic principles into historical or political discourse has certain practical consequences that should cause us to hesitate before applying such an approach to the analysis of political phenomena. Time and again Heidegger condemns as ignoble any contemplation of the kind of concrete political dilemmas that require negotiation and compromise. This is the way of weakness, of the social horde, of a pulling desire for security. The Heideggerian hero, who looks more and more like Nietzsche's superman, rejects all security to open himself to Being, to shatter himself upon the unknown. But we have already done that by opening up the unfamiliar world of the atom. It is now time for the unheroic activity of coping with our own discoveries.

> To put this another way, the Heideggerian critique cannot lead us to a realistic political criticism. Poetry is not going to solve the concrete problems of the nuclear age...(*Ibid.*, 241)

After rejecting contemporary neo-Marxism as an "essentially arbitrary" "prophetic ideology" Solomon falls back on what he calls "historical realism," which, though vague, at least sounds modest and amenable to common sense (*Ibid.*, 258-262).

47. O'Donovan 1989 traces historicism to the Machiavellian claim that "in extreme circumstances virtue is no guide to rational action" and to the Hobbesian "reduction of all rationality to the fear of [violent] death" (35-36). Nineteenth century writers added the secularized-religious notion of war as theophany, an irruption of 'God' (redefined as "the forces of history") into the course of events (45-46). "Under the protection of the romantic historicism of the nineteenth century...the idea took root that it was the destiny of war to cancel itself out of history by vast increases in scale and violence which would result in the increasing prevalence of peace" (48); that is, romantic historicism reinforced the protohistoricism of Kant. O'Donovan concludes:

> A war-weary civilization, eager to secure the goal of peace on terms that will cost no more bloodshed, dreams of an evolving historical necessity which will bring peace once and for all, and lays impatient claim to the world-conjuring powers of technology in order to conjure that peace into existence. The moral *askesis* that such a civilization needs is to turn away from the pursuit of peace and to attend to its responsibility for justice (116).

O'Donovan goes too far, succumbing to a theological form of 'poetic justice,' in contending that the historicist ethos that culminated in the use of nuclear deterrents has caused "the erosion and disappearance of the liberal political values which the West thought it was defending" (93): erosion, yes; disappearance, no — except among some of the elites.

48. See Ramsey 1983, 221.

49. See Walzer 1977, 1963.

50. Aron 1959, 11-12; Aron 1966, 162. For an example of the political and military character of the arms race — as sharply opposed to the technological 'action-reaction' model — recall that in early 1950 the United States Congress debated whether the military budget should be $14 million, $15 million, or $16 million; by June, after the North Koreans invaded South Korea, the budget was brought in at $60 million (Kahn 1962, 206).

51. See Jaspers 1961, 72-74.

52. Crosser 1972, 50.

53. Cited in Russell 1962, 100-101, and perhaps endorsed at *Ibid.*, 119. For a sound contemporary critique of Snow, see Kahn 1962, 25-26.

54. Caldicott 1980, 64; Caldicott 1986, 4, 7. As early as 1979 Caldicott, upon returning to the United States after a visit to the Soviet Union,

> ...often wandered into the labs at the Harvard Medical School, where brilliant young doctors conducted experiments on rare and diverse diseases. I thought, "What are they doing that for? We have three years before the world is out of control. Don't they know that?" (Caldicott 1986, 5)

They didn't 'know' it, and it is a good thing for those who suffered from rare and diverse diseases that the doctors didn't believe it.

55. See Jervis 1989, 224-225.

56. Jaspers 1961, 318.

57. "The twentieth Century — Its Promise and Its Realization," March 31, 1949, in Churchill 1974, VII, 7806-7807.

58. Aron 1959, 71.

59. Lang 1986 naively supposes that the notion of human omnicide occurred to people only after technology sufficient to the task had been invented, forgetting the Emperor Caligula, who long ago wished that humanity had one throat, that he might strangle it.

60. Schell 1983 argues, similarly, that "Epistemologically, the earth is a special object" because there are no "spare earths" on which to experiment and therewith to determine the effects of a large-scale nuclear war (76).

61. E.g., Caldicott 1986, 1 ("We live on a planet that is terminally ill"); Forcey 1986a, 4 ("We...know that nuclear war would settle nothing and lead to a fiery end to all life on earth"); Cohen and Lee 1986b, 1-2 ("Nuclear holocaust would be the human event to end all human events"); Stahl 1986, 106. For the contrary view, see Kennedy and Hatfield 1982, 67; Lackey 1984, 93-94; Ehrlich and Ehrlich 1986, 100.

62. Russell 1959, 7, 11, 32; italics in original. For a Marxist version of the politics of survival see Somerville 1975, 31-33.

63. Schell 1983, 45, 113, 115-130, 137-147. See also Stahl 1986, 106. Notice that the phrase "mortal god" is that of Hobbes for his Leviathan; Schell avoids the phrase while borrowing the concept. He is Hobbes democratized and 'humanized,' as is Russell.

64. "I can understand the dread of secular humanists over the alleged possible destruction of all human life on 'planet earth,' since for them that would be the end of all known *purpose* in the universe" (Ramsey 1988, 21).

65. Routley 1985, 22.

66. Nye, 1986, 45-46.

67. See O'Riordan 1981 *passim*; Schell 1983, 100-102, 113-114; Devall and Sessions 1985, *passim*.

68. *A Discourse: What Is the Origin of Inequality Among Men, and Is It Authorized by Natural Law?* In Rousseau 1950, 200-222, 234-235.

69. Shepard 1973, 4-7, 90, 97, 123, 126. It should be noted that Shepard gives no sign of having read Rousseau; it is possible that he has retraced a portion of Rousseau's thought independently.

70. For the "Gaia hypothesis" — that the earth itself is a living entity whose good ought to be served by all the species inhabiting it — see Lovelock 1988. Lovelock does not claim that the earth has always been alive (by "life" he means simply the reversal of the law of entropy (*Ibid.*, 3-4), but rather that it has become alive as smaller life-forms evolved and exerted progressively greater influence upon it. The earth of "gaia" is the sum total of these counter-entropic modifications (*Ibid.*, 128). Lovelock thus has no way to distinguish a living organism from a system of living organisms and non-living things. It should be noted that although Lovelock's hypothesis wins acclaim from ecologists as a metaphor or even as a theory, the details of the argument are unsettling to them; Lovelock shrugs off pollution as "an inevitable consequence of life at work" that may displease or harm some species but "may be irrelevant on the Gaian context" (*Ibid.*, 27, 110). For the "living planet" see Berry 1988, 22, 45-48; for "global ecopolitics" see Lifton and Markusen 1988, 276.

71. Berry 1988, 216-220. Naess 1989, 29, 127. It is important to notice Berry's hostility to the American regime, which is slated for revolutionizing in his project. Berry condemns the American founding as an event in the Baconian nature-conquest project (Berry 1988, 40-41) and links the regime with Christianity also, as a doctrine that commands the conquest of nature (109-113).

72. The problem of environmental pollution exemplifies this dilemma. "Polluting for whom? For this or that species or system?" (Naess 1989, 139).

73. See for example Schell 1983, 219; Lifton and Markusen 1988, 256; Naess 1989, 37; Devall and Sessions 1985, ix. The "species consciousness" of Lifton and Markusen is really little more than the old humanitarianism, and therefore rather narrow and retrograde from the ecopolitical perspective.

74. Naess 1989, 37. Notice the confusion of the Greek *sophia* with *phronesis*, typical of historicist doctrine.

75.   Devall and Sessions 1985, 80-90. The authors also claim to write in the Socratic tradition, but betray no knowledge of what that might be, beyond the "asking of searching questions about human life, society, and Nature" (*Ibid.*, 65); in fact their enterprise has nothing whatsoever to do with Socrates who did not participate in egalitarian political 'movements.'

On the connections between 'Deep Ecology' and Heidegger, see Zimmerman 1990, 241-244. Much of the same metamorphosis of the will-to-power from its form as the 'conqueror's' self-assertion to a new form and a new art, a 'drawing-forth' of 'Being,' is of course anticipated in the course of Heidegger's thought. As Zimmerman accurately observes, although Heidegger abandoned the "rhetoric of hardness," of conquest, as early as the mid-1930's, he still dreamed of the Overman as late as 1955 (*Ibid.*, 89-92). As seen in Chapter Five, above, this metamorphosis had already been formulated by Gandhi, and is consistent with certain passages in Nietzsche.

76.   Naess 1974, 24, 29; Naess 1989, 194; Roney 1988, 97-98; Devall and Sessions 1985, 196, 232-235.

77.   Naess 1989, 195. Naess's project does, however, require that a certain human type will rule or at least predominate. Although Naess 1986 says he writes "as a plain member of humanity" (424), he actually appeals to "us," i.e., "responsible citizens" (426); there is indeed a 'them' for Naess, despite his rhetoric of inclusion.

78.   Naess 1974, 14ff., 90. Concretely, Naess advocates the introduction of anti-nuclear and non-violent defense proposals within the North Atlantic Treaty Organization force structure (Naess 1989, 160) as a transition measure.

79.   Naess 1989, 182-183.

80.   *Ibid.*, 85, 165-175, 197-203.

81.   *Ibid.*, 176.

82.   Shepard 1973, 153, 239-244, 256-262, 276. It is important to note that Shepard does not want to abandon all scientific advances; for example, he wants to encourage the development of more nourishing vegetation as a human food source (*Ibid.*, 256-262). It is not clear how small tribes of hunter-gatherers would be able to sustain scientific research.

83.   Naess 1974, 9-10; Naess 1989, 99, 110-113, 132-133, 144-158.

84.   See Devall and Sessions 1985, 22; Berry 1988, 163-170.

85.   Naess 1989, 118-122.

86. Naess 1972, 13-21, 43, 50-61, 92-95, 107, 130-132. Naess rejects Hegel as too absolutist and Thomas S. Kuhn as too relativistic (*Ibid.*, 117-118).

87. *Ibid.*, 69-76, 130.

88. *Ibid.*, 127.

89. Schell 1983, 226.

90. Speech, August 15, 1945, in Churchill 1974, VII, 7211; "The Sinews of Power," March 5, 1946, in *Ibid.*, VII, 7287.

91. "Atomic War or Peace," Einstein 1960, 347. Still vaguer appeals may be seen in Russell 1954, 69; Russell 1962, 79; and Kahn 1962, 145-150. It should be remarked that Russell's initial reaction to the news of the United States deployment of nuclear weapons was much less neutralist. "Communism must be wiped out, and world government established," he wrote to American professor Walter Marseille as late as May 1948 (cited in Clark 1976, 524). In 1949 Russell advocated "bring[ing] pressure to bear upon Russia and even, if necessary, to go so far as to threaten war on the sole issue of internationalizing nuclear weapons;" "I have never been a complete pacifist and have at no time maintained that all who wage war are to be condemned" (Russell 1959, 89-90).

92. Russell 1954, 60. On the other hand, the withdrawal of U. S. and Soviet troops would have given an immense military advantage to the Soviets, who after all are *in* Europe. A temporary withdrawal might well have been in the Soviets' interest — hence the lack of interest in such proposals among the commercial republics.

93. Jaspers 1961 more or less foresees that this is what would need to happen to order to establish a world government. A "supreme legal authority" should guarantee free elections, "equal rights," and majority rule (19). He has no illusions about the means of obtaining such a government, although he is somewhat less than explicit in spelling them out:

> Bur the appeal of the rights of man is politically ineffective. It could become effective only if a great nation were to adopt the rights of man (not only human rights for its own citizens) as part of its constitution and to proclaim them as rights of all men. For without power to insure it there can be no rights.... Today the unity of mankind is an idea imposed upon us by reality itself. It can be wrought only by unanimity about the rights of man (*Ibid.*, 34-35).

94. This may be seen by considering the argument of Fischer 1984. Beginning with the standard observation "nuclear holocust...could lead to human extinction" and positing the standard remedy — to prevent

nuclear holocaust "we must abolish war as a human institution" — he recommends a "legal framework at the global level" without the abolition of "nation states" (*Ibid.*, 4-5). As an example he cites the United States and Japan, France and Germany — countries once at war, now at peace. But of course the only "legal framework" shared by those pairs of countries is treaty law. It is commercial republicanism, not a legal framework easily abrogated or ignored, that makes them peaceful.

95. Aron 1959, 133-134. Accordingly, Aron insisted that "The scientists who enjoin us to create the universal state or perish in a monstrous holocaust do not strengthen our will but drive us to despair. Political wisdom can offer no more hopeful prospect than survival through moderation" (*Ibid.*, 140). On the point that weapons of mass destruction are not necessarily the most effective instruments of regime change. See Brodie 1959, 132-142, on the limitations of air power in this respect.

96. As late as the mid-1980's, on public opinion poll showed that 41% of Americans preferred to die in a nuclear war than to live under communism (Nye 1986, 3) — a rather more firm position than even the calculation that one is unlikely so to perish in any event and so the risk is worth taking in defense of political liberty.

97. Fischer 1984, 3. Child 1986 contrasts Locke and Montesquieu with Hobbes on this point (105, 136), and concludes that "To forswear resistance and put ourselves into the hands of a nuclear-armed and aggressive adversary is something very like selling ourselves into slavery" (102); "as soon as I attempt to trade my slavery for my life and safety, I have handed over my life and safety to the complete discretion of another" (105).

Codevilla 1983 rightly observes that "History's cruelest battles have never proved to be nearly so destructive as cruel rulers. The worst slaughters have been accomplished without a fight" (85). Reilly 1983 remarks that "more people were killed in Southeast Asia since the withdrawal of the United States than during the entire war" in "a peace worse than war" (6).

98. In the eight Marxist oligarchies of Europe in the mid-1980's 13.8 persons per thousand population were in the military; in the commercial republics of Europe, the figure was 7.6 per thousand. The Soviet Union at that time had 16.3 persons per thousand under arms; the United States had 9.1 per thousand. See James L. Payne: "Marxism and Militarism," cited in Martino 1988, 58. Similar and quite possibly even more disproportionate ratios might have existed in comparing such categories as intelligence and secret police or even, on a more mundane level, government bureaucrats.

99. Cf. Churchill:

> Well, how is it then — that [the Kremlin] have
> deliberately united the free world against them? It is, I
> am sure, because they feared the friendship of the West
> more than they do its hostility. They can't afford to
> allow free and friendly intercourse between their country
> and these they control, and the rest of the world... Their
> motive is self-preservation — not for Russia — but for
> themselves ("The Communist Menace," March 25, 1949,
> in Churchill 1974, VII, 7797).

Reilly 1983 suggests that the Soviet Union "fear[ed] truth far more
than radiation" (26).

100.   Churchill writes:

> It's no good trying to convert a Communist, or persuade
> him. You can only deal with him on the following
> basis...by having superior force on your side on the
> matter in question — and they must also be convinced
> that you will use — you will not hesitate to use — these
> forces, if necessary, in the most ruthless manner. You
> have not only to convince the Soviet Government that
> you have superior force — that they are confronted by
> superior force — but that you are not restrained by any
> moral consideration if the case arose from using that
> force with complete material ruthlessness. And that is
> the greatest chance of peace, the surest road to peace.
> Then the Communists will make a bargain...[W]e stop at
> nothing that honor allows. ("The Communist Menace,"
> March 5, 1949, in Churchill 1974, VII, 7797).

Compare the last sentence with the aristocratic standard of the final
sentence of the United States Declaration of Independence, in which
the signatories pledge to each other their lives, fortunes, and sacred
honor.

101.   For Soviet policy with respect to the use of nuclear weapons, see
Carnesdale et. al. 1983, 136; Wieseltier 1986, 31-36. For a dissenting
view see Caldicott 1986, 107.

102.   Kardelj 1960, 122.

103.   Butler 1985 sees that

> Peaceful coexistence among Marxist-Leninists is very
> explicitly not a moral end-in-itself. It openly has an
> instrumental, strategic justification. It gives socialism
> breathing space in which to grow and eclipse capitalism
> (181).

Thus one should view with suspicion such locutions as "Acceptance of long-term coexistence between capitalists and socialists is a precondition to cooperation, and an essential ingredient of global thinking" (Gromyko and Hellman 1988b, 9).

104. Somerville 1975, 96, 106, 135-139, 158, 180, 212.

105. See Kenny 1985, 36; Levine 1990, 4.

106. Martino 1988, 276.

107. Wieseltier 1986 states this eloquently:

> The surprising thing about life since Hiroshima, however, is the extent to which it has not changed. There has been a great deal of moral and political continuity. Nor can this be all attributed to denial. The nuclear peril has never been really denied, as Schell and others have claimed. (The notion of denial, though, is a useful way to discredit psychologically the view of those with whom you disagree). It has just never taken over. People went on living for the old purposes, and politics remained as premised on these purposes as it ever was. The values of democracy were still good, and the values of totalitarianism were still evil. The struggle between democracy and totalitarianism did not end in 1945, because it is a struggle between different answers to some of the most fundamental questions of human life. The nuclear danger has not robbed these questions of their urgency (6).

108. Dummet 1984, 39.

109. Caldicott 1986, 167. Caldicott attempts to prove this by recalling the shifts in American alliances since the 1940's, when the Germans and Japanese were enemies, the Soviets and Chinese friends, to the postwar period when the character of these relationships reversed (*Ibid.*, 183). It never occurs to her that regime changes in three of these four countries may have had something to do with the change in their relations with the United States.

110. Falk 1986, 438, 442.

111. Russell 1959, 88. See for related statements *Ibid.*, 37, 75, 92; see also Russell 1969a, 161; Arendt 1970, 13; Schell 1983, 229. Russell also advances the much weaker argument that those who adhere to the opposite position, that it is better to be dead than Red, have no right "to impose their opinion upon those who do not hold it by the infliction of the death penalty upon all of them" (*Ibid.*, 88). It would indeed have been unjust had Lord Russell and his colleagues been hanged for expressing their opinions, but there was never any serious danger of

this. As for the imposition of the 'death penalty' upon Lord Russell by means of nuclear attack, evidently no one intended to do that, either; at least, it never happened.

112. Russell 1962, 39, 78.

113. Kenny 1984, 14, 18-19; Kenny 1985, 35. See also Brodie 1959, 336; Kahn 1962, 79; Blackett 1962, 95; Routley 1985, 30 n. 1; Stahl 1986, 125.

114. For what is in my view an excessively optimistic view recommending the nuclear disarmament of the commercial republics coupled with "democratic political warfare" see King-Hall 1959, 9-10, 48, 68, 77-79, 116. For the contention that technology in the hands of tyrants will lead to a "scientific Gehenna" worse even than nuclear war, see Hook 1969, 166.

115. Schall 1983, 34. For typically unsound assertions that the United States in the 1980's planned to initiate nuclear war against the Soviets see Caldicott 1986, 107-108, 138-139, 298. Caldicott also claims that from 1945 to 1971, the United States "acted as a global nuclear bully, threatening total death and destruction to hundreds of millions of Soviet people" (*Ibid.*, 164) − raising the question of why the U.S. never bothered to strike first when it had the chance to do so with relative impunity.

Brodie 1959 rejects 'Better dead than Red' but finds in that rejection "little upon which we can erect a national policy," that is, a political and military policy:

> Armed aggression by one nation against another is an old story, and there is not much reason to suppose that we have seen the last of it. We have thus far found no way to control it except by the threat or the action of opposing it with sufficient force (Brodie 1959, 336).

116. O'Donovan 1989, 94.

117. *Ibid.*, 95. This notwithstanding, O'Donovan is right to warn of the threat to commercial republicanism posed by populist egalitarianism, on the one hand, and by the encroachments of the judicial upon the legislative power, on the other. "[I]s it not, at least, worthy of observation that in the very era when we have claimed to defend Western liberalism by resort to ultimate sanction, the context of that liberalism has undergone unprecedented change and become subject to far-reaching uncertainty?" (*Ibid.*, 96).

O'Donovan's underestimation of the political character (particularly the political endurance and attractiveness) of commercial republicanism may be seen in his false prophecy: "The empires must crumble some day, yet it is almost inconceivable that they can do so without nuclear war" (*Ibid.*, 90). This was quite conceivable to such Europeans as de Gaulle even at the height of the 'Cold War,' and became increasingly conceivable to Europeans living under Marxist oligarchies in the 1980's and 1990's. Indeed, it had been conceivable if not achievable all along, as the aborted revolutions of Hungary in 1956 and Czechoslovakia in 1968 should have demonstrated to everyone. The same kind of factual refutation may be leveled at O'Donovan's claim that "the achievement of [nuclear] deterrence has been to make international policies exceedingly dangerous" (91). For the same mistake see Hampsch 1985: "[N]either ideological bloc can realistically expect the other bloc to relinquish its ideological principles or goals as a pre-condition for cooperation for peace..." (129). On the contrary, the extreme danger of nuclear weapons has evidently made their use quite unlikely, and has contributed to making war itself less likely among countries that possess them. That is why the second half of the twentieth century proved so much less bloody than the first, so much safer if you will, among the 'nuclear powers.'

O'Donovan's fundamental objection to unclear deterrence has nothing to do with these political and military concerns. He objects to "the wrongfulness of the deterrent will" − that is, the conditional intention to kill innocents (*Ibid.*, 91).

118. Hook 1969, 163-167. See also Jaspers 1961, 3-4, 166-167, who concludes:

> Man is born to be free, and the free life that he tries to save by all possible means is more than mere life. Hence, life in the sense of existence − individual life as well as all life − can be staked and sacrificed for the sake of the life that is worth living (*Ibid.*, 169).

119. "The Deterrent Nuclear Warfare," March 1, 1955, in Churchill 1974, VIII, 8624, 8629-8630.

120. Kahn 1968, 277. See also Jervis 1989, 9; Waltz 1990, 732. Fischer 1984 distinguishes deterrence from dissuasion, whereby country A convinces B that mutually beneficial peaceful relations are more in B's self-interest that A's destruction is.

121. Carnesdale *et. al.* 1983, 31-37. Brodie 1959 observes that "The development of Russian nuclear capability was decisive in quashing the [American] school urging preventive war precisely because it reinforced the moral argument against preventive war with one founded on fear" (238).

122. See Crosser 1972, 152-153; Lifton and Markusen 1982, 23-24; Holmes 1989, 260-263; Boulding 1989, 145. O'Donovan 1989 argues illogically that nuclear deterrence "gives us no *permanent* security, and *therefore* no security at all" (105).

123. O'Donovan 1989, 7, 107. O'Donovan writes that he has been "unable to imagine" an instance of "nuclear blackmail" (195) and that "badly contaminated territories are not conquerable" – overlooking the expedited surrender of Japan to the United States in 1945.

124. King-Hall 1959, 108. Green 1966 puts it more colorfully: Arguments for nuclear deterrence "amount to not much more than a wildly hopeful prophecy that nuclear weapons are too horrible ever to be used" (xii).

125. Cohen and Lee 1986b, 7-9.

126. Child 1986, 132; Clark 1988, 124; Jervis 1989, 45.

127. Brodie 1959, 304; Aron 1966, 649; Clark 1989, 127.

128. On this 'cooperation' see Jervis 1984, 13-14; Jervis 1989, 7. Carnesdale et. al. 1983 observe that between 1945 and 1965 there were seventeen crises in which nuclear "signaling" occurred; by contrast, between 1966 and 1973 there were only two, with none at all in subsequent years (151). The Soviet Union could not reach the continental United States with nuclear weapons until the late 1950's; see Sloan and Gray 1982, 9. For an account of the United States nuclear weapons program in the first decade see Polmar 1982, 1-5. Geyer 1982 dismisses this as *post hoc ergo propter hoc* reasoning (37-38), which is of course what most historical arguments must be. It is a sound warning to use them with caution.

129. See Joffe 1985, 238.

130. Ruston 1984, 47. See also Catudal 1985, 39, 73.

131. Carnegie Panel on Security and the Future of Arms Control 1983, 71. For an excellent, succinct argument maintaining the "deeply stable" character of nuclear deterrence see Waltz 1990, 733-738. It should be remarked, however, that the paradoxical character of nuclear deterrence, particularly the apparentness of its fragility, must be maintained if nuclear deterrence is to continue to work. Kahn 1968 warns that "in any long period of peace, there may be a tendency for governments to become more intransigent as the thought of war becomes unreal" (11). See also Hehir 1976, 39. This is not to say that deterrence of *all* military threats can be achieved by the deployment of nuclear weapons; see "The Deterrent – Nuclear Warfare," March 1, 1955, in Churchill 1974, VIII, 8631-8632; see also Blackett 1962, 33, 45.

132. Ullman 1985 calls nuclear deterrence "by its nature probabilistic" (194). Goodin calls it "incorrigibly probabilistic" and therefore "simply inappropriate" – reckless and irresponsible (268-270). See also O'Donovan 1989, 57-58, 63. For the contrary view see Kavka 1987, 39-41.

133. Williams 1984, 107-108.

134. Jaspers 1961 claims that the use of 'tactical' nuclear weapons by NATO would "instantly result in total atomic war," as "expressly stated by the Russians" (65). In fact Soviet statements have been unambiguous with respect to attacks on Soviet territory, but not with respect to battlefields outside that territory. It would be usually foolish of the Soviets to launch an all-out nuclear strike in response to a nuclear attack outside Soviet territory. Martino 1988 is right to argue that "because nuclear weapons *can* be used in a disproportionate or unjust manner does not mean that all use of them is inherently disproportionate or unjust" (110). The battlefield use of short-range nuclear weapons clearly can fall within just war rules.

135. See Kahn 1968, 201; Wieseltier 1986, 53.

136. Crosser 1972, 99.

137. Kahn 1960, 19, 132; Kahn 1962, 51.

138. Blackett 1962, 134-135.

139. Brodie 1959, 293.

140. See Kahn 1962, 68.

141. Russell 1959, 33. See also Green 1966, 237; Bok 1989, 11.

142. Osgood and Tucker 1967, 320; see also Tucker 1985, 53-65.

143. Kenny 1984, 21. See also Wasserstrom 1985, 26-30. The intendedly pragmatic segment of Kenny's argument, in contrast to the moral side, deserves to be dismissed with contempt. If the United States were to retaliate in kind in response to a Soviet nuclear attack, he writes, this will preclude Soviet "medical assistance and economic aid" to the U.S. survivors. "[T]his hostile but kindred society [the U.S.S.R.]...would provide the best hope, in the long run, of any eventual reconstruction of the U.S.A. along the lines of the rehabilitating of Germany and Japan by the allied powers after the Second World War" (Kenny 1984, 21). The "allied powers" who actually rehabilitated the Axis powers were the commercial republics; the "allied power" that perpetuated the ruin of the countries it got its hands on was the Soviet Union.

144. See Gauthier 1985, 113. Gauthier goes on to argue that a world in which such deterrence is unnecessary for survival would be even more rational, and urges that citizens work for it (116-117).

The most succinct statement of deterrence policy may be found in Brodie 1959:

> Known ability to defend our retaliatory force constitutes the only unilaterally attainable situation that provides potentially a perfect defense of our homeland. Conversely, a conspicuous inability or unreadiness to defend our retaliatory force must tend to provoke the opponent to destroy it...(185).

From a moral standpoint, Nye argues, the commercial republics do not intend to commit nuclear war but rather intend to prevent it by the only means that evidently work − the threat of retaliation (Nye 1986, 54). The British news magazine *The Economist* once editorialized in a similar vein, "the most utterly horrible war that does not happen is preferable to the most humane war that does" (cited in Groom 1974). See also Walzer 1977, 272-274. Lackey 1984 concurs but then objects that such a threat is still immoral "if it involves an irrecoverable commitment to carrying it out" (176), as he supposes the nuclear threat to do; see however Lackey 1989, 101.

145. Heering 1943 was premature in supposing that bomber-delivered poison gas attacks would render cities indefensible (149). But, despite anti-aircraft and 'civil defense' shelters, it has long been evident that nuclear missiles have made existing defenses inadequate: see Jaspers 1961, 59; Blackett 1962, 22.

146. Fischer 1984, 37-38, 86. Fischer also argues that it is possible to design a military force structure that can be judged defensive by reasonable outsiders without sacrificing the capacity to retaliate against a country that launched a first strike (*Ibid.*, 6, 38, 66).

147. Brodie 1959, 156-162; Roszak 1985, 75-78; Catudal 1985, 148-187; Caldicott 1986, 109-110; Jervis 1989, 117. There is another argument often used against 'counterforce' that is presented as commonsensical but in fact is based upon ignorance. "There is little point," according to Ford, Kendall, and Nadis 1982, "in having a weapon capable of destroying the enemy's ICBM silos unless you intend to use it first. After all, the silos would presumably be empty if the other side started the war" (59). See also Roszak 1985, 72. The silos might be empty but they would also be reloadable; their destruction would ensure that enemy ICBM stockpiles would be useless until new silos were constructed. The attacked country might find this cold comfort; other countries around the world might find it an indispensable opportunity.

148. Ramsey 1983, 362. Hehir 1976 also suggests that bluff may be useful in maintaining deterrence without forming an evil intention.

149. Kenny 1984, 22-24; see also Kenny 1985, 54. On the alleged impracticality of bluff see Ruston 1984, 44; Morris 1985, 83; Nye 1986, 53. On the immorality of requiring subordinates to intend to commit mass murder see Morris 1985, 83; Nye 1986, 54; Hare 1986, 192-196; Martino 1988, 39-41; O'Donovan 1989, 82-83.

150. Wells 1979, 260.

151. Nietzsche 1986, I, 54.

152. Gray 1970 writes that "the man who kills from a distance and without consciousness of the consequence of his deeds feels no need to answer to anyone or to himself;" such men "are those who make our age a monstrous one" (xviii).

153. Grotius 1925, III, i, 599.

154. Fussell 1988, 31-33.

155. Walzer 1977, 145.

156. Fussell 1988, 19. Fussell dismisses Gray's argument (note #152, above) as an example of "error occasioned by remoteness from experience" (29); Gray never engaged in actual combat. Any writer "who dilate[s] on the special wickedness of the A-bomb droppers...was not socially so unfortunate as to find himself down there with the ground forces, where he might have had to compromise the purity and clarity of his moral system by the experience of weighing his own life" − to be sure, the life of a dangerous man, a soldier − "against someone else's" − even if an innocent civilian's (34).

157. Walzer 1977, 264.

158. Green 1966, 225, 239. See also Ruston 1984, 49-52; Lackey 1984, 163; Cohen 1986b, 25 (who, however, do not endorse the argument).

159. Sidney 1990, I, ii, 10.

160. Russell 1936, 202.

161. Green 1966, 168.

162. Ramsey 1978, 72-79; Boyle 1985, 10.

163. Nye 1986 asks, "At what point does the principle of not taking an innocent life collapse before the consequentialist burden?" One life to save a thousand? One to save a million? "Absolutist ethics bear a heavier burden of proof in the nuclear age than ever before" (18-19):

> Given the enormity of the potential effects, moral reasoning about nuclear weapons must pay primary attention to consequences. In the nuclear era a philosophy of pure integrity that would 'let the world perish' is not compelling. But given the unavoidable uncertainties in the estimation of risks, consequentialist arguments will not support precise or absolute moral judgements. (*Ibid.*, 91).

O'Donovan argues that one might want an enemy to fear civilian deaths as the result of a 'counter*force*' attack, just as one might remind a would-be criminal that his imprisonment would result in the undeserved misery of his wife and children. A judge who then sentenced the convicted criminal could be said to intend to jail the man but not to harm the wife and children, who surely will be harmed (15-16).

164. Lackey 1985, 22. See also Lee 1985, who claims that "a slave economy would not be justified even by great economic productivity" (175); indeed not, but what if slavery were necessary to the very survival of the society, i.e., to the survival of masters and slaves alike?

165. · This becomes obvious in Lackey 1984, who argues that "*history* teaches that the common good is best served by an absolute injunction against killing the innocent;" without such an injunction people "lose their inhibitions about killing" (163).

166. Nardin 1986 follows the Kantian line of refusing to 'confuse' the right, the obligatory, one's duty, with the good, the desirable, one's purpose. To do so would be "subversive of morality as a distinctive form of thought and conduce" (301). In the religions duty follows from obedience to God's will, which as such is right and also all-powerful. Duty as absolute obligation makes perfect sense in that framework. Remove God and it no longer makes sense, as the laws have no infallibility either conceptually or in sanction.

167. Reilly 1983 writes that "modern ideology decided to accept as real only that which man could change" or create: this results in the abolition of truth and the worship of a power that is not in fact all-powerful (13). "The old-fashioned tyranny is not ordered on anything but the boundless passion of the tyrant's will," but the new tyrannies 'systematize' that will by invoking 'creative' and supposedly scientific 'method' (16).

168. This argument is that of Morris 1985, 89-98.

169. Lackey 1984, 163ff.; Lee 1985, 179.

170. Nye 1986, 56-57.   One of the most entertainingly wrongheaded arguments ever produced during the course of the debate over nuclear weapons and regime politics in the 'nuclear age' is that of Thompson 1982. The existence of mutual assured destruction, he claims, "fixes indefinitely the tension which makes the resolution of differences improbable," "postponing war" but also "postponing the resolution of peace" (12). Thompson goes on to deride "Western ideologists" who "suppose that the Soviet economy will collapse under the burden of increasing arms allocations, with internal nationalist and dissident movements, and with insurrection and near-insurrection throughout Eastern Europe;" even were these improbabilities to occur, they would

only "precipitate the resolution of war" (18). For a Marxist, Thompson is surprisingly undialectical.

171. See Walzer 1977, 282-283; Hoffmann 1981, 51-52, 74, 81-83; Lackey 1985, 24; Lackey 1989, 67; and Nye 1986, 49. McCormick 1978 argues that the principle of 'double effect,' as it is called, which allows harm to be done in order to achieve a greater good, does not apply to *moral* evils, which usually may not be done no matter what moral or other goods may accrue. However, a lesser moral evil may be *permitted* if unavoidable in order to achieve a greater *moral* good (30-35).

172. See for discussion Schell 1983, 153; Kenny 1985, 45-50; Kavka 1987, 46-54; Lifton and Markusen 1988, 207; O'Donovan 1989, 79-81.

173. Holmes 1989, 211.

174. Holmes 1989 offers the analogy that "Interracial marriage is no more rendered wrong by the reaction of bigots than Christianity was rendered wrong by the feeding of Christians to lions" (208); similarly, murder is wrong under any circumstances. To which one may reply that the point is undeniable in principle but not in practice. If marriage is intended to be a framework for a stable family life, and if one lives in an extremely bigoted society where such stability would be entirely denied to interracial couples, the marriage would best be avoided (unless the couple's intention is not to have a stable marriage but to try to change the bigots' hearts and minds). As for the martyrdom of early Christians, it was justified in their own minds by the conviction that Christianity was the one thing absolutely needful to save their immortal souls; there was a hierarchy of moral goods to which they faithfully adhered.

175. Kenny 1985, 56. For a similar appeal to emotions see Schell 1983, who instructs his readers that "reason must [now] sit at the knee of instinct and learn reverence for the miraculous instinctual capacity for creation" (156). Reason sitting at the knee of instinct might also learn reverence for the not-so-miraculous instinctual capacity for destruction.

176. Grotius 1925, III, iv, 648-651; III, x, 716-719.

177. Walzer 1977, 42, 152; Nye 1986, 55.

178. Lackey 1989, 21.

179. Thus Lackey 1989 writes: "Antiwar pacifists speak on behalf of the enemy dead, and on behalf of all those millions who would have lived if the war had not been fought. On this silent constituency they rest their moral case" (24). He offers no articulation of why these (hypothetical) silent millions morally outweigh other (hypothetical) silent millions dead from an unanswered unclear attack by a tyrant, or the not-so-

hypothetical silent millions dead at the hands of tyrants who were not effectively opposed.

Seabury and Codevilla 1989 argue, by contrast, that "the corollary of the rule that armies may not make war on cities full of civilians is the rule that armies may not hide behind civilians" (225). If armies do not in fact use civilians as shields, enemy armies may morally strike through that shield; the blame rests squarely and exclusively on the hostage-taker.

180. See for example Dummett 1984, 31-36. Insofar as Dummett attempts a rational argument, he claims that if mass murder is not immoral then nothing is; that permission to commit mass murder entails nihilism or the broadest permission to pursue 'self-interest' at any cost. In fact it entails no such thing; to commit mass murder of a million to prevent mass murder of two million is wrong by certain absolute standards or rules but it can scarcely be described as nihilistic or even, necessarily, self-interested.

181. Axinn 1989, 150. Axinn nonetheless goes on to make his own questionable prediction, namely, that "a nuclear war would not be a war; it would be omnicide" (154). See also Wasserstrom 1985, 24.

182. Lackey 1984, 150. For a conflation of the emotionalist and 'human rights' assertions wherein 'human rights' assertions wherein 'human rights' are reduced to an emotionalist/subjectivist foundation see Murphy 1979, 351., 357.

183. *Ibid.*, 153. Child 1986 argues that the defended is simply "saying that he is not worth *less* than the aggressor" (27).

184. Lackey 1985, 20. In other words, "it is wrong to intend an act that is wrong" (Cohen and Lee 1986b, 25).

185. Lackey 1984, 158.

186. For example, Kenny 1985 objects to Allied bombings of civilians in Europe and Asia in World War II. Even if these bombings were necessary to win the war, "Can we be certain that the war did more good than harm, in the sense that the world was a better place in 1946 than it was in 1938, or even than it would have been in 1946 had there been no war [but instead, presumably, surrender to the Nazis]?" (42). In my opinion we can indeed be certain of the war's doing more good than surrender would have done, *as certain as one can be* in answering this kind of question. Of course, the defense of this 'certainty' would require much evidence and reasoning, and would be revisable. But in secular rationalist terms, provisional 'certainty' is the only kind we have. This may leave one dissatisfied with secular rationalism, but that is another matter.

187. Wasserstrom 1985, 23.

188. Martino 1988, 167-168.

189. Ramsey 1978, 35. See also Lackey 1989, 40-41. On this ground Lackey answers the question, "How many innocent people am I entitled to kill if their deaths are necessary for my own survival?" with a moderate "not many!" (43). See also Ruston 1984, 57.

190. See Ruston 1984 on Ramsey, 58. Ruston's objections to Ramsey's arguments are entirely prudential. Ruston later argues that "mutual annihilation − even when it is brought about by the system itself − would always be a better fate than Soviet domination" is "a belief...[that] would put us outside rational argument altogether" (45). This is most likely so, but few argue *for* mutual annihilation.

> Osgood and Tucker 1967 writes:

> Given sufficient faith in the effectiveness of deterrence, then, we are left with the argument that an act which would be unjust to commit ought never to be threatened, however remote the contingency that the act will ever be committed and whatever the consequences that may follow if the threat is not made. When reduced to this rather pure form, however, the argument seems singularly unpersuasive (251).

191. Lackey 1985, 31.

192. See for example Cohen and Lee 1986b, 20-24; Clark 1988, 47-48.

193. Dworkin 1985, 49.

194. Dworkin himself offers an entirely unsatisfactory account of the issue:

> ...if one has to choose between risking a nuclear war and fighting one, it is preferable to choose risking. If one had to choose between firing a pistol with six bullets in the chamber at a baby and firing a pistol with five bullets, one would choose the latter. But both are morally impermissible (47).

One reason why shooting at babies with a loaded gun is morally impermissible is that there is a morally worthy alternative, namely, not shooting at all. In the case of nuclear deterrence it is not intuitively obvious that not shooting at all, much less not threatening to shoot, is the morally worthy alternative. Not shooting may well be morally worthy even under the nuclear gun, but this conclusion requires prudence, not simple deduction from evident premises, in order to be reached on rational and secular grounds.

195. Lewis 1940, 78-81.

196. *Ibid.*, 82-84.

197. See Barnet 1982, 63; Lackey 1984, 144-150. Dworkin 1985 goes so far as to claim that if the United States could develop a machine that would cause any enemy's nuclear missiles to "bounce back" from our skies, we might with equal morality deflect the missiles onto Switzerland as onto the territory of the attacker, because "the noncombatants of the aggressor nation are no more responsible for the attack of the leaders than are the citizens of Switzerland" (45).

198. Nardin 1986, 295.

199. See Boorstin 1991, 41.

200. Child 1986, 144-147. Obviously, this is also the case, and even more strongly, with respect to citizens who elect their governors; see *Ibid.*, 140-143; Markus 1962, 77; Kenny 1985, 32.

201. See Martino 1988, 152.

202. As usual, Caldicott 1980 takes the plunge: "I believe that the Russian people are so frightened of nuclear war that they would heave a momentous sigh of relief" at the commercial republics' disarmament "and would want their own leaders to follow America's moral initiative toward nuclear disarmament" (78). Why Soviet "leaders" would have indulged their captive nations in this sentiment is not clear, but it seems to have something to do with the Caldicott's claim that "Nothing is more disarming than vulnerability" (234) – a pretty notion belied, among other things, by statistics on child abuse, rape, murder, and war. Caldicott argues additionally that "The Soviets are paranoid, so we mustn't do anything to frighten them" (230); one might have thought that humoring the paranoid is no way to cure him. See also Fromm 1962, *passim.*

203. King-Hall 1959 advocates unilateral nuclear disarmament by Great Britain, to be replaced by "defense without arms" (145) – i.e., political and economic resistance to threats and invasions. World opinion, "as echoed in the United Nations" (185), would be outraged by any attack on Great Britain in such circumstances. "Echoed" is about right; King-Hall under-estimates the degree to which "world opinion" follows the correlation of forces, including military as well as economic and political forces. See also Naess 1986, 427.

204. Lackey, 1984, 127, 143.

205. Kenny 1985, 72-78; Kenny 1984, 24-27. It should be noted that Kenny wants the commercial republics to retain their submarine-based nuclear weapons in the hope that retaining the possibility of counterattacking would deter enemy attack even if there was no intention to use those weapons (Kenny 1985, 79). This argument

presumes that one's enemy could not reasonably probe one's intentions.

206. Martino 1988 observes that "Ukrainizing the United States would result in over 91 million deaths" (48).

207. See for discussion Kahn 1960, 230; O'Connor 1983, 342-343; Carnesdale *et. al.* 1983, 247; Krauthammer 1984, 16.

208. Kenny 1985, 5.

209. Dougherty 1985, 46. See also Hardin 1986, 205-207; Wieseltier 1986, 73-76; Nye 1986, 42; Martino 1988, 43-44.

210. Martino 1988, 51.

211. See for a related point Williams 1984, 101.

212. Sidney 1990, III, vii, 358.

213. Franklin 1988, 3-4.

214. Gray 1985, 298.

215. See for example Schell 1984: "On the one side stands human life and the terrestrial creation. On the other side stands a particular organization of life — the system of independent, sovereign nation-states" (218). Bok 1985 speaks of "mutual distrust between the nuclear powers" (340), overlooking the friendly relations among those nuclear "powers" that are also commercial republics. Trachtenberg 1985 perfectly expresses this misconception:

> There is a political conflict at the heart of U.S.-Soviet tension. This is not to be over-defined as a conflict between a threatening Evil Empire and a beleaguered Free World but is rather to be understood in more classic terms as a rivalry between two very great powers whose interests do not coincide (365).

For the same error see also Narveson 1985, 215.

216. Schell 1984, 56. See also Kenny 1985, 66; Nardin 1986, 303.

217. Catudal 1985, 73-74.

218. Holmes 1989, 243-244.

219. Green 1966, 247-251. See also Lifton and Markusen 1988, 82-97.

220. O'Donovan 1989, 61.

221.　For example, Wells 1967 intones:

> If war is indeed the only alternative to national
> obliteration, or if war is required for the survival of what
> we call culture, then it may be that, faced with
> thermonuclear devastation, we would choose the better
> part to cast our fate with Providence and to die
> gracefully.　If eschatology is the correct metaphysics,
> then self-abnegation may be the noblest ethics (137).

And if eschatology is not the correct metaphysics, what then?

222.　*The Spirit of Conquest*, in Constant 1989, 128.　This leads to irreligion, to the supposition that "no just being watches over [humanity's] destiny" (128).　See also Platt 1991, 427-438, on the relation of "the loss of the semipiternity of the species" on the occasion of the invention of nuclear weapons to the degradation of Americans' longing for eternal things.　If there seems to be not time for *longing*, for desires whose fulfillment may not come even during a lifetime, will the human soul not 'flatten out' or weaken?

223.　Walzer 1977, 271.　Walzer generously suggests that "If we had to keep millions of people under restraint in order to maintain the balance of terror, or if we had to kill millions of people (periodically) in order to convince our adversaries of our credibility, deterrence would not be accepted for long" (271).　Perhaps.

224.　Lifton and Falk 1982, 64-71.

225.　Blackett 1962 complains of the "Jupiter complex" among airmen who would deliver "atomic thunderbolts" (93).

226.　Lifton and Markusen 1988, 3.

227.　Fromm 1962, 130-131.　See also Green 1966, 218; Kovel 1983, 27-31, 51, 88.

228.　Thus McMahon 1985 argues that the conditional intention to use nuclear weapons does not corrupt the majority of commercial republican citizenry because most people "give no thought to the policy" (146).

229.　Tucker 1985, 69.

230.　Blackett 1962, 94.

CONCLUSION

1. Gentili 1933, 7. Gentili's only consolation is that he finds the circumstance inevitable.

2. See Goodall 1986, 530-534; Alexander 1987, *passim*.

3. Huxley 1937, 178.

4. Jaspers 1961, 67.

5. Hocking 1923, 375, 378. Berns 1951 observes that for devotees of a Creator-God Who is providential, "There is no necessary conflict between the love of one's own and the good, if the love of one's own is sanctified by the ultimate principle of the universe. Particularly is not disparaged; the ultimate principle of the universe reveals itself in personal address to particular men, particular families and nations, on particular occasions. If their souls are immortal, each individual is of everlasting importance" (51).

6. Hocking 1923, 377.

7. On historicism as the final result of the breakdown of the Aristotelian and Scriptural ethos, and the tyranny that must result from historicism, see Brunner 1945, 15-17.

8. John Adams, Letter to Thomas Jefferson, February 2, 1812, in Cappon 1959, 298.

9. See Strauss 1964, 209.

10. Tocqueville 1945, II, 129-135. Tocqueville rightly associates this attitude with Montaigne, that most cautious early defender of the commercial republican ethos.

BIBLIOGRAPHY

Abelson, Raziel, ed. 1969. *Ethics and Metaethics: Readings in Ethical Philosophy*. New York: St. Martin's Press.

Abrams, Ray H. 1933. *Preachers Present Arms: A Study of the War-Time Attitudes and Activities of the Churches and the Clergy in the United States, 1914-1918*. Philadelphia: Round Table Press.

Adams, Henry. 1986. *History of the United States of America during the Administrations of James Madison*. New York: The Library of America.

Adams, John. 1851. *The Works of John Adams*. 10 vols. Ed. Charles Francis Adams. Boston: Little, Brown and Company.

Addams, Jane. 1907. *Newer Ideals of Peace*. London: The Macmillian Company.

-----. 1922. *Peace and Bread in Time of War*. London: The Macmillan Company.

Adler, Mortimer J. 1944. *How To Think About War and Peace*. New York: Simon and Schuster.

Ahrensdorf, Peter. 1989. "Socrates' Understanding of the Problem of Religion and Politics." In Baumann and Jensen 1989b.

Airaksinen, Timo and Bertman, Martin A. 1989. *Hobbes: War Among Nations*. Aldershot: Averbury.

Aland, Kurt. 1968. "The Relation Between Church and State in Early Times: A Reinterpretation." *Journal of Theological Studies*. XIX: 115-127.

Alberdi, Juan Bautista. 1913. *The Crime of War*. Trans L.J. MacConnell. London: J.M. Dent and Sons.

Alexander, Horace G. 1928a. "Mr. Gandhi's Ashram: Some Impressions." *The Friend*. Vol. LXVIII, No. 18: 371-372.

-----. 1928b. "India: The Work of Reconciliation." *The Friend*. Vol. LXVIII, No. 24: 540-541.

-----. 1930. "Gandhi and the Burning of Foreign Cloth." *The Friend*. Vol. LXIX, No. 19: 410-411.

Alexander, Richard D. 1987. *The Biology of Moral Systems*. Hawthorne: Aldine de Gruyter.

Alfarabi. 1969. *The Philosophy of Plato: Its Parts, the Ranks of Order of Its Parts, from the Beginning to the End.* In Mahdi 1973.

-----. 1973a. *The Enumeration of the Sciences.* In Lerner and Mahdi 1973.

-----. 1973b. *The Attainment of Happiness.* In Lerner and Mahdi 1973.

Alighieri, Dante. 1949. *De Monarchia.* Trans. Herbert W. Schneider. Indianapolis: The Bobbs-Merrill Company.

-----. 1966. *The Divine Comedy.* 3 vols. Trans. John D. Sinclair. New York: Oxford University Press.

Allen, Devere, ed. 1929. *Pacifism in the Modern World.* Garden City: Doubleday, Doran and Company.

Allen, E. L. 1946. *Pacifism as an Individual Duty.* London: Central Board for Conscientious Objectors.

Allen, W.B., ed. 1988. *George Washington: A Collection.* Indianapolis: Liberty Classics.

-----. 1990. "The Constitutionalism of The Federalist." *The Political Science Reviewer.* XIX: 145-176.

Alves, Rubem. 1986. "From Paradise to the Desert: Autobiographical Musings." In Ferm 1986.

Alvis, John and West, Thomas G. 1981. *Shakespeare as Political Thinker.* Durham: Carolina Academic Press.

Ambrose. 1961a. *Exposition of the Christian Faith.* In *A Select Library of Nicene and Post-Nicene Fathers of the Christian Church.* Second Series, Part I. Vol. X. See Schaff and Wace 1961.

-----. 1961b. *On the Duties of the Clergy.* See Schaff and Wace 1961.

American Fellowship of Reconciliation. 1930. "Statement on India." *Reconciliation.* Vol. 7, No. 8: 151.

American Friends Service Committee. 1955. *Speak Truth to Power: A Quaker Search for an Alternative to Violence.* New York: American Friends Service Committee.

Anastaplo, George. 1985. "An Introduction to Hindu Thought: The *Bhagavad Gita.*" In *The Great Ideas Today.* Chicago: Encyclopedia Britannica, Inc.

-----. 1986. "Political Philosophy of the Constitution." In Levy, Karst, and Mahoney 1986.

-----. 1989. *The Constitution of 1787: A Commentary.* Baltimore: John Hopkins University Press.

Andreski, Stanislav. 1968. *Military Organization and Society.* London: Routledge and Kegan Paul.

Andrews, C.F. 1930. *Mahatma Gandhi's Ideas.* New York: The Macmillan Company.

Angell, Norman. 1913. *The Great Illusion: A Study of the Relation of Military Power to National Advantage.* Fourth ed. New York: G.P. Putnam's Sons.

-----. 1935. *Peace and the Plain Man.* New York: Harper and Brothers.

-----. 1938. *Peace With the Dictators?* New York: Harper and Brothers.

-----. 1939. *For What Do We Fight?* New York: Harper and Brothers.

-----. 1943. *Let the People Know.* New York: The Viking Press.

Anonymous. 1798. *The Lawfulness of Defensive War Upon Christian Principles Impartially Considered.* London: Darton and Harvey.

Anonymous. 1810. *The Duty of a Christian in a Trying Situation.* New York: D. McDermut.

Anonymous. 1837. *The Spirit of Despotism.* Darby: Alexander M. Kemble.

Anonymous. 1921. "India's Problems." *The Friend.* Vol. LXI, No. 36: 586.

Anonymous. 1930a. "The Society of Friends in India." *The Friend.* Vol. LXX, No. 25: 565-568.

Anonymous. 1930b. "India." *Reconciliation.* Vol. 7, No. 8: 141-142.

Anonymous. 1969. *La Chanson de Roland.* Trans. Dorothy L. Sayers. Baltimore: Penguin Books.

Anonymous. 1973. *Epistle of Methetes to Diognetus.* In *The Ante-Nicene Fathers.* Vol. I. See Roberts and Donaldson 1973.

Anonymous. n.d. *A Modest Plea in Behalf of the People Call'd Quakers.* London: C. Corbett.

Anscombe, G.E.M. 1961. "War and Murder." In Stein 1961a

Appleton, Lewis. 1889. *Henry Richard: Apostle of Peace.* London: Trubner and Company

Arendt, Hannah. 1970. *On Violence.* New York: Harcourt, Brace and World.

-----. 1971. *The Origins of Totalitarianism* New York: World publishing Company.

Aristophanes. 1962. *The Complete Plays of Aristophanes*. Trans. Moses Hadas et. al. New York: Bantam Books.

Aristotle. 1941. *The Works of Aristotle*. Trans. Richard McKeon. New York: Random House.

-----. 1984. *The Politics*. Trans. Carnes Lord. Chicago: University of Chicago Press.

Arnnobius. 1973. *The Seven Books of Arnobius Against the Heathen*. In *The Ante-Nicene Fathers*. Vol. VI. See Roberts and Donaldson 1973.

Arnold, Thurman W. 1935. *The Symbols of Government*. New Haven: Yale University Press.

Aron, Raymond. 1954. *The Century of Total War*. Garden City: Doubleday and Company.

-----. 1959. *On War*. Trans. Terence Kilmartin. Garden City: Doubleday and Company

-----. 1966. *Peace and War: A Theory of International Relations*. Trans. Richard Howard and Annette Baker Fox. Garden City: Doubleday and Company.

Aronoff, Myron J., ed. 1984. *Religion and Politics*. New Brunswick: Transaction Book.

Assmann, Hugo. 1975. *Practical Theology of Liberation*. Trans. Paul Burns. London: Search Press.

-----. 1986. "The Christian Contribution to Liberation in Latin America." In Ferm 1986.

-----. 1987. "The Improvement of Democracy in Latin America." In Novak 1987.

Athanasius. 1961a. *To Amun. In a Select Library of Nicene and Post-Nicene Fathers of the Christian Church*. Series Two, Part I. Vol. IV. See Schaff and Wace 1961.

-----. 1061a. *Incarnation of the Word*. See Schaff and Wace 1961.

Athenagoras. 1973. *A Plea for the Christians*. In *The Ante-Nicene Fathers*. Vol. II. See Roberts and Donaldson 1973.

Aubert, Roger, ed. 1965. *Concilium: Theology in the Age of Renewal*. Vol. 7. Glen Rock: Paulist Press.

Augustine of Hippo. 1950. *The Christian Combat*. Trans. Robert P. Russell. In *The Fathers of the Church*. Vol. 2. See DeFerrari 1950-1968.

-----. 1961a. *Against the Epistle of Manichaeus Called Fundamental*. In *A Select Library of Nicene and Post-Nicene Fathers of the Christian Church*. Series Two, Part I. Vol. IV. See Schaff and Wace 1961.

-----. 1961b. *Contra Faustum Manichaeum*. See Schaff and Wace 19661.

-----. 1961c. *Of the Morals of the Catholic Church*. Trans. Richard Strothert. See Schaff and Wace 1961.

-----. 1961d. *Our Lord's Sermon on the Mount, According to Matthew*. Trans. William Findley. See Schaff and Wace 1961.

-----. 1964. *Letters*. 5 vols. Trans. Wilfred Parsons. In *The Fathers of the Church*. See DeFerrari 1950-1968.

-----. 1966. *The City of God Against the Pagans*. 7 vols. Trans. George E. McCracken *et. al.* Cambridge: Harvard University Press.

-----. 1968. *Retractions*. Trans. Mary Inez Bogan. In *The Fathers of the Church*. Vol. 60. See DeFerrari 1950-1968.

Aukerman, Dale. 1981. *Darkening Valley: A Biblical Perspective on Nuclear War*. New York: The Seabury Press.

Averroes. 1973. *The Decision Treatise, Determining What the Connection is Between Religion and Philosophy*. In Lerner and Mahdi 1973.

-----. 1974. *Commentary on Plato's "Republic."* Trans. Ralph Lerner. Ithaca: Cornell University Press.

-----. 1977a. *Short Commentary on Aristotle's "Topics."* In Butterworth 1977.

-----. 1977b. *Short Commentary on Aristotle's "Rhetoric."* In Butterworth 1977.

Axinn, Sidney. 1989. *A Moral Military*. Philadelphia: Temple University Press.

Babst, Dean. 1972. "A Force of Peace." *Industrial Research*: 55-58.

Bacon, Benjamin W. 1918. *Non-Resistance: Christian or Pagan?* New Haven: Yale University Press.

Bacon, Francis. 1968a. *Advertisement Touching a Holy War*. In *The Works of Francis Bacon*. Vol. VII. See Spedding, Ellis.

-----. 1968b. *Consideration Touching a Holy War With Spain.* In *The Works of Francis Bacon.* Vol. XIV. See Spedding, Ellis, and Heath 1968.

Bagehot, Walter. 1968. *The English Constitution.* London: Oxford University Press.

Bailey, Alice. 178. *The Destiny of the Nations,* New York: Lucis Publishing Company.

Bailyn, Bernard. 1967. *The Ideological Origins of the American Revolution.* Cambridge: Harvard University Press.

Bainton, Roland. 1960. *Christian Attitudes Toward War and Peace: A Historical Survey and Critical Re-Evaluation.* New York: Abingdon Press.

-----. 1969. *Erasmus of Christendom.* New York: Charles Scribner's Sons.

Baldwin, Alice M. 1958. *The New England Clergy and the American Revolution.* New York: Frederick Ungar Publishing Company.

Baldwin, Roger N., ed. 1927. *Kropotkin's Revolutionary Pamphlets.* New York: Dover Publications.

Ballou, Adin. 1839. *Non-Resistance in Relation to Human Governments.* Boston: Non-Resistance Society.

-----. 1854. *Practical Christian Socialism: A Conversational Exposition of the True System of Human Society.* New York: Fowlers and Wells.

-----. 1860. *A Discourse on Christian Non-Resistance in Extreme Cases.* Milford: Hopedale.

-----. 1862. *Christian Non-Resistance Defended Against Rev. Henry Ward Beecher.* Milford: Hopedale.

-----. 1870-1900. *Primitive Christianity and Its Corruptions.* 3 vols. Boston: Universalist Publishing House.

-----. 1896. *Autobiography.* Lowell: Thompson and Hill.

-----. 1910. *Christian Non-Resistance In All Its Important Bearings, Illustrated and Defended.* Philadelphia: Universal Peace Union.

Bancroft, Joseph and Barclay, Robert, eds. 1879. *A Persuasive to Unity.* Philadelphia: Thomas William Stuckey.

Barbé, Dominique. 1987. *Grace and Power: Base Communities and Non-violence in Brazil.* Trans. John Pairman Brown. Maryknoll: Orbis Books.

Barbour, Hugh. 1964. *The Quakers in Puritan England.* New Haven: Yale University Press.

Barbour, Hugh and Roberts, Arthur O., eds. 1973. *Early Quaker Writings, 1650-1700.* Grand Rapids: William B. Eerdmans Publishing Company.

Barclay, Robert. 1733. *The Anarchy of the Ranters and Other Libertines, The Hierarchy of the Romanists and other pretended Churches, equally Refused and Refuted, in a Two-Fold Apology for the Church and People of God called in Derision Quakers.* London: F. Sowle.

-----. 1879. *Universal Love Considered and Established upon Its Right Foundation.* In *A Persuasive to Unity.* See Bancroft and Barclay 1879.

-----. n.d. *An Apology for the True Christian Divinity: Being an Explanation and Vindication of the Principles and Doctrines of the People Called Quakers.* Philadelphia: Friend's Book Store.

Baker, Ernest. 1949. "Gandhi, as Bridge and Reconciler." In Radhakrishnan 1949.

Barkun, Michael. 1968. *Law without Sanctions: Order in Primitive Societies and the World Community.* New Haven Yale University Press.

Barnett, Richard, 1982. "Lies Clearer Than Truth." In Wallis 1982.

Barraclough, Geoffrey. 1958. "History, Morals, and Politics." *International Affairs.* Vol. XXXIV, No. 1: 1-15.

Barrès, Maurice. 1971. *Scènes et Doctrines du Nationalisme.* In McLelland 1971.

Barry, Brian. 1987. "Can States Be Moral? International Morality and the Compliance Problem." In Myers 1987.

Barth, Karl. 1944. *The Church and the War.* Trans. Antonia H. Froendt. New York: The Macmillan Company.

-----. 1961. *Church Dogmatics.* Vol. III. Part 4. Tran. A. T. MacKay et.al. Edinburgh: T. & T. Clark.

Baumann, Fred and Jensen, Kenneth M., eds. 1989a. *American Defense Policy and Liberal Democracy.* Charlottesville: University Press of Virginia.

-----. 1989b. *Religion and Politics.* Charlottesville: University Press of Virgina.

Bayly, William. 1676. *A Collection of the Several Wrightings of that True Prophet, Faithful Servant of God and Sufferer for the Testimony of Jesus, William Bayly*. No publisher listed.

Beales, A.C.F. 1931. *The History of Peace: A Short Account of the Organized Movements for International Peace*. New York: The Dial Press.

Beard, Charles A. 1954. *An Economic Interpretation of the Consitution of the United States*. New York: The Macmillan Company.

Beaumont, George. 1808. *The Warrior's Looking Glass; Wherein is shewn from many High Authorities, the Trivial Causes, Cruel Nature, Direful Effects, and Anti-Christian Spirit and Practices of War*. Sheffield: J. Crome.

Beck, Lewis White, ed. 1963. *Kant on History*. Indianapolis: The Bobbs-Merrill Company.

Becker, Carl L. 1942. *The Declaration of Independence: A Study in the History of Political Ideas*. New York: Vintage Books.

Beckwith, George C., ed. 1945. *The Book of Peace: A Collection of Essays on War and Peace*. Boston: George C. Beckwith.

-----. 1847. *The Peace Manual or, War and Its Remedies*. Boston: The American Peace Society.

Bellers, John. 1935. *John Bellers, 1654-1725: Quaker, Economist, and Social Reformer*. London: Cassell and Company Ltd.

Belz, Herman. 1988. "Abraham Lincoln and American Constitutionalism" *The Review of Politics* Vol. 50, No. 2: 169-193

Bemis, Samuel Flagg. 1967. *The Diplomacy of the American Revolution*. Bloomington: Indiana University Press.

Bernadete, Seth. 1984. *The Being of the Beautiful: Plato's Theaetetus, Sophist, and Statesmen*. Chicago: University of Chicago Press.

-----. 1989. *Socrates' Second Sailing*. Chicago: University of Chicago Press.

Benda, Julien. 1959. *The Betrayal of the Intellectuals*. Trans. Richard Richard Aldington. Boston: Beacon Press.

Benezet, Anthony, 1766. *Collection of Religious Tracts*. Philadelphia: Henry Miller.

-----. 1782. *The Plainness and Innocent Simplicity of the Christian Religion, With Its Salutary Effects, compared to the Corruption of Nature and dreadful Effects of War*. Philadelphia: Joseph Crukshank.

Bennett, John C. 1958. *Christians and the State*. New York: Charles Scribner's Sons.

-----. ed. 1962. *Nuclear Weapons and the Conflict of Conscience*. New York: Charles Scribner's Sons.

Bentham, Jeremy. 1939. *Plan for a Universal and Perpetual Peace*. London: Peace Book Company.

Berdyaev, Nicolas. 1960. *The Origin of Russian Communism*. Trans. R.M. French. Ann Arbor: University of Michigan Press.

Berger, Morroe. 1965. *Madame de Staël on Politics, Literature, and National Character*. Garden City: Doubleday and Company.

Bernard of Clairvaux. 1954. *On the Christian Year*. Trans. "A Religious of C.S.M.V." London: A.R. Mowbray and Company.

Bernhardi, Fredrich von. 1914. *Germany and the Next War*. Trans. Allen H. Powles. New York: Charles A. Eron.

Berns, Walter. 1969. "The New Left and Liberal Democracy." In *How Democratic Is America? Responses to the New Left Challenge*. See Goldwin 1969.

-----. 1984. *In Defense of Liberal Democracy*. Chicago: Gateway Editions.

Berry, Thomas. 1988. *The Dream of the Earth*. San Francisco: Sierra Club Books.

Berryman, Phillip. 1987. *Liberation Theology: Essential Facts About the Revolutionary Movement in Latin America -- and Beyond*. Philadelphia: Temple University Press.

Bespaloff, Rachel. 1962. *On the Iliad*. Trans. Mary McCarthy. New York: Harper and Row.

Besse, Joseph 1747. *An Enquiry into the Validity of a late Discourse, intituled the Nature and Duty of Self-Defence*. London: T. Sowle Raylton.

-----. 1753. *A Collection of the Sufferings of the People called Quakers, for the Testimony of a Good Conscience*. London: Luke hinde.

Bidegun, Ana María. 1989. "Women and the Theology of Liberation." In Tamez 1989.

Billias, George Athen, ed. 1990a. *American Constitutionalism Abroad: Selected Essays in Comparative Constitutional History*. Westport: Greenwood Press.

780

-----. 1990b. "American Constitutionalism in Europe, 1776-1848." In Billias 1990a.

Bing, Anthony G. 1989. "Peace Studies as Experiential Education." In Lopez 1989.

Blackett, P.M.S. 1962. *Studies of War: Nuclear and Conventional*. New York: Hill and Wang.

Blainey, Geoffrey. 1988. *The Causes of War*. Melbourne: The Macmillan Company.

Blake, Nigel and Pole, Kay, eds. 1984. *Objections to Nuclear Defence: Philosophers on Deterrence*. London: Routledge and Kegan Paul.

Blalock, Hubert M. 1989. *Power and Conflict: Toward a General Theory*. Newbury Park: SAGE Publications.

Blanchard, Joshua P. 1845. *Principles of the Revolution: Showing the Perversion of Them and the Consequent Failure of Their Accomplishments*. Boston: Press of Damrell and Moore.

-----. 1848. *Communications on Peace Written for the Christian Citizen*. Boston: C.C.P. Moody.

Bloch, Jean de. 1972. *The Future of War in Its Technical, Economic and Political Relations*. Trans. R.C. Long. New York: Garland Publishing Company.

Blotner, Joseph. 1974. *Faulkner: A Biography*. 1 vols. New York: Random House.

Blum, Léon. 1932. *Peace and Disarmament*. Trans. Alexander Werth. London: Jonathan Cape.

Blunden, Edmund. 1956. *Undertones of War*. London: Oxford University Press.

Bodin, Jean. 1962. *The Six Books of the Commonweale*. Trans. Robert Knolles. Cambridge Harvard University Press.

Boehme, Jacob. 1969. *A Dialogue between a Scholar and His Master concerning the Supersensual Life*. Cambridge: James Clarke and Company.

Boétie, Etienne de la. 1975. *The Politics of Obedience: The Discourse of Voluntary Servitude*. Trans. Harry Kurz. Montreal: Black Rose Books.

Boff, Leonardo. 1978. *Jesus Christ Liberator: A Critical Christology for Our Time*. Trans. Patrick Hughes. Maryknoll: Orbis Books.

-----. 1979. "Christ's Liberation via Oppression: An Attempt at Theological Construction from the Standpoint of Latin America." In Gibellini 1979.

-----. 1982a. *Way of the Cross -- Way of Justice*. Trans. John Drury. Maryknoll: Orbis Books.

-----. 1982b. *Saint Francis: A Model for Human Liberation*. Trans. John W. Diercksmeier. New York: Crossroad.

-----. 1986. *Ecclesiogenesis: The Base Communities Reinvent the Church*. Trans. Robert R. Barr. Maryknoll: Orbis Books.

-----. 1987. *The Maternal Face of God: The Feminine and Its Religious Expression*. Trans. Robert R. Barr and John W. Diercksmeier. San Francisco: Harper and Row.

-----. 1988a. "Liberation Theology: A Political Expression of Biblical Faith." *Christian Jewish Relations*. Vol. 21, No. 1: 12-21.

----- and Boff, Clodovis. 1987. *Introducing Liberation Theology*. Maryknoll: Orbis Books.

Bogue, David. 1845. *Universal Peace*. In *The Book of Peace: A Collection of Essays on War and Peace*. See Beckwith 1945.

Bok, Sissela. 1985. "Distrust, Secrecy, and the Arms." In Hardin et. al. 1985.

-----. 1989. *A Strategy for peace: Human Values and the Threat of War*. New York: Pantheon Books.

Bondurant, Joan V. 1958. *Conquest of Violence: The Gandhian Philosophy of Conflict*. Princeton: Princton University Press.

Bonino, José Miquez. 1983. *Doing Theology in a Revolutionary Situation*. Philadelphia: Fortress Press.

Bonpane, Blase. 1985. *Guerrillas of Peace: Liberation Theology and the Central American Revolution*. Boston: South End Press.

Boorne, James. 1846. *On the Unlawfulness and Impolicy of War*. Newcastle: P.S. MacLiver.

Boorstin, Daniel J. 1991. "Myths of Popular Innocence." *U.S. News and World Report*. Vol. 110, No. 8: 41.

Borman, William. 1986. *Gandhi and Non-Violence*. Albany: State University of New York Press.

Boserup, Anders and Mack, Andrew. 1975. *War Without Weapons: Non-Violence in National Defense*. New York: Schocken Books.

Boucher, Jonathan. 1899. *Letters of Jonathan Boucher to George Washington.* Brooklyn: Historical Printing Club.

-----. 1967a. *Reminiscences of an American Loyalist, 1738-1789.* Port Washington: Kennikat Press.

-----. 1967b. *A View of the Causes and Consequences of the American Revolution; in Thirteen Discourses, Preached in North America between the Years 1763 and 1775; with an Historical Preface.* New York: Russell and Russell.

Boulding, Kenneth E. 1962. *Conflict and Defense: A General Theory.* New York: Harper and Row.

-----. 1985. *The World as a Total System.* Beverly Hills: SAGE Publications.

-----. 1989. *Three Faces of Power.* Newbury Park: SAGE Publications.

Bourne, Randolph S. 1964. *War and the Intellectuals: Essays, 1915-1919.* New York: Harper and Row.

Bowman, Rufus D. 1944. *The Church of the Brethren and War, 1708-1941.* Elgin: Brethren Publishing Company.

-----. 1945. *Seventy Times Seven.* Elgin: Brethren Publishing Company.

Bowsky, William M., ed. 1964. *Studies in Medical and Renaissance History.* Vol. I. Lincoln University of Negraska Press.

Boyle, Jr., Joseph M. 1985. "War: The Normative Alternatives." In Jones and Griesbach 1985.

-----. 1986. "The Challenge of Peace and the Morality of Nuclear Deterrence." In Reid 1986.

Bradford, M.E. 1979. *A Better Guide than Reason: Studies in the American Revolution.* La Salle: Sherwood Sugden and Company.

Bradford, William. 1952. *Of Plymouth Plantation, 1560-1647.* Ed. Samuel Eliot Morison. New York: Alfred A. Knopf.

Braithwaite, William C. 1912. *The Beginnings of Quakerism.* London: Macmillan and Company.

-----. 1919. *The Second Period of Quakerism.* London: Macmillan and Company.

Brandon, S.G.F. 1967. *Jesus and the Zealots: A Study of the Political Factor in Primitive Christianity.* New York: Charles Scriber's Sons.

Brann, Eva T.H. 1984. "Madison's 'Memorial and Remonstrance': A Model of American Eloquence." In *Rhetoric and American Statesmanship.* See Thurow and Wallin 1984.

Brée, Germaine and Brenauer, George, eds. 1970. *Defeat and Beyond: An Anthology of French Wartime Writing, 1940-1943.* New York: Pantheon Books.

Breig, Joseph A. 1976. "Gandhi and Christ." In Chatfield 1976.

Breuer, Isaac. 1974. *Concepts of Judaism.* Jerusalem: Israel Universities Press.

Brewer, William C. 1940. *Permanent Peace.* Philadelphia: Dorrance and Company.

Brezhnev, Leonid I. 1978. *Leonid I. Brezhnev: Pages From His Life.* New York: Simon and Schuster.

Brierly, J.L. 1963. *The Law of Nations: An Introduction to the International Law of Peace.* New York: Oxford University Press.

Briffault, Robert. 1963. *The Mothers.* Ed. Gordon Rattray Taylor. New York: Grosset and Dunlap.

Brinton, Howard. 1939. Untitled address, in "How Should Religion Deal with Totalitarianism?" In *Town Meeting: Bulletin of America's Town Meeting of the Air.* Vol. 4, No. 8. New York: Columbia University Press.

-----. 1941. *Sources of the Quaker Peace Testimony.* Wallingford: Pendle Hill Historical Studies.

-----. 1943. *Critique By Eternity and Other Essays.* Wallingford: Pendle Hill Historical Studies.

-----. 1958. *The Peace Testimony of the Society of Friends.* Philadelphia: American Friends Service Committee.

Brock, Peter. 1957. *The Political and Social Doctrines of the Unity of Czech Brethren in the Fifteenth and Sixteenth Centuries.* The Hague: Moutan and Company.

-----. 1968. *Pacifism in the United States: From the Colonial Era to the First World War.* Princeton University Press.

-----. 1970. *Twentieth-Century Pacifism.* New York: Van Nostrand Reinhold Company.

-----. 1972. *Pacifism in Europe to 1914.* Princeton: Princeton University Press.

Brodie, Bernard. 1959. *Strategy in the Missile Age*. Princeton: Princeton University Press.

Brookes, George S. 1937. *Friend Anthony Benezet*. Philadelphia: University of Pennsylvania Press.

Brown, Bernard Edward. 1951. *American Conservatives: The Political Thought of Francis Lieber and John W. Burgess*. New York: Columbia University Press.

Brown, Dale W. 1986. *Biblica Pacifism: A Peace Church Perspective*. Elgin: Brethren Press.

Brown, Judith M. 1972. *Gandhi's Rise to Power: Indian Politics*, 1915-1922. Cambridge: Cambridge University Press.

-----. 1977. *Gandhi and Civil Disobedience: The Mahatama in Indian Politics, 1928-1934*. Cambridge: Cambridge University Press.

Brown, P.R.L. 1964. "St. Augustine's Attitude to Religious Concern." *Journal of Roman Studies* LIV: 107-116.

Brown, Seyom. 1987. *The Causes and Prevention of War*. New York: St. Martin's Press.

Brown, Wendy. 1988. *Manhood and Politics: A Feminist Reading in Political Theory*. Totowa: Rowman and Allanheld.

Bruce, F.F. *The Hard Sayings of Jesus*. Downers Grove: Inter Varsity Press.

Brundage, James A. 1986. "The Limits of the War-Making Power: The Contributions of the Medieval Canonists." In Reid 1986.

Brunner, Emil. 1945. *Justice and the Social Order*. Trans. Mary Hottinger. London: Lutterworth Press.

-----. 1947. *The Divine Imperative*. Trans. Olive Wyon. Philadelphia: The Westminster Press.

Bruun, Geoffrey. 1927. *The Enlightened Despot*. New York: Henry Holt and Company.

Bryan, William Jennings. 1909. *Speeches of William Jennings Bryan: Revised and Arranged by Himself*. 2 vols. New York: Funk and Wagnalls Company.

-----. 1917. *Heart to Heart Appeals*. New York: Fleming H. Revell Company.

Brzezinski, Zbigniew, ed. 1978. *The Relevance of Liberalism*. Boulder: Westview Press.

Bühler, Georg. ed. 1969. *The Laws of Manu.* Trans. George Bühler. New York: Dover Publications.

Bueno de Mesquita, Bruce. 1981. *The War Trap.* New Haven: Yale University Press.

-----. and Lalman, David 1990. "Dyadic Power, Expectations, and War." In Gochman and Sabtusky, 1990.

Burckhardt, Jacob. 1951. *The Civilization of the Renaissance in Italy.* Trans. S.G.C. Middlemore. London: Phaidon Press.

-----. 1979. *Reflections on History.* Trans. M.D. Hottinger. Indianapolis: Liberty Classics.

Burgess, John W. 1890. *Political Science and Comparative Constitutional Law.* 2 vols. Boston: Ginn and Company.

Burke, Edmund. 1887. *The Works of the Right Honourable Edmund Burke.* 12 vols. London: John C. Nimmo.

-----. 1961. *Reflections on the Revolution in France.* Garden City: Doubleday and Company.

-----. 1982. *A Vindication of Natural Society, or, a View of the Miseries and Evils Arising to Mankind from Every Species of Artificial Society.* Indianapolis: Liberty Classics.

Burritt, Elihu. 1856. *Thoughts and Things at Home and Abroad.* Boston: Phillips, Sampson and Company.

Burrough, Edward. 1660. *A Declaration to All the World of Our Faith, and what we believe who are called Quakers.* London: Thomas Simmons.

-----. n.d. *A Message to All Kings and Rulers in Christendom.* Swarthmore: Friends Historical Library.

Burtchaell, James Tunstead. 1988. "How Authentically Christian Is Liberation Theology?" *The Review of Politics.* Vol. 50 No. 2: 266-274.

Butler, Clark. 1985. "Peaceful Coexistence and the Nuclear Traumatization of Humanity." In Jones and Griesbach 1985.

Butterworth, Charles E., ed. 1977. *Averroes' Three Short Commentaries on Aristotle's "Topics," "Rhetoric," and "Poetics."* Trans. Charles E. Butterworth, Albany: State University of New York Press.

Byrd, Robert O. 1960. *Quaker Ways in Foreign Policy.* Toronto: University of Toronto Press.

786

Cadbury, Henry J. 1018. "The Basis of Early Christian Antimilitarism" *Journal of Biblical Literature* 37:66-94.

Cadoux, C. John. 1919. *The Early Christian Attitude to War: A Contribution to the History of Christian Ethics.* London: Headley Brothers Publishers, Ltd.

-----. 1925. *The Early Church and the World: A History of the Christian Attitude to Pagan Society and the State Down to the Time of Constantine.* Edinburgh: T. & T. Clark.

-----. 1940. *Christian Pacifism Re-Examined.* Oxford: Basil Blackwell.

Cady, Duane L. 1989. *From Warism to Pacifism: A Moral Continuum.* Philadelphia: Temple University Press.

Caldicott, Helen. 1980. *Nuclear Madness: What You Can Do!* New York: Bantum Books.

-----. 1986. *Missile Envy: The Army Race and Nuclear War.* Toronto: Bantum Books.

Calhoun, John C. 1883. *The Works of John C. Calhoun.* 6 vols. Ed. Richard K. Cralle. New York: D. Appleton and Company.

-----. 1957. *A Disquisition on Government.* Indianapolis: The Bobbs-Merrill Company.

Calhoun, Robert L. *et. al.* 1946. *Atomic Warfare and the Christian Faith: Report of the Commission on the Relation of the Church to the War in the Light of the Christian Faith.* New York: Federal Council of the Churches of Christ of America.

Calvin, John. 1960. *Institutes of the Christian Religion.* Trans. Ford Francis Battles. Philadelphia: The Westminister Press.

-----. 1982. *Treatises Against the Anabaptists and Against the Libertines.* Trans. Benjamin Wirt Farley. Grand Rapids: Baker Book House.

Cambridge Women's Peace Collective. 1984. *My Country Is the Whole World: An Anthology of Women's Work on Peace and War.* London: Pandora Press.

Camus, Albert. 1955. *The Myth of Sisyphus and Other Essays.* Trans. Justin O'Brien. New York: Random House.

-----. 1958. *The Fall and Exile and the Kingdom.* Trans. Justin O'Brien. New York: The Modern Library.

Canby, Henry Seidel, ed. 1943. *Prefaces to Peace.* New York: Simon and Schuster.

Cantor, Paul. 1976. *Shakespeare's Rome: Republic and Empire*. Ithaca and London: Cornell University Press.

Cappon, Lester J., ed. 1959. *The Adams-Jefferson Letters*. Chapel Hill: University of North Carolina Press.

Capra, Fritjof and Spretnak, Charlene. 1984. *Green Politics*. New York: E. P. Dutton.

Carey, George W. 1987a. "James Wilson's Political Thought and the Constitutional Convention." *The Political Science Reviewer*. XVII: 49-107.

-----. 1987b. "James Madison on Federalism: The Search on Abiding Principles." *Benchmark: A Bimonthly Report on the Consitution and the Courts*. Vol. III, Nos. 1, 2: 27-57.

Carey, H. C. 1872. *The Past, the Present, and the Future*. Philadelphia: Henry Carey Baird.

Carnegie Panel on U.S. Security and the Future of Arms Control. 1982. *Challenges for U.S. National Security*. Washington: Carnegie Endowment for International Peace.

Carnesdale, Albert; Doty, Paul; Hoffmann, Stanley; Huntington, Samuel P.; Nye, Jr., Joseph S.; Sagan, Scott. 1983. *Living With Nuclear Weapons*. New York: Bantam Books.

Carter, April. 1967. "Political Conditions for Civilian Defense." In Roberts 1967.

Carter, Jimmy. 1976. *Why Not the Best?* New York: Bantam Books.

-----. 1977. *A Government as Good As Its People*. New York: Simon and Schuster.

-----. 1984. *Keeping Faith: A Presidential Memoir*. New York: Bantam Books.

Carter, Paul A. 1956. *The Decline and Revival of the Social Gospel: Social and Political Liberalism in American Protestant Churches, 1920-1940*. Ithata: Cornell University Press.

Case, Clarence Marsh. 1923. *Non-Violent Coercion: A Study in the Methods of Social Pressure*. New York: The Century Company.

Caspary, Gerard E. 1979. *Politics and Exegesis: Origen and the Two Swords*. Berkley: University of California Press.

Cassidy, Richard J. 1978. *Jesus, Politics, and Society: A Study of Luke's Gospel*. Maryknoll: Orbis Books.

Castro, Emilio. 1969. "Conversion and Social Transformation." In Cox 1969.

Caws, Peter, ed. 1989. *The Causes of Quarrel: Essays on Peace, War, and Thomas Hobbes*. Boston: Beacon Press.

Catudal, Honoré M. 1985. *Nuclear Deterrence: Does It Deter?* Berlin: Berlin Verlag Arno Spitz.

Ceadel, Martin, 1987. *Thinking About War and Peace*. Oxford: Oxford University Press.

Chalmers, Thomas. 1816. *Thoughts on Universal Peace: A Sermon Delivered on Thursday, January 18, 1816, The Day of National Thanksgiving for Restoration and Peace*. Secont edition. Edinburgh: Andrew Balfour.

Chan, Steve. 1984. "Mirror, Mirror on the Wall: Are the Freer Countries More Pacific?" *Journal of Conflict Resolution*. Vol. 28, No. 4: 617-648.

Channing, William Ellery. 1903. *Discourses on War*. Boston: Ginn and Company.

Chamfort. 1963. *Maximes et Pensées*. Paris: Union Général d'Editions.

Charney, Anne. 1988. "Spiritedness and Piety in Aristotle." In Zuckert 1988.

Chatfield, Charles. 1971. *For Peace and Justice: Pacifism in America, 1914-1941*. Knoxville: University of Tennessee Press.

-----. ed. 1976. *The Americanization of Gandhi: Images of the Mahatma*. New York: Garland Publishing Company.

-----. 1989. "Misplaced Crisis." In Cromartie 1989.

Chatterjee, Margaret. 1983. *Gandhi's Religious Thought*. Norre Dame: University of Notre Dame Press.

Chelcický, Petr. 1964a. *Statement about the triple division of the people, and about the clergy and laity*. Trans. R. Holinka. In *Studies in Medieval and Renaissance History*. See Bowsky 1964.

-----. 1964b. *On The Holy Church*. Trans. R. Holinka. In *Studies in Medieval and Renaissance History*. See Bowsky 1964.

Chickering, Roger. 1975. *Imperial Germany and a World Without War: The Peace Movement and German Society, 1892-1914.* Princeton: Princeton University Press.

Child, James W. 1986. *Nuclear War: The Moral Dimension*. New Brunswick: Transaction Books.

Childress, James F. 1971. *Civil Disobedience and Political Obligation: A Study in Christian Social Ethics*. New Haven: Yale University Press.

-----. 1982. *Moral Responsibility in Conflicts: Essays on Nonviolence, War, and Conscience*. Baton Rouge: Louisiana State University Press.

Churchill, Winston S. 1931. *India: Speeches and an Introduction*. London: Thornton Butterworth Ltd.

-----. 1948-1953. *The Second World War*. 6. vols. Boston: Houghton Mifflin Company.

-----.1974. *Winston S. Churchill: His Complete Speeches, 1897-1963*. 8 vols. Ed. Robert Rhodes James. New York: Chelsea House.

Cicero. 1880. *Academic Questions*. Trans. C.D. Yonge, London: Henry G. Bohn.

-----. 1968. *The Offices*. Trans. Walter Miller. Cambridge: Harvard University Press.

-----. 1970, *De Re Publica*. Trans. C.W. Keyes. Cambridge: Harvard University Press.

Clancy, William, ed. 1961. *The Moral Dilemma of Nuclear Weapons*. New York: The Church Peace Union.

Clark, David Lee, ed. 1966. *Shelly's Prose, or The Trumpet of a Prophecy*. Albuquerque: University of New Mexico Press.

Clark, Ian. 1982. *Limited Nuclear War: Political Theory and War Limitations*. Oxford: Martin Robertson.

-----. 1988. *Waging Wars: A Philosophical Introduction*. Oxford: Clarendon Press.

Clark, Ronald W. 1976. *The Life of Bertrand Russell*. New York: Alfred A. Knopf.

Clark, Stephen R.L. 1989. *Civil Peace and Sacred Order: Limits and Renewals I*. Oxford: Clarendon Press.

Clarkson, Thomas, 1806. *A Portraiture of Quakerism*. 3 vols. New York: Samuel Stansbury.

-----. n.d. *An Essay on the Doctrines and Practices of the Early Christians as the Relate to War*. Ipswich: J. King.

Clastres, Pierre. 1987. *Society Against the State: Essays in Political Anthropology*. Trans. Robert Hurley and Abe Stein. New York: Zone Books.

Clausewitz, Carl von. 1976. *On War*. Trans. Michael Howard and Peter Paret. Princeton: Princeton University Press.

Clemençeau, Georges. 1930. *Grandeur and Misery of Victory*. Trans. F.M. Atkinson. New York: Harcourt, Brace and World.

Clement of Alexandria. 1973a. *Exhortation to the Heathen*. Trans. Marcus Dods. In *The Ante-Nicene Fathers*. Vol I. See Roberts and Donaldson 1973.

-----. 1973b. *The First Epistle of Clement*. Trans. Alexander Roberts and James Donaldson. In *The Ante-Nicene Fathers*. Vol. I. See Roberts and Donaldson 1973.

-----. 1973c. *Pedagogus*. Trans. Marcus Dods. In *The Ante-Nicene Fathers*. Vol. III. See Roberts and Donaldson 1973.

-----. 1973c. *Pedagogus*. Trans. Marcus Dods. In *The Ante-Nicene Fathers*. Vol. III. See Roberts and Donaldson 1973.

-----. 1973d. *Protrepticus*. Trans. Marcus Dods. In *The Ante-Nicene Fathers*. Vol. II. See Roberts and Donaldson 1973.

-----. 1973e. *The Stromata*. Trans. Marcus Dods. In *The Ante-Nicene Fathers*. Vol. II. See Roberts and Donaldson 1973.

Cobden, Richard. 1973. *The Political Writings of Richard Cobden*. New York: The Garland Publishing Company.

Cochrane, Charles Norris. 1972. *Christianity and Classical Culture*. London: Oxford University Press.

Codevilla, Angelo. 1983. "Justice, War, and Active Defense." In Lawler 1983.

Cohen, Avner and Lee, Steven, eds. 1986a. *Nuclear Weapons and the Future of Humanity: The Fundamental Questions*. Totowa: Rowman and Allanheld.

-----. 1986b. "The Nuclear Predicament." In Cohen and Lee 1986a.

Cohen, Eliot A. 1985. *Citizens and Soldiers: The Dilema of Military Service*. Ithata: Cornell University Press.

Cohen, Carl, ed. 1962. *Communism, Fascism and Democracy*. New York: Random House.

Cohen, Morris R. 1946. *The Faith of a Liberal*. New York: Henry Holt and Company.

Cohn, Carol. 1989. "Sex and Death in the Rational World of Defense Intellectuals." In Forcey 1989b.

Colet, John. 1965. *An Exposition of St. Paul's Epistle to the Romans.* Ridgewood: The Gregg Press.

Colman, Benjamin. 1991. *Government thePillar of the Earth.* In Sandoz, 1991.

Combee, Jerry H. 1989. "Religious Roots of the Rights of Man in America." In Baumann and Jensen 1989b.

Comblin, José. 1979. *The Church and the National Security State.* Maryknoll: Orbis Books.

Comenius, John Amos. n.d. *The Angel of Peace.* Trans. anonymous. New York: Pantheon Books.

Conquest, Robert. 1991. *The Great Terror: A Reassessment.* New York: Oxford University Press.

Constant, Benjamin. 1090. *Political Writings.* Trans. Biancamaria Fontana. Cambridge: Cambridge University Press.

Cooper, Thomas. 1826. *Two Essays.* Columbia: D. & J.M. Faust.

Cotta, Sergio. 1978. *Why Violence? A Philosophical Interpretation.* Trans. Giovanni Gullace. Gainesville: University of Florida Press.

Coulton, G.G. 1016. *The Main Illusions of Pacifism: A Criticism of Mr. Norman Angell and of the Union of Democratic Control.* Cambridge: Bowes and Bowes.

Council on Religion and International Affairs. 1976. *The New Nuclear Debates.* New York: Council on Religion and International Affairs.

Cousins, Norman. 1945. *Modern Man Is Obsolete.* New York: The Viking Press.

-----. 1953. *Who Speaks for Man?* New York: The Macmillan Company.

Cox, Harvey C., ed. 1969a. *The Church Amid Revolution.* New York: Association Press.

-----. 1969b. "Introduction." In Cox 1969a.

Cox, Richard H. 1982. *Locke on War and Peace.* Lanham: University Press of America.

-----. 1987. "Aristotle and Machiavelli on Liberty." In *The Crisis of Liberal Democracy: A Straussian Perspective.* See Deutsch and Soffer 1987.

Crèvecoeur, J. Hector St. John de. 1957. *Letters From an American Farmer.* New York: E.P. Dutton.

Cromartie, Michael, ed. 1989. *Peace Betrayed? Essays on Pacifism and Politics.* Washington: Ethics and Public Policy Center.

Crook, John, 1660. *An Epistle of Love to all that are in present Sufferings, whether Inwardly, or Outwardly, whether they are, or have been Officers or Soldiers of the Army, or, Rulers or Governors of these Nations, or Public Preachers, or any other, who by reason of the Fear of the Loss of Life, Liberty or Estate; or any other Suffering that is likely to come upon them; Read these Lines in the fear of the Lord, and receive them as the Testimony of a Friend in love to all your souls.* London: Robert Wilson.

Cropsey, Joseph. 1957. *Policy and Economy: An Interpretation of the Principles of Adam Smith.* The Hague: Martinus Nijhoff.

-----. 1977. *Political Philosophy and the Issues of Politics.* Chicago: University of Chicago Press.

-----. 1986. "The United States as Regime and the Sources of the American Way of Life." In Horwitz 1986.

Crosser, Paul K. 1972. *War Is Obsolete: The Dialectics of Military Technology and Its Consequences.* Amsterdam: B. R. Grüner N.V.

Crossman, Richard, ed. 1949. *The God That Failed.* New York: Harper and Brothers.

Crucé, Eméric. 1972. *The New Cineas: Discourse on Opportunities and Means for Establishing a General Peace and Freedom of Trade Throughout the World.* Trans. C. Frederick Farrell, Jr. and Edith R. Farrell. New York: Garland Publishing Company.

Cuadra, Pablo Antonio. 1990. "Reclaiming the Revolution." *Journal of Democracy.* Vol. 1, No. 3: 39-47.

Cullmann, Oscar. 1956. *The State in the New Testament.* New York: Charles Scribner's Sons.

-----. 1970. *Jesus and the Revolutionaries.* Trans. Gareth Putnam. New York: Harper and Row.

Cunningham, William. 1910. *Christianity and Social Questions,* New York: Charles Scribnr's Sons.

-----. 1915. *Christianity and Politics.* Boston: Houghton Mifflin Company.

Curti, Merle E. 1929. *The American Peace Cursade, 1915-1860.* Durham: Duke University Press.

-----. 1959. *Peace or War: The American Peace Struggle, 1636-1936*. Boston: J.S. Cannes and Company.

Cyprian. 1973. *To Donatus*. In *The Ante-Nicene Fathers*. Vol. V. See Roberts and Donaldson 1973.

Dahl, Robert A. 1956. *A Preface to Democratic Theory*. Chicago: University of Chicago Press.

Dakin, D. Martin. 1956. *Peace and Brotherhood in the Old Testament*. London: Bannisdale Press.

Dallas, Alexander. 1815. *An Exposition of the Causes and Character of the Late War Between the United States and Great Britain*. Middlebury: William Slade, Jr.

Daly, Mary. 1978. *Gyn/Ecology: The Metaethics of Radical Feminism*. Boston: Beacon Press.

-----. 1985. *Beyond God the Father: Toward a Philosophy of Women's Liberation*. Boston: Beacon Press.

Dannhauser, Werner J. 1983. Untitled review of *The Longer War: Israel in Lebanon* by Jacobo Timerman. *The American Spectator*. Vol. 16, No. 4: 34-35.

Darby, W. Evans. 1908. *The Christ Method of Peace Making*. London: Headley Brothers.

Darrow, Clarence. 1903. *Resist Not Evil*. Chicago: Charles H. Kerr and Company.

-----. and Lewis, Arthur M. 1911. *Marx versus Tolstoy: A Debate*. Chicago: Charles H. Kerr and Company.

Datta, Dhirendra Mohan. 1961. *The Philosophy of Mahatma Gandhi*. Madison: University of Wisconsin Press.

Davies, Samuel. 1755. *Religion and Patriotism the Constituents of a Good Soldier*. Philadelphia: James Chattin.

-----. 1757. *The Crisis*. London: J. Buckland.

-----. 1758. *The Curse of Cowardice*. London: J. Buckland.

-----. 1761. *Religion and Public Spirit*. London: James Parker and Company.

Davis, Rebecca Harding. 1984. "The Civil War." In Cambridge Peace Collective 1984.

Day, Dorothy, 1959. *The Long Loneliness*. Garden City: Doubleday and Company.

-----. 1963. *Loaves and Fishes*. New York: Harper and Row.

De Benedetti, Charles. 1978. *Origins of the Modern American Peace Movement*. Millwood: KTO Press.

Debs, Eugene V. 1927. *Walls and Bars*. Chicago: The Socialist Party.

DeFerrari, Joseph, ed. 1950-1964. *The Fathers of the Church*. New York: Fathers of the Church, Inc.

De Gaulle, Charles. 1934. *Vers l'armée de métier*. Paris: Plon.

-----. 1973. *La discorde chez l'ennemi*. Paris: Plon.

Demosthenes. 1967. *Public Orations*. Trans. John Warrington. London: J.M. Dent and Sons Ltd.

De Quincey, Thomas. 1897. *The Collected Writings of Thomas De Quincey*. 8 vols. London: A. & C. Black.

Destro, Robert A. 1986. Pastoral Politics and Public Policy: *Reflections on the Legal Aspects of the Catholic Bishops' "Pastoral Letter on War and Peace."* In Reid 1986.

Deutsch, Karl W. and Hoffmann, Stanley, eds. 1968. *The Relevance of International Law: Essays in Honor of Leo Gross*. Cambridge: Schenkman Publishing Company.

Deutsch, Kenneth L. and Soffer, Walter, eds. 1987. *The Crisis of Liberal Democracy: A Straussian Perspective*. Albany: State University of New York Press.

Devall, Bill, and Sessions, George. 1985. *Deep Ecology*. Salt Lake City: Peregrine Smith Books.

Dewey, John. 1946. *Problems of Men*. New York: Philadelphia Library.

Diamond, Martin. 1986. "Ethics and Politics: The American Way." In Horwitz 1986.

-----. 1987. "The Federalist." In Strauss and Cropsey 1987

Dickinson, G. Lowes. 1925. *War: Its Nature, Cause and Cure*. New York: The Macmillan Company.

Diggins, John P. 1984. *The Lost Soul of American Politics: Virtue, Self-Interest, and the Foundations of Liberalism*. New York: Basic Books.

Diwaker, R.R. n.d. Untitled essay. In Kumar n.d.

Dobson, James O. 1925. "The Political Thought of Young India. *The Friend*. Vol. LXV, No. 14: 282-283.

Dodge, David L. 1810. *Remarks Upon an Anonymous Letter*. New York: Williams and Whiting.

-----. 1816. *Observations on the Kingdom of Peace, Under the Benign Reign of the Messiah*. New York: J. Seymour.

-----. 1854. *Memorial of Mr. David Low Dodge, Consisting of an Autobiography, prepared at the Request and for the Use of His Children; with a Few Selections from His Writings*. Boston: S.K. Whipple.

-----. 1905. *War Inconsistent with the Religion of Jesus Christ*. Boston: Ginn and Company.

Doke, Joseph J. 1909. *M.K. Gandhi: An Indian Patriot in South Africa*. London: The London Indian Chronicle.

Dolci, Danilo. 1965. *A New World in the Making*. Trans. R. Munroe. New York: Monthly Review Press.

Dombrowski, Daniel A. 1991. *Christian Pacifism*. Philadelphia: Temple University Press.

Donne, John. 1953-1962. *Sermons*. 10 vols. George R. Potter and Evelyn M. Simpson, eds. Berkeley: University of California Press.

Dougherty, James E. 1985. "The Environment of Nuclear Deterrence: Empirical Factors and Moral Judgments." In Jones and Griesbach 1985.

Douglass, James W. 1968. *The Non-Violent Cross: A Theology of Revolution and Violence*. New York: The Macmillan Company.

-----. 1972. *Resistance and Contemplation: The Way of Liberation*. New York: Doubleday and Company.

-----. 1983. *Lightning East and West: Jesus, Gandhi, and the Nuclear Age*. New York: Crossroads.

Doyle, Michael. 1983. "Kant, Liberal Legacies, and Foreign Affairs." *Philosophy an Foreign Affairs*. Vol. 12, Nos. 3 and 4: 205-235, 323-353.

-----. 1986. "Liberalism and World Politics." *American Political Science Review*. Vol. 80, No. 4: 1151-1169.

Dresner, Samuel H. 1961. "Man, God, and Atomic War." In Keys 1961.

796

Dresser, Amos. 1849. *The Bible Against War*. Oberlin: Amos Dresser.

Drumont, Edouard. 1976. *La France Juive*. In McLelland 1976.

Duffield, Marcus. 1933. "Our Quarreling Pacifists." *Harpers Magazine*. No. 166: 688-696.

Dumm, Thomas L. 1987. *Democracy and Punishment: Disciplinary Origins of the United States*. Madison: University of Wisconsin Press.

Dummett, Michael. 1984. "Nuclear Warfare." In Blake and Pole 1984.

Dunne, Pete. 1990. "In the Natural State." *The New York Times*. March 7, Section 12:17.

Durkheim, Emile. 1951. *Suicide*. Trans. John Spaulding and George Simpson. New York: The Free Press.

Dye, Thomas R. and Zeigler, Harmon. 1989. "Socialism and Militarism." *PS: Political Science and Politics*. Vol. 22, No. 4: 800-813.

Dymond, Jonathan, 1855. *Essays on the Principles of Morality, and on the Private and Political Rights and Obligations of Mankind*. New York: Harper and Brothers.

-----. 1892. *An Inquiry into the Accordancy of War with the Principles of Christianity, and Examination of the Philosophical Reasoning by which It is Defended, with some Observations on Some of the Causes of War and on Some of Its Effects*. Philadelphia: Friends' Book Store.

Easton, Loyd and Guddat, Kurt H., eds. 1967. *The Writings of the Young Marx on Philosophy and Society*. Garden City: Doubleday and Company.

Eckhardt, William 1976. *A Manual on the Development of the Concept of Compassion and Its Measurement, 1963-1975*. Oakville: Canadian Peace Research Institute.

Edwardes, Michael. 1986. *The Myth of the Mahatma: Gandhi, the British and the Raj*. London: Constable and Company.

Ehrlich, Paul R. and Ehrlich, Anne H. 1986. "Ecology of Nuclear War: Population, Resources, Environment." In Cohen and Lee 1986a.

Eidelberg, Paul. 1968. *The Philosophy of the American Constitution: A Reinterpretation of the Intentions of the Founding Fathers*. New York: The Free Press.

-----. 1974. *A Discourse on Statesmanship: The Design and Transformation of the American Policy*. Urbana: University of Illinois Press.

-----. 1976. *On the Silence of the Declaration of Independence*. Amherst: University of Massachusetts Press.

-----. 1977. *Beyond Detente: Toward an American Foreign Policy*. La Salle: Sherwood Sugden and Company.

-----. 1983. *Jerusalem vs. Athens: In Quest of a General Theory of Existence*. Lanham: University Press of America.

----- and Morrisey, Will. 1992. *Our Culture 'Left' or 'Right'*. Lewiston: The Edwin Mellen Press.

Einstein, Albert. 1960. *Einstein on Pace*. Eds. Otto Nathan and Heine Norden. New York: Simon and Schuster.

Eisler, Riane. 1988. *The Chalice and the Blade: Our History, Our Future*. San Francisco: Harper and Row.

Elliot, Jonathan, ed. 1845. *Debates on the Adoption of the Federal Constitution, Convention Held at Philadelphia in 1787: with a Diary of the Debates of the Congress of the Confederation; as Reported by James Madison*. Philadelphia: J.B. Lippincott and Company.

Ellul, Jacques. 1967. *The Political Illusion*. Trans. Konrad Kellen. New York: Alfred A. Knopf.

-----. 1969. *Violence*. Trans. Cecelia Gaul Kings. New York: The Seabury Press.

-----. 1976. *The Ethics of Freedom*. Trans. Geoffrey W. Bromiley. Grand Rapids: William B. Eerdmans Publishing Company.

Elshtain, Jean Bethke. 1983. "On Beautiful Souls, Just Warriors, and Feminist Consciousness." In Stiehm 1983.

-----. 1986a. "Critical Reflections on Realism, Just Wars, and Feminism in a Nuclear Age." In Cohen and Lee 1986a.

-----. 1986b. *Meditations on Modern Political Thought: Masculine/Feminine Themes from Luther to Arendt*. New York: Praeger.

-----. 1987. *Women and War*. New York: Basic Books.

Emerson, Ralph Waldo. 1929. *The Complete Writings of Ralph Waldo Emerson*. New York: William H. Wise and Company.

Emmert, Kirk. 1989. *Winston S. Churchill on Empire*. Durham: Carolina Academic Press.

Enz, Jacob J. 1972. *The Christian and Warfare: The Roots of Pacifism in the Old Testament*. Scottdale: Herald Press.

Eppstein, John. 1935. *The Catholic Tradition of the Law of Nations*. Washington: Catholic Association for International Peace.

Epstein, David F. 1984. *The Political Theory of the Federalist*. Chicago: University of Chicago Press.

Erasmus. 1972. *Adages*. Trans. Margaret Mann Phillips. New York: Garland Publishing Company.

-----. 1986. *The Collected Works of Erasmus*. 66 vols. Ed. A.H.T. Levi. Toronto: University of Toronto Press.

Erikson, Eric. 1969. *Gandhi's Truth: On the Origins of Militant Non-Violence*. New York: W.W. Norton and Company.

Eusebius Pamphilus. 1961a. *The Life of the Blessed Emperor Constantine*. In *A Select Library of Nicene and Post-Nicene Fathers of the Christian Church*. Series Two, Vol. I. See Schaff and Wace 1961.

-----. 1961b. *The Oration of the Emperor Constantine*. In *A Select Library of Nicene and Post-Nicene Fathers of the Christian Church*. Series Two, Vol. I. See Schaff and Wace 1961.

-----. 1961c. *The Oration of Eusebius Pamphilus in Praise of the Emperor Constantine Pronounced on the Thirtieth Anniversary of His Reign*. In *A Select Library of Nicene and Post-Nicene Fathers of the Church*. Series Two, Vol. I. See Schaff and Wace 1961.

Faguet, Emile. 1908. *Le Pacifisme*. Paris: Société Française D'Imprimerie de la Librairie.

-----. 1914. *The Cult of Imcompetence*. Trans. Beatrice Barstow. New York: E.P. Dutton.

Falk, Richard A. 1970. *The Status of Law in International Society*. Princeton: Princeton University Press.

-----. 1975. *A Study of Future Worlds*. New York: The Free Press.

-----. 1986. "Nuclear Weapons and the Renewal of Democracy." In Cohen and Lee 1986a.

Fallows, James. 1981. *National Defense*. New York: Random House.

Fanon, Frantz. 1968. *The Wretched of the Earth*. Trans. Constance Farrington. New York: Grove Press.

Farmer, Herbert H. 1948. "The Christian and War." In Jones 1948.

Farrand, Max, 1913. *The Framing of the Constitution of the United States*. New Haven: Yale University Press.

Fast, Howard A. 1959. *Jesus and Human Conflict*. Scottdale: Herald Press.

Fedoseyev, Pyotor. 1985a. "Preventing Nuclear War Is the Prime Task of Humanity." Trans. In *Peace and Disarmament: Academic Studies*. See Fedoseyev 1985b.

-----, ed. 1985b. *Peace and Disarmament: Academic Studies*. Moscow: Progress Publishers.

Ferguson, John. 1974. *The Politics of Love: The New Testament and Nonviolent Revolution*. Cambridge: James Clarke and Company.

-----. 1978. *War and Peace in the World's Religions*. New York: Oxford University Press.

-----. and Pitt-Watson, Ian. 1956. *Letters on Pacifism*. London: SCM Press Ltd.

Ferguson, Marilyn. 1980. *The Aquarian Conspiracy: Personal and Social Transformation in the 1980's*. Los Angeles: J.P. Tarcher, Inc.

Ferm, Deane William, ed. 1986. *Third World Liberation Theologies: A Reader*. Maryknoll: Orbis Books.

Ferrero, Guglielmo. 1933. *Peace and War*. Trans. Bertha Pritchard. London: Macmillan and Company.

Feuer, Lewis S., ed. 1959. *Marx and Engels: Basic Writings on Politics*. Trans. Leonard E. Mins. Garden City: Doubleday and Company.

Field, G.C. 1945. *Pacifism and Conscientious Objection*. Cambridge: Cambridge University Press.

Figgis, J.N. 1921. *The Political Aspects of S. Augustine's 'City of God.'* London: Longmans, Green, and Company.

-----. 1960. *Political Thought from Gerson to Grotius, 1414-1625*. New York: Harper and Borthers.

Filmer, Robert. 1949a. *The Anarchy of a Limited or Mixed Monarchy*. In Laslett 1949.

-----. 1949b. *Directions for Obedience to Government in Dangerous or Difficult Times*. In Laslett 1949.

-----. 1949c. *The Freeholder's Grand Inquest Touching the King and His Parliament*. In Laslett 1949.

-----. 1949d. *Observations concerning the Original of Government*. In Laslett 1949.

-----. 1949e. *Observations Upon Aristotle's Politics Touching Forms of Government*. In Laslett 1949.

-----. 1949f. *Patriarcha: A Defense of the Natural Power of Kings Against the Unnatural Liberty of the People*. In Laslett 1949.

Finch, Richard. 1746. *The Nature and Duty of Self-Defence: Addressed to the People called Quakers*. London: M. Cooper.

-----. 1775. *Second Thoughts Concerning War: Wherein That Great Subject, Is Candidly Considered, and Set in a New Light, in Answer to, and by the Author of a late Pamphlet, entitled The Nature and Duty of Self Defence, addressed to the People called Quakers*. London: M. Cooper.

Finn, James. 1967. *Protest: Pacifism and Politics*. New York: Random House.

Finnis, John, Boyle, Jr., Joseph M. and Grisez, Germain. 1987. *Nuclear Deterrence, Morality and Realism*. Oxford: Clarendon Press.

Fiorenza, Elisabeth Schüssler. 1983. *In Memory of Her: A Feminist Theological Reconstruction of Christian Origins*. New York: Crossroad Publishing Company.

Fischer, Dietrich. 1984. *Preventing War in the Nuclear Age*. Totowa: Rowman and Allanheld.

Fischer, Louis. 1938. "Fascist Pacifism. *The Nation*, Vol. 147: 446-448.

-----. 1949. (Untitled). In Crossman 1949.

Flaumenhaft, Harvey. 1976. "Hamilton on the Foundation of Government." *The Political Science Reviewer*. Vol. VI: 143-214.

Floy, James. 1841. *The Republicanism of Christianity*. Brooklyn: Thomas R. Mercein.

Foch, Ferdinand. 1931. *Memoirs*. Trans. T. Bentley Mott. Garden City; Doubleday, Doran and Company.

Fontaine, Arturo. 1987. "It Is Not Easy to Argue with Liberation Theologians." In Novak 1987.

Fontaine, Jacques. 1965. "Christians and Military Service in the Early Church." Trans. Theodore L. Westow, In Aubert 1965.

Forcey, Linda. 1989a. "Introduction ot Peace Studies." In Forcey 1989b.

-----. 1989b. *Peace: Meanings, Politics, Strategies*. Newyork: Praeger.

Ford, Daniel; Kendall, Henry; and Nadis, Steven. 1982. *Beyond the Freeze: The Road to Nuclear Sanity*. Boston: Beacon Press.

Fornari, Franco. 1974. *The Psychoanalysis of War*. Trans. Alenka Pfeifer. Garden City: Doubleday and Company.

Fortin, Ernest L. 1972. *Political Idealism and Christianity in the Thought of St. Augustine*. Villanova: Villanova University Press.

-----. 1981. *Dissidence et philosophie au Moyen Age*. Paris: J. Vrin.

-----. 1989. "Church Activism in the 1980's: Politics in the Guise of Religion?" In Baumann and Jensen 1989b.

Foster, Mary Le Cron and Rubinstein, Roberts A., eds. 1986. *Peace and War: Cross Cultural Perspectives*. New Brunswick: Transaction Books.

Fox, George. 1659. *To the Council of Officers of the Army, and the Heads of the Nation; and for the Inferior Officers and Soldiers to Read*. Swarthmore: Friends Historical Library.

-----. 1660. *A Declaration from the Harmless and Innocent People of God, called Quakers, against all the Plotters and Fighters in the World*. Swarthmore: Friends Historical Library.

-----. 1661. *An Answer to the Arguments of the Iewes, in which they go about to prove, that the Messiah is not come*. Swarthmore: Friends Historical Library.

-----. 1706. *Gospel-Truth Demonstrated, in a Collection of Doctrinal Books, Given Forth by that Faithful Minister of Jesus Christ, George Fox: Containing Principles, Essential to Christianity and Salvation, held among the People called Quakers*. London: T. Soule.

-----. 1911. *The Journal of George Fox*. Ed. Norman Penny, Cambridge: Cambridge University Press.

Fox, Margret. 1660. *A Declaration and an Information From us the People of God called Quakers, to the present Governors, the King, and Both Houses of Parliament, And all whom it may Concern*. London: Thomas Simmons and Robert Wilson.

Fox, Richard Wightman. 1985. *Reinhold Niebuhr: A Biography*. New York: Pantheon Books.

Franklin, Benjamin. 1945. *Autobiographical Writings*. Ed. Carl Van Doren. New York: The Viking Press.

-----. 1959-1988. *The Papers of Benjamin Franklin*. Ed. Leonard W. Labarea. New Haven: Yale University Press.

-----. 1987. *Writings*. J.A. Leo LeMay. New York: The Library of America.

Franklin, H. Bruce. 1988. *War Stars: The Superweapon and the American Imagination*. New York: Oxford University Press.

Freire, Paulo. 1974. *Pedagogy of the Oppressed*. Trans. Myra Bergman Ramos. New York: The Seabury Press.

Freud, Sigmund. 1962. *Civilization and Its Discontents*. Trans. James Strachey. New York: W.W. Norton and Company.

Fried, Alfred H. 1912. *The German Emperor and the Peace of the World*. Trans. anonymous. New York: Hodder and Staughton.

-----. 1916. *The Restoration of Europe*. Trans. Lewis Stiles Gannett. New York: The Macmillan Company.

Friedel, Frank. 1947. *Francis Lieber: Nineteenth-Century Liberal*. Baton rouge: Louisiana State University.

Friedrich, Carl J. 1969. *Inevitable Peace*. New York: Greenwood Press.

Frisch, Morton J. and Stevens, Richard G., eds. 1973. *The Political Thought of American Statesmen: Selected Writings and Speeches*. Itasca: F.E. Peacock, Publishers.

Fromm, Erich. 1962. "Explorations into the Unilateral Disarmament Position." In Bennett 1962.

Fry, Joan Mary. 1904. *The Way of Peace and Other Essays*. London: Headley Brothers.

-----. ed. 1915. *Christ and Peace: A Discussion of Some Fundamental Issues Raised by the War*. London: Headley Brothers.

Fussell, Paul. 1975. *The Great War and Modern Memory*. New York: Oxford University Press.

-----. 1988. *Thank God for the Atom Bomb and Other Essays*. New York: Summit Books.

-----. 1989. *Wartime: Understanding and Behavior in the Second World War*. New York: Oxford University Press.

Fustel de Coulanges, Numa Denis. n.d. *The Ancient City*. Trans. anonymous. Garden City: Doubleday and Company.

Gabriel, Richard A. 1987. *No More Heroes: Madness and Psychiatry in War.* New York: Hill and Wang.

-----. 1990. *The Culture of War: Invention and Early Development.* Westport: Greenhood Press.

Gaismayr, Michael. 1975. *Plan of Reform.* In Zuck 1975.

Galilea, Segundo. 1979. "Liberation Theology and New Tasks Facing Christians." In Gibellini 1979.

Gallie, W. B. 1978. *Philosophers of Peace and War: Kant, Clausewitz, Marx, Engels and Tolstoy.* Cambridge: Cambridge University Press.

Galtung, Johan. 1980. *The True Worlds: A Transnational Perspective.* New York: The Free Press.

Galston, William A. 1975. *Kant and the Problem of History.* Chicago: University of Chicago Press.

Gandhi, Mohandas K. 1958-1984. *The Collected Works of Mahatma Gandhi.* 90 vols. Delhi: The Publications Division, Ministry of Information and Broadcasting, Government of India.

Gardner, M. B. 1944. *Christianity vs. Marxism, or The Christian's Recall to Foundational Principles.* Philadelphia: M. B. Gardner.

Gargaz, Pierre-André. 1922. *Conciliator of all the Nations of Europe, or A Project of Perpetual Peace, between all the Sovereigns Europe and their Neighbors.* New York: George Simpson Eddy.

Garrison, William Lloyd, ed., 1861. *TheAbolition of Slavery and the Right of the Government Under the War Power.* Boston: F. Wallcut.

-----. 1862. *The Abolitionists, and Their Relations to the War.* n.p.

-----. 1885. *William Lloyd Garrison, 1805-1879: The Story of His Life as Told by His Children.* 4 vols. New York: The Century Company.

-----. 1966. *Selections from the Writings and Speeches of William Lloyd Garrison.* New York: Negro University Press.

-----. 1975. *The Letters of William Lloyd Garrison.* Ed. Louis Ruchamer and Walter M. Merrill. Cambridge: Harvard University Press.

Garrity, Patrick J. 1987. "Foreign Policy and *The Federalist*." In Kesler 1987.

Gauthier, David. 1985. "Deterrence, Maximization, and Rationality." In Hardin *et. al.* 1985.

Gay, William C., ed. 1984. *Philosophy and the Debate on Nuclear Weapons Systems and Policy.* In *Philosophy and Social Criticism.* Vol. 10, No. 3-4.

Geach, P. T. 1961. "Conscience in Commission." In Stein 1961.

Gellner, Ernst. 1988. *Plough, Sword, and Book: The Structure of Human History.* London: Collins Harvill.

Genovés, Santiago. 1972. *Is Peace Inevitable? Aggression, Evolution, and Human Destiny.* London: George Allen and Unwin.

Gentili, Albertico. 1933. *De Iure Belli Libri Tres.* Trans. John C. Rolfe. Oxford Clarendon Press.

Gentz, Friedrich. 1959. *The French and American Revolution Compared.* Trans. John Quincy Adams. Chicago: Henry Regnery Company.

George, S.K. 1939. *Gandhi's Challenge to Christianity.* London: George Allen and Unwin.

-----. 1976. "Gandhi Lifts the Cross." In Chatfield 1976.

Geyer, Alan. 1982. *The Idea of Disarmament! Rethinking the Unthinkable.* Elgin: The Brethren Press.

-----. 1986. "Two and Three-Fourths Cheers for the Bishops' Pastoral: A Peculiar Protestant Perspective." In Reid 1986.

Gibbon, Edward, n.d. *The Decline and Fall of the Roman Empire.* 3 vols. New York: The Modern Library.

Gibellini, Rosino, ed. 1979. *Frontiers of Theology in Latin America.* Maryknoll: Orbis Books.

Gide, André. 1949. In Crossman 1949.

Gilbert, Felix. 1961. *To the Farewell Address Ideas of Early American Foreign Policy.* Princeton: Princeton University Press.

Gildin, Hilail. 1983. *Rousseau's Social Contract: The Design of the Argument.* Chicago: University of Chicago Press.

Gillespie, Michael. 1988. "Death and Desire: War and Bourgeoisification in the Thought of Hegel. In Zuckert 1988.

Ginzburg, Natalia. 1988. "The Son of Man." In Gioseffa 1988.

Gioseffi, Daniela, ed., 1988. *Women on War: Essential Voices for the Nuclear Age.* New York: Simon and Schuster.

Gish, Arthur G. 1970. *The New Left and Christian Radicalism*. Grand Rapids: William B. Eerdmans Publishing Company.

Givry, Grillot de. 1924. *Le Christ et la Patrie*. Paris: André Delpeuch.

Glidden, C. Paul. 1948. "The Gospel Basis of Pacifism" In Jones 1948.

Gochman, Charles S. and Sabrosky, Alan Ned, eds. 1990. *Prisoners of War? Nation-States in the Modern Era*. Lexington: D.C. Heath and Company.

Godwin, William. 1946. *Enquiry Concerning Political Justice and Influence on Morals and Happiness*. Toronto: University of Toronto Press.

Goldman, Emma. 1969. *Anarchism and Other Essays*. Port Washington: Kennikat Press.

-----. n.d. *Preparedness, the Road to Universal Slaughter*. New York: The Mother Earth Publishing Association.

Goldschmidt, Walter, 1986. "Personal Motivation and Institutionalized Conflict." In Foster and Rubinstein 1986.

Goldwin, Robert A. 1969. *How Democratic Is America? Responses to the New Left Challenge*. Chicago: Rand McNally Company.

-----. 1986. "Religion and the Founding Principle." In *The Moral Foundations of the American Republic*. See Horwitz 1986.

-----, and Schambra, William A., eds. 1981. *How Democratic Is the Constitution*? Washington: American Enterprise Institute.

-----, and Schamhra, William A., eds. 1985. *How Does the Constitution Secure Rights*? Washington: American Enterprise Institute.

Goldschmidt, Walter. 1986. "Personal Motivation and Institutionalized Conflict." In Foster and Rubinstein 1986.

Gollancz, Victor. 1959. *The Devil's Repertoire, or Nuclear Bombing and the Life of Man*. Garden City: Doubleday and Company.

Goltz, Colman von der. 1913. *The Nation in Arms: A Treatise on Modern Military Systems and the Conduct of the War*. Trans. Philip A. Ashworth. London: Hugh Ress Ltd.

Goodall, Jane. 1986. *The Chimpanzees of Gombe*. Cambridge: Harvard University Press.

Goodin, Robert E. 1985. "Nuclear Disarmament as a Moral Certainty." In Hardin *et. al.* 1985.

Gottfried, Paul. 1991. "Confronting *The Challenge of the Exception*: George Schwab as an Interpreter of Carl Schmitt." *The Political Science Reviewer*. Vol. XX: 264-285.

Gottwald, Norman K. 1961. "Nuclear Realism or Nuclear Pacifism?" In Keys 1961.

-----. 1979. *The Tribes of Yahweh: A Sociology of Religion of Liberated Israel: 1250-1050 B.C.E.* Maryknoll: Orbis Books.

Graham, John W. 1928. "Christianity in India." *The Friend*. Vol. LXVIII, No. 13: 255-257.

-----. 1929. "India: The Case for the English." *The Friend*. Vol. LXIX, No. 50: 1157-1158.

-----. 1930. "British Government in India." *Reconciliation*. Vol. 7, No. 8: 145-147.

Graves, Robert. 1970. *The White Goddess: A Historical Grammar of Poetic Myth*. New York: Farrar, Straus and Giroux.

Gray, Colin. 1985. "Strategic Defense, Deterrence, and the Prospects for Peace." In Hardin *et.al*. 1985.

Gray, J. Glenn. 1970. *The Warriors: Reflections on Men in Battle*. New York: Harper and Row.

Grebel, Conrad. 1975. *A Letter of Thomas Muentzer*. In Zuck 1975.

Green, Martin. 1986. *The Origins of Nonviolence: Tolstoy and Gandhi in Their Historical Settings*. University Park: The Pennsylvania State University Press.

Green, Philip. 1966. *Deadly Logic: The Theory of Nuclear Deterrence*. New York: Schocken Books.

Green, T. H. 1967. *Lectures on the Principles of Political Obligation*. Ann Arbor: University of Michigan Press.

Green, Thomas F. 1952. "The Basis of Christian Pacifism." *The Friends' Quarterly*. Vol. 6, No. 2: 91-99.

Greenhouse, Carol J. 1986. "Fighting for Peace." In Foster and Rubinstein 1986.

Gregg, Richard B. 1966a. "Pacifist Program in Time of War, Threatened War, or Facism." In Lynd 1966.

-----. 1966b. *The Power of Nonviolence*. New York: Schocken Books.

Gremillion, Joseph. 1976. *The Gospel of Peace and Justice: Catholic Social Teaching Since Pope John.* Maryknoll: Orbis Books.

Grenier, Richard. 1983. *The Gandhi Nobody Knows.* Nashville: Thomas Nelson Publishers.

Grimké, Thomas S. 1832. *Address on the Truth, Dignity, Power and Beauty of the Principles of Peace, and on the Unchristian Character and Influence of War and the Warrior.* Hartford: C.F. Olmsted.

Grisez, Germain and Boyle, Jr., Joseph M. 1979. *Life and Death With Liberty and Justice: A Contribution to the Euthanasia Debate.* Notre Dame: University of Notre Dame Press.

Griswold, Charles L. 1989. "War, Competition, and Religion: Hobbes and the American Founding." In Caws 1989.

Griswold, Stanley. 1991. *Overcoming Evil with Good.* In Sandoz, 1991.

Gromyko, Anatoly and Hellman, Martin, eds. 1988a. *Breakthrough: Emerging New Thinking.* New York: Walker and Company.

-----. 1988b. "The Challenge to Change." In Gromyko and Hellman 1988a.

Groom, A.J.R. 1974. *British Thinking About Nuclear Weapons.* London: Frances Pinter.

Grose, Peter. 1984. *Israel in the Mind of America.* New York: Alfred A. Knopf.

Grotius, Hugo. 1925. *The Law of War and Peace, Three Books.* Trans. Francis W. Kelsey et. al Oxford: Clarendon Press.

Guevara, Ché. 1969. *Guerrilla Warfare.* Trans. J.P. Murray. New York: Vintage Books.

Gurney, Joseph John. 1845. *War Unlawful under the Christian Dispenstion.* In The Book of Peace. See Beckwith 1845.

-----. 1869. *An Essay on War, and Its Lawfulness Under the Christian Dispensation.* New York: Peace Association of Friends in America.

-----. n.d. *An Address to the Ministers of the Gospel, and to all Professors of Christianity, on the Subject of War and Peace.* London: Harvey and Darton.

Gutierrez, Gustavo. 1979. "Liberation Praxis and Christian Faith." In Gibellini 1979.

808

-----. 1985. *On Job: God-Talk and the Suffering of the Innocent.* Trans. Matthew J. O'Connell. Maryknoll: Orbis Books.

Hackett, John Winthrop. 1979. "The Military in the Service of the State." In Wakin 1979.

Häring, Bernard. 1970. *A Theology of Protest.* New York: Farrar, Straus and Giroux.

Hamilton, Alexander; Madison, James; and Jay, John. 1961. *The Federalist.* New York: The New American Library.

Hamlin, C.H. 1927. *The War Myth in United States History.* New York: Vanguard Press.

Hampsch, George H. 1985. "Nuclear Deterrence and World Peace." In Jones and Griesbach 1985.

Harakas, Stanley 1986. "The N.C.C.B. Pastoral Letter, *The Challenge of Peace*: An Eastern Orthodox Response." In Reid 1986.

Hardin, Russell. 1986. "Risking Armageddon." In Cohen and Lee 1986a.

Hare, John. 1986. "Credibility and Bluff." In Cohen and Lee 1986a.

Harnack, Adolf. 1981. *Militia Christi: The Christian Religion and the Military in the First Three Centuries.* Trans. Dennis McInnes Gracie. Philadelphia: Fortress Press.

Harries, Richard. 1986. *Christianity and War in a Nuclear Age.* London: Mowbray.

Harstock, Nancy. 1983. "The Barracks Community in Western Political Thought: Prolegomena to a Feminist Critique of War and Politics." In Stiehm 1983.

Hartill, Percy 1948. "The Philosophy of Christian Pacifism." In Jones 1948.

Harvey, Cyrus W. 1921. *The Prince of Peace, or the Bible on Non-Resistance and War.* Galena: Elbruck Printing Company.

Haskell, Frank A. 1958. *The Battle of Gettysburg.* Boston: Houghton Mifflin Company.

Hauerwas, Stanley. 1983. *The Peaceable Kingdom: A Primer in Christian Ethics.* Notre Dame: University of Notre Dame Press.

-----. 1985. *Against the Nations: War and Survival in a Liberal Society.* Minneapolis: Winston Press.

-----. 1989. "Pacifism: A Form of Politics." In Cromartie 1989.

Haynes, Sylvanus. 1824. *A Brief Reply to the Friend of Peace, or a Concise Vindication of Defensive War. In Which is Shown the Importance of Civil Government, and a Line of Distinction is Drawn Between the Kingdoms of This World, and the Kingdoms of Christ*. Auburn: Richard Oliphant.

Hazelton, John H. 1906. *The Declaration of Independence: A History*. New York: Dodd, Mead and Company.

Heath, J. St. George. 1915. "Christianity and Civilization." In Fry 1915.

Heering, Gerrit Jan. 1943. *The Fall of Christianity: A Study of Christianity, the State, and War*. Trans. J.W. Thompson. New York: Fellowship Publication.

Hegel, G.W.F. 1900. *Philosophy of History*. Trans. J. Sibree. London: Colonial Press.

-----. 1954. *Philosophy of History*. Trans. Carl J. Friedrich and Paul W. Friedrich. New York: The Modern Library.

-----. 1966. *Preface to the Phenomenology of Spirit*. Trans. Walter Kaufmann. Garden City: Doubleday and Company.

-----. 1967. *The Phenomenology of Mind*. Trans. J.B. Baillie. New York: Harper and Row.

-----. 1973. *Philosophy of Right*. Trans. T.M. Knox. London: Oxford University Press.

Hehir. J. Bryan. 1976. "Political and Ethical Considerations." In Council on Religion and International Affairs 1976.

-----. 1986. "The Context of the Moral-Strategic Debate and the Contribution of the U.S. Catholic Bishops." In Reid 1986.

Heimert, Alan. 1966. *Religion and the American Mind from the Great Awakening to the Revolution*. Cambridge: Harvard University Press.

Helgeland, John. 1986. "The Early Church and the Sociology of Idolatry." In Reid 1986.

-----; Daly, Robert J. and Burns, J. Patout. 1985. *Christians and the Military*. Philadelphia: Fortress Press.

Hembleben, Sylvester John. 1943. *Plans for World Peace through Six Centuries*. Chicago: University of Chicago Press.

Hendel, Charles W., ed. 1953. *David Hume's Political Essays*. New York: Liberal Arts Press.

810

Heraclitus. 1967. *Fragments*. Trans. W.H.S. Jones. See Hippocrates 1967.

Herodotus. 1942. *Histories*. Trans. George Rawlinson. New York: The Modern Library.

Herreshoff, David. 1967. *American Disciples of Marx: From the Age of Jackson to the Progressive Era*. Detroit: Wayne State University.

Hershberger, Betty Ann. 1951. "A Pacifist Approach to Civil Government: A Comparison to the Participant Quaker and Mennonite View." B.A. Thesis. Swarthmore College.

Hershberger, Guy F. 1969. *War, Peace, and Nonresistance*. Scottdale: Herald Press.

Hesburgh, Theodore M. 1989. *The Nuclear Dilemma: The Greatest Moral Dilemma of All Time*. New York: Carnegie Council on Ethics and International Affairs.

Hibbert, Christopher. 1962. *Il Duce: The Life of Benito Mussolini*. Boston: Little, Brown and Company.

Hindmarsh, Albert E. 1933. *Force in Peace: Force Short of War in International Studies*. Cambridge: Harvard University Press.

Hinshaw, Cecil E. 1954. *Toward Political Responsibility*. Wallinford: Pendle Hill.

-----. 1956. *Nonviolent Resistance: A Nation's Way to Peace*. Wallingford: Pendle Hill.

Hippocrates. 1967. *Hippocrates IV*. Ed. W.H.S. Jones and E.T. Withington. Cambridge: Harvard University Press.

Hirsh, Richard G. 1974. *The Most Precious Gift: Peace in the Jewish Tradition*. New York: Commission on Social Action of Reform Judaism.

Hirst, Francis. 1906. *The Arbiter in Council*. New York: The Macmillan Company.

Hirst, Margaret E. 1923. *The Quakers in War and Peace: An Account of Their Peace Principles and Practice*. New York: George H. Doran Company.

Hitler, Adolf. 1941. *My New Order*. Ed. Raoul de Roussy de Sales. New York: Reynal and Hitchcock.

-----. 1943. *Mein Kampf*. Trans. Ralph Manheim. Boston: Houghton Mifflin Company.

Hobbes, Thomas. 1962. *Leviathan: Or the Matter, Form and Power of a Commonwealth Ecclesiastical and Civil.* New York: Collier Books.

-----. 1971. *A Dialogue Between a Philosopher and a Student of the Common Laws of England.* Chicago: University of Chicago Press.

-----. 1990. *Behemoth, or The Long Parliament.* Chicago: University of Chicago Press.

Hobhouse, Stephen. 1949. "The Significance of Gandhi for the Outlook of the Christian Pacifistl" In Radhakrishnan 1949.

Hobhouse, Walter. 1909. *The Church and the World in Idea and in History.* London: Macmillan and Company.

Hocking, William Ernest. 1923. *Human Nature and Its Remaking.* New Haven: Yale University Press.

Hodgkin, Henry. 1915. "The Christian Basis for Society." In Fry 1915.

Hoffman, Piotr. 1986. *Doubt, Time, Violence.* Chicago: University of Chicago Press.

-----. 1989. *Violence in Modern Philosophy.* Chicago: University of Chicago Press.

Hoffman, Robert L. 1972. *Revolutionary Justice: The Social and Political Theory of P.J. Proudhon.* Urbana: University of Illinois Press.

Hoffman, Stanley. 1965. *The State of War: Essays on the Theory and Practice of International Politics.* New York: Frederick A. Praeger, Publisher.

-----. 1968. "International Law and the Control of Force." In Deutsch and Hoffmann 1968.

-----. 1981. *Duties Beyond Borders: On the Limits and Possibilities of Ethical International Politics.* Syracuse: Syracuse University Press.

Hofstadter, Richard, 1948. *The American Political Tradition and the Men Who Made It.* New York: Vintage Books.

Holcombe, Arthur N. *et. al.*, eds. 1975. *Orgnaizing Peace in the Nuclear Age.* Westport: Greenwood Press.

Holcombe, Henry. 1923a. *The Advocate of Peace, including Decisive Proof that war is inconsistent with Christianity.* Philadelphia: Pennsylvania Peace Society.

-----. 1923b. *The Martial Christian's Manual.* Philadelphia: Pennsylvania Peace Society.

Holdeman, John. 1891. *A Treatise on Magistracy with War: Millenium, Holiness, and the Manifestation of Spirit*. Carthage: Press Book and Job Publishing House.

Hollenbach, David. 1983. *Nuclear Ethics: A Christian Moral Argument*. New York: Paulist Press.

-----. 1988. *Justice, Peace, and Human Rights: American Catholic Social Ethics in a Pluralistic Context*. New York: Crossroad Publishing Company.

Hollins, Harry B.; Powers, Averill 1. and Sommer, Mark. 1989. *The Conquest of War: Alternative Strategies for Global Security*. Boulder: Westview Press.

Holmes, John Haynes. 1916. *New Wars for Old: Being a Statement of Radical Pacifism in terms of Force versus Non-Resistance, with Special Reference to the Facts and Problems of the Great War*. New York: Dodd, Mead and Company.

-----. 1953. *My Gandhi*. New York: Harper and Brothers.

-----. 1976a. "Who is the Greatest Man in the World Today." In Chatfield 1976.

-----. 1976b. "The Return of Mahatma Gandhi and the Renaissance of India." In Chatfield 1976.

Holmes, Robert L. 1989. *On War and Morality*. Princeton: Princeton University Press.

Homer, 1967. *The Iliad*. Trans. Richmond Lattimore. Chicago: University of Chicago Press.

-----. 1974. *The Odyssey*. Trans. Albert Cook. New York: W.W. Norton and Company.

Hook, Sidney. 1969. "A Free Man's Choice." In Abelson 1969.

Hoover, Herbert and Gibson, Hugh. 1943. *The Problems of Lasting Peace*. In *Preface to Peace*. See Canby 1943.

Hornus, Jean-Michel. 1980. *It Is Not Lawful for Me to Fight: Early Christian Attitudes toward War, Violence, and the State*. Trans. Alan Kreider and Oliver Coburn. Scottdale: Herald Press.

Horowitz, Asher. 1987. *Rousseau, Nature, and History*. Toronto: University of Toronto Press.

Horsburgh, H.J.N. 1968. *Non-Violence and Aggression: A Study of Gandhi's Moral Equivalent of War*. London: Oxford University Press.

Horsch, Johm. 1924. *Modern Religious Liberalism: The Destructiveness and Irrationality of Modernist Theology*. Chicago: The Bible Institute Colpartage Association.

-----. 1927. *The Principle of Nonresistance As Held by the Mennonite Church: A Historical Study*. Scottdale: Mennonite Publishing House.

-----. 1931. *The Hutterian Brethren 1528-1931: A Story of Martyrdom and Loyalty*. Goshen: The Mennonite Historical Society.

Horwitz, Robert H. 1962. "Scientific Propaganda: Harold D. Lasswell." In Storing 1962.

-----. ed. 1986. *The Moral Foundations of the American Republic*. Third edition. Charlottesville: University Press of America.

Howard, Michael. 1978. *War and the Liberal Conscience*. London: Temple Smith.

-----. 1983. *The Causes of War and Other Essays*. Cambridge: Harvard University Press.

Howard, Simeon. 1983. "A Sermon Preached to the Ancient and Honourable Artillery Company in Boston." In Hyneman and Lutz 1982, Vol. I.

Howe, Irving. 1978. "Socialism and Liberalism: Articles of Conciliation?" In Brzezinski 1978.

-----. 1986. *The American Newness: Culture and Politics in the Age of Emerson*. Cambridge: Harvard Unviersity Press.

Hoyland, John S. 1922a. "Movements in India." *The Friend*. Vol LXII, No. 5: 73-74.

-----. 1922b. "India: The Arrest." *The Friend*. Vol. LXII, No. 14: 233.

-----. 1922c. "The Trial of Gandhi." *The Friend*. Vol. LXII, No. 18: 305.

-----. 1023a. "The Interpretation of Christ to India." *The Friend*. LXIII, No. 9: 151-154.

-----. 1923b. "The Inner Meaning of the Gandhi Movement." *The Friend*. Vol. LXIII, No. 33: 631-633.

-----. 1929a. "India and England." *The Friend*. Vol. LXIX, No. 30: 667-668.

-----. 1929b. "India: Religious and Social Life." *The Friend*. Vol. LXIX, No. 41: 924-926.

-----. 1929c. "India: Caste and Womanhood." *The Friend*. Vol. LXIX, No. 42: 949.

-----. 1929d. "Britain and India." *The Friend*. Vol LXIX, No. 43: 967-968.

-----. 1929e. "Problems of Government in India." *The Friend*. Vol. LXIX, No. 44: 989-990.

-----. 1929f. "Indian Aspirations." *The Friend*. Vol. LXIX, No. 45. 1009-1010.

-----. 1929g. "Britain and India." (letter). *The Friend*. Vol. LXIX, No. 47: 1957.

-----. 1929h. "Mr. Gandhi's Ideas." *The Friend*. Vol. LXIX, No. 49: 1107.

-----. 1930. "The Situation of India." *Reconciliation*. Vol. 7, No. 8: 143-144.

-----. 1949. "Gandhi's Satyagraha and the Way of the Cross." In Radhakhrishnan 1949.

Hoyt, Herman A. 1956. *Then Would My Servants Fight*. Winona Lake: Brethren Missionary Herald Company.

Hubbard, Geoffrey. 1974. *Quaker By Convincement*. Baltimore: Penguin Books.

Hubmaier, Balthasar. 1957. *On Free Will*. In *Christianity and Revolution: Radical Christian Testimonies, 1520-1650*. See Zuck 1975.

-----. 1971. *On the Sword*. In *Balthasar Hubmaier: The Leader of the Anabaptists*. See Vedder 1971.

Hughan, Jessie Wallace. 1942. *Pacifism and Invasion*. New York: War Resisters League.

Hugo, John J. 1944. *The Gospel of Peace*. New York: privately printed.

Hugo, Victor. 1887. *William Shakespeare*. Trans. Melville B. Anderson. Chicago: A.C. McClurg and Company.

Hume, David. 1957. *An Enquiry Concerning the Principles of Morals*. Indianapolis: Bobbs-Merrill Company.

-----. 1968. *A Treatise of Human Nature*. Oxford: Oxford University Press.

-----. 1985. *Essays: Moral, Political and Literary*. Indianapolis Liberty Classics.

Hungerland, Isabel. 1989. "Hobbes and the Concept of World Government." In Airaksinen and Bertman 1989.

Hunt, James D. 1986. *Gandhi and the Nonconformists: Encounters in South Africa*. New Delhi: Promilla and Company.

Hunter, David R. and Sydnor, William, eds. 1956. *What Is Christian Courage? Junior High School Resource Book*. Greenwich: The Seabury Press.

Hurd, John Codman. 1968. *The Law of Freedom and Bondage in the United States*. 2 vols. New York: Negor University Press.

Hutchinson, Thomas. 1776. *Strictures upon the Declaration of the Congress at Philadelphia*. London: Privately Printed.

Huth, Paul K. 1988. "Extended Deterrence and the Outbreak of War." *American Political Science Review*. Vol. 82, No. 2: 423-443.

Huxley, Aldous. 1937. *End and Means: An Inquiry into the Nature of Ideals and into the Methods Employed for their Realization*. New York: Harper and Brothers.

Huyghe, Bernard. 1986. "Toward a Structural Model of Violence: Male Intiation Rituals and Tribal Warfare." In Foster and Rubinstein 1986.

Hyneman, Charles S. and Lutz, Donald S., eds. 1983. *American Political Writings during the Founding Era, 1760-1805*. 2 vols. Indianapolis: Liberty Classics.

Iglehart, Charles W. 1941. "Modern War and the World Christian Mission." In Jones 1941.

Inge, William Ralph. 1926. *Lay Thoughts of a Dean*. New York: G.P. Putman's Sons.

Ingram, Kenneth. 1939. *The Defeat of War: Can Pacifism Achieve It?* London: George Allen and Unwin Ltd.

Irenaeus. 1973. *Against Heresies*. Trans. Alexander Roberts and James Donaldons. In *The Ante-Nicene Fathers*. Vol. I. See Roberts and Donaldson 1973.

Isaac-Diaz, Ada Maria and Tarango, Yolanda. 1988. *Hispanic Women, Prophetic Voice in the Church: Toward a Hispanic Woman's Liberation Theology*. San Francisco: Harper and Row.

Iyer, Raghaven N. 1973. *The Moral and Political Thought of Mahatma Gandhi*. New York: Oxford University Press.

Jackson, John. 1846. *Reflections on Peace and War*. Philadelphia: T. Ellwood Chapman.

Jaeger, Werner. 1945. *Paideia: The Ideals of Greek Culture*. 3 vols. Trans. Gilbert Highet. New York: Oxford University Press.

Jaffa, Harry V. 1965. *Equality and Liberty: Theory and Practice in American Politics*. New York: Oxford University Press.

-----. 1975. *The Conditions of Freedom: Essays in Political Philosophy.* Baltimore: John Hopkins University Press.

-----. 1978. *How to Think About the American Revolution: A Bicentennial Celebration.* Durham: Carolina Academic Press.

-----. 1979. *Thomism and Aristotelianism: A Study of the Commentary by Thomas Aquinas on the Nicomachean Ethics.* Westport: Greenwood Press.

-----. ed. 1981. *Statesmanship: Essays in Honor of Sir Winston S. Churchill.* Durham: Carolina Academic Press.

-----. 1984. *American Conservatism and the American Founding.* Durham: Carolina Academic Press.

-----. 1987a. "Equality, Liberty, Wisdom, Morality and Consent in the Idea of Political Freedom." *Interpretation: A Journal of Political Philosophy.* Vol. 15, No. 1: 2-27.

-----. 1987b. "What Were the 'Original Intentions' of the Framers of the Constitution of the United States?" *University of Puget Sound Law Review.* Vol 10, No. 3: 351-448.

James, Patrick. 1988. *Crisis and War.* Kingston: McGill-Queens University Press.

James, William. 1967. *The Writings of William James: A Comprehensive Edition.* Ed. John J. McDermott. New York: Random House.

Janney, Samuel M. 1871. *The Life of William Penn.* Philadelphia: J.B. Lippincott and Company.

Jaspers, Karl. 1961. *The Future of Mankind.* Trans. E.B. Ashton. Chicago: University of Chicago Press.

-----. 1967. *The Future of Germany.* Trans. E.B. Ashton, Chicago: University of Chicago Press.

Jay, John. 1893. *The Correspondence and Papers of John Jay.* 4 vols. Ed. Henry P. Johnston. New York: G.P. Putman's Sons.

Jefferson, John. 1832. *The Unlawfulness of War: A Discourse.* London: H. Teape and Son.

Jefferson, Thomas. 1903. *The Writings of Thomas Jefferson.* 20 vols. Ed. Andrew A. Lipscomb. Washington: The Thomas Jefferson Memorial Association of the United States.

-----. 1944. *The Life and Selected Writings of Thomas Jefferson*. Ed. Adrienne Koch and William Peden. New York: The Modern Library.

Jellinek, Georg. 1902. *La Déclaration des Droits de L'Homme et du Citoyen: Contributions à l'Histoire du Droit Constitutionnel Moderne*. Trans. George Fardis. Paris: Albert Fontremoing.

Jeremias, Joachim. 1971. *New Testament Theology*. New York: Charles Scribner's Sons.

Jervis, Robert. 1984. *The Illogic of American Nuclear Strategy*. Ithaca: Cornell University Press.

-----. 1989. *The Meaning of the Nuclear Revolution: Statecraft and the Prospect of Armageddon*. Ithaca: Cornell University Press.

Jesudasan, Ignatius. 1984. *A Gandhian Theology of Liberation*. Maryknoll: Orbis Books.

Joad, C.E.M. 1939. *Why War?* London: Penguin Books.

Joffe, Josef. 1985. "Nuclear Weapons, No First Use, and European Order." In Hardin *et. al.* 1985.

Johnson, James Turner. 1975. *Ideology, Reason, and the Limitation of War: Religious and Secular Concepts, 1200-1740*. Princeton: Princeton University Press.

-----. 1981. *Just War Tradition and the Restraint of War: A Moral and Historical Inquiry*. Princeton: Princeton University Press.

-----. 1987. *The Quest for Peace: Three Moral Traditions in Western Cultural History*. Princeton: Princeton University Press.

Johnson, Ralph Arthur. 1976. "Nonviolence: A Commitment to Civil Discourse." Ph.D. diss. Indiana University.

Johnstone, Brian. 1986. "Noncombatant Immunity and the Prohibition of the Killing of the Innocent." In Reid 1986.

Jonas, Gerlad. 1971. *On Doing Good*. New York: Charles Scribner's Sons.

Jones, A.H.M. 1964. "The Social Background of the Struggle between Paganism and Christianity." In Momigliano 1964.

Jones, Alun Gwynne. 1967. "Forms of Military Attack." In Roberts 1967.

Jones, E. Stanley. 1948. *Mahatma Gandhi: An Interpretation*. New York: Abingdon-Cokesbury Press.

818

Jones, John D., and Griesbach, Marc F. eds. 1985. *Just War Theory in the Nuclear Age*. Lanham: University Press of America.

Jones, Mary Hoxie. 1971. *Swords Into Ploughshares: An Account of the American Friends Service Committee, 1917-1937*. Westport: Greenwood Press.

Jones, Rufus M. 1914. *Spiritual Reformers in the Sixteenth and Seventeenth Centuries*. London: Macmillan and Company.

-----. 1923. *Studies in Mystical Religion*. New York: Macmillan and Company.

-----. 1932. *Mysticism and Democracy in the English Commonwealth*. Cambridge: Harvard University Press.

-----. ed. 1948. *The Church, the Gospel, and War*. New York: Harper and Brothers.

Jouvenel, Bertrand de. 1957 *Sovereignty: An Inquiry into the Political Good*. Trans. J.F. Huntington, Chicago: University of Chicago Press.

-----. 1962. *On Power: Its Nature and the History of Its Growth*. Trans. J.F. Huntington. Boston: Beacon Press.

Judd, Sylvester, 1842. *A Moral Review of the Revolutionary War, or Some of the Evils of that Event Considered*. Hallowell: Glazier, Masters and Smith.

Julian. 1962. *Works*. 3 vols. Trans. Wilmer Cave Wright. Cambridge: Harvard University Press.

Julius Caesar. 1887. *Caesar's Commentaries on the Gallic and Civil Wars: With the Supplemental Books attributed to Hirtius; Including the Alexandrian, African, and Spanish Wars*. Trans. W.A. McDevitte and W.S. Bohn. New York: Harper and Row.

Justin Martyr. 1973a. *Dialogue of Justin, Philosopher and Martyr, with Trypho, a Jes*. Trans. Alexander Roberts and James Donaldson. In *The Ante-Nicene Fathers*. Vol. I. See Roberts and Donaldson 1973.

-----. 1973b. *The Discourse to the Greeks*. Trans. Marcus Dods. In *The Ante-Nicene Fathers*. Vol. I. See Roberts and Donaldson 1973.

-----. 1973c. *The First Apology of Justin Martyr*. Trans. Alexander Roberts and James Donaldson. In *The Ante-Nicene Fathers*. Vol. I. See Roberts and Donaldson 1973.

-----. 1973d. *Justin's Hortatory Address to the Greeks*. Trans. Marcus Dods. In *The Ante-Nicene Fathers*. Vol. I. See Roberts and Donaldson 1973.

-----. 1973e. *The Second Apology of Justin for the Christians, Addressed to the Roman Senate*. Trans. Alexander Roberts and James Donaldson. In *The Ante-Nicene Fathers*. Vol. I. See Roberts and Donaldson 1973.

Kagawa, Toyohiko. 1929. *Love the Law of Life*. Trans. J. Fullerton Gressitt. Philadelphia: The John C. Winston Company.

-----. 1936. *Brotherhood Economics*. New York: Harper and Brothers.

Kahn, Herman. 1960. *On Thermonuclear War*. Princeton: Princeton University Press.

-----. 1962. *Thinking About the Unthinkable*. New York: Horizon Books.

-----. 1968. *On Escalation*. Baltimore: Penguin Books.

Kainz, Howard P., ed. 1987. *Philosophical Perspectives on Peace: An Anthology of Classical and Modern Sources*. London: Macmillan Press.

Kallas, James. 1965. "Romans xiii. 1-7: An Interpretation." *New Testament Studies*. Vol. II, No. 4: 365-374.

Kaminsky, Howard. 1964. "Petr Chelcický: Treatises on Christianity and the Social Order." In *Studies in Medieval and Renaissance History*. Vol. I. See Bowsky 1964.

Kant, Immanuel. 1964. *The Critique of Judgment*. Trans. James Creed Meredith. London: Oxford University Press.

Kardelj, Edvard. 1960. *Socialism and War: A Survey of Chinese Criticism of the Policy of Coexistence*. Trans. Alec Brown. Belgrade: Jugoslavija.

Karsner, David. 1919. *Debs: His Authorized Life and Letters from Woodstock Prison to Atlanta*. New York: Roni and Liveright.

Kaufman, Gordon D. 1985. *Theology for a Nuclear Age*. Manchester: Manchester University Press.

Kaunda, Kenneth. 1980. *The Riddle of Violence*. San Francisco: Harper and Row.

Kautsky, Karl. 1953. *Foundation of Christianity*. Trans. Henry F. Mins. New York: S.A. Russell.

-----. 1973. *Terrorism and Communism: A Contribution to the Natural History of Revolution*. Trans. W.H. Kerridge. Westport: Hyperion Press.

Kavka, Gregory S. 1987. *Moral Paradoxes of Nuclear Deterrence*. Cambridge: Cambridge University Press.

820

Kecskemeti, Paul. 1984. *Strategic Surrender: The Politics of Victory and Defeat*. New York: Atheneum.

Kellerman, O. 1901. *War and Peace: A Moral Study Dedicated to the Members of the Hague Conference*. London: Headley Brothers.

Kelsen, Hans. 1968. "The Essence of International Law." In Deutsch and Hoffmann 1968.

Kelsey, Alice Geer. 1956. "The Declaration of Dependence." In Hunter and Sydnor 1956.

Kendall, Willmoore. 1989. "Equality: Commitment or Ideal?" *The Intercollegiate Review*. Vol. 24, No. 2: 25-33.

Kennedy, Edward M. and Hatfield, Mark O. 1982. *Freeze! How You Can Help Prevent Nuclear War*. New York: Bantam Books.

Kenny, Anthony. 1984. "Better Dead than Red." In Blake and Pole 1984.

-----. 1985. *The Logic of Deterrence*. Chicago: University of Chicago Press.

Kersey, Jesse. 1815. *A Treatise on Fundamental Doctrines of the Christian Religion: In Which are Illustrated the Profession, Ministry, Worship, and Faith of the Society of Friends*. London: William Phillips.

Kesler, Charles R., ed. 1987. *Saving the Revolution: The Federalist Papers and the American Founding*. New York: The Free Press.

Key, Ellen. 1972. *War, Peace, and the Future: A Consideration of Nationalism and Internationalism, and the Relation of Women to War*. Trans. Hildegard Norberg. New York: Garland Publishing Company.

Keys, Donald, ed. 1961. *God and the H-Bomb*. New York: Bellmeadow Press.

-----. 1982. *Earth at Omega: Passage to Planetization*. Boston: The Brandon Press.

King, Jr., Martin L. 1961. *Stride Toward Freedom: The Montgomery Story*. New York: Ballantine Books.

-----. 1963. *Strength to Love*. New York: Harper and Row.

-----. 1964a. *A Martin Luther King Treasury*. Yonkers: Educational Heritage, Inc.

-----. 1964b. *Why We Can't Wait*. New York: New American Library.

-----. 1967a. *The Trumpet of Conscience*. New York: Harper and Row.

-----. 1967b. *Where Do We Go From Here: Chaos or Community?* New York: Harper and Row.

-----. 1968. *The Measure of Man.* Philadelphia: Pilgrim Press.

King-Hall, Stephen. 1959. *Defence in the Nuclear Age.* Nyack: Fellowship Publications.

Kirk, Ilse. 1987. "Images of Amazons: Marriage and Matriarchy." In Macdonald, Holden and Ardener 1987.

Kirk, J. Andrew. 1979. *Liberation Theology: An Evangelical View from the Third World.* Atlanta: John Knox Press.

Kirk, Russell. 1977. *The Roots of American Order.* Malibu: Pepperdine University Press.

Kissinger, Henry. 1957. *Nuclear Weapons and Foreign Policy.* New York: Harper and Row.

-----. 1962. *The Necessity for Choice: Prospects of American Foreign Policy.* Garden City Doubleday and Company.

Kittel, Gerhard, ed. 1964. *Theological Dictionary of the New Testament.* Trans. Geoffrey W. Bromiley. Grand Rapids: William B. Eerdmans Publishing Company.

Klenicki, Leon. 1988. "God's Intervening Action." *Christian Jewish Relations.* Vol. 21, No. 1: 5-11.

Knorr, Klaus. 1966. *On the Use of Military Power in the Nuclear Age.* Princeton: Princeton University Press.

Koestler, Arthur. 1949. Untitled. In Crossman 1949.

Kohn, Hans. 1960. *The Mind of Germany: The Education of a Nation.* New York: Charles Scribner's Sons.

Kortunov, Andrei V. 1988. "Realism and Morality in Politics." In Gromyko and Hellman 1988a.

Kot, Stanislas. 1957. *Socinianism in Poland: The Social and Political Ideas of the Polish Antitrinitarians in the Sixteenth and Seventeenth Centuries.* Trans. Earl Morse Wilbur. Boston: Starr King Press.

Kovel, Joel. 1983. *Against the State of Nuclear Terror.* Boston: South End Press.

Krauthammer, Charles. 1984. "On Nuclear Morality." In Woolsey 1984.

Kropotkin, Peter. 1972. *Mutual Aid: A Factor of Evolution*. New York: New York University Press.

-----. 1978. *Memoirs of a Revolutionist*. London: The Folio Society.

Kueshana, Eklal. 1982. *The Ultimate Frontier*. Stelle: The Stelle Group.

Kumar, Krishna, ed. n.d. *Democracy and Nonviolence: A Study of Their Relationship*. New Delhi: Gandhi Peace Foundation.

Lackey, Douglas P. 1984. *Moral Principles and Nuclear Weapons*. Totowa: Rowman and Allanheld.

-----. 1989. *The Ethics of War and Peace*. Englewood Cliffs: Prentice Hall.

Lackner, Stephen. 1984. *Peaceable Nature: An Optimistic View of Life on Earth*. San Francisco: Harper and Row.

Lactantius. 1973a. *The Divine Institutes*. In *The Ante-Nicene Fathers*. Vol. VII. See Roberts and Donaldson 1973.

-----. 1973b. *Of the Manner in Which the Persecuted Died*. In *The Ante-Nicene Fathers*. Vol. VII. See Roberts and Donaldson 1973.

-----. 1973c. *A Treatise on the Anger of God*. In *The Ante-Nicene Fathers*. Vol. VII. See Roberts and Donaldson 1973.

Ladd, William. 1827. *The Essays of Philadelphia on Peace*. Exeter: John T. Burnham.

La Fontaine, Jean de. 1965. *The Fables*. Trans. Marianne Moore. New York: The Viking Press.

Lalor, John C., ed. 1895. *Cyclopedia of Political Science, Political Econimy and of the Political History of the United States By the Best American and European Writers*. 3 vols. New York: Maynard, Merrill, and Company.

Lamb, Beatrice Pitney. 1968. *India: A World in Transition*. New York: Frederick A. Praeger.

Lang, Berel. 1986. "Genocide and Omnicide: Technology at the Limits." In Cohen and Lee 1986a.

Lang, Daniel G. and Russell, Greg. 1991. "The Ethics of Power in American Diplomacy: The Statecraft of John Quincy Adams." *The Review of Politics*. Vol 52, No. 1: 3-31.

Laslett, Peter. 1949. *Patriarcha, or, the Natural Powers of the Kings of England Asserted, and Other Political Works of Sir Robert Filmer*. Oxford: Basil Blackwell.

Lasserre, Jean. 1962. *War and the Gospel*. Trans. Oliver Coburn. Scottdale: Herald Press.

Lasswell, Harold. 1927. *Propaganda Technique in the World War*. New York: Alfred A. Knopf.

Latin American Episcopal Council. 1986. *The Church in the Present-Day Transformation of Latin America in the Light of the Council*. In Rosso 1986.

Lauterpacht, Hersch. 1970. *International Law*. 4 vols. Cambridge: Cambridge University Press.

Lawler, Philip F., eds. 1983. *Justice and War in the Nuclear Age*. Lanham: University Press of America.

Lea, Home. 1909. *The Valor of Innocence*. New York: Harper and Brothers.

Lee, Steven. 1985. "The Morality of Nuclear Deterrence: Hostage Holding and Consequences." In Hardin *et.al.* 1985.

Lee, Umphrey. 1943. *The Historic Church and Modern Pacifism*. New York: Abingdon-Cokesbury Press.

Leads, Josiah W. 1876. *The Primitive Christians' Estimate of War and Self-Defense*. New Vienna: Peace Association of Friends in America.

Lefever, Ernest W. 1961. "Facts, Calculation and Political Ethics." In Clancy 1961.

Legnano, Giovanni da. 1917. *Tractatus De Bello, De Representalis et De Duello*. Trans. James Lesley Brierly Oxford: Oxford University Press.

Lenin, V.I. 1929. *Collected Works*. New York: International Publishers.

-----. 1966. *Collected Works*. Moscow: Progress Publishers.

-----. 1968. *Selected Works*. Moscow: Progress Publishers.

Lenski, R.C.H. 1961. *Commentary on the New Testament*. 12 vols. Minneapolis: Augsberg Publishing House.

Lerner, Ralph. 1987. *The Thinking Revolutionary: Principle and Practice in the New Republic*. Ithaca: Cornell University Press.

-----, and Mahdi, Muhsin, eds., 1973. *Medieval Political Philosophy*. Ithaca: Cornell University Press.

Levine, Daniel H. 1988. "Assessing the Impact of Liberation Theology in Latin America." *The Review of Politics*. Vol. 50, No. 2: 241-263.

Levine, Robert. 1990. *Still the Arms Debate*. Aldershot: Dartmouth Publishing Company.

Levy, Leonard W.; Karst, Kenneth L., and Mahoney, Dennis J. 1986. *Encyclopedia of the American Constitution*. New York: The Macmillan Company.

Lévy-Bruhl, Lucien. 1966. *Primitive Mentality*. Trans. Lillian A. Clare. Boston: Beacon Press.

Lewis, C.S. 1980. *The Weight of Glory and Other Addresses*. New York: Macmillan Publishing Company.

Lewis, John. 1940. *The Case Against Pacifism*. London: George Allen and Unwin.

Lewis, Jr., Marlo. 1981. "On War and Legitimacy in Shakespeare's Henry V." In Jaffa 1981.

Lewy, Guenter. 1988. *Peace and Revolution: The Moral Crisis of American Pacifism*. Grand Rapids: William B. Eerdmans Company.

Liddel Hart, B.H. 1967. "Lessons from Resistance Movements – Guerrilla and Non-Violent." In Roberts 1967.

Lieber, Francis. 1874. *On Civil Liberty and Self-Government*. Philadelphia. J.B. Lippincott and Company.

-----. 1881. *Manual of Political Ethics, Designed Chiefly for the Use of Colleges and Students of Law*. 1 vols. Philadelphia: J.B. Lippincott and Company.

Liebknecht, Karl. 1972. *Militarism and Anti-Militarism*. Trans. Alexander Sirnis. New York: Dover Publications.

Lienesch, Michael. 1988. *New Order of the Ages: Time, the Constitution, and the Making of Modern American Political Thought*. Princeton: Princeton University Press.

Lifton, Robert Jay and Falk, Richard. 1982. *Indefensible Weapons: The Political and Psychological Case Against Nuclearism*. New York: Basic Books.

Lifton, Robery Jay and Markusen, Eric. 1988. *The Genocidal Mentality: Nuclear Holocaust and Nuclear Threat*. New York: Basic Books.

Ligt, Barthelmy de. 1938. *The Conquest of Violence: An Essay on War and Revolution*. Trans. Honor Tracy. New York: E.P. Dutton and Company.

Lincoln, Abraham. 1953. *The Collected Works of Abraham Lincoln.* 7 vols. Ed. Roy P. Basler. New Brunswick: Rutgers University Press.

Lind, Millard. 1980. *Yahweh Is a Warrior: The Theology of Warfare in Ancient Israel.* Scottdale: Herald Press.

Lively, Jack, ed. 1965. *The Works of Joseph de Maistre.* New York: The Macmillan Company.

Livermore, Abiel Abbot. 1850. *The War with Mexico Reviewed.* Boston: William Crosby and H.P. Nichols.

Livingston, Donald W. 1988. "David Hume: Ambassador from the World of Learning to the World of Conversation." *The Political Science Reviewer.* Vol XVIII: 35-84.

Livy, 1962. *A History of Rome.* Trans. Moses Hadas and Joe P. Poe. New York: The Modern Library.

Locke, John. 1959. *Essay Concerning Human Understanding.* 2 vols. New York: Dover Publications.

-----. 1963. *Two Treatises of Government.* Ed. Peter Laslett. New York: New York: New American Library.

-----. 1968. *Epistola de Tolerantia.* Trans. J.W. Gough. London: Oxford University Press.

-----. 1990. *Questions Concerning the Law of Nature.* Trans. Jenny Strauss Clay. Ithaca: Cornell University Press.

Long, Edward Leroy. 1950. *The Christian Response to the Atomic Crisis.* Philadelphia: The Westminster Press.

-----. 1968. *War and Conscience in America.* Philadelphia: The Westminster Press.

-----. 1983. *Peace Thinking in a Warring World.* Philadelphia: The Westminster Press.

Lopez, George A., ed. 1989. *Peace Studies: Past and Future.* New York: SAGE Publications.

Lopez, Mauricio. 1969. "The Political Dynamics of Latin American Society Today." In Cox 1967.

Lord, Carnes. 1983. *Education and Culture in the Political Thought of Aristotle.* Ithaca: Cornell University Press.

-----. 1989a. "American Strategic Culture." In Baumann and Jensen 1989a.

-----. 1989b. *The Presidency and the Management of National Security.* New York: The Free Press.

Lorenz, Konrad. 1966. *On Aggression.* Trans. Marjorie Kerr Wilson. New York: Harcourt, Brace and World.

Lothian, P.H.K. 1941. *Pacifism Is Not Enough: Nor Patriotism Either.* London: Oxford University Press.

Lowenthal, David. 1988. "Locke on Conquest." In Zuckert 1988.

Lovelock. J.E. 1988. *Gaia: A New Look at Life on Earth.* New York: Oxford University Press.

Luard, Evan. *Peace and Opinion.* New York: Oxford University Press.

Luther, Martin 1956. *Luther's Works.* Ed. Jaroslav Pelikan. New York: Concordia Publishing House.

Luttwak, Edward N. 1986. "Catholics and the Bomb: The Perspective of a Non-Catholic Strategist." In Reid 1986.

-----. 1987. *Strategy: The Logic of War and Peace.* Cambridge: Harvard University Press.

Lutz, Donald S. 1988. *The Origins of the American Constitution.* Baton Rouge: Louisiana State University Press.

Lynd, Staughton, ed. 1966. *Nonviolence in America: A Documentary History.* Indianapolis: Bobbs-Merrill Company.

-----. 1968. *Intellectual Origins of American Radicalism.* New York: Vintage Books.

Maaranen, Steven A. 1981. "The Struggle for a New World Order: The Foreign Policy of the British Left, 1932-1939." In Jaffa 1981.

Macdonald, Sharon. 1987. "Drawing the Lines -- Gender, Peace and War: An Introduction." In Macdonald, Holden and Ardener 1987.

-----; Holden, Pat and Ardener, Shirley, eds. 1987. *Images of Women in Peace and War: Cross-Cultural and Historical Perspectives.* London: Macmillan Education Ltd.

Macgregor, G.H.C. 1960. *The New Testament Basis of Pacifism and The Relevance of an Impossible Ideal.* Nyack: Fellowship Publications.

Machiavelli, Niccolò. 1950. *Discourses on the First Ten Books of Titus Livius.* Trans. Christian E. Detmod. New York: The Modern Library.

-----. 1965. *The Art of War*. Trans. Ellis Farneworth and Neal Young. Indianapolis: The Bobbs-Merrill Company.

-----. 1985. *The Prince*. Trans. Harvey C. Mansfield, Jr. Chicago: The University of Chicago Press.

Mackenzie, Compton. 1961. "Thy Neighbor as Thyself." In Keys 1961.

Mackinder, Halford J. 1962. *Democratic Ideals and Reality*. New York: W.W. Norton and Company.

MacLaren, James H. 1900. *Put Up Thy Sword*. Chicago: Fleming H. Revell Company.

Macmillan, Harold. 1972. *Pointing the Way, 1959-1961*. New York: Harper and Row.

MacNamara, H.T.J. 1841. *Peace, Permanent and Universal: Its Practicability, Value, and Consistency with Divine Revelation*. London: Saunders and Otley.

Madan, Spencer. 1805. *The Fatal Use of the Sword: Considered in a Sermon Preached in St. Cecelia's Church, Birmingham*. London: E. Piercy.

Madison, James 1962. *The Papers of James Madison*. 14 vols. to date. Ed. Robert A. Rutland and Thomas A. Mason. Charlottesville: Univerisity Press of Virginia.

Mahan, Alfred Thayer. 1890. *The Influence of Sea Power Upon History, 1660-1783*. Boston: Little, Brown.

Mahdi, Muhsin, ed. 1969. *Alfarabi's Philosophy of Plato and Aristotle*. Trans. Muhsin Mahdi. Ithaca: Cornell University Press.

Maimonides, Moses. 1963. *The Code of Maimonides*. Trans. Abraham M. Hershman. New Haven: Yale University Press.

Maistre, Joseph de. 1965. *The Saint Petersburh Dialogues*. In Lively 1965.

-----. 1974. *Considerations on France*. Trans. Richard A. Lebrun. Montreal: McGill-Queens University Press.

Manicas, Peter T. 1989. *War and Democracy*. Cambridge: Basil Blackwell.

Mansfield, Jr., Harvey C. 1965. *Statesmanship and Party Government: A Study of Burke and Bolingbroke*. Chicago: University of Chicago Press.

-----. 1978. *The Spirit of Liberalism*. Cambridge: Harvard University Press.

-----. 1983. "On the Impersonality of the Modern State: A Comment on Machiavelli's Use of *Stato*." *American Political Science Review*. Vol. 77, No. 4: 849-357.

-----. 1989. *Taming the Prince: The Ambivalence of Modern Executive Power*: New York: The Free Press.

Maoz, Zeev. 1990. *Paradoxes of War: On the Art of National Self-Entrapment*. Boston: Unwin Hyman.

----- and Abdolai, Nasrin. 1989. "Regime Types and International Conflict." *Journal of Conflict Resolution*. Vol. 33, No. 1: 3-35.

Margolis, Joseph. 1986. "The Peculiarities of Nuclear Thinking." In Cohen and Lee 1986a.

Maritain, Jacques. 1935. *Freedom in the Modern World*. Trans. Richard O'Sullivan. London: Sheed and Ward.

-----. 1957. *Man and the State*. Chicago: University of Chicago Press.

Markus, R.A. 1961. "Conscience and Deterrence. In Stein 1961a.

Marrs, Texe. 1987. *Dark Secrets of the New Age: Satan's Plan for a One World Religion*. Westchester: Crossway Books.

Marsilius of Padua. 1967. *The Defensor Pacis*. Trans. Alan Gerwirth. New York: Harper and Row.

Martin, David. 1966. *Pacifism: An Historical and Sociological Study*. New York: Schocken Books.

Martino, Joseph P. 1988. *A Fighting Chance: The Moral Use of Nuclear Weapons*. San Francisco: Ignatius Press.

Marx, Karl. 1906. *Capital: A Critique of Political Economy*. Trans. Samuel Moore and Edward Aveling. New York: The Modern Library.

-----. 1971. *The Poverty of Philosophy*. New York: International Publishers.

Marzials, Frank. 1965. *Memoirs of the Crusades*. Trans. Frank Marzials. New York: E.P. Dutton.

Mashruwala, K.G. 1946. *Practical Non-Violence and Ideology of Non-violence*. Ahmedabad: Navajivan Publishing House..

-----. 1960. *Gandhi and Marx*. Ahmedabad: Navajivan Publishing House.

Mather, Moses. 1991. *America's Appeal to an Impartial World*. In Sandoz, 1991.

Maurer, Marvin. 1986. "Quakers and Changing Concepts of Pacifism." Paper presented at the Annual Meeting of the American Political Science Association. August 28-31, 1986.

Mavrodes, George I. 1979. "Conventions and the Morality of War." In Wakin 1979.

Mayer, Milton. 1944. *Conscience and the Commonwealth*. New York: The Plowshare Press.

Mayhew, Jonathan. 1750. *A Discourse Concerning Unlimited Submission and Non-Resistance to the Higher Powers*. Boston: D. Fowle.

-----. 1991. *The Snare Broken*. In Sandoz, 1991.

McCormick, Richard A. 1978. "Ambiguity in Moral Choice." In McCormick and Ramsey 1978.

-----. 1983. "Nuclear Deterrence and the Problem of Intention: A Review of the Positions." In Murnion 1983.

-----, and Ramsey, Paul, eds. 1978. *Doing Evil to Achieve Good; Moral Choice in Conflict Situations*. Chicago: Loyola University Press.

McDonald, Forrest. 1979. *E Pluribus Unum: The Formation of the American Republic, 1776-1790*. Indianapolis: Liberty Press.

-----. 1985. *Novus Ordo Seclorum: The Intellectual Origins of the Constitution*. Lawrence: University of Kansas Press.

M'Cree, George Wilson. 1845. *War Incompatible with Christianity*. London: Charles Gilpin.

McGiffert, Arthur Cushman. 1915. "Christianity and War: A Historical Sketch." *The American Journal of Theology*. Vol. XIX, No. 3: 323-345.

McGuinness, Celia. 1989. "*The Fundamental Constitutions of North Carolina* as a Tool for Lockean Scholarship." *Interpretation: A Journal of Political Philosophy*. Vol. 17, No. 1: 127-143.

McGuinness, Diane, ed. 1987. *Dominance, Aggression and War*. New York: Paragon House.

McLelland, J.S., ed. 1976. *The French Right From Maistre to Maurras*. New York: Harper and Row.

McMahon, Jeff. 1985. "Deterrence and Deontology." In Hardin *et. al.* 1985.

McSorley, Richard. 1979. *New Testament Basis of Peacemaking*. Washington: Center for Peace Studies.

McWilliam, Wilson Carey. 1973. *The Idea of Fraternity in America*. Berkley: University of California Press.

-----. 1984. "The Bible in the American Political Tradition." In *Religion and Politics*. See Arnoff 1984.

Mead, Edwin D. 1903. *The Principles of the Founders: Oration Before the City Government and Citizens of Boston, at Faneuil Hall, July 4, 1900*. Boston: American Unitarian Association.

Mead, Lucia Ames. 1912. *Swords and Plousghshares: The Supplanting of the System of War by the System of Law*. New York: G.P. Putman's Sons.

Meador, Roy. 1986. "In Chess and Politics, Franklin Believed That There Was No Substitute for Victory." *Chess Life*. May 1986: 11-12.

Mee, Jr. Charles L. 1987. *The Genius of the People*. New York: Harper and Row.

Meinecke, Friedrich 1957. *Machiavellianism: The Doctrine of Raison d'État and Its Place in Modern History*. Trans. Douglas Scott. New Haven: Yale University Press.

Merleau-Ponty, Maurice. 1964. *Sense and Non-Sense*. Trans. Hubert L. Dreyfus and Patricia A. Dreyfus. Evanston: Northwestern University Press.

-----. 1969. *Humanism and Terror: A Essay on the Communist Problem*. Trans. John O'Neill. Boston Beacon Press.

Merton, Thomas 1966. *Reflections of a Guilty Bystander*. Garden City: Doubleday and Company.

-----. 1968. *Faith and Violence: Christian Teaching and Christian Practice*. Notre Dame. University of Notre Dame Press.

-----. 1980. *The Nonviolent Alternative*. Ed. Gordon C. Zahn. New York: Farrar Straus Giroux.

Meyers, Marvin, ed. 1973. *The Mind of the Founder: Sources of the Political Thought of James Madison*. Indianapolis: The Bobbs-Merrill Company.

Michelet, Jules. 1973a. *History of the French Revolution*. Trans. Charles Cocks. Chicago: University of Chicago Press.

-----. 1973b. *The People*. Trans. John P. McKay. Urbana: University of Illinois Press.

Michnik, Adam 1985. *Letters from Prison and Other Essays*. Trans. Maya Latynski. Berkeley: University of California Press.

Mill, John Stuart. 1911. *The Subjection of Women*. New York: Frederick A. Stokes Company.

-----. 1951. *Utilitarianism, Liberty and Representative Government* New York: E.P. Dutton and Company.

-----. 1963. *Essays on Politics and Culture*. Garden City: Doubleday and Company.

Miller, Charles A. 1988. *Jefferson and Nature: An Interpretation*. Baltimore: The Johns Hopkins University Press.

Miller, Richard B. 1991. *Interpretations of Conflict: Pacifism and the Just-War Tradition*. Chicago: The University of Chicago Press.

Miller, William Robert. 1964. *Nonviolence: A Christian Interpretation*. New York: Association Press.

Millis, Walter. 1956. *Arms and Men: A Study of American Military History*. New York: G.P. Putnam's Sons.

Mills, Paul M. 1968. *The Bible and War*. Newberg: The Barclay Press.

Milne, A.A. 1934. *Peace With Honor*. New York: E. P. Dutton and Company.

Minucius, Felix. 1973. *The Octavius*. In *The Ante-Nicene Fathers*. Vol. IV. See Roberts and Donaldson 1973.

Miranda, José. 1986. "Christianity Is Communism." In Ferm 1986.

Molander, Roger C. and Molander, Earl A. 1982. *Nuclear War: What's In It For You?* New York: Pocket Books.

Molnar, Thomas. 1978. *Le modèle défiguré: L'Amérique de Tocqueville à Carter*. Paris: Presses Univeritaires de France.

-----. 1981. "Is a Theory of International Relations Formulable?" *Revue européene des sciences sociales*. Vol. XIX, Nos. 54-55: 225-231.

-----. 1987. "Morality, the State and America." *This World: A Journal of Religion and Public Life*. No. 16, 70-76.

Momigliano, Arnaldo, ed. 1964. *The Conflict Between Paganism and Christianity in the Fourth Century*. Oxford: Oxford University Press.

Monroe, James. 1987. *The People, the Sovereigns: Being a Comparison of the Government of the United States with Those of the Republics Which Have Existed Before, with the Causes of their Decadence and Fall*. Cumberland: James River Press.

Montesquieu, Charles Louis de Secondat. 1968a. *The Persian Letters*. Trans. J. Robert Loy. New York: World Publishing Company.

-----. 1968b. *Considerations on the Causes of the Greatness of the Romans and Their Decline*. Trans. David Lowenthal. Ithaca: Cornell University Press.

-----. 1898. *The Spirit of the Laws*. Trans. Anne M. Cohler, Basia Carolyn Miller, Harold Samuel Stone. Cambridge: Cambridge University Press.

More, Thomas. 1946. *Utopia*. New York: E.P. Dutton.

Morris, Christopher W. 1985. "A Contractarian Defense of Nuclear Deterrence." In Hardin *et. al*. 1985.

Morris, David. 1949. *China Changed My Mind*. Boston: Houghton Mifflin Company.

Morris-Jones, W.H. 1960. "Mahatma Gandhi: Political Philosopher?" *Political Studies*. Vol. VIII, No. 1: 16-36.

Morrisey, Will. 1983. *Reflections on De Gaulle: Political Founding in Modernity*. Lanham: University Press of America.

-----. 1984a. *Reflections on Malraux: Cultural Founding in Modernity*. Lanham: University Press of America.

-----. 1984b. *The Politics of Compassion*. Dollard des Ormeaux: Dawn Publishing Company.

-----. 1986. Review of *Jerusalem vs. Athens: In Quest of a General Theory of Existence*. *Interpretation: A Journal of Political Philosophy*. Vol. 14 No. 2-3: 441-447.

-----. 1987a. "The Founding and Perpetuation of the American Republic." *Interpretation: A Journal of Political Philosophy*. Vol. 15, No. 1: 148-153.

-----. 1987b. "Public Morality, and Public Moralism." *This World: A Journal of Religion and Public Life*. No. 16: 77-85.

-----. 1992. Untitled review of Tucker and Hendrickson: *Empire of Liberty: The Statecraft of Thomas Jefferson*. *Interpretation: A Journal of Political Philosophy*. Vol.

Mott, James. 1814. *The Lawfulness of War for Christians, Examined*. New York: Samuel Wood.

Moynihan, Daniel P. 1990. *On the Law of Nations*. Cambridge: Harvard University Press.

Mueller, John. 1989. *Retreat From Doomsday: The Obsolescence of Major War*. New York: Basic Books.

Mulford, Elisha. 1887. *The Nation: The Foundation of Civil Order and Political Life in the United States*. Boston: Houghton Mifflin Company.

Muller, Robert. 1982. *New Genesis: Shaping a Global Spirituality*. Garden City: Doubleday and Company.

-----. 1985. *What War Taught Me About Peace*. Garden City: Doubleday and Company.

Mumford, Lewis. 1972. *Interpretations and Forecasts, 1922-1972: Studies in Literature, History, Biography, Technics and Contemporary Society*. New York: Harcourt Brace Jovanovich.

Murphy, Jeffrie G. 1979. "The Killing of the Innocent." In Wakin 1979.

Murnion, Philip J. ed. 1983. *Catholics and Nuclear War: A Commentary on the Challenge of Peace, The U.S. Catholic Bishops' Pastoral Letter on War and Peace*. New York: Crossroad Publishing Company.

Murray, John Courtney. 1960. *We Hold These Truths: Catholic Reflections on the American Proposition*. New York: Sheed and Ward.

Murry, John Middleton. 1932. *The Necessity of Communism*. London: Jonathan Cape.

-----. 1937. *The Necessity of Pacifism*. London: Jonathan Cape.

-----. 1941, *The Betrayal of Christ by the Churches*. London: Andrew Dakers Ltd.

-----. 1948. *The Free Society*. London: Andrew Dakers Ltd.

Musser, Daniel. 1878. *The Reformed Mennonite Church, Its Rise and Progress, with its Principles and Doctrines*. Lancaster: Inquirer Printing and Publishing Company.

Mussolini, Benito. 1928. *My Autobiography*. New York: Charles Scribner's Sons.

-----. 1949. *Memoirs 1942-1943*. Trans. Frances Lobb. London: George Weidenfeld and Nicolson Ltd.

-----. 1962. "The Doctrine of Fascism." In Cohen 1962.

Muste, A.J. 1940. *Non-Violence in an Aggressive World*. New York: Harper and Brothers.

834

-----. 1947. *Not By Might: Christianity, the Way of Human Decency*. New York: Harper and Brothers.

-----. 1967. *The Essays of A.J. Muste*. Ed. Nat Hentoff. Indianapolis: The Bobbs-Merrill Company.

Myers, Robert J. ed. 1987. *International Ethics in the Nuclear Age*. Lanham: University Press of America.

Naess, Arne. 1972. *The Pluralist and Possibilist Aspect of the Scientific Enterprise*. London: Allen and Unwin.

-----. 1974. *Gandhi and Group Conflict: An Exploration of Satyagraha*. Oslo: Universitetsforlaget.

-----. 1986. "Consequences of an Absolute NO to Nuclear War." In Cohen and Lee 1986a.

-----. 1989. *Ecology, Community, and Lifestyle: Outline of an Ecosophy*. Trans. David Rothenberg. Cambridge: Cambridge University Press.

Nakamura, Hajime. 1974. "Violence and Nonviolence in Buddhism." In Wiener and Fisher 1974.

Nanada, B.R. 1985. *Gandhi and His Critics*. Delhi: Oxford University Press.

Nardin, Terry. 1983. *Law, Morality, and the Religion of States*. Princeton: Princeton University Press.

-----. 1986. "Nuclear War and the Argument from Extremity." In Cohen and Lee 1986a.

Narveson, Jan. 1965. "Pacifism: A Philosophical Analysis." In Wasserstrom 1965.

-----. 1985. "Getting on the Road to Peace: A Modest Proposal." In Hardin et. al. 1985.

Nash, Jr., Howard P. *The Forgotten Wars: The Role of the U.S. Navy in the Quasi War with France and the Barbary Wars 1798-1805*. South Brunswick: A.S. Barnes and Company.

National Conference of Catholic Bishops. 1983. *The Challenge of Peace: God's Promise and Our Response*. Washington: United States Catholic Conference.

Navarrete, Sergio. 1990. "Voices from Nicaragua." *Christian Anti-Communism Crusade Newsletter*. Vol. 30, No. 15: 5-6.

Nearing, Scott and Russell, Bertrand. 1924. *Debate, Resolved: That the Soviet Form of Government is Applicable to Western Civilization.* New York: The League for Public Discussion.

Nehru, Jawaharlal. 1961. *Toward Freedom.* Boston: Beacon Press.

Newlin, Claude M. 1962. *Philosophy and Religion in Colonial America.* New York: Philosophical Library.

Nicolai, G.F. 1919. *The Biology of War.* Trans. Constance and Julian Grande. New York: The Century Company.

Niebuhr, H. Richard. 1959. *The Kingdom of God in America.* New York: Harper and Row.

Niebuhr, Reinhold. 1932. *Moral, Man and Immoral Society: A Study in Ethics and Politics.* New York: Charles Scribner's Sons.

-----. 1934. *Reflections on the End of an Era.* New York: Charles Scribner's Sons.

-----. 1940. *Christianity and Power Politics.* New York: Charles Scribner's Sons.

-----. 1944. *The Children of Light and the Children of Darkenss; A Vindication of Democracy and a Critique of Its Traditional Defense.* New York: Charles Scribner's Sons.

-----. 1949. *Faith and History: A Comparison of Christian and Modern Views of History.* New York: Charles Scribner's Sons.

-----. 1952. *The Irony of American History.* New York: Charles Scribner's Sons.

-----. 1953. *Christian Realism and Political Problems.* New York: Charles Scribner's Sons.

-----. 1958. *The World Crisis and American Responsibility.* New York: Association Press.

-----. 1959. *The Structure of Nations and Empires: A Study of the Recurring Patterns and Problems of the Political Order in Relation to the Unique Problems of the Nuclear Arms.* New York: Charles Scribner's Sons.

-----. 1964. *The Nature and Destiny of Man.* 1964. 2 vols. New York: Charles Scribner's Sons.

-----, and Eddy, Sherwood. 1936. *Doom and Dawn.* New York: Eddy and Page.

-----, and Heimert, Alan. 1963. *A Nation So Conceived: Reflections of the History of America from Its Early Visions to Its Present Power.* New York: Charles Scribner's Sons.

-----, and Sigmund, Paul E. 1969. *The Democratic Experience: Past and Prospects.* New York: Frederick A. Praeger, Publishers.

Nietzsche, Fredrich. 1966. *Basic Writings of Nietzsche.* Ed. and Trans. Walter Kaufmann. New York: The Modern Library.

-----. 1968. *The Portable Nietzsche.* Ed. and Trans. Walter Kaufmann. New York: The Viking Press.

-----. 1974. *The Gay Science.* Trans. Walter Kaufmann. New York: Random House.

-----. 1986. *Human, All Too Human: A Book for Free Spirits.* Trans. R.J. Hollingdale. Cambridge: Cambridge University Press.

Nkrumah, Kwame. 1969. *Handbook of Revolutionary Warfare: A Guide to the Armed Phase of the African Revolution.* New York: International Publishers.

North, Helen. 1966. *Sophrosyne: Self-Knowledge and Self-Restraint in Greek Literature.* Ithaca: Cornell University Press.

Novak, Michael. 1986a. "Realism, Dissuasion, and Hope in the Nuclear Age." In Reid 1986.

-----. 1986b. *Will It Liberate? Questions About Liberation Theology.* New York: Paulist Press.

-----. ed. 1987. *Liberation Theology and the Liberal Society.* Washington: American Enterprise Institute.

Novikov, Jakov A. 1911. *War and Its Alleged Benefits.* Trans. Thomas Selzer. New York: Henry Holt and Company.

Nowell, Samuel. 1678. *Abraham in Arms.* Boston: John Foster.

Nuñez, Emilio A. 1985. *Liberation Theology.* Trans. Paul E. Sywulka. Chicago: Moody Press.

Nuttall, Geoffrey F. 1958. *Christian Pacifism in History.*

Nye, Sr., Joseph S. 1986. *Nuclear Ethics.* New York: The Free Press.

-----. 1990. "The Changing Nature of World Power." *Political Science Quarterly.* Vol. 105, No. 2: 179-192.

Nygren, Anders. 1941. *Agape and Eros: A Study of the Christian Idea of Love.* 2 vols. Trans. A.G. Hebart. London: Society of Promoting Christian Knowledge.

O'Brien, William V. 1967. *Nuclear War, Deterrence, and Morality.* Westminster: Newman Press.

O'Connell, Robert L. 1989. *Of Arms and Men: A History of War, Weapons, and Aggression.* New York: Oxford University Press.

O'Connor, John J. 1983a. "The Morality of Defense." In Zagano 1983.

-----. 1983b. "Traditional Western Criteria for Justice in War." In Lawler 1983.

Octavius Felix. 1973. *The Octavius.* In Roberts and Donaldson 1973, IV.

O'Donovan, Oliver. 1989. *Peace and Certainty: A Theological Essay on Deterrence.* Grand Rapids: William B. Eerdmans Publishing Company.

Olsen, Mancur. 1982. *The Rise and Decline of Nations: Economic Growth Stagflation, and Social Rigidities.*

Onuf, Peter S. and Onuf, Nicholas G. 1990. "American Constitutionalism and the Emergence of a Liberal World Order." In Billias 1990.

Origen. 1960. *Homélies Sur Josué.* Trans. Annie Jaubert. Paris: Editions du Cerf.

-----. 1965. *Contra Celsum.* Trans. Henry Chadwick. Cambridge: Cambridge University Press.

-----. 1973a. *Commentary on the Gospel of John.* In *The Ante-Nicene Fathers.* Vol. X. See Roberts and Donaldson 1973.

-----. 1973b. *Commentary on the Gospel of Matthew.* In *The Ante-Nicene Fathers.* Vol. X. See Roberts and Donaldson 1973.

-----. 1973c. *De Principiis.* In *The Ante-Nicene Fathers.* Vol. IV. See Roberts and Donaldson 1973.

O'Riordan T. 1981. *Environmentalism.* London: Pion.

Orwell, George 1968. *The Collected Essays, Journalism and Letters of George Orwell.* 4 vols. New York: Harcourt, Brace and World.

Osgood, Robert E. and Tucker, Robert W. 1967. *Force, Order and Justice.* Baltimore: The Johns Hopkins University Press.

O'Toole, George Barry. 1941. *War and Conscription at the Bar of Christian Morals*. New York: The Catholic Worker Press.

Ovid. 1963. *Metamorphoses*. Trans. Rolfe Humphries. Bloomington: Indiana University Press.

Page, Kirby. 1931. *National Defense: A Study of the Origins, Results and Prevention of War*. New York: Farrar and Rinehart.

-----. 1937. *Must We Go to War? A Book for Men with a Sub-Title for Women: Must American Women Send Their Men to Fight in Europe or Asia?* New York: Farrar and Rinehart.

-----. 1948. "Atomic Slaughter Confronts Christian Churches." In Jones 1948.

-----. 1976. "Is Mahatma Gandhi the Greatest Man of the Age?" In Chatfield 1976.

Pagels, Elaine. 1988. *Adam, Eve, and the Serpent*. New York: Random House.

Paine, Thomas. 1961. *The Rights of Man*. Garden City: Doubleday and Company.

Palmer, Michael. 1982. "Love of Glory and the Common Good." *American Political Science Review*. Vol. 76, No. 4: 825-836.

Pangle, Thomas L. 1973. *Montesquieu's Spirit of Liberalism: A Commentary on the Spirit of the Laws*. Chicago: University of Chicago Press.

-----. ed. 1987. *The Roots of Political Philosophy: Ten Forgotten Socratic Dialogues*. Ithaca: Cornell University Press.

-----. 1988. *The Spirit of Modern Republicanism: The Moral Vision of the American Founders and the Philosophy of Locke*. Chicago: University of Chicago Press.

Panter-Brick, Simone. 1966. *Gandhi Against Machiavellianism: Non-violence in Politics*. Trans. P. Leon. Bombay: Asia Publishing House.

Parekh, Bhiku. 1986. "Gandhi and His Translators." *Gandhi Marg: Journal of the Gandhi Peace Foundation*. Vol. 8, No. 3: 163-172.

-----. 1989a *Colonialism, Tradition and Reform: An Analysis of Gandhi's Political Discourse*. New Delhi: SAGE Publications.

-----. 1989b. *Gandhi's Political Philosophy*. London: Macmillan Press.

Parel, Anthony. 1971. "Gandhian Satyagraha and Machiavellian Virtù." In Powers 1971.

Parsons, Thomas. 1913. *Christianity a System of Peace.* Burlington: David Allinson.

Paupert, Jean-Marie. 1969. *The Politics of the Gospel.* Trans. Grego Roy. New York: Holt, Rinehart and Winston.

Payne, Thomas F. 1983. "The Amorality of Arms Control." In Lawler 1983.

Peabody, Andrew P. 1943. *The Nature and Influence of War.* Boston: American Peace Society.

Penington, Isaac. 1653. *A Considerable Question About Government Briefly Considered.* London: Giles Calvert.

-----. 1661. *Somewhat Spoken to a Weighty Question, Concerning the Magistrates protection of the Innocent, wherein is held forth the blessing and peace which Nations ought to wait for an embrace in their later days.* London: Thomas Simmons.

-----. 1663. *A Weighty Question, Proposed to the King, And both Houses of Parliament: Together with some Queries About Religion, for the good of mens Souls, that they may seek after, and be established in that which gives life.* London: Robert Wilson.

-----. n.d. *To the Army.* Pamphlet Vol. 72. Swarthmore: Friends Historical Library.

Penn, William. 1882. *No Cross, No Crown: A Discourse showing the Nature and Discipline of the Holy Cross of Christ; and that the Denial of Self, and Daily Bearing of Christ's Cross, Is the Alone Way to the Rest and Kingdom of God.* Philadelphia: Friends' Book Association.

-----. 1912. *An Essay Toward the Present and Future Peace of Europe.* Washington: The American Peace Society.

Perret, Geoffrey. 1989. *A Country Made By War.* New York: Random House.

Perrin, Noel. 1979. *Giving Up the Gun: Japan's Reversion to the Sword, 1543-1879.* Boston: David R. Godine.

Perry, Ralph Barton. 1915. "What Is Worth Fighting For?" *Atlantic Monthly.* Vol. CXVI, No. 6: 822-831.

-----. 1916. *The Free Man and the Soldier: Essay on the Reconciliation of Liberty and Discipline.* New York: Charles Scribner's Sons.

-----. 1919. *The Present Conflict of Ideals: A Study of the Philosophical Background of the World War.* New York: Longmans, Green and Company.

Pickett, Clarence E. 1953. *For More Than Bread: An Autobiographical Sketch of Twenty-Two Years' Work with the American Friends' Service Committee.* Boston: Little, Brown and Company.

Pierson, Ruth Roach. 1987. "'Did Your Mother Wear Army Boots?' Feminist Theory and Women's Relation to War, Peace and Revolution." In Macdonald, Holden and Ardener 1987.

Plato. 1937. *The Dialogues.* 2. vols. Trans. Benjamin Jowett. New York: House.

-----. 1968. *The Republic of Plato.* Trans. Allan Bloom. New York: Basic Books.

-----. 1980. *The Laws of Plato.* Trans. Thomas L. Pangle. New York: Basic Books.

Platt, Michael. 1981. "Shakespearean Wisdom?" In Alvis and West 1981.

-----. 1983. *Rome and Romans According to Shakespeare.* Lanham: University Press of America.

-----. 1987. "Leo Strauss: Three Quarrels, Three Questions, One life." In Deutsch and Soffer 1987.

-----. 1988. "Nature as an Order of Rank (according to Nietzsche)." *The Journal of Value Inquiry.* Vol. XXII: 147-165.

-----. 1991. "Souls Without Longing." *Interpretation: A Journal of Political Philosophy.* Vol. 18, No. 3: 415-465.

Plattner, Marc F. 1979. *Rousseau's State of Nature: An Interpretation of the Discourse on Inequality.* DeKalb: Northern Illinois University Press.

Plautus. 1968. *The Pot of Gold and Other Plays.* Trans. E.F. Watling. Baltimore: Penguin Books.

Plutarch, n.d. *The Lives of the Noble Greeks and Romans.* Trans. John Dryden. New York: The Modern Library.

Polin, Raymond. 1974. "Nietzschean Violence." In Wiener and Fisher 1974.

Pollard, Francis E. 1930. "Pacifism and Mr. Gandhi." *Reconciliation.* Vol. 7, No. 8: 147-148.

-----. 1946. *Pacifism as a Policy.* London: Central Board for Conscientious Objectors.

Polmar, Norman. 1982. *Strategic Weapons: An Introduction.* New York: Crane Russak.

Pompe. C.A. 1953. *Aggressive War an International Crime.* The Hague: Martinus Nijhoff.

Pottenger, John R. 1989. *The Political Theory of Liberation Theology: Toward a Reconvergence of Social Values and Social Science.* Albany: State University of New York Press.

Potter, Ralph B. 1973. *War and Moral Discourse.* Richmond: John Knox Press.

Powers, Paul F., ed. 1971. *The Meanings of Gandhi.* Honolulu: University of Hawaii.

Price, Richard. 1970. *A Discourse on the Love of Our Country.* Boston: Edward E. Powers.

Proudhon, Pierre-Joseph. 1861. *La Guerre et la Paix: Recherches sur le Principle et la Constitution des Droits des Hommes.* Paris: E. Dentu.

-----. 1927. *La Guerre et la Paix: Recherches sur le Principle et la Constitution des Droits des Hommes.* Paris: Libraires des Sciences Politiques et Sociales.

Pseudo-Aristotle. 1987. *Epistle to Alexander the Great on World Government.* In Kainz 1987.

Puri, Balraj. n.d. (Untitled). In Kumar n.d.

Puri, Rashmi-Sudha. 1987. *Gandhi on War and Peace.* New York: Frederick A. Praeger, Publishers.

Radhakrishnan S., ed. 1949. *Mahatma Gandhi: Essays and Reflections on His Life and Work.* London: George Allen and Unwin Ltd.

Rahe, Paul. 1993. *Republics Ancient and Modern.* Chapel Hill: University of North Carolina Press

Ramsey, Paul. 1961a. *War and the Christian Conscience: How Shall Modern War Be Conducted Justly?* Durham: Duke University Press.

-----. 1961b. *Christian Ethics and the Sit-In.* New York: Association Press.

-----. 1961c. "Right and Wrong Calculation." In Clancy 1961.

-----. 1978. "Incommensurability and Indeterminacy in Moral Choice." In McCormick and Ramsey 1978.

-----. 1983. *The Just War: Force and Responsibility.* Lanham: University Press of America.

-----. 1988. *Speak Up for Just War or Pacifism: A Critique of the United Methodist Bishops' Pastoral Letter "In Defense of Creation."* University Park: The Pennsylvania State University Press.

Raskin, Marcus G. 1989. "From National Security State to Democracy." In Baumann and Jensen 1989a

Ratcliffe, K.M. 1929. "M.K. Gandhi: Patriot, Saint, Reformer." *The Friend.* Vol. *No. 41: 914-915.*

Ratzinger, Joseph, 1988. *Church Ecumenism and Politics: New Essays in Ecclesiology.* New York: Crossroad.

Rauschenbusch, Walter. 1964. *Christianity and Social Crisis.* New York: Harper and Row.

Rauschning, Hermann. 1939. *The Revolution of Nihilism: Warning to the West.* New York: Longmans, Green and Company.

Raven, Charles E. 1940. *The Cross and the Crisis.* London: The Fellowship of Reconciliation.

-----. 1948. "The Renunciation of War." In Jones 1948.

-----. 1951. *The Theological Basis of Christian Pacifism.* New York: Fellowship Publications.

Read, Herbert. 1943. *The Politics of the Unpolitical.* London: George Routledge and Sons.

Reardon, Betty A. 1985. *Sexism and the War System.* New York: Teachers College Press.

-----. 1989. "Toward a Paradigm of Peace." In Forcey 1989a.

Reding, Andrew, ed. 1987. *Christianity and Revolution: Tomás Borge's Theology of Life.* Trans. Andrew Reding. Maryknoll: Orbis Books.

Régamey, P. 1966. *Non-Violence and the Christian Conscience.* London: Darton, Longman and Todd.

Reid, Jr., Charles J. ed. 1986. *Peace in a Nuclear Age: The Bishops' Pastoral Letter in Perspective.* Washington: Catholic University of America Press.

Reilly, Rober R. 1983. "The Nature of Today's Conflict." In Lawler 1983.

-----. 1986. "In Proportion to What? The Problem with the Pastoral." In Reid 1986.

Revel, Jean François. 1971. *Without Marx or Jesus: The New American Revolution Has Begun*. Trans. J.F. Bernard. Garden City: Doubleday and Company.

Reynolds, Reginald. 1956. "What Are Pacifists Doing." *Peace News*. No. 1, 047: 5.

Rhys, J. Bradley. 1798. *An Answer to Some Passages in a Letter from the Bishop or Rochester to the Clergy upon the Lawfulness of Defensive War*. London: Darton and Harvey.

Richard, Henry. 1846. *Defensive War*. London: Charles Gilpin.

Richards, Glyn. 1982. *The Philosophy of Gandhi: A Study of His Basic Ideas*. London: Curzon Books.

Richardson, Lewis. 1960a. *Arms and Insecurity*. Pittsburgh: The Boxwood Press.

-----. 1960b. *Statistics of Deadly Quarrels*. Pittsburgh: The Boxwood Press.

Rifkin, Jeremy. 1991. *Biosphere Politics*. New York: Crown Publishers.

Roberts, Adam, ed. 1967. *The Strategy of Civilian Defense: Non-Violent Resistance to Aggression*. London: Faber and Faber Ltd.

-----. 1986. *Nations in Arms: The Theory and Practice of Territorial Defense*. New York: St. Martin's Press.

Roberts, Alexander and Donaldson, James, eds. 1973. *The Ante-Nicene Fathers*. Grand Rapids: William B. Eerdmans Publishing Company.

Roberts, Owen J., Schmidt, John F., and Streit, Clarence K. 1987. "The New Federalist." In Kainz 1987.

Roberts, Richard 1915. "The Question of Christian Duty in Wartime." In Fry 1915.

Rocco, Alfredo. 1962. "The Political Doctrine of Fascism." In Cohen 1962.

Roche, John 1961. "The Founding Fathers: A Reform Caucus in Action." *American Political Science Review*. Vol. 55: 799-816.

Rochietti, Arcelay de 1989. "Women and the People of God." In Tamez 1989.

Rock, Stephen R. 1989. *Why Peace Breaks Out: Great Power Rapprochement in Historical Perspective*. Chapel Hill: University of North Carolina Press.

Rodgers, Daniel T. 1987. *Contested Truths: Keywords in American Politics Since Independence*. New York: Basic Books.

Roelofs, H. Mark. 1988. "Liberation Theology: The Recovery of Biblical Radicalism." *American Political Science Review*. Vol. 82, No. 2: 549-565.

Rolland, Romain. 1916. *Above the Battle*. Trans. C.K. Ogden. Chicago: The Open Court Publishing Company.

-----. 1924. *Mahatma Gandhi: The Man Who Became One with the Universal Being*. Trans. Catherine D. Groth. New York: The Century Company.

Roney, Richard T. 1988. "Beyond War: A New Way of Thinking." In Gromyko and Hellman 1988a.

Roosevelt, Grace G. 1990. *Reading Rousseau in the Nuclear Age*. Philadelphia: Temple of University Press.

Rosen, Stanley. 1974. *G.W.F. Hegel: An Introduction to the Science of Wisdom*. New Haven: Yale University Press.

Rosso, Alberto ed. 1986. *The Theology of Liberation*. Quezon City: Claretion Publications.

Roszak, Theodore. 1985. "A Just War Analysis of Two Types of Deterrence." In Hardin *et. al.* 1985.

Rothbard, Murray N. 1973. *For a New Liberty*. New York: The Macmillan Company.

Rougement, Denis de. 1983. *Love in the Western World*. Trans. Montgomery Belgion. Princeton: Princeton University Press.

Rousseau, Jean-Jacques. 1927. *A Project of Perpetual Peace*. London: Richard Cobden-Sanderson.

-----. 1950. *The Social Contract and Discourses*. Trans. G.D.H. Cole. New York: E.P. Dutton and Company.

-----. 1968. *Politics and the Arts: Letter to M. D'Alembert on the Theatre*.

-----. 1979. *Emile or On Education*. Trans. Allan Bloom. New York: Basic Books.

-----. n.d. *Les Confessions*. Paris: Librairie Garnier Frères.

Routley, Richard 1985. "Metaphysical Fallout from the Nuclear Predicament." In Jones and Griesbach 1985.

845

Rowbatham, Sheila. 1972. *Women, Resistance and Revolution*. London: Allen Lane The Penguin Press.

Rowntree, William. 1900. *War and Christianity*. London: West, Newman and Company.

Roy, Ramashray. 1984. *Gandhi: Soundings in Political Philosophy*. Delhi: Chanakys Publishers.

Royden, A. Maude. 1915. "The Nature of Christian Obedience." In Fry 1915.

Ruddick, Sara. 1989. *Maternal Thinking: Toward a Politics of Peace*. Boston: Beacon Press.

Ruether, Rosemary. 1972. *Liberation Theology: Human Hope Confronts Christian History and American Power*. New York: Paulist Press.

Ruitenbeek, Hendrik M. 1963. *Varieties of Classic Social Theory*. New York: E.P. Dutton and Company.

Rule, James B. 1988. *Theories of Civil Violence*. Berkeley: University of Californial Press.

Runciman, Steven. 1965. *Byzantine Civilization*. Cleveland: Meridian Books.

Rush, Benjamin. 1951. *Letters of Benjamin Rush*. Ed. L.H. Rutterfield. Princeton: Princeton University Press.

Ruskin, John n.d. *The Crown of Wild Olive: Three Lectures on Work, Traffic and War*. In John Ruskin's Works. Boston: Dana Estes and Company.

Russell, Bertrand. 1915. "The War and Non-Resistance: A Rejoinder to Professor Perry." *International Journal of Ethics*. Vol. XXV, No. 3: 23-30.

-----. 1917a. *Justice in War Time*. Chicago: The Open Court Publishing Company.

-----. 1917b. *Why Men Fight: A Method for Abolishing the International Duel*. New York: The Century Company.

-----. 1920. *Bolshevism: Theory and Practice*. New York: Harcourt, Brace and Howe.

-----. 1936. *Which Way to Peace?* London: Michael Joseph Ltd.

-----. 1959. *Common Sense and Nuclear Warfare*. New York: Simon and Schuster.

-----. 1960. *Authority and the Individual*. Boston: Beacon Press.

-----. 1962. *Has Man a Future?* New York: Charles Scribner's Sons.

-----. 1969. "World Communism and Nuclear War." In Abelson 1969.

Russell, Frederick H. 1975. *The Just War in the Middle Ages.* Cambridge: Cambridge University Press.

-----. 1986. "The Historical Perspective of the Bishops' Pastoral Letter: The View of One Medievalist." In Reid 1986.

Russett, Bruce M. 1970. *What Price Vigilance? The Burdens of National Defense.* New Haven: Yale University Press.

-----. 1972. *No Clear and Present Danger: A Skeptical View of United States Entry into World War Two.* New York: Harper and Row.

-----. 1983. *The Prisoners of Insecurity: Nuclear Deterrence, the Arms Race, and Arms Control.* New York: W.H. Freeman and Company.

Ruston, Roger. 1984. "Nuclear Deterrence and the Use of the Just War Doctrine." In Blake and Pole 1984.

Rutenber, Culbert G. 1950. *The Dagger and the Cross: An Examination of Christian Pacifism.* New York: Fellowship Publications.

Ryan, Edward S. 1952. "The Rejection of Military Service by the Early Christians." *Theological Studies.* Vol XIII, No. 1: 1-32.

Ryan, John K. 1933. "Modern War and Basic Ethics." Ph.D. diss. The Catholic University of America.

Sagan, Carl. 1978. *The Dragons of Eden.* New York: Ballantine Books.

Saint-Simon, Louis de Rouvroy. 1901. *Memoirs of Louis XIV.* 3 vols. Trans. Bayle St. John Washington: M. Walter Dunne.

Sampson, Ronald V. 1966. *The Psychology of Power.* New York: Pantheon Books.

-----. 1973. *The Discovery of Peace.* New York: Pantheon Books.

Sanders, E.P. 1985. *Jesus and Judaism.* Philadelphia: Fortress Press.

Sandoz, Ellis, ed. 1991. *Political Sermons of the American Founding Era, 1730-1835.* Indianapolis: Liberty Press.

Santhanam, K. n.d. (Untitled). In Kumar n.d.

Santoni, Ronald E. 1984. "The Arms Race, Genocidal Intent and Individual Responsibility." In Gay 1984.

Sartre, Jean-Paul. 1968. "Preface." In Fanon 1968.

Satin, Mark. 1977. *New Age Politics: The Emerging New Alternative to Liberalism and Marxism*. Vancouver: Fairweather Press.

Sattler, Michael. 1975. "The Scheitheim Comfession of Faith." In Zick 1975.

Saxonhouse, Arlene. 1983. "An Unspoken Theme in Plato's *Gorgias*: War." *Interpretation: A Journal of Political Philosophy*. Vol. 11, No. 2: 139-169.

Scargill, William Pitt. 1815. *An Essay on the Impolicy of War*. London: Darton, Harvey, and Darton.

Schaff, Philip and Wace, Henry, eds. 1961. *A Select Library of Nicene Post-Nicene Fathers of the Christian Church*. Grand Rapids: William B. Eerdmans Publishing Company.

Schall, James V. 1982. *Liberation Theology in Latin America*. San Francisco: Ignatius Press.

-----. 1983. "Intellectual Origins of the Peace Movement." In Lawler 1983.

Schaull, Richard. 1969. "Revolutionary Change in Theological Perspective." In Cox 1969.

Scheiders, Susan M. 1983. "New Testament Reflections on Peace and Nuclear Arms." In Murnion 1983.

Schell, Jonathan. 1982. *The Fate of the Earth*. New York: Avon Books.

-----. 1984. "The Abolition." *The New Yorker*. Vol. 59, Nos. 1, 2: 36-44, 43-44+.

Schlegel, Friedrich von. 1849. *The Aesthetic and Miscellaneous Works of Frederich von Schlegel*. Trans. E.J. Millington. London: Henry G. Bohn.

Schlesinger, Jr., Arthur M. 1987. "National Interests and Moral Absolutes." In Myers 1987.

Schmitt, Carl. 1976. *The Concept of the Political*. Trans. George Schwab. New Brunswick: Rutgers University Press.

Schopenhauer, Arthur. 1974. *Of the Fourfold Root of the Principle of Sufficient Wisdom*. Trans. E. F. J. Payne. LaSalle: Open Court Publishing Company.

Schreiner, Olive. 1914. *Women and War*. New York: Frederick A. Stokes.

Schweitzer, Albert. 1960. *The Quest of the Historical Jesus: A Critical Study of Its Progress from Reimarus to Wrede.* Trans. W. Montgomery. New York: The Macmillan Company.

-----. 1968. *The Kingdom of God and Primitive Christianity.* Trans. L.A. Garrard. New York: The Seabury Press.

Scott, John. 1800. *War Inconsistent with the Doctrine and Example of Jesus Christ.* New Bedford: Abraham Shearman, Jr.

Scott-Craig, T.J.K. 1938. *Christian Attitudes to War and Peace.* Edinburgh: Oliver and Boyd.

Seabury, Paul and Codevilla, Angelo. 1989. *War: Ends and Means.* New York: Basic Books.

Segundo, Juan Luis. 1976. *Liberation of Theology.* Trans. John Drury. Maryknoll: Orbis Books.

-----. 1978. *The Hidden Motives of Pastoral Action: Latin American Reflections.* Trans. John Drury. Maryknoll: Orbis Books.

-----. 1985. *Theology and the Church: A Response to Cardinal Ratzinger and a Warning to the Whole Church.* Trans. John W. Diercksmeier. Minneapolis: Winston Press.

Seifert, Harvey. 1961. "A Reappraisal of Realism in Foreign Policy." In Keys 1961.

Seifert, Harvey. 1965. *Conquest by Suffering: The Process and the Politics of Nonviolent Resistance.* Philadelphia: The Westminster Press.

Senghaas, Dieter. 1987. "Transcending Collective Violence, the Civilizing Process and the Peace Problem." In Värynen 1987.

Sewall, Joseph. 1991. *Ninevah's Repentance and Deliverance.* In Sandoz, 1991.

Sharp, Gene. 1973. *The Politics of Nonviolent Action.* Boston: Porter Sargent Publishers.

-----. 1979. *Gandhi as a Political Strategist: With Essays on Ethics and Politics.* Boston: Porter Sargent Publishers.

-----. 1980. *Social Power and Political Freedom.* Boston: Porter Sargent Publishers.

-----, and Jenkins, Bruce. 1990. "People Power' Takes Center Stage." *United States Institute of Peace Journal.* Vol. III, No. 1: 7-9.

Sheehan, Colleen. 1990. "Madison's Party Press Essays." *Interpretation: A Journal of Political Philosophy.* Vol. 17, No. 3: 355-377.

Sheen, Fulton J. 1961. "Is Nuclear Warfare Justifiable?" In Keys 1961.

Shelley, Percy B. 1966. *Shelley's Prose, or The Trumpet of Prophecy.* Ed. David Lee Clark. Albuquerque: The University of New Mexico Press.

Shepard, Paul. 1973. *The Tender Carnivore and the Sacred Game.* New York: Charles Scribner's Sons.

Shinn, Rober. 1972. *Wars and Rumors of Wars.* Nashville: Abingdon Press.

Shridharani, Krishnalal. 1939. *War without Violence: A Study of Gandhi's Method and Its Accomplishment.* New York: Harcourt, Brace and Company.

Sibley, Mulford Q. 1944. *The Political Theories of Modern Pacifism.* Philadelphia: The Pacifist Research Bureau.

-----, ed. 1968. *The Quiet Battle: Writings on the Theory and Practice of Non-Violent Resistance.* Boston: Beacon Press.

Sider, Ronald J. 1979. *Christ and Violence.* Scottdale: Herald Press.

Sidgwick, Henry. 1909. *Practical Ethics: A Collection of Essays and Addresses.* London: Swan Sonnenschein and Company.

Sidney, Algernon. 1989. *Discourses Concerning Government.* Indianapolis: Liberty Classics.

Sikes, W.E. 1976. "Gandhi Converts a Missionary." In Chatfield 1976.

Simmel, Georg. 1963. "The Sociology of Conflict." In Ruitenbeek 1963.

Simons, Menno. 1966. *The Complete Writings of Menno Simons.* Trans. Leonard Verduin. Scottdale: Herald Press.

Singer, Milton. 1972. *When a Great Tradition Modernizes: An Anthropoligical Approach to Indian Civilization.* New York: Praeger Publishers.

Singer, Peter. 1973. *Democracy and Disobedience.* Oxford: Clarendon Press.

Singh, Nagendra. 1981. *Human Rights and the Future of Mankind.* New Delhi: Vanity Books.

-----. 1986. *Enforcement of Human Rights in Peace and War and the Future of Humanity.* Dordrecht: Martinus Nijhoff.

Singha, Shoran S. 1924. "India's Contact with the West." *The Friend.* Vol. LXIV, No. 38: 807-808.

-----. 1925. "Gandhi and the Gospels: An Indian Christian View." *Reconciliaition.* Vol. 2, No. 12: 221-222.

Siverson, Randolph M. and Starr, Harvey. 1990. "Opportunity, Willingness, and the Diffusion of War." *American Political Science Review.* Vol. 84, No. 1: 47-67.

Skodvin, Magne. 1967. "Norwegian Non-Violent Resistance During the German Occupation." In Roberts 1967.

Sloan, Stanley R. and Gray, Robert C. 1982. *Nuclear Strategy and Arms Control.* New York: Foreign Policy Association.

Smith, Adam. 1965. *An Inquiry into the Nature and Causes of the Wealth of Nations.* New York: The Modern Library.

-----. 1976. *The Theory of Moral Sentiments.* Indianapolis: Liberty Classics.

Smith, Anthony D. 1972. *Theories of Nationalism.* New York: Harper and Row.

Smith, John. 1748. *The Doctrine of Christianity, as held by the People called Quakers, Vindicated: In Answer to Gilbert Tennent's Sermon on the Lawfulness of War.* Philadelphia: Benjamin Franklin and David Hall.

Smith, Steven B. 1989. *Hegel's Critique of Liberalism: Rights in Context.* Chicago: University of Chicago Press.

Smith, William. 1675. *Balm from Gilead.* Privately printed.

Smoke, Richard and Harman, Willis. 1987. *Paths to Peace: Exploring the Feasibility of Sustainable Peace.* Boulder: Westview Press.

Soderlund, Jean, ed. 1983. *William Penn and the Founding of Pennsylvania 1680-1684: A Documentary History.* Philadelphia: University of Pennsylvania Press.

-----. 1985. *Quakers and Slavery: A Divided Legacy.* Princeton: Princeton University Press.

Solomon, J. Fischer. 1988. *Discourse and Reference in the Nuclear Age.* Norman: University of Oklahoma Press.

Soloveitchik, Joseph B. 1983. *Halakhic Man.* Trans. Lawrence Kaplan. Philadelphia: Jewish Publication Society of America.

-----. 1986. *The Halakhic Mind: An Essay on Jewis Tradition and Modern Thought.* New York: Seth Press/Free Press.

Somerville, John. 1954. *The Philosophy of Peace.* New York: Liberty Press.

-----. 1975. *The Peace Revolution: Ethos and Social Process.* Westport: Greenwood Press.

-----, ed. 1981. *Soviet Marxism and Nuclear War: An International Debate.* Westport: Greenwood Press.

Sorabji, Mary. 1922. "What India Needs." *The Friend.* Vol. LXII, No. 17: 282-282.

Sorel, Georges. 1957. *Reflections on Violence.* Trans. T.E. Hulme and J. Roth. New York: Collier Books.

Soto, Hernando de. 1989. *The Other Paths: The Invisible Revolution in the Third World.* June Abbott. New York: Harper and Row.

Spangler, David. 1984. *Emergencies: The Rebirth of the Sacred.* New York: Delta/Merloyd Lawrence.

Spedding, James; Ellis, Robert Leslie; and Heath, Douglas Denon, eds. 1968. *The Works of Francis Bacon.* 14 vols. New York: Garrett Press.

Spender, Stephen. 1949. Untitled. In Crossman 1949.

Spengler, Oswald. 1929. *The Decline of the West: Form and Actuality.* 2 vols. Trans. Charles Francis Atkinson. New York: Alfred A. Knopf.

Spinoza, Benedict. 1951. *Works and Spinoza.* 2 vols. Trans R.H.M. Elwes. New York: Dover Publications.

Spretnak, Charlene. 1982a. *The Politics of Women's Spirituality: Essays on the Spiritual Power within the Feminist Movement.* Garden City: Doubleday and Company.

-----. 1982b. "Introduction." In Spetnak 1982a.

Stackhouse, Max. 1971. *The Ethics of Necropolis: An Essay on the Military-Industrial Complex and the Quest for Peace and Justice.* Boston: Beacon Press.

Stahl, Gary. 1986. "Remembering the Future." In Cohen and Lee 1986a.

Stalin, Joseph. 1939. *Foundations of Leninism.* New York: International Publishers.

-----. 1971. *Selected Works.* Davis: Cardinal Publishers.

Starhawk. 1982. Witchcraft as Goddess Religion." In Spretnak 1982a.

Starrett, Barbara. 1982. "The Metaphors of Power." In Spretnak 1982a.

Staub, Ervin. 1989. *The Roots of Evil: The Origins of Genocide and Other Group Violence*. Cambridge: Cambridge University Press.

Steel, Ronald. 1967. *Pax Americana*. New York: Viking Press.

Stein, Walter, ed. 1961a. *Nuclear Weapons and Christian Conscience*. London: Merlin Press.

-----. 1961b. "Introductory: The Defense of the West:" In Stein 1961a.

-----. 1961c. "Prudence, Conscience and Faith." In Stein 1961a.

Stepan, Alfred. 1988. *Rethinking Military Politics: Brazil and the Southern Cone*. Princeton: Princeton University Press.

Stephen, Caroline Emelia. 1890. *Quaker Strongholds*. London: Kegan Paul, Trench, Trübner and Company.

Stephenson, Carolyn M. 1983. "Feminism, Pacifism, Nationalism, and the United Nations Decade of Women." In Stiehm 1983.

Sternstein, Wolfgang. 1967. "The Ruhrkampf of 1923: Economic Problems of Civilian Defense." In Roberts 1967.

Stevens, Richard G. 1987. "The Constitutional Completion of the Liberal Philosophy of Hobbes and Locke." *The Political Science Reviewer*. Vol. XVII: 167-184.

Stevenson, Jr. William R. 1987. *Christian Love and Just War: Moral Paradox and Political Life in Saint Augustine and His Modern Interpreters*. Macon: Mercer University Press.

Stiehm, Judith, ed. 1983. *Women and Men's Wars*. Oxford: Pergamon Press.

Stirner, Max. n.d. *The Ego and His Own*. Trans. Steven T. Byington. New York: The Modern Library.

Stone, Merlin. 1978. *When God Was a Woman*. New York: Harcourt Brace Jovanovich.

Storing, Herbert J., ed. 1962. *Essays on the Scientific Study of Politics*. New York: Holt, Rinehart and Winston.

-----. 1981. *What the Anti-Federalists Were FOR*. Chicago: University of Chicago Press.

-----. 1985. "The Constitution and the Bill of Rights." In *How Does the Constitution Secure Rights*? See Goldwin and Schambra 1985.

Stratmann, Franziskus. 1928. *The Church and War: A Catholic Study*. London: Sheed and Ward.

Straus, Oscar S. 1887. *The Origin of the Republican Form of Government in the United States*. New York: G.P. Putman's Sons.

Strauss, Leo. 1953. *Natural Right and History*. Chicago: University of Chicago Press.

-----. 1964. *The City and Man*. Chicago: Rand McNally and Company.

-----. 1965. *Spinoza's Critique of Religion*. New York: Schocken Books.

-----. 1968. *On Tyranny*. Ithaca: Cornell University Press.

-----. 1969. *Thoughts on Machiavelli*. Seattle: University of Washington Press.

-----. 1970. *Xenophon's Socratic Discourse*. Ithaca: Cornell University Press.

-----. 1973. *What Is Political Philosophy? and Other Studies*. Westport: Greenwood Press.

-----, and Cropsey, Joseph, eds. 1987. *History of Political Philosophy*. Thir Edition. Chicago: The University of Chicago Press.

Stringfellow, William 1982. "The Nuclear Principalities." In Wallis 1982.

Struckmeyer, Frederick R. 1979. "The 'Just War' and the Right of Self-Defense." In Wakin 1979.

Students for a Democratic Society. 1969. *The Port Huron Statement*. In *How Democratic is America? Responses to the New Left Challenge*. See Goldwin 1969.

Stuart, Reginald C. 1982. *War and American Thought: From the Revolution to the Monroe Doctrine*. Kent: Kent State University Press.

Suarez, Francisco. 1044. *Selections from Three Works*. Trans. Gladys L. Williams, Ammi Brown and John Waldron. Oxford: Clarendon Press.

Sumner, Charles. 1969. *Charles Sumner, His Complete Works*. 10 vols. New York: Negro University Press.

Sun Tzu. 1963. *The Art of War*. Trans. Samuel B. Griffith. New York: Oxford University Press.

Sutherland, G.A. 1946. *Society and the Conscientious Objector*. London: Central Board Conscientious Objectors.

Suttner, Bertha von. 1914. *Lay Down Your Arms: The Autobiography of Martha von Tilling*. Trans. T. Holmes. New York: Longsman, Green and Company,

Swift, Louis J. 1983. *The Early Fathers on War and Military Service.* Wilmington: Michael Glazier, Inc.

-----. 1986. "Search the Scriptures: Patristic Exegesis and the Ius Belli." In Reid 1986.

Synesius of Cyrene. 1926. *Letters.* Trans. Augustine Fitzgerald. London: Oxford University Press.

Tacitus. 1942. *The Complete Works of Tacitus.* Trans. Alfred J. Church and W. J. Brodribb. New York: The Modern Library.

Taft, William Howard and Bryan, William Jennings. 1917. *World Peace: A Written Debate Between William Howard Taft and William Jennings Bryan.* New York: George H. Doran and Company.

Tähtinen, Unto. 1964. *Non-Violence as an Ethical Principle: With Special Reference to the Views of Mahatma Gandhi.* Turku: Turum Yliopisto.

Tamez, Elsa, ed. 1989a. *Through Her Eyes: Women's Theology from Latin America.* Maryknoll: Orbis Books.

-----. 1989b. "The Power of the Naked." In Tamez 1989a.

Tarcov, Nathan. 1984. *Locke's Education for Liberty.* Chicago: University of Chicago Press.

-----. 1985. "American Constitutionalism and Individual Rights." *In How Does the Constitution Secure Rights?* See Goldwin and Schambra 1985.

-----. 1988. "The Spirit of Liberty and Early American Foreign Policy." In Zuckert 1988.

-----. 1989. "Principles and Prudence: The Use of Force from the Founders' Perspective." In Baumann and Jensen 1989a.

-----. 1990. "War and Peace in The Federalist." *The Political Science Reviewer.* XIX: 87-106.

Tasso, Torquato. 1982. *Tasso's Dialogues: A Selection, with the Discourse on the Art of the Dialogue.* Trans. Carnes Lord and Dain Trafton. Berkeley: University of California Press.

Tatian the Assyrian. 1973. *Address to the Greeks.* Trans. J.E. Ryland. In *The Ante-Nicene Fathers.* Vol. II. See Roberts and Donaldson 1973.

Taylor, A.J.P. 1957. *The Trouble Makers: Dissent Over Foreign Policy, 1792-1939.* London: H. Hamilton.

Taylor, Joseph. 1920. "Thirty Years of Missionary Effort in India." *The Friend.* Vol. LX, No. 26: 393-394.

-----. 1921. "India in Transition." *The Friend*. Vol. LXI, No. 51: 876-877.

-----. 1922. "The New Movement in India: Mr. Gandhi's Policy." *The Friend*. Vol. , No. 4: 55.

Taylor, Thomas. 1697. *Truths Innocency and Simplicity Shining*. London: T. Sowle.

Teichman, Jenny. 1986. *Pacifism and the Just War: A Study in Applied Philosophy*. London: Basil Blackwell.

Templin, Ralph T. 1965. *Democracy and Nonviolence: The Role of the Individual in World Crisis*. Boston: Porter Sargent, Publisher.

-----. n.d. Untitled essay. In Dumar n.d.

Tennent, Gilbert. 1748a. *The Late Association for Defence, Encourag'd, or, the Lawfulness of Defensive War*. Second edition. Philadelphia: William Bradford.

-----. 1748b. *The Association for Defence Further Encouraged: or, Defensive War Defended; and Its Consistency with True Christianity Represented*. Philadelphia: Benjamin Franklin and D. Hall.

-----. 1765. *The Blessedness of Peace-Makers Represented; and the Dangers of Persecution considered; in Two Sermons on Mat. v. 9*. Philadelphia: William Bradford.

Tertullian. 1973a. *Apology*. Trans. S. Thelwall. In *The Ante-Nicene Fathers*. Vol. III. See Roberts and Donaldson 1973.

-----. 1973b. *De Corona*. Trans. S. Thelwall. In *The Ante-Nicene Fathers*. Vol. III. See Roberts and Donaldson 1973.

-----. 1973c. *On Idolatry*. Trans. S. Thelwall. In *The Ante-Nicene Fathers*. Vol. III. See Roberts and Donaldson 1973.

-----. 1973d. *Of Patience*. Trans. S. Thelwall. In *The Ante-Nicene Fathers*. Vol. III. See Roberts and Donaldson 1973.

Tewari, S.M. n.d. "Gandhi's Concept of Democracy: A Doctrine of Ten Meanings." In Kumar n.d.

Thayer, John. 1991. *A Discourse, delivered at the Roman Catholic Church in Boston*. In Sandoz, 1991.

Theophilus of Antioch. 1973. *Letter to Autolycus*. Trans. Marcus Dods. In *The Ante-Nicene Fathers*. Vol. II. See Roberts and Donaldson 1973.

Thomas Aquinas. 1949. *On Kingship: To the King of Cyrus*. Trans. Gerald B. Phelan and I. Eschmann. Toronto: The Pontifical Institute of Mediaeval Studies.

-----. 1963. *Summa Theologiae*. 60 vols. Trans. Thomas Gilby. New York: McGraw-Hill Book Company.

-----. 1975. *Summa Contra Gentiles*. Trans. James F. Anderson, Vernon J. Bourke, and Charles J. O'Neill. Notre Dame: University of Notre Dame Press.

Thomas, Evan. 1974. *The Radical "No": The Correspondence and Writings of Evan Thomas on War*. Ed. Charles Chatfield. New York: Garland Publishing Company.

Thomas, M.M. 1969. *The Acknowledged Christ of the Indian Renaissance*. London: SCM Press, Ltd.

Thomas, Norman. 1917. *The Christian Patriot*. Philadelphia: Walter H. Jenkins.

-----. 1923. *The Conscientious Objector in America*. New York: B.W. Huebsch, Inc.

-----. 1931. *America's Way Out: A Program for Democracy*. New York: The Macmillan Company.

-----. 1934. *The Choice Before Us: Mankind at the Crossroads*. New York: Macmillan Company.

-----. 1925. *War: No Glory, No Profit, No Need*. New York: Fredrick A. Stokes.

-----. 1941. *We Have a Future*. Princeton: Princton University Press.

-----. 1944. *What Is Our Destiny*. Garden City: Doubleday, Doran and Company.

-----. 1959. *The Prerequisites of Peace*. New York: Garland Publishing Company.

-----. 1974. *Norman Thomas on War*. Ed. Bernard K. Johnpoll. New York: Garland Publishing Company.

Thompson, E.P. 1982. *Beyond the Cold War: A New Approach to the Arms Race and Nuclear Annihilation*. New York: Pantheon Books.

Thompson, Kenneth W. 1959. *Christian Ethics and the Dilemmas of Foreign Policy*. Durham: Duke University Press.

Thompson, William R. 1988. *On Global War: Historical-Structural Approaches to World Politics.* Columbia: University of South Carolina Press.

Thoreau, Henry David. 1966. *Civil Disobedience.* In *Walden and Civil Disobedience.* Ed. Owen Thomas. New York: W.W. Norton and Company.

Thucydides. 1934. *The Peloponnesian War.* Trans. R. Crawley. New York: The Modern Library.

Thurow, Glen. 1976. *Abraham Lincoln and American Political Religion.* Albany: State University of New York Press.

-----, and Wallin, Jeffrey D., eds. 1984. *Rhetoric and American Statesmanship.* Durham: Carolina Academic Press.

Tocqueville, Alexis, de. 1945. *Democracy in America.* 2 vols. Trans. Henry Reeve, Francis Bowen, and Phillips Bradley. New York: Vintage Books.

-----. 1959. *"The European Revolution" and Correspondence with Gobineau.* Trans. John Lukacs. Garden City: Doubleday and Company.

-----. 1965. *Recollections.* Trans. Alexander Teixcira de Mattos. Cleveland: World Publishing Company.

Tolstoy, Lew. 1904. *Bethink Yourselves.* Trans. V. Tchertkoff. New York: Thomas Y. Crowell and Company.

-----. 1905. *The Complete Works of Count Tolstoy.* 29 vols. Trans. Leo Weiner. Boston: Dana Estes and Company.

-----. 1960. *The Kingdom of God and Peace Essays.* Trans. Aylmer Maude. London: Oxford University Press.

-----. 1968. *Tolstoy's Writings on Civil Disobedience and Nonviolence.* Trans. Anonymous. London: Peter Owen.

-----. 1970. *The Law of Love and the Law of Violence.* Trans. Mary Koutouzow Tolstoy. New York: Holt, Rinehart and Winston.

Tomkinson, Leonard. 1940 *Studies in the Theory and Practice of Peace War in Chinese History and Literature.* Shanghai: Christian Literature Society.

Topel, L. John. 1982. *The Way to Peace: Liberation Through the Bible.* Maryknoll: Orbis Books.

Trachtenberg, Marc. 1985. "Strategists, Philosophers, and the Nuclear Question." In Hardin *et. al.* 1985.

Tracy, James D. 1978. *The Politics of Erasmus: A Pacifist Intellectual and His Intellectual Milieu*. Toronto: University of Toronto Press.

Trocmé, André. 1973. *Jesus and the Nonviolent Revolution*. Trans. Michael H. Shank and Marlin E. Miller. Scottdale: Herald Press.

Troeltsch, Ernst. 1949. *The Social Teaching of the Christian Churches*. 2 vols. Trans. Olive Wyon. New York: Macmillan and Company.

Trotter, W. 1922. *Instincts of the Herd in Peace and War*. London: T. Fisher and Unwin.

Trotsky, Leon. 1918. *The Bolsheviki and World Peace*. New York: Boni and Liveright.

-----. 1930. *My Life*. New York: Grosset and Dunlap.

-----. 1936. *Défense du Terrorisme*. Paris: Editions de la Nouvelle Revue Critique.

Tucker, Benjamin R. 1893. *Instead of a Book by a Man Too Busy to Write One: A Fragmentary Exposition of Philosophical Anarchism*. New York: Benjamin R. Tucker, Publisher.

Tucker, Robert W. 1960. *The Just War: A Study in Contemporary American Doctrine*. Baltimore: The Johns Hopkins University Press.

-----. 1977. *The Inequality of Nations*. New York: Basic Books.

-----. 1985. "Morality and Deterrence." In Hardin *et. al*. 1985.

-----, and Hendrickson, David C. 1990. *Empire of Liberty: The Statecraft of Thomas Jefferson*. New York: Oxford University Press.

Tully, Alan 1977. *William Penn's Legacy: Politics and Social Structure in Provinical Pennsylvania*.

Ullman, Richard H. 1985. "Denuclearizing International Relations." In Hardin *et. al*. 1985.

Upham, Thomas. 1936. *The Manual of Peace*. New York: Leavitt, Lord and Company.

Upton, Emory 1904. *The Military Policy of the United States*. Washington: Government Printing Office.

van Braght, Thieleman J. 1950. *The Bloody Theater or Martyrs Mirror of the Defenseless Christians Who Baptized only Upon Confession of Faith, and Who Suffered and Died for the Testimony of Jesus, Their Saviour, From the Time of Christ to the Year A.D. 1600*. Trans. Joseph F. Sohm. Scottdale: Herald Press.

Van Buren, Martin. 1918. *Autobiography*. Ed. J.C. Fitzpatrick. Annual Report of the American Historical Association for the Year 1918. Washington: Government Printing Office.

Van Kirk, Walter W. 1934. *Religion Renounces War*. Chicago: Willett, Clark and Company.

Vann, Gerald. 1939. *Morality and War*. London: Burns, Oates and Washbourne Ltd.

Varma, Vishwanath Prasad. 1965. *The Political Philosophy of Mahatma Gandhi and Sarvodaya*. Agra: Lakshmi Naraja Agarwal.

Värynen, Raimo, ed. 1987. *The Quest for Peace: Transcending Collective Violence and War among Societies, Cultures, and States*. London: SAGE Publications.

Vasto, Lanza del. 1972. *Definitions of Nonviolence*. South Ackworth: Greenleaf Books.

-----. 1974. *Warriors of Peace: Writings on the Technique of Nonviolence*. Trans. Jean Sidgwick. New York: Alfred A. Knopf.

Vattel, Emmerich de. 1916. *The Law of Nations or The Principles of Natural Law Applied to the Conduct and to the Affairs of Nations and of Sovereigns*. Trans. Charles G. Fenwick. Washington: The Carnegie Institution.

Vauban, Sebastien Le Pestre de. 1968. *A Manual of Siegecraft and Fortification*. Trans. George A. Rothrock. Ann Arbor: University of Michigan Press.

Veblen, Thorstein. 1917. *An Inquiry into the Nature of Peace and the Terms of Its Perpetuation*. New York: Macmillan and Company.

Vedder, Henry C. 1971. *Balthasar Hübmaier: The Leader of the Anabaptists*. New York: AMS.

Victoria, Franciscus de. 1917. *Reflectiones theologicae XII*. Ed. Herbert Francis Wright. Washington: Carnegie Endowment for International Peace.

Vincent, Marvin R. 1903. *Word Studies in the New Testament*. 4 vols. New York: Charles Scribner's Sons.

Vining, Elizabeth Gray. 1956. "A Legend of St. Francis." In Hunter and Sydnor 1956.

Voegelin, Eric. 1952. *The New Science of Politics*. Chicago: University of Chicago Press.

-----. 1956-1974. *Order and History*. 4 vols. Baton Rouge: Louisiana State University Press.

-----. 1978. *Anamnesis*. Trans. Gerhart Niemeyer. Notre Dame: University of Notre Dame Press.

Voltaire. 1962. *Philosophical Dictionary*. Trans. Peter Gay. New York: Harcourt, Brace and World.

Wagner, Murray. 1983. *Peter Chelcikÿ: A Radical Separatist in Hussite Bohemia*. Scottdale: Herald Press.

Wakin, Malham M., ed. 1979. *War, Morality, and the Military Profession*. Boulder: Westview Press.

Wallace, Henry. 1970. *Toward World Peace*. Westport: Greenwood Press.

Wallace, Michael D. 1990. "Racing Redux: The Arms Race-Escalation Debate." In Gochman and Sabrosky.

Wallis, Jim, ed. 1982. *Waging Peace: A Handbook for the Struggle to Abolish Nuclear Weapons*. San Francisco: Harper and Row.

Walsh, Walter. 1916. *The Moral Damage of War*. Boston: World Peace Foundation.

Walters, Jr., Leroy Brandt. 1971. "Five Classic Just-War Theories: A Study in the Thought of Thomas Aquinas, Victoria, Suarez, Gentili, and Grotius." Ph.D. diss. Yale University.

Waltz, Kenneth N. 1965. *Man, the State and War: A Theoretical Analysis*. New York: Columbia University Press.

-----. 1967. *Foreign Policy and Democratic Politics: The American and British Experiences*. Boston: Little, Brown and Company.

-----. 1990. "Nuclear Myths and Nuclear Realities." *American Political Science Review*. Vol. 84, No. 3: 731-744.

Walzer, Michael. 1970. *Obligations: Essays on Disobedience, War and Citizenship*. New York: Simon and Schuster.

-----. 1977. *Just and Unjust Wars: A Moral Argument with Historical Illustrations*. New York: Basic Books.

Warner, H.E. 1905. *The Ethics of Force*. Boston: Ginn and Company.

Warner, Richard. 1805. *War Inconsistent With Christianity: A Fast-Sermon*. London: Cuthell and Martin.

Warren, Josiah. 1863. *True Civilization an Immediate Necessity, and Last Ground of Hope for Mankind*. Boston: J. Warren.

Washburn, John M. 1873. *Reason vs. The Sword, a Treatise; in Which It Is Shown that Man Has No Right to Take Human Life; and that War is Violative of the Laws of Nature and of Revelation, and Destructive of Self-Government*. New York: G.P. Putnam and Son.

Wasserstrom, Richard A., ed. 1970. *War and Morality*. Belmont: Wadsworth Publishing Company.

-----. 1985. "War, Nuclear War, and Nuclear Deterrence: Some Conceptual and Moral Issues." In Hardin *et. al.* 1985.

Watkins, C.H. 1924. "Nationalism and Non-Violence." *Reconciliation*. Vol. I, No. 2: 26-28.

Wayland, Francis. 1847. *The Duty of Obedience to the Civil Magistrate: Three Sermons Preached in the Chapel of Brown University*. Boston: Charles C. Little and James Brown.

-----. 1868. *The Elements of Moral Science*. Revised edition. Boston: Gould and Lincoln.

Weart, Spencer R. 1988. *Nuclear Fear: A History of Images*. Cambridge: Harvard University Press.

Weber, Max. 1958. *The City*. Trans. Don Martindale and Gertrud Neuwirth. New York: The Free Press.

Webking, Richard. 1985. "Virtue and Individual Rights in John Adams' Defence." *Interpretation: A Journal of Political Philosophy*. Vo. 13. No. 2: 177-193.

Webster, Noah. 1991. *The Revolution in France Considered in Respect to Its Progress and Effects*. In Sandoz, 1991.

Weede, Erich. 1984. "Democracy and War Involvement. *Journal of Conflict Resolution*. Vol. 28, No. 4: 649-664.

Weigel, George. 1987. *Tranquillitas Ordinis: The Present Failure and Future Promise of American Catholic Thought on War and Peace*. Oxford: Oxford University Press.

-----. 1989. "Five Theses for a Pacifist Reformation." In Cromartie 1989.

Weigert, Kathleen Maes. 1989. "Peace Studies as Education for Nonviolent Social Change." In Lopez 1989.

Weil, Simone. 1970. "The Iliad, or the Poem of Force." In *Defeat and Beyond: An Anthology of French Wartime Writing. 1940-1943.* Brée and Bernauer 1970.

-----. 1973. *Oppression and Liberty.* Trans. Arthur Wills and John Petrie. Amherst: University of Massachusstts Press.

Weinberger, Jerry. 1981. "On Bacon's Advertisement Touching a Holy War." *Interpretation: A Journal of Political Philosophy.* Vol. 9, Nos. 2 and 3: 191-206.

Weiner, Myron 1988. "How Nations Become Democratic." *This World: A Journal of Religion and Public Life.* No. 22: 23-29.

Weiner, Philip P. and Fisher, John, eds. 1974. *Violence and Aggression in the History of Ideas.* New Brunswick: Rutgers University Press.

Wells, Donald A. 1967. *The War Myth.* New York: Pegasus.

-----. 1979. "How Much Can the 'Just War' Justify?" In Wakin 1979.

Wells, John I. 1810. *An Essay on War.* Baltimore: Joseph W. Miller.

Wells, Seth Youngs. 1831. *A Brief Illustration of the Principles of War and Peace.* Albany: Packard and Van Benthuysen.

West, Thomas G. 1988. "The Protestant Ethic and the Spirit of the Gun Range." *The Proposition.* December 1988: 1-3.

-----. 1990. "Foreword." In Sidney 1990.

Weston, Jessie L. 1957. *From Ritual to Romance.* Garden City: Doubleday and Company.

Whelpley, Samuel. 1818. *Letters Addressed to Caleb Strong, Esq., Late Governor of Massachusetts: Showing War to be Inconsistent with the Laws of Christ, and the Good of Mankind.* Third edition. Philadelphia: Benjamin and Thomas Kite.

Whipple, Charles K. 1860. *Non-Resistance applied to the Internal Defense of a Community.* Boston: R.F. Wallcutt.

White, Howard B. 1978. *Antiquity Forget: Essays on Shakespeare, Bacon, and Rembrandt.* The Hague: Martinus Nijhoff.

White, Morton. 1987. *Philosophy, The Federalist, and the Constitution.* New York: Oxford University Press.

Whitman, Cedric. 1958. *Honor and the Heroic Tradition.* Cambridge: Harvard University Press.

Wiecek, William M. 1977. *The Sources of Antislavery Constitutionalism in America, 1760-1848*. Ithaca: Cornell University Press.

Wiesel, Elie. 1968. *Legends of Our Time*. New York: Avon Books.

Wieseltier, Leon. 1983. *Nuclear War, Nuclear Peace*. New York: Holt, Rinehart and Winston.

Wilder, Amos Niven. 1939. *Eschatology and Ethics in the Teaching of Jesus*. New York: Harper and Brothers Publishers.

Wilhelmsen, Frederick D. 1978. *Christianity and Political Philosophy*. Athens: University of Georgia Press.

Wilken, Robert L. 1984. *The Christians as the Romans Saw Them*. New Haven: Yale University Press.

Will, George. 1983. *Statecraft as Soulcraft: What Government Does*. New York: Simon and Schuster.

Willard, Charity Cannon, ed. 1958. *The "Livre de la Paix" of Christine de Pisan*. The Hague: Mouton and Company.

Williams, Bernard. 1984. "Morality, Skepticism and the Nuclear Arms Race." In Blake and Pole 1984.

Williams, Elisha. 1991. *The Essential Rights and Liberties of Protestants*. In Sandoz, 1991.
Williams, George H., ed. 1957. *Spiritual and Anabaptist Writers: Documents Illustrative of the Radical Reformation*. Philadelphia: the Westminister Press.

Willkie, Wendell. 1943. *One World*. In *Prefaces to Peace*. See Canby 1943.

Willms, Bernard. 1989. "World-State or State-World: Thomas Hobbes and the Law of Nations." In Airaksinen and Bertram 1989.

Wills, Garry. 1978. *Inventing America: Jefferson's Declaration of Independence*. Garden City: Doubleday and Company.

Wilson, Edward O. 1978. *On Human Nature*. Cambridge: Harvard University Press.

Wilson, William E. 1914. *Christ and War: The Reasonableness of Disarmament on Christian Humanitarian and Economic Grounds*. London: James Clarke and Company.

-----. 1918. *The Foundations of Peace: A Discussion of Pacifism and the Prevention of Wars*. London: Headley Brothers, Publishers.

-----. 1923. *Atonement and Non-Resistance*. London: The Swarthmore Press.

864

Wilson, Woodrow. 1896. *Mere Literature and Other Essays*. Boston: Houghton Mifflin and Company.

-----. 1898. *The State: Elements of Historical and Practical Politics*. Boston: D.C. Heath and Company.

-----. 1966-1986. *The Papers of Woodrow Wilson*. 54 vols. Ed Arthur S. Link. Princeton: Princeton University Press.

Windass, Stanley. 1964. *Christianity Versus Violence: A Social and Historical Study of War and Christianity*. London: Sheed and Ward.

Winslow, Jack C. 1949. "Mahatma Gandhi and Aggressive Pacifism" Radhakrishna 1949.

Witthoff, Tardis. 1985. *Five Questions on World Peace*. Stockholm: Women's International League for Peace and Freedom, Swedish Section.

Wittner, Lawrence S. 1969. *Rebels Against War: The American Peace Movement, 1941-1960*. New York: Columbia University Press.

Wollstonecraft, Mary. 1988. *A Vindication of the Rights of Woman with Strictures on Political and Moral Subjects*. New York: W.W. Norton and Company.

Wood, Gordon S. 1972. *The Creation of the American Republic, 1776-1787*. New York: W.W. Norton and Company.

-----. 1981. "Democracy and the Constitution." In Goldwin and Schambra 1981.

-----. 1986. "The Democratization of Mind in the American Mind in the American Revolution." In Horwitz 1986.

Woolf, Virginia. 1963. *Three Guineas*. New York: Harcourt, Brace and World.

Woolman, John. 1922. *The Journal and Essays of John Woolman*. Ed. Amelia Mott Gummere. New York: The Macmillan Company.

Woolsey, R. James, ed. 1984. *Nuclear Arms: Ethics. Strategy, Politics*. San Francisco: ICS Press.

Worcester, Noah. 1815. *A Solemn Review of the Custom of War; Showing, That War is the Effect of Popular Delusion, and Proposing a Remedy*. New York: Samuel Wood and Sons.

Wright, Esmond. 1986. *Franklin of Philadelphia*. Cambridge: Harvard University Press.

865

Wright, Henry C. 1841. *Man-Killing, by Individuals and Nations, Wrong – Dangerous in All Cases*. Boston: Moses A. Dow.

-----. 1845. *Six Months at Graefenber; with Conversations in the Saloon, on Nonresistance and Other Subjects*. London: Charles Gilpin.

-----. 1846. *Evils of the Revolutionary War*. Boston: New England Non-Resistance Society.

-----. 1888. *A Kiss for a Blow; A Collection of Stories for Children inculcating the Principles of Peace*. Boston: Lee and Shepard Publishers.

Wright, Quincy. 1965. *A Study of War*. Chicago: University of Chicago Press.

-----. 1975. "The Role of Law in the Organization of Peace." In Holcombe *et. al.* 1975.

Wright, Richard. 1949. Untitled. In Crossman 1949.

Xenophon. 1855. *Anabasis*. Trans. J.W. Watson. London: Henry G. Bohn.

-----. 1947. *Cyropaedia*. 2 vols. Trans. Walter Miller. Cambridge: Harvard University Press.

-----. 1962. *Scripta Minora*. Trans. E.C. Marchant. Cambridge: Harvard University Press.

-----. 1968a. *Hiero*. Trans. Marvin Kendrick. In Strauss 1968.

-----. 1968b. *Memorabilia*. Trans. E.C. Marchant. Cambridge: Harvard University Press.

Yarrow, C.H. Mike. 1978. *Quaker Experience in International Conciliation*. New Haven: Yale University Press.

Yoder, John Howard. 1970. *Karl Barth and the Problem of War*. Nashville: Abingdon Press.

-----. 1971. *The Original Revolution: Essays on Christian Pacifism*. Scottdale: Herald Press.

-----. 1972. *The Politics of Jesus: Vicit Agnus Noster*. Grand Rapids: William B. Eerdmans Publishing Company.

-----. 1976. *Nevertheless: The Varieties and Shortcomings of Religious Pacifism*. Scottdale: Herald Press.

-----. 1983. *What Would You Do? A Serious Answer to a Standard Question*. Scottdale: Herald Press.

-----. 1984. *When War Is Unjust: Being Honest in Just-War Thinking*. Minneapolis: Augsburg Publishing House.

-----. 1986. "The Challenge of Peace: A Historic Peace Church Perspective." In Reid 1986.

-----. 1990. "The Wider Setting of Liberation Theology." *The Review of Politics*. Vol. 52, No. 2: 285-296.

-----. n.d. *Reinhold Niebuhr and Christian Pacifism*. Evanston: CONCERN.

Young, Nigel. 1987. "Peace Movements in Industrial Societies: Genesis, Evolution, Impact." In Värynen 1987.

Yudkin, Marcia. 1983. "Reflections on Woolf's *Three Guineas*. In Stiehm 1983.

Zagano, Phyllis, ed. 1983. *The Nuclear Arms Debate*. Book Forum. Vol. III, No. 3.

Zahn, Gordon C. 1967. *War, Conscience and Dissent*. New York: Hawthorn Books.

-----. 1987. "Pacifism and the Just War." In Murnion 1987.

Zampaglione, Geraldo. 1973. *The Idea of Peace in Antiquity*. Trans. Richard Dunn. Notre Dame: University of Notre Dame Press.

Zetterbaum, Marvin. 1967. *Tocqueville and the Problem of Democracy*. Stanford: Stanford University Press.

Zimmerman, Chaim. 1979. *Torah and Reason: Insiders and Outsiders of Torah*. Jerusalem: "HED" Press.

-----. 1986. *Torah and Existence: Insiders and Outsiders of Torah*. Jerusalem: Privately printed.

Zimmerman, Michael E. 1990. *Heidegger's Confrontation with Modernity: Technology, politics, and Art*. Bloomington: Indiana University Press.

Zuck, Lowell H., ed 1975. *Christianity and Revolution: Radical Christian Testimonies, 1520-1650*. Philadelphia: Temple University Press.

Zuckert, Catherine H., ed. 1988. *Understanding the Political Spirit: Philosophical Investigations from Socrates to Nietzsche*. New Haven: Yale University Press.

INDEX

Caton, Hiram, 470 n.35, 484 n.80

Catudal, Honoré, 758 n.130, 760 n.147, 767 n.217

Ceadel, Martin, 453 n.4, 629 n.521, 707 n.244

Ceaser, James, 484 n.78, 490 n.106, 540 n.49

Celsus, 234

Cervantes, Miguel de, 572-573 n.17

Chalmers, Thomas, 592 nn.216, 218

Chamfort, 307

Chan, Steve, 455 n.23

Channing, William Ellery, 76-77, 81, 521-522 nn.137-140

Charlemagne, 71, 383, 580 n.87

Charles I, 501 n.21, 618 n.441

Charney, Anne, 599 n.285

Chatfield, Charles, 255, 455n.31, 532 nn.1, 3, 638 n.69

Chatterjee Margaret, 640 n.89, 644 n.120, 648 nn.145, 153, 650 n.159, 659 n.321

Chauncy, Charles, 499 n.5

Chelcický, Petr, 575 n.45, 587 n.168, 590 n.194, 624-625 nn.492, 493, 631 n.537, 706 n.241

Chicherin, G.V., 374, 727 n.397

Chickering, Roger, 705 n.235

Child, James W., 743 n.23, 753 n.97, 758 n.126, 764 n.183, 766 n.200

Childress, James F., 573 n.29, 613 n.406, 615 n.412, 616 n.425, 632 n.1, 645 n.129, 649 n.154, 652 n.174, 658 n.215

Christine de Pisan, 619-620 n.458

Chryseis, 171

Chryses, 171

Churchill, Winston S., 244-247, 248, 253, 404-405, 412-413, 586 n.153, 633 nn.9-19, 740 n.414, 742 nn.5, 7, 747 n.42, 749 n.57, 752 n.90, 753-754 nn.99, 100, 757 n.119, 758 n.131

Cicero, 65, 69, 141, 338, 479 n.61, 550 n.76, 596 n.264, 605 n.337, 609 n.374, 617 n.436, 620 n.461, 703, n.223

Clark, Ian, 675 nn.20, 21, 758 n.126, 765 n.192

Clark, Ronald W., 373 nn.612, 752 n.41

Clark, Stephen R.L., 684 n.91, 758 n.127

Clarkson, Thomas, 579 n.76, 589 n.185, 612 n.395, 630 n.529, 631 n.538

Clastres, Pierre, 319, 476 n.49, 679 nn.61, 65-67

Clausewitz, Carl von, 151, 571 n.238, 726 n.395, 739 n.508

Clay, Henry, 42, 496 n.124

Clemenceau, Georges, 389, 735 n.474

Clement of Alexandria, 206, 207, 595 n.252, 601 n.302, 602 n.308, 603 n.315, 604 nn.320, 322, 605 n.331

Clifford, John, 636 n.58, 637 n.65

Cobden, Richard, 347, 613 n.404, 704 nn.233, 234, 705 n.239

Cochrane, Charles Norris, 598 n.281

Codevilla, Angelo, 453 n.10, 686 n.106, 703 n.228, 709 n.275, 743 n.23, 753 n.97, 764 n.179

Cohen, Avner, 749 n.61, 758 n.125, 761 n.158, 764 n.184, 765 n.192

Cohen, Carl, 739 n.510

Cohen, Eliot A., 497 n.125, 533

SYMPOSIUM SERIES